Windows
PowerShell® 2.0 Bible

Windows PowerShell® 2.0 Bible

Thomas Lee

Karl Mitschke

Mark E. Schill

Tome Tanasovski

WILEY

John Wiley & Sons, Inc.

Windows PowerShell® 2.0 Bible

Published by
John Wiley & Sons, Inc.
10475 Crosspoint Boulevard
Indianapolis, IN 46256
www.wiley.com

Copyright © 2011 by John Wiley & Sons, Inc., Indianapolis, Indiana

Published simultaneously in Canada

ISBN: 978-1-118-02198-9

ISBN: 978-1-118-18326-7 (ebk)

ISBN: 978-1-118-18328-1 (ebk)

ISBN: 978-1-118-18327-4 (ebk)

Manufactured in the United States of America

10 9 8 7 6 5 4 3 2 1

For general information on our other products and services, please contact our Customer Care Department within the United States at (877) 762-2974, outside the United States at (317) 572-3993 or fax (317) 572-4002.

Wiley also publishes its books in a variety of electronic formats. Some content that appears in print may not be available in electronic books.

Library of Congress Control Number: 2011936812

My work on this project is dedicated to Susan, my wife, for her patience, affection, and outstanding proofreading skills. I could not have done it without her. To my godmother, Alberta Stehle, and my aunt, Mrs. James Wright, for their inspiration.
— Thomas Lee

My work on this book is dedicated to my best friend, the love of my life, my bride, Sherry. Without your faith and constant support, I'd still be staring at a blank Word document. Thanks for always believing in me.
— Karl Mitschke

My work on this book is dedicated to my wife, Carla. It is with her support and constant encouragement that I have been able to be where I am today.
— Mark E. Schill

My work on this book is dedicated to my ladies. To my wife, Heather, who is and will always be the love of my life and my best friend, I'm sorry if you felt like a single mother at times while I was working on this. To my daughter Elora, who made sure that I took breaks from writing, and to my unborn daughter who we have yet to name, I hope this book serves as an inspiration that you can do anything you want in this world with enough hard work and commitment.
— Tome Tanasovski

About the Authors

Thomas Lee is an IT industry veteran. Thomas graduated from Carnegie Mellon University in 1973, and has had a number of interesting assignments over the decades. Today, he consults, writes, and provides training mainly on Microsoft technologies, including Lync and Windows PowerShell. He has also been a speaker at major IT conferences over the past two decades.

A Microsoft Certified Trainer for 17 years and an MVP for 16 of the past 17 years, Thomas was the first person in the world to blog about Windows PowerShell in 2003. He has also been involved with the Windows PowerShell community since its inception and is a director of PowerShellCommunity.org.

Thomas was part of the team that wrote both official Microsoft Windows PowerShell classes and has taught clients around the world to use the product. He writes two blogs, Under The Stairs (at `http://tfl09.blogspot.com`) and PowerShell Scripts Blog (at `http://pshscripts.blogspot.com`), is active on Twitter (`@doctordns`), and hosts online forums. In his spare time, he lives in an old cottage in the English countryside with his wife Susan, daughter Rebecca, a fine wine cellar, and large collection of Grateful Dead live recordings.

Karl Mitschke is a Systems Engineer for the State of Montana. His primary focus is Microsoft Exchange Server administration, with a strong emphasis on Windows PowerShell. Karl was awarded the Microsoft Community Contributor award for his contributions in Microsoft online community forums.

With more than 25 years of IT experience and extensive experience creating utility programs in C# and Visual Basic, Karl has been working with Windows PowerShell since the public beta was available. He has worked with Microsoft Exchange since Version 5.0 and was a Banyan Vines email administrator previous to that. Karl currently works with Microsoft Exchange Server 2010 SP1, System Center Operations Manager 2007 R2, and SQL Server 2008.

Karl is a frequent contributor on multiple scripting forums and blogs. You can follow his comments on `http://unlockpowershell.wordpress.com/`.

Mark E. Schill, a graduate of the Georgia Institute of Technology, is an IT veteran with 13 years of experience specializing in Windows server and Citrix technologies. He started scripting with a Y2K project that required the creation of thousands of new NT domain accounts and has been automating ever since. He made the switch to Windows PowerShell in July 2007 with his first Citrix MFCOM script for publishing desktops, which is still in production to this day. Mark spends his workdays as an all-in-one scripter, C# developer, SQL Server database administrator, and Windows system administrator.

About the Authors

He is currently the president of the Atlanta PowerShell User Group and the Atlanta Citrix User Group, as well as the vice president of the Virtual PowerShell User Group.

When possible, Mark hangs out with the Virtual PowerShell User Group on the #PowerShell IRC channel on `irc.freenode.net`. You can track Mark at his blog at `www.cmschill.net/StringTheory`, contact him via email at `Mark.Schill@cmschill.net`, or follow him on twitter `@meson3902`.

 **Tome Tanasovski** is a Windows engineer for a market-leading, global financial services firm in New York City. He has worked in the IT industry as both an IT professional and a developer for more than 15 years. He is the founder and leader of the New York City PowerShell User Group, a cofounder of the NYC Techstravaganza, a blogger, a speaker, and a regular contributor to the Windows PowerShell forum at Microsoft. He is a recipient of the MVP award for Windows PowerShell.

About the Technical Editors

Marco Shaw has worked in the IT industry for more than 12 years. He currently is an IT consultant in Canada with CGI (www.cgi.com), a global IT consulting firm. Marco works daily with Microsoft products, VMware, and other products that heavily rely on Windows PowerShell for automation of their tasks.

Marco has been awarded the Microsoft Most Valuable Professional award in the Windows PowerShell category for the past four years, and he continues to be active in the online Windows PowerShell community. He has spoken at TechMentor in the U.S. and has given several sessions at Microsoft's TechDays annual conference in Canada (www.techdays.ca) on various IT topics. Marco has already coauthored a book and appeared in Microsoft's *TechNet Magazine* a few years ago. He blogs at http://marcoshaw.blogspot.com and tweets as @MarcoShaw.

Shay Levy is a four-year Windows PowerShell MVP and a System Administrator for a government institute in Israel. He has worked with Microsoft platforms for more than 20 years, focusing on Microsoft Exchange and Active Directory.

As a longtime Windows PowerShell community supporter, Shay has become a moderator of multiple forums and is a codirector of the PowerShellCommunity.org website. He is the creator of the popular Windows PowerShell Community browser toolbar, a one-stop shop for various Windows PowerShell resources, including downloads, webcasts, videos, podcasts, and more.

Shay often covers Windows PowerShell topics on his blog at http://powershay.com. You can also follow him on Twitter at http://twitter.com/ShayLevy.

We appreciate the assistance of the following individuals for lending their expertise to the technical editing of specific chapters: Niklas Goude (Microsoft MVP) for the SharePoint chapter, Chad Miller (Microsoft MVP) for the SQL chapter, and Christian Gehring (Citrix) for the two Citrix chapters.

Credits

Acquisitions Editor
Paul Reese

Project Editor
Linda Harrison, Harrison Ridge Services

Technical Editor
Marco Shaw

Production Editor
Rebecca Anderson

Copy Editor
Kim Cofer

Editorial Manager
Mary Beth Wakefield

Freelancer Editorial Manager
Rosemarie Graham

Associate Director of Marketing
David Mayhew

Business Manager
Amy Knies

Production Manager
Tim Tate

Vice President and Executive Group Publisher
Richard Swadley

Vice President and Executive Publisher
Neil Edde

Associate Publisher
Jim Minatel

Project Coordinator, Cover
Katie Crocker

Proofreaders
Edmund Berrigan, Word One New York
Paul Sagan, Word One New York

Indexer
J & J Indexing

Cover Designer
LeAndra Young

Cover Image
Joyce Haughey

Acknowledgments

Collectively, we would like to thank Linda Harrison and Paul Reese at Wiley for being so patient with our drivel; oftentimes, we're sure it felt more like babysitting than publishing. We would also like to thank Marco Shaw for putting the four of us together. Finally, thanks to Pete Zerger and Aaron Nelson for their amazing contributions to this work.

— THOMAS LEE, KARL MITSCHKE, MARK E. SCHILL, AND TOME TANASOVSKI

I'd like to say thanks to Jeffrey Snover, one of the most inspiring people I have ever met. His vision, combined with his presentation and technical skills, continue to inspire me on a near-daily basis. I'd also like to say a *huge* thank you to the entire Windows PowerShell development team — an utterly amazing group of incredibly talented people. You have all made Windows PowerShell a reality! And no book would be complete without our fantastic team at Wiley. Thanks to Paul Reese, and a double thanks to superstar editor Linda Harrison.

— THOMAS LEE

I'd like to thank all the pioneers in Windows PowerShell. I'd be nowhere without following in the footsteps of Brandon Shell, Shay Levy, Marc van Orsouw, Glen Scales, and of course, who could forget Jeffrey Snover and Lee Holmes? You've all been an inspiration to me, and I am sure I have forgotten more people than I've mentioned. For this, I'm sorry.

Marco Shaw gets a special thanks, as it was he who first pushed me into creating a blog, and then into working on this book. Thanks, Marco!

Of course, without my coauthors Mark E. Schill, Tome Tanasovski, and Thomas Lee, this book would be many hundreds of pages slimmer, and still unfinished. Thanks, guys!

Thanks are due to our editor, Linda; without your help, we'd have a book that no one could read. You've turned my near random thoughts into a cohesive series of paragraphs. Thanks, Linda! I know I put you through a lot.

— KARL MITSCHKE

I want to thank Marco Shaw who first introduced me to the opportunity of writing this book. I also want to thank Ed Wilson for introducing me to the much larger scripting community. Without Jeffrey Snover, the father of Windows PowerShell, and the Windows PowerShell team, there, of course, wouldn't have been anything to write about. Without Linda Harrison, our editor, none of this would have made any sense.

— MARK E. SCHILL

Thank you to Marco Shaw and Ed Wilson for noticing me and my writing.

— TOME TANASOVSKI

Contents at a Glance

Introduction xxxiii

Part I: Introduction 1
Chapter 1: Introduction to Windows PowerShell 3
Chapter 2: What's New in Windows PowerShell V2 43

Part II: Windows Desktop 69
Chapter 3: Managing Windows 7 71
Chapter 4: Managing Microsoft Office 2010 95
Chapter 5: Managing Security 123
Chapter 6: Managing and Installing Software 151

Part III: Server Management 163
Chapter 7: Managing Windows Server 2008 R2 165
Chapter 8: Performing Basic Server Management 189
Chapter 9: Performing Advanced Server Management 203
Chapter 10: Managing Active Directory 229
Chapter 11: Managing Group Policy 257

Part IV: Server Applications 269
Chapter 12: Managing Microsoft Exchange Server 271
Chapter 13: Managing SQL Server 2008 R2 341
Chapter 14: Managing Microsoft SharePoint 2010 Server 371
Chapter 15: Managing Internet Information Services 7 389
Chapter 16: Managing System Center Operations Manager 2007 R2 409
Chapter 17: Managing Microsoft Deployment Toolkit 2010 441
Chapter 18: Managing Citrix XenApp 6 455
Chapter 19: Managing Citrix XenDesktop 5 479

Part V: Virtualization and Cloud Computing 511
Chapter 20: Managing Hyper-V 2008 R2 513
Chapter 21: Managing System Center Virtual Machine Manager 2008 R2 523
Chapter 22: Managing Windows Azure 541
Chapter 23: Managing VMware vSphere PowerCLI 557

Contents at a Glance

Part VI: Beyond the Console. 579
Chapter 24: Creating User Interfaces 581
Chapter 25: Using the Windows PowerShell ISE 597

Index 623

Contents

Introduction xxxiii

Part I: Introduction   1

Chapter 1: Introduction to Windows PowerShell 3

Managing Windows — The Challenges of the Past.............................3
   Management in the Early Days 3
   Management with Windows NT 4
   Management with Windows Server 2003.................................4
   Introducing Windows PowerShell.....................................5
What Is Windows PowerShell?..5
   Windows PowerShell as a Task Automation Platform....................5
   Windows PowerShell's Scripting Language.............................6
   Windows PowerShell in Production Scripts and Admin GUIs 7
Key Windows PowerShell Concepts 8
   Cmdlets...8
   Objects...9
   The Pipeline 10
Discovery and the Community 10
   Get-Help 11
   Get-Command.. 11
   Get-Member... 12
   The Windows PowerShell Community 12
Windows PowerShell Language Constructs 13
   Variables.. 13
   Operators..14
   Expressions.. 16
   Providers.. 18
Formatting Output... 18
   Default Formatting... 19
   Formatting Using Format-Table and Format-List 20
   Formatting with Windows PowerShell Hashtables 22
Scripting... 23
   What Is a Script?.. 23
   Alternation or Conditional Execution 24
   Iteration — Operating on a Collection or Array.................... 27
   Error and Exception Handling....................................... 30

Contents

Extending Windows PowerShell with Snap-ins and Modules 34
    Windows PowerShell Snap-ins 35
    Windows PowerShell Modules 36
Installing Windows PowerShell 36
    Windows PowerShell Version Support 37
    Getting Windows PowerShell for Downlevel OSs 37
    Script Security and Execution Policy 37
Customizing Windows PowerShell with Profiles 39
    What Is a Profile? 39
    Where Are Your Profiles? 40
    Managing Profiles in the Enterprise 41
Summary 42

Chapter 2: What's New in Windows PowerShell V2 . . . . **43**
The Road to V2 43
    The Version 2 Betas 43
    V2 in Windows 7/R2 44
    V2 on Downlevel OSs 45
Using Remoting 45
    What Is Remoting? 46
    Windows PowerShell Remoting Architecture 46
    Setting Up Remoting 48
    Using Remoting 48
    Serialization 50
Working with Jobs 50
    What Is a Job? 51
    Using Jobs 51
    Potential Glitches Associated with Jobs 52
Using Advanced Functions 52
    What's New with Advanced Functions? 53
    Comment-Based Help 54
    Cmdlet Binding 55
    Splatting 56
Working with Modules 57
    What Is a Module? 57
    Script Modules 57
    Manifest Modules 59
    Implicit Modules 59
Making Use of Eventing 61
    What Is Eventing? 61
    Using Eventing 61
Using the Integrated Scripting Environment 63
Supporting Transactions 63
    The Need for Transactions 63
    Transaction Support for V2 64

Debugging and Error Handling 65
    Debugging from the Command Line 65
    Using Try/Catch/Finally 66
New Cmdlets 67
Summary 67

Part II: Windows Desktop   69

Chapter 3: Managing Windows 7 71

Troubleshooting Windows 7 with Windows PowerShell 71
Managing Windows Search 77
    Discovering Which Folders Are Currently Indexed 77
    Adding Folders to the Index 79
    Removing Folders from the Index 81
    Re-Indexing the Search Catalog 82
Checking HotFix Status 84
Managing Files and Folders 84
    Setting Security on Files and Folders 84
    Listing Unique File Extensions 87
    Counting a Specific Type of Files 88
    Finding Empty Folders 89
    Searching with Windows Search 89
    Opening a File Using Its Default Handler 91
Summary 92

Chapter 4: Managing Microsoft Office 2010 95

Introducing the Office COM Objects 96
    The Office Application Objects 96
    Cleaning Up after Your Office Scripts 97
Automating Microsoft Word 98
    Creating or Opening a Document 98
    Adding Content 98
    Searching for Text 102
    Formatting Text 103
    Spell Checking 105
    Printing 106
    Saving a Document 106
Working with Microsoft Excel Spreadsheets 107
    Creating and Opening a Workbook 107
    Worksheets 107
    Working with Cells 108
    Managing Data 111
    Generating Charts and Graphs 112
    Searching Spreadsheets 113
Navigating Microsoft Outlook 113
    A Word about Security 114

Contents

Traversing Folders 114
Working with Outlook Items 116
Working with an Outlook MailItem. 116
Working with an Outlook AppointmentItem. 117
Working with an Outlook ContactItem 118
Working with an Outlook TaskItem 119
Additional Office COM Examples 119
Summary 121

Chapter 5: Managing Security 123

NTFS Permissions. 124
Retrieving Current NTFS Permissions. 124
Modifying NTFS Permissions 126
Share Permissions 127
Retrieving Current Share Permissions 127
Modifying Share Permissions 132
Registry Settings 135
Retrieving Current Registry Permissions 136
Modifying Registry Permissions 137
Managing the Windows Firewall 139
Checking Firewall Status. 139
Opening and Closing Ports 144
Enabling Remote Desktop. 147
Checking the Status of Remote Desktop 148
Summary 149

Chapter 6: Managing and Installing Software 151

Listing Software 151
Using WMI 152
Using the Windows Registry 153
Creating Software Baselines 155
Installing Software 157
Using Restore Points 157
Using WMI 158
Removing Software. 159
Removing Software Using WMI 159
Removing Software Using Windows Registry 159
Dealing with Spaces. 160
Summary 162

Part III: Server Management   163

Chapter 7: Managing Windows Server 2008 R2 165

What's New in Server 2008 R2 165
Default Installation of Windows PowerShell. 165

Windows PowerShell Included in Server Core 166

Managing Server Features and Roles 167

Running Best Practice Analyzer Scans 169

Running Scans Locally 169

Running Scans Remotely 172

Enabling Remoting 173

Managing Windows Backup 174

Installing the Cmdlets 174

Configuring New Backup Jobs 174

Checking the Status of Backup Jobs 176

Deleting Backup Jobs 177

Starting and Stopping Backup Jobs 178

Scheduling Backup Jobs 178

Limitations in the Cmdlets 179

Managing Server Migration 180

Installing the Cmdlets 180

Discover What Can Be Migrated 182

Exporting Features 183

Importing Features 184

Managing AppLocker 186

Summary 187

Chapter 8: Performing Basic Server Management 189

Discovering Server Configuration 189

Managing Scheduled Tasks 191

Checking Hotfix Status 194

Checking Hotfixes on Multiple Computers 194

Checking for a Specific Hotfix 195

Gathering Data from Event Logs 195

Using System Time 198

Retrieving the Date and Time 198

Setting the Date and Time 200

Summary 201

Chapter 9: Performing Advanced Server Management 203

Managing Command-Line Services 203

Listing Running Services on Multiple Servers 204

Finding Servers Running a Specific Service 204

Listing Stopped Services That Are Set to Start Automatically 205

Managing Processes 207

Listing All Processes on Multiple Servers 207

Stopping Processes on Remote Servers 208

Reading the Registry 209

Using the Registry Provider Locally 210

Using Microsoft.Win32.RegistryHive Remotely 210

Contents

Setting Registry Values 211
    Locally Using the Registry Provider. 212
    Remotely Using Microsoft.Win32.RegistryHive 212
Validating Network Configuration on Remote Servers. 213
    Retrieving the DNS Settings. 214
    Validating That Servers Use the Same DNS Settings 214
    Changing the Network Configuration 215
Gathering Data from Performance Counters. 217
Modifying Regional Settings on Multiple Computers 218
Managing Local Accounts 219
    Modifying Local Users and Groups 219
    Creating and Deleting Local Users and Groups 220
Configuring Remote DCOM. 221
    Viewing DCOM Permissions. 222
    Granting a Domain User Remote DCOM Access 226
Summary 227

Chapter 10: Managing Active Directory 229
Installing and Using the Cmdlets. 230
    Prerequisites 230
    A Word About Remoting 231
    Installation 231
Using the Active Directory Provider. 232
Querying Active Directory 234
    Users, Groups, and Computers 234
    Querying Group Membership 238
User and Group Administration 240
    Creating Users and Groups 240
    Modifying Properties 242
    Working with Group Membership 243
    Common Tasks 244
    Managed Service Accounts. 246
Managing Organizational Units 247
    Moving Active Directory Objects. 247
    Creating Organizational Units 248
    Removing Active Directory Objects 249
Password Policies. 249
    Viewing Password Policies. 250
    Creating a Fine-Grained Policy 251
    Modifying Password Policies. 251
Managing the Rest of Active Directory 252
Managing Active Directory with the ActiveRoles Management Shell. 253
    Installing the Cmdlets. 253
    Using the Cmdlets. 253
Summary 255

Chapter 11: Managing Group Policy **257**

Installing and Using the Cmdlets 257
   Enabling the Module on Windows Server 2008 R2. 257
   Installing the Module on Windows 7 258
   A Word about Remoting 258
Getting Policy Information 258
   Group Policy Objects (GPOs) 258
   Group Policy Links 261
   Resultant Set of Policy (RSOP) 262
Creating and Configuring GPOs 262
Backing Up and Restoring GPOs 264
Group Policy Security 265
   Getting Security Information 265
   Setting Permissions 265
Summary 266

Part IV: Server Applications   **269**

Chapter 12: Managing Microsoft Exchange Server **271**

Installing the Cmdlets on a Workstation 271
   Microsoft Exchange Server 2007 272
   Microsoft Exchange Server 2010 272
What's New in Microsoft Exchange Server 2010 273
Managing Microsoft Exchange Server Permissions 274
   Microsoft Exchange Server 2007 274
   Microsoft Exchange Server 2010 275
Administering Objects 276
   Administering Recipients 279
Managing Databases 309
   Microsoft Exchange Server 2007 310
   Microsoft Exchange Server 2010 310
   Finding Mailbox Database White Space 311
Discovering Space Used by Disabled Mailboxes 313
Managing Quotas 316
Managing Microsoft Exchange Server Remotely 320
Email Address Policies 322
Interoperating with Earlier Versions of Microsoft Exchange 324
   Microsoft Exchange Server 2007 325
   Microsoft Exchange Server 2010 326
Using Filters 328
   Using Client-Side Filters 328
   Using Server-Side Filters 329
Managing Recipient Scope 330
   Managing Scope in Microsoft Exchange Server 2007 331
   Managing Scope in Microsoft Exchange Server 2010 331

Contents

Managing Role Based Access Control..332
Introducing Microsoft Exchange Web Services 335
Summary 339

Chapter 13: Managing SQL Server 2008 R2 341

PowerShell Basics for SQL Server 341
Managing SQL Server Services 343
    Working with Snap-ins...344
    Working with Assemblies 345
    Changing the Service Account..346
Querying SQL Server...347
    Using a Quoted String to Query SQL Server......................................347
    Returning Data into a Datatable...348
    Using an Input File to Query SQL Server 349
Loading Data..350
    Loading SQL Server Data...350
    Loading Non-SQL Server Data 351
Getting SQL Server Information..351
    Getting Version Information 352
    Getting Service Pack Information 352
    Getting Instance Uptime Information 352
Gathering Performance Counters 354
Scripting Objects...357
Scheduling Windows PowerShell SQL Server Agent Job Steps.........................362
Getting Space Usage Information 363
    Getting Volume Space Usage 363
    Getting Database Space Usage..363
    Getting Table Space Usage...365
Managing Registrations in SQL Server Management Studio...........................366
    Leveraging Registrations to Query Multiple Registered Servers.............367
    Leveraging Registrations to Query Multiple Central
      Management Servers..369
Summary 369

Chapter 14: Managing Microsoft SharePoint 2010 Server 371

Installing and Using the Cmdlets..371
    SharePoint 2010 Management Shell 372
    PipeBind Parameters 372
    SPAssignment..372
Remoting with SharePoint 373
    Limitations of the SharePoint Cmdlets 373
    Memory Limits in WS-Man..373
Automating Site Administration 374
    Creating Site Collections 374
    Connecting to Sites 374
    Removing Sites 375

Contents

Using SharePoint Lists 375
   Browsing Lists. 375
   Viewing List Data 376
   Updating List Data 376
   Adding Items to a List. 376
   Working with Views 377
   Creating Lists 378
   List Settings 378
   Managing Permissions 378
   Managing Document Libraries 379
Creating a Web Application 381
Deploying Developer Code 381
Administering Workflows 382
   Manually Kicking Off Workflows 382
   Monitoring Workflows 382
   Cancelling Workflows. 383
Backing Up and Restoring. 384
   The Configuration Database 384
   Farms 385
   Site Collections 385
   Lists and Libraries 386
Search and Timer Jobs 386
   Modifying Crawls 387
   Kicking Off Crawls 387
Summary 388

Chapter 15: Managing Internet Information Services 7 389

Installing the Necessary Components 390
   Installing the Snap-in 390
   Installing the Web Server Role 390
   Loading the WebAdministration Cmdlets and Provider 391
   Installing the WMI Provider 392
Browsing IIS:\ 393
Scripting Deployments and Changes 394
   Using New-Item 394
   Creating Sites 395
   Creating Virtual Directories. 396
   Creating Web Applications 397
   Creating Application Pools 398
   Configuring SSL. 398
   Using the Provider to Make Changes 399
   Removing IIS Objects with the Cmdlets 400
   Advanced WebConfiguration Settings. 400
Managing IIS. 403
   Controlling IIS Services 404
   Backing Up and Restoring Configurations 405

Contents

Digesting Log Files..406
    ConvertFrom-Csv..406
    Filtering Tips 407
Summary 407

Chapter 16: Managing System Center Operations Manager 2007 R2 409

Exploring the Available Cmdlets 409
Working with Alerts 410
    Processing Alerts in Bulk 410
    Updating Custom Fields in Alert Properties in Bulk 413
Automating Maintenance Mode 415
    Adding and Removing Objects and Groups 415
    Automating Client-Side (Remote) Maintenance Mode.................417
Deploying and Configuring OpsMgr Agents and Network Devices 418
    Configuring Agent Failover Without AD Integration.................419
    Managing SNMP Device Failover 419
    Automating Agent Discovery and Deployment......................421
    Verifying Agent Load Balance Across Management Servers.................422
Exploring Discovered Inventory Data 423
    Enumerating Classes and Discovered Instances 423
    Enumerating Monitored Objects and Relationships 425
Windows PowerShell and the Command Notification Channel....................426
    Performing Simple Event and Log File Creation from
        the Command Channel 427
    Forwarding SNMP Traps with Windows PowerShell........................429
Overrides...431
    Retrieving and Converting Overrides into Readable
        Reporting Format 431
    Creating Overrides Programmatically...............................434
Notifications...435
    Enabling and Disabling Notifications...............................435
    Working with Notification Recipients 435
Monitoring Scripts in Windows PowerShell 436
Sample OpsMgr Scripts and Other Community Resources 437
    Where to Find and Share Samples on the Web.........................438
    Where to Find Free Support on Authoring Windows
        PowerShell Scripts for OpsMgr 438
Summary 439

Chapter 17: Managing Microsoft Deployment Toolkit 2010 441

Installing and Using the Cmdlets...441
    Exploring the MDT Windows PowerShell Provider 442
    Using the GUI to Create Your Scripts 442

Contents

Creating and Populating the Deployment Share 443
   Initializing the Deployment Share... 443
   Creating the MDT Database 444
   Importing Operating Systems... 444
   Importing Device Drivers 445
   Importing Applications 446
   Creating Task Sequences 449
Managing the Deployment Share.. 451
   Configuring the Deployment Share....................................... 451
   Updating the Deployment Share.. 452
   Managing Media 452
Summary 454

Chapter 18: Managing Citrix XenApp 6 .... **455**
Installing and Using the Cmdlets... 455
What's New in XenApp 6 456
Working with Administrators 456
   Retrieving Administrators.. 456
   Adding and Removing Administrators 457
   Enabling and Disabling Administrators 458
   Modifying Privileges 459
Providing Applications 462
   Retrieving Applications... 462
   Publishing New Applications.. 463
   Modifying Application Properties.. 465
   Importing/Exporting Applications....................................... 465
   Adding and Removing Assigned Accounts 466
   Removing and Disabling Applications 466
Managing Sessions 467
   Enumerating Sessions 467
   Managing Session Processes 469
   Managing Sessions 469
Maintaining Servers 470
   Managing Server Logons... 470
   Getting Server Load.. 471
   Managing Load Evaluators.. 471
   Changing Server Zones... 473
Applying Load-Balancing Policies 473
   Creating Load-Balancing Policies 473
   Configuring Load-Balancing Policies 474
   Applying Filters to Load-Balancing Policies 474
Worker Groups 475
   Adding and Removing Worker Groups 475
   Modifying Worker Groups 476
Summary 477

Contents

Chapter 19: Managing Citrix XenDesktop 5 . . . . **479**

Introducing Citrix XenDesktop 5 479

Examining the Windows PowerShell Tab 480

Exploring the Snap-Ins 481

Performing an Automated Environment Setup 481

Administrators 486

Explaining Access Control 486

Creating Administrators 487

Catalogs 488

Creating Catalogs 488

Managing Catalogs 496

Removing Catalogs 497

Provisioning 497

Introducing Machine Creation Services 498

Updating Master Images 498

Desktop Groups 499

Creating Desktop Groups 499

Creating Application Desktop Groups 502

Hosts 505

Hosts PSProvider 505

Adding Hosts 506

Removing Hosts 508

Summary 509

Part V: Virtualization and Cloud Computing   511

Chapter 20: Managing Hyper-V 2008 R2 . . . . **513**

Hyper-V Management Interfaces 513

WMI Management Classes 513

Windows PowerShell Management Library for Hyper-V 515

Managing Hosts 516

Retrieving Information 516

Using Show-HypervMenu 516

Managing Virtual Machines 517

Creating and Modifying Virtual Machines 517

Controlling Virtual Machines 518

Summary 521

**Chapter 21: Managing System Center Virtual Machine
Manager 2008 R2** **523**

Working with System Center Virtual Machine Manager 2008 R2 523

Installing and Loading the Cmdlets 523

Backing Up the VMM Database 524

Using the VMM Administrator Console to Write Scripts 524

Connecting to VMM 525

Working with Host Servers 526
    Adding Hosts to VMM 526
    Organizing Hosts 528
Managing Clusters 528
    Adding Clusters 528
    Performing Maintenance on Host Servers 530
Working with Virtual Machines 531
    Creating and Modifying Virtual Machines 531
    Removing Virtual Machines 535
    Controlling Virtual Machines 535
    Managing Checkpoints 536
Libraries 537
    Creating a Library 538
    Finding Dependent Objects 539
Summary 539

Chapter 22: Managing Windows Azure **541**
Installing and Using the Windows Azure Service Manager Cmdlets 541
    Installing the WASM Cmdlets 542
    Creating and Registering Your Certificate 542
Managing Hosted Services 544
    Getting Hosted Service Information 544
    Starting and Stopping Deployments 545
    Get-OperationStatus 546
    Deploying New Code 546
    Scaling Services 548
Managing Certificates 548
Windows Azure Diagnostics 549
    Getting Logging Configuration 549
    Configuring Logging 551
    Forcing Logs to Transfer to Storage 553
Summary 554

Chapter 23: Managing VMware vSphere PowerCLI **557**
Installing and Using the Cmdlets 557
    Installing PowerCLI 557
    Loading PowerCLI 558
    Connecting to a Host or vCenter Instance 558
    Retrieving Hosts and VMs 559
Managing ESX and ESXi 560
    Putting Hosts in Maintenance Mode 560
    Inspecting Host Properties 560
    Managing Storage 562
    Managing Host Networks 563
    Configuring NTP Servers 564
    Working with Host Profiles 565

Contents

Getting Logs 566
Gathering Performance Data from a Host. 567
Managing Virtual Machines 568
Deploying New VMs. 568
Removing VMs 569
Working with Virtual Hardware 569
Managing VM Resource Configuration 571
Updating VM Tools. 571
Starting and Stopping VMs. 572
Using Snapshots. 572
Invoking Scripts 573
Managing vCenter. 573
Clusters. 573
Migrating VMs 574
Managing Folders, Resource Pools, and Datacenters. 575
Getting Log Data 575
Getting Performance Data. 576
Everything Else. 576
Summary 577

Part VI: Beyond the Console — 579

Chapter 24: Creating User Interfaces 581
Working with Text Mode UI 581
Getting Credentials 582
Getting Strings. 583
Validating Input. 583
Building a Simple UI in Windows PowerShell Using Windows Forms 584
Using Windows Forms 585
Building a GUI with Windows Forms — the Basics 585
Using Windows Forms Controls. 586
Label Control 586
Button Control 588
Textbox Control. 589
Using Windows PowerShell and PrimalForms. 593
Using Windows Presentation Foundation 595
Summary 596

Chapter 25: Using the Windows PowerShell ISE 597
Key Features of the ISE. 597
Screen Layout. 598
Modifying the ISE Layout 606
Using the ISE. 607
The ISE as an Alternative to the Windows
PowerShell Console 607

Using the ISE to Edit Windows PowerShell Scripts/Modules..............607
ISE Profile Files 608
Debugging with the ISE 608
Setting and Using Breakpoints in the ISE................................609
Debugging 609
Extending the ISE...610
Overview of the ISE Object Model 610
What's in $PsISE 617
Sample Windows PowerShell ISE Add-On 620
Third-Party Alternatives to the ISE 620
Summary 622

Index **623**

Introduction

Welcome to *Windows PowerShell 2.0 Bible*. We hope that through reading this book and working through the sample code we provide, you will learn a great deal about using Windows PowerShell. This standard automation tool is sure to be one of the most useful tools in your administration toolbox. Join us as, together, we explore this powerful tool and how you can use it.

Overview of the Book and Technology

When the authors of this book got together to discuss the content of the book, we came to a consensus that this book had to follow a new direction. We wanted to create a book that was different from all of the existing Windows PowerShell books. And with "Bible" in the name, we knew we had to really step it up.

All of the existing Windows PowerShell books fell into one of two categories:

- Core fundamentals books that explained the Windows PowerShell language itself, but rarely demonstrated real-world application examples.
- Application-oriented books that explained how to use Windows PowerShell to manage a single specific application.

We wanted this book to be unique among all of the other Windows PowerShell books. We cover the core language fundamentals for users who are new to Windows PowerShell and/or Version 2, but we also take a selection of some of the most prevalent applications in the IT ecosystem and dedicate an entire chapter to them. This book serves as a reference guide for any system administrator managing Windows computers.

How This Book Is Organized

This book is organized into six parts. The first part of the book is the Introduction. This section covers the basics of the Windows PowerShell language as well as the new features added in the second version. If you are new to Windows PowerShell and/or Version 2, you should start at the beginning.

Part II covers the desktop environment. In this section, the focus of the chapters is the management of the Windows desktop and related technologies. Part III switches focus to the server side of things to provide a thorough coverage of Windows Server 2008 R2 and its various components, as well as coverage of server management.

Part IV looks at the applications that provide valuable additional capabilities to the server environment. Virtualization and the cloud are hot topics in the server space today, so an entire section is devoted to this topic in Part V.

Part VI takes Windows PowerShell beyond the console and shows some of the ingenious ways to use Windows PowerShell. It describes how to take advantage of the capabilities of a brand-new integrated scripting environment.

Part I: Introduction

Part I consists of Chapters 1 and 2 and covers Windows PowerShell basics. In Chapter 1, you are introduced to the key components of the Windows PowerShell language. Here, you learn the true power of the language. Next, in Chapter 2, you learn about the new enhancements to Windows PowerShell and how such a powerful tool can be made even better.

Part II: Windows Desktop

Part II consists of Chapters 3 through 6 and includes information for the management of desktop environments.

Chapter 3 focuses on the Windows 7 desktop operating system and how it can be effectively managed by Windows PowerShell. Chapter 4 covers Microsoft's office productivity suite, Office 2010. Chapter 5 discusses the always important topic of security. Finally, Chapter 6 demonstrates Windows PowerShell's various options for managing software on Windows operating systems.

Part III: Server Management

Part III consists of Chapters 7 through 11 and covers the management of Windows Server 2008 R2 and core infrastructure.

Beginning with Chapter 7, you learn about the core Windows Server 2008 R2 operating system. Chapters 8 and 9 cover server management starting with basic management concepts and proceeding to more advanced management. Chapter 10 demonstrates the advanced capability of managing Active Directory with Windows PowerShell. In Chapter 11, Active Directory management is extended with the management of Group Policy.

Part IV: Server Applications

Part IV consists of Chapters 12 through 19 and includes coverage of several applications that augment the server environment.

In Chapter 12, both Microsoft Exchange Server 2007 and Microsoft Exchange Server 2010 are covered. Chapter 13 covers SQL Server 2008 R2, and Chapter 14 covers the management of Microsoft SharePoint 2010 Server.

Chapter 15 expands to cover Internet Information Services (IIS). Chapter 16 enters the Microsoft System Center space with System Center Operations Manager (SCOM) 2007 R2. Chapter 17 discusses the Microsoft Deployment Toolkit 2010 and helps you manage your deployment scenarios.

Chapters 18 and 19 cover the two most popular technologies created by Citrix Systems, Inc. Chapter 18 covers the Citrix server application, Citrix XenApp 6, and Chapter 19 covers the still-hot Citrix XenDesktop 5.

Part V: Virtualization and Cloud Computing

Virtualization and cloud computing is a technology area that has seen tremendous growth and visibility in recent months. Chapters 20 through 23 cover key products in this area.

Chapter 20 deals with the Microsoft hypervisor Hyper-V, which is built into Windows Server 2008 R2 and only has to be enabled for you to begin using. System Center Virtual Machine Manager is Microsoft's enterprise solution for managing Hyper-V and is covered in Chapter 21.

Chapter 22 discusses Windows Azure, Microsoft's cloud-based solution for hosting applications. Chapter 23 presents on overview of how Windows PowerShell works as a scripting language for use with VMware's vSphere PowerCLI.

Part VI: Beyond the Console

Part VI introduces two key concepts that augment the scripts and the creation of scripts in Windows PowerShell. Chapter 24 demonstrates the task of creating user interfaces and Chapter 25 covers the Windows PowerShell ISE.

Who Should Read This Book

If you are someone who is interested in applying Windows PowerShell to real-world environments, *Windows PowerShell 2.0 Bible* is definitely a book you should read.

This book assumes that you have basic networking skills and a basic understanding of Windows. Chapter 1 covers the basics of Windows PowerShell so if you are just starting out, by all means, start at the beginning. Chapter 2 covers the new features introduced in Windows PowerShell Version 2 if you need a refresher on what's new.

Each of the remaining chapters covers an independent topic. Read through them to gain a thorough knowledge of the capabilities of Windows PowerShell in managing the different components and applications of the Windows environment. Or you can use each chapter as a reference for learning how to script against a specific topic.

Tools You Will Need

At the bare minimum, you will need Windows PowerShell 2.0 installed on your system.

For the desktop section, you will need Windows 7, which includes Windows PowerShell 2.0 built in. You can download a 90-day evaluation copy of Windows 7 Enterprise Edition from the Technet Evaluation Center at `http://technet.microsoft.com/en-us/evalcenter/cc442495`. To install the Windows 7 operating system from the download, you will need a system with the following general configuration:

- 1 GHz or faster 32-bit (x86) or 64-bit (x64) processor
- 1 GB of RAM (32-bit)/2 GB RAM (64-bit)
- 16 GB available disk space (32-bit)/20 GB (64-bit)
- DirectX 9 graphics processor with WDDM 1.0 or higher driver
- DVD-compatible drive
- Internet access (fees may apply)

For the server section, you will need Windows Server 2008 R2, which includes Windows PowerShell 2.0 built in. You can download a 180-day evaluation copy of Windows Server 2008 R2 from the Technet Evaluation Center at `http://technet.microsoft.com/en-us/evalcenter/ee175713.aspx`. To install Windows 2008 R2 from the download, you will need a system with the following general configuration:

- 1.4 GHz or faster 64-bit (x64) processor
- 512 MB of RAM
- 32 GB available disk space
- Super VGA (800 × 600) or higher-resolution monitor
- DVD-compatible drive
- Internet access (fees may apply)

Conventions Used in This Book

Throughout the book, special typography indicates code and commands. Commands and code are shown in a monospaced font:

```
This is how code looks.
```

In the event that an example includes both input and output, the monospaced font is still used, but input is presented in bold type to distinguish the two. Here's an example:

```
$ ftp ftp.handsonhistory.com
Name (home:jake): jake
Password: ******
```

In a number of examples, you'll see a variable in italics. The previous command might be displayed as the following:

```
$ ftp hostname
```

In this case, you should replace "hostname" with the name of a particular host on your network.

Finally, there are a number of examples in this book in which a block of code is followed by the result of that code. The code appears as it would in the examples above. The result of the code is what you would see returned on your screen and is displayed with a screen covering the code:

```
State            :  Connected
Connection State :  Connected
PowerState       :  PoweredOn
```

The following features are used to call your attention to points that are particularly important:

Note
A note box provides extra information to which you need to pay special attention. ■

Tip
A tip box shows a special way of performing a particular task. ■

Caution
A caution box alerts you to take special care when executing a procedure, or damage to your computer hardware or software could result. ■

Cross-Reference
A cross-reference box refers you to further information, outside the existing chapter, about a subject. ■

What's on the Website

The authoring team has taken great pains to provide a wide range of code samples throughout the book. We know how frustrating it can be to have to rekey lengthy code listings. So, we've provided them for you on the book's website at `www.wiley.com/go/windowspowershell2bible`. You'll find the code listings from the book as well as additional code examples and a variety of reference information.

Summary

We hope you will get your hands dirty and learn to manage many key software systems through Windows PowerShell. If you do, we know that you will come to appreciate the powerful tool at your disposal. Along the way, be sure to get involved in the Windows PowerShell community.

To help you further your PowerShell learning, we have included several key websites that will complement this book:

- Microsoft Script Center: `http://technet.microsoft.com/en-us/scriptcenter`
- PowerShell Groups: `http://powershellgroup.org/`
- The PowerShellCommunity.org: `http://powershellcommunity.org/`

You'll find them to be excellent resources. We look forward to seeing you on the forums and in the user groups.

Good luck!

Windows
PowerShell® 2.0 Bible

Part I

Introduction

IN THIS PART

Chapter 1
Introduction to Windows
PowerShell

Chapter 2
What's New in Windows
PowerShell V2

CHAPTER

1

Introduction to Windows PowerShell

W indows PowerShell is Microsoft's strategic administrative task automation platform. It began life over 10 years ago and has now become mainstream. Before looking at all of the wonderful things that Windows PowerShell can do, this chapter starts by looking at how we got here, and then examining what Windows PowerShell is. This includes a brief overview of the language and syntax of Windows PowerShell.

Cross-Reference

The contents of this chapter mainly refer to Windows PowerShell Version 1. Version 2 added some great new features, and those are described more in Chapter 2, "What's New in Windows PowerShell V2." The features described in this chapter are all contained within Version 2, so everything you learn in this chapter is fully usable in Version 2. ∎

Managing Windows — The Challenges of the Past

The path to Windows PowerShell has been a long but steady one that really started with the launch of the IBM PC in 1981. Since then management of systems has grown from something of a rarity to where we are today. This book starts by looking at where we have come from and the challenges that have arisen.

Management in the Early Days

Microsoft entered the PC operating system (OS) field in 1981, with the launch of the IBM PC. The original PC was a non-networked floppy

IN THIS CHAPTER

Managing Windows — the challenges of the past

Introducing Windows PowerShell

Understanding key Windows PowerShell concepts

Discovering by leveraging the community

Formatting with Windows PowerShell

Automating administrative functions with scripting

Extending Windows PowerShell with snap-ins and modules

Installing Windows PowerShell

Customizing Windows PowerShell with Profiles

disk–based machine. Those who had more than one machine managed by carrying around floppy disks, copying them as needed. There was no hard disk to hold either programs or data. Subsequent versions of the DOS operating system added hard disk support, and eventually, there was local area networking capability.

The growth in corporate networks was greatly enhanced by the introduction of Windows. But management was more an afterthought than designed as a feature. This, of course, led to tools like Symantec's Ghost to help to manage DOS and Windows systems. While the need to manage the systems was increasing, a number of architectural constraints of the older 16-bit architecture made this more difficult. And of course, at that time, Microsoft was not quite as focused on management as is the case today.

Management with Windows NT

The release of Windows NT 3.1 in the summer of 1993 marked a huge advance both in terms of the product and also the start of focusing on enterprise management. Not only was there a networking stack built in, but there was also a server version that enabled domains. In those days, most management tasks were conducted with GUI applications (for example, File Manager or User Manager). There was a rudimentary shell with a few commands, but coverage was far from complete.

Subsequent releases of NT (Windows NT 3.5 and 3.51) added features, but there was no real change in the overall management approaches within Windows NT itself. Microsoft was embarking on the creation of the Systems Management Server, but the creation of what we now know as System Center Configuration Manager took a number of years.

By the release of Windows 2000, some things had begun to change. Microsoft was pushing hard into the enterprise market where manageability was a prerequisite. As any Unix administrator would tell you, to manage large numbers of systems, you need automated scripting. To some degree, it felt like the mandate changed from "You manage from the GUI" to "You manage from the GUI and the command line." There was finally some acceptance that all those Unix guys had been right all along. But management was still very much piecemeal, with no overarching strategy or consistent toolset.

For Windows 2000, and more so for Windows Server 2003 and Windows XP, there was a push for command-line parity. If you can do something from the GUI, you should be able to do it from the command line. This led to a plethora of command-line tools from each different product group and subgroup. This change was highly welcome, of course, but not without challenges. None of the tools resembled any of the other tools, so what you learned about one was definitely not transferrable.

Management with Windows Server 2003

During the Windows 2003 days, things continued on — much as with Windows 2000 — but with improved feature parity between the command line and GUI. There were really no fundamental changes in the approach to managing Windows desktop and server systems, at least for public consumption.

By the time Microsoft released XP and Windows Server 2003, the very earliest version of Windows PowerShell, or Monad as it was then called, had begun to surface. But Monad wasn't really enterprise-ready. Some groups within Microsoft began talking up this new approach, but the mainstream audiences were not taking much heed at that point.

Another key aspect of managing this generation of systems was the huge number of Group Policies added into the client OS (XP). Microsoft also beefed up the Windows Management Instrumentation (WMI) components, although to some degree, this was probably more useful to folks writing management tools than to IT professionals.

During this time period, Microsoft was pushing Systems Management Server (SMS, later to be renamed System Center Configuration Manager), which was homegrown, as well as Microsoft Operations Manager (renamed later to System Center Operations Manager), which Microsoft acquired from a purchase. However, in those days, the individual products (that is, Operations Manager and SMS) were very distinct and separate products. The package we now recognize as Systems Center, and the other members of the family, were still some years off.

Introducing Windows PowerShell

To some degree, the death knell of the Management By GUI age was the publication of the Monad Manifesto in August 2002. You can download this document from `http://blogs` `.msdn.com/b/powershell/archive/2007/03/19/monad-manifesto-the-origin-of-` `windows-powershell.aspx`.

The manifesto suggested that the key issue was the lack of "administrator-oriented composable tools to type commands and automate management," which were the domain of scripting languages. The main scripting tools of the day, however, worked by using "very low level abstractions such as complex object models, schemas and APIs."

The paper goes on to suggest a broad architecture of components. Though a lot of details have changed since that document was written, Windows PowerShell today delivers on the promise.

A year later, in September 2003, Microsoft demonstrated Monad in public for the first time at the Professional Developers Conference. Though it took a number of years to get from Monad to where Windows PowerShell is today, the result has made the journey worthwhile.

What Is Windows PowerShell?

Before you begin to use Windows PowerShell, you must understand a bit about it. This section takes a look at what Windows PowerShell is and what it contains.

Windows PowerShell as a Task Automation Platform

Windows PowerShell is, first and foremost, Microsoft's strategic administrative task automation platform. It aims to help the administrator, the IT professional, to manage all aspects of a Windows system and the applications that run on them as efficiently as possible, both locally and remotely. Such a tool needs to be focused on the administrator and work with high-level task-oriented abstractions. For example, rather than worrying about bits inside a file, the tool should work at the level of a user, process, service, and so on.

Since 2009, Windows PowerShell has been a part of Microsoft's Common Engineering Criteria (CEC) for Windows and Windows applications. The CEC mandates that all new applications and all parts of Windows must have at least adequate Windows PowerShell support. If a product or component does not meet those criteria, it does not ship. At least that's the theory.

Note
You can read more about the CEC and look at the details and scorecards at Microsoft's Common Engineering website: www.microsoft.com/cec/en/us/cec-overview.aspx. ∎

Windows PowerShell has several components:

- **Rich administrative shell:** On a par with the best of Unix shells in terms of both ease of use and power
- **Powerful scripting language:** As rich and powerful as Perl, Ruby, and VBScript
- **Production orientation:** Aimed at IT professionals running large enterprise environments where there is a strong need for secure, robust, and scalable scripting
- **Focus on Windows and Windows applications:** Works across all supported versions of Windows and has to support all the applications

Although not stated in the Monad Manifesto, but noted at the first public outing of Monad a year later, there was also a need for a rich, vibrant community. The community needed to, and indeed has, focused Microsoft on doing the right things with Windows PowerShell and has filled the gaps in terms of additional features you can just plug into Windows PowerShell. The staggering support provided by the community is nothing short of amazing.

This book examines every aspect of Windows PowerShell and shows you the product, warts and all. But before diving deep, it's necessary to review some of the key concepts behind Windows PowerShell. If you are new to Windows PowerShell, you should take the time to read this, but if you have a good basic understanding of Windows PowerShell, feel free to skip over this next section.

Windows PowerShell's Scripting Language

Windows PowerShell provides both a shell and a shell scripting language. In the Windows PowerShell console, you can enter individual lines of Windows PowerShell's language constructs (for example, `Create-AdUser`, to create a new Active Directory account). But you can also add a number of Windows PowerShell statements together into a script file to automate more complex administrative tasks such as provisioning a user into your environment (creating the Active Directory account, adding a SharePoint Site, adding the users to groups, and so on).

Windows PowerShell's language is broadly based on C#, with concepts (for example, the pipeline) taken from other great scripting languages. Windows PowerShell is, as Microsoft points out, "on the glide scope" to C#. If you know Windows PowerShell, then reading C# should be relatively straightforward and vice versa. Having said that, a number of constructs in C# have not been added to Windows PowerShell because the focus of the two languages is quite different: C# is aimed at professional programmers building applications, whereas Windows PowerShell is aimed at IT professionals who manage those applications.

Later, this chapter presents the basics of this language. The description is brief and provides only the basics. To really understand and use Windows PowerShell, you need practice. Later chapters expand on the introduction you get in this chapter.

In writing this book, the authors wish to concentrate on using and leveraging Windows PowerShell in Windows, and all the key applications you're likely to run into. To avoid hundreds of pages describing the details of the syntax and language in minute detail, we prefer to let you refine that on the job. What follows here are the basics of the Windows PowerShell language.

Note

Microsoft has done a fantastic job in adding great documentation on Windows PowerShell's fundamentals into the product. You can find these topics by typing `Get-Help about_*` at the Windows PowerShell prompt. There are more than 90 help files that contain great details of each of the specific language features, including examples. ∎

Windows PowerShell in Production Scripts and Admin GUIs

Windows PowerShell was designed for use both at the command line and in production-oriented scripts. This requirement gives rise to the need to be very pithy at the command-line console while verbose and rich in a production script. At the command line, you can issue terse commands, making use of Windows PowerShell's alias and parameter naming conventions, which enable you to specify only the minimum. In production-oriented scripts, spelling things out in full, along with providing rich validation and error-handling features, becomes much more important.

Another aspect of Windows PowerShell is the ability to use it in building GUI administration tools. In this approach, the key administrative functions are actually built as cmdlets. The GUI just gathers enough data to call these cmdlets and then renders the output. This enables you to create a simple GUI for the most common administrative tasks, which are often performed by less skilled individuals. The less common administrative tasks, which are usually performed by more skilled administrators, are carried out solely using cmdlets.

A great example of this is Microsoft Exchange. With Exchange 2007 and Exchange 2010, the GUI (the Exchange Management Console) is relatively simple (certainly when compared with the Microsoft Management Console snap-in that was included in earlier versions of

Microsoft Exchange!). Adding a mailbox, for example, is done by the GUI gathering the information (mailbox name and so on) and constructing a call to the New-Mailbox cmdlet. The output from this cmdlet is then returned to Exchange. Exchange can then show the results (i.e., an updated list of mailboxes).

With Exchange, at any rate, the command issued to create a new mailbox is shown once the administrative action is complete. This allows you to copy it and then use it as the basis for writing scripts to add more users. Other products, notably Microsoft Lync Server 2010, do not provide such a feature. But in both cases, everything you can do at the GUI can be done from a Windows PowerShell console. And from the Windows PowerShell console, you can do more than you can in the GUI.

Next, you take a look at the concepts of Windows PowerShell and how you can take advantage of them.

Key Windows PowerShell Concepts

Within Windows PowerShell are three core conceptual pillars: cmdlets, objects, and the pipeline. It's hard to talk about one without talking about the other two, so the definitions of these pillars, these key concepts, intertwine to some degree.

Cmdlets

A *cmdlet* is a small bit of executable code that performs some administrative task such as deleting a file, adding a user, or changing the registry. Cmdlets are named with a verb-noun syntax with strict guidelines for verb naming. An example cmdlet is Get-Process, which returns information about processes running on a machine.

To ensure consistency, the set of verbs that developers can use is restricted through the use of formal guidance (and runtime checking that emits an error if unapproved verbs are used in a cmdlet). That helps to ensure that the "get" verb has the same semantics in Active Directory as in Exchange — and that's the same semantics for Get-Process.

Cmdlet nouns can vary more because they are task-specific. A cmdlet's noun, however, should always be singular, possibly with a prefix to avoid *collision* (where two product groups produce similarly named cmdlets that do potentially different things). Quest's Active Directory tools use the noun prefix QAD, whereas Microsoft's Active Directory cmdlets use the prefix AD. So, although both cmdlet sets provide a way to get a user in the AD, Quest's tool uses Get-QADuser, whereas Microsoft's cmdlet is Get-AdUser.

To some degree, learning the verbs Windows PowerShell uses for any given task domain is easy — these are standard (Get, New, Remove, and so on). What differs are the nouns, which are in effect the task domain objects. Thus, in Active Directory (AD), you work with users (Get-AdUser), groups (Get-AdGroup), and domains (Get-AdDomain), whereas in Lync

Server you work with topology (`Enable-CSTopology`), analog device (`Get-CSAnalogDevice`), location policy (`Get-CSLocationPolicy`), and so on.

Cmdlets can have aliases — shortcut names to simplify typing, particularly at the command prompt. Thus, `GPS` is an alias for `Get-Process`. Windows PowerShell comes with some built-in aliases, but you can easily add your own aliases in profile files that run each time you run Windows PowerShell.

Cmdlets can take parameters that tell the cmdlet how to work. The `Get-Process` cmdlet has a property, `-Name`, which is used to tell Windows PowerShell the name of the processes you want information about. Cmdlet property names always begin with a hyphen (-) and are separated from the parameter value and other parameters by a space.

Windows PowerShell provides you with *parameter value globbing*; that is, specifying a parameter value with wildcards to match potentially more than one object. Thus, you could issue the cmdlet `Get-Process -Name P*W` to get all the processes that begin with a "p" and have a "w" somewhere later in the process name.

Parameter full names, which can get long in some cases, can also be abbreviated. Windows PowerShell lets you use the fewest number of characters necessary to distinguish one parameter name from all the others.

Objects

Cmdlets consume and produce objects — we say Windows PowerShell is object-oriented. An *object* is a computer representation of some tangible thing, such as a process running on a computer, or a user in the Active Directory. The `Get-Process` cmdlet produces a set of zero, one, or more process objects. In the absence of any direction from you, Windows PowerShell renders the objects produced onto the screen in a format defined by Microsoft.

An object has some definition, or class, that defines what each object occurrence contains. `Get-Process` produces objects belonging to the .NET class `System.Diagnostics.Process`. A cmdlet can produce zero, one, or more occurrences of the class — `Get-Process` can return any number of process instances, each representing a single process.

Note

Windows Powershell is built on top of .NET, but you don't need to be a .NET expert to use Windows PowerShell. As you learn more about Windows PowerShell, you will naturally learn more about .NET, including the details of .NET objects. ■

Class instances have members that include properties, methods, and events. A *property* is some attribute of the instance, for example, the CPU time used by a particular process. A *method* is some function that the class knows how to do on an instance; for example, to kill a specific process, you could call that instance's `Kill()` method. *Events* are specific things that an object can trigger and that you detect using `Register-ObjectEvent`.

Classes can also have both static methods and static properties. These are properties and methods of the class in general as opposed to a particular instance. For example, the `[System.Int32]` class has a static property called `MaxValue`, which is the largest value of a 32-bit integer. This class also contains a static method called `TryParse`, which attempts to parse a string into a 32-bit value (and returns a value to indicate if the parsing was successful).

Note

For some help on objects, type `Get-Help About_Objects` in Windows PowerShell. ■

The Pipeline

The pipeline is a device in Windows PowerShell that takes the output objects produced by one cmdlet and uses them as input to another cmdlet. For example, taking the output of `Get-Process` and sending it to `Sort-Object` to change the order of the process objects would look like this in Windows PowerShell:

```
Get-Process -Name * | Sort-Object -Property Handles
```

The pipeline is not really a new concept. The Unix and Linux operating systems have had this feature for decades. However, with Unix/Linux, the pipeline is most often used to pass just text — with Windows PowerShell, the pipeline uses objects. That means when the `Sort-Object` cmdlet in this pipeline gets a set of process objects to sort, it can tell exactly what kind of object is being passed and precisely where to find the field(s) to sort on (that is, it knows what the `Handles` property is and how to sort it).

By comparison, with Unix, you'd need to take the text output produced by one command and do some text parsing, often called prayer-based parsing, and hopefully get the right answer. Thanks to a cool feature in .NET called Reflection, a cmdlet can look at actual objects passed and not have to rely on pure text parsing.

Note

See www.codeproject.com/KB/dotnet/Reflection.aspx for more information on reflection. ■

The pipeline is an amazingly powerful construct, although it does take a bit of time for many administrators to understand the concept and to start to use it efficiently.

Note

For more information on the pipeline in Windows PowerShell, type `Get-Help About_Pipeline` in Windows PowerShell. ■

Discovery and the Community

Discovery is a central component of Windows PowerShell, because it enables you to find out more about Windows PowerShell by using it. Windows PowerShell is in many ways self-documenting, which is of huge benefit to new and seasoned users alike.

Windows PowerShell includes three key discovery-related cmdlets: Get-Help and Get-Command. Get-Help displays help information about Windows PowerShell cmdlets and Windows PowerShell concepts and Get-Command gets basic information about cmdlets and other commands. A third cmdlet, Get-Member, enables you to harness .NET's reflection capability to see what's inside an object.

Get-Help

The Get-Help cmdlet provides a good introduction to individual Windows PowerShell cmdlets. Get-Help provides details on each cmdlet, including how it works, its syntax, parameter information, and examples of the cmdlet in use.

Get-Help can also provide information about Windows PowerShell concepts. More than 90 built-in "About_" files describe Windows PowerShell language constructs and concepts. The conceptual help built into Windows PowerShell is an important part of discovery — Get-Help really is your friend!

Every cmdlet in Windows PowerShell supports the -? switch, which gives basic help information about that cmdlet. This enables you to type the following to get basic help information about the Get-Process cmdlet:

```
Get-Process -?
```

Get-Command

The Get-Command cmdlet returns related, but different, discovery information. With Get-Command, you can find out the names of the command that meet a certain criteria, such as having a particular verb or noun, or coming from a particular add-in module.

For example, to find the name of the cmdlets that have a "Get" verb, you could type:

```
Get-Command -Verb Get
```

To find all the cmdlets that were added when you imported the Bitstransfer module (a set of cmdlets shipped with Windows 7 and Windows Server 2008 R2), you could type:

```
Import-Module BitsTransfer
Get-Command -Module BitsTransfer
```

Note

Modules and the Import-Module cmdlet are features that are added with Version 2. Modules provide a simple way of adding new sets of cmdlets into Windows PowerShell. Get-Command provides a great way to discover the cmdlets added by a particular module. ∎

If you are about to start using some new module, one key way to discover the nouns that belong to the module, such as `BitsTransfer`, is to type:

```
Get-Command -Module BitsTransfer | Group-Object -Property Noun |↵
 Sort-Object Count -Descending
Count Name              Group
----- ----              -----
    7 BitsTransfer      {Complete-BitsTransfer, Get-BitsTransfer...}
    1 BitsFile          {Add-BitsFile}
```

Get-Member

The `Get-Member` is another key discovery-based cmdlet. `Get-Member` takes any object and tells you what's inside. Thus, if you pipe the output of `Get-Process` to `Get-Member`, Windows PowerShell returns details about the members of the `System.Diagnostic.Process` objects that are produced by `Get-Member`. This description includes the methods and properties supported by that object. By piping an unfamiliar object to `Get-Member`, you can discover what it contains and how to interact with it.

The Windows PowerShell Community

Windows PowerShell was designed from the outset to be extensible. The Windows PowerShell team alone could not produce all the cmdlets needed to manage Windows and all the Windows applications. From the very beginning, Windows PowerShell had an add-in model, the `PsSnapin`, that enabled developers to create new cmdlets and other extensions. A developer could write a Windows PowerShell snap-in, known as a `PsSnapin`, in a .NET language, typically C#. This could then be loaded and used on any system that has Windows PowerShell loaded. Writing cmdlets was relatively easy and developers both inside and outside Microsoft jumped at the challenge.

With Version 2 of Windows PowerShell, Microsoft added a new model for adding functionality into Windows PowerShell: the module. A module enables you to do nearly everything a snap-in could, but also enables you to write what are in effect script cmdlets — functions that act like fully featured cmdlets. These functions could be used standalone as well as in a pipeline, and could support the `Get-Help` facilities noted earlier.

The community has produced a number of outstanding additions to Windows PowerShell — a full description of all the various add-ons would require a small book! Two noteworthy examples are the PowerShell Community Extension (PSCX) and the Quest AD tools. PSCX adds a number of highly useful cmdlets, for example, a set that works with Microsoft's message queuing feature. An even larger add-in was the Windows PowerShell Pack, a mega-module that shipped as part of the Windows 7 resource kit (and is available for free for download). This add-in provides hundreds of additional functions for use in a variety of situations.

Note

You can get the PowerShell Community Extensions from `http://pscx.codeplex.com`, the Quest tools from `www.quest.com/powershell/activeroles-server.aspx`, and the PowerShellPack from `http://archive .msdn.microsoft.com/PowerShellPack`. ∎

The community is also a valuable resource for any IT professional or any Windows PowerShell user when they come up with questions or issues. A variety of community websites have sprung up that offer forums to help Windows PowerShell users. Third-party sites include `www.Powershell.com`, `www.PowerShellCommunity.org`, and `www.PowerGui.org`. A key Microsoft-sponsored site is The Scripting Guys Official Forum at `http://social.technet.microsoft.com/Forums/en/ITCG/threads`.

In addition, countless blogs and other areas provide great community support. Pretty much anywhere someone can ask a question, or provide an answer to a question, you'll find passionate Windows PowerShell advocates. This includes Twitter, the microblogging site, where you can ask simple questions and get answers in near–real time.

As with other Microsoft technologies, Microsoft has rewarded a number of Windows PowerShell community members with the coveted Microsoft Most Valuable Professional (MVP) award. If there's somewhere someone can add to the Windows PowerShell evangelism, you'll probably find MVPs!

The community has played, and continues to play, a vital role in both guiding the future of Windows PowerShell and in providing great resources to anyone who wants, or needs, to find out more.

Windows PowerShell Language Constructs

As with any scripting or programming language, there is an underlying set of language constructs you need to learn in order to use Windows PowerShell. You can divide these into two broad camps: the basics of Windows PowerShell when operating from the keyboard, and the extra features you use when writing production-oriented scripts. This section introduces the key concepts.

Variables

Like most languages, Windows PowerShell supports the concept of a *variable*, a named object you assign a value to and then use in other aspects of Windows PowerShell. Variables are indicated in a script or from the command line by a $ and a variable name. Thus, `$A` and `$ThisIsALongVariable` are both variables.

To assign a value to a variable, you use the assignment operator =. The following are examples of creating variables:

```
$MagicNumber = 42
$MyName = "Rebecca Marie"
$Files = Get-ChildItem C:\PowerShellScripts
```

The first example sets a variable to the value of 42. Windows PowerShell sets the value of $MyName to the string "Rebecca Marie" in the second example, and in the third example, the $Files variable (which most Windows PowerShell users just call $files) gets the output of Get-ChildItem cmdlet on a particular folder.

In Windows PowerShell, you can use a variable to hold any sort of object, from simple objects like numbers or strings to more complex objects like a Windows service or process, In fact, because the data types come from .NET, a variable can hold any .NET data type you assign to the variable. In .NET, each object you can create is known as a *class*. Classes are at the core of .NET, and you use them all the time with Windows PowerShell to do all the detailed work.

In the first part of the preceding example, Windows PowerShell sets the type of $MagicNumber to be a 32-bit integer, System.Int32, and in the second example, Windows PowerShell sets the type to string, or more formally, System.String. The third example is a little harder because a folder can hold two different types of .NET objects: folders (System.IO.DirectoryInfo) and files (System.IO.FileInfo). In these three cases, Windows PowerShell works out what is the most appropriate type for a given assignment.

If you want to override the type, you can specify the type name explicitly. To assign a value of 42 to $MagicNumber, but have that number be a 64-bit integer (to enable the use of much larger numbers), you would use:

```
[System.Int64] $BigMagicNumber = 424242424242424242
```

If you create a variable in this way, you cannot assign another type (for example, System.Int32) to the variable because the type is set for the duration of the Windows PowerShell session.

Note

For more help on variables, type **Get-Help about_Variables** in Windows PowerShell. ∎

Operators

Operators act on variables and constants to produce new values that you can use in Windows PowerShell scripts either to control the flow of execution or to assign to a variable. Like most programming and scripting languages, Windows PowerShell supports a rich set of operators, which include:

- **Arithmetic operators:** These operators perform basic arithmetic on numeric types and include + (addition), – (subtraction), * (multiplication), \ (division), and % (modulo). Note that you can add two strings and you can multiply a string by a number. See the about_Arithmetic_Operators help file for more information on these operators.

- **Assignment operators:** These operators assign the value of an expression to a variable. Assignment operators include = (simple assignment) and +=, -=, *=, /=,

and `%=`. The latter operators assign a variable the value of that variable plus the expression to the right of the assignment operator. `$s += 10`, for example, adds 10 to the value of `$s` and assigns the results back to `$s`. You can use the same approach to multiply (`$a *= 3`), subtract (`$a -= 32`) or divide (`$a /+ 10`). See the `about_Assignment_Operators` help file for more information on these operators.

- **Comparison operators:** These operators compare two expressions and return true (if the two expressions compare appropriately) or false. The comparison operators include `-eq` (equal), `-ne` (not equal), `-lt` (less than), `-ge` (greater than or equal), `-like` (wildcard match), `-notlike` (wildcard nonmatch), `-match` (regular expression match), `-notmatch` (regular expression nonmatch), `-band` (Boolean and), `-bor` (Boolean or), `-bxor` (Boolean `exclusive or`) and `-bnot` (Boolean not). See the `about_Comparison_Operators` help file for more information on these operators.

- **Logical operators:** These enable you to build more complex expressions and include `-and`, `-or`, `-xor` (exclusive or), and `-not` (the alias for `-not` is `!`). See the `about_Logical_Operators` help file for more information on these operators.

Windows PowerShell also has a number of more specialized operators, as follows:

- **Redirection operators:** These operators enable you to redirect output to a file and include `>` (send output to a file), `>>` (append output to a file), `2>` (send error stream to a file), `2>>` (append error stream to a file), and `2>&1` (send error and regular output to the same file). See the `about_Redirection` help file for more information on the redirection operators.

- **Split operator:** This operator splits one or more strings into substrings. See the `about_Split` help file for more detail on the `Split` operator.

- **Join operator:** This operator joins one or more strings. See the `about_Join` help file for more information on this operator.

- **Type operators:** These operators enable you to check if a variable or expression is (or is not) of a particular type, and to convert an expression to another type. See the `about_type_operators` help file for more details on the type operators.

- **Contains operator:** This operator returns true if an element is contained within an array, or false otherwise. For more information on arrays and the contains operator, see the `about_Arrays` help file.

- **Unary operators:** These two operators (`++` and `--`) add and subtract one from a variable and store the result back into the variable. `$a++` is the same as `$a=$a+1` (and `$a+=1`), and `$a −` is the same as `$a=$a=1` (or `$a-=1`).

- **Format operator:** The `-f` operator is used to format a composite format string, which precedes the `-f` operator using values from the array following the operator.

Expressions

An *expression* is a set of operators and operands that result in a value. An *operand* is some value that an operator can act on. Adding two numbers involves two operands (the numbers) and an operand (that tells Windows PowerShell to add the two numbers).

In some cases, the resultant value can be a simple Boolean (that is, either true or false), and in other cases it may be a numeric or some other value. Like most modern programming languages, you can affect the order of calculation by enclosing sub-expressions in parentheses. For example, here are some simple expressions:

```
$a=1; $b = $a * 10          # $b is assigned an expression based on the
                            # value of $a
$a -gt 100 -or $b -le 21    # expression is true if a is more than
                            # or $b is less than 22.
-not  (1,2,3) -contains 3   # returns false
$area = $pi * ($radius *$radius) # area of a circle with a radius of $radius
```

Wildcards (–like) and Regular Expressions (–match)

As noted earlier, Windows PowerShell provides two types of special string comparison operators, -like and -match (plus their alter egos of -notlike and -notmatch). The -like and -notlike operators compare a string with a wildcard string returning true if there is a match. The -match and -notmatch operators do much the same thing, but match against a .NET regular expression. If you are not familiar with regular expressions, they are explained later in this chapter.

You can specify wildcards to match on both one or multiple characters and also range. In addition to "*" to match zero or more characters, and "?" to match either zero or one character, Windows PowerShell wildcards also enable you to specify a range of characters [a-b] or a set of characters [asfl] to compare. Here are some examples:

```
'Cookham' -like 'C*'                 # true
'Cookham' -like 'Cook*'              # true
'Cookham' -like 'C*kh?m'             # true
'Cookham' -like 'C[aeiou][a-o]?ham'  # true
```

Windows PowerShell also supports the -match and -notmatch operators, which perform regular expression matching. Regular expressions are a way of specifying rich pattern-matching criteria that Windows PowerShell can use to match (or not) against another string. People are easily able to differentiate strings like doctordns@gmail.com, 131.107.2.200, and \\lon-dc1\documents\letter.docx. Simple wildcards are not adequate to do this sort of rich pattern matching. Instead, Windows PowerShell uses .NET regular expressions.

For example:

```
'rmlt@psp.co.uk' -match '[A-Z0-9._%+-]+@[A-Z0-9.-]+\.[A-Z]{2,4}' # true
'131.107.2.200' -match '\d{1,3}\.\d{1,3}\.\d{1,3}\.\d{1,3}' # true
```

Note

Regular expressions are a valuable skill and are complex in their own right. To learn more about regular expressions, see the `About_RegularExpressions` help file. Also take a look at `www.regular-expressions .info` for a tutorial on regular expressions, as well as a wealth of examples. ∎

Case Sensitivity — or Not

For the most part, Windows is a case-insensitive operating system, in regard to the various names and naming conventions used (for example, DNS names, NetBios names, filenames, registry key names, and UPN names, to name a few). With very few exceptions, names are case-insensitive. Windows does remember the case used and tries to preserve it for display purposes, but in operation, Windows does not differentiate on the basis of case. That means that a filename `C:\FOO\FooBarXXyyXX.txt` is the "same" as `c:\foo\foobarxxyyxx.TXT`. The exceptions to case-insensitivity are small (you run across one case when accessing Windows Active Directory using the ADSI interface).

Because Windows is, in effect, case-insensitive, it makes sense that, by default, Windows PowerShell should be case-insensitive. And it is. The various comparison operators noted earlier are case-insensitive. And in most cases, that makes sense. Most scripters use the default comparison operators, which are case-insensitive. This can confuse users who have more experience with Unix and Linux, where case sensitivity does matter.

For most administrative tasks in Windows and Microsoft applications, case sensitivity is rarely important, although there may be cases where it does matter. Windows PowerShell caters to those instances by providing case-sensitive versions of all the comparison operators. This is done by adding a "c" to the start of the operator, to give us `-ceq` (case-sensitive equal), `-cne` (not equal), `-clt` (less than), `-cge` (greater than or equal), `-clike` (wildcard match), `-cnotlike` (wildcard nonmatch), `-cmatch` (regular expression match), and `-cnotmatch` (regular expression nonmatch).

But case sensitivity does not end there. Because you have the ability to explicitly state case sensitivity in a comparison operation, there's an argument that says you should have the ability to explicitly perform operations in a case-insensitive way. There is some symmetry (being able to explicitly compare with case-insensitivity and case-sensitivity). To support that, Windows PowerShell uses an "i" instead of a "c" at the start of each operator; thus, you have `-ieq` (case-sensitive equal), `-ine` (not equal), `-ilt` (less than), `-ige` (greater than or equal), `-ilike` (wildcard match), `-inotlike` (wildcard nonmatch), `-imatch` (regular expression match), and `-inotmatch` (regular expression nonmatch).

This is demonstrated in the example here:

```
'a' -eq 'A'                    # True
'a' -ceq 'A'                   # False
'a' -ieq 'A'                   # True
'COOKHAM' -eq  'cookham'       # True
'COOKHAM' -ceq 'cookham'       # False
'COOKHAM' -ieq 'cookham'       # True
```

```
'COOKHAM' -like  'c*'          # True
'COOKHAM' -clike 'c*'          # False
'Cookham' -ilike 'c*'          # True
```

Providers

Providers are Windows PowerShell data access components that provide a consistent interface to different data stores. This enables you to use a consistent set of cmdlets to access any data store for which a provider exists. Windows PowerShell comes with a set of Providers, including:

- **Alias:** Provides access to the set of cmdlet aliases you have defined (using `New-Alias` or `Set-Alias`)
- **Environment:** Provides access to the Windows environment variables set on your computer
- **FileSystem:** Provides access to the file store in a way similar to how both Unix shells and the Windows `cmd.exe` program display the file store
- **Function:** Provides access to the set of functions defined on your computer
- **Registry:** Provides access to the Windows registry
- **Variable:** Provides access to the set of variables in use
- **Certificate:** Provides access to the certificate store

Each provider enables you to create provider-specific drives. When you use them, Windows PowerShell accesses the different underlying data stores. To see Windows PowerShell's Provider coverage, try running the following on your computer:

```
Cd c:\
Dir
Ls
Get-ChildItem
Cd hkcu:
Ls
Cd cert:
Ls
Ls alias:dir
```

Note

For more information on Providers, see the `about_Providers` built-in help file. ■

Formatting Output

Unlike other scripting or programming languages, such as VBScript, Windows PowerShell was designed from the outset to create output by default, thus keeping the user from having to do a lot of work to get sensible output. This can dramatically simplify both command-line ad hoc usage as well as production scripts. You can also override Windows PowerShell's default formatting to create as complex an output as you might wish to.

Default Formatting

Whenever you run a cmdlet/pipeline/script, that action can leave objects in the pipeline. For example, when you call `Get-Process` on its own, you leave a set of process objects in the pipeline. Even just typing the name of a Windows PowerShell variable leaves object(s) in the pipeline (that is, the object contained in the pipeline). In such cases, Windows PowerShell attempts to format the objects using a set of simple rules that are supported by customizable XML.

Windows PowerShell supports formatting XML, which describes how a particular object class should be output, by default. Additionally, Windows PowerShell supports type XML, which can state the properties that are to be output when a given object is displayed (the type XML includes the properties to be output and not the specific format to be used). Microsoft's default formatting and type XML are loaded each time you run Windows PowerShell and provide a good default starting set. You can, of course, write your own to either add to or improve what Windows PowerShell does by default.

When Windows PowerShell finishes a pipeline (which can be one or more commands), it looks to see if any objects are left over. If so, Windows PowerShell first looks at the loaded format XML to see if there is a view of the objects (in the pipeline). For example, if you run `Get-Process`, Windows PowerShell produces a set of `System.Diagnostics.Process` objects. Windows PowerShell would then look to see if there is a view that's been defined of these objects in any of the loaded format XML files. If so, that view is chosen and defines how Windows PowerShell formats the remaining objects.

If there are no view declarations, Windows PowerShell has to work out how to format the properties. Via the .NET reflection capability, Windows PowerShell can "see" what objects are in the pipeline and what properties they have, so this is relatively straightforward.

If there is a `PropertySet` declaration in any of the registered type XML files, this defines the specific properties to be displayed. If there is no `PropertySet` declaration, Windows PowerShell uses all the properties in the objects.

Finally, Windows PowerShell has to work out whether to format the objects in a table or a list. If the number of properties to be displayed is four or less, Windows PowerShell formats them as a table; with five or more, Windows PowerShell formats the objects as a list. When formatting a list, Windows PowerShell, by default, determines the width to be used for each column (unless there is display XML that specifies a specific column width). Windows PowerShell also uses the property name as the column header.

When formatting the `System.Diagnostics.Process` objects, Windows PowerShell discovers a view for that object class in one of the predefined format XML files that directs Windows PowerShell to generate a table with a set of predefined properties. This format

XML also gets Windows PowerShell to perform some calculations on the underlying property, for example, displaying the virtual memory used by a process in megabytes (versus bytes) to improve readability.

Formatting Using Format-Table and Format-List

When composing a pipeline, rather than leaving objects in the pipeline for Windows PowerShell to format by default, you can pipe them to either `Format-Table` or `Format-List`. This enables you to override the properties displayed, their order, and whether to display the objects as a table or list.

With both `Format-Table` and `Format-List`, you specify the specific properties to be displayed. Thus, you could do the following:

```
Get-Process -Name * | ↵
Format-Table -Property ProcessName, StartTime, Workingset64, CPU
```

This would produce the output you see in Figure 1-1.

FIGURE 1-1

Formatting a table with Format-Table

As you can see, this simple pipeline produces a nice output, although Windows PowerShell is quite generous with the amount of space between each column. To avoid using so much space, you can specify the `AutoSize` parameter. When you specify this parameter, `Format-Table` first works out the largest width for a column (based on the actual data being displayed) and then uses the minimum number of characters to ensure only the minimum of space is left between each column in the table, as you can see in Figure 1-2.

FIGURE 1-2

Formatting a table with Format-Table and -AutoSize

By using `Format-Table` or `Format-List`, you can display any property of any object in either a table or list format. If you don't know an object's property names (that is, the names you specify to `Format-Table` or `Format-List`), then pipe the object to `Get-Member`. This outputs a list of all the properties, their types, and whether you can get (only) or both get and set that property on an instance of the object's class. Piping `Get-Process` to `Get-Member` shows you the properties of the `System.Diagnostics.Process` class, such as `Priorityclass` and `Starttime`, but also that `Priorityclass` can be set and read, but `Starttime` is read-only.

Windows PowerShell offers a third useful format cmdlet, `Format-Wide`. This cmdlet displays the values of just a single property of the object being displayed, for example, the process name for each process that is returned by `Get-Process`. Figure 1-3 shows the use of `Format-Wide` to format the process name of the processes.

FIGURE 1-3

Formatting a table with Format-Wide

Something you notice when using the format cmdlets is that the default format used to display each property and the column/row labels are fixed. Windows PowerShell, again by default, chooses the best display format based on the data type being output and uses the property name for the column/row header.

Formatting with Windows PowerShell Hashtables

Windows PowerShell supports an object called a *hashtable*, a special sort of array that contains entries with just a key and a value. Hashtables are discussed in more detail later in this chapter. But for now, the hashtable(s) you use has a predefined set of keys, making setting up a hashtable simple (although the syntax is a bit on the ugly side for most new to Windows PowerShell, and is probably ugly for the rest of us, too).

You use a hashtable to tell `Format-Table` or `Format-List` how to format a particular column or row. You can use what are known as *calculated properties* to include a row or column title, an expression defining the actual value to display (for example, VM as megabytes), and detailed format instructions on how to format numbers/dates. For use with `Format-Table`, the hashtable can also contain a column width and a justification (right/left).

To format a table of processes that contains process name, CPU time, and virtual memory used when using a hashtable to alter the column headers and to specify how each property is calculated and used, you could use the following script — with the results as shown in Figure 1-4:

```
$ProcessHT = @{Label="Process Name";
               Expression={$_.Name};
               Alignment="Right"
               Width=25}
$CpuHT      = @{Label="CPU Used";
               Expression={$_.Cpu};
               FormatString="N2";
               Width=10}
$VmmHT      = @{label="Virtual Memory (MB)";
               Expression={$_.VirtualMemorySize64/$(1mb)}
               FormatString="N1";
               Alignment="Center";
               Width=15}
Get-Process notepad| Format-Table $ProcessHT,$CpuHT,$VmmHT
```

FIGURE 1-4

Formatting a table with hashtables

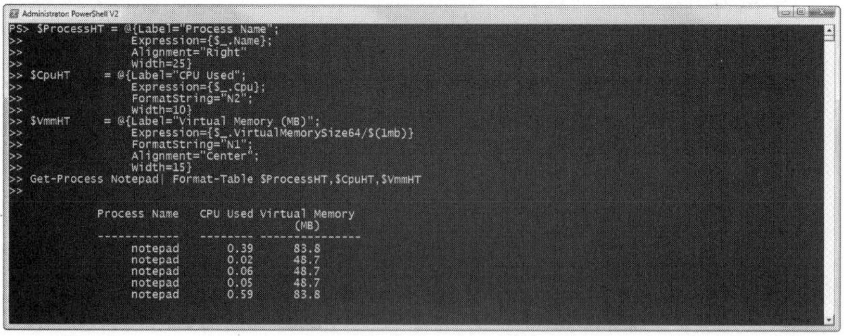

22

In this example, you create three hashtables, each describing a column you want `Format-Table` to display. The first column is 25 characters wide and uses the process's name property as the data, which is right-aligned in the column. The second hashtable, `$CpuHT`, uses "Virtual Memory" as the header of a 10 character–wide column that displays the object's CPU time. When this value is converted to a display string, the .NET format string `N2` (numeric with two digits of precision) is used to neatly format the result. The last hashtable displays a final column entitled "Virtual Memory (MB)." This column contains the virtual memory size, divided by 1 MB, that is left-centered in a 15-character column.

This example, which is a bit advanced, shows you how you can take advantage of the .NET formatting and `Format-Table` or `Format-List` to format nearly any table or list just the way you like it. There are other ways to create complex output, but I leave those as an exercise you can complete once you have more experience with Windows PowerShell.

The way that you tell Windows PowerShell how to convert numbers and dates into text is via the `FormatString` hashtable key. The format of what goes into the key is based on .NET. You can get the full details of .NET's numeric format strings at `http://msdn.microsoft .com/en-us/library/427bttx3(VS.71).aspx` and .NET's date and time format strings at `http://msdn.microsoft.com/en-us/library/97x6twsz(VS.71).aspx`. Of course, as an administrator, you might not want to take the time to customize the output because the default output may be good enough.

Scripting

In this section, you look at the concept of Windows PowerShell scripts, what they contain, and how you use them.

What Is a Script?

A script is nothing more than a text file of Windows PowerShell commands. *Scripting* is the art and science of creating these files of commands and then executing them as a single entity. You could create a script to provision a new user into your organization. This script might take data from an Excel spreadsheet about the users, and might include creating a new AD user account, adding that account to some security groups, adding a mailbox, a Unified Messaging mailbox, a Lync account, or a SharePoint site, plus setting all the necessary ACLs.

This complex script, the details of which are a matter of company business policy, is just a set of calls to cmdlets (for example, `New-AdUser`, `New-Mailbox`, and so on) or calls to functions you develop locally. They are all things you could do, a step at a time, from the console. The only problem with that is it could take a long time, even assuming you typed every statement perfectly each time. If your boss walks in with a spreadsheet containing 1000 new users he needs to get created as soon as possible, the thought of all that typing would drive most folks over the edge!

The beauty of a script is, once it is created, you can just run it, sit back, and watch it do all the work. The script completes the same actions you might have performed at the console far faster and more reliably. Scripting is the key to repeated and reliable automation, which is, after all, the primary focus of Windows PowerShell.

Scripts can be of virtually any length, and generally consist of some or all of the following components:

- **Business logic:** What the script is meant to do through the use of cmdlets and associated processing pipelines. In the case of the provisioning script noted earlier, it might add a user to the AD using `New-ADUser` (an AD cmdlet), then create a mailbox for that account using `New-Mailbox` (an Exchange cmdlet), and so on.

- **Error handling:** Every cmdlet can fail based on a large variety of factors. Trying to add a user to AD might fail if you already have an account with the same name as you are trying to add, or if AD is for some reason down.

- **User input validation:** Any time you get input from any user (even you!), treat it with suspicion until you validate it thoroughly.

- **Logging:** Creating a detailed log that can be audited at some later date. If nothing else, the logging can show your boss that you just added the 1,000 new users he asked you to add 10 minutes ago.

- **Windows PowerShell language constructs:** You use these to orchestrate the individual actions the script performs. These provide the rich glue that binds a script together.

Two important programming constructs that you use in most scripts are known as *alternation* and *iteration*. A script can do different things, that is, *alternate*, based on some condition (create a special set of log entries if the creation of the user was not successful). Also, scripts often process groups of objects (those 1,000 users you just added), *iterating* through one or more individual objects one at a time, for example, creating each user for each line on the Excel spreadsheet using the values on that spreadsheet line. Windows PowerShell has rich syntax to enable you to do both of these.

Alternation or Conditional Execution

As noted, alternation happens when a script takes a different action depending on a condition. Windows PowerShell provides several language control features for managing alternation, namely the `if` statement and the `switch` statement. The `if` statement, which has several variations, involves evaluation and expression, and depending on the value, it performs different actions.

The basic form of an `if` statement is `if ( <condition> ) { <action>}`. For example:

```
if ($a -gt 100) {Write-Host  '$a is big'}
```

The second form uses an `else` clause, taken if the condition is *not* true. For example:

```
if ($a -gt 100) {Write-Host  '$a is big'} else {Write-Host '$a is small'}
```

A third form enables you to have multiple mutually exclusive `if` clauses:

```
if      ($A -gt 100){Write-Host '$a is big'}`
elseif ($A -gt 50) {Write-Host '$a is fairly big'}`
elseif ($A -gt 18) {Write-host '$a is fairly small'}`
else    {'$A is small or tiny'}
```

When writing more complex `if` statements, you may need to use the line continuation character (`) at the end of the line, as in the preceding example. This stops Windows PowerShell from just executing the first line of the `if` statement and enables the `elseif` and final `else` statement in this example.

The second alternation construct supported by Windows PowerShell is the `switch` statement (also known as the `case` statement in VB and other languages). This statement takes a value and repeatedly compares it with a set of values — and takes the indication action when these values are the same. Several variations on the `switch` statement make it really preferable to the `if` statement for handling complex types of alternation.

The `switch` statement has the basic syntax:

```
switch (<expression} {
 <value 1> {<action for expression = value 1}
 <value 2> {<action for expression = value 2}
 <etc.>
 default {<action take for expression not equal to any value}
 }
```

To see this in action, here's a more real-life example that makes use of the PowerShell Community Extensions:

```
$a = 1..4 | Get-Random -count 1
Switch ($a) {
1 {Write-host 'number chosen is 1'}
2 {Write-host 'number chosen is 2'}
3 {Write-host 'number chosen is 3'}
4 {Write-host 'number chosen is 4'}
Default {Write-Host 'some other number chosen'}
 }
```

This example assigns $a to a random number between 1 and 4 and then tests its value using the `switch` statement. Of course, as long as the random number generator in `Get-Random` is working, this snippet can only generate a random number greater than or equal to 1 and less than or equal to 4, thus the default action can never be taken, so you could probably omit that last line in the `switch` statement.

With the `switch` statement, each potential value is checked. Thus, after checking if $a is 1 (and taking the action in the script block if so), by default, the `switch` statement then checks if $a is 2, and so on. In some cases, $a may end up matching multiple values, for example:

```
$a = Read-Host 'enter Y/yes or N/No'
switch ($a.toupper()) {
   'Y'     {$response = 'YES'}
   'YES'   {$response='YES'}
   'N'     {$Response='NO'}
   'NO'    {$Response='NO'}
  default {$Response='Unknown'}}
```

In most situations, however, you want to avoid multiple comparisons because the values you are checking against are mutually exclusive. In those cases, you can end the script block with a `break` statement, which tells Windows PowerShell to jump to the end of the `switch` statement. For example, the earlier `switch` statement might be more efficiently coded as:

```
$a = 1..4 | get-random -count 1
switch ($a) {
1 {Write-Host 'number chosen is 1'; break}
2 {Write-Host 'number chosen is 2'; break}
3 {Write-Host 'number chosen is 3'; break}
4 {Write-Host 'number chosen is 4'; break}
Default {Write-Host 'some other number chosen'}
}
```

In this case, if $a is 1, Windows PowerShell performs the `Write-Host`, then jumps to the line after the end of the `switch` statement. If $a is 1, then it can't be equal to 2, 3, or 4, so the additional checking is redundant. The `break` statement gives you flexibility to handle mutually exclusive values sensibly.

Two alternatives to the `switch` statement make use of wildcards and regular expressions. In these variations, Windows PowerShell uses either a wildcard or regular expression comparison: Does the value match the wildcard expression or the regular expression? Examples of this are:

```
$a = read-host 'enter Yes or No'
switch -wildcard ($a.ToLower())

{
   'y*' { $response = 'You entered Yes'}
   'n*' { $response = 'You entered No' }
     default { "You entered something else" } }
```

and

```
$a = read-host 'Enter Yes or No'; $reponse = ""
switch -regularexpression ($a.ToLower())
{
```

```
"^y" { $response = 'You entered Yes'; break}
"^n" { $response = 'You entered No' ; break}
default { "You entered something else" } }
```

In the first of these two examples, Windows PowerShell did a wildcard comparison between the expression $a.tolower() and the wildcard string 'y*'. In the second example, Windows PowerShell did a regular expression match between the expression $a.tolower() and the regular expression '^y'. As you can see, you are free to use the break statement as and when appropriate.

Iteration — Operating on a Collection or Array

As noted earlier, iteration involves looking at a number of objects one at a time. Windows PowerShell has rich iteration support with a variety of syntax to carry out iteration.

Iteration is a programming construct present in every scripting or programming language worth discussing. The idea is quite simple: you create some collection or array (all the files in the folder M:\GratefulDeadShows, or all the processes that are consuming either over 1000 handles or 500 MB of virtual memory), then do some action or set of actions for the members of that collection.

There are four basic iteration operators in Windows PowerShell (more than adequate for all situations). Two of these have two alternative methods of use:

- for loop
- do until / do while loop
- while loop
- ForEach-Object and foreach statement

The for loop is one a number of programming languages have, and has the basic syntax:

```
for (<expression 1>; <expression 2>; <expression 3>) {<statements>}
```

The for loop starts by evaluating the expression <expression 1>. Typically, this initializes a loop counter. Then, <expression 2> is evaluated and, if true, the statement block is executed. Finally, <expression 3> is evaluated (typically, this just advances the loop counter that was set in <expression 1>). The loop continues by reevaluating <expression 2>, running the script block if it's still true, and so on. Here's an example:

```
For ($i=0; $i -lt 100; $i++){
    $i
}
```

In this example, $i is initialized to zero. Windows PowerShell then evaluates the expression and, because $i is less than 100, the loop body is executed (which just prints out the current value of $i, which the first time is zero). After the loop body is executed,

$i is incremented by 1, then tested again to see if it's still less than 100. In summary, this loop prints out the numbers from 0 to 99. Many old-school programmers find this loop contrast similar to what much earlier programming languages had.

The next three iteration constructs are really just variations on the theme of running a script block until or while some condition is true.

The first, the do...until loop, runs a script block until some condition is true. For example:

```
$i=0
Do {
  $i
  $i++
} until ($i -ge 100)
```

This example does the same thing as the for loop earlier. A simple variant on this is the do...while loop, which outputs the numbers 1 through 99:

```
$i=0
Do {
  $i
  $i++
} while ($i -lt 100)
```

A third variation is the while loop, which looks like this:

```
$i=0
While ($i -lt 100)
  {
     $i
     $i++
  }
```

All of these looping constructs do broadly the same thing: run some script block multiple times, ending when some condition is true. In the case of the for loop and the while loop, depending on how you construct it, the script block may not run, whereas for the do... while or do...until case, the script block is always run at least once. These iteration constructs work just fine and may ease you into Windows PowerShell. But none of them makes use of the pipeline, which is Windows PowerShell's secret weapon against complex scripting!

With the foreach constructs, Windows PowerShell runs a script block inside a pipeline — once for each member of the pipeline. Rather than having to construct some means to determine when the loop should terminate, Windows PowerShell can simply run a script block for each member.

The first foreach construct is the ForEach-Object cmdlet, which has a syntax like this:

```
ForEach-Object (<name> in <collection>) {<script block}
```

In this construct, Windows PowerShell runs the script block for every object in the collection. Suppose you had a set of music files in a single folder — some were `.mp3`, some text (`.txt`), plus other files. Using the `ForEach-Object` statement, you could categorize these like so:

```
#Initialize variables
$txtfile = $mp3file = $m4a = $other = 0
#Look at all files in c:\music
ForEach-Object ($file in (Get-Childitem c:\music) {
  switch ($file.extension) {
     ".txt"   {$Txtfile++}
     ".mp3"   {$Mp3file++}
     default {$other++}} }
#Display results
"$txtfile text files"
"$mp3file MP3 files"
"$other other files"
```

For a well-populated MP3 collection, the output might look like:

```
232 text files
12323 MP3 files
280  other files
```

In this `foreach` variant, you state the name you are going to use for the current object being evaluated. Each time the preceding `ForEach-Object` loop is executed, the `$file` variable is set to be the current object (that is, the current file in the `C:\Music` folder).

A simplified version of `foreach`, the `foreach` statement, is used within a pipeline only. In this variant, there is no "name in collection-name" clause. Instead, each time the loop runs, the current object is represented by the variable `$_`. To recast the preceding example, you might have this:

```
#Initialize variables
$txtfile = $mp3file = $m4a = $other = 0
#Look at all files in c:\music
Get-Childitem c:\music | foreach {
  switch ($_.Extension)
  {
  ".txt"   {$Txtfile++}
  ".mp3"   {$Mp3file++}
  default {$other++}
  }
}
#Now Display results
"$txtfile text files"
"$mp3file MP3 files"
"$other other files"
```

In this example, each time through the loop, the current file object is represented by `$_`, and therefore has a file extension property of `$_.Extension`.

It is these last two constructs that are most commonly used with Windows PowerShell. The `ForEach-Object` cmdlet is, at least for some, preferable for more complex script blocks, whereas the second is more appropriate in short one-liner type pipelines. But both can be used interchangeably.

Error and Exception Handling

In the world of administrative scripting, errors occur. Some are minor and can be fixed easily as you develop a script. Others can be anticipated, trapped, and possibly worked around. Although writing business logic is going to be your focus, you need to anticipate and manage the rich possibility today's computing environment provides as a source of error.

You can divide these errors into three broad classes. First are the *syntax errors*, where you just typed the wrong syntax or perhaps misspelled a variable or cmdlet. For the most part, these syntax errors are corrected pretty easily because Windows PowerShell won't run the script until the basic syntax is right and terminates if you try to access nonexistent cmdlets, providers, and so on. Reasonable testing of your script exposes these issues for you to correct.

The second type of error is a *logic error* — your script runs fine, but it produces the wrong results. Logic errors can be hard to find, especially as the script grows in size and complexity, though sometimes, you can look at a script and just see the error and quickly fix it. Other cases may be much harder to work out and discover the underlying issue.

The final type of error is the *runtime error* — something that *should* work, but doesn't. For example, if you use the `Get-AdUser` cmdlet from the `Active Directory` module, you should get the relevant user(s) returned. But what if the domain controller is down, or the network between you and the domain controller is down?

For pretty much any cmdlet that does something outside the local box, there is the potential for a runtime error. The same applies for operations on your own computer — for example, the comma-separated value file containing users you want to add to the Active Directory does not exist, and so on.

Using an Advanced IDE

One thing that really helps you to detect and correct syntax errors is an advanced Interactive Development Environment (IDE) in which you develop your code. Two specific features that really help you to eliminate syntax and possibly some logic errors are syntax color coding and IntelliSense.

Color coding occurs when the code editor you are using displays different syntax tokens using different colors. For example, if your strings are all color-coded dark red, and suddenly you see a huge block of dark red characters, chances are you have missed either a closing or opening string delimiter.

IntelliSense is where the editor "knows" Windows PowerShell's syntax and helps you type it. For example, if you start to type the cmdlet `Get-WmiObject`, a suitably smart IDE would recognize you've typed `Get-`, and pop up all the `Get-` cmdlets available. In effect, this is tab completion on steroids and can save you a lot of time and effort — not only should it be a bit quicker to type your scripts because the tool does the typing, but you also ensure the tool types the syntax correctly and in full.

In terms of tools you can use, you can start using the Windows PowerShell's Interactive Script Environment (ISE). This comes as part of the installation of Windows PowerShell on most systems. Windows PowerShell ISE is loaded by default on Windows 7 and when you install Windows PowerShell on earlier client operating systems. For server systems, particularly Server 2008 R2, you need to add this component separately. Sadly, Windows PowerShell ISE is not supported on Server Core. Other tools you can use include Idera's Windows PowerShell Plus Professional, Quest's PowerGui (free), and Sapien's Primal Script.

Cross-Reference

See Chapter 25, "Using the Windows PowerShell ISE," for more information on both the ISE and alternative products. ∎

Set-StrictMode Cmdlet

The `Set-StrictMode` cmdlet finds a number of instances of incorrect syntax that might otherwise work (albeit incorrectly) and reports at runtime on the error. For example, you can call a cmdlet using .NET method invocation syntax and, though Windows PowerShell may not complain when you enter such a statement, it almost certainly will not call the cmdlet in the way you intended. Also, you might type a variable name incorrectly and refer to a nonexistent and noninitialized variable, or perhaps a nonexistent property of an object. These are easy mistakes to make, and can be hard to see in a large script.

Using `Set-StrictMode` causes Windows PowerShell's parser to be extra strict and report on issues like these (and others). When `StrictMode` is turned on, Windows PowerShell generates a terminating error if best-practice coding rules are violated (that is, your script stops when such things happen).

Using `Set-StrictMode` is a great idea while you are developing your script. You might consider setting it in your profile. See the "Customizing Windows PowerShell with Profiles" section later in this chapter for more information about using profiles.

Debugging

Debugging is the process of removing logic and other errors from your script. Windows PowerShell (both from the console and using the ISE) and other third-party tools provide you a wealth of runtime debugging tools.

Although Windows PowerShell is "new," the concept and practice of debugging has been a part of the computing environment ever since Grace Hopper removed a moth from a valve-based computer in the mid-1950s.

You can take two broad approaches to runtime debugging. First, you can add diagnostic statements to your script that display key information as your script runs. For example, if you issue a `Get-AdUser` cmdlet, the diagnostic information output might include the number of users returned and the names of the users. This might help you fix a problem in the filter (filtering which users you want to get out of AD).

The second approach is to use debugger to step through your program line by line — stopping now and again to look at the values of certain variables (perhaps even setting some values temporarily). Windows PowerShell, both Windows PowerShell console and Windows PowerShell ISE, have a debugging platform you can use.

To produce debug output, Windows PowerShell provides the `Write-Debug` cmdlet. This cmdlet writes debug information to the console when directed. The neat thing about `Write-Debug` is that it prints information only when you set the variable `$PSDebugPreference`.

Windows PowerShell's core debugging features are provided via seven core cmdlets:

- **`Set-PsDebug`:** Turns script debugging on and off, sets trace level, and can set a strict level

- **`Set-PsBreakpoint`:** Enables you to set a breakpoint. You can break at a line/column in a script, whenever a variable is used/set, or whenever a function/script is called

- **`Get-PsBreakpoint`:** Gets a list of breakpoints currently set

- **`Disable-PsBreakpoint`:** Disables a particular breakpoint, but does not remove it

- **`Enable-PsBreakpoint`:** Enables a previously disabled breakpoint

- **`Remove-PsBreakpoint`:** Removes a previously set breakpoint

- **`Get-PsCallStack`:** Gets details on how a particular function or script was called (that is, who called who to call who, and so on)

Note

For more information on the debugging features inside Windows PowerShell, see the `about_Debuggers` help file. Also, run `Get-Help` on each of the preceding cmdlets for more information on how to use them. ∎

Trapping Runtime Errors

As mentioned earlier, runtime errors can affect almost any script/function/cmdlet, even if that bit of code ran thousands of times previously without issue. As Murphy's Law posits: anything that can go wrong, does so at the most inopportune time; Mrs. Murphy's corollary was that Murphy was an optimist.

Two Windows PowerShell syntax components enable you to catch and handle errors that would otherwise be fatal. One is the `trap` statement and the other `try/catch/finally` construct.

The `trap` statement enables you to specify a set of commands, a script block to run when an otherwise fatal error has occurred. For example, if you have a script that iterates through a list of, say, 500 systems and does something with those systems — if one system is down, the script would fail. In your script, you can trap such errors, write the information away to a log file, or perhaps send mail or a page alert to an administrator, then continue. This turns fatal errors into recoverable errors.

The `trap` statement on its own traps all errors in any code that follows, such as:

```
Trap {
     "Error Encountered in script - continuing"
     $Error[0]                | out-file c:\scriptlog.txt -append
     "In {0}"           -f    | out-file c:\scriptlog.txt -append
     "On {0}, at {1}" -f $(hostname, $(get-date) |
                               out-file c:\scriptlog.txt -append
     Continue
}
...
```

In this example, the script can go along executing and, if any error occurs, the `trap` statement catches that error, prints out some information to a log file, and then continues.

Note

For more information on errors in general, see the **about_Errors** help file. For more information on the **trap** statement, see the **about_Trap** help file. And see the **about_Try_Catch_Finally** help file for how to use the **try/catch/finally** blocks to trap and handle runtime terminating errors. ■

Nonterminating Errors

In the preceding text, the errors discussed were terminating errors — that is, when the script encountered an error, Windows PowerShell terminated the execution of that script. However, a lot of errors that occur can be nonterminating. That means that Windows PowerShell displays error information at the console and then continues to execute your script.

Suppose you had a simple script that takes a file of file names and deletes them. This might look something like this:

```
$Files = Get-Contents C:\Del.txt
Foreach ($File in $Files) {
  Remove-Item $file
}
```

Next, let's suppose that one of the files (`c:\foo\Foobar.txt`) did not actually exist. In that case, Windows PowerShell would produce an error like this:

```
Remove-Item : Cannot find path 'C:\foo\foobar.txt' because it does not exist.
At line:1 char:12
```

```
   + remove-item <<<<  foobar.txt
      + CategoryInfo          : ObjectNotFound: (C:\foo\foobar.txt:String) ↵
   [Remove-Item], ItemNotFoundException
      + FullyQualifiedErrorId : ↵
   PathNotFound,Microsoft.PowerShell.Commands.RemoveItemCommand
```

You have two options as to how to handle these nonterminating errors. First, you could use the -ErrorAction parameter. Or you could use the -ErrorVariable parameter.

The -ErrorAction parameter is a common parameter (available on all cmdlets) that tells Windows PowerShell what to do with nonterminating errors. When you call a cmdlet, in this case Remove-Item, you can specify four different values of -ErrorAction:

- **SilentlyContinue:** Windows PowerShell ignores the error, displays no error text, and continues.
- **Stop:** Windows PowerShell stops, in effect turning a nonterminating error into a terminating error.
- **Continue:** Windows PowerShell displays the error message and then continues, which is the default action.
- **Inquire:** Windows PowerShell asks you want to do next.

You can also use the -ErrorVariable common parameter, typically in conjunction with -ErrorAction. If you specify the -ErrorVariable parameter and provide a variable name, Windows PowerShell stores any nonterminating errors in the variable name. If you precede the variable name with a plus sign ("+"), Windows PowerShell appends any errors to the variable, thus creating an array of errors found. Note that you must specify the variable name without using a "$," as follows:

```
Remove-Variable x
$Files = Get-Contents C:\Del.txt
Foreach ($File in $Files) {
   Remove-Item $file -ErrorAction SilentlyContinue -ErrorVariable +x
}
If ($x.count) {Write-Host ("{0} errors deleting files" -f $x.count)}
Elseif ($x)   {Write-Host "1 Error deleting files"}
Else  {Write-Host "All files deleted OK"}
```

Extending Windows PowerShell with Snap-ins and Modules

Windows PowerShell was designed from the start to be extensible, which allows product teams, third parties, and the community to create extensions. This section introduces the snap-in, which came with V1, and shows a sample snap-in.

Cross-Reference

The Module construct, added with Windows PowerShell V2, is another way to add functionality into Windows PowerShell. Modules are explained in more detail in Chapter 2, "What's New in Windows PowerShell V2." ■

Windows PowerShell Snap-ins

When Windows PowerShell shipped, as Version 1, there was a single method of adding functionality — the snap-in, or PsSnapIn. The PSSnapin enabled developers to create installable packages of cmdlets and providers, which could be used on other machines and within other organizations. These extra cmdlets could be free (for example, the Active Directory toolset from Quest) or commercial (for example, /n Software's networking cmdlets). Or they could be provided by some product or operating system component (for example, the System Migration cmdlets included with Windows Server 2008 R2).

Each snap-in has a full name (for example, Quest's add-in tools for Active Directory: Quest.ActiveRoles.ADManagement). You can use the Add-PsSnapIn cmdlet to add the snap-in and the Remove-PsSnapIn cmdlet to remove the snap-in. Adding the snap-in makes the cmdlets etc. available for use at the console or within a script.

From your Windows PowerShell console, you can find out what snap-ins have already been added by using Get-PsSnapIn. Unless you have customized your environment by using profile files, if you run Get-PsSnapIn, you can see that Windows PowerShell has loaded a core set of seven Windows PowerShell snap-ins:

- Microsoft.PowerShell.Diagnostics
- Microsoft.WSMan.Management
- Microsoft.PowerShell.Core
- Microsoft.PowerShell.Utility
- Microsoft.PowerShell.Host
- Microsoft.PowerShell.Management
- Microsoft.PowerShell.Security

To find out what cmdlets are inside each of the snap-ins, you can use the Get-Command cmdlet, and specify a module name (that is, Microsoft.Powershell.Core). The results are shown in Figure 1-5.

FIGURE 1-5

Cmdlets contained in Microsoft.PowerShell.Core PsSnapIn

Windows PowerShell Modules

The snap-in was a good way of adding functionality, but it had several weaknesses:

- It was a compiled add-on, requiring developers to use a .NET language such as C#. This made it difficult for nondevelopers to construct.

- It had to be installed, so developers needed to create an installer (which fortunately was pretty easy to do!) and the user had to run the installation process.

- It had to be registered in the system registry — for some locked-down workstations, this meant the installation process failed.

For these key reasons, Microsoft created the module, which is part of Version 2. Windows PowerShell modules are discussed in more detail in Chapter 2.

Installing Windows PowerShell

Before you can use Windows PowerShell, you need to install it. This ranges from the trivial (it's already there!) to the impossible (it's not supported on Windows 2000 or earlier).

Windows PowerShell Version Support

Basically, you need to do two things to get Windows PowerShell loaded on your system. These two things vary a bit depending on what OS you have. The first thing is getting the binary bits, and the second is installing them. Depending on your operating system, here's how to proceed:

- **Windows 2000 (workstation or server) and earlier:** Windows PowerShell is not available or supported for these versions of Windows. There is some anecdotal evidence that you can hack Windows PowerShell into Windows 2000, but it's only going to be a hack — there are missing components that make your experience with Windows PowerShell on this OS extremely suboptimal.

- **Windows XP, Windows Embedded, Windows Server 2003/Windows Server 2003 R2, and Windows Vista:** For these operating systems, you can download an OS Patch and install it.

- **Windows Server 2008**: Server 2008 includes Windows PowerShell V1 as a feature you can install (but not in Server Core installations). You should just download V2 and use that, unless there is some business reason why you need V1.

- **Windows 7 and Server 2008 R2 (Full install):** Windows PowerShell is included and is installed on these OSs. For Server 2008 R2, there's even a shortcut icon to Windows PowerShell prepopulated on the Start bar. For Server 2008 R2, the ISE is included as a separate feature, which you can add. The ISE requires the .NET Framework 3.5 SP1, which is also included if you choose to install the ISE.

- **Server 2008 R2 (Server Core):** For this version of Server Core, Windows PowerShell V2 is included in the binaries, but you need to add Windows PowerShell (and the .NET Framework to support it) before you can use it. Use the `Sconfig.exe` program to add these two components. After starting `Sconfig`, just enter 42 to add Windows PowerShell (some may find that amusing — after all, isn't Windows PowerShell the answer to everything?).

Getting Windows PowerShell for Downlevel OSs

Windows PowerShell is now part of the Windows Management Framework Core (WMFC) component as described in KB article 968930 (see `http://support.microsoft.com/kb/968930`). To add Windows PowerShell to your downlevel system, you need to add the latest version of this component, which you can obtain from the KB page on Microsoft's website.

When finding the version for your system, be careful, because there are seven separate versions of the WMFC component for different versions of the OS and for different hardware platforms. Sadly, there is no support for Itanium.

Script Security and Execution Policy

After installing either the latest OS or installing the WMFC component onto an older OS, you are ready to start running and using Windows PowerShell. You can use either the Windows

PowerShell console (`PowerShell.exe`), Windows PowerShell ISE (`PowerShellISE.exe`) on supported platforms, or any of the Windows PowerShell third-party applications such as Windows PowerShell Plus, PowerGUI, and so on.

However, the first time you try to run a script within Windows PowerShell, you see the ugly error message shown in Figure 1-6.

FIGURE 1-6

Scripts being blocked by Windows PowerShell's default execution policy

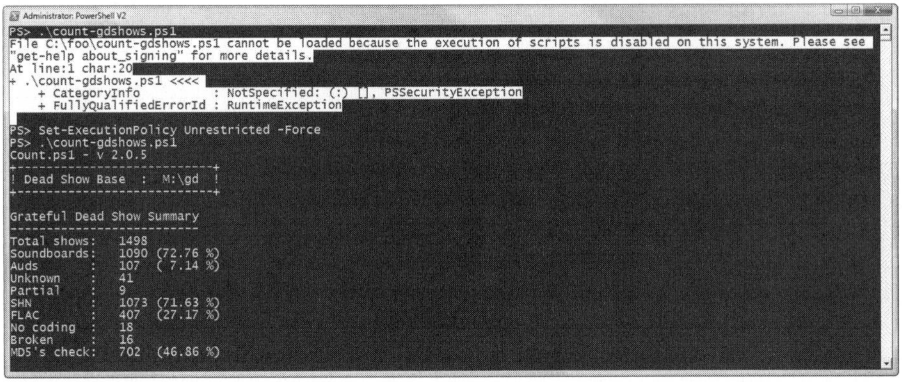

Windows PowerShell has an execution policy that applies to each system on which you install Windows PowerShell. This policy tells what scripts can run (all, signed, or none). It is set up to be restrictive by default, but it is very easy for you to change.

The idea behind this is that it might be easy for a malware site to drop a malicious script on your system that you could then be persuaded to execute. So far, there has been no reported case of this vulnerability, but for naïve users, it may be safer to not have the ability to run scripts until they know enough to not be too dangerous. In some higher-security environments, you might want to prevent any but signed (and therefore well-scrutinized) scripts.

However, turning on a restrictive execution policy does not stop determined administrators — they can easily just cut the script from the file in Notepad, and paste it into a Windows PowerShell console. Even if execution policy is restricted, there are plenty of ways a rogue user with administrative privileges can damage a system. Don't forget, cmdlets are only dangerous if you have the necessary permissions — Windows PowerShell just makes it more efficient to do damaging things for those who already can!

The execution policy can take one of the following values:

- **Unrestricted:** You can run any script.
- **RemoteSigned:** You can run any local script, but scripts from a remote source must be digitally signed (and that signature must be valid).

- **AllSigned:** You can only run scripts that were digitally signed.
- **Restricted:** You can run NO scripts.

You can set the execution policy in three ways:

- **Specify an ExecutionPolicy parameter when starting Windows PowerShell:** This allows you to set the policy for this invocation of Windows PowerShell.
- **Enter Windows PowerShell and run Set-ExecutionPolicy and select a less restricted policy (for example, RemoteSigned or Unrestricted):** From then on, all Windows PowerShell consoles obey this setting.
- **Use Group Policy:** By setting a group policy object (gpo), you can be granular in which execution policy applies to which systems. Note that group policy overrides any manual setting.

If you are going to use group policy, you need to either create your own group policy administrative template or add the administrative template for Windows PowerShell as published by Microsoft. You can get this template from www.microsoft.com/downloads/en/details.aspx?FamilyID=2917a564-dbbc-4da7-82c8-fe08b3ef4e6d&DisplayLang=en.

Once you download and install this template, you can use it to set Windows PowerShell's default execution policy. Once set for a given machine, users on that machine can run any scripts allowed by the execution policy you have set (and they can't change it without changing or removing the GPO).

Customizing Windows PowerShell with Profiles

Windows PowerShell has four scripts it can run at startup. Known as *profiles*, these scripts are run in "dot source" mode — thus, variables, functions, and so on that you create in the profile are persisted in the Windows PowerShell console. Most users create profile files to customize their Windows PowerShell console or ISE usage.

What Is a Profile?

A *profile* is a file that Windows PowerShell runs as part of starting up a Windows PowerShell session. You can take advantage of four profiles, each of which runs before you see the prompt in your Windows PowerShell window. Any variable, alias, or function you define or any provider you load is available for your use in the Windows PowerShell session. For more information on scope, see the about_Scopes help file.

A profile file is where you can put all the variables you want to persist in a session, define small functions or aliases, and where useful, create new provider drives. If you are going to be developing large functions that you want to be made available within your PowerShell console (or for a script), it might be preferable to bundle them up into a module and then just load that module either in your profile or script, or only when you actually need it. This might be a way to speed up your startup times!

Windows PowerShell enables you to use four separate profiles. These enable you to best manage the Windows PowerShell environment. The four are known as:

- **AllUsersAllHosts:** This profile runs for every user and for every Windows PowerShell host.
- **AllUsersCurrentHost:** This profile runs for every user running this specific Windows PowerShell host (for example, `PowerShell.exe`, `PowerShell_ISE.exe`, and so on).
- **CurrentUserAllHosts:** This profile runs for the current user only but for all hosts.
- **CurrentUserCurrentHost:** This profile runs for the current user within only the current host.

This flexibility enables you to have, for example, different profiles when you run `PowerShell.exe` versus the ISE and to have different profiles for different users. It also enables system-wide profiles (that is, for any user using this system) and individual user profiles.

When Windows PowerShell starts, it creates a variable for you, `$profile`, which points to the `CurrentUserCurrentHost` profile, which means you could have two — one for `PowerShell.exe` and the other for `PowerShellISE.exe`. For most users, this is sufficient. For multiuser systems, the `AllUsers` profiles can be useful over and above the per-user profile.

Where Are Your Profiles?

The four profile files for use with `PowerShell.exe` are listed in Table 1-1. If you installed Windows to a different drive, the location would change.

TABLE 1-1

Default Windows PowerShell Profiles for PowerShell.exe

Profile Name	Profile Location
AllUsersAllHosts	C:\Windows\System32\WindowsPowerShell\v1.0\profile.ps1
AllUsersCurrentHost	C:\Windows\System32\WindowsPowerShell\v1.0\Microsoft.PowerShell_profile.ps1
CurrentUserAllHosts	C:\Users\<username>\Documents\WindowsPowerShell\profile.ps1
CurrentUserCurrentHost	C:\Users\<username>\Documents\WindowsPowerShell\Microsoft.PowerShell_profile.ps1

The profiles available for use with Windows PowerShell ISE are listed in Table 1-2.

Default Windows PowerShell Profiles for PowerShell_ISE.exe

Profile Name	Profile Location
AllUsersAllHosts	C:\Windows\System32\WindowsPowerShell\v1.0\profile.ps1
AllUsersCurrentHost	C:\Windows\System32\WindowsPowerShell\v1.0\ Microsoft.PowerShellISE_profile.ps1
CurrentUserAllHosts	C:\Users\<username>\Documents\WindowsPowerShell\ profile.ps1
CurrentUserCurrentHost	C:\Users\tfl\Documents\WindowsPowerShell\Microsoft .PowerShellISE_profile.ps1

If you have other Windows PowerShell hosts, they may or may not implement additional CurrentHost profiles. Once you've started up your Windows PowerShell host, you can find out the profile files for that host easily. Just run the following:

```
$profile | format-list *host* -force
```

Managing Profiles in the Enterprise

You have options as to how you use profiles, how you coordinate them, and how you keep them up to date. This can provide flexibility for large and small organizations alike. Some things you could do include:

- Letting your Windows PowerShell users do their own thing and not control profiles centrally.

- Putting all key corporate functions, aliases, and any locally developed scripts and providers into a module.

- Using the AllUsersAllHosts profile for common corporate standards, letting users further customize their per-user profiles.

- Using group policy to deploy a startup script or a logon script that copies your corporate AllUsersAllHosts profile to the appropriate folder on administrative workstations.

- Creating multiple profile files for the different hosts used in your organization and deploying these with group policy (startup or login script), depending on the level of control you want to maintain.

- Providing a sample set of profile contents and letting users download and use them as appropriate.

Summary

In this chapter, you looked at the basics of Windows PowerShell. You reviewed the path leading to the release of Windows PowerShell, and you learned about the core components of Windows PowerShell's language. These components — cmdlets, objects, and the pipeline — are the fundamentals on which the rest of this book rests.

You learned that you can use these concepts to create rich production-oriented scripts to run your enterprise. Scripts can be a mixture of cmdlets, and existing console applications that are combined with iteration and alternation processes. Add in a mixture of user input validation and error handling to resolve the unpredictability inevitable in automation of your computer environment, and you have rich tools to perform all manner of task automation.

This chapter finished with a look at both installing Windows PowerShell and how you might extend your Windows PowerShell environment with snap-ins and modules. These additions come from a variety of places: some are built in, whereas others are either commercially provided or have been created by Windows PowerShell's vibrant community. You also examined how you install Windows PowerShell (for those operating systems where Windows PowerShell is not automatically loaded) as well as how to customize Windows PowerShell using profile files.

In the next chapter, you learn about the features added to Windows PowerShell's Version 2. One could devote an entire book to just what's new in V2, but Chapter 2 avoids this by providing a concise look at key features.

What's New in Windows PowerShell V2

This chapter looks at what's new in Windows PowerShell Version 2 (V2). The chapter begins with a short look at how we got to V2 before looking at key features added in Version 2. Like Chapter 1, this chapter does not go into a huge amount of detail about these features. You can take advantage of the about_* text files to read additional conceptual information that can help you to understand more about the new features.

The Road to V2

The road from Windows PowerShell Version 1 to Version 2 was an interesting one. Microsoft went from V1 to V2 via a set of Community Technology Preview (CTP) releases, which were supported by an active newsgroup. Initially, V2 was an out-of-band project; but for the final release, Microsoft also took Windows PowerShell into Windows as a full component. This move was great news for the future of Windows PowerShell!

Like most product teams at Microsoft, shipping a version of a product is a cause for celebration; but after a day or two, it's back to work on the next version. And so it was for the Windows PowerShell team on their road to V2. Hardly any time seemed to elapse between shipping V1 and the release of the V2 interim, prerelease builds.

The Version 2 Betas

Microsoft showed off the emerging V2 through three Community Technology Preview (CTP) releases. These CTP releases were

IN THIS CHAPTER

Getting to Version 2

Introducing remoting and jobs

Reviewing advanced functions

Introducing modules

Utilizing eventing

Introducing the ISE

Reviewing transactions

Using debugging and error handling

Describing new cmdlets in V2

downloadable, fully featured beta versions. Although Microsoft used the term CTP as opposed to Beta, these interim builds were ready for production. But they did provide a great snapshot of the progress the team had made at the time each interim build shipped.

Each CTP got progressively richer and included more features. The final CTP shipped in late December 2008. The CTPs were supported by a rich and vibrant online newsgroup wherein the features were dissected and improvements suggested. The discussions with the product team were amazingly productive and helped to shape many of the features.

Perhaps the best news that emerged from the team was how Windows PowerShell would be supported and released going forward, namely that Windows PowerShell was to become a component of Windows and be issued and serviced just like other Windows components.

With Windows PowerShell moving into Windows, Windows PowerShell is now a full component of Windows, much like Control Panel, the Active Directory, and so on. That's great news, but at the same time, there is some bad news.

Whenever any component becomes part of Windows, the servicing model for that component is the normal Windows service model: hotfixes for critical issues, roll-up patches in some cases, and occasional service packs. Thus, errors in Windows PowerShell that might once have been fixed with interim releases of Windows PowerShell can no longer be shipped as easily. Instead, new features are only released with new versions of the Windows operating system. Being part of the Windows operating system benefits Windows PowerShell and its users at one level, but waiting for operating system releases also hampers the Windows PowerShell team's ability to be agile.

What this means to you is that, at least until there's a new version of the Windows operating system, Windows PowerShell remains constant (aside from any high-priority bug fixes). This allows you to really get to know how Windows PowerShell benefits you without having to worry about regular feature upgrades.

V2 in Windows 7/R2

In August 2009, Microsoft released both Windows Server 2008 R2 and Windows 7 (although the formal marketing launch was some months later). Windows 7 got the lion's share of press attention, but the updated version of Windows Server was a major step forward in terms of Windows PowerShell.

As part of this release, Windows PowerShell is installed by default into all versions of both Windows Server 2008 R2 and Windows 7. On Windows 7, Windows PowerShell console and Windows PowerShell Integrated Scripting Environment (ISE) are both installed — just hit Start, type **Windows PowerShell**, and away you go with the console.

For Windows Server 2008 R2, Windows PowerShell V2 is not only installed, but there's a shortcut placed on the Start bar. But for this server version, only the Windows PowerShell console is installed by default. If you want to install the Windows PowerShell ISE, you need to use Server Manager (or the Server Manager cmdlets) to add this feature. Note the ISE requires the .NET Framework 3.5 SP1 — if you select Windows PowerShell ISE, Server Manager automatically installs the updated version of the .NET Framework.

Windows PowerShell is not installed in any Windows 2008 Server R2 Server Core installation. However, you can add both the .NET Framework and Windows PowerShell. You easily add both by using `sconfig.exe` and specifying "42" (no doubt, Douglas Adams fans will be amused by this). As you might expect, you do not get the ISE in Server Core — only the console edition is available.

Tip

For the most part, managing Server Core installations is best done remotely, either using Server Manager or using Windows PowerShell on the server core installation. Adding Windows PowerShell to each Server Core installation does give you the option of "local management" should you need it. So, consider adding Windows PowerShell to all Server Core installations at installation time. ■

V2 on Downlevel OSs

Shortly after the release of Server 2008 R2 and Windows 7, Microsoft also released Windows PowerShell Version 2 for downlevel operating systems (i.e., older version of Windows). Specifically, support is provided for Windows XP, Windows Vista, Windows Server 2003, Windows Server 2003 R2, and Windows Server 2008. All of these versions of Windows PowerShell come for both x64 and i386 OSs.

There is no version of V2 for any Itanium-based version of Windows. Additionally, there is no support for Windows 2000. There has been some anecdotal evidence that you can hack V2 onto a Windows 2000 system, but there is sufficient missing functionality in the OS to make such an attempt relatively futile even if it is an interesting science project.

So what key features did Microsoft add in Version 2? The following sections look at the key new features, starting with one of the most important new features: remoting.

Using Remoting

One of the key features needed to manage just about every computing environment is the ability to manage and control systems remotely. This is a requirement that grows increasingly critical as the number of computers in your organization grows. Though you can easily manage one or two systems from a GUI, managing thousands or tens of thousands becomes progressively more difficult — and, at some point, probably impossible — at least at a reasonable cost (think how long it would take you to create a terminal services connection to 10,000 computers one at a time in order to install a hotfix!).

Windows PowerShell Version 1 did have remoting capabilities — that is, the ability to access functions and features of some other remote computer. But V1's remoting capability was provided cmdlet by cmdlet and not across the board. Also, V1 used a different set of underlying technologies based on Remote Procedure Calls (RPCs) to achieve the level of remoting. Besides being fairly firewall-unfriendly, the implementation of remote management in V1 was patchy and inconsistent. Of all the new features in Version 2, a universal remoting capability is perhaps the biggest addition.

What Is Remoting?

Remoting is a set of Windows PowerShell features that enables you to run scripts and commands on another system, and return the results to a local system. Remoting enables you to open up a connection to one, or more than one, system and work as though these systems were local. You can load modules, use Providers, and run cmdlets and scripts on the remote system(s). Results can be processed either remotely or locally.

With Windows PowerShell remoting, you can create a session to a remote computer, say, from your desktop to your Lync server, using the `New-PsSession` cmdlet. You can use this session to run a single command (for example, get a list of Lync users assigned to the Cookham pool) and dispense with it upon completion. Or you can create and enter the session and run commands on the remote system (including all data processing) as though you were logged on to the remote machine from its local console.

Following are the three broad types of remoting in Windows PowerShell:

- **1:1:** This is where you open a session to a remote machine, do some administrative work, and then close the session. You might, for example, want to get mailbox statistics from an Exchange mailbox by remoting into your Exchange server and running the appropriate cmdlet(s).

- **Fan-out:** This is where you want to run a set of commands on multiple, perhaps thousands or tens of thousands of computers. For example, you might want to use Active Directory (AD) to determine all the computers in your domain, then remote to each one and ensure that a particular hotfix has been applied.

- **Fan-in:** This is where multiple administrators are all actively remoting in to a particular machine. For example, suppose you are in the process of setting up Lync. You might have two or three administrators from around your company all remoting into the Lync server(s) to do some of the setup.

Windows PowerShell Remoting Architecture

Remoting in Windows PowerShell V2 makes use of several components beyond `PowerShell.exe`. In Figure 2-1, you see a block diagram of the Windows PowerShell remoting architecture.

FIGURE 2-1

Windows PowerShell remoting architecture

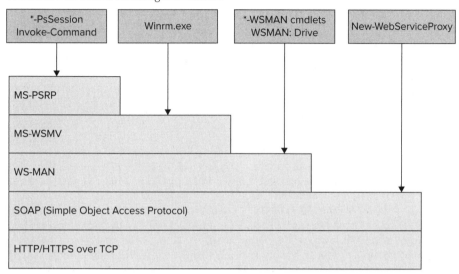

As you can see in Figure 2-1, the remoting stack contains five key elements:

- **TCP/IP and HTTP/S:** The transport layer for remoting is HTTP/S run over TCP/IP. This makes the remoting stack much more firewall-friendly.

- **SOAP:** Simple Object Access Protocol, an XML-based remote object access protocol, running over HTTP/S. This is the basis for XML web services as well as for WS-MAN.

- **WS-MAN:** Web Services Management layer standardized across platforms — WS-MAN enables you to create and utilize endpoints on other machines. WinRM is Microsoft's implementation of WS-MAN.

- **MS-WSMV:** Web Service Management For Vista — defines, in effect, how WS-MAN is done over WinRM in the Microsoft stack.

- **MS-PSRP:** The Windows PowerShell Remoting protocol. This is a stateful protocol instantiating remote instances of Windows PowerShell, sending pipelines to those instances, and getting results back. MS-PSRP runs over MS-WSMV and WS-MAN.

The Windows TCP/IP stack, along with the HTTP/S suite, provides basic transport features for all remoting activities. Although we refer to web services here, you do not need to implement IIS to support Remoting. HTTP/S is merely the transport protocol used to utilize WS-MAN and related management services.

Sitting on top of TCP/IP and HTTPS is SOAP. SOAP is an XML-based messaging protocol. It enables you to set up a sender and receiver and send XML-formatted messages to and from the local and remote system. For the most part, SOAP is part of the management transport, but you can use `New-WebServiceProxy` and call an XML web service directly (and get a response!).

WS-MAN is a standard, and on Windows, it is implemented by WinRM. With WS-MAN, you can set up remote endpoints and, using SOAP, send messages back and forth. MS-WSMV is used by Windows to manage this layer.

Windows PowerShell remoting sits on top of WS-MAN/WinRM. MS-PSRP enables a local Windows PowerShell session to create a remote session on some remote machine and both send pipelines to be evaluated and get the data returned from that processing.

Setting Up Remoting

Setting up remoting is relatively straightforward: you just run the `Enable-PsRemoting` cmdlet on each remoting client and server. When you run this cmdlet, you are doing two things:

- Setting up the WinRM service. `Enable-PsRemoting` does this by calling the `Set-WsManQuickConfig` cmdlet, which starts the WinRM service and sets the system startup type to Automatic so that WinRM service starts each time the OS starts. Next, it creates a listener to accept inbound requests on all IP addresses. Finally, it enables firewall exceptions for WS-MAN communication. This step enables basic WinRM functionality on the local machine.

- Enabling Windows PowerShell remoting to listen for and receive management instructions from a remote system. The setup process creates session configuration objects that define how a particular remote session is to work and sets the Access Control Lists (ACLs) on these objects. Finally, the WinRM service is restarted with these new endpoints defined and the new endpoint configuration objects active.

Session configuration objects provide you with a considerable amount of flexibility in controlling remoting sessions. Each time you create a remote session, Windows PowerShell connects to a remote session configuration object that defines how the remote Windows PowerShell session is to act. You can set ACLs to these objects to lock down certain users, enabling them to use only the specific session configuration you want to supply to that user. You can also constrain what cmdlets the user can use in a remote session.

Using Remoting

You use remoting in two basic ways:

- To create a remote session using the `*-PsSession` cmdlets, and then enter that session and use the remote system. These sessions are called *persistent* sessions.

- To run a script block or a script file on the remote system using `Invoke-Command`. The short-lived sessions used in this case are referred to as *ad-hoc* or *temporary* sessions.

You create a persistent session on a remote machine by using the `New-PsSession` cmdlet and specifying the remote machine and the appropriate credentials for that remote machine, as needed. Once the session is created, you use `Enter-PsSession` to enter the session, after which any commands entered are sent directly to the remote machine. This is shown in Figure 2-2.

FIGURE 2-2

A remoting session

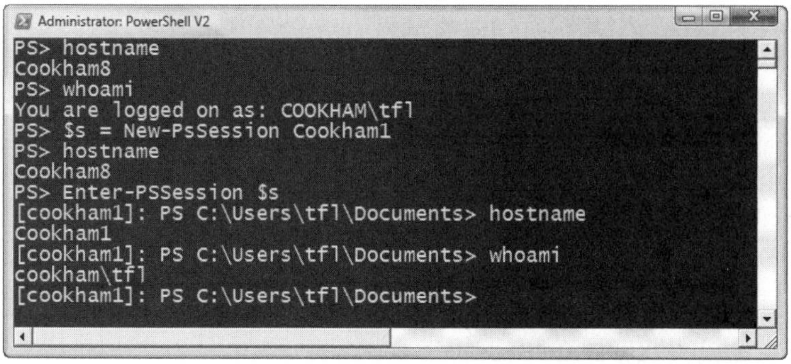

```
Administrator: PowerShell V2
PS> hostname
Cookham8
PS> whoami
You are logged on as: COOKHAM\tfl
PS> $s = New-PsSession Cookham1
PS> hostname
Cookham8
PS> Enter-PSSession $s
[cookham1]: PS C:\Users\tfl\Documents> hostname
Cookham1
[cookham1]: PS C:\Users\tfl\Documents> whoami
cookham\tfl
[cookham1]: PS C:\Users\tfl\Documents>
```

In the example illustrated, we created a persistent session to the computer `Cookham1`. You can then see we ran the `Hostname` command and it returned the local workstation name. After entering the persistent session, you can run cmdlets and scripts, load and use modules — in fact, you can do everything you can do in a local session, subject to the constraints of the session configuration object you use to create the remote session.

Storing the session object as a variable ($s) allows easy use of that session as long as the current Windows PowerShell session (on the local system) exists.

To run a one-off command or script on a remote machine, you could also use `Invoke-Command`, as shown in Figure 2-3. You can also use `Invoke-Command` to run a command in an existing session.

FIGURE 2-3

Remoting using Invoke-Command

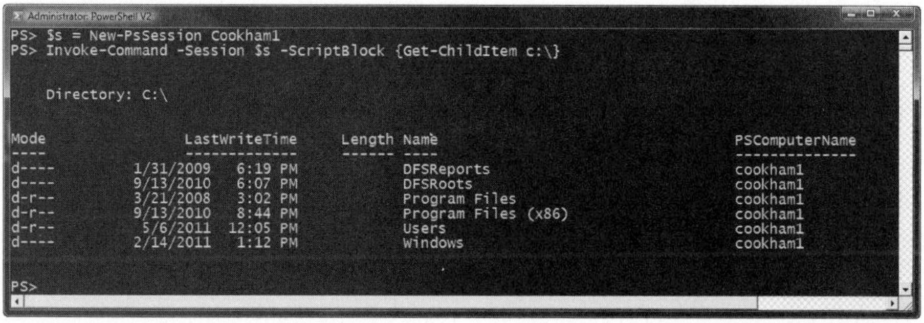

```
Administrator: PowerShell V2
PS> $s = New-PsSession Cookham1
PS> Invoke-Command -Session $s -ScriptBlock {Get-ChildItem c:\}


    Directory: C:\


Mode                LastWriteTime     Length Name                        PSComputerName
----                -------------     ------ ----                        --------------
d----         1/31/2009   6:19 PM            DFSReports                  cookham1
d----         9/13/2010   6:07 PM            DFSRoots                    cookham1
d-r--         3/21/2008   3:02 PM            Program Files               cookham1
d-r--         9/13/2010   8:44 PM            Program Files (x86)         cookham1
d-r--          5/6/2011  12:05 PM            Users                       cookham1
d----         2/14/2011   1:12 PM            Windows                     cookham1


PS>
```

A less common form of remoting is known as implicit remoting. With *implicit remoting*, you set up a session to a remote machine as normal, and then import cmdlets from that remote session into your local session. To use implicit remoting, you first create a persistent remote session with the target server. Over that session, you can optionally load additional Windows PowerShell modules. Then, you use the `Import-PsSession` cmdlet to import the session. Typically, you will limit the importation to just the cmdlets that are within a module. For example, you could create a remote session to your Lync 2010 server, load the Lync module, use `Import-PsSession,` and just return the Lync-related cmdlets.

When you import a remote session, Windows PowerShell converts the remote cmdlets into local functions (with the same name and parameters). When you call these functions, Windows PowerShell invokes the remote cmdlets for you. This would allow you, for example, to have remote sessions to your Domain Controller, Exchange Server, and Lync Server and use all the related cmdlets as though they existed on the local machine.

Cross-Reference
For more information on setting up remoting, see the `about_remote` and `about_remote_requirements` help files. For more information on all aspects of Windows PowerShell remoting, see The Administrator's Guide to Remoting at `http://powershell.com/cs/media/p/4908/download.aspx`. ■

Serialization

When you retrieve data from a remote server to your workstation, PSRP serializes the data into XML and deserializes it at the receiving end. Because of this, objects returned to your workstation lose their methods. For example, if you set up a remote session and then send a `Get-Process` to the remote machine, the remote machine takes the outputs left in the pipeline and serializes them before the serialized objects are transported back to the remoting client. Once at the remoting client, PSRP deserializes the objects automatically. The upshot is that all the methods, for example, the process's `Kill()` method, are lost and cannot be used on the local machine.

This is not really an issue, and it is easy to work around where you need to. If you need, for example, to kill a process on a remote machine, just execute the `Kill()` method on the remote machine. By ensuring all the necessary processing is carried out remotely and data returned only when it's appropriate, you also tend to improve performance by avoiding transporting data across the wire that is never actually used.

Working with Jobs

Another key feature in V2 is jobs. Jobs are related to (and often carry out) remoting tasks.

What Is a Job?

A Windows PowerShell *job* is a script or script block that is executed in the background to a given Windows PowerShell console. Like any script or script block, the execution can create output that can be viewed once the job has completed.

Jobs enable you to run long-running scripts in the background, leaving the foreground available. Jobs also enable you to keep the job's output (again, as long as you keep the foreground window open).

You manage jobs using the `*-Job` cmdlets. These enable you to create a new job, view all jobs, stop a running job, wait (block) until a particular job has completed, and get the results of a job's execution.

Using Jobs

To create a new job, you use the `Start-Job` cmdlet. This cmdlet enables you to specify either a script file or a script block as the source of the job. You can also specify parameters including credentials and authentication providers, initialization scripts (scripts to run before the job itself — sort of a profile for the job), and input objects (which can also come from the pipeline). For example:

```
Start-Job -Name WMI1 -File C:\Foo\Wmi1sto.ps1
```

You use `Get-Job` to view jobs within the current Windows PowerShell window. To stop a job, use `Stop-Job`, and to remove all details of a job, use `Remove-Job` and specify the ID or name of the job. When you run a job, any output is saved, in memory, by Windows PowerShell. Once the job is finished, you can get the job's results by using `Receive-Job`.

You can see the code to create a job, retrieve the results, and remove a job in Figure 2-4.

FIGURE 2-4

Using jobs

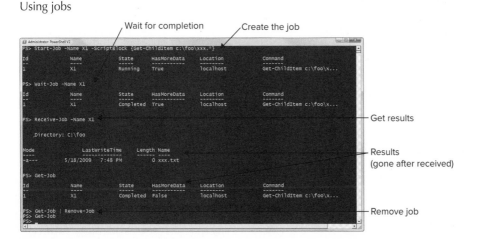

In addition to using the `*-Job` cmdlets, some cmdlets support an `-AsJob` parameter that runs the cmdlet as a job. You can then manage the job and retrieve the output in the normal way!

Potential Glitches Associated with Jobs

Jobs are a wonderful addition with V2, but two small issues might catch you unaware.

First, as noted earlier in this chapter, jobs are associated with a Windows PowerShell instance (the command line or a runspace in ISE). If that instance closes, all jobs and all the related information are lost. So, if you have just finished 10 jobs spanning thousands of machines and you close Windows PowerShell, all the existing jobs — completed, in action, and waiting to start — are gone, along with any unprocessed results from the completed jobs. Be careful to complete your processing of any job or jobs before you close the Windows PowerShell window.

The second potential problem you may encounter is that the `Receive-Job` cmdlet, by default, displays the results and then removes them. If you wanted to look at the results a second time, you can't. To avoid this happening, use the `Keep` parameter to `Receive-Job`. That way, Windows PowerShell keeps the job's output for reuse. For example:

```
Start-Job -file C:\Longjob.ps1 -name Longjob
Receive-Job -Name Longjob -Keep
```

Caution

It may be tempting to run lots of jobs in parallel. Assuming the computer was infinitely powerful, this might make sense. Windows PowerShell always starts any new job as soon as it's created (for example, after a `Start-Job` cmdlet). If you have too many jobs, especially those that run for a long time, you could slow your machine down significantly. Modern versions of Windows handle multiple jobs with ease, especially on today's multiprocessor, multithreaded computer systems. But only up to a point. Running larger numbers of jobs causes a lot of paging because each job fights all the other jobs for limited resources. As a rule of thumb, keep the number of active jobs at, or just below, the number of cores on your computer. ■

For more information on Windows PowerShell jobs, look at the content help topics `about_jobs`, `about_job_details`, and `about_remote_jobs`.

Using Advanced Functions

Windows PowerShell V1 was fairly simple and provided a limited set of features, especially when compared with cmdlets. Windows PowerShell V2 introduces advanced functions, which are much richer and enable you to, in effect, write cmdlets purely in script. In particular, you can also now write functions that function fully in a pipeline.

This section describes these new functions and looks at two key aspects of advanced functions: comment-based help and parameter bindings.

What's New with Advanced Functions?

A *function* is a named script block that you can execute. Functions can take parameters, which can come from a pipeline; functions can also produce output. In V2, there is no real difference between a function and an advanced function. The *advanced* refers to the extra things you can now do with features (e.g., comment-based help).

A function might look like this:

```
Function hello { Write-Host "Hello World"}
```

If you enter that function definition into Windows PowerShell, nothing appears to happen until you run it by entering `hello` in Windows PowerShell. You can see the results in Figure 2-5. This is the same behavior as you saw with functions in Version 1.

FIGURE 2-5

Running a function

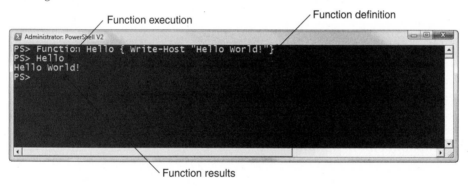

Functions can take a parameter block that identifies and describes the parameters that you can pass to a function. You name each parameter, and can optionally type them and get Windows PowerShell to conduct some degree of validation on the parameters by adding .NET attributes to a parameter. For example, here's a parameter block and accompanying function body:

```
Function Foo {
Param (
  [string] $name = $(Throw "You must specify name"),
  [ValidateSet("A", "B", "C")]
  [string] $class,
  [ValidateRange(2,7)]
  [int]    $version )

"Name    =    {0}" -f $name
"Class    =    {0}" -f $class
```

```
"Version =    {0}" -f $version

}
```

If you call this function, you must specify at least the name parameter. If you do specify either the class or version parameters, then Windows PowerShell validates what you enter based on the Validation attributes. If you specify the class parameter, you must specify either A, B, or C, while the version number, if specified, has to be between 2 and 7.

Note

For more information on advanced functions, see the about_functions, about_functions_advanced, about_functions_advanced_methods, and about_functions_advanced_parameters help files. ∎

Comment-Based Help

Comment-based help (CBH) is a feature of V2 where you add comments to function and/ or scripts. These comments can be understood and used by Get-Help so that scripts and functions you develop can have the same rich help experience that cmdlets can enjoy. This is a major improvement in usability/discovery.

With CBH, you enter a set of comments to a script or function file. These comments contain specific Windows PowerShell help keywords, preceded by a dot (.) and associated help content. You can enter the help comments either using a *comment block* (a block of text surrounded by a <# and a #>) or a block of comments, where each comment line begins with a pound sign (#). The keywords and their related information can appear in any order within the comment block.

Comment-based help must appear either at the beginning of a function or a script body, at the end of a function body, or before the function keyword. Note, there cannot be more than one blank line between the last line of the function help and the line containing the function keyword. Help is kind of brittle in that if you make a mistake such as using an incorrect help keyword, you do not get an error message or a full set of help information.

Here's a sample help block for the Foo function shown earlier:

```
<#
.SYNOPSIS
  This script demonstrates use of Windows PowerShell validation parameters in
  a param block.
.DESCRIPTION
  This script defines three parameters and displays the values
  passed. You can use this to test out validation of the parameters
.PARAMETER Name
  The first parameter - any string
.PARAMETER Class
  Second parameter - must be a string of either A, B, or C
.PARAMETER Version
  Third parameter - must be a number between 2 and 7 inclusive.
.EXAMPLE
  Foo -Name "hello" -Class "C" -version 4
```

```
       Illustrates a correct call
.EXAMPLE
   Foo "hello" D 3
   Illustrates an erroneous call
#>
```

If you combine this help block with the function `Foo` noted earlier and load it, you can then use `Get-Help` to get help on the function, as illustrated in Figure 2-6.

FIGURE 2-6

Using comment-based help

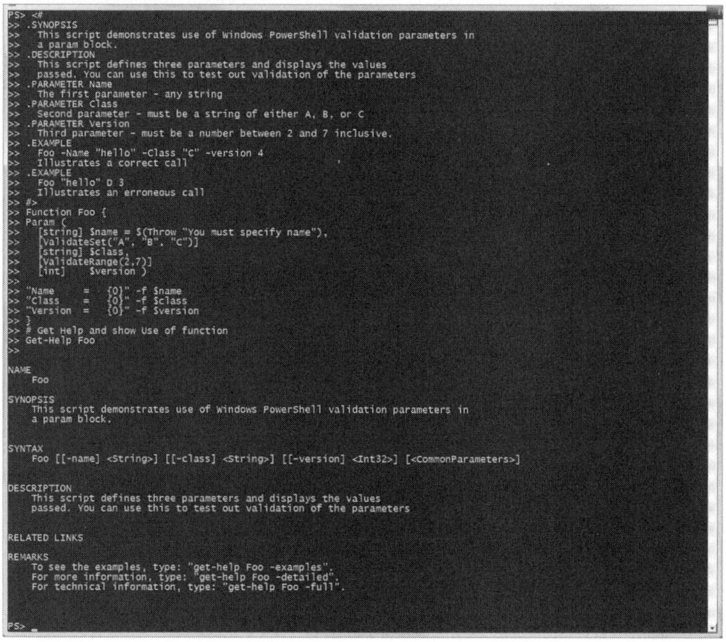

Note

For more information about using comment-based help in Windows PowerShell, see the Windows PowerShell help topic `about_Comment_Based_Help`. ■

Cmdlet Binding

Cmdlet binding is a term referring to how function parameters are bound at runtime. With cmdlet binding, a function is able to act like a cmdlet and get parameter(s) from the pipeline as well as from the command line. Cmdlet binding also enables you to implement confirmation, where the function asks for confirmation before carrying out some possibly risky operation in your function, and to specify a default parameter set name, which can be useful if you have functions with multiple parameter sets, especially where most parameters end up taking default values.

To invoke cmdlet binding, you need to add the `CmdletBinding()` attribute to the start of the function body, like this:

```
Function foo{
[CmdletBinding(SupportsShouldProcess=<Boolean>
  ConfirmImpact=<String>,
  DefaultParameterSetName=<String>)]
Parm ...
Rest of function ...
}
```

Note

For more details on cmdlet binding and how it works, see the `about_functions_CmdletBindingAttribute` help file. For more information about confirmation requests, see the MSDN page `http://go.microsoft .com/fwlink/?LinkId=136658`. ■

Splatting

An interesting new feature with V2 is splatting. *Splatting* is a technique that uses a hashtable to pass parameters to advanced functions (and cmdlets). The idea is fairly simple: instead of having multiple parameters and their values specified on a call to a function or cmdlet, you can create a hashtable and just pass the hashtable instead. The hashtable would have a row for every parameter you want to pass, where the row's key is the parameter name and the row's value is the value for that parameter. Consider a really simple function:

```
Function F1 {
Param ($P1, $P2, $P3, $P4)
...
}
```

In V1 (and V2) you could invoke the parameter like this:

```
F1 -P1 "P1 value" -P2 42 -P3 "P3 value" -P4 $Xxx
```

If there are a lot of parameters, or if the parameter values are long, this approach becomes hard to read. With splatting, you would first create a hashtable and then call the function like this:

```
# Create hashtable for F1
$F1ht=@{P1 = "P1 value"
        P2 = 42
        P3 = "P3 value"
        P4 = $Xxx}   # where $Xxx was calculated earlier
# Now call F1 passing the hashtable
F1 @F1ht
```

This approach is certainly a cool feature. It allows you to make calls to complex cmdlets or functions in a more readable way. For example, creating a new user in Active Directory could require more than five parameters — which means very long lines or adding line breaks to aid readability. With splatting, this becomes a lot easier to read. Splatting also enables you to programmatically add parameters (as you parse user input) more simply.

Working with Modules

Modules are a way of packaging Windows PowerShell scripts and cmdlets for distribution and reuse. This section describes modules and looks at the three types of modules: script modules, manifest modules, and implicit modules. Modules both supersede snap-ins as a way of adding new cmdlets and Providers into Windows PowerShell and provide a great way for enterprises and others to manage sets of related code. Because, in effect, cmdlets can now be written in script, modules provide a great way to package related functions, cmdlets, Providers, and so on into manageable units that can be leveraged by other Windows PowerShell users in your organization.

What Is a Module?

In Windows PowerShell, a module is a unit of code that you can add in, or remove, from your Windows PowerShell console (or other Windows PowerShell host). You use the `Import-Module` cmdlet to import the module into your console and `Remove-Module` to unload the module. Modules can contain cmdlets, Providers, script, functions, variables, and other tools/files.

The three types of modules are script modules, manifest modules, and implicit modules. Each of these module types enables you to package code, provide different features, and have different use cases.

Modules are, by default, located in one of two places: `C:\Users\<user>\Documents\ Windows PowerShell\Modules` (for user-specific modules) and `C:\Windows\system32\ Windows PowerShell\v1.0\Modules\` (for system-wide modules). In both cases, this assumes you install Windows using the normal installation folder defaults. You create a module by creating a folder in one of these two folders. The name of the folder is the name of the module. The contents of this folder vary depending on the module type. You can explicitly load modules from other locations by providing a full path to `Import-Module`.

Tip

If you are going to be using profiles extensively, you might want to create two variables (such as $mod and $sysmod) and two drives (such mod: and sysmod:) in your profile to point, respectively, to the default user module folder and the default system module folder. You can do this as follows:

```
$mod    = (Dir Env:PsModulePath).Value.Split(";")[0]
$sysmod = (Dir Env:PsModulePath).Value.Split(";")[1]
New-PSDrive -Name mod -Root $mod -PSProvider FileSystem
New-PSDrive -Name Sysmod -Root $sysmod -PSProvider FileSystem ∎
```

Script Modules

A *script module* is essentially a Windows PowerShell script defining functions (and variables) that is saved as a `.psm1` file. The file is saved under one of your module folders with the same name as the folder. Thus, a script module called `Module1` would live in `C:\Users\<user>\ Documents\Windows PowerShell\Modules\Module1\Module1.psm1`.

When you import a script module, Windows PowerShell runs the script to define functions, create variables, and so on. You use a script module where you want to create and use a set of related script cmdlets.

An excellent example of a script module is the Windows PowerShell Management Library for Hyper-V. Written by James O'Neill (and downloadable free from http://pshyperv .codeplex.com/), this module has around 80 functions that enable you to manage Hyper-V without the need for Microsoft's System Center Virtual Machine Manager product. If you are using Hyper-V, then take a look at this module!

A key difference between scripts and script modules is that you can control which functions, variables, and so on created in the .psm1 file are visible after the import is complete. By controlling the objects exported, using Export-ModuleMember, you can have helper functions and internal variables that your (exported) functions use, but that are not exposed to the module's user.

Here is a very simple module with three functions, only one of which is exported:

```
# Module 1 - Really simple module
Write-Host "Loading Module 1"
Function Foobar      { "In module1"}
Function Foobar2     {"Also in Module"}
Function Barfoo      { foobar; foobar2}
Export-ModuleMember -Function Barfoo
```

This script module is saved as C:\Users\tfl\Documents\Windows PowerShell\Modules\ module1\module1.psm1. Figure 2-7 shows this module, Module1, in use — the example first imports the module and then invokes the functions inside the module. Note that the function Foobar cannot be called after the module is loaded (because it's not exported). However, the function Barfoo can be called. Because it was exported, you can use it, and it can call the two nonexported functions, as you can see.

FIGURE 2-7

Simple script module

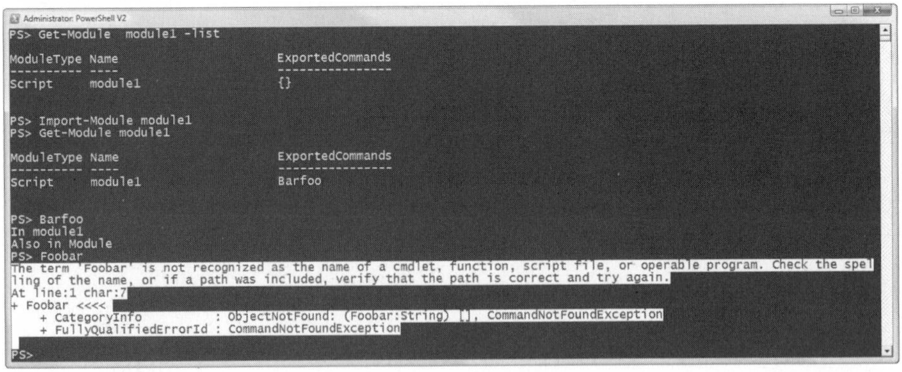

Manifest Modules

A *manifest module* is a module that contains a module manifest that specifies the module content and other components (typically, but not always, other compiled code). Manifest modules, in effect, replace the snap-in from V1, although for compatibility reasons, snap-ins continue to be supported.

A module manifest contains a hashtable with predefined keys, which is stored in a .psd1 file underneath a module folder. The hashtable can be manually created, or you can use New-ModuleManifest to create the manifest.

Here is a simple module manifest:

```
#
# Module manifest for module 'mmodule1'
@{
ModuleToProcess = 'Mmodule1'
ModuleVersion = '1.0'
GUID = '051c7eb1-01f1-4813-a821-83f111e791d3'
Author = 'Thomas Lee'
CompanyName = 'PS Partnership'
Copyright = '2011'
Description = 'Module 1 converted to Manifest Module'
FunctionsToExport = 'BARFOO'
}
```

In the manifest, you see the basic documentation (author, company name, and so on), along with a module to process. This module manifest (which is saved as Mmodule1.psm1) is found in the same folder as Mmodule1.psd1. This enables you to convert a simple script module into a richer manifest module by just adding a manifest (and possibly other files as needed).

Manifest modules allow you to specify a number of attributes about a module by adding keys to the manifest's hashtable. The preceding example shows eight of the more common attributes you can specify.

Note

For a more complete list of the module attributes, see http://msdn.microsoft.com/en-us/library/dd878337%28VS.85%29.aspx. ∎

Implicit Modules

Implicit modules are modules created by Windows PowerShell when you use the Import-PsSession cmdlet to import the cmdlets from a remote session into your local session, as noted earlier in this chapter. Windows PowerShell creates an implicit module and converts the remote cmdlets into local (proxy) functions. Thus, when you use the functions that Windows PowerShell autogenerates when it creates the implicit module, you actually run the cmdlets on the remote machine.

For example, suppose you have two machines, a local system and a remote server, and you want to use cmdlets from the `ServerManager` module on the remote server. You first create a remote session to the remote server, as follows:

```
$S = New-PsSession -Computer Cookham11
```

Once the session is created, you can load the `ServerManager` module as follows:

```
Invoke-Command -Session $S -ScriptBlock {Import-Module ServerManager}
```

Finally, you can import the remote `ServerManager` module into the local session by typing:

```
Import-PSSession $S -Module ServerManager
```

Once completed, you can run any of the cmdlets contained in the `ServerManager` module from your local machine. When these cmdlets run, Windows PowerShell runs them on the remote machine (`Cookham2`) rather than locally. You can see this in Figure 2-8.

FIGURE 2-8

Implicit remoting

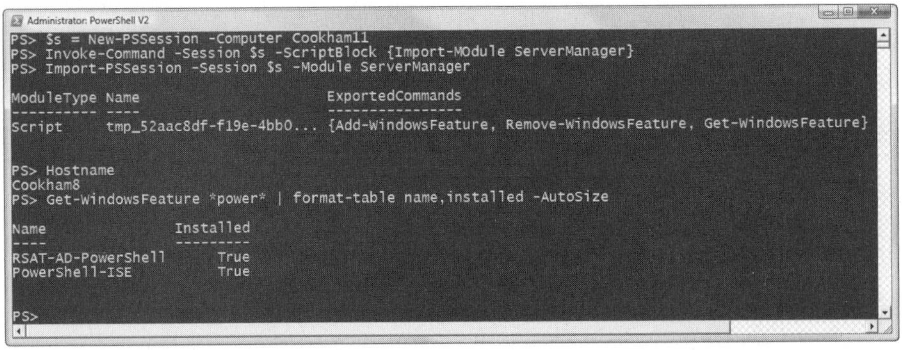

As you can see in Figure 2-8, the implicit module is created when you import the remote session. It has a name that is generated by Windows PowerShell that incorporates a Globally Unique Identifier (GUID). And as you can also see, only the three cmdlets in the `Servermanager` module are imported into the local session.

You can, if you want, import an entire `PsSession` from a remote machine. That means, however, all the cmdlets you normally run could be overwritten by proxy functions. Windows PowerShell detects this and does not create command proxies for remote commands that would override, or "clobber," local commands. Should you want this to happen, you could use the `-AllowClobber` parameter to `Import-PsSession`, as follows:

```
Import-PsSession $s -AllowClobber
```

For more information on `Import-PsSession` and implicit modules, see the help text for `Import-PsSession`.

Making Use of Eventing

Eventing is the ability to register for events that occur in Windows and when these events occur, execute the code you registered. For example, each time a process starts, you could get Windows PowerShell to dump information about the new process to assist in troubleshooting. This section first describes eventing, then looks at how you could use it.

What Is Eventing?

Eventing enables you to respond to asynchronous event notifications that Windows and many .NET and Windows Management Instrumentation (WMI) objects support. Events are a fundamental part of programming in Windows, albeit possibly less useful for administrators who use Windows PowerShell.

The concept behind eventing is fairly simple. With eventing, you have two pieces of code. For example, you might have a script that is running based on a scheduled task. That script might encounter some condition and can raise (or signal) an event, perhaps that it has completed its work. A second bit of code, perhaps a second script running on that same system, can register for events. When the first bit of code raises the event, the second can handle the event and do something appropriate to the event, perhaps just log the successful completion of the first script, or maybe invoke an additional script.

Using Eventing

To use eventing in Windows PowerShell, you first subscribe to events generated by .NET, WMI, or the Windows PowerShell engine itself. To subscribe (or register, as Windows PowerShell calls it) for an event, you use `Register-ObjectEvent` (to register for a .NET Object event), `Register-EngineEvent` (to register for a Windows PowerShell engine event or an event raised by `New-Event`), or `Register-WmiEvent` (to subscribe to a WMI event).

After subscribing to an event, for example, subscribing to the elapsed timer event from the `System.Timers.Timer` class, you can poll the event queue using the `Get-Event` cmdlet. Each time you call this cmdlet, you can specify to get all the events, or you can be more specific and use the `-EventIdentifier` parameter to get events of a specific type or the `-SourceIdentifier` to get events from a specific event source.

In general, polling can be somewhat tedious, especially because you have to wait until the event occurs anyway. Polling also means you have to write a loop to check to see if there's an event, then wait a bit and try again, and again, and again. This approach wastes CPU cycles.

To avoid polling, you can use the `Wait-Event` cmdlet in your script to wait until the event has occurred. Once the event fires, your script continues, and you can process the event. This is an improvement on polling, but still means your script/session is blocked until the event occurs and Windows PowerShell returns from `Wait-Event`.

Another eventing technique is to use the `-Action` parameter in conjunction with one of the `Register-*Event` cmdlets. This enables you to specify a script block that Windows PowerShell runs when the event fires. This is illustrated by the following script fragment:

```
# Run notepad (code assumes 1 copy of notepad running)
notepad
# Now get the process object for this process
$process = Get-Process -Name Notepad
# Register for the 'exited' event
Register-ObjectEvent -Input $process -EventName Exited `
 -Action {Write-Host "notepad has exited"}
```

When you run this code, you first start a copy of Notepad and then get the process details for Notepad. When you use `Register-ObjectEvent`, Windows PowerShell runs the script block when the process completes and the exited event is raised. This script block then writes a message to the host. You can see the results of this in Figure 2-9.

FIGURE 2-9

Eventing with Windows PowerShell

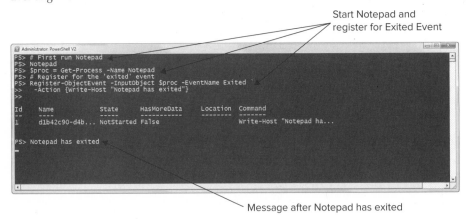

Start Notepad and
register for Exited Event

Message after Notepad has exited

Eventing is a fairly advanced feature and tends to be used only in more complex scenarios. For example, you might create a script that runs other scripts on multiple machines, raising events as the script executes. You could then have a separate dashboard script that handles the events raised and displays progress of the scripts.

Using the Integrated Scripting Environment

The Integrated Scripting Environment, or ISE, is a Unicode-based GUI alternative to the Windows PowerShell console. It offers a basic set of IDE features — much easier to use than Notepad and the console, but without some of the richer features in third-party tools.

Cross-Reference

This section is just a quick introduction because there's more information later in this book in Chapter 25, "Using the Windows PowerShell ISE." In that chapter, you find more information on the ISE and how to customize and extend it for your own use. ∎

You can use the ISE both to access Windows PowerShell and to develop scripts. The ISE is designed to be a better scripting environment than Notepad, and specifically supports Unicode, which is of great value in those countries where the local language is rendered in Unicode. The ISE also enables you to create customizations to further improve your productivity.

Supporting Transactions

The basic ability to support transactions was added to V2, but has not really been widely used. With V2, the registry Provider is the only Provider that supports transactions. This section introduces the idea of transactions and shows how transactions are supported in V2.

The Need for Transactions

The idea of transactions comes from databases but can be used in almost any IT scenario. A *transaction* is a set of changes that are atomic — either they all happen or none of them happen. Transactions are essential in banking environments, for example, where you move money between two accounts. There needs to be a debit and a credit — and both have to occur for the transaction to make sense.

With Windows PowerShell, individual Providers are able to implement transactions (although only the Registry Provider actually does). With a transaction-enabled Provider, you can begin a transaction, perform any number of updates to the data in the Provider, and then either commit the transaction (and publish all the changes), or roll the transaction back.

In task administration, there is often a desire to implement transactions across the product, for example, to transaction complex provisioning — either the object is fully provisioned or not. Unfortunately, such global support of transactions is not implemented yet, although this may happen in a future version of Windows PowerShell. If you need such functionality in your scripts, you have to write your own more complex scripts to implement any required transactioning.

Transaction Support for V2

Transactions, in general, are supported in two ways. First, a set of standard transaction cmdlets lets you define a transaction and then use it. Second, these cmdlets only work against a Provider that supports transactions. You can see which Providers on your system are capable of supporting transactions by typing `Get-PsProvider`.

Using the registry Provider's transaction support, you would start the transaction by using the `Start-Transaction` cmdlet. Subsequent registry operations (for example, creating a new key or value entry) are done as normal using the `*-Item` cmdlets, but each registry update is done specifying the `-UseTransaction` property. Once the transaction is complete, you signal completion to Windows PowerShell by using the `Complete-Transaction` cmdlet. If you find some reason why the transaction should be rolled back (and, in effect, undone), you signal that by calling the `Undo-Transaction` cmdlet.

Figure 2-10 shows a simple example of a registry handling with transactions.

FIGURE 2-10

Registry transactions

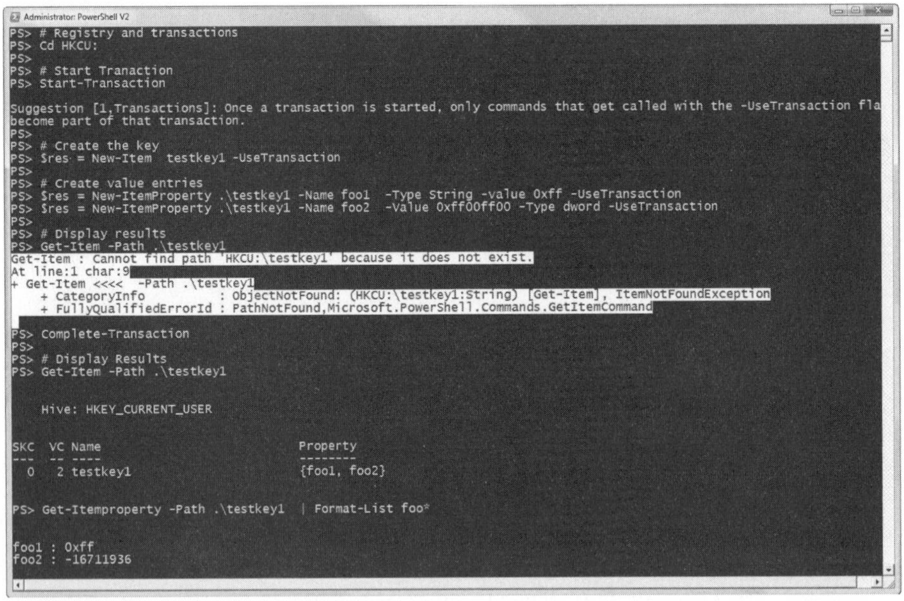

Cross-Reference

For more information on setting up transactions in Windows PowerShell, see the `about_remote` and `about_transactions` help file. ∎

Debugging and Error Handling

Debugging scripts was difficult in V1. With V2, Microsoft added 10 debugging-related cmdlets you can use at the console and the ISE, along with ISE menu items you can use to debug your scripts. In addition to the specific debugging-related cmdlets, you can also use the Windows PowerShell ISE to debug your scripts.

Debugging from the Command Line

The debugging cmdlets in V2 revolve around the concept of *breakpoints* — points in a script where Windows PowerShell should stop and let you examine what the script has done so far, look at variables, and so on.

As with most traditional debugging environments, you can set a breakpoint at a particular line in a script. You can also set a breakpoint on a command (stop when you hit the command) or on a variable (break when a variable is used). This provides a rich set of debugging features.

The breakpoint-related cmdlets in Windows PowerShell V2 are:

- `Set-PSBreakpoint`: Sets a breakpoint in a script.
- `Get-PSBreakpoint`: Gets the breakpoints set in the current Windows PowerShell session.
- `Disable-PSBreakPoint`: Disables a breakpoint but does not remove it.
- `Enable-PSBreakPoint`: Enables a previously disabled breakpoint.
- `Remove-PSBreakpoint`: Disables and removes a breakpoint.

After setting breakpoints, you run your script(s), which run as normal until a breakpoint is reached. What happens then is based on using the `Set-PSDebug` cmdlet. This cmdlet lets you turn script debugging on or off and can toggle `StrictMode`.

`StrictMode` is a V2 Windows PowerShell feature that you use to tell Windows PowerShell how strict to be when running a script. `StrictMode` is similar to using `Option Explicit` in Visual Basic.

With `StrictMode` on, and set to Version 2 (`Set-StrictMode -Version 2`), Windows PowerShell enforces coding rules in any code that you try to execute. If you use these Version 2 settings with `Set-StrictMode`, Windows PowerShell prohibits references to uninitialized variables, nonexistent properties of an object, function calls that use the syntax for calling object methods, and variables without any name.

Here is an example of turning on `StrictMode` and trapping a coding error:

```
# Set StrictMode
Set-StrictMode -Version 2
```

```
# Define a function
# function uses a variable that has not yet been defined
Function X {$x = $foo}
# Call this function
X
The variable '$foo' cannot be retrieved because it has not been set.
At line:1 char:22
+ Function X {$x = $foo <<<< }
    + CategoryInfo          : InvalidOperation: (foo:Token) [],
RuntimeException
      + FullyQualifiedErrorId : VariableIsUndefined
```

The situations detected by Set-StrictMode typically come about as the result of a typo — typing a variable name or property name *almost* correctly. Setting StrictMode is a great way to find the typos that could render a script runnable, but not useful.

Two other V2 debugging-related cmdlets are Write-Debug and Write-Verbose. You can use these cmdlets in any script you write, but they will output information only if you've enabled output. To enable Write-Debug to output, you turn on debugging by using Set-PsDebug. To enable verbose output, either set $VerbosePreference or use the -Verbose parameter in any cmdlet. You can set $VerbosePreference to one of four values:

- **SilentlyContinue:** Write-Verbose produces no output, and your script continues.
- **Stop:** Write-Verbose produces the verbose output, and your script stops.
- **Continue:** Write-Verbose produces the verbose output and your script continues.
- **Enquire:** Write-Verbose produces the verbose output, and Windows Powershell inquires as to what you want to do (i.e., stop, continue).

If you use the -Verbose parameter in any cmdlet, Windows PowerShell displays verbose output in the same way as with Write-Verbose.

With Write-Debug, you can add write statements throughout your scripts, which would result in output only if you set debugging on — the rest of the time, Windows PowerShell just skips over them.

Note
For more information about the Windows PowerShell debugger, see the about_Debuggers help file. ∎

Using Try/Catch/Finally

Handling errors with Version 1 was pretty basic — you could just use the Trap command and trap any terminating errors. But with Windows PowerShell V2, Microsoft added some new error-handling syntax: Try/Catch/Finally. These operators, which come from C#, enable you to try to run some potentially breakable cmdlet or sequence of cmdlets and catch (and handle) errors that might occur, particularly runtime errors (for example, disk not found, network host not available, and so on). This can make error reporting a lot easier as well as enabling you to recover more easily for certain types of errors.

Here's a simple example of `Try/Catch`:

```
Try {
$computers = import-csv c:\foo\computers.csv
"number of rows: {0}" -f $computers.count
} Catch {
"c:\foo\computers.csv file not found";
}
```

In this example, the code first tries to open the file `c:\computer.csv` and then displays how many rows were created in the file. If this file exists, the code prints out how many lines were in the file, but if the file does not exist, then that error is trapped and a suitable error message is written out.

The `Try/Catch` blocks can be used in conjunction with a third syntax block, `Finally`. This enables you do something whether or not an error was captured. Typically, this is where you might do cleanup based on work done in the `Try` block.

New Cmdlets

Windows PowerShell V2 added over 100 new cmdlets. This chapter has introduced you to many of the more important ones.

Some of the additional new cmdlets include `Get-Hotfix`, `Send-MailMessage`, `Get-ComputerRestorePoint`, `Add-Computer`, `Reset-ComputerMachinePassword`, and `Get-Random`.

Note
Perhaps the best way to discover all the new cmdlets in Windows PowerShell V2 is to use Bing's Visual Search feature to look at all Windows PowerShell cmdlets at `www.bing.com/visualsearch?g=Windows PowerShell_cmdlets#toc=0&version_rbid=1`. ∎

Summary

In this chapter, you looked at what's new in Windows PowerShell V2 and saw how this version of Windows PowerShell adds a wealth of valuable new features and cmdlets. Version 2 added a lot of very powerful features, including remote management, background jobs, advanced functions, modules, eventing, the ISE, transactions, and debugging.

In the next section of this book, you examine the use of Windows PowerShell from your client desktop, including interoperating with Microsoft Office 2010. Chapter 3 looks at Windows PowerShell in Windows 7.

Part II

Windows Desktop

IN THIS PART

Chapter 3
Managing Windows 7

Chapter 4
Managing Microsoft Office 2010

Chapter 5
Managing Security

Chapter 6
Managing and Installing Software

Managing Windows 7

IN THIS CHAPTER

Troubleshooting Windows 7

Managing Windows Search

Checking hotfix status

Managing files and folders

W indows PowerShell allows you to troubleshoot Windows 7 problems and verify that patches have been installed. You are also able to manage Windows Search, performing searches and adding or removing folders in the search catalog. Finally, you can use Windows PowerShell to manage files and folders in Windows 7.

Troubleshooting Windows 7 with Windows PowerShell

Windows 7 comes with over 100 built-in scripts designed to facilitate troubleshooting. The number of scripts may vary, depending on which applications or service pack level your computer is running. You will need to import the scripts before you can use them. Because the scripts are provided in a module, you use the `Import-Module` cmdlet with the required parameter `Name`, and the name of the module, which is `TroubleshootingPack`. The following example imports the `TroubleshootingPack` module, which enables you to access any of the built-in troubleshooting packs:

```
Import-Module -Name TroubleshootingPack
```

The built-in scripts are located in the `C:\Windows` directory, in a subfolder named `Diagnostics`. The actual scripts are in separate subfolders under the `System` subfolder of the `Diagnostics` folder.

To get a list of the available troubleshooting packs, you use the `Get-ChildItem` cmdlet, with the parameter `Path`. The following example shows the current troubleshooting packs located under the `Windows\Diagnostics\System` folder. The output is shown in Figure 3-1.

```
Get-ChildItem -Path $Env:WinDir\Diagnostics\System
```

FIGURE 3-1

Default troubleshooting packs

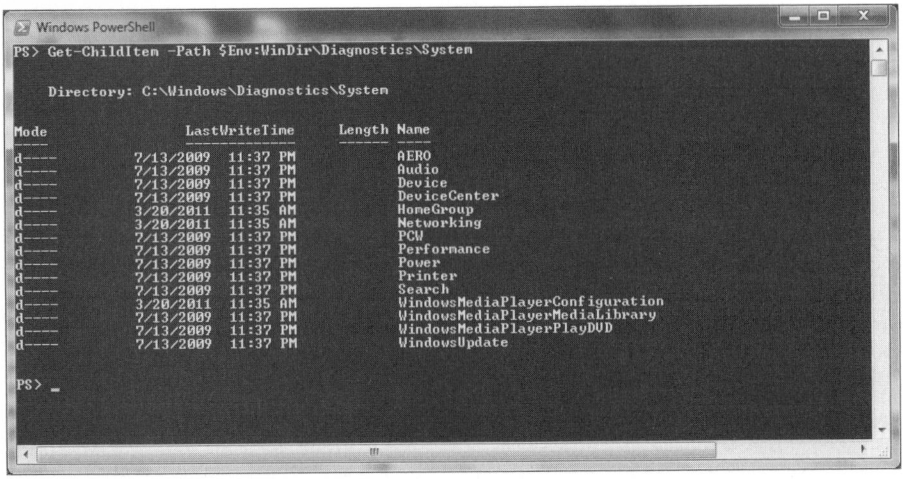

You can find more information about any of the listed troubleshooting packs using the `Get-TroubleshootingPack` cmdlet, along with the required parameter `Path`. The following example shows the default information returned by the `Get-TroubleshootingPack` cmdlet. The default information returned is the troubleshooting pack's `Id`, `Name`, `Publisher`, and `Version`.

```
$TroubleshootingPack = @{
Path = "$Env:WinDir\Diagnostics\system\aero"
}
Get-TroubleshootingPack @TroubleshootingPack
```

Id	Name	Publisher	Version
--	----	---------	-------
AeroDiagnostics	Aero	Microsoft Windows	1.0

You can get more detailed information about the troubleshooting pack by piping the output of the `Get-TroubleshootingPack` cmdlet to either the `Format-List` cmdlet or the `Select-Object` cmdlet. The next example shows that the troubleshooting pack `Aero` troubleshoots "Display aero effects such as transparency":

```
$TroubleshootingPack = @{
Path = "$Env:WinDir\Diagnostics\system\aero"
}
```

```
Get-TroubleshootingPack @TroubleshootingPack | Select-Object Description
Description
-----------
Display Aero effects such as transparency.
```

If you are not sure which troubleshooting pack will help with a particular problem, you can show the description of all currently installed troubleshooting packs. The following example first sets the variable $PackPath to the directory where the troubleshooting packs are stored, and then lists the name and description for each one:

```
$PackPath = "$Env:WinDir\Diagnostics\System"
ForEach ($Pack in Get-ChildItem $PackPath)
{
Get-TroubleshootingPack -Path $PackPath\$Pack | Select-Object Name, Description
}
```

You can run any of the troubleshooting packs using the Invoke-TroubleshootingPack cmdlet, with the required parameter Pack. The Pack parameter does not take a file path; you need to either pipe the results of a Get-TroubleshootingPack cmdlet, or save that result into a variable and use that variable as the Pack parameter's value. The following example runs the printer troubleshooting pack with the default options. When run without options, a troubleshooting pack sends the output to the console only, and you will typically be prompted to choose one or more options.

```
$TroubleshootingPack = @{
Path = "$Env:WinDir\Diagnostics\System\Printer"
}
$PrinterPack = Get-TroubleshootingPack @TroubleshootingPack
Invoke-TroubleshootingPack -Pack $PrinterPack
```

To save the output to a file, you can add the optional Result parameter. The Result parameter specifies the path where you would like the result files saved. Output is saved in two files: DebugReport.xml and ResultReport.xml. A third file, results.xsl, will be saved in the same path. This file is an XLS style sheet, defining how to display the two XML report files. You can view either of the report files by double-clicking them in Windows Explorer or by using the Invoke-Item cmdlet described later in this chapter.

A further parameter to the Invoke-TroubleshootingPack cmdlet is the AnswerFile parameter. An answer file allows the script to bypass questions the troubleshooting pack asks. You create the answer file with the Get-TroubleshootingPack cmdlet, passing the required parameters Pack and AnswerFile. The AnswerFile value can be either a path and filename, or just a filename. If you do not specify a path, the file will be saved in the current working directory.

The following example creates an answer file for the search troubleshooting pack, which troubleshoots Windows Search. The output of the example shows the steps involved in creating the answer file.

```
$TroubleshootingPack = @{
Path = "C:\Windows\Diagnostics\System\Search"
AnswerFile = "SearchAnswerFile.xml"
}
$Search = Get-TroubleshootingPack @TroubleshootingPack
PS> $Search = Get-TroubleshootingPack @TroubleshootingPack

Please answer the following questions
You will be asked a series of questions from the specified package.
The answers you provide will be stored in an answer file that
  you can use to automate question responses during package execution

Press enter to continue



What problems do you notice?
Select all that apply.

[1] Files don't appear in search results.
[2] E-mail doesn't appear in search results.
[3] Search or indexing is slowing down the computer.
[4] My problem isn't listed above. (Please provide a description
  on the next page.)
[5] None of the above

[?] Help
[x] Exit
:1

Please describe your problem
Enter a brief description of your problem in the box below:
:missing files
PS>
```

Once you have the answer file created, you pass it to the `AnswerFile` parameter of the `Invoke-TroubleshootingPack` cmdlet. This is shown in the following example, using the answer file you created in the previous example:

```
$myPack = @{
Path = "C:\Windows\Diagnostics\System\Search"
}
$Options = @{
AnswerFile = "SearchAnswerFile.xml"
}
Get-TroubleshootingPack @myPack | Invoke-TroubleshootingPack @Options
```

You can get the path and description for all troubleshooting packs by modifying the previous example. The next example lists all current troubleshooting packs, removing the

`$Env:WinDir\Diagnostics\System` part of the path, and displaying the folder name and description. This output is shown in Figure 3-2.

```
$PackPath = "$Env:WinDir\Diagnostics\System"
$Format =@{Label='Name';Width=35;Expression={Split-Path $_.Path -Leaf}},
"Description"
$Packs = @()

ForEach ($Pack in Get-ChildItem $PackPath)
{
$Packs += Get-TroubleshootingPack -Path $PackPath\$Pack
}
$Packs |Format-Table $Format
```

FIGURE 3-2

Default troubleshooting packs

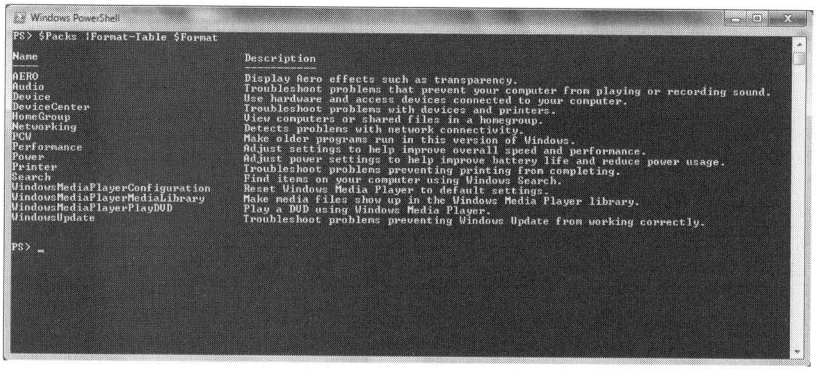

Because the `Get-TroubleshootingPack` cmdlet requires the entire path, you still need to add the `$Env:WinDir\Diagnostics\System` part of the path to the string you pass to the `Path` parameter.

You can create a function to get the troubleshooting pack and invoke it in one call. This makes using the troubleshooting packs more convenient. Listing 3-1 provides a sample function.

LISTING 3-1

The Use-TroubleshootingPack Function

```
Function Use-TroubleshootingPack
{
param ([string]$Pack,
[string]$AnswerFile = $null,
[string]$Result = $null)
```

continues

75

LISTING 3-1   *(continued)*

```
if (!(Get-Module troubleshootingpack))
{
Import-Module TroubleshootingPack
}
$packPath = "$Env:WinDir\Diagnostics\System\$pack"
$myPack = @{
Path = $packPath
}
$Options = @{
}
if ($Result)
{
$Options += @{
Result = $Result
}
}
if ($AnswerFile)
{
$Options += @{
AnswerFile = $AnswerFile
}
}
Get-TroubleshootingPack @myPack |Invoke-TroubleshootingPack @Options
}
```

You can use this function by passing the required parameter `Pack`. The following example runs the search troubleshooting pack, prompting for input:

```
Use-TroubleshootingPack -Pack search
```

The next example runs the troubleshooting pack `Audio`, saving the results in `c:\scripts\results`:

```
Use-TroubleshootingPack -Pack Audio -Result c:\Scripts\Results
```

This final example runs the troubleshooting pack `Search`, using a previously created answer file, saving the results in the folder `C:\scripts\Results`:

```
$TroubleshootingPack = @{
Pack = "search"
AnswerFile = "C:\scripts\AnswerFiles\Search.xml"
Result = "C:\scripts\Results"
}
Use-TroubleshootingPack @TroubleshootingPack
```

Managing Windows Search

Managing Windows Search requires that you download the Interop DLL from Microsoft. An Interop DLL allows you to use a COM library as a .NET class. The DLL is part of the Microsoft Windows Search 3.x SDK, which you can download from www.microsoft .com/downloads/en/details.aspx?FamilyID=645300AE-5E7A-4CE7-95F0-49793F8F76E8&displaylang=en.

The SDK is a self-extracting zip file. The SDK extracts to C:\Windows Search 3x SDK by default. Examples in this chapter use this path.

Once you have downloaded and extracted the SDK, you can load the DLL into Windows PowerShell. The following example loads the Windows Search DLL. These two lines will need to be included at the top of any script designed to manage Windows Search.

```
$dllpath = "C:\Windows Search 3x SDK\Managed\Microsoft.Search.Interop.dll"
Add-Type -Path $dllpath
```

Discovering Which Folders Are Currently Indexed

You can discover which folders are currently indexed within any Windows PowerShell console.

After the DLL is loaded, you need to create an instance of the search manager class. This class is called CSearchManagerClass. Because you need to reference this class within the script, load the instance into a variable, as shown here:

```
$Search = New-Object -TypeName Microsoft.Search.Interop.CSearchManagerClass
```

This results in an object of the CSearchManagerClass class pointed to by the $Search variable. Once you have the search class loaded into the $Search variable, you need to load the search catalog into another variable. Currently, the only catalog is the SystemIndex. The following line shows an example of loading the search catalog:

```
$Catalog = $Search.GetCatalog("SystemIndex")
```

Now that you have the catalog loaded, you need to create an interface to the scope rule manager, again storing the interface in a variable, as shown here:

```
$ScopeManager = $catalog.GetCrawlScopeManager()
```

You have now loaded the DLL and created all the necessary objects. From this point on, you will need to initialize a few variables, and then you can run your search.

First, you need to define an array to hold the returned scope rules, as well as a Boolean variable ($true or $false) to indicate the beginning of the enumeration. You also have to create a variable to hold the output of each loop through the enumeration process. These steps are shown here:

```
$ScopeRules = @()
$FirstLoop = $true
[Microsoft.Search.Interop.CSearchScopeRule]$CurrentScope = $null
$Enumeration = $ScopeManager.EnumerateScopeRules()
```

Note

Enumeration refers to the procedure of listing all members of a set. ■

You can handle the enumeration of the scopes in a Do-While loop. The search returns an object for each rule in the system index. You can output them to an array for later processing, as shown here, or just output them to the standard output if you are not interested in manipulating the objects.

In the following example, the results of the enumeration are stored in the array variable $ScopeRules. To examine the results, you can simply enter $ScopeRules in the console. The type accelerator [ref] is a pointer to the System.Management.Automation .PSReference .NET type. This type defines an object that is a value or variable reference.

```
Do
{
$Enumeration.Next(1,[ref]$CurrentScope,[ref]$null)
$FirstLoop = $false
$ScopeRules += $CurrentScope
}While ($CurrentScope -ne $null -or $FirstLoop)
PS> $ScopeRules
```

PatternOrURL	IsIncluded	IsDefault
csc://{S-1-5-21-2223528128...	1	1
file:///*\$RECYCLE.BIN*	0	1
file:///*\DfsrPrivate*	0	1
file:///*\System Volume In...	0	1
file:///C:\ProgramData*	0	1
file:///C:\ProgramData\Mic...	0	1
file:///C:\ProgramData\Mic...	1	1
file:///C:\Users\	1	1
...		

Patterns and URLs that are indexed are indicated with a 1 in the IsIncluded field. Patterns and URLs that are specifically excluded are indicated with a 0 in the IsIncluded field.

You can filter the output to list just patterns that are indexed by Windows search by piping $ScopeRules to the Where-Object cmdlet, as shown here:

```
$ScopeRules |Where-Object {$_.IsIncluded} |Select-Object PatternOrUrl
```

Logically, therefore, you can list the patterns that are specifically excluded from Windows search by using the `Where-Object` cmdlet and specifying `!$.IsIncluded`:

```
$ScopeRules |Where-Object {!$_.IsIncluded} |Select-Object PatternOrUrl
```

The entire script to list all patterns of currently indexed folders is shown in Listing 3-2.

LISTING 3-2

Determining Which Folders Are Currently Indexed

```
$dllpath = "C:\Windows Search 3x SDK\Managed\Microsoft.Search.Interop.dll"
Add-Type -path ($dllpath)
$Search = New-Object Microsoft.Search.Interop.CSearchManagerClass
$Catalog = $Search.GetCatalog("SystemIndex")
$ScopeManager = $catalog.GetCrawlScopeManager()
$ScopeRules = @()
$FirstLoop = $true
[Microsoft.Search.Interop.CSearchScopeRule]$CurrentScope= $null
$Enumeration = $ScopeManager.EnumerateScopeRules()
Do
{
$Enumeration.Next(1,[ref]$CurrentScope,[ref]$null)
$FirstLoop = $false
$ScopeRules += $CurrentScope
}while ($CurrentScope -ne $null -or $FirstLoop)
$Filter = @{
FilterScript = {$_.IsIncluded}
}
$ScopeRules |Where-Object @filter |Select-Object -Property PatternOrUrl
```

You can show which patterns of folders are explicitly excluded from indexing by switching the `$Filter` hash, as shown here:

```
$Filter = @{
FilterScript = {!$_.IsIncluded}
}
```

Adding Folders to the Index

You need to load the DLL and create references to the catalog as if you were searching the index before you can add items to the index. Let's put the relevant code into a function. The complete `Load-Search` function is shown in Listing 3-3. You will need to dot source the function when you call it, as shown in the following code:

```
. Load-Search
```

Tip

Dot sourcing refers to the practice of placing a period and a blank space in front of a Windows PowerShell script or function. This causes all variables within the script or function to be global variables. Global variables are available to every script, function or cmdlet run within the current Windows PowerShell session. ■

LISTING 3-3

The Load-Search Function

```
Function Load-Search
{
$dllpath = "C:\Windows Search 3x SDK\Managed\Microsoft.Search.Interop.dll"
Add-Type -path ($dllpath)
$Search = New-Object Microsoft.Search.Interop.CSearchManagerClass
$Catalog = $Search.GetCatalog("SystemIndex")
$ScopeManager = $catalog.GetCrawlScopeManager()
}
```

Once you have the DLL and references loaded, you add folders to the index with the `AddUserScopeRule()` method of the `ScopeManager` class. The following example, when used in conjunction with the `Load-Search` function, adds the folder `c:\Scripts` to the user's scope rules. This means that the folder `C:\Scripts` will be searchable as well.

```
. Load-Search
$ScopeManager.AddUserScopeRule("file:///c:\Scripts\*",$true,$false,$null)
$ScopeManager.SaveAll()
```

You can also add default scope rules with the `AddDefaultScopeRule()` method of the `ScopeManager` class. The following example adds the default scope rule for the filesystem `C:\ArchiveFiles\*`, and all files in that path:

```
. Load-Search
$ScopeManager.AddDefaultScopeRule("file:///C:\ArchiveFiles\*",$true,$null)
$ScopeManager.SaveAll()
```

In both the `AddUserScopeRule()` and the `AddDefaultScopeRule()` methods, the first parameter is the path that you want to add to the scope rules. The second parameter is a Boolean that determines if the path is included in indexing (`true`), or explicitly excluded from indexing (`false`). For the `AddUserScopeRule()` method, the third parameter is another Boolean that indicates whether to overwrite child rules. If set to `$true`, existing child rules will in effect be deleted. The final parameter of both methods is a flag parameter, `FOLLOW_FLAGS`, which indicates whether the path is to be indexed or just followed.

Both previous examples have added a local folder to the search index. You can add a network shared folder by replacing the `file:///` handler with the `otfs://` file handler. The following example adds the network shared folder `\\karl-pc\shared` to the user scope rules:

```
. Load-Search
$ScopeManager.AddUserScopeRule("otfs://karl-pc\shared\*",$true,$true,$null)
$ScopeManager.SaveAll()
```

You can verify that the folders have been added by running the script in Listing 3-2, or by running just the search part of the script in Listing 3-2. You could create a function for that part of the script as well. This is shown in Listing 3-4. Notice that this function requires the Load-Search function from Listing 3-3.

LISTING 3-4

List-Scope Function

```
Function List-Scope
{
param ([bool]$Included = $true)
. Load-Search
$ScopeRules = @()
$FirstLoop = $true
[Microsoft.Search.Interop.CSearchScopeRule]$CurrentScope= $null
$Enumeration = $ScopeManager.EnumerateScopeRules()
Do
{
$Enumeration.Next(1,[ref]$CurrentScope,[ref]$null)
$FirstLoop = $false
$ScopeRules += $CurrentScope
}while ($CurrentScope -ne $null -or $FirstLoop)
$Filter = @{
FilterScript = {$_.IsIncluded -eq $Included}
}
$ScopeRules |Where-Object @filter |Select-Object -Property PatternOrUrl
}
```

By default, the List-Scope function will show patterns included in the index. You can add the Included parameter with a value of $false to show patterns that are not included in the index as shown in the following example:

```
List-Scope -Included $false
```

Removing Folders from the Index

Once again, you need to load the DLL and create references to the catalog as if you were searching the index before you can remove items from the index.

You will continue to use the Load-Search function shown in Listing 3-3. Don't forget to dot source the function.

Once the Load-Search function is loaded, the relevant methods of the ScopeManager class are RemoveScopeRule(), RemoveDefaultScopeRule(), and RevertToDefaultScope(). The following example removes the default scope rule file:///C:\ArchiveFiles*:

```
. Load-Search
$ScopeManager.RemoveDefaultScopeRule("file:///C:\ArchiveFiles\*")
$ScopeManager.SaveAll()
```

The next example removes the network shared folder \\karl-pc\shared from the user scope rules:

```
. Load-Search
$ScopeManager.RemoveScopeRule("otfs://karl-pc\shared\*")
$ScopeManager.SaveAll()
```

The final example removes all user scope rules:

```
. Load-Search
$ScopeManager.RevertToDefaultScopes()
$ScopeManager.SaveAll()
```

Re-Indexing the Search Catalog

After adding or removing rule scopes, you can force a re-index all of the URLs in your catalog or specific URLs in the catalog. While the index is in process, the catalog retains the old data until it is overwritten by new data, or removed.

Once again, you will use the Load-Search function shown in Listing 3-3 to load the DLL and create references to the catalog:

```
. Load-Search
```

Now that the search function is loaded, you can re-index the catalog with the Reindex(), ReindexMatchingURLs(), or ReindexSearchRoot() methods of the Catalog interface. The following example re-indexes all URLs in the catalog:

```
$Catalog.Reindex()
```

Note

Both the Reindex() and Reset() methods of the Catalog interface require that you are running in an elevated shell. Right-click on the Windows PowerShell icon and select "Run as Administrator." ∎

The ReindexMatchingURLs() method re-indexes only matching URLs and takes one parameter, the URL to be re-indexed. The following example re-indexes the network shared folder \\karl-pc\shared*:

```
. Load-Search
$Catalog.ReindexMatchingURLs("otfs://karl-pc\shared\*")
```

You use the `ReindexSearchRoot()` method to re-index a search root. This method also takes one parameter. In this case, the parameter is the URL on which the search is rooted.

Before you can re-index a search root, you will need to discover your search roots. You do this with the `EnumerateRoots()` method of the search root class.

As always, you will need to load the DLL and create references to the catalog. Because listing roots is similar to listing scope rules, the `List-Root` function in Listing 3-5 will look familiar.

LISTING 3-5

List-Root Function

```
Function List-Root
{
param ([bool]$Included = $true)
. Load-Search
$ScopeRoots = @()
$FirstLoop = $true
[Microsoft.Search.Interop.CSearchRootClass]$CurrentRoot= $null
$Enumeration = $ScopeManager.EnumerateRoots()
Do
{
$Enumeration.Next(1,[ref]$CurrentRoot,[ref]$null)
$FirstLoop = $false
$ScopeRoots += $CurrentRoot
}while ($CurrentRoot -ne $null -or $FirstLoop)
$ScopeRoots |Select-Object -Property RootURL
}
```

Again, remember to dot source the function:

```
. List-Root
```

Now that you have your roots, you can call the `ReindexSearchRoot()` method of the Catalog interface. The following example re-indexes the network shared folder \\karl-pc\shared*:

```
$Catalog.ReindexSearchRoot("otfs://karl-pc\shared\*")
```

You can also reset the catalog. When you reset the catalog, all URLs are re-indexed. This can take a long time, and should be done only if there is an issue with the search index, as identified by the search troubleshooting pack.

Once again, you will use the `Load-Search` function from Listing 3-3 to load the DLL and create references to the catalog.

Once the search function is loaded, you can reset the catalog with the `Reset()` method of the Catalog interface. The `Reset()` method takes no parameters. The following example resets the catalog:

```
. Load-Search
$Catalog.Reset()
```

Checking HotFix Status

You can list updates supplied by Microsoft's Component-Based Servicing that are installed on your Windows 7 computer with the `Get-HotFix` cmdlet. These updates are commonly referred to as Quick Fix Engineering updates. Specifically, this does not include updates provided by Windows Update, or via an MSI installer.

The `Get-HotFix` cmdlet, when run without parameters, returns a list of all these updates. You can pass the optional parameters `Id` or `Description` to specify which hotfix to examine, or what type of hotfix to list. A further parameter, `ComputerName`, enables you to search for hotfixes on remote computers.

Cross-Reference
Searching for hotfixes on remote computers is examined in depth in Chapter 8, "Performing Basic Server Management." ■

The following example retrieves all hotfixes installed on the local computer. The default data displayed is the computer name, hotfix description, hotfix ID, who installed the hotfix, and when the hotfix was installed. The hotfixes are not sorted in any particular order.

```
Get-HotFix
```

The following code shows two examples. The first example returns information on the hotfix with the `Id` of `KB975467`, and the second example returns information on all hotfixes with the `Description` of `update`, sorted by the install date:

```
Get-HotFix -Id KB975467
Get-HotFix -Description "update" |Sort-Object InstalledOn
```

Managing Files and Folders

In this section, you manage security on files and folders. You learn to search for files using built-in cmdlets and Windows Search. You also learn how to open files from Windows PowerShell.

Setting Security on Files and Folders

Windows PowerShell includes two cmdlets for managing file and folder security descriptors: `Get-Acl` and `Set-Acl`. The `Get-Acl` cmdlet retrieves objects that represent the current security descriptor for the file or folder. Once you have the security descriptor, you can either use it as is, or modify it and then apply it with the `Set-Acl` cmdlet. It is easier to copy a security descriptor or modify one and then apply it with the `Set-Acl` cmdlet than it is to create a new security descriptor.

Tip
Security descriptors, in this case, represent the file and folder permissions. ■

Copying Security from One File or Folder to Another

Copying security from one file or folder to another can be accomplished by passing the output of the `Get-Acl` cmdlet to the `Set-Acl` cmdlet, specifying the parameter `Path` to each cmdlet. The following example copies the security descriptor from the folder `c:\scripts` to the folder `d:\scripts`:

```
Get-Acl -Path c:\scripts\book | Set-Acl -Path d:\scripts\test
```

If you only want to copy security from one file to another, you specify the full path to each file. The next example copies the security descriptor from the file `c:\scripts\test.ps1` to the file `d:\scripts\test.ps1`:

```
Get-Acl -Path c:\scripts\test.ps1 | Set-Acl -Path d:\scripts\test.ps1
```

As you can see, copying security from one folder to another, or one file to another, is quite simple with Windows PowerShell.

Modifying Security on a File or Folder

You can also modify security on an existing file or folder with the `Get-Acl` and `Set-Acl` cmdlets.

First, you get the current security descriptor with the `Get-Acl` cmdlet. Then, you can build a new access rule and add it to the previously retrieved security descriptor. Finally, you write the new security descriptor to the file or folder. The following example adds the user `Karl-Laptop\Sherry` to the security descriptor for the path `c:\scripts`, giving that user `ReadData` rights:

```
$CurrentAcl = Get-Acl -Path c:\scripts
$User = "Karl-Laptop\Sherry"
$AccessRight = "ReadData"
$Object = @{
TypeName = "System.Security.AccessControl.FileSystemAccessRule"
ArgumentList = $User,$AccessRight,'Allow'
}
$AccessRule = New-Object @Object
$CurrentAcl.SetAccessRule($AccessRule)
Set-Acl -Path c:\scripts -AclObject $CurrentAcl
```

Note

More information on the System.Security.AccessControl.FileSystemAccessRule class is available on MSDN: `http://msdn.microsoft.com/en-us/library/system.security.accesscontrol .filesystemaccessrule.aspx`. ∎

If you wanted to give this user access to all files in a folder that did not have inheritance set, you would pass the output of the `Get-ChildItem` cmdlet through a `foreach` loop. The next example adds the user `Karl-Laptop\Sherry` to the security descriptor for all files in the path `c:\scripts`, giving that user `ReadAndExecute` rights. You re-create the `$CurrentAcl` security descriptor for each file, because each file could potentially have different permissions, and you only want to add the new security descriptor to each file.

```
$User = "Karl-Laptop\Sherry"
$AccessRight = "ReadAndExecute"
$Object = @{
TypeName = "System.Security.AccessControl.FileSystemAccessRule"
ArgumentList = $User,$AccessRight,'Allow'
}
$AccessRule = New-Object @Object
foreach ($file in Get-ChildItem c:\scripts -Recurse )
{
$CurrentAcl = Get-Acl -Path $file.FullName
$CurrentAcl.SetAccessRule($AccessRule)
Set-Acl -Path $file.FullName -AclObject $CurrentAcl
}
```

Note

For more information on inheritance, see TechNet: `http://technet.microsoft.com/en-us/library/ cc758779(WS.10).aspx`. ∎

Table 3-1 lists the possible values for the `$AccessRight` variable.

TABLE 3-1

Access Rights

ListDirectory	ReadData	WriteData	CreateFiles
CreateDirectories	AppendData	ReadExtendedAttributes	WriteExtendedAttributes
Traverse	ExecuteFile	DeleteSubdirectoriesAndFiles	ReadAttributes
WriteAttributes	Write	Delete	ReadPermissions
Read	ReadAndExecute	Modify	ChangePermissions
TakeOwnership	Synchronize	FullControl	

Listing Unique File Extensions

You can list unique file extensions in a folder by combining the output of the `Get-ChildItem`, an array, and the `Select-Object` cmdlet. The following example lists all unique file extensions in `c:\scripts`, sorted from a to z:

```
$Extensions = @()
$Item = @{
Path = "C:\scripts"
Recurse = $true
}
$Where = @{
FilterScript = {!$_.psIsContainer -AND $_.Extension}
}
$files = Get-ChildItem @Item | Where-Object @Where
foreach ($file in $files)
{
$Extensions += $file.Extension.SubString(1).ToLower()
}
$Extensions |Select-Object -Unique |Sort-Object
```

You can modify this example to provide a count of each extension by removing the `Select-Object` cmdlet, and sending the results through the `Group-Object` cmdlet. The `NoElement` parameter provides the quantity and name of the extensions, without listing each extension in a group. This is shown in the following example:

```
$Extensions = @()
$Item = @{
Path = "C:\scripts"
Recurse = $true
}
$Where = @{
FilterScript = {!$_.psIsContainer -AND $_.Extension}
}
$files = Get-ChildItem @Item | Where-Object @Where
foreach ($file in $files)
{
$Extensions += $file.Extension.SubString(1).ToLower()
}
$Extensions | Group-Object -NoElement
Count Name
----- ----
  499 ps1
  487 txt
  149 csv
  313 htm
   32 vbs
   15 xml
```

The following example lists all unique file extensions in `c:\scripts`, listing the quantity of each, and sorting by count:

```
$Extensions = @()
$Item = @{
Path = "C:\scripts"
Recurse = $true
}
$Where = @{
FilterScript = {!$_.psIsContainer -AND $_.Extension}
}
$Grp = @{
NoElement = $true
}
$Table = @{
Property = @{Label="Extension";Expression ={$_.Name}},
@{Label="Quantity";Expression ={$_.Count}}
AutoSize = $true
}
$files = Get-ChildItem @Item | Where-Object @Where
foreach ($file in $files)
{
$Extensions += $file.Extension.SubString(1).ToLower()
}
$Extensions |Group-Object @Grp |Sort-Object Count |Format-Table @Table
```

Counting a Specific Type of Files

You may be interested in knowing exactly how many of a specific file extension you have on your computer. Once again, you accomplish this with the `Get-ChildItem` and `Group-Object` cmdlets. This example shows the count of `.ps1` files in `c:\scripts`:

```
$Item = @{
Recurse = $true
Force = $true
ErrorAction = "SilentlyContinue"
}
$Grp = @{
Property = {$_.Extension}
NoElement = $true
}
Get-ChildItem -Path C:\scripts -Include "*.ps1" @Item |Group-Object @Grp
```

The final example shows the count of `.psm1` and `.ps1` files in `c:\scripts`:

```
$ChildItem = @{
Path = "C:\scripts"
Include = "*.psm1","*.ps1"
}
Get-ChildItem @ChildItem @Item |Group-Object @grp
```

Finding Empty Folders

Another task that you may need to perform is to find empty folders on your hard drive. If you define empty folders as folders that have neither files nor folders in them, you can list them with a combination of the `Get-ChildItem`, `Where-Object`, and `Select-Object` cmdlets. The following example shows all folders in `C:\Scripts` and subfolders that are empty:

```
$Item = @{
Path = "C:\Scripts"
Recurse = $true
Force = $true
}
$Filter = @{
FilterScript = {$_.PSIsContainer -eq $True}
}
$Where = @{
FilterScript = {($_.GetFiles().Count -eq 0) -and
($_.GetDirectories().Count -eq 0)}
}
$a = Get-ChildItem @Item |Where-Object @Filter
$a |Where-Object @Where |Select-Object FullName
```

Searching with Windows Search

You can also search using the Windows Search catalog introduced earlier in the chapter. This search will be much quicker than the previous searches because the results are already cataloged, and you need to query only that catalog. The downside to searching via Windows Search is that the search will only retrieve the list of files that are indexed. If you are looking for a list of `.json` files, which are in `c:\json`, and that folder is either not included in the index or specifically excluded, the search will return no data.

The search syntax can be either a form of SQL known as *Windows Search SQL*, or a syntax known as *Advanced Query Syntax*, which is actually the default search syntax for Windows Search. The examples in this chapter use Windows Search SQL.

Create a function that takes the search criteria as parameters. You could include this function in your `$profile` script to ensure that the function is always available. The Find-Files function is shown in Listing 3-6.

LISTING 3-6

Find-Files Function

```
function Find-Files
{
param(
```

continues

LISTING 3-6 *(continued)*

```
[CmdletBinding(DefaultParametersetName="p2")]
[Parameter(ParameterSetName="P1")]
[string]$Sql,
[Parameter(ParameterSetName="P2")]
[string[]]$Output,
[Parameter(ParameterSetName="P2")]
[string]$Type,
[Parameter(ParameterSetName="P2")]
[string]$Modifier)
if (!$Sql)
{
$sql = "Select $Output from SystemIndex Where System.$Type $Modifier"
}
$cnx = "Provider=Search.CollatorDSO;Extended Properties='Application=Windows';"
$connection = New-Object System.Data.OleDb.OleDbConnection $cnx
$command = New-Object System.Data.OleDb.OleDbCommand $sql,$connection
$connection.Open()
$adapter = New-Object System.Data.OleDb.OleDbDataAdapter $command
$dataset = New-Object System.Data.DataSet
[void] $adapter.Fill($dataSet)
$connection.Close()
$dataSet.Tables |Select-Object -Expand Rows
}
```

This simple function enables you to search the catalog by specifying the output you want, along with the type of search, and the specific items you are interested in. The function requires that you pass either the Sql parameter, or all three of the parameters Output, Type, and Modifier. The Sql parameter is a complete Structured Query Language string. The Output parameter defines the data you want to see, the Type parameter defines the specific type of file you are looking for, and the Modifier parameter describes the specific file or files you are looking for.

The following example finds all music files by the artist John Mellencamp. The data you send to the function is case-insensitive. You could also search for john mellencamp or for the type of music.artist.

```
$Files = @{
Output = "filename, path, size"
Type = "Music.Artist"
Modifier = "= 'John Mellencamp'"
}
Find-Files @Files
```

The following example finds all files that are over the size of 1000000000 bytes:

```
$LargeFiles = @{
Output = "path, size"
Type = "Size"
Modifier = "> 1000000000"
}
Find-Files @LargeFiles
```

The next example finds all files with a file extension of .jpg:

```
$PictureFiles = @{
Output = "filename, path"
Type = "FileExtension"
Modifier = "= '.jpg'"
}
Find-Files @PictureFiles
```

Note that in all these examples, the Modifier parameter needs the SQL comparison operator to operate.

You can also specify a complete Windows Search SQL string for the search. The following example finds all files that are larger than 10000 bytes. This example returns the System.ItemUrl and System.ItemNameDisplay. The System.ItemNameDisplay is a cleaner version of the filename used in previous examples.

```
$FindSql = @{
Sql = "SELECT System.ItemUrl,System.ItemNameDisplay
FROM SystemIndex WHERE System.Size >= 10000"
}
Find-Files @FindSql
```

All of these examples can be piped to any of the Export cmdlets or any of the Format cmdlets.

For more information on searching the index with Windows Search SQL, see http://msdn .microsoft.com/en-us/library/bb231256(v=VS.85).aspx.

Opening a File Using Its Default Handler

You can open a file with its default handler using the Invoke-Item cmdlet, passing the required parameter Path or LiteralPath. This will enable you to open a script file in your default editor from within Windows PowerShell. Normally, if you enter the name of a script file in a Windows PowerShell console, the script will run. Of course, that's what you would normally want.

If you want to edit that script file, you can navigate to it via Windows Explorer and double-click it, or you can use the Invoke-Item cmdlet. The following example opens the script file c:\scripts\test.ps1 in your default script editor:

```
Invoke-Item -Path c:\scripts\test.ps1
```

The default script editor is Windows Notepad. However, this can be changed by third-party tools such as PowerGui. Another interesting use of the `Invoke-Item` cmdlet is to edit your Windows PowerShell profile. Normally, entering `$Profile` in the Windows PowerShell console will output the path to the profile. The following example opens your Windows PowerShell profile in your default script editor. You can then modify the `$profile` script and save it. The updated `$profile` script will be loaded the next time you start Windows PowerShell.

```
Invoke-Item -Path $Profile
```

Caution

When first installed, Windows 7 does not create the folder or file that contains a user's profile. In this case, `Invoke-Item -Path $Profile` will generate an error. You would need to create the folder and a new file first. This can be done with the `New-Item` cmdlet. The code line `New-Item -ItemType File -Path $Profile -Force` will overwrite an existing profile, so use caution. ∎

You can also open all files in a specific path at once using `Invoke-Item`. The next example opens all files in the path `c:\scripts\results` that were created earlier in the troubleshooting section of this chapter:

```
Invoke-Item -Path C:\scripts\results\*
```

Usually, you'd only be interested in the two `.xml` files returned when running the troubleshooting pack, and not the `.xsl` file because it only describes how to display the `.xml` files. You can open only the `.xml` files by specifying the file extension as part of the `Path` parameter. The following example opens all `.xml` files in the path `c:\scripts\results`:

```
Invoke-Item -Path C:\scripts\results\*.xml
```

The previous two examples will work only if the default handler for that file type allows more than one instance to run. Assuming your default media player is Windows Media Player, this example plays only the first `.wma` file in the path:

```
Invoke-Item -Path C:\Music\Journeyman\*.wma
```

The proper way to play all the `.wma` files would be to use a playlist. The final example plays all the music files in the playlist `C:\Music\Journeyman\Journeyman.wpl`:

```
Invoke-Item -Path C:\Music\Journeyman\Journeyman.wpl
```

Summary

In this chapter, you learned how to take advantage of Windows 7's built-in troubleshooting scripts and created a function to facilitate troubleshooting Windows 7. You learned how to add and remove folders in Windows Search, creating additional functions to manage Windows Search.

You explored managing security on files and folders, finding all files of a specific type, and discovered how to find empty folders on your computer. You also explored searching the Windows Search catalog for specific files, creating another function that allows you to quickly search the catalog.

You learned how to find out which hotfixes are installed on the local computer, and how to search for a specific hotfix. Finally, you learned how to open files with their built-in file handlers.

Next, you learn to leverage Microsoft Office 2010 with Windows PowerShell and work with Excel, Word, and Outlook.

Managing Microsoft Office 2010

Microsoft's suite of Office applications is utilized heavily in most organizations. It is because of this widespread usage that there is a natural tendency to want to automate tasks with the different Office applications. Scripts have a tendency to fall into two categories when working with Microsoft Office.

The first category of script types covers output and reporting. You may find that you want a script to do some processing and then create a file in one of the Office formats like a Word document, Excel spreadsheet, OneNote, or PowerPoint presentation. With a script in this category, you often want to format the data in specific ways. For example, you may want to output a set of data to Excel and then automatically generate a graph or chart from this data set.

The second type of script is based on making it easier to complete repetitive tasks. Everyone in the modern age has encountered a task where they need to go back through a document and fix something. This may or may not be a good enough reason for you to want to write a script to tackle a problem. However, if you had to fix the same problem in millions of documents, writing a script to handle the task would be essential.

Windows PowerShell enables you to create the logic that can handle your requirements regardless of the type of script you need to create. In this chapter, you explore some of the ways you can use Windows PowerShell to interact with the Microsoft Office suite.

IN THIS CHAPTER

Working with the COM objects

Scripting against Word

Scripting against Excel

Scripting against Outlook

Introducing the Office COM Objects

Scripting against Microsoft Office is done primarily through a series of Component Object Model (COM) interfaces. The wonderful thing about this object model is that most of the code that has been around since 2000 is still usable. The bad news is that it is hardly ever written in Windows PowerShell and will require you to be keen with transcribing code to make use of it. Even the indispensible MSDN documentation for the interfaces that is available doesn't always explain everything you need to know to use the objects. This chapter keeps things as simple as possible by providing you with solutions to common tasks that you can use right away.

Note

In addition to the object model you will see in this chapter, there are other techniques that allow you to interact directly with the documents. These techniques are based on the fact that most of the Microsoft Office 2010 applications use an XML-based document format that can be modified directly. This chapter does not explore these methods. ■

The Office Application Objects

The first step in scripting Office is to create the COM object that represents the application you are going to script against. Each Office application has its own `Application` object you must create or bind to.

- `Access.Application`
- `Excel.Application`
- `InfoPath.Application`
- `OneNote.Application`
- `Outlook.Application`
- `PowerPoint.Application`
- `Publisher.Application`
- `Visio.Application`
- `Word.Application`

Note

Microsoft Project can also be scripted against, but in order to do so, you must use native .NET objects instead of COM. For the purpose of this book, you will be looking at Word and Excel with a few examples of some of the other applications near the end of the chapter. ■

Depending on your requirements, a script can create a new application or it can bind to an instance of an Office application that has already been started.

Creating a New Application

You create the `Application` object by using the `ComObject` parameter of the `New-Object` cmdlet. Most of the time, the first thing you will do after you receive the object is to make the application visible. This is not always needed, but it definitely helps during the development of an Office script so that you can see what your script is doing as you try different methods.

```
$app = New-Object -ComObject 'Word.Application'
$app.Visible = $True
```

Binding to Existing Applications

If the Office application was already launched manually and you want to bind to the application object, you can use the `GetActiveObject` static method of `System.Runtime.InteropServices.Marshal` to do so:

```
$marshal = [System.Runtime.InteropServices.Marshal]
$app = $marshal::GetActiveObject('Word.Application')
```

Cleaning Up after Your Office Scripts

When you are done using an Office application, it is common to call the `Quit()` method of the application object to close the Office application. Sometimes, this will close the window, but it will not completely stop the process from running. This can lead to problems in some applications. To handle this, you can use the `ReleaseComObject()` static method of `System.Runtime.InteropServices.Marshal`. It is also necessary to call the `Collect()` and `WaitForPendingFinalizers()` static methods of the `GC` class. This class, also known as the *garbage collector*, controls the release of memory by the system. In addition, it is good practice to remove the variable for the application object because it is no longer in use. Listing 4-1 shows an example of how to bind to an open Excel application and close it cleanly.

LISTING 4-1

Binding to an Open Excel Application, Exiting the App, and Performing Cleanup

```
$marshal = [System.Runtime.InteropServices.Marshal]
# Bind to an already opened Excel application
$app = $marshal::GetActiveObject('Excel.Application')
# Close the application
$app.Quit()
# Clean up
$marshal::ReleaseComObject($app)
[gc]::Collect()
[gc]::WaitForPendingFinalizers()
Remove-Variable -Name app
```

Automating Microsoft Word

Many of the scripts people create to automate Microsoft Word revolve around formatting the look and feel of a document. Sometimes, a script will also perform inline editing of the document's content. This section looks at some examples of these common tasks.

Note

As with all of the Microsoft Office applications, it is possible to automate nearly every task that you can perform manually given enough time and research. When working with these objects, you will find that the documentation on MSDN is indispensible. The normal Windows PowerShell introspection using cmdlets like `Get-Member` will take you only so far. Each of the objects you will work with has an enormous number of properties, methods, and events, and many of them are not easy to figure out without doing a bit of reading. Unfortunately, the code in the documentation is not normally in Windows PowerShell so it can require interpretation at times. ■

Creating or Opening a Document

Documents are created by using the `Add()` method of the `Documents` property of your `Application` object. The following line of code is used to invoke this method:

```
$doc = $app.Documents.Add()
```

Note

The samples in this chapter build upon variables that were created in previous sections. For example, the preceding snippet uses the `$app` variable. Though this variable is not explicitly created in the snippet, it was created earlier in the chapter. You should expect to see the `$doc` variable again soon, and you should be on the lookout for `$selection` as well. ■

You open a document by invoking the `Open()` method of the `Documents` property of your `Application` object:

```
$doc = $app.Documents.Open('c:\doc1.docx')
```

Adding Content

With a document created or opened, you can now begin to add or manipulate the text and formatting within the document.

Adding Text

You can use the `Text` property found within the `Content` property of a `Document` object to set or read the text within a Word document as follows:

```
# Set the contents of the document
$doc.Content.Text = "Hello World!`r`n"
```

```
# Read and display the contents of the document
$doc.Content.Text
```

It is more common, however, to use the `Selection` property of the `Application` object to manipulate the contents of a document. The `Selection` object indicates the cursor position in a document as you are typing. For example, the following will write "Hello World" in the position where the cursor is within the Word document:

```
$selection = $app.Selection
$selection.TypeText("Hello World!")
```

The advantage to using this method to insert text over setting `$doc.Content.Text` is that you can set the selection to different positions or ranges within your text, just as you would when editing a Word document with a mouse. For example, if you wanted to remove the exclamation point in the "Hello World!" text you entered above, you could highlight the exclamation point by holding the Shift key and pressing the arrow once to the left followed by hitting the Backspace key. Programmatically, we can set the selection by defining a new start position for the selection that is one character back from its current position. A `Selection` object has a `Start` property you can use to do this.

```
$selection.Start = $selection.start - 1
```

In order to use Windows PowerShell to mimic the behavior of hitting the Backspace key, you can use the `TypeBackspace()` method of the `Selection` object.

```
$selection.TypeBackspace()
```

Here is another example that shows how you can explicitly set both the start and end position of the `Selection` object by using the `SetRange()` method. These two lines of code select the word *Hello* and change it to *Goodbye*:

```
$selection.SetRange(0,5)
$selection.TypeText("Goodbye")
```

Finally, here are two more examples that demonstrate how the `Selection` object allows you to create scripts that emulate the behavior of a user who is working in Word with a keyboard and mouse. This example invokes the `EndKey()` method to move the selection to the end of the line and then calls on the `TypeParagraph()` method to start a new paragraph.

```
$selection.EndKey()
$selection.TypeParagraph()
```

Working with Bullets

Bullets are managed by modifying the properties of the range that makes up a paragraph you are interested in converting to or from a bullet list. `Paragraph` objects are obtained as a property of a `Document` object. Listing 4-2 details the technique.

LISTING 4-2

Creating a Bulleted List

```
$app = New-Object -ComObject 'Word.Application'
$app.visible = $true
$doc = $app.Documents.Add()
$selection = $app.Selection

$selection.TypeText("Bullet List:")
$selection.TypeParagraph()

# Select the second paragraph and turn it into a bulleted list
$range = $doc.Paragraphs.item(2).Range
$range.ListFormat.ApplyBulletDefault()

$selection.TypeText("Item1")
$selection.TypeParagraph()
$selection.TypeText("Item2")
$selection.TypeParagraph()

# Select the fourth paragraph and set its style to normal
$range = $doc.Paragraphs.item(4).Range
$range.Style = "Normal"

$selection.TypeText("Back To Normal")
```

Creating Hyperlinks

Hyperlinks are stored in the Document object. To create one, you must select a range of text and then add a new hyperlink to the collection within the Document object. The following snippet shows an example of how to do this:

```
$text = 'website'
$url = 'http://www.wiley.com'
$selection.TypeText($text)
$selection.Start -= $text.Length
$range = $selection.Range
$doc.HyperLinks.Add($range, $url, $null, $null, $null) |Out-Null
```

Note

In the previous example, the last line uses the Out-Null cmdlet to suppress the output of the cmdlet. The Add() method of HyperLinks creates a HyperLink object. If you do not use Out-Null, the object will be displayed to the screen when the script is run. This is not necessarily a bad thing, but it is worth noting in case you would like to suppress any unexpected output while using Windows PowerShell. ∎

Inserting Images

Images, like hyperlinks, are stored in the Document object. Images live in a larger collection of different shapes that exist in the document. To add an image, you must use the AddPicture() method of the Shapes property of a Document object. The following shows how this is done:

```
$x = 0
$y = 30
$wrap = [Microsoft.Office.Interop.Word.WdWrapType]::wdWrapTopBottom
$linkToFile = $false
$saveWithFile = $true
$doc.Shapes.AddPicture('C:\ps.jpg',$linkToFile,$SaveWithFile,$x,$y)
$doc.Shapes.Range(1).WrapFormat.Type = $wrap
```

Note

Two colons in a row have been used after a class name in brackets a few times in this chapter as a way of invoking static methods. However, the preceding example uses this to access the values in an enumeration. One great thing about the tab completion in Windows PowerShell is that you can use it to help you see what values are available within an enumeration. If you type [Microsoft.Office.Interop.Word.WdWrapType]:: followed by the tab key over and over, you will see every option that is available. This can be an extremely useful method of self-discovery in Windows PowerShell, especially when dealing with the Office COM objects that use these enumerations. ■

Adding Tables

Tables also belong to the Document object. They are created by passing a range, number of rows, and number of columns to the Add() method of the Tables property within the Document object. Listing 4-3 shows how this is done.

LISTING 4-3

Inserting the Output of Get-Process into a Table

```
$app = New-Object -ComObject 'Word.Application'
$app.visible = $true
$doc = $app.Documents.Add()
$selection = $app.Selection

$processes = get-process
$selection.TypeText("Processes:")
$selection.TypeParagraph()

$range = $doc.Paragraphs.item(2).Range
$table = $doc.Tables.Add($Range,$processes.count,2)
$table.cell(1,1).Range.Text = "PID"
```

continues

LISTING 4-3 *(continued)*

```
$table.cell(1,2).Range.Text = "ProcessName"
$row = 2
foreach ($process in $processes) {
  $table.cell($row,1).Range.Text = $process.ID
  $table.cell($row,2).Range.Text = $process.ProcessName
  $row++
}
```

Headers and Footers

The `Headers` and `Footers` collections belong to the `Section` object for each document. This makes sense because in Word, a section can have a different set of headers and footers. The following shows how you can grab the first section of a document and create a header and footer:

```
$section = $doc.Sections.Item(1)

$header = $section.headers.item(1)
$header.Range.Text = "Here is my header"

$footer = $section.Footers.Item(1)
$footer.Range.Text = "Here is my footer"
```

Searching for Text

The `Selection` object contains a `Find` property, which enables you to set the properties of a search and then execute the search. Here is an example of how it can be used:

```
$find = $selection.Find
$find.Text = 'psbible'
$find.Forward = $False
$find.MatchWholeWord = $False
$find.Execute()
```

Replacing Words

When using the `Find` object to find the text you want to replace, it will automatically place the selection over the word that you have found. This makes it easy enough to just execute `$selection.TypeText('ReplacementWord')` to replace what you have just searched for. However, you can also invoke the `Execute()` method with specific parameters to let Word handle the replacement for you. Listing 4-4 shows an example of how this can be used to replace text in a document.

LISTING 4-4

Replacing All Text in a Word Document with Different Text

```
$app = New-Object -ComObject 'Word.Application'
$app.visible = $true
$doc = $app.Documents.Open('C:\psbible.docx')
$selection = $app.Selection

$find = $selection.Find
$word = 'psbible'
$matchcase = $false
$matchwholeword = $false
$matchwildcards = $false
$matchsoundslike = $false
$matchallwordforms = $false
$forward = $true
$wrap = [Microsoft.Office.Interop.Word.WdFindWrap]::wdFindContinue
$format = $null
$replacewith = 'wiley'
$replace = [Microsoft.Office.Interop.Word.WdReplace]::wdReplaceAll

$find.Execute($word,$matchcase,$matchwholeword,$matchwildcards,↵
$matchsoundslike,$matchallwordforms,$forward,$wrap,$format,↵
$replacewith,$replace)
```

Copy and Paste

When you have text in a selection, you can use the `Copy()`, `Cut()`, and `Paste()` methods of a selection object to manipulate the data in the clipboard:

- `$selection.Copy()`
- `$selection.Cut()`
- `$selection.Paste()`

Note

Office COM scripts can be fun to watch because of the speed at which the tasks occur; they are relatively slow. It almost feels like you are watching someone type and work on a document at superhuman speed — obviously, not fast for a computer, though. One shortcut to entering data into an Office application is to populate the clipboard in Windows PowerShell by piping text into `clip.exe` and then using the `Paste()` method to quickly put the data into your document. ∎

Formatting Text

Text formatting is applied to a section of text by calling the appropriate method or by modifying the appropriate properties of a range object.

Using Fonts

`Font` is the name of a property that exists in a `Range` object. By simply changing one of the properties of the `Font` object, you can modify the font for the range of text:

```
$text = "PowerShell Rules!"
$selection.TypeText($text)
$selection.Start -= $text.length

$selection.Range.Font.Name = 'Lucida Console'
$selection.Range.Font.Size = 20
$selection.Range.Font.Bold = $true
$selection.Range.Font.Italic = $true
$uvalue = [Microsoft.Office.Interop.Word.WdUnderline]::wdUnderlineSingle
$selection.Range.Font.Underline = $uvalue
```

Note

The COM objects are very robust. You can oftentimes accomplish a task in more than one way. For example, the underline can be set directly by setting the underline property of a range rather than doing it through the font. It's also possible to access the **Font** directly from a selection object rather than using the **Range** property to get to it. Combine this with the fact that the COM objects are so comprehensive, and it is very easy to get confused and lost when exploring this object model. All the more reason to keep things as simple as possible for this chapter. ■

Highlighting Text

Highlighting text is simply done by specifying the `HighlightColorIndex` of a range. The values for this property come from the `WdColorIndex` enumeration. For example, to highlight the first paragraph in a document with yellow, you would do the following:

```
$range = $doc.Paragraphs.Item(1).Range
$color = [Microsoft.Office.Interop.Word.WdColorIndex]::wdYellow
$range.HighlightColorIndex = $color
```

Applying Styles

You can set a selection of text to be one of the default style types by setting the `Style` property of a `Range` object to a value in the `WdBuiltInStyle` enumeration. The following shows how this can be accomplished to convert an entire document to the normal style:

```
$selection.SetRange(0,$doc.Content.End)
$norm = [Microsoft.Office.Interop.Word.WdBuiltinStyle]::wdStyleNormal
$selection.range.style = $norm
```

Style Sets

To switch the style set for the document, you must invoke the `ApplyQuickStyleSet()` method of the `Document` object. For example, you can change the style set to modern by using the following:

```
$doc.ApplyQuickStyleSet('Modern')
```

Spell Checking

You can tap into the Word spell checker for your current document or for any String you want to validate. You can determine whether or not a bit of text is valid by passing the text to the CheckSpelling() method of the application object:

```
$app.CheckSpelling($doc.Content.Text)
```

In addition, you can ask for suggestions for a particular word by passing the word to the GetSpellingSuggestions() method of an application object. Listing 4-5 shows a snippet of code that enables you to create a report of the suggestions to correct each misspelled word in a Document object.

LISTING 4-5

Creating a Report of Misspelled Words in a Word Document

```
$app = New-Object -ComObject 'Word.Application'
$app.visible = $true
$doc = $app.Documents.Add()
$doc.Content.text = 'The anser to the meening of lief is PowerShel.'

$selection = $app.Selection

$report = @()
foreach ($word in ($doc.Words |Select -ExpandProperty Text)){
  if (!($app.CheckSpelling($word))) {
    $result = New-Object -TypeName psobject -Property @{Mispelled=$word}
    $sug = $app.GetSpellingSuggestions($word) |Select -ExpandProperty name
    if ($sug) {
      $report += New-Object psobject -Property @{
        Misspelled = $word;
        Suggestions = $sug
      }
    }
    else {
      $report += New-Object -TypeName psobject -Property @{
        Misspelled = $word;
        Suggestions = "No Suggestion"
      }
    }
  }
}
$report |Select -Property Misspelled, Suggestions
```

The following shows a sample of the report that Listing 4-5 creates:

```
Misspelled                    Suggestions
----------                    -----------
anser                         {answer, anger, answers}
meening                       {meaning, meeting, mining}
lief                          {life, lie, lied, lies...}
PowerShel                     PowerShell
```

Printing

Printing can be done by calling the `PrintOut()` method for either a `Document` or `Application` object. This method takes a large number of parameters. Listing 4-6 provides an example of how to use this method along with some examples for the common parameters you may need to change when printing a document.

LISTING 4-6

Printing a Word Document

```
$app = New-Object -ComObject 'Word.Application'
$app.visible = $true
$doc = $app.Documents.Open('C:\psbible.docx')

$background=[ref]$False
$append=[ref]$False
$range=[ref][Microsoft.Office.Interop.Word.WdPrintOutRange]::wdPrintAllDocument
$outputfilename=[ref] [System.Reflection.missing]::Value
$from=[ref][System.Reflection.missing]::Value
$to=[ref] [System.Reflection.missing]::Value
$is=[ref][Microsoft.Office.Interop.Word.WdPrintOutItem]::wdPrintDocumentContent
$copies=[ref] 1
$pages=[ref][System.Reflection.missing]::Value
$patype=[ref][Microsoft.Office.Interop.Word.WdPrintOutPages]::wdPrintAllPages

$doc.PrintOut($background,$append,$range,$outputfilename,$from,$to,$items,↵
$copies,$pages,$pagetype)
```

Saving a Document

You save a document by invoking either the `Save()` or `SaveAs()` method of a `Document` object. The `Save()` method takes no parameters.

```
$doc.Save()
```

The `SaveAs()` method can be invoked simply by specifying the full path to the file you would like to save the document as:

```
$file = 'C:\psbible\doc1.docx'
$doc.SaveAs([ref] $file)
```

The `SaveAs()` method has a number of parameters you may optionally use, but the most common one is to specify a different file type. You do that by specifying the appropriate type in the `WdSaveFormat` enumeration. For example, if you wanted to save the document as an HTML file, you could do so with the following:

```
$type = [Microsoft.Office.Interop.Word.WdSaveFormat]::wdFormatHTML
$file = 'C:\psbible\doc1.html'
$doc.SaveAs([ref] $file, [ref] $type)
```

Working with Microsoft Excel Spreadsheets

Working with Word had you using `Application`, `Document`, `Selection`, and `Range` objects. Excel uses `Application`, `Workbook`, `Worksheet`, `Cell`, and `Range` objects.

Creating and Opening a Workbook

After you have retrieved an `Excel.Application` COM object, you can invoke the `Add()` method of the `Workbooks` property to create a new workbook:

```
$app = new-object -ComObject Excel.Application
$app.Visible = $true
$wb = $app.Workbooks.add()
```

To open an existing workbook, you can use the `Open()` method on the same `Workbooks` property. You should specify the full path to the Excel document you want to open when you call this method.

```
$wb = $app.Workbooks.Open('c:\psbible.xlsx')
```

Worksheets

For each workbook, there is a `Worksheets` property you can use to select the worksheet you would like to work with. You select a specific worksheet by invoking the `Item()` method of the `Worksheets` property. This method enables you to enter the ordinal item number or the worksheet name you would like to select. For example, when you create a new workbook, it is created with three worksheets by default. You could use either of these two lines of code to get access to the second worksheet, which is named Sheet2 by default:

```
$ws = $wb.Worksheets.Item(2)
$ws = $wb.Worksheets.Item('Sheet2')
```

You can also inspect the `Name` property of a workbook to see what worksheets it contains:

```
$wb.Worksheets |Select Name
```

In addition to the `Worksheets` property, you can also get the sheet that is currently active in Excel by using the `ActiveSheet` property of a workbook object:

```
$ws = $wb.ActiveSheet
```

Adding a New Worksheet

Worksheets can be added by invoking the `Add()` method on the `Worksheets` property:

```
$ws = $wb.Worksheets.Add()
```

Removing a Worksheet

There is a `Delete()` method you can invoke on a workbook or a worksheet. The only problem with this method is that it will prompt the user for confirmation of whether or not this is what they want to do.

```
$ws.Delete()
```

Caution

If you run this example, you will delete the worksheet. The **$ws** variable is used throughout the remaining examples of the book. Make sure that you add a worksheet back before continuing if you are following along with the examples. ∎

Working with Cells

Once a `Worksheet` object has been obtained, you can begin working with the underlying cells. There is a `Cells` property that you can use, but working with a `Range` object for either a single cell or a set of cells makes your code more consistent.

Selecting a Cell

Obtaining a single cell involves passing a cell name to the `Range()` method of a `Worksheet` object:

```
$cell = $ws.Range('A1')
```

Writing to a Cell

The value of the cell can be set or viewed by using the `Value2` property of the `cell` object:

```
# Set the cell value to psbible
$cell.Value2 = 'psbible'
# View the value of the cell
"The cell value is: " + $cell.Value2
```

You can use Excel functions within a cell as you normally would when you are working in Excel. This is done by setting the value of the cell to a string of text that contains the formula for the cell. For example, to set the value of A1 to the number 1 and then the value of B1 to A1 plus one, you would do the following:

```
$ws.Range('A1').Value2 = 1
$ws.Range('B1').Value2 = '=A1+1'
```

Selecting Ranges of Cells

A range is created by specifying more than one cell when invoking the `Range()` method. To select the group of four cells from A1 to B2, you would use the following:

```
$range = $ws.Range('A1','B2')
```

Because this `Range` object is the same as the one used to select a single cell, you can use the `Value2` property to set all of the cells to a single value:

```
$range.Value2
```

However, do not try to view the `Value2` property if the values are not identical or it will break all of your COM objects. Rather than doing that, you need to inspect the `Value2` property of each cell in the range:

```
$range.cells |Select value2
```

Caution

During the development of a script that interacts with the Office COM objects, it is possible to throw everything out of whack for seemingly no reason. These types of problems are due to known issues, but they are never documented or they are hidden in a forum post well away from where you are working. These manifest as nuisances that can make the development of a script a very excruciating process. Many times, the only way to fix these types of problems is to kill the executable for the Office application via Task Manager and then start over. For example, the `excel.exe` or `outlook.exe` process would need to be killed if you are having problems with Excel or Outlook. ■

It is common to write to a range of cells by looping through the cells in a range. Listing 4-7 shows an example of this technique.

LISTING 4-7

Writing the Output of Get-Process to Excel

```
$app = New-Object -ComObject 'Excel.Application'
$app.visible = $True

$wb = $app.Workbooks.Add()
```

continues

LISTING 4-7   *(continued)*

```
$ws = $wb.Worksheets.Item(1)

$columns = @('Name','Id','CPU')
$processes = Get-Process

$endcolumn = [char]([int][char]'A' + $columns.Count - 1)
$endrow = $processes.Count + 1
$endcell = "$endcolumn$endrow"
$range = $ws.Range('A1',$endcell)

$currentcell = 1

# Add the header row
foreach ($column in $columns) {
  $range.Cells.Item($currentcell).Value2 = $column
  $currentcell++
}

#Insert the data
foreach ($process in $processes) {
  foreach ($column in $columns) {
    $range.Cells.Item($currentcell).Value2 = $process.($column)
    $currentcell++
  }
}
```

Note

Faster techniques exist that you can use to get data into a range of cells. You can use the Paste function to input data, or you can convert an object to a multidimensional array and then supply it to the range. The method outlined in Listing 4-7 is a much simpler method to wrap your head around. Just remember that if speed becomes an issue, there are options you can explore. ∎

Cell Properties and Formatting

Styles can be applied to a range of cells through the Styles property of a Range object:

```
$range.Style = 'Title'
$range.Style = 'Normal'
```

Ranges also have a Font property where you can control the font of the data within the range of cells:

```
$range.Font.Size = 20
$range.Font.Name = 'Lucida Console'
```

You can access a number of other properties within a `Range` to set different characteristics about the range of cells:

```
$range.ColumnWidth = 20
$range.RowHeight = 50
$range.WrapText = $True
$range.MergeCells = $True
$range.NumberFormatLocal = '$0.00'
```

In addition to standard ranges, it can also be helpful to grab a range of rows or columns. Fortunately, it is easy to grab a row or column directly from a worksheet. `Range` objects that represent a row or a column also have a special `Autofit()` method that you can call to set the row or column to automatically adjust its size based on the size of the data inside of it.

```
# Set column A to autofit
$ws.Columns.Item(1).Autofit()

# Set all of the columns in a worksheet to autofit
$ws.Columns.Autofit()
```

Managing Data

A very common automation task within Excel is to sort or filter data. Sorting and filtering are done by invoking either the `Sort()` or `AutoFilter()` method on a `Range` object.

Sorting

Sorting a range of cells requires you to specify the column that should act as the key on which the range will be sorted. In addition, you can specify the order in which you would like to sort the data:

```
$order = [Microsoft.Office.Interop.Excel.XlSortOrder]::xlDescending
$sortcolumn = $ws.Columns.Item(1)
$range.Sort($sortcolumn,$order)
```

In addition to a simple sort on a single column, you can specify additional columns to sort on. Here's an example of a sort that sorts on column A, then column B, and finally on column C. This sort also uses another optional parameter that allows you to specify whether or not the first row is a header row.

```
$range = $ws.range('A1','C6')
$order = [Microsoft.Office.Interop.Excel.XlSortOrder]::xlDescending
$hasHead = [Microsoft.Office.Interop.Excel.XlYesNoGuess]::xlYes
$scol1 = $ws.Columns.Item(1)
$scol2 = $ws.Columns.Item(2)
$scol3 = $ws.Columns.Item(3)
$range.Sort($scol1,$order,$scol2,$null,$order,$scol3,$order,$hasHead)
```

Note

There is one $null placed in the middle of the method invocation in this example that seems out of place. This argument is used only when working with pivot tables. ∎

Filtering

When you click the filter button on an Excel document, it turns your first row into a drop-down list that enables you to filter the data in the spreadsheet. You can enable and disable this filter mechanism in Windows PowerShell by using the following line of code:

```
$ws.Range('A1').Autofilter()
```

You can use the same method to perform the actual filtering. The most common type of filtering requires you to pass two arguments to the method. The first argument indicates the column number you would like to filter on. The second argument specifies what you would like to filter for. For example, to filter the first column for all instances of the number 30, you would do the following:

```
$ws.Range('A1').Autofilter(1,'30')
```

If you want to filter for all blank entries, use the equals sign (=) as the argument:

```
$ws.Range('A1').Autofilter(1,'=')
```

If you want to filter for all of the non-blank entries, you would use <>:

```
$ws.Range('A1').Autofilter(1,'<>')
```

To clear the filter, omit the second argument:

```
$ws.Range('A1').Autofilter(1)
```

Generating Charts and Graphs

Generating charts and graphs from sets of data is an extremely useful automation task. This can be a very powerful reporting engine for your scripts. To get access to the charts and graphs in a worksheet, you must invoke the ChartObjects() method of the Worksheet. You can then invoke the Add() method to create a new chart of a specified dimension. After the chart is created, you can adjust the type of chart it is and finally set its data source to a range in the worksheet. Here's an example of how to create a simple line chart that uses the data in the range between cells B2 and C6:

```
$x = 100
$y = 100
$width = 300
$height = 200

$chart = $ws.ChartObjects().add($x,$y,$width,$height).chart
$chart.ChartType = [Microsoft.Office.Interop.Excel.XlChartType]::xlLine
```

```
$datarange = $ws.Range('B2','C6')
$chart.SetSourceData($datarange)
```

Searching Spreadsheets

You can search a range of cells by invoking the `Find()` method on a `Range` object. For example, if you wanted to make all instances where the cell value is 100 bold, you would do the following:

```
$range = $ws.Range('A1').CurrentRegion
foreach ($cell in ($range.Find('100'))) {
  $cell.font.bold = $true
}
```

Note

`CurrentRegion` is a handy property of a range object that you have not seen before. It returns a range of cells surrounding the current range that expands until it finds blank cells. This can be a very useful shortcut when you are unsure of how large the range needs to be. ■

Navigating Microsoft Outlook

The Outlook object model is an entirely different beast from Word or Excel. It has an application object like the others, but it introduces a whole array of new objects that represent different parts of Outlook. Table 4-1 lists a few of the key objects.

TABLE 4-1

Important Outlook Objects

Object	Description
Explorer	Represents the window where folder contents are displayed
Inspector	Represents a window where data such as an email or appointment is shown to the user
Namespace	Represents the root for a data source — primarily used to provide you access to the root set of folders in MAPI
MAPIFolder	A folder, such as the inbox or deleted items
MailItem	An email
AppointmentItem	A calendar entry
TaskItem	A task
ContactItem	A contact

A Word about Security

When people first think about everything they can automate with Outlook, their minds usually turn to automated emails, contact management, manipulation of folders, and anything else that might be tedious when it is done manually. Unfortunately, very early in the life of the COM interface for Outlook, the object model was quickly exploited by people who wrote malicious code to easily automate tasks like distributing your contact list or sending email from your account without your knowledge. Because of this, Microsoft quickly plugged the security hole. The object model is still accessible. However, if you try to access secure data or perform a secure operation, a prompt is given to the user of the computer asking if they'd like to grant permission to the application or script that is trying to access the sensitive data or method. This security feature can only be disabled temporarily and it will return over time.

Note

If you absolutely must perform Outlook tasks in an automated fashion without a security prompt, there is a well-known way to do this. There is a DLL you can purchase called redemption.dll from Dr. Dimitry Streblechenko, Outlook MVP, that will provide you with a set of objects that is extremely similar to the Outlook object model provided by Microsoft. The DLL also provides some additional functionality that cannot be performed with the COM objects. If this book inspires you to script heavily against Outlook, it is definitely worth understanding what this DLL is capable of doing. It is a fairly safe DLL to use in small instances, but if you are thinking of deploying it to your entire organization, you will want to understand how you can protect your users from malicious code and attackers that know of its existence. ■

Traversing Folders

All of the different types of items in Outlook are stored within folders. To access the data within them, you will first need to retrieve the objects that represent the folders in Outlook. Before that, here are the two lines of code discussed at the beginning of the chapter that will provide you with an Application object for an already opened instance of Outlook:

```
$marshal = [System.Runtime.InteropServices.Marshal]
$app = $marshal::GetActiveObject('Outlook.Application')
```

Working with the Major Folders

To get the MAPIFolderItem that represents one of the default folders in Outlook, you must bind to the namespace for MAPI. You can do this two ways, neither of which is superior to the other. The first involves calling the GetNamespace() method of the application object:

```
$ns = $app.GetNamespace('MAPI')
```

The second involves getting the active Explorer object from the Application object. An Explorer object has a Session property that is a Namespace object.

```
$ns = $app.ActiveExplorer().Session
```

The `Namespace` object has methods that enable you to get the folder objects you are looking for. If you are trying to work in one of the major folders, such as the Inbox, Deleted Items, Calendar, and Contacts, you use the `GetDefaultFolder()` method. For example, to get the `MAPIFolder` that represents the Inbox, you would do the following:

```
$ftype = [Microsoft.Office.Interop.Outlook.OlDefaultFolders]::olFolderInbox
$inbox = $ns.GetDefaultFolder($ftype)
```

Working with Subfolders

You can view the folders within a folder by using the `Folders` property of a `MAPIFolder` object. For example, to list all of the folders within a folder, you can do this:

```
$inbox.Folders |Select name
```

Because the `Namespace` object acts as the root, there is also a `Folders` property there. This enables you to get access to things such as PSTs, which live outside of the primary set of folders.

```
$ns.Folders |Select name
```

If you want to return a specific folder from the `Folders` collection, you can use the `Item()` method to do so. For example, this returns a folder in the Inbox that is called `psbible`:

```
$subfolder = $inbox.Folders.Item('psbible')
```

Creating Folders

You create folders by invoking the `Add()` method on the `Folders` property of a folder object:

```
$inbox.Folders.Add('PowerShell E-Mails')
```

Creating a PST

PST files are created by invoking the `AddStore()` method of the namespace. You must specify a full path to the PST. If the PST exists, it will mount it; otherwise, it will create the PST file in the location specified. Once it is mounted, it can be accessed via the `Folders` property of the `Namespace` object. Here is an example of how you can create a PST and rename it from Outlook Data File to something more useful:

```
$explorer = $app.ActiveExplorer()
$ns = $explorer.Session

$ns.AddStore('C:\psbible.pst')
if ($explorer.Session.Folders.Item('Outlook Data File')) {
  $pst = $explorer.Session.Folders.Item('Outlook Data File')
  $pst.name = 'PSbible Archive'
}
```

Working with Outlook Items

Items within folders are obtained by using the `Items` property of a `MAPIFolder` object. For example, to see all of the subject lines for each item within your Inbox, you would do the following:

```
$inbox.Items |Select TaskSubject
```

Every item and folder in Outlook has an associated ID string. Folders have a `StoreID` property and items have an `EntryID` property. Because these are static, you can store this information for later use or subsequent runs of a script. To retrieve the object using the ID, you can invoke the `GetFolderFromID()` or `GetItemFromID()` methods. For example, if you store an item's `StoreID` to disk with something like this:

```
$item.StoreID |Out-File -FilePath c:\mail1.txt
```

you can then restore it during another session by performing this line of code:

```
$ns.GetItemFromID((Get-Content -Path c:\mail1.txt))
```

Moving Items

To move an item from one folder to another, you invoke the `Move()` method on the item. For example, if you wanted to move all of the items in your Inbox to a subfolder in your Inbox named `psbible`, you would do the following:

```
$target = $inbox.Folders.Item('psbible')
foreach ($item in $inbox.Items) {
  $item.Move($target) |Out-Null
}
```

Deleting Items

You delete items by invoking the `Delete()` method of an item. For example, to delete all of the mail in your Inbox (a dangerous proposition), you would do the following:

```
foreach ($item in $inbox.Items) {
  $item.Delete()
}
```

Working with an Outlook MailItem

The item objects are a series of layered objects that inherit base properties from their parent, `Item`. These items all share certain methods like `Move()` and `Delete()`. However, each item type will return a whole range of new properties and methods that are specific to that type. For example, if you are in your Inbox and are inspecting the `Items` property of the Inbox, you will retrieve a collection of `MailItems`. A `MailItem` has properties like `Subject`, `Body`, `HTMLBody`, `Attachments`, `To`, `Sender`, and `Unread`.

Sending a MailItem

To send a `MailItem`, you must first create one using the `CreateItem()` method of the `Application` object. Once you have added the appropriate properties to the `MailItem`, you can invoke the `Send()` method on the item.

```
$itemtype = [Microsoft.Office.Interop.Outlook.OlItemType]::olMailItem
$mailitem = $app.CreateItem($itemtype)
$mailitem.Subject = 'You should read this book!'
$mailitem.Body = 'The PowerShell Bible Rocks!'
$mailitem.To = 'yourbestfriend@wiley.com'
$mailitem.Send()
```

Note

If your only intention is to send email, there is a much simpler way to do this than using the Outlook object model. **Send-MailMessage** is a cmdlet that comes with Windows PowerShell for the purpose of sending email via Windows PowerShell scripts. ∎

Working with Attachments

To add attachments to an email you are about to send, invoke the `Add()` method on the collection of attachments for the `MailItem`:

```
$mailitem.Attachments.Add('C:\psbible.zip')
```

If you have a `MailItem` in a folder and you want to save its attachments to disk, you can invoke the `SaveAsFile()` method on the `Attachment` object. Here is an example of how you can save the attachments in a `MailItem` to disk:

```
$savefolder = 'C:\attachments'
foreach ($attachment in $mailitem.Attachments) {
  $path = Join-Path $savefolder $attachment.FileName
  $attachment.SaveAsFile($path)
}
```

Working with an Outlook AppointmentItem

An `AppointmentItem` represents an item in your calendar. An `AppointmentItem` is created using the same `CreateItem()` method used to create an email. However, the type of item that is created is an `olAppointmentItem`.

```
$itemtype = [Microsoft.Office.Interop.Outlook.OlItemType]::olAppointmentItem
$appointment = $app.CreateItem($itemtype)
```

Once you have a new or existing `AppointmentItem`, you can modify its properties and then invoke the `Save()` method of the item to apply it to your calendar:

```
$appointment.Start = (Get-Date).AddHours(4)
$appointment.End = (Get-Date).AddHours(5)
```

```
$appointment.Subject = "Dentist"
$appointment.Save()
```

Working with an Outlook ContactItem

A `ContactItem` represents an entry in your Contacts list.

Creating a New Contact

A `ContactItem` is created using the same method you've already seen for both email and appointments. The major difference, of course, is that different properties exist for a contact than for an email or an appointment.

```
$itemtype = [Microsoft.Office.Interop.Outlook.OlItemType]::olContactItem
$contact = $app.CreateItem($itemtype)
$contact.FirstName = 'NYC PowerShell User Group'
$contact.Email1Address = 'powershellnyc@gmail.com'
$contact.WebPage = 'http://powershellgroup.org/nyc'
$contact.Save()
```

Finding a Contact

Searching is done by invoking the `Find()` method on a collection of items. The method requires a filter that enables you to define what you are looking for. The constructs for the filter can get a little overwhelming. However, if you have a simple exact-match filter with no special characters, a filter can be very easy to write. For example, this bit of code finds the contact that was created for the NYC PowerShell User Group and displays its contents in Outlook:

```
$ftype = [Microsoft.Office.Interop.Outlook.olDefaultFolders]::olFolderContacts
$folder = $ns.GetDefaultFolder($ftype)

$filter = "[FirstName]='NYC PowerShell User Group'"
$items = $folder.Items
$item = $items.Find($filter)
$item.Display()
```

It is possible to have more than one item returned from a contact. If that is the case, you can use the `FindNext()` method on the `Items` collection to continue searching for additional items. A very common utility loop to handle this is as follows:

```
$item = $items.Find($filter)
while ($item) {
  # Do something with $item here
  $item = $items.FindNext()
}
```

Note

Searching for any type of item in Outlook is not as simple as it should be in the object model. The **Find()** method allows you to filter using operators like greater than and less than, but it does not allow partial matches. Partial matches require you to invoke the **AdvancedSearch()** method of the application object. ∎

Note

You can find more information about the filters accepted by the `Find()` method and the `AdvancedSearch()` method at the following links to Microsoft's official documentation on the subjects:

- `http://msdn.microsoft.com/en-us/library/bb147590(office.12).aspx`
- `http://msdn.microsoft.com/en-us/library/microsoft.office.interop.outlook._
  application.advancedsearch.aspx` ■

Working with an Outlook TaskItem

The `TaskItem` follows suit with the rest of the item types. A task item is of the type `olTaskItem`. Here is a sample of how to add a task to your to-do list in Outlook:

```
$itemtype = [Microsoft.Office.Interop.Outlook.OlItemType]::olTaskItem
$task = $app.CreateItem($itemtype)
$task.Subject = 'Write some PowerShell'
$task.Save()
```

Additional Office COM Examples

Here are some additional examples of the COM objects in action on some of the other Office applications. Listing 4-8 provides an example of some Microsoft PowerPoint automation to create a new presentation.

LISTING 4-8

Creating a PowerPoint Presentation

```
# Create the application object
$app = New-Object -ComObject PowerPoint.Application
$app.Visible = [Microsoft.Office.Core.MsoTriState]::msoTrue
# Create a new presentation
$presentation = $app.Presentations.Add()

# Add a Title slide
$numberofslides = 1
$stype = [Microsoft.Office.Interop.PowerPoint.PpSlideLayout]::ppLayoutTitle
$slide = $presentation.Slides.Add($numberofslides,$stype)
$slide.Shapes.Item(1).TextFrame.TextRange.Text = 'The PowerShell Bible'
$slide.Shapes.Item(2).TextFrame.TextRange.Text = 'Rocks!'

# Apply the Black Tie theme to the presentation
$theme = 'C:\Program Files\Microsoft Office\Document Themes 14\Black Tie.thmx'
$presentation.ApplyTheme($theme)

#View the slide show in full screen
$presentation.SlideShowSettings.Run()
```

PowerPoint scripts have a very similar look and feel to Word and Excel. Unfortunately, not all of the Office applications follow the same set of rules. For example, the OneNote model gives you interfaces to a lot of XML data that must be manipulated to produce the desired effect. Listing 4-9 shows an example of how you can create a new OneNote page and add some data to it.

LISTING 4-9

Creating a New OneNote Page and Adding Data to It

```
 # Get the application object
$app = New-Object -ComObject OneNote.Application

# Get the structure of the notebooks in OneNote
$struct = [ref]""
$scope = [Microsoft.Office.Interop.OneNote.HierarchyScope]::hsPages
$app.GetHierarchy($null, $scope, $struct)
$struct = [xml]$struct.Value

# Find the Personal notebook
$notebook = $struct.Notebooks.Notebook |where {
  $_.name -match "Personal"
}
# Find the Unfiled Notes section
$OneSection = $notebook |select -ExpandProperty section |where {
  $_.name -match "Unfiled Notes"
}

# Create a new OneNote Page
$id = [ref]""
$app.CreateNewPage($OneSection.id,$id)

# Get the XML that represents the new page
$OnePage = [ref]""
$app.GetPageContent($id.value,$OnePage)
$OnePage = [xml]$OnePage.Value

# Insert a new section into the page using XML
$frag = $OnePage.CreateDocumentFragment()
$frag.InnerXml = @'
<one:Outline xmlns:one="http://schemas.microsoft.com/office/onenote↵
/2010/onenote">
 <one:OEChildren>
  <one:OE>
   <one:T>
    <![CDATA[{0}]]>
   </one:T>
  </one:OE>
```

```
  </one:OEChildren>
</one:Outline>
'@ -f "This is the text I would like to insert"
$OnePage.Page.AppendChild($frag)

# Update the page with the new XML
$app.UpdatePageContent($OnePage.OuterXml)
```

Summary

The breadth of the Microsoft Office COM model cannot be understated. The ability to programmatically control all aspects of an Office application comes with a large degree of complexity. Some tasks are intuitive, whereas others will have you scratching your head for an hour or so. The lack of documentation available to the Windows PowerShell scripter can make an automation task against Office a daunting one. Even with this labyrinth of objects, methods, and properties, you can take the small usable snippets from this chapter to accomplish many of the common requirements you will be given when you are asked to automate some part of Word, Excel, or Outlook.

The next chapter leaves applications for a while and returns to some of the core desktop functionality. Specifically, you will be looking at how Windows PowerShell can be used to manage permissions, the firewall, and other security-related tasks.

Managing Security

IN THIS CHAPTER

Using NTFS, file share, and registry permissions

Working with the Windows Firewall

Configuring Remote Desktop

You can manage permissions on file, folder, and registry objects with the Get-Acl and Set-Acl cmdlets. As the names imply, these cmdlets retrieve or modify the access control list (ACL) for a file, folder, or registry key. The object returned by the Get-Acl cmdlet is actually a security descriptor, which includes the access control list. The Get-Acl cmdlet, when run on its own, returns nearly useless data unless piped through to either the Format-List cmdlet or one of the export cmdlets like Export-Csv. All of the examples in this chapter that require you to view the ACL use Format-List, whereas all of the examples that save the ACL to a file use the Export-Csv cmdlet. If you are going to modify the ACL, and then reapply it with the Set-Acl cmdlet, you will not necessarily output the result of the Get-Acl cmdlet to screen.

The first part of this chapter builds on the section "Setting Security on Files and Folders" introduced in Chapter 3, "Managing Windows 7."

Table 5-1 lists some of the inheritance and propagation flags that can be set on various objects. The Set-Acl cmdlet writes the security descriptor to an object.

Common Inheritance and Propagation Flags for Use with the Set-Acl Cmdlet

Object	InheritanceFlags	PropagationFlags
Subfolders and Files only	ContainerInherit, ObjectInherit	InheritOnly
This Folder, Subfolders, and Files	ContainerInherit, ObjectInherit	None
This Folder, Subfolders, and Files	ContainerInherit, ObjectInherit	NoPropagateInherit
This Folder and Subfolders	ContainerInherit	None
Subfolders only	ContainerInherit	InheritOnly
This Folder and Files	ObjectInherit	None
This Folder and Files	ObjectInherit	NoPropagateInherit

Note

For more on propagation and inheritance flags, see the `System.Security.AccessControl` namespace documentation on MSDN: `http://msdn.microsoft.com/en-us/library/tbsb79h3.aspx`. ■

NTFS Permissions

NTFS permissions are applied to every file and folder. NTFS permissions affect local and domain users when logged in on a specific computer.

Retrieving Current NTFS Permissions

You retrieve NTFS permissions with the `Get-Acl` cmdlet, passing the parameter `Path`. This cmdlet retrieves the current security descriptor for a file or folder. Later in the chapter, you examine permissions as they apply to the registry. The `Path` parameter takes wildcards, so you could retrieve the ACL for a group of files at once. The first line in the following example retrieves the security descriptor for the folder `C:\scripts`, and the second retrieves the security descriptor for all files in the folder `C:\scripts`:

```
Get-Acl -Path C:\scripts
Get-Acl -Path C:\scripts\*
```

As mentioned at the beginning of the chapter, the output of the `Get-Acl` cmdlet is nearly useless unless passed through the `Format-List` cmdlet. Figure 5-1 displays the difference between the default output of the `Get-Acl` cmdlet and the same output piped through the `Format-List` cmdlet.

FIGURE 5-1

Output from the Get-Acl cmdlet compared to the Format-List cmdlet

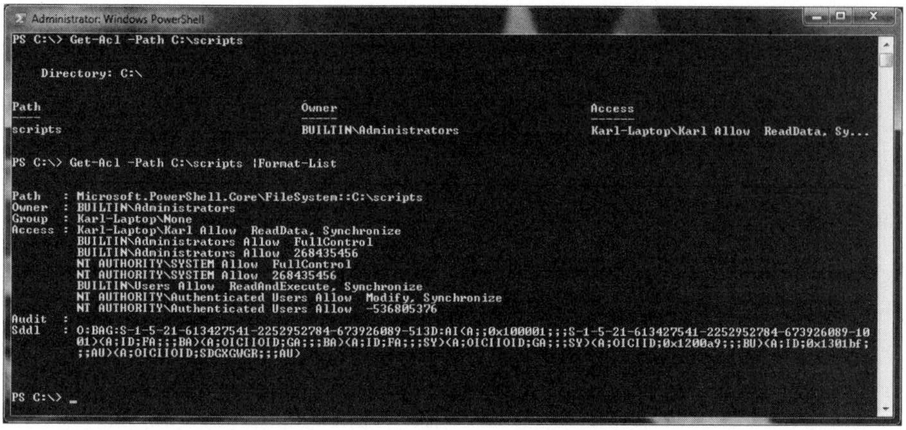

Unfortunately, the `Get-Acl` cmdlet does not have a `Recurse` parameter, so if you want to get the security descriptor for all the files in multiple subfolders, you will need to combine the `Get-ChildItem` cmdlet with the `Get-Acl` cmdlet. If you have more than two or three files, or a complex security descriptor, you would pass the output through the `Export-Csv` cmdlet. To view the output onscreen, you would pass the output through the `Out-Host` cmdlet, specifying the switch parameter `Paging`. The following example saves the security descriptors for all files and folders under `c:\docs` to the file `test.csv` in your current path:

```
$ChildItem = @{
Path = "c:\docs\*"
Recurse = $true
}
$Csv = @{
Path=test.csv = $true
NoTypeInformation = $true
}
Get-ChildItem @ChildItem | Get-Acl | Export-Csv @Csv
```

The following example displays the same information onscreen as the previous example, pausing after each page:

```
Get-ChildItem -Path c:\docs\* -Recurse | Get-Acl | Out-Host -Paging
```

Caution

The `Paging` parameter generates an error in the Integrated Scripting Environment. You should use this parameter only in the Windows PowerShell console. ■

Modifying NTFS Permissions

As mentioned previously, you can modify NTFS permissions with the Set-Acl cmdlet, passing the required parameters Path and AclObject. You can create a completely new ACL object to pass to the AclObject parameter, or modify an ACL object retrieved with the Get-Acl cmdlet. The following example adds the user Contoso\johnb to the access control list for the folder c:\Scripts\Test, and propagates those rights to all files in that folder. Subfolders in the folder will not have their access control lists modified unless they have inheritance turned on. The inheritance flags and propagation flags were shown in Table 5-1 earlier in the chapter.

```
$User = "Contoso\johnb"
$Folder = "c:\Scripts\Test"
$Inheritance = [System.Security.AccessControl.InheritanceFlags]`
"ContainerInherit, ObjectInherit"
$Propagation = [System.Security.AccessControl.PropagationFlags]"None"
$acl = Get-Acl -Path $Folder
$Object = @{
TypeName = "System.Security.AccessControl.FileSystemAccessRule"
ArgumentList = $User,"Modify", $Inheritance, $Propagation, "Allow"
}
$Rule = New-Object @Object
$acl.AddAccessRule($Rule)
Set-Acl -Path $Folder -AclObject $acl
```

You can modify permissions on files only by getting a list of files with the Get-ChildItem cmdlet, filtering out directories with the Where-Object cmdlet. Once you have the list of files, you get the current ACL with the Get-Acl cmdlet, build and add a new rule to the ACL, and finally write the updated ACL to the file with the Set-Acl cmdlet. The following example allows the user contoso\gmayes to access all files in the folder c:\scripts\test and its subfolders:

```
$User = "contoso\gmayes"
$Folder = "c:\Scripts\Test"
$Filter = @{
FilterScript = {!$_.PSIsContainer}
}
$FileRights = [System.Security.AccessControl.FileSystemRights]"Read","Write"
$Inheritance = [System.Security.AccessControl.InheritanceFlags]"None"
$Propagation = [System.Security.AccessControl.PropagationFlags]"InheritOnly"
$AceType =[System.Security.AccessControl.AccessControlType]"Allow"
$Files = Get-ChildItem $Folder -Recurse | Where-Object @Filter
foreach ($File in $Files)
{
$acl = Get-Acl -Path $File.FullName
$Object = @{
TypeName = "System.Security.AccessControl.FileSystemAccessRule"
ArgumentList = $User,$FileRights, $Inheritance, $Propagation, $AceType
}
$Rule = New-Object @Object
```

```
$acl.AddAccessRule($Rule)
Set-Acl -Path $File.FullName -AclObject $acl
}
```

You can also remove or modify a user's access to files or folders with the Get-Acl and Set-Acl cmdlets. First, you get the ACL with the Get-Acl cmdlet, then get the specific rule to remove with the Where-Object cmdlet. Once you have the rule, you remove it from the ACL object using the RemoveAccessRuleSpecific() method of the ACL object, and write the ACL back to the file or folder with the Set-Acl cmdlet. The following example removes the user contoso\bballard from the ACL for all files in the folder c:\Scripts\Test and its subfolders, when those rights are not inherited:

```
$User = "contoso\bballard"
$Folder = "c:\Scripts\Test"
$Filter = @{
FilterScript = {!$_.PSIsContainer}
}
$RuleFilter = @{
FilterScript = {$_.IdentityReference -eq $user}
}
$Files = Get-ChildItem $Folder -Recurse | Where-Object @Filter
foreach ($File in $Files)
{
$acl = Get-Acl -Path $File.FullName
$Rule = $acl.Access | Where-Object @RuleFilter
$acl.RemoveAccessRuleSpecific($Rule)
Set-Acl -Path $File.FullName -AclObject $acl
}
```

Share Permissions

Share permissions are different from NTFS permissions. NTFS permissions define accounts that have access to files and folders on a local machine, whereas *share permissions* define who has access to shared folders and files on remote machines. Every file and folder on a disk with the NTFS format is secured with NTFS permissions, whereas only files and folders that are explicitly shared will have share permissions. If a shared folder is set to allow a user full control and has NTFS permissions that allow that user only Read access, the NTFS permissions take precedence. Additionally, share permissions can only be set on the root of the share. Any subfolders under the shared folder will have the same permissions unless they are overridden via NTFS permissions. Viewing and modifying share permissions can be accomplished with Windows Management Instrumentation (WMI) calls.

Retrieving Current Share Permissions

You can retrieve share permissions with the Get-WmiObject cmdlet, passing the parameters Class and ComputerName. The Class value used to retrieve share permissions is Win32_LogicalShareSecuritySetting. The output from the Get-WmiObject cmdlet is a collection of security objects and will be fairly useless without further processing. The next example lists the share permissions for all shares on the server Server01. The permissions and the AceType are numeric. The AceType is the Access Control Entry (ACE) type, which can be set to Allow (0) or Deny (1).

```
$ShareObject = @{
Class = "Win32_LogicalShareSecuritySetting"
ComputerName = "Server01"
}
$SelectObject = @{
Property = "Share","Domain","ID","Permission","AceType"
}
$Security = Get-WmiObject @ShareObject
$RightsCollection = @()
ForEach ($ShareSecurity in ($Security))
{
  ForEach ($DACL in $ShareSecurity.GetSecurityDescriptor().Descriptor.DACL)
  {
    $DACLObject = "" | Select-Object @SelectObject
    $DACLObject.Share = $ShareSecurity.Name
    $DACLObject.Domain = $DACL.Trustee.Domain
    $DACLObject.ID = $DACL.Trustee.Name
    $DACLObject.Permission = $DACL.AccessMask
    $DACLObject.AceType = $DACL.AceType
    $RightsCollection += $DACLObject
  }
}
$RightsCollection | Format-Table -AutoSize
```

Note

For more on access control, see http://msdn.microsoft.com/en-us/library/aa374872(VS.85).aspx. ∎

Unless you have a listing of the possible permissions handy, the integer returned will be fairly useless. The AceType is easier to translate because there are only two possibilities. The possible permission access masks are defined in Table 5-2, and the ACE type is defined in Table 5-3.

TABLE 5-2

Share Permissions Access Mask Definitions

Access Mask	Definition
1179817	Read
1245631	Change
2032127	FullControl

TABLE 5-3

Share Permissions ACE type Definition

ACE Type	Definition
0	Allow
1	Deny

It would make sense to have Windows PowerShell convert the `AccessMask` and `AceType` with a simple hashtable. The following snippet converts the `AccessMask` and `AceType` to the more human-friendly versions:

```
$SharePermission = @{}
$SharePermission.Add(1179817, "Read")
$SharePermission.Add(1245631, "Change")
$SharePermission.Add(2032127, "FullControl")
$AceType = @{}
$AceType.Add(0,"Allow")
$AceType.Add(1,"Deny")
```

The example in Listing 5-1 retrieves the share permissions for all shares on the server `Server01`. Data output will be the share name, domain name for the group or user, the group or user's name, the permissions for that user or group, and whether the permissions allow or deny access to the share. The `AccessMask` and `AceType` are shown in the human-friendly format from the preceding snippet.

LISTING 5-1

Retrieve Share Permissions for All Shares on Server01

```
$ShareObject = @{
Class = "Win32_LogicalShareSecuritySetting"
ComputerName = "Server01"
}
$SharePermission = @{}
$SharePermission.Add(1179817, "Read")
$SharePermission.Add(1245631, "Change")
$SharePermission.Add(2032127, "FullControl")
$AceType = @{}
$AceType.Add(0,"Allow")
$AceType.Add(1,"Deny")
$Security = Get-WmiObject @ShareObject
$RightsCollection = @()
$Select = @{
Property = "Share","Domain","ID","Permission","AceType"
}
```

continues

LISTING 5-1 *(continued)*

```
ForEach ($ShareSecurity in ($Security))
{
  $Descriptor = $ShareSecurity.GetSecurityDescriptor()
  ForEach ($DACL in $Descriptor.Descriptor.DACL)
  {
    $DACLObject = "" | Select-Object @Select
    $DACLObject.Share = $ShareSecurity.Name
    $DACLObject.Domain = $DACL.Trustee.Domain
    $DACLObject.ID = $DACL.Trustee.Name
    $DACLObject.Permission = $SharePermission[([INT]$DACL.AccessMask)]
    $DACLObject.AceType = $AceType[([int]$DACL.AceType)]
    $RightsCollection += $DACLObject
  }
}
$RightsCollection |Format-Table -AutoSize
```

You could replace the final line of the script in Listing 5-1 with a call to the `Export-Csv` cmdlet to save a copy of current share permissions. An example of this would be `$RightsCollection | Export-Csv -Path SharePermission.csv -NoTypeInformation`.

An alternative to the script in Listing 5-1 would be a function that allows you to specify the computer and share to retrieve permissions from. The script in Listing 5-2 provides this functionality. The `Get-SharePermission` function requires the parameters `ComputerName` and `ShareName`, and returns the domain, ID, permission, and `AceType` for each account that is allowed or denied access to the share.

LISTING 5-2

Get-SharePermission Function

```
function Get-SharePermission
{
  param(
  [Parameter(Mandatory = $true)]
  [string]$ComputerName,
  [Parameter(Mandatory = $true)]
  [string]$ShareName
  )
  $ShareObject = @{
  Class = "Win32_LogicalShareSecuritySetting"
  ComputerName = $computername
  }
```

```
$WhereObject = @{
FilterScript = {$_.Name -eq "$sharename"}
}
$SelectObject = @{
Property = "Domain","ID","Permission","AceType"
}
$Security = Get-WmiObject @ShareObject | Where-Object @WhereObject
$SharePermission = @{}
$SharePermission.Add(1179817, "Read")
$SharePermission.Add(1245631, "Change")
$SharePermission.Add(2032127, "FullControl")
$AceType = @{}
$AceType.Add(0,"Allow")
$AceType.Add(1,"Deny")
ForEach ($ShareSecurity in ($Security))
{
  $Descriptor = $ShareSecurity.GetSecurityDescriptor()
  $RightsCollection = @()
  ForEach ($DACL in $Descriptor.Descriptor.DACL)
  {
    $RightsObject = "" | Select-Object @SelectObject
    $RightsObject.Domain = $DACL.Trustee.Domain
    $RightsObject.ID = $DACL.Trustee.Name
    $RightsObject.Permission  = $SharePermission[([INT]$DACL.AccessMask)]
    $RightsObject.AceType = $AceType[([int]$DACL.AceType)]
    $RightsCollection += $RightsObject
  }
}
  Return $RightsCollection
}
```

The following example displays the current share permissions for the share AccountingFiles on the computer Server02:

```
Get-SharePermission -ComputerName Server02 -ShareName AccountingFiles
```

The next example saves the share permissions for the share UserFiles on the computer Server03 to the file UserFiles.csv in the current path:

```
$SharePermission = @{
ComputerName = "Server03"
ShareName = "UserFiles"
}
$Csv = @{
Path = "UserFiles.csv"
NoTypeInformation = $true
}
Get-SharePermission @SharePermission | Export-Csv @Csv
```

Modifying Share Permissions

Modifying share permissions is considerably more difficult than retrieving them. First, you need to define a custom type using the Add-Type cmdlet. The Add-Type cmdlet allows you to embed code from a .NET programing language directly into Windows PowerShell. This type defines the security settings for the share. As with NTFS permissions, you will need to retrieve the current permissions with the Get-WmiObject cmdlet, calling the Win32_Share class. Once you get a pointer to the share with the Win32_Share class, you create a new object using the New-Object cmdlet passing the custom type you created earlier as the TypeName parameter. This custom object holds information about the share for use later. Now you retrieve the current share permissions with the Get-WmiObject cmdlet, using the Win32_LogicalShareSecuritySetting class. You then build a new access control list, copying the current settings, and adding the new permissions. Finally, you need to save the new access control list to the share using the SetShareInfo() method of the Win32_Share class.

This top-level overview only scratches the surface of the problem. The script in Listing 5-3 gives the complete program for setting permissions on a local or remote computer.

LISTING 5-3

Set-SharePermission.ps1 Script

```
param(
[Parameter(Mandatory = $true, Position = 0)]
[string]$User,
[Parameter(Mandatory = $true, Position = 1)]
[ValidateSet("Allow","Deny")]
[string]$AccessType,
[Parameter(Mandatory = $true, Position = 2)]
[ValidateSet("FullControl","Change","Read")]
[string]$Permission,
[Parameter(Mandatory = $true, Position = 3)]
[String]$ShareName,
[Parameter(Mandatory = $false, Position = 4)]
[String]$ComputerName = $env:COMPUTERNAME
)
#Inspired by Vadims Podans
#http://en-us.sysadmins.lv/Lists/Posts/Post.aspx?ID=28
Add-Type @'
namespace Utility
{
namespace SecurityDescriptor
{
public enum AccessType : int
{
Allow,
Deny
}
```

```
public enum Right : int
{
Read,
Change,
FullControl
}
public struct SD
{
public string User;
public string SIDString;
public string Domain;
public AccessType AccessType;
public Right Permission;
public int AccessMask;
public int AceType;
public int AceFlags;
}
}
public class ShareInfo
{
public string ComputerName;
public string Name;
public string Path;
public string Description;
public bool AllowMaximum;
public int MaximumAllowed;
public SecurityDescriptor.SD[] SecurityDescriptor;
}
}
'@
$AccessType = [Utility.Securitydescriptor.AccessType]$AccessType
$Permission = [Utility.Securitydescriptor.Right]$Permission
$WmiShareObject = @{
Class = "Win32_Share"
ComputerName = $ComputerName
Filter = "name LIKE '$($ShareName.Replace("*","%"))'"
}
$Share = Get-WmiObject @WmiShareObject
if ($Share -eq $null -or $Share.Type -ne 0){
  Write-host "Share '$ShareName' is not found on '$ComputerName'"
}
if ($Share){
  $ShareInfo = New-Object -TypeName Utility.ShareInfo
  $ShareInfo.ComputerName = $Share.__SERVER
  $ShareInfo.Name = $Share.Name
  $ShareInfo.Path = $Share.Path
  $ShareInfo.Description = $Share.Description
  $ShareInfo.AllowMaximum = $Share.AllowMaximum
```

LISTING 5-3   *(continued)*

```
$ShareInfo.MaximumAllowed = [int]$Share.MaximumAllowed
$WmiShareSecurity = @{
Class = "Win32_LogicalShareSecuritySetting"
ComputerName = $ShareInfo.ComputerName
Filter = "Name='$($Share.name)'"
}
$ShareSec = Get-WmiObject @WmiShareSecurity
if ($shareSec){
  $SD = $sharesec.GetSecurityDescriptor()
  $SD.Descriptor.DACL | ForEach-Object{
    $Descriptor = New-Object Utility.SecurityDescriptor.SD
    $Descriptor.User = $_.trustee.Name
    $Descriptor.SIDString = $_.trustee.SIDString
    $Descriptor.Domain = $_.trustee.Domain
    $Descriptor.AccessMask = $_.AccessMask
    $Descriptor.AceFlags = $_.AceFlags
    $Descriptor.AceType = $_.AceType
    $ShareInfo.SecurityDescriptor += $Descriptor
    }
}
else{
  Write-Error "You may not have rights to access the share."
}
}
else{
  Write-Error "No security information could be retrieved from the share."
}
$Masks = @{}
$Masks.Add("FullControl",2032127)
$Masks.Add("Change",1245631)
$Masks.Add("Read",1179817)
$Types = @{}
$Types.Add("Allow",0)
$Types.Add("Deny",1)
$Object = @{
TypeName = "Security.Principal.NTAccount"
ArgumentList = $User
}
$OldSD = $ShareInfo.SecurityDescriptor
$Descriptor = New-Object Utility.SecurityDescriptor.SD
$Descriptor.SIDString = (New-Object @Object).Translate(
[Security.Principal.SecurityIdentifier]).Value
$Descriptor.Domain = $null
$Descriptor.User = $User
$Descriptor.AccessMask = $Masks[[string]$Permission]
$Descriptor.AceFlags = 0
```

```
$Descriptor.AceType = $Types.$AccessType
$ShareInfo.SecurityDescriptor = @($Descriptor) + $OldSD
$SD = ([wmiclass]'Win32_SecurityDescriptor').CreateInstance()
$ace = ([wmiclass]'Win32_Ace').CreateInstance()
$Trustee = ([wmiclass]'Win32_Trustee').CreateInstance()
$SD.DACL = @()
foreach ($Descriptor in $ShareInfo.SecurityDescriptor){
  $SID = New-Object Security.Principal.SecurityIdentifier($Descriptor.SIDString)
  [Byte[]]$SIDArray = ,0 * $SID.BinaryLength
  $SID.GetBinaryForm($SIDArray, 0)
  $Trustee.Name = $Descriptor.User
  $Trustee.SID = $SIDArray
  $ace.AccessMask = $Descriptor.AccessMask
  $ace.AceType = $Descriptor.AceType
  $ace.AceFlags = $Descriptor.AceFlags
  $ace.Trustee = $Trustee
  $SD.DACL += $ace.psobject.baseobject
  }
$Share.SetShareInfo(
$ShareInfo.MaximumAllowed, $ShareInfo.Description, $SD) | Out-Null
```

The `Set-SharePermission` script requires the parameters `User`, which is the user that you are granting permissions to; `AccessType`, which can be set to either `Allow` or `Deny` access to the share; `Permission`, which can be set to `FullControl`, `Change`, or `Read`; and `ShareName`, which is the share to set permissions on. The optional parameter `ComputerName` defaults to the local computer if omitted. You can specify a user with a domain name or as just the username. If you do not specify the domain, the script will attempt to find the user in the current domain.

The following example allows the user `cmccarley` to `Read` the share named `UserFiles` on the server `FileServer01`:

```
$SharePermission = @{
User = "cmccarley"
AccessType = "Allow"
Permission = "Read"
ShareName = "UserFiles"
ComputerName = "FileServer01"
}
.\Set-SharePermission.ps1 @SharePermission
```

Registry Settings

You use the .NET classes to view or modify registry permissions on remote computers, and the `Get-Acl` and `Set-Acl` cmdlets to view and modify local registry permissions. By default, the `Get-Acl` and `Set-Acl` cmdlets work only on the HKEY_CURRENT_USER and

HKEY_LOCAL_MACHINE registry hives, because Windows PowerShell has built-in providers for those hives. The code samples using .NET classes will work locally or remotely, but if you are interested in the security in the previously mentioned hives on the local machine, the Get-Acl and Set-Acl examples will be quicker to type from the command line.

As an alternative to using .NET classes locally, you could also create drives pointing to the other registry hives with the New-PSDrive cmdlet, passing the required parameters Name, PSProvider, and Root. The following example creates a new drive called HKCR, which points to the HKEY_CLASSES_ROOT hive:

```
New-PSDrive -Name HKCR -PSProvider Registry -Root HKEY_CLASSES_ROOT | Out-Null
```

The previous example pipes the output of the New-PSDrive cmdlet to the Out-Null cmdlet. This simply prevents the output of the New-PSDrive cmdlet from showing onscreen.

Retrieving Current Registry Permissions

As mentioned, you can retrieve the current permissions for a local registry key with the Get-Acl cmdlet. For viewing onscreen, you pipe the output through the Format-List cmdlet. The following example shows the current permission for the registry key PowerShell in the path HKLM:\SOFTWARE\Microsoft on the local machine:

```
Get-Acl -Path HKLM:\SOFTWARE\Microsoft\PowerShell | Format-List
```

As with the Get-Acl examples in the NTFS section, you could pass the output of a Get-ChildItem cmdlet to the Get-Acl cmdlet to gather the current security settings for an entire hive or key. The following example exports the security permissions for the path HKCU:\AppEvents to the .csv file C:\Logs\HKCU.csv:

```
$Item = @{
Path = "HKCU:\AppEvents"
Recurse = $true
}
$Acl = @{
ErrorAction = "SilentlyContinue"
}
$Object = @{
Property = "Path","Owner","Group"
ExpandProperty = "Access"
}
$Csv = @{
Path = "C:\Logs\HKCU.csv"
NoTypeInformation = $true
}
Get-ChildItem @Item | Get-Acl @Acl | Select-Object @Object | Export-Csv @Csv
```

You can retrieve registry permissions for remote machines with the .NET classes Microsoft.Win32.RegistryKey and Microsoft.Win32.RegistryHive. You first assign the classes to variables, and instantiate them as needed. The following two script lines assign the needed classes to variables:

```
$classKey = [Microsoft.Win32.RegistryKey]
$classHive = [Microsoft.Win32.RegistryHive]
```

Once the classes are assigned to variables, you can call the methods or properties of the classes. The following example shows the current permission for the registry key PowerShell in the path HKLM:\SOFTWARE\Microsoft on the file server named File-Server:

```
$Server = "File-Server"
$classKey = [Microsoft.Win32.RegistryKey]
$classHive = [Microsoft.Win32.RegistryHive]
$RemoteKey = $classKey::OpenRemoteBaseKey($classHive::LocalMachine, $server)
$regKey = $RemoteKey.OpenSubKey("SOFTWARE\Microsoft\PowerShell")
$regKey.GetAccessControl() | Format-List
```

Modifying Registry Permissions

As with other permissions in this chapter, you must first retrieve the current permissions for a registry key before creating a new ACL, add the new ACL to the current ACL, and finally, write the new ACL to the registry key.

The following example grants the user contoso\sherrym full control of the registry key PowerShell in the path HKLM:\SOFTWARE\Microsoft\PowerShell on the local machine. The permission will be granted on only that key. The RegistryAccessRule class also enables you to specify inheritance and propagation flags, as shown in Table 5-4 and Table 5-5.

```
$RegistryAcl = Get-Acl "HKLM:\SOFTWARE\Microsoft\PowerShell"
$RuleObject = @{
TypeName = "System.Security.AccessControl.RegistryAccessRule"
ArgumentList = "contoso\sherrym","FullControl","Allow"
}
$RegistryRule = New-Object @RuleObject
$RegistryAcl.SetAccessRule($RegistryRule)
$RegistryAcl | Set-Acl -Path $RegistryAcl.Path
```

TABLE 5-4

Registry Inheritance Flags

Inheritance Flag	Definition
None	The ACE is not inherited by child objects.
ContainerInherit	The ACE is inherited by child container objects.
ObjectInherit	The ACE is inherited by child leaf objects.

TABLE 5-5

Registry Propagation Flags

Propagation Flag	Definition
None	Specifies that no inheritance flags are set.
NoPropagateInherit	Specifies that the ACE is not propagated to child objects.
InheritOnly	Specifies that the ACE is propagated only to child objects. This includes both container and leaf child objects.

Now that you have the inheritance and propagation flags, you can create a registry access control list that allows the specific permission you want. Suppose you wanted the user contoso\gmitschke to have full permission to the key in the previous example and all child objects. You would set the inheritance flag to ContainerInherit and ObjectInherit, and the propagation flag to None. This is shown in the following example:

```
$RegistryAcl = Get-Acl "HKLM:\SOFTWARE\Microsoft\PowerShell"
$User = "contoso\gmitschke"
$Right = "FullControl"
$Inherit = "ContainerInherit,ObjectInherit"
$Propagation = "None"
$Access = "Allow"
$ArgumentList = @($User,$Right,$Inherit,$Propagation,$Access)
$RuleObject = @{
TypeName = "System.Security.AccessControl.RegistryAccessRule"
ArgumentList = $ArgumentList
}
$RegistryRule = New-Object @RuleObject
$RegistryAcl.SetAccessRule($RegistryRule)
$RegistryAcl | Set-Acl -Path $RegistryAcl.Path
```

You modify registry permissions for remote machines with the .NET classes Microsoft .Win32.RegistryKey and Microsoft.Win32.RegistryHive. You first assign the classes to variables, and instantiate them as needed. The following two script lines assign the needed classes to variables:

```
$classKey = [Microsoft.Win32.RegistryKey]
$classHive = [Microsoft.Win32.RegistryHive]
```

Once the classes are assigned to variables, you can call the methods or properties of the classes. The following example retrieves the current permission for the registry key PowerShell in the path HKLM:\SOFTWARE\Microsoft on the file server named File-Server. Once the permissions are retrieved and stored in the $Acl variable, you create a new object of the System.Security.AccessControl.RegistryAccessRule class. You then add the new rule object to the existing permission list by calling the AddAccessRule() method of the System.Security.AccessControl.RegistrySecurity class.

Finally, you need to remove protection on the access rules by calling the SetAccessRuleProtection() method of the System.Security.AccessControl .RegistrySecurity class. This method takes two Boolean values. The first determines if inheritance is allowed to the permissions list, and the second determines if currently inherited rules are preserved. When both values are set to true, inheritance will be prevented, but the current inheritance will be preserved.

The following example grants the user contoso\gmitschke full control of the registry key PowerShell in the path HKLM:\SOFTWARE\Microsoft\PowerShell on the server File-Server, and all child objects:

```
$ComputerName = "File-Server"
$Key = [Microsoft.Win32.RegistryKey]
$Hive = [Microsoft.Win32.RegistryHive]
$RemoteKey = $Key::OpenRemoteBaseKey($Hive::LocalMachine, $ComputerName)
$regKey = $RemoteKey.OpenSubKey("SOFTWARE\Microsoft\PowerShell", $true)
$Acl = $regKey.GetAccessControl()
$User = "contoso\gmitschke"
$Right = "FullControl"
$Inherit = "ContainerInherit,ObjectInherit"
$Propagation = "None"
$Access = "Allow"
$ArgumentList = @($User,$Right,$Inherit,$Propagation,$Access)
$RuleObject = @{
TypeName = "System.Security.AccessControl.RegistryAccessRule"
ArgumentList = $ArgumentList
}
$RegistryRule = New-Object @RuleObject
$Acl.AddAccessRule($RegistryRule)
$Acl.SetAccessRuleProtection($true,$true)
$regKey.SetAccessControl($Acl)
$regKey.Close()
```

Managing the Windows Firewall

Using Windows PowerShell, you can verify that the Windows Firewall is enabled, you can disable or enable the firewall, and you can open and close ports. Additionally, you can allow or disallow applications. In this section, you explore all of these tasks, and create a script that lists all active rules.

Checking Firewall Status

Microsoft Windows XP has two firewall profiles: the domain and private profile. Microsoft Windows Vista and newer versions have the previously mentioned profiles and a third profile, the public profile. The public profile is in effect when you connect a Windows Vista or newer machine to a public network. The domain profile is active when you are connected to a work domain, and the private profile is active when you are connected to a home network or workgroup.

Locally

You can check that the firewall is enabled in the private and domain profiles by loading a COM object known as HNetCfg.FwMgr. The following example shows which firewall types are enabled on the local machine, and which firewall profile is active.

```
$Object = @{
ComObject = "HNetCfg.FwMgr"
}
$FirewallPolicy = (New-Object @Object).LocalPolicy
$CurrentFirewall = $FirewallPolicy.CurrentProfile.Type
$Domain = $FirewallPolicy.GetProfileByType(0).FirewallEnabled
$Private = $FirewallPolicy.GetProfileByType(1).FirewallEnabled
switch ($Domain)
{
  "False" {$Domain = "Disabled"}
  "True" {$Domain = "Enabled"}
}
switch ($Private)
{
  "False"  {$Private  = "Disabled"}
  "True" {$Private = "Enabled"}
}
switch ($CurrentFirewall)
{
  0 {$CurrentFirewall = "Domain"}
  1 {$CurrentFirewall = "Private"}
}
Write-Output "The local computer Domain firewall is $Domain."
Write-Output "The local computer Private firewall is $Private."
Write-Output "The $CurrentFirewall profile is active."
```

Tip

The COM object **HNetCfg.FwMgr** only shows settings for the domain and private profile, so if you are running Microsoft Vista or a newer operating system, you'd want to use the code in the section on checking the firewall status "Remotely Via the Registry" to determine which firewall is active. The rest of the code in this section works with Windows XP and newer. ■

Using the same COM object, you can list the applications and services that are authorized through the firewall, as well as any globally open ports. Additionally, you can view the Internet Control Message Protocol (ICMP) settings. The example in Listing 5-4 creates a function to load the COM object and retrieves the values requested.

LISTING 5-4

Get-FirewallSetting Function

```
function Get-FirewallSetting
{
param(
[Parameter(Mandatory = $true)]
[ValidateSet("Status",
"Applications",
"Services",
"Ports",
"ICMP")]
[String[]]$Value
)
$Object = @{
ComObject = "HNetCfg.FwMgr"
}
  $FirewallPolicy = (New-Object @Object).LocalPolicy
  foreach ($ValueName in $Value)
  {
    switch ($ValueName)
   {
      "Status"
      {
        $CurrentFirewall = $FirewallPolicy.CurrentProfile.Type
        switch ($CurrentFirewall)
        {
          0 {$Firewall = "Domain"}
          1 {$Firewall = "Private"}
        }
        $FirewallState = $FirewallPolicy.GetProfileByType($CurrentFirewall)
        switch ($FirewallState.FirewallEnabled)
        {
          "False" {$Current = "Disabled"}
          "True" {$Current = "Enabled"}
        }
        Write-Output "The current firewall is the $Firewall firewall."
        Write-Output "The firewall is $Current."
      }
      "Applications"
     {
        $Apps = $FirewallPolicy.CurrentProfile.AuthorizedApplications
        if ($Apps.Count -gt 0)
        {
          Write-Output "Authorized applications are:"
         $Apps | Select-Object -Property Name, Enabled
        }
```

continues

LISTING 5-4   *(continued)*

```
   else
   {
     Write-Output "There are no authorized applications."
   }
 }
 "Services"
 {
   $Services = $FirewallPolicy.CurrentProfile.Services
   if ($Services.Count -gt 0)
   {
     Write-Output "Authorized services are:"
      $Services
   }
   else
   {
     Write-Output "There are no authorized services."
   }
 }
 "Ports"
 {
   $Ports = $FirewallPolicy.CurrentProfile.GloballyOpenPorts
   if ($Ports.Count -gt 0)
   {
     Write-Output "Globally open ports are:"
      $Ports
   }
   else
   {
     Write-Output "There are no globally open ports."
   }
 }
 "ICMP"
 {
   $Icmp = $FirewallPolicy.CurrentProfile.IcmpSettings
   Write-Output "ICMP settings are:"
    $Icmp
 }
}
$Domain = $FirewallPolicy.GetProfileByType(0).FirewallEnabled
$Private = $FirewallPolicy.GetProfileByType(1).FirewallEnabled
switch ($Domain)
{
  "False" {$Domain = "Disabled"}
  "True" {$Domain = "Enabled"}
}
```

```
    switch ($Private)
    {
      "False"  {$Private  = "Disabled"}
      "True" {$Private = "Enabled"}
    }
    switch ($CurrentFirewall)
    {
      0 {$CurrentFirewall = "Domain"}
      1 {$CurrentFirewall = "Private"}
    }
  }
}
```

The Get-FirewallSetting function takes the required parameter Value. The Value parameter takes a string or array of strings for the data. ValidateSet in the param() block indicates that the Value parameter accepts only the strings Status, Applications, Services, Ports, or ICMP.

The following example shows the firewall setting for Applications:

```
Get-FirewallSetting -Value Applications
```

Remotely Via the Registry

You can check that the firewall is enabled on a remote machine by reading three remote registry keys. The keys are DomainProfile, PublicProfile, and StandardProfile in the path System\ControlSet001\Services\SharedAccess\Parameters\FirewallPolicy\ DomainProfile, which is in the hive HKEY_LOCAL_MACHINE. Each of those keys has a dword value named EnableFirewall, which is 1 if the firewall is enabled for that profile, and 0 if it is not enabled. The following example shows the firewall status for all three profiles for the computer Server05, if you have permission on that server:

```
$Computer = "Server05"
$Hive = "LocalMachine"
$RegKey = $null
$Key = "System\ControlSet001\Services\SharedAccess\Parameters\FirewallPolicy"
$DomainKey = "$Key\DomainProfile"
$StandardKey = "$Key\StandardProfile"
$Publickey = "$Key\PublicProfile"
$ValueName = "EnableFirewall"
$RegHive = [Microsoft.Win32.RegistryHive]$hive
$RegKey = [Microsoft.Win32.RegistryKey]::OpenRemoteBaseKey($RegHive,$Computer)
if ($RegKey)
{
  $Domain = ($RegKey.OpenSubKey($DomainKey)).GetValue("EnableFirewall")
  $Private = ($RegKey.OpenSubKey($StandardKey)).GetValue("EnableFirewall")
  $Public = ($RegKey.OpenSubKey($PublicKey)).GetValue("EnableFirewall")
```

```
    switch ($Domain)
    {
      0 {$Domain = "Disabled"}
      1 {$Domain = "Enabled"}
    }
    switch ($Private)
    {
      0 {$Private  = "Disabled"}
      1 {$Private = "Enabled"}
    }
    switch ($Public)
    {
      0 {$Public  = "Disabled"}
      1 {$Public = "Enabled"}
    }
    Write-Output "The computer $Computer Domain firewall is $Domain."
    Write-Output "The computer $Computer Private firewall is $Private."
    Write-Output "The computer $Computer Public firewall is $Public."
}
Else
{
    Write-Output "Cannot read registry on $Computer."
}
```

As mentioned at the beginning of the section, Windows Vista and newer operating systems provide a private firewall profile. You cannot specifically determine if the private firewall profile is enabled using the `HNetCfg.FwMgr` COM object. To do this on the local machine, you'd want to check the registry as illustrated previously in the section on checking the firewall status locally. Conversely, you can gather more information with the `HNetCfg.FwMgr` COM object.

Opening and Closing Ports

You can open ports with the `HNetCfg.FwMgr` and `HNetCfg.FwOpenPort` objects. Before you can create a new port, you need to get a pointer to the current ports collection, which is in the current firewall profile. You then create the new port object, and finally add the new port object to the ports collection. Before opening a port, it would be a good idea to see which ports are already open. The following example uses the `HNetCfg.FwMgr` object to retrieve a list of currently open ports. The protocol will be displayed as an integer, where 6 represents TCP and 17 represents UDP.

```
$Firewall = (New-Object -ComObject HNetCfg.FwMgr).LocalPolicy.CurrentProfile
$Firewall.GloballyOpenPorts | Format-Table -AutoSize
```

Once you have seen that the port you need opened is not on the list of open ports, you can add it by creating a collection of ports and using the `Add()` method of the ports collection. Ports can be opened for the TCP protocol or the UDP protocol, or both. Additionally, a single application could have multiple ports open for each protocol. The simple function in the next example opens a single port for either the TCP or UDP protocol. You can open a port by calling the function and passing the required parameters `PortName`, `PortNumber`, and `Protocol`. The function must be run from an elevated Windows PowerShell console.

```
function Open-FirewallPort
{
param(
[string]$PortName,
[int]$PortNumber,
[string]$Protocol
)
switch ($Protocol){
  "TCP" {$ProtocolNumber = 6}
  "UDP" {$ProtocolNumber = 17}
}
$Firewall = (New-Object -ComObject HNetCfg.FwMgr).LocalPolicy.CurrentProfile
$Ports = $Firewall.GloballyOpenPorts
$AddPort = New-Object -ComObject HNetCfg.FwOpenPort
$AddPort.Port = $PortNumber
$AddPort.Name = $PortName
$AddPort.Enabled = $true
$AddPort.Protocol = $ProtocolNumber
$Ports.Add($AddPort)
}

Open-FirewallPort -PortName "SCOMAction" -PortNumber 1270 -Protocol "TCP"
```

With this line of code, you would open the port named SCOMAction, allowing TCP traffic, through port 1270. The port name is arbitrary, and can be whatever you choose.

You can close a firewall port using the same basic function, but calling the `Remove()` method of the ports collection. The following function, when run from an elevated Windows PowerShell console, closes all ports for the specified port name:

```
function Close-FirewallPort
{
param(
[string]$PortName
)
$Profile = (new-object -com HNetCfg.FwMgr).LocalPolicy.CurrentProfile
$openPorts = $Profile.GloballyOpenPorts
$Ports = @($openPorts | Where-Object -FilterScript {$_.Name -eq $PortName})
$Ports | ForEach-Object -Process {$openPorts.Remove($_.Port,$_.Protocol)}
}
```

The Windows Firewall can also allow a range of ports through for a specific protocol. The enhanced function shown in the following code opens a single or multiple ports for either or both protocols. As with the previous example, you will need to run this function from an elevated Windows PowerShell console. If you need to open a range of ports, the port numbers will need to be enclosed in parentheses, with two dots between the numbers: for example, (1200..1255).

```
function Open-FirewallPort
{
  param(
  [Parameter(Mandatory = $true)]
  [string]$PortName,
  [Parameter(Mandatory = $true)]
  [int[]]$PortNumber,
  [Parameter(Mandatory = $true)]
  [ValidateRange("TCP","UDP")]
  [string[]]$Protocol
  )
  $ProtocolNumber = @()
  switch ($Protocol)
  {
    "TCP" {$ProtocolNumber += 6}
    "UDP" {$ProtocolNumber += 17}
  }
  $Firewall = (New-Object -ComObject HNetCfg.FwMgr).LocalPolicy.CurrentProfile
  $Ports = $Firewall.GloballyOpenPorts
  foreach ($ProtocolType in $ProtocolNumber)
  {
    foreach ($Port in $PortNumber)
    {
      $AddPort = New-Object -ComObject HNetCfg.FwOpenPort
      $AddPort.Port = $Port
      $AddPort.Name = $PortName
      $AddPort.Enabled = $true
      $AddPort.Protocol = $ProtocolType
      $Ports.Add($AddPort)
    }
  }
}
```

The following code would open the ports between 1270 and 1300, inclusive, and allow traffic on UDP and TCP, for the port named SCOMAction.

```
$Port = @{
PortName = "SCOMAction"
Protocol = "UDP","TCP"
}
Open-FirewallPort @Port -PortNumber (1270..1300)

$Port = @{
PortName = "SCOMAction"
Protocol = "UDP","TCP"
}
Open-FirewallPort @Port -PortNumber 1270,1300
```

Enabling Remote Desktop

You can enable Remote Desktop locally or remotely via the registry. Remote Desktop settings are contained in two registry keys in the HKEY_LOCAL_MACHINE hive. The dword value fDenyTSConnections is in the path \System\CurrentControlSet\Control\Terminal Server, and the dword value UserAuthentication is in the path \System\CurrentControlSet\Control\Terminal Server\WinStations\RDP-Tcp.

If fDenyTSConnections is set to 1, Remote Desktop connections are denied. When fDenyTSConnections is set to 0, Remote Desktop connections are allowed. You can choose to allow connections from computers running any version of Remote Desktop by setting UserAuthentication to 0, or only allow connections from computers running Remote Desktop with network-level authentication by setting UserAuthentication to 1, which is more secure.

The script in Listing 5-5 sets the Remote Desktop configuration as specified on the local computer or a remote computer. When run without parameters, the script sets the local computer to allow Remote Desktop connections using network-level authentication. Optional parameters allow you to choose the computer and authentication level, or disable Remote Desktop connections. The script must be run in an elevated Windows PowerShell session.

LISTING 5-5

Set-RDPConnection Function

```
function Set-RDPConnection
{
param(
[string]$Computer = (Get-Childitem -path env:computername).Value,
[string]$Authentication = "High",
[switch]$Disable
)
  $Kind = [Microsoft.Win32.RegistryValueKind]
  $Key = [Microsoft.Win32.RegistryKey]
  $Hive = "LocalMachine"
  $RootKey = "System\CurrentControlSet\Control\Terminal Server"
  $AuthKey = "$RootKey\WinStations\RDP-Tcp"
  $Value = "fDenyTSConnections"
  $AuthValue = "UserAuthentication"
  switch ($Authentication){
    "High" {$AuthCode = 1;break}
    "Low" {$AuthCode = 0;break}
  }
  $EnableCode = 0
  if($Disable){
    $EnableCode = 1
  }
```

continues

LISTING 5-5 *(continued)*

```
$regKey = $Key::OpenRemoteBaseKey($Hive,$Computer)
$Cnx = $regKey.OpenSubKey($RootKey,$true)
$Cnx.SetValue($Value, $EnableCode,$Kind::DWord)
$Auth = $regKey.OpenSubKey($AuthKey,$true)
$Auth.SetValue($AuthValue, $AuthCode,$Kind::DWord)
}
```

The first example in the following code disables Remote Desktop connections on the computer Exch2010, and the second example enables Remote Desktop connections to the computer EntDc1, allowing only secure connections:

```
.\Set-RDPConnection -Computer Exch2010 -Disable
.\Set-RDPConnection -Computer EntDc1 -Authentication High
```

Checking the Status of Remote Desktop

You can check whether Remote Desktop is enabled by checking the same registry keys that are used to enable Remote Desktop. The script in Listing 5-6 displays the status of Remote Desktop for the local computer or a remote computer. Save the script as Get-RDPConfiguration.ps1. If you call the script with no parameters, the script shows the configuration for the local machine. If you call the script with the optional Computer parameter, the script retrieves data for that computer.

The script uses the try / catch method of error handling introduced in the "Trapping Run-Time Errors" section of Chapter 1. The try and catch blocks allow you to run the section of code in the try block and handle any errors in the catch block. This is a good method of preventing errors from displaying onscreen.

LISTING 5-6

Get-RDPConnection Function

```
function Get-RDPConnection
{
param(
$Computer = (Get-Childitem -path env:computername).Value
)
  $Key = [Microsoft.Win32.RegistryKey]
  $Hive = "LocalMachine"
  $ConnectionKey = "System\CurrentControlSet\Control\Terminal Server"
  $Value = "fDenyTSConnections"
  $RegHive = [Microsoft.Win32.RegistryHive]$hive
```

```
try
{
  $RegKey = $Key::OpenRemoteBaseKey($RegHive,$Computer)
  $Connection = ($RegKey.OpenSubKey($ConnectionKey)).GetValue($Value)
  if ($Connection -eq 1){
    Write-Output "$Computer does not allow connections"
  }
  else{
    $AuthKey = "$ConnectionKey\WinStations\RDP-Tcp"
    $AuthValue = "UserAuthentication"
    $Authentication = ($RegKey.OpenSubKey($AuthKey)).GetValue($AuthValue)
    if ($Authentication -eq 1){
      Write-Output "Only Secure Connections are allowed to $Computer."
    }
    else{
      Write-Output "All Connections are allowed to $Computer."
    }
  }
}
catch{
  Write-Output "Could not connect to $Computer."
}
}
```

Summary

In this chapter, you learned how to configure permissions in NTFS filesystems, on file shares, and on the registry locally and on remote computers. You also examined DCOM permissions on the local and remote computers. You learned how to manage the Windows Firewall, and how to configure Remote Desktop.

In the next chapter, you learn how to manage software, from listing the software that's already installed, to installing and uninstalling software.

Managing and Installing Software

Microsoft has not added any cmdlets to Windows PowerShell specifically intended for software management. However, the language does provide several interfaces to the operating system that allow for software management. This chapter covers three aspects of software management:

- Taking inventory of installed software
- Installing new software on a system
- Removing software from a system

There is usually more than one method to accomplish each task, so this chapter demonstrates the different methods. As each topic is covered, I point out the strengths and weaknesses of each method.

IN THIS CHAPTER

Understanding WMI

Using WMI to list software

Using the Windows Registry to list software

Getting software onto your computer

Removing software from your computer

Listing Software

The first software management task in your environment is to determine what software you have installed. This chapter covers two alternative methods for retrieving software installed on your systems: Windows Management Instrumentation and the Windows Registry.

Windows Management Instrumentation (WMI) is Microsoft's implementation of the Web-Based Enterprise Management (WBEM) and Common Information Model (CIM) standards for systems management as defined by the Distributed Management Task Force (DMTF, www.dmtf.org/standards/cim). The WMI environment is an object-oriented environment in which entities are represented as classes with properties and methods exposed, depending on the object being represented. WMI also includes support for SQL-like statements called the WMI Query Language (WQL) for interacting with the huge amount of data available.

Using WMI

The WMI class that represents the software components of a system is the `Win32_Product` class. However, Microsoft configured `Win32_Product` to manage only software that utilizes the Windows Installer Technology. If you need to list installed software that was not installed with a Windows Installer package (`.msi`), you will need to use the Windows Registry.

Note

The Windows Installer Provider is an optional component on Windows Server 2003 and is not installed by default. It can be installed using the Control Panel. Installing it on your servers will make sure it is available when you need it. On Windows Server 2008, it is available by default. ■

Begin with obtaining the list of software installed on the local system. For this task, you use the `Get-WmiObject` cmdlet. This cmdlet enables you to retrieve instances of a WMI class. The simplest method for retrieving information from `Get-WmiObject` is to specify the WMI Class. This will retrieve and present the default fields for the objects in the class specified. The default WMI namespace for `Get-WmiObject` is the `root\cimv2` namespace.

```
Get-WmiObject -Class Win32_Product
```

An alternative method for retrieving the same information is by using the WMI Query Language:

```
Get-WmiObject -Query "SELECT * FROM Win32_Product"
```

Both of these options give us the results shown in Figure 6-1, which is the default view for the class that includes *IdentifyingNumber*, *Name*, *Vendor*, *Version*, and *Caption*.

FIGURE 6-1

Default Get-WmiObject output

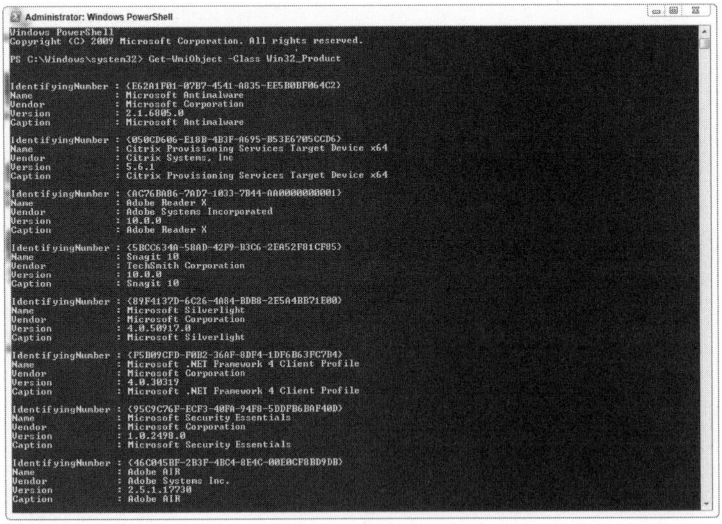

Typically, you are going to want more information than what is shown in the default view. To get that additional detail, select the properties that you are interested in. In this case, you select the name of the software (Name), the manufacturer of the product (Vendor), the version of the software (Version), and the date the product was installed (InstallDate):

```
Get-WmiObject -Class Win32_Product |
Select-Object Name, Vendor, Version, InstallDate
```

If you want to retrieve all of the properties, you can replace the property names with an asterisk (*).

Listing the software on remote systems couldn't be any easier than with WMI. The Get-WmiObject cmdlet has built-in support for remote operations that doesn't rely on Windows Remoting (WinRM), so you don't have to already have Windows Remoting enabled. Just add the ComputerName parameter to the previous statements to direct the command to operate on a remote system:

```
Get-WmiObject -Class Win32_Product -ComputerName Capella
```

Caution

WMI operates on top of the Distributed Component Object Model (DCOM). DCOM is Microsoft's proprietary technology for communications between networked computers. It utilizes Remote Procedure Call (RPC) to dynamically select a random port above 1024. This results in a tremendously large firewall exception required. DCOM also stores the destination IP address inside of the network packets, so address translation will break the communication because the final address doesn't match what the client thought was the destination IP Address. ∎

Caution

When you query the Win32_Product class, Windows actually performs a Windows Installer reconfiguration on every .msi package installed on the system. You can verify this by looking at the Application Event Log after you run a query. The issue with this is that it will perform a validation on the .msi package and repair if it finds any inconsistencies between the package and original .msi file. For example, if you disable a service or delete an icon, it will enable the service and/or restore the icon. It also makes this method slower than the alternative method of using the Windows Registry because you are forced to wait until this process completes. ∎

Using the Windows Registry

The second method to list the software installed is the Windows Registry. This method is not as simple as the WMI method, particularly for remote machines, but it performs much quicker than using WMI and without the noted side effect of reconfiguring the .msi package. It also lists all software installed, even non–Windows Installer installed packages.

When software is installed on a system, basic information about the software is recorded in a central location in the Windows Registry. This location, HKEY_LOCAL_MACHINE\SOFTWARE\Microsoft\Windows\CurrentVersion\Uninstall, is where the Control Panel retrieves its list of installed software.

Note

If you are working on a 64-bit Windows platform, to get complete information about software installed on your machine, you will also need to include `HKEY_LOCAL_MACHINE\SOFTWARE\Wow6432Node\Microsoft\Windows\CurrentVersion\Uninstall`. This is where Windows registers 32-bit software that is installed on 64-bit platforms. ■

Each piece of software installed has its own key underneath the root `Uninstall` key. Each of these keys has values that describe the software such as name, vendor, version, and uninstall command. For this step, you are going to enumerate the child keys of the root `Uninstall` key and retrieve the same corresponding properties as the last example you completed. In the Windows Registry are keys that exist without a `DisplayName`. You are not interested in those because they do not represent installed software, so exclude them from your results. Listing 6-1 provides the code to retrieve the software list.

LISTING 6-1

Retrieving Installed Software

```
Get-ChildItem HKLM:\SOFTWARE\Microsoft\Windows\CurrentVersion\Uninstall |
Get-ItemProperty | Where-Object {$_.DisplayName} |
Select-Object DisplayName, Publisher, DisplayVersion, InstallDate
```

If you have a large number of software packages installed on your system, you will no doubt have noticed a significant increase in performance with this method over the WMI method.

If you need to retrieve the same information from a remote system, you generally have two different methods for reading a remote Windows Registry. The first method, and probably the easiest, works if you have Windows Remote Management enabled and configured. To use Remoting, you simply pass the same code in Listing 6-1 to `Invoke-Command` with the `ComputerName` parameter, as shown in Listing 6-2. The code is executed on the remote system and the results are returned to the local system.

Cross-Reference

For more information on Windows Remote Management, refer to the "Remoting" section in Chapter 2, "What's New in Windows Powershell V2." ■

LISTING 6-2

Retrieving Installed Software with Remoting

```
Invoke-Command -ComputerName Capella -ScriptBlock {
   Get-ChildItem HKLM:\SOFTWARE\Microsoft\Windows\CurrentVersion\Uninstall |
   Get-ItemProperty | Where-Object {$_.DisplayName} |
   Select-Object DisplayName, Publisher, DisplayVersion, InstallDate }
```

The other method for reading the remote Windows Registry is to use the .NET class, `Microsoft.Win32.RegistryKey`. Listing 6-3 shows how to use the `OpenRemoteBaseKey()` method to create a connection to the `HKEY_LOCAL_MACHINE` tree on the remote machine. You then navigate to the Uninstall key and retrieve the child keys in a similar manner to your native Windows PowerShell methods.

One item to note is that this method relies on the Remote Registry service of Windows. On Windows 7, this service is set to manual, so you may have to start it in order to retrieve the information.

LISTING 6-3

Retrieving Installed Software with .NET

```
$RegistryKey = "SOFTWARE\Microsoft\Windows\CurrentVersion\Uninstall"
$RootKey = [Microsoft.Win32.RegistryKey]::OpenRemoteBaseKey(↩
        "LocalMachine","Capella")
$UninstalKey = $RootKey.OpenSubKey($RegistryKey)
$UninstalKey.GetSubKeyNames() |
ForEach-Object {
  $SoftwareKey = $UninstalKey.OpenSubKey($_)
  $Software = @{
    "DisplayName" = $SoftwareKey.GetValue("DisplayName")
    "Publisher" = $SoftwareKey.GetValue("Publisher")
    "DisplayVersion" = $SoftwareKey.GetValue("DisplayVersion")
    "InstallDate" = $SoftwareKey.GetValue("InstallDate")
  }
  $Software | Where-Object {$_.DisplayName}
}
```

Creating Software Baselines

Now you know how to list the software installed on your system. But what if you want to keep track of software that is added or removed from a system between two points in time? Or what if you want to compare your systems to make sure that they all have the same software installed? To accomplish this task, you create software baselines.

The first step you need to take is to create a baseline of all the software installed on the machine. The function in Listing 6-4 creates a software baseline for the local system. This function includes additional logic for detecting a 64-bit operating system and adds the additional Windows Registry key to list the 32-bit software that is installed. The magic of the function is in the `Export-CliXml` cmdlet. This powerful cmdlet takes any object or collection of objects and generates an XML-based representation that is then saved to a file. In this case, you create the name based on the machine on which it is run and the date at which it is run.

LISTING 6-4

Creating a Software Baseline

```
function New-SoftwareBaseline
{

  $RegLoc = @()
  $SnapshotTime = Get-Date -uformat "%Y-%m%-%d_%H-%M"
  $RegLoc += "HKLM:\SOFTWARE\Microsoft\Windows\CurrentVersion\Uninstall"
  if ( $env:PROCESSOR_ARCHITECTURE -eq 'AMD64' )
  {
    $RegLoc +=
      "HKLM:\SOFTWARE\Wow6432Node\Microsoft\Windows\CurrentVersion\Uninstall"
  }

  $Software = @()
  $Software += $RegLoc | Get-ChildItem | Get-ItemProperty |
    Where-Object { $_.DisplayName} |
    Select-Object DisplayName, Publisher, DisplayVersion, InstallDate

  $Software | Sort-Object DisplayName |
    Export-CliXml "$($Env:ComputerName)_$SnapshotTime.xml"

}
```

You now have your software baseline. The next step is to use the same script to obtain another baseline on another computer and/or the same computer at another point in time. Once you do that, you have two files that represent the software installed on two different systems and/or two different periods of time. To compare the baselines in an intelligible manner, you need to "rehydrate" the objects. For this, you use the Import-CliXml cmdlet, which is the inverse of the Export-CliXml cmdlet. It takes the XML-based representation and converts the XML-based representation into a Windows PowerShell object.

```
$Baseline = Import-CliXml .\CAPELLA_2010-11-22_17-13.xml
$SnapShot = Import-CliXml .\CAPELLA_2010-11-22_19-43.xml
```

Now that they are objects again, you use the Compare-Object cmdlet to compare the baselines. You want to use DisplayName as the property to compare.

```
Compare-Object $BaseLine $SnapShot -Property DisplayName
```

DisplayName	SideIndicator
Mozilla Firefox (3.6.12)	=>
7-Zip 9.20 (x64 edition)	<=

In this example, you can see that Mozilla Firefox appears in the second baseline and not the first, indicating that it was installed after the first baseline was taken. You can also see that 7-Zip was removed after the first baseline was taken.

Installing Software

This section covers the task of installing software. It introduces Restore Points and shows how they can be used when installing software.

Using Restore Points

Starting with Windows Me and continuing to the latest Microsoft operating system, Microsoft has included the System Restore component. Starting with Microsoft Vista, System Restore utilizes Microsoft's Shadow Copy technology where block-level changes are monitored and backed up prior to triggered events, and can be rolled back in the event of system malfunction or failure.

By default in Windows 7, System Restore snapshots are taken at system startup and at midnight every day as triggered by a Task Scheduler job. Also, Windows will take checkpoints when software is installed using Windows Installer, Windows Update installs a new update, or a user installs a driver that is not digitally signed by Windows Hardware Quality Labs. However, sometimes you might want to create your own System Restore checkpoint.

Windows PowerShell V2 offers several cmdlets for managing System Restore in Windows. The first one allows you to enable System Restore if it is not already enabled. You just need to specify which drive to enable, starting with your system drive, of course:

Caution

All of these cmdlets require administrator credentials to function. ∎

```
Enable-ComputerRestore -Drive "C:\"
```

Now that you have System Restore enabled, you are ready to create your own checkpoint:

```
Checkpoint-Computer -Description "Custom Application Install"
```

Once you execute this, you will see a progress bar detailing the progress of the cmdlet. When it is finished, you will have a checkpoint with the description specified.

Now you can list all of the system checkpoints by using the Get-ComputerRestorePoint cmdlet.

If you need to fall back to a Restore Point, you need the sequence number of the Restore Point, which you can pull using `Get-ComputerRestorePoint` and matching the description of the Restore Point:

```
Restore-Computer -RestorePoint ( Get-ComputerRestorePoint |
    Where-Object { $_.Description -eq "Custom Application Installation" } |
    Select-Object -ExpandProperty SequenceNumber )
```

After you execute this command, your system will immediately reboot to complete the restore.

Using WMI

When you need to install software, you have several options, including WMI, of course. If the software you want to install is a Windows Installer package, you can use the `Win32_Product` WMI class introduced earlier in this chapter. To install software, you use the `Install` method of the `wmiclass` class:

```
([wmiclass]"\\Capella\root\cimv2:Win32_Product").Install(↵
"C:\ProductInstall.msi", " ALLUSERS=YES",$True)
```

Note

[wmiclass] is a Windows Powershell type accelerator, essentially a shortcut that allows more direct access to the WMI class: `System.Management.ManagementClass`. ∎

A couple of limitations exist when using the `Install` method. First, you are limited to Windows Installer packages. Second, you are not able to specify any Windows Installer options. You can, however, specify transform properties like `ALLUSERS=YES`.

Not being able to specify Windows Installer options probably hinders you the most when you want to change the way you log the software installation so that you can see why your install fails or to gather more information during the installation. To work around the limitation of not being able to specify the command-line options, you utilize another WMI class, `Win32_Process`. The `Win32_Process` class includes a method, `Create`, for executing programs:

```
Invoke-WmiMethod Win32_Process -Name Create `
    -ComputerName Capella `   -ArgumentList "msiexec /i C:\7z920-x64.msi /qn"
```

This example calls the `msiexec.exe` executable directly on the remote machine, passing the install package as well as the `.msi` logging options. This example also demonstrates another way to call WMI methods. The `Invoke-WmiMethod` cmdlet is a built-in cmdlet for executing WMI methods. You could, in fact, use this method in the earlier example.

The final option for installing software remotely is Windows PowerShell Remoting. As you remember from the Remoting example earlier in the chapter, you need to pass a script block to `Invoke-Command`. If you have a complicated or changing command, you can always place the script block in a file and utilize the `filepath` parameter.

```
Invoke-Command -ComputerName Capella -ScriptBlock {
    msiexec /i C:\7z920-x64.msi /l*v C:\7zip.log }
```

As you can see from this example, you are installing the 7-zip software and logging the installation to a log file. The file path in the command is the path of the remote system, so you have to copy the file to the remote system before installing because you are unable to access remote files due to the restriction of Windows Remoting.

Removing Software

This section demonstrates the methods for removing software from a system. WMI is demonstrated first, followed by the Windows Registry method. Finally, a trick for working with spaces in software install paths is introduced.

Removing Software Using WMI

If the software you want removed is a Windows Installer package and is able to communicate with WMI, the `Win32_Product` class is what you want:

```
$Application = Get-WmiObject-Class Win32_Product -ComputerName "Capella" |
    Where-Object { $_.Name -match "My Application" }
$Application.Uninstall()
```

In this example, you retrieve the list of software from the remote computer and filter out the application that matches your application name. You then call the `Uninstall` method from the WMI class to uninstall the software.

Removing Software Using Windows Registry

The next series of actions is for removing software using the Windows Registry. To remove software, you need to know the command for the software that you want to uninstall. The easiest way to obtain the uninstall command is to pull it from the Windows Registry.

In the "Listing Software" section, you saw the method for using the Windows Registry to list the software installed on your system. To uninstall it, you modify that code just a little to get your desired outcome:

```
$Application = "My Application"
$UnInstall = Get-ChildItem ↵
  HKLM:\SOFTWARE\Microsoft\Windows\CurrentVersion\Uninstall |
Get-ItemProperty | Where-Object {$_.DisplayName -eq $Application } |
  Select-Object -ExpandProperty UninstallString
& $UnInstall
```

In this example, you supply the `DisplayName` matching the application you want to remove. You could have used one of the other fields present as well to filter the results. To get the command needed to uninstall the software, you want the `UninstallString` Windows Registry value. This is the command that the application registered with the system as its uninstall command. The final step of the example executes that string, thereby removing the software.

Dealing with Spaces

Depending on the location of the software you want to uninstall, you might have run into a problem. For example, the typical uninstall command for Microsoft Security Essentials is `C:\Program Files\Microsoft Security Essentials\setup.exe /x`. If you try the preceding code with this example, Windows PowerShell will spit out the error shown in Figure 6-2.

FIGURE 6-2

Windows PowerShell execution error

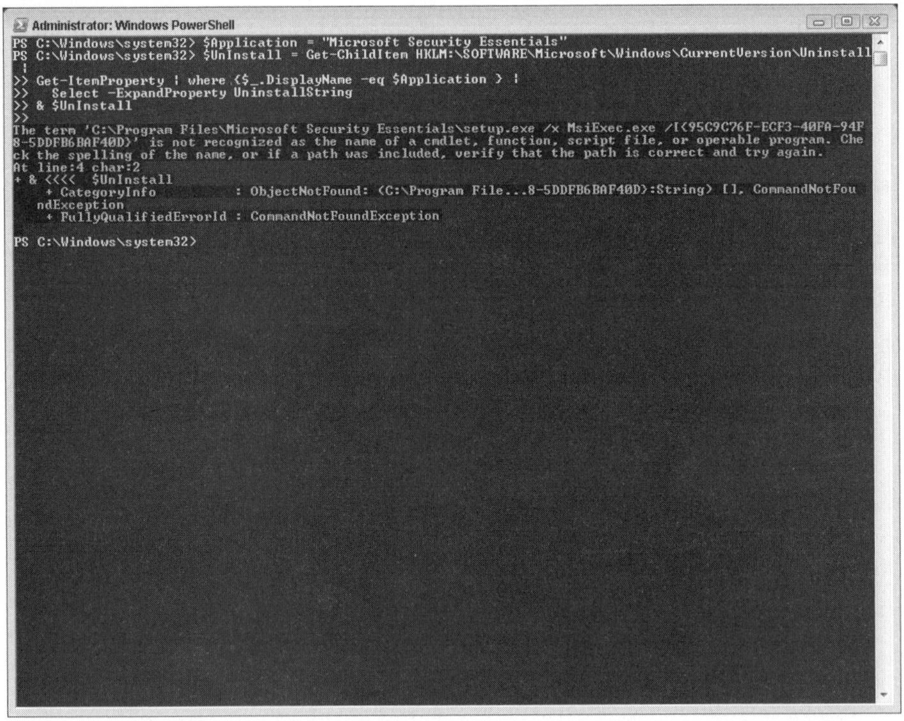

The problem lies in the fact that the path includes spaces, but the path is not enclosed in parentheses. Windows PowerShell reads the string up to the first space and assumes that segment is the path to the executable. To remedy this situation, you use a function called `Get-CommandLine`, as shown in Listing 6-5. It takes a command-line string that includes paths and arguments and splits the string up into the corresponding components while validating that the path to the executable exists. With this information, you are able to place the strings around the executable, as shown in the last line, and execute the uninstall program.

LISTING 6-5

Handling Spaces in the Uninstall Path

```
function Get-CommandLine
{
  param
  (
  [Parameter(Position=0,ValueFromPipeline=$True,Mandatory=$True)]
  [string]$Command
  )
  $Arguments = $TempPath = $CommandPath = ""
  $Command -split " " |
  %{
    $TempPath += " $_"
    $TempPath = $TempPath.Trim()
    if ( Test-Path $TempPath -PathType Leaf ) { $CommandPath = $TempPath }
  }
  if ($CommandPath)
  {
    $Arguments = ($Command.Substring( $CommandPath.Length,
      $Command.Length - $CommandPath.Length )).Trim()
    return New-Object -Type PSObject -Property @{
      Executable = $CommandPath
      Arguments = $Arguments
    }
  }
  else { Write-Error "Commandline Executable not Found!!!" }
}
```

With this function created, you can now use it to obtain the uninstall command and arguments as shown.

```
$Application = "Microsoft Security Essentials"
$Uninstall = Get-CommandLine    (
  Get-ChildItem HKLM:\SOFTWARE\Microsoft\Windows\CurrentVersion\Uninstall |
    Get-ItemProperty | where {$_.DisplayName -eq $Application } |
    Select -ExpandProperty UninstallString
  )
& "$($Uninstall.Executable)" $Uninstall.Arguments
```

With this function in your toolbox, you can easily handle removing software from your machine. In fact, this function would be a valuable addition to your profile. It can be used whenever you interact with file paths.

Cross-Reference

For a refresher on profiles, read the "Customizing Windows PowerShell with Profiles" section in Chapter 1, "Introduction to Windows PowerShell." ■

Summary

In this chapter, you explored the management of software using Windows PowerShell. You compared the process of adding, listing, and removing software using WMI and the Windows Registry.

In Part III, you will learn how to use Windows PowerShell to manage your server infrastructure, beginning with a look at Windows Server 2008 R2.

Part III

Server Management

IN THIS PART

Chapter 7
Managing Windows
Server 2008 R2

Chapter 8
Performing Basic Server
Management

Chapter 9
Performing Advanced Server
Management

Chapter 10
Managing Active Directory

Chapter 11
Managing Group Policy

Managing Windows Server 2008 R2

I n this chapter, you read about managing Windows Server 2008 R2 with Windows PowerShell. All versions of Windows Server 2008 R2 include Windows PowerShell Version 2.

What's New in Server 2008 R2

Server 2008 Release 2 (commonly known as R2) is much more than a cosmetic upgrade to Server 2008. This chapter focuses on the Windows PowerShell modules and snap-ins designed to manage Windows servers.

Cross-Reference

For an overview of the new features in Windows PowerShell Version 2, see Chapter 2, "What's New in Windows PowerShell V2." ∎

Default Installation of Windows PowerShell

Windows Server 2008 R2 includes Windows PowerShell Version 2, which is installed by default. Windows PowerShell V2 became available for other operating systems soon after Server 2008 R2 and Windows 7 shipped. Although Windows PowerShell is installed by default, if you want to use the Integrated Scripting Environment (ISE), you will need to enable it via Server Manager. The "Managing Server Features and Roles" section provides more information on this.

Windows Server 2008 R2 includes eight modules that automate common system administration tasks. These modules, listed in Table 7-1, provide hundreds of cmdlets for managing Windows Server 2008 R2.

IN THIS CHAPTER
Examining new features in Server 2008 R2
Managing Features and Roles
Running best practice scans
Remoting
Using Windows Backup
Managing server migration
Using AppLocker

TABLE 7-1

Modules Included in Server 2008 R2

Module Name	Cmdlet Count
ActiveDirectory	76
ADRMS	15
AppLocker	5
BestPractices	4
BitsTransfer	8
FailoverClusters	69
GroupPolicy	25
ServerManager	3

Additionally, Server 2008 R2 includes two snap-ins designed to manage Windows backup and Server Migration: `Windows.ServerBackup` and `Microsoft.Windows.ServerManager.Migration`. Some of these modules and snap-ins require that the corresponding role or feature be installed before you can use them. For instance, the ActiveDirectory module will not be available unless the server is a domain controller, or is running the Remote Server Administration Tools (RSAT) feature or either the Active Directory Domain Services (AD DS) or Active Directory Lightweight Directory Services (AD LDS) server roles.

Windows PowerShell Included in Server Core

Server 2008 R2 Core includes the .NET Framework and Windows PowerShell V2. This is a significant improvement over Server 2008 Core, which could not run Windows PowerShell because the .NET Framework was not available. Server Core is Microsoft's minimal server installation, which provides a limited set of roles. Windows Server Core does not have Windows PowerShell enabled as other versions of Windows Server 2008 R2 do. Additionally, the prerequisite .NET Framework is not enabled by default. You can enable .NET and Windows PowerShell with the Deployment Image Servicing and Management tool (DISM), which is itself new in Server 2008 R2 Core. The following example enables Windows PowerShell and adds the `ServerManager` and `BestPractices` modules that you use later in this chapter:

```
DISM /Online /Enable-Feature /FeatureName:NetFx2-ServerCore
DISM /Online /Enable-Feature /FeatureName:MicrosoftWindowsPowerShell
DISM /Online /Enable-Feature /FeatureName:ServerManager-PSH-Cmdlets
DISM /Online /Enable-Feature /FeatureName:BestPractices-PSH-Cmdlets
```

Managing Server Features and Roles

Features, roles, and role services are software packages that provide functionality in Server 2008 R2. *Roles* allow the server to perform a specific function, such as the File Server role. *Role services* allow installed roles to provide specific services. Roles are functional as soon as they are installed. *Features* can support or enhance roles, or act on their own. Unlike roles, features are not functional as soon as they are installed. Server features, roles, and role services can be managed with the ServerManager module. This module is not loaded by default, so you need to import the module into the current Windows PowerShell session. You do this with the Import-Module cmdlet, passing the required parameter Name. The following example loads the ServerManager module:

```
Import-Module -Name ServerManager
```

Note

Although you can import the **ServerManager** module and list the Windows features that are installed or available to be installed with the **Get-WindowsFeature** cmdlet in a normal Windows PowerShell console, installing or removing features with the **Add-WindowsFeature** or **Remove-WindowsFeature** cmdlets requires that you run an elevated Windows PowerShell console. ■

The ServerManager module provides three cmdlets: Get-WindowsFeature, Add-WindowsFeature, and Remove-WindowsFeature.

Note

Although the cmdlets' noun is **WindowsFeature**, all three of the cmdlets target features, roles, and role services. I will not differentiate between features, roles, and role services in my examples. The cmdlets function the same in all cases. ■

All three of these cmdlets provide a progress bar when they are running. Once the module is loaded, you can list the currently installed features, roles, and role services with the GetWindowsFeature cmdlet, filtering the output through the Where-Object cmdlet. The following example returns output with the currently installed features:

```
Get-WindowsFeature | Where-Object {$_.Installed -eq $True}
```

When you install a feature you need to know the name of the feature. The name is not the same name that is shown in the Server Manager console. To list all the available features and their installation status, you can pass the output of the Get-WindowsFeature cmdlet to the Select-Object cmdlet, choosing to output the name and installed fields. The following example returns all features sorted by name, and displays only the name and installation status:

```
$Sort = @{
Property = "Installed"
}
$Select = @{
```

```
Property = "Name","Installed"
}
Get-WindowsFeature | Sort-Object @Sort | Select-Object @Select
```

Adding Windows features is accomplished with the aptly named `Add-WindowsFeature` cmdlet, passing the required parameter `Name`. The following example installs the Windows PowerShell Integrated Scripting Environment:

```
Add-WindowsFeature -Name PowerShell-ISE
```

An additional parameter that the `Add-WindowsFeature` cmdlet accepts is the `IncludeAllSubFeature` switch parameter. Specifying this parameter installs the feature and any subfeatures. Windows PowerShell and the `ServerManager` module enable you to determine if a feature has subfeatures.

One of the properties returned by the `Get-WindowsFeature` cmdlet is the `SubFeatures` property. This property shows any subfeatures that would be installed via the `IncludeAllSubFeature` switch parameter. The following example shows that the Windows feature `RSAT-ADDS` contains the optional subfeatures `RSAT-ADDS-Tools`, `RSAT-ADDS-AdminCenter`, and `RSAT-ADDS-SNIS`:

```
Get-WindowsFeature -Name RSAT-ADDS | Select-Object -ExpandProperty SubFeatures
PS> Import-Module -Name ServerManager
PS> Get-WindowsFeature -Name RSAT-ADDS | Select-Object -Expand SubFeatures
RSAT-ADDS-Tools
RSAT-AD-AdminCenter
RSAT-SNIS
```

Running the `Add-WindowsFeature` cmdlet, specifying the name of the feature, and including the optional switch parameter `WhatIf` shows which additional features, if any, the feature depends on. Features that are already installed will not be shown. The following example returns the information that the `Backup-Tools` feature depends on the Windows Server `Backup` feature.

```
Add-WindowsFeature -Name Backup-Tools -WhatIf
PS> Add-WindowsFeature -Name Backup-Tools -WhatIf
What if: Checking if running in 'WhatIf' Mode.
What if: Performing operation "Add-WindowsFeature" on Target "[Windows
Server Backup Features] Command-line Tools".
What if: Performing operation "Add-WindowsFeature" on Target "[Windows
Server Backup Features] Windows Server Backup".
What if: This server may need to be restarted after the installation
completes.

Success Restart Needed Exit Code Feature Result
True    Maybe          Success   {}
```

When you install a subfeature that depends on a feature that is not already installed, the parent feature is also installed. Another optional switch parameter is the `Restart` parameter.

When this parameter is specified, the `Add-WindowsFeature` cmdlet reboots the server if necessary. The following example installs the `Backup-Tools` subfeature of the `Backup` feature, while also installing the `Backup` feature. Finally, the server is rebooted if needed.

```
Add-WindowsFeature -Name Backup-Tools -Restart
```

Removing features is accomplished with the `Remove-WindowsFeature` cmdlet. The cmdlet accepts the same parameters as the `Add-WindowsFeature` cmdlet, except the `IncludeAllSubFeature` parameter. If you remove a feature that has dependent subfeatures, the subfeatures are removed as well. The following example removes the `Migration` feature:

```
Remove-WindowsFeature -Name Migration
```

Running Best Practice Analyzer Scans

Running Best Practice Analyzer scans requires that the `BestPractices` module be imported into the current session. The `BestPractices` module provides four cmdlets: `Get-BpaModel`, `Get-BpaResult`, `Invoke-BpaModel`, and `Set-BpaResult`. The Best Practice Analyzer scans one or more server roles to ensure that the specific role is configured to Microsoft suggested settings. For instance, the server ports may be scanned to ensure that only needed ports allow traffic.

The `Get-BpaModel` cmdlet shows which roles you can run a Best Practice Analyzer scan against. The returned data shows the ID of the role and the last scan time. If the role has not been scanned, the last scan time shows Never.

The `Get-BpaResult` cmdlet returns the results of a previously run scan. If the role has not been scanned, the cmdlet returns an error.

The `Invoke-BpaModel` cmdlet actually runs the Best Practice Analyzer scan.

The `Set-BpaResult` cmdlet includes or excludes results of an existing Best Practice Analyzer scan to display only the information you are interested in.

Running Scans Locally

After importing the `BestPractices` module, you can get a list of the available roles for the Best Practice Analyzer with the `Get-BpaModel` cmdlet. When run without parameters, this cmdlet returns all roles for which a scan can be performed as well as the last scan time, if any. If you know the ID of the role you are interested in, you can pass that information to the cmdlet using the `BestPracticesModelId` parameter. The first example in the following code returns all roles, and the second example returns only the `Microsoft/Windows/WebServer` role:

```
Get-BpaModel
Get-BpaModel -BestPracticesModelId Microsoft/Windows/WebServer
```

```
PS> Get-BpaModel
Id                                          LastScanTime
Microsoft/Windows/DirectoryServices         Never
Microsoft/Windows/DNSServer                 5/23/2011 9:27:28 PM
Microsoft/Windows/WebServer                 Never
PS>
PS> Get-BpaModel -BestPracticesModelId Microsoft/Windows/WebServer
Id                                          LastScanTime
Microsoft/Windows/WebServer                 Never
```

Once you have the name of the role that you want to scan, you can start a new scan with the `Invoke-BpaModel` cmdlet, passing the ID of the role to the `BestPracticesModelId` parameter. The following example runs the Best Practice Analyzer for the Certificate Services role:

```
Invoke-BpaModel -BestPracticesModelId Microsoft/Windows/CertificateServices
```

You could also run scans for all available roles by passing the output of the `Get-BpaModel` cmdlet to the `Invoke-BpaModel` cmdlet:

```
Get-BpaModel | Invoke-BpaModel
```

After running a Best Practice Analyzer scan, you retrieve the results with the `Get-BpaResult` cmdlet. You either pass the ID of the role to the `BestPracticesModelId` parameter or pass the output of the `Get-BpaModel` cmdlet to the `Get-BpaResult` cmdlet to see the result of all Best Practice Analyzer scans. A single Best Practice Analyzer scan may have many results, corresponding to different sections of the role. The first example in the following code returns the results of the web server Best Practice Analyzer scan, and the second example shows the results for all Best Practice Analyzer scans:

```
Get-BpaResult -BestPracticesModelId Microsoft/Windows/WebServer
```

```
PS> Get-BpaResult -BestPracticesModelId Microsoft/Windows/WebServer

ResultNumber : 1
ModelId      : Microsoft/Windows/WebServer
RuleId       : 1
ResultId     : 1122680488
Severity     : Information
Category     : Security
Title        : Grant a handler execute/script or write permissions, but not both
Problem      :
Impact       :
```

```
Resolution   :
Compliance   : The IIS Best Practices Analyzer scan has determined that you are
in compliance with this best practice.
Help         :
Excluded     : False
...
Get-BpaModel | Get-BpaResult
```

The `Set-BpaResult` cmdlet excludes or includes scan results being displayed in the Best
Practices Analyzer GUI. Excluded results are displayed in the Excluded tab of the Best
Practices Analyzer GUI, while included results are displayed in either the Compliant or
Noncompliant tabs. All results, including excluded results, are displayed in the All tab and
when running the `Get-BpaResult` cmdlet.

The following example excludes the results of a previously run Best Practices Analyzer
scan for the `BestPracticesModelId Microsoft/Windows/WebServer` where the severity
of the result is listed as `Information`.

```
$BpaResult = @{
BestPracticesModelId = "Microsoft/Windows/WebServer"
}
$Exclude = @{
FilterScript = {$_.Severity -eq "Information"}
}
$Result = Get-BpaResult @BpaResult | Where-Object @Exclude
Set-BPAResult @BpaResult -Exclude $True -Results $Result
```

You can display only included results of a Best Practices Analyzer scan by passing the
output of the `Get-BpaResult` cmdlet through the `Where-Object` cmdlet. The following
example displays only the included results from a previously run `Microsoft/Windows/`
`WebServer` scan:

```
Get-BPAResult @BpaResult | Where-object {$_.Excluded -ne $True}
PS> Get-BPAResult @BpaResult | Where-object {$_.Excluded -ne $True}
ResultNumber : 6
ModelId      : Microsoft/Windows/WebServer
RuleId       : 7
ResultId     : 2152644382
Severity     : Error
Category     : Security
Title        : Use SSL when you use Basic authentication
Problem      : Basic authentication is enabled for configuration path
                 'MACHINE/WEBROOT/APPHOST' but it lacks a required
                 SSL binding.
Impact       : If you use Basic authentication without SSL, credentials
                 will be sent in clear text that might be intercepted
                 by malicious code.
```

```
Resolution    : Use Basic authentication with an SSL binding, and make
                sure that the site or application is set to require SSL.
                Alternatively, use a different method of authentication.
Compliance    :
Help          : http://go.microsoft.com/fwlink/?LinkId=130717
Excluded      : False
```

Running Scans Remotely

You can run Best Practice Analyzer scans on remote Server 2008 R2 machines that have Windows PowerShell remoting enabled. The script in Listing 7-1 runs Best Practice Analyzer scans against every model available on each server in the file `c:\scripts\servers.txt`. The results are stored in comma-separated value (`.csv`) files in the path `\\Workstation\c$\BpaScanResults` and are named with the run date and time, and the scan name.

LISTING 7-1

Example Best Practice Analyzer Scan Script

```
$OutputPath = "\\Workstation\c$\BpaScanResults"
foreach ($Server in Get-Content c:\scripts\servers.txt)
{
Write-Host "Working on $Server"
try
{
$Command = @{
Computer = $Server
ArgumentList = $Server,$OutputPath
ScriptBlock = {
param (
$server,
$OutputPath
)
Import-Module -Name ServerManager
Import-Module -Name BestPractices
foreach ($Model in Get-BpaModel)
{
$RunDate = Get-Date -Format "MM-dd-yyyy-hhmm"
#I set the date to show as the 2-digit month, 2-digit day, 4-digit year
#and 2-digit hour and minute with a dash for separators.
#You can format the date as you like.
$ScanName = $Model.Id.Replace("Microsoft/Windows/","")
$FilePath = "$OutputPath\$Server-$ScanName$RunDate.csv"
Write-Host -Object "Running $ScanName scan on $Server"
Invoke-BpaModel -BestPracticesModelId $Model.Id | Out-Null
$BPAResults = Get-BpaResult -BestPracticesModelId $Model.Id
$BPAResults | Export-Csv -Path $FilePath -NoTypeInformation
}
```

```
}
}
Invoke-Command @Command
}
catch [PSRemotingTransportException]
{
#Catch the PSRemotingTransportException error to determine which servers
#experience trouble with remote PowerShell
$ErrorObject = @{
Object = "The following error occurred while attempting to connect to $Server:"
ForegroundColor = "red"
BackgroundColor = "black"
}
Write-Host @ErrorObject
$ErrorMessage = @{
Object = "($error[0]).ErrorDetails.Message"
ForegroundColor = "red"
BackgroundColor = "black"
}
Write-Host @ErrorMessage}
catch
{
#Catch all errors other than PSRemotingTransportException errors caught above
$ErrorObject = @{
Object = "The following error occurred when connecting to $Server:"
ForegroundColor = "red"
BackgroundColor = "black"
}
Write-Host @ErrorObject
$ErrorMessage = @{
Object = "($error[0]).ErrorDetails.Message"
ForegroundColor = "red"
BackgroundColor = "black"
}
Write-Host @ErrorMessage
}
}
```

Enabling Remoting

To enable remoting, run the `Enable-PSRemoting` cmdlet on the local host. You need to run the cmdlet in an elevated Windows PowerShell console. This cmdlet allows remote connections to the local host. You do not need to run it if you are only going to be accessing other remote hosts. The cmdlet accepts the optional parameter `Force`, which will bypass prompts. The following example enables remoting:

```
Enable-PSRemoting -Force
```

You can disable remoting on the local host with the `Disable-PSRemoting` cmdlet. This cmdlet does not stop the WinRM service, however. As with the `Enable-PSRemoting` cmdlet, `Disable-PSRemoting` accepts the `Force` parameter.

To enable remoting on multiple machines at once, you can use a Group Policy object. See `http://powertoe.wordpress.com/2011/05/16/enable-winrm-with-group-policy-but-use-powershell-to-create-the-policy/` for an example of creating the policy with Windows PowerShell.

Managing Windows Backup

Windows Backup is a feature that can be installed using the `Add-WindowsFeature` cmdlet. The feature name is `Backup-Features`. This feature allows you to perform backup and recovery operations on the local server and on remote servers. To enable Windows Backup to be scripted, you will need to add the `Backup-Tools` subfeature of the Windows Backup feature. See the "Managing Server Features and Roles" section earlier in the chapter for a refresher if needed.

The account used to run the cmdlets needs to be in either the local Backup Operators or Administrators group, or have been delegated the right to perform backups on that server. Additionally, you need to run an elevated Windows PowerShell console.

Installing the Cmdlets

Once the required Windows Backup Tools feature is installed, you can load the cmdlets by adding the `Windows.ServerBackup` snap-in. The following example loads the cmdlets:

```
Add-PSSnapin -Name Windows.ServerBackup
```

Once the cmdlets are loaded, you can get a list of them using the `Get-Command` cmdlet with the parameters `Name` and `CommandType`. The following example returns all the cmdlets in the `Windows.ServerBackup` snap-in:

```
Get-Command -Name *wb* -CommandType Cmdlet
```

Configuring New Backup Jobs

Creating new backup jobs is a multistep process. This requires multiple cmdlets, with their associated parameters. To cover this process, first I describe the cmdlets and parameters. Once the cmdlets and parameters are described, I will show examples that pull it all together. A backup job is called a *policy*. The first step is to create a new policy with the `New-WBPolicy` cmdlet. You will need to assign the new policy to a variable. Once you have the new policy object, you add a *backup target* (the path where the backups will be saved) and files or volumes to be included in the backup set. As an option, you can also set files to be excluded. In either instance, you have the option of setting a schedule for the backup.

Note

Windows Server Backup allows only one policy to be created at a time. This means that if you have multiple drives for which you would like to schedule separate backups, you will need to manipulate the system. For ideas, see the "Limitations in the Cmdlets" section later in this chapter. ■

You can get a list of volumes on the local computer with the `Get-WBVolume` cmdlet. This cmdlet requires one of the following parameters: `AllVolumes`, `CriticalVolumes`, `Disk`, or `VolumePath`. The switch parameter `AllVolumes` is fairly self-explanatory. The switch parameter `CriticalVolumes` includes volumes that contain operating system files. The `Disk` parameter takes the output from the `Get-WBDisk` cmdlet. The `VolumePath` parameter allows you to directly specify a volume by drive letter.

The first example returns all volumes on the current server, while the second example returns only critical volumes on the local server:

```
Get-WBVolume  -AllVolumes
Get-WBVolume  -CriticalVolumes
```

The `Get-WBDisk` cmdlet returns the online disks that are attached to the local server. The following example returns local disks whose `Properties` do not match `ValidTarget`. Disks whose `Properties` match `ValidTarget` may be used as a backup target:

```
Get-WBDisk | Where-Object {$_.Properties -match 'ValidTarget'}
```

The following example shows how you can combine the `Get-WBDisk` and `Get-WBVolume` cmdlets to set the volume to be used for the backup target. Note that both cmdlets have their output saved to variables. You will need these variables later on when you create the backup policy.

```
$Disk = Get-WBDisk | Where-Object {$_.Properties -notmatch 'ValidTarget'}
$Volume = Get-WBVolume -Disk $Disk
```

The `New-WBFileSpec` cmdlet allows you to specify files to include or exclude. The required `FileSpec` parameter specifies which files to back up, and the optional `Exclude` parameter specifies files to exclude. A further optional switch parameter, `NonRecursive`, specifies that only files in the path specified in the `FileSpec` parameter will be backed up.

The following example specifies that all `.ps1` files in the path `C:\Scripts` should be backed up. As the `NonRecursive` parameter was not specified, all `.ps1` files in any subdirectories of `C:\Scripts` will also be included in the backup.

```
$filespec = New-WBFileSpec -FileSpec C:\Scripts\*.ps1
```

The backup target is created with the `New-WBBackupTarget` cmdlet. This cmdlet requires one of the following parameters: `Disk`, `NetworkPath`, `Volume`, or `VolumePath`. As with the `Get-WBVolume` cmdlet, the `Disk` parameter takes the output from the `Get-WBDisk` cmdlet. The `NetworkPath` parameter takes a Universal Naming Convention (UNC) path for the target. The `Volume` parameter takes the output of the `Get-WBVolume` cmdlet. Finally, the `VolumePath` parameter takes a drive letter for the target.

The following example sets a backup target to a `ValidTarget` returned by the `Get-WBDisk` cmdlet. The returned disk object is stored in the variable `$Disk`, which is then passed to the `New-WBBackupTarget` cmdlet, which stores the returned backup target object in the `$BackupTarget` variable for later use.

```
$Disk = Get-WBDisk | Where-Object {$_.Properties -match 'ValidTarget'}
$BackupTarget = New-WBBackupTarget -Disk $Disk
```

Once you have the volumes or file specification you need, you add them to the blank policy you previously created with the `Add-WBVolume` or `Add-WBFileSpec` cmdlets. You add the target to the policy with the `Add-WBBackupTarget` cmdlet. At this point, you can run the backup or schedule it for later. Once the backup is scheduled, it will run on a daily basis.

The following example script creates a new backup policy, adds all critical volumes, sets the target to \\BackupServer01\backup\ in a subfolder named for the local server, and sets the backup to run daily at 7:00 p.m.:

```
$Credential = Get-Credential
$Policy = New-WBPolicy
$Volumes = Get-WBVolume -CriticalVolumes
$BackupDir = "\\BackupServer01\backup\$env:computername"
if (!(Test-Path -Path $BackupDir))
{
New-Item -Path $BackupDir -ItemType Directory | Out-Null
}
$WBBackupTarget = @{
NetworkPath = $BackupDir
Credential = $Credential
}
$BackupTarget = New-WBBackupTarget @WBBackupTarget
Add-WBVolume -Policy $Policy -Volume $Volumes
Add-WBBackupTarget -Policy $Policy -Target $BackupTarget
Set-WBSchedule -Policy $Policy -Schedule 19:00:00
Set-WBPolicy -Policy $Policy
```

Checking the Status of Backup Jobs

You can check the status of a local backup job with the `Get-WBJob` cmdlet. When run without parameters, the cmdlet returns the status of a currently running backup job. If no job is currently running, the cmdlet returns an empty object, as shown:

```
PS> Get-WBJob
JobType          : None
StartTime        :
EndTime          :
```

```
JobState            : Unknown
CurrentOperation    :
HResult             : 0
DetailedHResult     : 0
ErrorDescription    :
JobItems            :
VersionId           :
SuccessLogPath      :
FailureLogPath      :
```

You can view the status of a previous job or jobs by specifying the parameter `Previous` along with the number of previous jobs to display. The following example returns the status of the previous four backup jobs:

```
Get-WBJob -Previous 4
```

You can check the status of backups stored on a remote location with the `Get-WBBackupSet` cmdlet. You can pass a backup target to the cmdlet with the `BackupTarget` parameter. The backup target can be defined with the `New-WBBackupTarget` cmdlet. If there are backups for multiple machines on the target location, you can limit the results to only one server with the `MachineName` parameter. The following example outputs the backup information for the server `FileServer` on the target `\\Backup-Server\Backup`:

```
$Machine = "FileServer"
$Target = "\\Backup-server\Backup\$Machine"
$Targetpath = New-WBBackupTarget -NetworkPath $Target
Get-WBBackupSet -BackupTarget $Targetpath -MachineName $Machine
```

Deleting Backup Jobs

Use the `Remove-WBPolicy` cmdlet to delete backup jobs. To use this cmdlet, you will need to specify the specific policy you want to delete in the `Policy` parameter, or specify the parameter `All` to delete the backup job without specifying the policy name. The cmdlet will prompt for confirmation unless you specify the `Force` parameter.

The following example combines the `Get-WBPolicy` cmdlet with the `Remove-WBPolicy` cmdlet to delete the current policy. Note that the policy retrieved by the `Get-WBPolicy` cmdlet must be opened in editable mode with the `Editable` parameter, and that the returned policy object is stored in the variable `$Policy`, which is passed to the `Remove-WBPolicy` cmdlet:

```
$Policy = Get-WBPolicy -Editable
Remove-WBPolicy -Policy $Policy -Force
```

The next example removes the current policy:

```
Remove-WBPolicy -All -Force
```

Starting and Stopping Backup Jobs

You can start an existing backup job, whether it is a scheduled or one-time job, using the `Start-WBBackup` cmdlet and passing the required parameter `Policy`. You can retrieve the current policy with the `Get-WBPolicy` cmdlet. The following example starts an existing backup job:

```
$Policy = Get-WBPolicy
Start-WBBackup -Policy $Policy
```

Unfortunately, the `Windows.ServerBackup` snap-in does not provide a method to stop a currently running backup. To stop a currently running backup, you will need to use another command-line utility known as `wbadmin.exe`. The following example stops the current backup job:

```
wbadmin stop job
```

Scheduling Backup Jobs

You can schedule a job when you create it or schedule an existing job. In either case, you create the schedule with the `Set-WBSchedule` cmdlet, and only one job can be scheduled. Once the schedule is created, you add it to the policy with the `Set-WBPolicy` cmdlet. A schedule can be set to run a backup at multiple times. The times must be entered in HH:MM format using a 24-hour clock format, or HH:MM AM/PM to use the 12-hour format. Multiple times would be separated with a comma.

The following example schedules the backup job retrieved by the `Get-WBPolicy` cmdlet. As described in the "Deleting Backup Jobs" section, the policy must be opened in editable mode with the `Editable` parameter, and that the returned policy object is stored in the variable `$Policy`, which is passed to the `Set-WBSchedule` cmdlet.

```
$Policy = Get-WBPolicy -Editable
Set-WBSchedule -Policy $Policy -Schedule 19:00:00
```

For an example of creating a schedule for a new policy, see the "Configuring New Backup Jobs" section earlier in the chapter.

Checking the Schedule

You can check the schedule for the current backup profile using the `Get-WBSchedule` cmdlet. This cmdlet requires the `Policy` parameter. You can retrieve the current profile using the `Get-WBProfile` cmdlet. The following example returns the schedule for the current backup profile:

```
$Policy = Get-WBPolicy
Get-WBSchedule -Policy $Policy
PS> $Policy = Get-WBPolicy
PS> Get-WBSchedule -Policy $Policy

Tuesday, July 12, 2011 7:00:00 PM
```

Modifying the Schedule

Before you can modify the schedule for an existing policy, you need to pass the policy into a variable with the `Get-WBProfile` cmdlet. Because you will need to modify the policy, you need to specify the `Editable` parameter. You then create a schedule with the `Set-WBSchedule` cmdlet, and write it back to the current policy with the `Set-WBPolicy` cmdlet. The following example modifies the existing policy to perform backups at noon and 11:59 p.m.:

```
$Policy = Get-WBPolicy -Editable
Set-WBSchedule -Policy $Policy -Schedule 12:00, 23:59
Set-WBPolicy -Policy $Policy
```

You may need to pass credentials that have permission to access the backup target. If so, you will need to retrieve the current backup target using the `Get-WBBackupTarget` cmdlet, and then you can use the `Get-Credential` cmdlet, saving the credentials to a variable, which you will pass to the `New-WBBackupTarget` cmdlet. A backup policy can have only one target, so you will need to specify the switch parameter `Force` to the `New-WBBackupTarget` cmdlet. The following example extends the previous example to specify the credentials needed to access the backup target:

```
$Credential = Get-Credential
$Policy = Get-WBPolicy -Editable
$Target = Get-WBBackupTarget -Policy $Policy
$WBBackupTarget = @{
NetworkPath = $Target.Path
Credential = $Credential
}
$BackupTarget = New-WBBackupTarget @WBBackupTarget
Add-WBBackupTarget -Policy $Policy -Target $BackupTarget -Force
Set-WBSchedule -Policy $Policy -Schedule 12:00, 23:59
Set-WBPolicy -Policy $Policy
```

Limitations in the Cmdlets

For all the power of the `Windows.ServerBackup` cmdlets, they have some glaring omissions:

- You can set only one scheduled backup. This is a limitation of the backup program itself.

- As mentioned, you cannot stop a currently running backup using the cmdlets. The older command-line tool provides this functionality.

- You cannot back up to tape or any other form of removable storage. This is less of a problem than it used to be, with the relative low cost of disk-based storage.

- If you set the backup target to a remote shared folder, subsequent backups will overwrite previous backups. If there is an error during a backup, you will have no backup.

- Finally, although you can schedule a backup, or create and run a backup, there is no mechanism that allows you to restore an existing backup using the cmdlets.

You can mitigate some of these limitations with some creative scripting. For instance, to overcome the problem of having only one scheduled backup, you could create separate scripts for each desired backup, and run them via scheduled tasks. You could also move the previous backup via script before creating a new backup. The script in Listing 7-2 provides a sample script that renames the target path with the date of the last backup. Once the path is renamed, a new empty folder is created.

LISTING 7-2

Sample Script to Rename Backup Path

```
$Policy = Get-WBPolicy
$Path = $($Policy.BackupTargets).Path
if (Test-Path $Path)
{
$File = Get-ChildItem -Path $Path -Recurse -Include BackupSpecs.xml
$PathRenameDate = $File.LastWriteTime.Date.ToString("yyyy-MM-dd")
Rename-Item -Path $Path -NewName "$Path-$PathRenameDate"
}
New-Item -ItemType Directory -Path $Path | Out-Null
```

Managing Server Migration

Microsoft Windows Server 2008 R2 includes server migration functionality. Server migration simplifies creation of new servers. This also allows you to upgrade your infrastructure from previous versions of Windows Server to Windows Server 2008 R2. Certain roles and features, along with local users and groups, network settings, and other operating system features, can be migrated from servers running Server 2003 Service Pack 2, Server 2003 R2, full installations of Server 2008, and full or server core installations of Server 2008 R2.

Installing the Cmdlets

Server migration is managed with the `Microsoft.Windows.ServerManager.Migration` snap-in. This snap-in is part of the `Migration` feature, which can be installed with the `Add-WindowsFeature` cmdlet. Once the feature is installed, you add the snap-in with the `Add-PSSnapin` cmdlet, specifying the name of the snap-in. The following example adds the required feature and loads the snap-in:

```
Add-WindowsFeature -Name Migration
Add-PSSnapin -Name Microsoft.Windows.ServerManager.Migration
```

For Server 2003 and 2008, you will need to ensure that Windows PowerShell is installed on the source server. You then need to create a deployment folder on the target Server

2008 R2 server. The script in Listing 7-3 creates the migration folder for the operating system and architecture in the path you specify. The script requires the `Architecture`, `OS`, and `Path` parameters to be specified. An optional parameter allows you to specify the `ComputerName` to copy the deployment folder to. The source server is the server you will be migrating from. This parameter can take an array of servers. The folder will be copied to the root of the C: drive.

LISTING 7-3

Create-MigrationFolder.ps1

```
param(
 [Parameter(Mandatory = $True)]
[ValidateSet("x86","amd64")]
#ValidateSet allows ONLY the listed values to be passed to the script.
#other values will cause an error condition.

[string]$Architecture,
[Parameter(Mandatory = $True)]
[ValidateSet("WS03","WS08")]
[string]$OS,
[Parameter(Mandatory = $True)]
[string]$Path,
[Parameter(Mandatory = $False)]
[string[]]$Target
)
$Alias = @{
Name = "SetMigDeploy"
Value = "$env:windir\System32\ServerMigrationTools\SmigDeploy.exe"
}
$Command = @{
ScriptBlock = {
SetMigDeploy /Package /Architecture $Architecture /OS $OS /Path $Path
}
}
Set-Alias @Alias
Invoke-Command @Command
if ($Target)
{
foreach ($TargetServer in $Target)
{
$OutPath = "\\$TargetServer\C$\SMT_$OS"
$OutPath += "_$Architecture"
$InPath = "$Path\SMT_$OS"
$InPath += "_$Architecture"
```

continues

LISTING 7-3   *(continued)*

```
robocopy $InPath $OutPath /E | Out-Null
#use robocopy as it is quicker than the Copy-Item cmdlet,
#and there are varying amounts of files and folders to copy.
#robocopy is Microsoft's Robust File Copy utility, built into
#Windows Server.
}
}
```

The following example creates a migration folder for an x86 version of Server 2003 in the folder C:\MigrationFolder:

```
.\Create-MigrationFolder.ps1 -Architecture x86 -OS ws03 -Path C:\MigrationFolder
```

Once the migration folders are created, you need to copy them to the source servers. You can either do that when they are created with the script in Listing 7-1 or copy existing migration folders to the source servers. Once the folders are copied to the source servers, you will need to run the SmigDeploy.exe program within that folder on the source servers. Server 2003 R2 and above require that the program be run from an elevated command prompt or Windows PowerShell session.

The following example creates a migration folder for a 64-bit version of Server 2008 in the folder C:\MigrationFolder. Once the migration folder is created, it will be copied to the server DC02.

```
$Folder = @{
Architecture = "amd64"
OS = "ws08"
Path = "C:\MigrationFolder"
Target = "DC02"
}
.\Create-MigrationFolder.ps1 @Folder
```

Discover What Can Be Migrated

Once you have the required feature and snap-in installed, you can discover which features can be migrated by running the Get-SmigServerFeature cmdlet. When run without parameters, the cmdlet returns the list of exportable features on the local computer. The optional Path parameter points the Get-SmigServerFeature cmdlet to a migration store on a local or remote location. If the migration store is on a remote location, that path must be configured with a drive letter on the local machine. The example shown here shows which features can be migrated from the local machine:

```
Get-SmigServerFeature
```

When you specify the path of a migration store, you will need to provide the password for that migration store. The following example returns which features in the migration store on the path R: can be imported into the local server. The features that cannot be imported will not be displayed.

```
$Prompt = @{
Prompt = "Enter the password:"
AsSecureString = $True
}
Get-SmigServerFeature -Path "R:" -Password (Read-Host @Prompt)
```

Exporting Features

Exporting features is accomplished with the Export-SmigServerSetting cmdlet. This cmdlet exports features to a migration store or directly to another server. You can export some or all features, depending on your needs. If you do not know which features can be exported, you will need to discover them. See the "Discover What Can Be Migrated" section for a refresher.

To a Migration Store

Once you know which features can be migrated from the local machine, you can export them with the Export-SmigServerSetting cmdlet. You can export specific features by specifying the FeatureId parameter. This cmdlet also requires the Path parameter and the Password parameter. The password will need to be passed as a secure string. The following example exports the Hyper-V feature from the current server to the path C:\MigrationStore. The password is created as a secure string previous to calling the Export-SmigServerSetting cmdlet.

```
$Password = Read-Host -Prompt "Enter the password:" -AsSecureString
$SmigServerSetting = @{
FeatureId = "Hyper-V"
Path = "C:\MigrationStore"
Password = $Password
}
Export-SmigServerSetting @SmigServerSetting
```

As mentioned previously, you can also export local users and groups along with other operating system settings. Local users are exported by specifying the User parameter along with the qualifier of All, Enabled, or Disabled. For the user accounts, only the name and account status are exported. The password will need to be specified on first login. Likewise, groups are exported by specifying the Group parameter. Additionally, you can export the server's IP configuration information with the `IPConfig` parameter, specifying either `All`, `NIC`, or `Global` for the value, where `NIC` would export the IP configuration settings for network interface cards that are enabled and connected to the network, `Global` would export Windows IP configuration information, and `All` would export both.

To Another Server

You can export server information directly to another server with the `Send-SmigServerData` cmdlet. The destination server needs to be in the same IP subnet as the source server and must be running the `Receive-SmigServerData` cmdlet, which is described in the next section. The data is sent via TCP over port 7000. The data sent can be only file share information, including permissions, files and folders, and share properties. Other features, roles, and user information cannot be migrated directly to another server.

The `Send-SmigServerData` cmdlet requires that the type of data be specified with the `Include` parameter, with a valid value of either `All`, `Data`, or `Share`. If the `Include` parameter is set to either `All` or `Data`, this cmdlet also requires that the local source of the data be specified with the `SourcePath` parameter. The switch parameter `Recurse`, when included, will cause the data or share permissions in subfolders of the `SourcePath` to be migrated as well. Finally, you need to specify the `DestinationPath` and `ComputerName` parameters, which specify the target server, and a `Password` to encrypt the data transfer.

The following example migrates all files, folders, and share properties from the local path `C:\UserFiles` to the remote path `C:\UserFiles` on the server `FileServer02`, using the password of `P@ssW0rd` to secure the transfer:

```
$String = @{
String = "P@ssW0rd"
AsPlainText = $True
Force = $True
}
$Password = ConvertTo-SecureString @String
$SmigServerData = @{
Include = "All"
ComputerName = "FileServer02"
SourcePath = "C:\UserFiles"
DestinationPath = "C:\UserFiles"
Recurse = $True
Password = $Password
}
Send-SmigServerData @SmigServerData
```

Importing Features

Importing features is accomplished with the `Import-SmigServerSetting` cmdlet. This cmdlet imports features from a migration store, or directly from another server. You can import some or all features, depending on your needs.

From a Migration Store

Only features that have been previously exported to the migration store and are valid features for the target server can be imported. You can get a list of available features in the migration store with the `Get-SmigServerFeature` cmdlet, specifying the `Path` to the migration store as well as the `Password` for the migration store. The following example returns which features are available in the migration store located on `\\Server01\MigrationStore`. Because no password is specified, you will be prompted for the password.

```
Get-SmigServerData -Path \\Server01\MigrationStore
```

Now that you have the list of features available on the migration store, you can choose to import one or more. The following example imports the `Hyper-V` feature and IP configuration from the migration store located on `\\Server01\MigrationStore` after prompting for the password. The configuration for the network adaptor with the MAC address of `00-1F-3B-93-05-73` will be migrated to the local network adaptor with the MAC address of `BC-AE-C5-33-6E-EB`. The configuration for the network adaptor with the MAC address of `00-15-5D-01-0A-02` will be migrated to the local network adaptor with the MAC address of `00-15-5D-01-0A-01`. You will be prompted for a password.

```
$MigrationSetting = @{
Feature = "Hyper-V"
IPConfig = "All"
SourcePhysicalAddress = "00-1F-3B-93-05-73","00-15-5D-01-0A-02"
TargetPhysicalAddress = "BC-AE-C5-33-6E-EB","00-15-5D-01-0A-01"
Path = "\\Server01\MigrationStore"
}
Import-SmigServerSetting @MigrationSetting
```

The next example imports all features on the migration store `\\Server01\MigrationStore` that are applicable to the current server, after prompting for the password:

```
$Feature = @{
Path = "\\Server01\MigrationStore"
}
Get-SmigServerFeature @Feature | Import-SmigServerSetting @Feature
```

From Another Server

You can import file share data from another server with the `Receive-SmigServerData` cmdlet. This cmdlet requires that the source server be running the `Send-SmigServerData` cmdlet at the same time and that the source server be on the same subnet. The `Receive-SmigServerData` cmdlet accepts only the required `Password` parameter. All configuration is accomplished via the `Send-SmigServerData` cmdlet. The following example receives data that is currently being sent from another server:

```
$String = @{
String = "P@ssW0rd"
AsPlainText = $True
Force = $True
```

```
}
$Password = ConvertTo-SecureString @String
Receive-SmigServerData -Password $Password
```

Managing AppLocker

AppLocker is an application control feature available in Windows 7 ultimate and Enterprise editions and Windows Server 2008 R2 in all versions except the Web Server and Foundation editions that helps prevent the execution of unwanted and unknown applications within an organization's network. Windows 7 and Windows Server 2008 R2 ship with a module designed to manage AppLocker. The `AppLocker` cmdlets are imported into the current session with the `Import-Module` cmdlet. `Import-Module -Name AppLocker` imports the cmdlets.

The AppLocker module includes five cmdlets that work with the AppLocker policy in the local or domain-based group policy objects. These cmdlets enable you to retrieve, create, apply, or test an AppLocker policy. You will need to run the cmdlets in an elevated Windows PowerShell console.

Creating an AppLocker policy is accomplished with the `New-AppLockerPolicy` cmdlet. This cmdlet creates a policy for the specified user or group, based on file publisher, hash, or path information. You will gather file information with the `Get-AppLockerFileInformation` cmdlet to pass to the `New-AppLockerPolicy` cmdlet.

The `Get-AppLockerFileInformation` cmdlet requires the `FileType` parameter, which can be `Script`, `Exe`, `WindowsInstaller`, or `Dll`. You will also need to supply the `Directory` or `Path` to the files from which file information is to be retrieved. If you specify a `Directory`, you can also specify the optional Boolean parameter `Recurse`. The following example retrieves information for all script files in the directory `C:\scripts` and subfolders:

```
$Files = @{
FileType = "Script"
Directory = "C:\Scripts"
Recurse = $True
}
Get-AppLockerFileInformation @Files
```

As mentioned, you will need to pass this information to the `New-AppLockerPolicy` cmdlet. This cmdlet accepts the `RuleType` parameter, which specifies the type of rules to be created. The rules can be `Publisher`, `Hash`, or `Path` rules. By default, `Publisher` and `Hash` rules are created, which will apply hash rules when publisher information is not available. You can also specify the `User` parameter, which specifies which user or groups the rules will be applied to. The parameter `RuleNamePrefix` applies the specified prefix to each rule. The `Optimize` parameter groups similar rules, and the `Xml` parameter instructs the cmdlet to provide the output as XML data.

The following example builds on the previous example, creating a new AppLocker policy that creates `Hash` and `Publisher` rules for the group `Everyone`, and prefixes the rules with the string `Scripts`. Rules will be grouped together, and the data will be output as a `.xml` file.

```
$Policy = @{
RuleType = "Publisher,Hash"
User = "Everyone"
RuleNamePrefix = "Scripts"
Optimize = $True
Xml = $True
FileInformation = $Files
}
New-AppLockerPolicy @Policy | Out-File -FilePath C:\ScriptsPolicy.xml
```

Now that you have the new AppLocker policy saved in the file `C:\ScriptsPolicy.xml`, you can test the policy with the `Test-AppLockerPolicy` cmdlet. Because you have the XML data saved in a file, you specify the `XmlPolicy` parameter, passing the path of the file from the previous example, along with the `Path` parameter, which specifies a file to test. The following example tests the effect of the policy in `C:\ScriptsPolicy.xml` on the script file `C:\Scripts\Add-Firewallport.ps1`:

```
$TestPolicy = @{
XmlPolicy = "C:\ScriptsPolicy.xml"
Path = "C:\Scripts\Add-Firewallport.ps1"
}
Test-AppLockerPolicy @TestPolicy
```

Once you are satisfied with the AppLocker policy, you apply it with the `Set-AppLockerPolicy` cmdlet. To complete the previous examples, you can pass the XML file saved previously to the `XmlPolicy` parameter. The following example applies the previously created policy:

```
Set-AppLockerPolicy -XmlPolicy C:\ScriptsPolicy.xml
```

The preceding examples create an AppLocker policy on the local machine. You can apply the policy to a domain group policy object by specifying the LDAP parameter to the `Set-AppLockerPolicy` cmdlet, passing the LDAP path of the group policy object.

Cross-Reference

See Chapter 11, "Managing Group Policy," for information on retrieving the group policy object's LDAP path. ∎

Summary

In this chapter, you learned what's new in Server 2008 R2, with new cmdlets and functionality. You learned to manage features and roles, including discovering which are already installed and which are available to be installed.

You learned how to run best-practice scans against the local server or a list of remote servers, and examined how to enable remoting on the local server.

You examined the benefits of managing Windows Backup with the supplied cmdlets, as well as the limitations of the cmdlets, along with a few ways to mitigate the limitations. You learned how to migrate features, roles, users and groups, and other server information to a migration store, as well as how to migrate share information directly to another server.

Finally, you learned to manage AppLocker on local machines and on a domain group policy object.

In the next chapter, you learn basic server management, which is fairly version-independent. You discover how servers are configured, examine scheduling Windows PowerShell scripts, and explore managing the task scheduler.

You explore how to examine hotfix information locally and on remote servers, which will include checking that specific hotfixes are installed. You also learn to gather data from local and remote event logs, filtering for the data you are interested in.

Finally, you learn to manipulate time information on servers.

Performing Basic Server Management

I n this chapter, you read about performing basic server management with Windows PowerShell. This will be done by using a combination of built-in cmdlets and the `Get-WmiObject` cmdlet, which returns information from Windows Management Instrumentation (WMI) classes inherent to the operating system.

Discovering Server Configuration

You can discover your server configuration with the built-in Windows Management Instrumentation (WMI) interface. WMI is installed by default on all server operating systems from Windows Server 2000 and newer. Although WMI has been preinstalled since Windows Server 2000, Microsoft adds new classes and extends current classes with every operating system release. An example of this is the `MfrAssignedRevisionLevel` property of the `Win32_CDROMDrive` class, which is not available in Windows Server 2003 or earlier.

Note

For a complete reference to the WMI classes, see `http://msdn.microsoft` `.com/en-us/library/aa394554(v=VS.85).aspx.` ■

By now, you've seen multiple examples of using the `Get-WmiObject` cmdlet to gather data from various classes remotely and against the local computer. Rather than rehashing how to use the `Get-WmiObject` cmdlet, you learn how to discover which classes are available on a particular server for whatever information you are looking for.

The `Get-WmiObject` cmdlet accepts the switch parameter `List`, which lists available classes for a particular namespace. By default, the

IN THIS CHAPTER

Discovering how your server is configured

Working with the task scheduler

Checking for hotfixes

Examining event logs

Managing system time

List parameter displays all classes for the root\CIMV2 namespace. Using the Namespace parameter enables you to retrieve other classes.

Suppose you want to gather power settings from the namespace root\CIMV2\power. Knowing which classes the root\CIMV2\power namespace contains relating to power could help design a script to gather information from the server. The following example returns all classes whose name matches Win32_Power* in the root\CIMV2\power namespace on the server Karl-Server:

```
$WmiObject = @{
Namespace = "root\CIMV2\power"
List = $true
ComputerName = "Karl-Server"
}
$Filter = @{
FilterScript = {$_.name -match "Win32_Power*"}
}
Get-WmiObject @WmiObject | Where-Object @Filter | Select-Object -Property Name
Name
Win32_PowerMeterEvent
Win32_PowerSettingElementSettingDataIndex
Win32_PowerSettingCapabilities
Win32_PowerSettingDataIndexInPlan
Win32_PowerSettingInSubgroup
Win32_PowerSettingDefineCapabilities
Win32_PowerSettingDefinitionPossibleValue
Win32_PowerPlan
Win32_PowerSettingDefinitionRangeData
Win32_PowerSettingDataIndex
Win32_PowerSettingSubgroup
Win32_PowerSetting
Win32_PowerMeter
Win32_PowerSupply
Win32_PowerSettingDefinition
Win32_PowerMeterConformsToProfile
```

The preceding example works fine if you know which namespace you want to query, but what if you don't know which namespaces are installed on a specific server? As it turns out, the Get-WmiObject cmdlet can discover this for you as well. One of the parameters to the Get-WmiObject cmdlet is the Query parameter. This parameter takes a WMI Query Language (WQL) statement as its value. You can use the following example to display all namespaces under the root namespace on the server Karl-Server:

```
$NamespaceObject = @{
Query = "select * from __namespace"
Namespace = "root"
ComputerName = "Karl-Server"
}
Get-WmiObject @NamespaceObject | Select-Object -Property Name
```

Now that you know which namespace and class you want to query, it's easy to gather information from WMI on any server. The following example returns which power plan is active on the server Karl-Server:

```
$PowerObject = @{
Namespace = "root\CIMV2\power"
Class = "Win32_PowerPlan"
ComputerName = "Karl-Server"
}
$Filter = @{
FilterScript = {$_.IsActive -eq $true}
}
Get-WmiObject @PowerObject | Where-Object @Filter
```

For further examples, see the book's website.

Managing Scheduled Tasks

You can retrieve a list of running tasks on local or remote servers using the COM object Schedule.Service. After connecting to the scheduler service on the remote server using the Connect() method, you can retrieve the tasks by calling the GetRunningTasks() method. If the account used has local Administrator permission on the remote server, GetRunningTasks() returns a collection of all running tasks. If the account is only a member of the Users group on the remote server, GetRunningTasks() returns a collection of tasks running under that security context.

The Connect() method accepts four optional parameters. The first optional parameter is the name of the remote server. The next three parameters are the username, domain, and password for a user who has permission on the remote server. If the account used to start your Windows PowerShell session has permission on the remote server, you can either pass $null for these last three parameters, or ignore them altogether.

The GetRunningTasks() method requires a flag parameter that specifies which tasks to retrieve. Passing a 0 displays currently running tasks that are not hidden. Passing a 1 displays all currently running tasks.

Running the following code displays all running tasks on the server Karl-Server that the current user has permission to manage:

```
$TaskService = New-Object -ComObject Schedule.Service
$TaskService.Connect("Karl-Server")
$TaskService.GetRunningTasks(1)
```

When passing a password to a .NET method such as the Connect() method of the Schedule.Service object, the password must be passed as plain text. This can be accomplished by creating a credential object with the Get-Credential cmdlet and calling the GetNetworkCredential() method of the credential object. This method returns the username, domain, and password for the credential object. The following example prompts for the credentials for the user `Contoso\sherrym` and then uses those credentials to connect to the server `Karl-Server`, displaying all running tasks that `Contoso\sherrym` has permission to manage:

```
$Credential = Get-Credential -Credential "Contoso\sherrym"
$TaskService = New-Object -ComObject Schedule.Service
$User = $Credential.GetNetworkCredential().UserName
$Domain = $Credential.GetNetworkCredential().Domain
$Password = $Credential.GetNetworkCredential().Password
$TaskService.Connect("Karl-Server",$User,$Domain,$Password)
$TaskService.GetRunningTasks(1)
```

Scheduling a new task is accomplished with the `NewTask()` method of the `Schedule.Service` object. This method requires a parameter specifying flags for the method. At this time, the parameter is reserved for future use and must be set to 0. Once you have your `$TaskService` object, you create a new task by calling the method as `$NewTask = $TaskService.NewTask(0)`. You then define the properties for the new task and register the task.

Properties for the new task include the `Actions`, `Data`, `Principal`, `RegistrationInfo`, `Settings`, `Triggers`, and `XmlText`. Of these properties, `Data` and `XmlText` are optional.

Note

The full description of these properties and their associated values is beyond the scope of this chapter. For a full description, see `http://msdn.microsoft.com/en-us/library/aa383614(v=VS.85).aspx`. ∎

Once you have assigned the properties that define the task you want to create, you create a task folder reference by calling the `GetFolder()` method of the `Schedule.Service` object. You then register the task with the `RegisterTaskDefinition()` method of the folder object. The simple example shown next starts Windows PowerShell and runs the script in the `C:\Scripts\Get-SharePermission.ps1` directory on the `Karl-Server` server at 8:00 a.m. Daily for five years under the security context of the user who runs the script, if that user is logged on to the server:

```
$TaskService = New-Object -ComObject Schedule.Service
$TaskService.Connect("Karl-Server")
$TriggerTypeDaily = 2
$ActionType = 0
$NewTask = $TaskService.NewTask(0)
$Registration = $NewTask.RegistrationInfo
$Registration.Description = "Start PowerShell on a daily basis"
$Registration.Author = "Karl Mitschke"
$principal = $NewTask.Principal
$principal.LogonType = 3
$settings = $NewTask.Settings
$settings.Enabled = $True
```

```
$settings.StartWhenAvailable = $True
$settings.Hidden = $False
$StartTime = [datetime]::now.Date.AddMinutes(5)
$EndTime = $StartTime.AddYears(5)
$triggers = $NewTask.Triggers
$trigger = $triggers.Create($TriggerTypeDaily)
$trigger.StartBoundary = $StartTime.ToString("yyyy-MM-dd'T'HH:mm:ss")
$trigger.EndBoundary = $EndTime.ToString("yyyy-MM-dd'T'HH:mm:ss")
$trigger.DaysInterval = 1
$trigger.Id = "Daily PowerShell Task"
$trigger.ExecutionTimeLimit = "PT5M"
$trigger.Enabled = $True
$Action = $NewTask.Actions.Create($ActionType)
$Action.Path = "C:\Windows\System32\WindowsPowerShell\v1.0\powershell.exe"
$Action.Arguments = "C:\Scripts\Get-SharePermission.ps1"
$Action.WorkingDirectory = "C:\Scripts"
$rootFolder = $TaskService.GetFolder("\")
$rootFolder.RegisterTaskDefinition("PowerShell", $NewTask, 6,"","",3)| Out-Null
```

Stopping a currently running task is accomplished with the Stop() method of the task. You first gather a collection of running tasks with the GetRunningTasks() method of the Schedule.Service object. At this point, you loop through each task, examining it to ensure that it is the one you want to stop, and finally call the Stop() method on the proper task. The following example stops the currently running task PowerShell on the server Karl-Server:

```
$TaskService = New-Object -ComObject Schedule.Service
$TaskService.Connect("Karl-Server")
$Tasks = $TaskService.GetRunningTasks(1)
Foreach ($Task in $Tasks)
{
If ($Task.Name -eq "PowerShell")
{
$Task.Stop()
}
}
```

You can delete a scheduled task by retrieving the collection of tasks within a folder with the GetFolder() method of the Schedule.Service object. Once you have the list of scheduled tasks, you can loop through each task until the current task is the one you want to remove. You then call the DeleteTask() method of the folder object, passing the task name as the first parameter, and a 0 for the second parameter, which is an unused parameter. The following example results in deleting the scheduled task with the name PowerShell from the root folder on the server Karl-Server:

```
$TaskService = New-Object -ComObject Schedule.Service
$TaskService.Connect("Karl-Server")
$Folder = $TaskService.GetFolder("\")
```

```
$Tasks = $Folder.GetTasks(1)
Foreach ($Task in $Tasks)
{
If ($Task.Name -eq "PowerShell")
{
$Folder.DeleteTask($Task.Name,0)
}
}
```

For more examples, including passing arguments to the scheduled program, and scheduling tasks to run whether or not the user is logged in, see the book's website.

Checking Hotfix Status

PowerShell Version 2 includes the new cmdlet Get-HotFix, which enables you to see which hotfixes have been installed on the local computer or remote computers. The data returned is limited to hotfixes installed via Component-Based Servicing. Component-Based Servicing provides installer packages the ability to install, update, or uninstall operating system components. This specifically excludes patches installed via the Windows update site and patches installed by a .msi file. The Get-HotFix cmdlet is a wrapper for the WMI class Win32_QuickFixEngineering.

Hotfixes installed by Component-Based Servicing are designed to fix specific issues that may not be applicable to all servers. For instance, an Exchange 2010 Client Access Server running on Windows Server 2008 R2 requires four hotfixes that would not necessarily be required on a file server.

Running Get-HotFix without any parameters returns a list of all hotfixes on the current computer. Data returned is the source, which is the computer name; the description, which shows the type of hotfix; the hotfix ID, which usually points to a Knowledge Base article; who the hotfix was installed by; and the date the hotfix was installed.

Checking Hotfixes on Multiple Computers

One of the parameters the Get-HotFix cmdlet accepts is the ComputerName parameter. This parameter takes a string or array of strings. By default, the cmdlet uses the credentials of the current user. If you are running Windows PowerShell with an account that does not have WMI privileges on the computers for which you wish to retrieve hotfix information, you can pass the Credential parameter. The following example retrieves all hotfixes installed on the four servers ExchCAS01, ExchCAS02, ExchCAS03, and ExchCAS04, while running under the credentials of the current user:

```
Get-HotFix -ComputerName ExchCAS01,ExchCAS02,ExchCAS03,ExchCAS04
```

As previously mentioned, the first property returned is the computer name, so you can easily see which hotfix is installed on each server.

Checking for a Specific Hotfix

The `Get-HotFix` parameter accepts the `Id` parameter, which also accepts a string or array of strings. When combined with the `ComputerName` parameter, this enables you to check multiple servers for a list of hotfixes.

In the previous section, I alluded to the fact that Exchange 2010 Client Access Servers running on Server 2008 R2 require four hotfixes. The Exchange installation program will inform you of missing hotfixes after copying a large number of files to your server. Luckily, you can easily see which of the four required hotfixes are missing with a quick call to the `Get-HotFix` cmdlet. The following example returns which of the four required hotfixes are installed on each of the four servers — ExchCAS01, ExchCAS02, ExchCAS03, and ExchCAS04 — running under the credentials of the user `Contoso\karlm`. If you were to run this code, you would be prompted for a password.

```
$HotFix = @{
ComputerName = "ExchCAS01","ExchCAS02","ExchCAS03","ExchCAS04"
Id = "KB979099","KB979744","KB983440","KB977020"
Credential = "Contoso\karlm"
}
Get-HotFix @HotFix
```

Gathering Data from Event Logs

Almost every application run on Windows servers makes entries in one or more event logs. These entries have differing levels of severity. Suppose you have run Windows Update on a series of servers hosting user files and users are now unable to retrieve data. You can discover which updates were installed on these servers with Windows PowerShell. This example is shown later in this section.

PowerShell Version 2 includes two cmdlets for retrieving data from event logs: `Get-WinEvent` and `Get-EventLog`. The `Get-WinEvent` cmdlet retrieves data from the new event logs in Windows Server 2008 R2 and Windows 7, as well as the classic event logs on Windows Server 2008 and Windows Vista, and from `.etl`, `.evt`, and `.evtx` files, which are created by Tracelog (`.etl`), Windows 7 and Windows Server 2008 R2 Event Viewer (`.evtx`), and previous event viewers or legacy application logs in Windows 7 and Windows Server 2008 R2 (`.evt`). `Get-EventLog`, on the other hand, can retrieve data only from classic event logs. Both of these cmdlets accept the `ComputerName` parameter, enabling you to retrieve data from remote servers with ease. The `Get-WinEvent` cmdlet enables you to pass credentials via the `Credential` parameter, whereas the `Get-EventLog` cmdlet requires the current user to have permission to read event logs on the current host and remote servers.

If you have examined the newer event logs with the Event Viewer GUI in Windows Server 2008 or newer, you have seen that there is an abundance of log files. Luckily, the

`Get-WinEvent` cmdlet provides a way to determine which log files would potentially contain data you are interested in. For instance, a server hosting the Hyper-V role would have different event logs than a server hosting the Web Server role. Using the `ListLog` parameter enables you to determine which logs are available for a specific role, feature, or application. This parameter accepts the wildcard character *, so you can discover which logs are created specifically for the Hyper-V role on a local or remote server with one quick call to the `Get-WinEvent` cmdlet. The following example retrieves a list of the log files specific to the Hyper-V role on the server `HyperSrv01`:

```
$ListLog = @{
ListLog = "*Hyper*"
ComputerName = "HyperSrv01"
}
Get-WinEvent @ListLog | Select-Object -Property LogName
```

One of the most powerful parameters associated with the `Get-WinEvent` cmdlet is the `FilterHashTable` parameter. This parameter enables you to pass a query in hashtable format to the `Get-WinEvent` cmdlet. The hashtable consists of a series of key-value pairs. This query is evaluated on the server before the data is returned to the Windows PowerShell console. This parameter is the equivalent of the `Filter` parameter that is available in many other cmdlets. Table 8-1 shows the key-value pairs and provides a description for each.

TABLE 8-1

Key-Value Pairs for the FilterHashTable Parameter

Key	Value	Description
LogName	String[]	The name of a log or logs
ProviderName	String[]	The name of a provider or providers
Path	String[]	The path to .etl, .evt, and .evtx log files
Keywords	Long[]	The keyword or keywords to return
ID	Int32[]	The ID or IDs of events to return
Level	Int32[]	The severity of the event
StartTime	DateTime	The date and time of the oldest event to return
EndTime	DateTime	The date and time of the newest event to return
UserID	SID	A user's SID or valid domain account
Data	String[]	Used for events in classic event logs
*	String[]	A named event data field

The `LogName` and `ProviderName` keys accept wildcard input for the values. You can create the hashtable in any manner you are accustomed to. The following example shows all events in the local computer log file `Windows PowerShell` with a severity of 3, which are warning events:

```
Get-WinEvent -FilterHashTable @{LogName='Windows PowerShell'; Level=3}
```

Table 8-2 shows the log-level enumeration.

TABLE 8-2

Log-Level Enumeration

Numeric	Name	Description
0	LogAlways	No filtering is done on the level during event publishing.
1	Critical	A serious error that has caused a major failure.
2	Error	Normal errors that signify a problem.
3	Warning	A warning event.
4	Information	An informational event.
5	Verbose	Lengthy events or messages.

The following example returns all error events within the last seven days for the Windows Update client on the server `Exch2010`:

```
$Failure = @{
FilterHashTable = @{ProviderName='Microsoft-Windows-WindowsUpdateClient';
Id = 20; StartTime = (Get-Date).AddDays(-7)}
ComputerName = "Exch2010"
}
$Format = @{Expression={$_.Message.Split(":")[1].Split()[-1]};Label="Error"},
@{Expression={$_.Message.Split(":")[2]};Label="Message"}
Get-WinEvent @Failure | Format-Table $Format -AutoSize
```

The following example returns all successful updates within the last seven days for the Windows Update client on the server `Exch2010`:

```
$Events = @{
FilterHashTable = @{ProviderName='Microsoft-Windows-WindowsUpdateClient';
ID = 19; StartTime = (Get-Date).AddDays(-7)}
ComputerName = "Exch2010"
}
Get-WinEvent @Events | Format-List TimeCreated, Message
```

The `FilterHashTable` parameter is valid only on Windows Server 2008 R2. For Windows Server 2008 and previous, you will want to explore the `FilterXml` parameter. This parameter takes an arcane XML statement for the value. A good method of discovering the proper XML structure is to first create the query in the GUI application Event Viewer. Once you have the query configured in Event Viewer, you can click the XML tab and copy the resulting code to a here-string.

The next example is the equivalent to the previous `FilterHashTable` example, using the `FilterXml` parameter:

```
$filterXml = @'
<QueryList>
<Query Id="0" Path="Microsoft-Windows-WindowsUpdateClient/Operational">
<Select Path="Microsoft-Windows-WindowsUpdateClient/Operational">*
[System[Provider[@Name='Microsoft-Windows-WindowsUpdateClient']
and (EventID=20) and TimeCreated[timediff(@SystemTime) &lt;= 604800000]]]
</Select>
<Select Path="System">*
[System[Provider[@Name='Microsoft-Windows-WindowsUpdateClient']
and (EventID=20) and TimeCreated[timediff(@SystemTime) &lt;= 604800000]]]
</Select>
</Query>
</QueryList>
'@
Get-WinEvent -FilterXml $filterXml -ComputerName exch2010
```

Note

For more on the XML query schema, see http://msdn.microsoft.com/en-us/library/ aa385760(v=VS.85).aspx. ∎

Using System Time

Time within a domain is of critical importance. If the time on a member server or PC is off by more than 5 minutes, the Kerberos network authentication protocol will not function correctly, which could prevent logins on the Server. Also, Active Directory replication and Windows Update rely on the time being correct. Although time is normally replicated to domain-joined computers with the W32Time Time Service tool, on some occasions, a system will have incorrect time. This section shows you how to display the system time for a list of computers, as well as how to set the time on a list of servers.

Retrieving the Date and Time

Retrieving the time from multiple servers can be accomplished with the `Get-WmiObject` cmdlet. The `Win32_OperatingSystem` class contains the `LocalDateTime` and the `CurrentTimeZone` properties. The `LocalDateTime` property needs to be converted from

Universal Time Coordinate format into the local time format. To do so, use the [wmi] type accelerator, calling the ConvertToDateTime() method. The following example retrieves the current date, time, and time zone for each server in the file C:\Scripts\Servers.txt after prompting for the credentials for a user who has permission to the remote servers:

```
$Credential = Get-Credential
foreach($Server in Get-Content -Path "C:\Scripts\Servers.txt")
{
$TimeObject = @{
ComputerName = $Server
Class = "Win32_OperatingSystem"
Credential = $Credential
}
$OutTZ = $Null
$Computer = Get-WmiObject @TimeObject
$Time = $Computer.LocalDateTime
$Zone = $Computer.CurrentTimeZone
$ServerTime = ([wmi]'').ConvertToDateTime($Time)
$TimeZone = [string][Math]::Floor($Zone /60)
([math]::DivRem($Zone,60,[ref]$OutTZ)) | Out-Null
$TimeZone += ":$($OutTZ.ToString("00"))"
$Output = "$Server time is $ServerTime."
$Output += " Timezone is $Timezone."
Write-Output -InputObject $Output
}
```

The preceding script will not show whether Daylight Saving Time is enabled or in effect. Adding this information requires a call to the Win32_ComputerSystem class. The following example builds on the previous example and adds the information on Daylight Saving Time:

```
$Credential = Get-Credential
foreach($Server in Get-Content -Path "C:\Scripts\Servers.txt")
{
$TimeObject = @{
ComputerName = $Server
Class = "Win32_OperatingSystem"
Credential = $Credential
}
$TimeZoneObject = @{
ComputerName = $Server
Class = "Win32_ComputerSystem"
Credential = $Credential
}
$OutTZ = $Null
$DaylightEnabled = " Daylight Saving Time is not enabled, and "
$DaylightInEffect = "is not in effect."
$ComputerTime = Get-WmiObject @TimeObject
$ComputerTimeZone = Get-WmiObject @TimeZoneObject
$Time = $ComputerTime.LocalDateTime
```

```
$Zone = $ComputerTime.CurrentTimeZone
$ServerTime = ([wmi]'').ConvertToDateTime($Time)
$TimeZone = [string][Math]::Floor($Zone /60)
([math]::DivRem($Zone,60,[ref]$OutTZ)) | Out-Null
$TimeZone += ":$($OutTZ.ToString("00"))"
if ($ComputerTimeZone.EnableDaylightSavingsTime)
{
$DaylightEnabled = " Daylight Saving Time is enabled, and "
}
if ($ComputerTimeZone.DaylightInEffect)
{
$DaylightInEffect = "in effect."
}
$Output = "$Server time is $ServerTime."
$Output += " Timezone is $Timezone."
$Output += $DaylightEnabled
$Output += $DaylightInEffect
Write-Output -InputObject $Output
}
```

Setting the Date and Time

As with retrieving time for multiple servers, setting the date and time is accomplished with the Get-WmiObject cmdlet. The time will need to be converted to the Universal Time Coordinate format from the local time format. Once again, this is accomplished with the [wmi] type accelerator, calling the ConvertFromDateTime() method. The time is set with the SetDateTime() method of the Win32_OperatingSystem WMI class. The following example sets the date and time for each server in the file C:\Scripts\Servers.txt after prompting for the credentials for a user who has permission to the remote servers. The date and time are set to the date and time of the local computer.

```
$Credential = Get-Credential
foreach ($Server in Get-Content -Path C:\Scripts\Servers.txt)
.{
$TimeObject = @{
Class = "Win32_OperatingSystem"
ComputerName = $Server
Credential = $Credential
EnableAllPrivileges = $true
}
$CurrentTime = ([wmi]'').ConvertFromDateTime($(Get-Date))
(Get-WmiObject @TimeObject).SetDateTime($CurrentTime)
}
```

Although this simple method sets the date and time on multiple servers at once, the servers have the potential to be off by a second or two. If you need more accuracy than this, you should have each server set to retrieve time either from an Internet time server, or from a domain time server. As an alternative, the previous example could be modified to retrieve the time from a local domain controller instead of the local computer. The following snippet retrieves the time from the domain controller DC-01. You can use this in place of the $CurrentTime in the previous example.

```
$DCTimeObject = @{
ComputerName = "DC-01"
Class = "Win32_OperatingSystem"
Credential = $Credential
}
$CurrentTime = (Get-WmiObject @DCTimeObject).LocalDateTime
```

Summary

In this chapter, you learned how to leverage your knowledge of WMI and the Get-WmiObject cmdlet to discover server configuration. You also learned how to work with scheduled tasks locally and remotely. Additionally, you learned how to check for hotfixes on local and remote servers, searching for all or a subset of hotfixes. You explored event logs with the new cmdlet Get-WinEvent. Finally, you learned how to retrieve and set the time and date on remote servers.

In the next chapter, you learn how to manage services and processes on multiple remote servers and learn to manage the registry with Windows PowerShell. You will verify and modify network configurations, retrieve data from performance counters, and modify regional settings. You will manage local accounts and groups on remote servers. Finally, you will configure remote DCOM.

Performing Advanced Server Management

This chapter covers a lot of ground because advanced server management is a complex subject. Microsoft has provided a hodgepodge of cmdlets in Windows PowerShell that can help with the various server management tasks. However, quite a few of these cmdlets are not designed to work against remote computers. In multiple cases, cmdlets within the same functional area will have different behaviors. For instance, the `Set-Service` cmdlet accepts a `ComputerName` parameter, whereas the rest of the `*-Service` cmdlets that modify services do not.

This chapter covers two options for managing remote servers. You can use remoting cmdlets such as the `Invoke-Command` cmdlet, or you can use WMI with a combination of methods. This chapter focuses on using WMI when a cmdlet does not accept the `ComputerName` parameter.

IN THIS CHAPTER

Managing Windows services

Managing processes

Reading and modifying the registry

Modifying network settings

Retrieving performance counters

Setting regional settings

Maintaining local accounts

Configuring remote DCOM

Managing Command-Line Services

You manage services with the `Get-Service`, `Stop-Service`, `Start-Service`, `Suspend-Service`, `Resume-Service`, `Restart-Service`, and `Set-Service` cmdlets. Of these, the `Get-Service` and `Set-Service` cmdlets accept the `ComputerName` parameter. The remaining cmdlets require the remote server to be configured for remoting. As an alternative to remoting, you can manage services with the `Get-WmiObject` cmdlet.

Listing Running Services on Multiple Servers

You can list services that are running on remote servers with the `Get-Service` cmdlet, passing the optional parameter `ComputerName`. Comparing running services can help when you are troubleshooting issues. The `Get-Service` cmdlet returns all services, so you need to provide a filter to return only running services. You do this with the `Where-Object` cmdlet. Finally, you will need to pass the output to the `Select-Object` cmdlet, one of the `Format-*` cmdlets, or one of the `Export-*` cmdlets to view the computer name. The following example displays all running services on the servers `ExchCAS01`, `ExchCAS02`, `ExchCAS03`, and `ExchCAS04`. The output shows the server name, the service name, and the service display name.

```
$Computers = "ExchCAS01","ExchCAS02","ExchCAS03","ExchCAS04"
$Filter = @{
FilterScript = {$_.Status -eq "Running"}
}
$Select = @{
Property = "MachineName","Name","DisplayName"
}
foreach ($Computer in $Computers)
{
Get-Service -ComputerName $Computer |
Where-Object @Filter |
Select-Object @Select
}
```

```
MachineName   Name                   DisplayName
-----------   ----                   -----------
ExchCAS01     AppHostSvc             Application Host Helper Service
ExchCAS01     Appinfo                Application Information
ExchCAS01     AudioEndpointBuilder   Windows Audio Endpoint Builder
ExchCAS01     AudioSrv               Windows Audio
ExchCAS01     BFE                    Base Filtering Engine
ExchCAS01     BITS                   Background Intelligent Transfer Service
ExchCAS01     CertPropSvc            Certificate Propagation
...
```

Finding Servers Running a Specific Service

The `Get-Service` cmdlet accepts the optional parameter `Name`, which enables you to retrieve only specific services. This parameter accepts wildcard input as well as an array of names. The following example returns a list of servers that have the Exchange Information Store and Exchange System Attendant services running:

```
$Computers = "ExchCAS01","ExchCAS02"
$Service = "MSExchangeIS","MSExchangeSA"
$Filter = @{
FilterScript = {$_.Status -eq "Running"}
}
$Select = @{
```

```
Property = "MachineName","Name","DisplayName"
}
$ServiceHash = @{
Name = $Service
ErrorAction = "SilentlyContinue"
}
foreach ($Computer in $Computers)
{
Get-Service @ServiceHash -ComputerName $Computer |
Where-Object @Filter | Select-Object @Select
}
```

```
MachineName      Name           DisplayName
-----------      ----           -----------
ExchCAS01        MSExchangeIS   Microsoft Exchange Information Store
ExchCAS01        MSExchangeSA   Microsoft Exchange System Attendant
ExchCAS02        MSExchangeIS   Microsoft Exchange Information Store
ExchCAS02        MSExchangeSA   Microsoft Exchange System Attendant
```

Listing Stopped Services That Are Set to Start Automatically

On many occasions, services may be set to start automatically, but fail to start. Unfortunately, the Get-Service cmdlet does not return information on the service start type. For this information, you need to use the Get-WmiObject cmdlet. The class you call is the Win32_Service class.

This class returns the service State and StartMode, among other properties. Those properties can be passed to the Filter parameter of the Get-WmiObject cmdlet to limit results to just services that are set to start automatically and are not running. The following example returns a list of services that are set to start automatically on the FileServer01 and FileServer02 servers and are not running:

```
$Computers = "FileServer01","FileServer02"
$WmiObject = @{
Class = "Win32_Service"
Filter = "StartMode='Auto' and State!='Running'"
}
foreach ($Computer in $Computers)
{
$Select = @{
Property = "SystemName","Name"
}
Get-WmiObject @WmiObject -ComputerName $Computer |
Select-Object @Select
}
```

```
SystemName                       Name
----------                       ----
FileServer01                     Ati External Event Utility
```

FileServer01	clr_optimization_v4.0.30319_32
FileServer01	clr_optimization_v4.0.30319_64
FileServer02	NetTcpActivator
FileServer02	sppsvc

Starting Stopped Services

The previous example shows which non-running services are set to run automatically. You can start services on remote servers with the StartService() method of the Win32_Service class. The following example extends the previous example to attempt to start all stopped services:

```
$Computers = "FileServer01","FileServer02"
$WmiObject = @{
Class = "Win32_Service"
Filter = "StartMode='Auto' and State!='Running'"
}
foreach ($Computer in $Computers)
{
foreach ($Svc in Get-WmiObject @WmiObject -ComputerName $Computer)
{
Write-Host "Starting the" $Svc.DisplayName "service on $Computer"
$Svc.StartService() | Out-Null
}
}
```

Setting Services to Disabled

Another method of the Win32_Service class is the ChangeStartMode() method. This method enables you to set a service to disabled, which will prevent it from starting. Suppose that you previously discovered that the service Windows Audio was running on one of your servers. Unneeded services provide a potential security problem, so you would probably want to disable and stop the Windows Audio service on that server. The following example accomplishes this task:

```
$ServiceObject = @{
Class = "Win32_Service"
Filter = "Name = 'AudioSrv'"
ComputerName = "DC01"
}
$Service = Get-WmiObject @ServiceObject
$Service.ChangeStartMode("Disabled")
$Service.StopService()
```

For more examples, which include waiting for the service to start as well as reporting on failures, see the book's website.

Managing Processes

Think of Windows processes as programs or specific parts of an program. For instance, an antivirus program might use several processes. Each processor on a server can run one process at a time. As the process is running, every other process is waiting for processor time.

A process that is not responding will, at best, stop a program from responding, and at worst, stop the entire server from responding. In this section, you learn how to discover and stop those processes.

Processes are managed with the `Get-Process`, `Stop-Process`, `Wait-Process`, `Debug-Process`, and `Start-Process` cmdlets. With the exception of `Get-Process`, these cmdlets manage processes on the local computer.

The `Get-Process` cmdlet supports the `ComputerName` parameter, so it does not require that remoting be enabled on the remote server. The other process cmdlets require that remoting is enabled on remote servers. As an alternative to enabling remoting, you can stop processes on remote servers with WMI. Both methods are covered in the section "Stopping Processes on Remote Servers."

Listing All Processes on Multiple Servers

The `Get-Process` cmdlet, when run without parameters, lists all processes on the local computer. To view processes on remote servers, you pass the server names to the `ComputerName` parameter. The default view that the `Get-Process` cmdlet returns does not include the computer name, so you will have to use the `Select-Object` cmdlets or one of the `Format-*` cmdlets to view the machine name onscreen, or pass the output through one of the `Export-*` cmdlets to save the data to disk. The following example returns all processes on the servers `FileServer01` and `FileServer02`:

```
$Process = @{
ComputerName = "FileServer01","FileServer02"
}
$Sort = @{
Property = "MachineName","ProcessName"
}
$Table = @{
Property = "MachineName","ProcessName","Id","NPM","PM","WS","VM"
AutoSize = $True
}
Get-Process @Process | Sort-Object @Sort | Format-Table @Table
```

Perhaps a more interesting exercise would be to list processes on remote servers that are not responding. One of the properties that the `Get-Process` cmdlet returns is the

`Responding` property. The following example returns which processes are not responding on the server `Server01`:

```
$Computer = "Server01"
$Process = @{
ComputerName = $Computer
}
$Filter = @{
FilterScript = {$_.Responding -ne $True}
}
Get-Process @Process | Where-Object @Filter
```

Handles	NPM(K)	PM(K)	WS(K)	VM(M)	CPU(s)	Id	ProcessName
965	13	2788	4940	45		496	csrss
192	13	19264	13400	58		568	csrss
404	34	20612	24344	342		1760	dfsrs
164	15	4440	8060	39		2068	dfssvc
5220	22171	314340	312252	349		1816	dns
444	29	48252	50488	154		4948	Dropbox

Stopping Processes on Remote Servers

Suppose you wanted to stop the `Dropbox` process from the previous example. If the process were running on the local computer, you could stop the process with the `Stop-Process` cmdlet, passing the process ID to the `Id` parameter as `Stop-Process -Id 4948`.

The `Stop-Process` cmdlet does not accept the `ComputerName` parameter, so you will need to use remoting to run the command on the remote server or use the `Get-WmiObject` cmdlet, which does accept the `ComputerName` parameter.

The following example stops the `Dropbox` process on the server `Server01` using the `Invoke-Command` cmdlet. This will only succeed on servers that have remoting enabled.

```
Invoke-Command -ComputerName Server01 -ScriptBlock {Stop-Process -Id 4948}
```

The `Get-WmiObject` cmdlet will work on any computer on which you have permission to run WMI queries. You call the `InvokeMethod()` method of the `Win32_Process` class to stop the process. The following example is the functional equivalent of using the `Invoke-Command` cmdlet in the previous example, rewritten to avoid the requirement for remoting:

```
$ProcessSplat = @{
Class = "Win32_Process"
Filter = "ProcessId = 4948"
ComputerName = "Server01"
}
(Get-WmiObject @ProcessSplat).InvokeMethod("Terminate", $null)
```

Certain processes will not allow you to stop them because they are required for Windows to function. In those cases, you would need to restart the server.

Note

You can also stop a process by name. I recommend using the process ID because each process has a unique ID, whereas you could have several processes with the same name. The examples shown in this section would fail if there were more than one process to stop. ■

Reading the Registry

Windows PowerShell includes a provider that enables you to read and write to the two most common registry hives on the local computer. With this provider, you can access the HKEY_Local_Machine and HKEY_Current_User registry hives as if they were a file system. *Registry hives* are a logical collection of keys, subkeys, and values within the registry.

You can also create your own provider to access the other registry hives. This is accomplished with the New-PSDrive cmdlet, passing the parameters Name, PSProvider, and Root. The following example creates the local provider named HKCR pointing to the Registry provider in the root HKEY_CLASSES_ROOT:

```
New-PSDrive -Name HKCR -PSProvider Registry -Root HKEY_CLASSES_ROOT
```

You can access the registry on a remote computer with the .NET classes Microsoft.Win32 .RegistryHive and Microsoft.Win32.RegistryKey. If you manage remote registries on an ongoing basis, you may want to create custom type accelerators for these classes. *Type accelerators* are a shortcut to an underlying .NET type name. The type accelerator [string] points to the .NET type System.String. Using a type accelerator allows you to reference the underlying type without typing the type name, or even necessarily knowing the name. The example in Listing 9-1 creates these type accelerators. You can either run the code in Listing 9-1 each time you work with remote registry, or put the code in your $Profile script so that it is available every time you load Windows PowerShell. The examples in this chapter use these type accelerators.

LISTING 9-1

Creating Type Accelerators for Registry Access

```
$accelerators = [type]::gettype("System.Management.Automation.TypeAccelerators")
$acceleratorRegHive = [type]::gettype("Microsoft.Win32.RegistryHive")
$acceleratorRegKey = [type]::gettype("Microsoft.Win32.RegistryKey")
$accelerators::Add("reghive", $acceleratorRegHive)
$accelerators::Add("regkey", $acceleratorRegKey)
```

You could also read remote registry values using the Invoke-Command cmdlet, if the remote servers have remoting enabled.

Using the Registry Provider Locally

As mentioned, you can read a local registry key by accessing the registry provider directly. The two included providers (HKLM and HKCU) can be accessed with the Set-Location cmdlet, passing the parameter Path. Once you have set the location to the registry key of your choice, you retrieve a value with the Get-ItemProperty cmdlet, passing the Path parameter.

The following example returns which version of Windows PowerShell is installed on the local computer:

```
Set-Location -Path HKLM:\SOFTWARE\Microsoft\PowerShell\1\PowerShellEngine
(Get-ItemProperty -Path .).PowerShellVersion
```

You could also gather the data without changing location to the registry path, by passing that information to the Path parameter of the Get-ItemProperty cmdlet. The following example shows this. The example uses the $Path variable to hold the name of the registry key, and passes the key to the Path parameter of the Get-ItemProperty cmdlet:

```
$Path = "HKLM:\SOFTWARE\Microsoft\PowerShell\1\PowerShellEngine"
(Get-ItemProperty -Path $Path).PowerShellVersion
```

Using Microsoft.Win32.RegistryHive Remotely

As previously mentioned, you read a registry value remotely with the .NET classes Microsoft.Win32.RegistryHive and Microsoft.Win32.RegistryKey. To read the value of a registry key, you first have to create a Microsoft.Win32.RegistryHive value pointing to the hive you are interested in. This can be ClassesRoot, CurrentUser, LocalMachine, Users, or PerformanceData.

Once you have your hive object, you open the remote hive with the OpenRemoteBaseKey() method of the Microsoft.Win32.RegistryKey class. This method takes the hive and computer name as parameters. Once you have the remote hive open, you open the subkey and read the value with the OpenSubKey() and GetValue() methods of the Microsoft .Win32.RegistryKey class, respectively.

The following example extends the previous example to show which version of Windows PowerShell is installed on the servers FileServer01 and FileServer02. This example uses the custom type accelerators created in Listing 9-1. If you have not loaded them, you will need to do that before running the example.

```
foreach ($Server in "FileServer01","FileServer02")
{
  $Version = $null
  $Message = $null
  $keyName = "SOFTWARE\Microsoft\PowerShell\1\PowerShellEngine"
  $valueName = "PowerShellVersion"
  $regHive = [reghive]"LocalMachine"
  try
```

```
  {
    $regKey = [regkey]::OpenRemoteBaseKey($regHive,$Server)
  }
  catch
  {
    $Message = "$Server cannot be contacted. Is it online?"
  }
  if ($Message -eq $null)
  {
    try
    {
      $Version = ($regKey.OpenSubKey($keyName)).GetValue($ValueName)
      $Message = "$Server has version $Version of Windows PowerShell"
    }
    catch
    {
      $Message = "$Server does not seem to have Windows PowerShell"
    }
  }
  Write-Output $Message
}
```

```
FileServer01 has version 2.0 of Windows PowerShell
FileServer02 does not seem to have Windows PowerShell
```

Setting Registry Values

Setting registry values is more complex than reading them, because you need to specify the type of value you are setting. Possible value types are listed in Table 9-1.

TABLE 9-1

Registry Value Types

ItemType	DataType	Description
String	REG_SZ	A string
ExpandString	REG_EXPAND_SZ	A string with environment variables that are resolved when invoked
Binary	REG_BINARY	Binary values
Dword	REG_DWORD	Numeric values
MultiString	REG_MULTI_SZ	Text of several lines
Qword	REG_QWORD	64-bit numeric values

Besides setting values for existing registry keys, Windows PowerShell provides methods to create new registry keys.

Locally Using the Registry Provider

Creating a new key on the local computer can be accomplished with the `New-Item` cmdlet, passing the `Path` and `ItemType` parameters. Registry keys are treated as directories by the built-in registry providers. Thus, the item type value is `Directory`. The following example creates the new key `PowerShellBible` in the `Software` key of the `HKEY_Local_Machine` hive:

```
New-Item -ItemType Directory -Path "HKLM:\Software\PowerShellBible"
```

Note
You may need to run Windows PowerShell in an elevated session to create a new registry key. ■

The new key contains an empty default value. If you want to create a new key with subkeys, you need to create it from the top level down. The following example creates the registry keys as shown under the previously created `PowerShellBible` key. If you attempted to create the second key first, the command would fail.

```
New-Item -ItemType Directory -Path "HKLM:\Software\PowerShellBible\First"
New-Item -ItemType Directory -Path "HKLM:\Software\PowerShellBible\First\Second"
```

Creating a registry value locally is accomplished with the `Set-ItemProperty` cmdlet, passing the `Path`, `Name`, `Type`, and `Value` parameters. The following example creates the new values as shown:

```
$Path = "HKLM:\Software\PowerShellBible"
Set-ItemProperty -Path $Path -Name "Example1" -Value 123 -Type Dword
Set-ItemProperty -Path $Path -Name "Example2" -Value "Test" -Type String
```

You modify an existing value in the same manner as creating a new value. Suppose you realized that the `Example1` value was supposed to be a string value. The following example changes the `Dword` value `123` to a `String` value of `q123`:

```
$Path = "HKLM:\Software\PowerShellBible"
Set-ItemProperty -Path $Path -Name "Example1" -Value "q123" -Type String
```

Remotely Using Microsoft.Win32.RegistryHive

Creating a new key on a remote computer can be accomplished with the .NET classes `Microsoft.Win32.RegistryHive` and `Microsoft.Win32.RegistryKey`. Examples shown use the custom type accelerators shown in Listing 9-1.

Once again, if remoting is enabled on the remote computers, you can create registry keys and values with the `Invoke-Command` cmdlet. The `Invoke-Command` cmdlet has the benefit of accepting credentials, which allows you to run Windows PowerShell as a nonprivileged user and invoke commands as an administrator.

The first step in creating a new key or value with the .NET classes is opening the parent key in read-write mode. You do this with the `OpenSubKey()` method of the `Microsoft.Win32.RegistryKey` class. This method has an overload that accepts a Boolean value as its second parameter. When this value is set to `$True`, the key is opened in read-write mode.

Note

An overload allows a programmer to have multiple methods with the same name that accept varying types or quantities of arguments. In this case, you can call the `OpenSubKey()` method with one, two, or three parameters. The first parameter is a string, and the second can be a `Boolean` as we used, or a `RegistryKeyPermissionCheck` object. The third parameter would be a `RegistryRights` object. ■

Creating a new key is accomplished with the `CreateSubKey()` method of the `Microsoft.Win32.RegistryKey` class, and creating a value is accomplished with the `SetValue()` method of the `Microsoft.Win32.RegistryKey` class. If not specified, the `SetValue()` method attempts to infer the value type.

The following example creates the new key `PowerShellBible` in the `Software` key of the `HKEY_Local_Machine` hive, and adds the values named `Example1` and `Example2` on both servers listed:

```
foreach ($Server in "FileServer01","FileServer02")
{
$keyName = "SOFTWARE"
$newKeyName = "PowerShellBible"
$value1Name = "Example1"
$value2Name = "Example2"
$value1 = 123
$value2 = "Test"
$value1Type = "Dword"
$value2Type = "String"
$regHive = [reghive]"LocalMachine"
$regKey = [regkey]::OpenRemoteBaseKey($regHive,$Server)
$key = $regKey.OpenSubKey($keyName,$True)
$key.CreateSubKey($newKeyName)
$key = $regKey.OpenSubKey("$keyName\$newKeyName",$True)
$key.SetValue($value1Name, $value1, $value1Type)
$key.SetValue($value2Name, $value2, $value2Type)
}
```

Validating Network Configuration on Remote Servers

Network configuration on remote servers can be retrieved with the `Win32_NetworkAdapterConfiguration` class of the `Get-WmiObject` cmdlet. By default, this class returns information on all network adapters on the computer. You can filter the returned data to only include adapters where IP is enabled to cut down on the extra data. The following example retrieves information on each enabled adapter on the server `Exch2010`:

```
$WmiObject = @{
Class = "Win32_NetworkAdapterConfiguration"
ComputerName = "Exch2010"
Filter = "IPEnabled = 'true'"
#The filter acts on the string 'true', not the
#Boolean $True.
}
Get-WmiObject @WmiObject
DHCPEnabled      : False
IPAddress        : {192.168.1.10, fe80::acee:78b3:604e:5b}
DefaultIPGateway : {192.168.1.1}
DNSDomain        :
ServiceName      : VMSMP
Description      : External
Index            : 16
```

As you can see, the information returned in the default view is rather sparse. Piping the output through the `Format-List` cmdlet, passing the `Property` parameter with the value of * returns all properties of each network adapter. On the network adapter on my server, this is 71 properties. Some of the properties, like the `DNSDomain` above, will be empty.

Retrieving the DNS Settings

DNS settings are stored in the properties of the `Win32_NetworkAdapterConfiguration` class. The following example shows the DNS settings for the server `Exch2010`:

```
$WmiObject = @{
Class = "Win32_NetworkAdapterConfiguration"
ComputerName = "Exch2010"
Filter = "IPEnabled = 'true'"
}
Get-WmiObject @WmiObject | Format-List -Property dns*
```

Validating That Servers Use the Same DNS Settings

You can build on the previous example to gather DNS settings for a group of servers in a `foreach` loop. Because there may be multiple network adapters in each server, the network adapters are also handled in a `foreach` loop. Finally, the `DNSDomainSuffixSearchOrder` and `DNSServerSearchOrder` properties are arrays that may have multiple values, so you cast those to a string type, and replace spaces with a semicolon and a space to make them more readable. This also allows those properties to be exported to a `.csv` file. The following example returns a list of the DNS settings for the servers `Exch2010`, `fileServer01`, and `PrintServer23`:

```
$Servers = "Exch2010","fileServer01","PrintServer23"
$ServerDNS = @()
```

```
foreach ($Server in $Servers)
{
$WmiObject = @{
Class = "Win32_NetworkAdapterConfiguration"
ComputerName = $Server
Filter = "IPEnabled = 'true'"
}
$DnsSettings = @(Get-WmiObject @WmiObject)
foreach ($DnsSetting in $DnsSettings)
{
$Dns = "" | Select-Object -Property DNSHostName, DNSDomain,
DNSDomainSuffixSearchOrder, DNSEnabledForWINSResolution,
DNSServerSearchOrder, DomainDNSRegistrationEnabled,
FullDNSRegistrationEnabled
$TempSuffixSearch = [string]$DnsSetting.DNSDomainSuffixSearchOrder
$TempServerSearch = [string]$DnsSetting.DNSServerSearchOrder
$Dns.DNSHostName = $DnsSetting.DNSHostName
$Dns.DNSDomain = $DnsSetting.DNSDomain
$Dns.DNSDomainSuffixSearchOrder = $TempSuffixSearch.Replace(" ","; ")
$Dns.DNSEnabledForWINSResolution = $DnsSetting.DNSEnabledForWINSResolution
$Dns.DNSServerSearchOrder = $TempServerSearch.Replace(" ","; ")
$Dns.DomainDNSRegistrationEnabled = $DnsSetting.DomainDNSRegistrationEnabled
$Dns.FullDNSRegistrationEnabled = $DnsSetting.FullDNSRegistrationEnabled
$ServerDNS += $Dns
}
}
$ServerDNS
```

This example could easily be extended to save the results to a file or to gather DNS settings for more servers.

Changing the Network Configuration

Changing the network configuration on remote servers can be accomplished with a combination of the Get-WmiObject and Invoke-WmiMethod cmdlets.

Caution

Care should be taken because you can easily cause a server to lose connection to the network by passing incorrect parameters, and the server may momentarily drop the network connection while changes take effect. ∎

Modifying the DNS Suffix Search Order

Modifying the DNS suffix search order is accomplished with the Invoke-WmiMethod cmdlet, passing the ComputerName, Class, Name, and ArgumentList parameters. The class used is the Win32_NetworkAdapterConfiguration class. The ArgumentList parameter requires an array of objects for the first value, and a $null for the second value. The method invoked is the SetDNSSuffixSearchOrder() method.

Note

The methods of the `Win32_NetworkAdapterConfiguration` class are documented at `http://msdn`
`.microsoft.com/en-us/library/aa394217(v=VS.85).aspx`. ∎

The following example sets the DNS suffix search order to `contoso.com`, `contoso.co.us`,
and the previous DNS suffix search order, in that order:

```
$WmiObject = @{
ComputerName = "Exch2010"
Class = "Win32_NetworkAdapterConfiguration"
}
$Nics = @(Get-WmiObject @WmiObject -Filter "IPEnabled = 'true'")
foreach ($Nic in $Nics)
{
$OldSuffix = $Nic.DNSDomainSuffixSearchOrder
$Suffix = "contoso.com", "contoso.co.us" + $OldSuffix
$InvokeObject = @{
Name = "SetDNSSuffixSearchOrder"
ArgumentList = @($Suffix), $null
}
Invoke-WmiMethod @WmiObject @InvokeObject
}
```

Modifying the Server's IP Address

Modifying an IP address can be accomplished by creating an object reference to the
network interface card with the `Win32_NetworkAdapterConfiguration` class of the
`Get-WmiObject` cmdlet, and calling the `EnableStatic()` method of that object.
The following example modifies the third octet of each IPv4 address to a 0. The third
octet of each DNS server IP address will also be changed to a 0.

```
$WmiObject = @{
ComputerName = "Exch2010"
Class = "Win32_NetworkAdapterConfiguration"
}
$ThirdOctet = 0
$NewDns = @()
$Nics = @(Get-WmiObject @WmiObject -Filter "IPEnabled = 'true'")
foreach ($Nic in $Nics)
{
[ipaddress]$OldIP = $($Nic.IPAddress -match "^\d.\d.\d.\d")
$NewIp = $OldIP.GetAddressBytes()[0..1] -join "."
# the -join operator concatenates strings in the order
# in which they appear. The "." causes them to be
# delimited by a dot as an IP address would be.
$NewIp = $NewIp, $ThirdOctet,$OldIP.GetAddressBytes()[3] -join "."
$Subnet = $Nic.IPSubnet[0].ToString()
$OldDNS = @($nic.DNSServerSearchOrder)
foreach ($Dns in $OldDNS)
```

```
{
[ipaddress]$InDns = $Dns
$OutDns = $InDns.GetAddressBytes()[0..1] -join "."
$OutDns = $OutDns, $ThirdOctet,$InDns.GetAddressBytes()[3] -join "."
$NewDns += $OutDns
}
$Nic.SetDNSServerSearchOrder($NewDns)
$Nic.EnableStatic($NewIp,$Subnet)
}
```

Gathering Data from Performance Counters

Microsoft Windows operating systems and applications provide performance counters designed to provide information on the health or usage of the application or operating system. Hundreds of performance counters are available on any given system. Windows PowerShell includes the `Get-Counter` cmdlet, which is designed to retrieve performance counter data from the local and remote computers. Because so many counters are available on any given computer, the `Get-Counter` cmdlet includes the `ListSet` parameter, which allows you to determine counters that may be of importance in a given situation. The following example shows which counter sets that target the processor are available on the local computer:

```
Get-Counter -ListSet "Processor*" | Select-Object -Property CounterSetName
CounterSetName
--------------

Processor Information
Processor
Processor Performance
```

Now that you know that the local computer includes the counter set `Processor`, you can see which counters that set includes by once again calling the `Get-Counter` cmdlet. This time, you target the specific set you are interested in and pipe the output through the `Select-Object` cmdlet to list just the counters.

```
Get-Counter -ListSet "Processor" | Select-Object -Expand Counter
\Processor(*)\% Processor Time
\Processor(*)\% User Time
\Processor(*)\% Privileged Time
\Processor(*)\Interrupts/sec
...
```

Finally, you can start gathering data from a counter. In this case, you will be gathering data from the `\Processor(*)\% User Time` counter. Once again, this is accomplished with the `Get-Counter` cmdlet, passing the `Counter` parameter. When run with just the `Counter` parameter, the `Get-Counter` cmdlet returns only one set of data. Further parameters enable you to set the `SampleInterval` and `MaxSamples` or to specify that the cmdlet gathers data continuously using the `Continuous` switch parameter. The following example gathers data from the local computer's `\Processor(*)\% User Time` counter every 3 seconds for 10 samples:

```
$Counter = @{
Counter = "\Processor(*)\% User Time"
SampleInterval = 3
MaxSamples = 10
}
Get-Counter @Counter
```

The parameter `ComputerName` enables you to gather data from remote computers. The following example modifies the previous example to retrieve the `\Processor(*)\% User Time` counter every 3 seconds for 10 samples from the server `Exch2010`:

```
$Counter = @{
Counter = "\Processor(*)\% User Time"
SampleInterval = 3
MaxSamples = 10
ComputerName = "Exch2010"
}
Get-Counter @Counter
```

You can use the `ListSet` parameter along with the `ComputerName` parameter to see which counters are available on a remote computer.

Modifying Regional Settings on Multiple Computers

Regional settings affect how the server processes numbers, dates, currency, keyboard input, and so on. Windows operating systems include predefined settings for most countries. As you can imagine, regional settings can be very complex. The regional settings are stored in the registry in the `HKEY_Current_User` hive, under the `Control Panel` key in the `International` subkey. Perhaps the simplest method of modifying regional settings on remote computers is copying valid settings from one computer to another. This can be easily accomplished with WMI. The following example copies the regional settings from `WinDC01` to `WinDC02` and `WinDC03`:

```
$hive ="CurrentUser"
$keyName = "Control Panel\International"
$Computers = "WinDC02", "WinDC03"
$Source = "WinDC01"
$Hive = [Microsoft.Win32.RegistryHive]$hive
```

```
$SourceKey = [Microsoft.Win32.RegistryKey]::OpenRemoteBaseKey($Hive,$Source)
$SourceSubkey = $SourceKey.OpenSubKey($keyName)
$valueNames = $SourceSubkey.GetValueNames()
Foreach ($Computer in $Computers)
{
$regHive = [Microsoft.Win32.RegistryHive]$hive
$regKey = [Microsoft.Win32.RegistryKey]::OpenRemoteBaseKey($regHive,$Computer)
$Subkey = $regKey.OpenSubKey($keyName,$True)
foreach ($valueName in $valueNames)
{
$SourceValue = $SourceSubkey.GetValue($valueName)
$Subkey.SetValue($valueName,$SourceValue)
}
}
```

Managing Local Accounts

Local accounts can be managed with the DirectoryEntry class of the System
.DirectoryServices namespace. Windows PowerShell includes the [adsi] type
accelerator for this class.

Modifying Local Users and Groups

Modifying local users and groups can be accomplished by creating an object pointing to
the user or group using the [adsi] type accelerator. Modifications to user accounts are
saved to the computer by calling the SetInfo() method of the user object. Modifications to
groups are written to the computer immediately.

Note
When you use a type accelerator, you enclose it in square brackets. ■

Once you have created a group object, you add members to the group by calling the Add()
method of the object. Group members can be either a local or domain user. A user can be
removed from a local group with the Remove() method of the group object. The following
example adds the domain user Contoso\karlm to the Backup Operators group on the
server FileServer01:

```
$Computer = "FileServer01"
$Member = "karlm"
$Domain = "Contoso"
$GroupName = "Backup Operators"
([ADSI]"WinNT://$Computer/$GroupName,group").Add("WinNT://$Domain/$Member")
```

Modifying the final line to remove the domain reference adds a local user to the group. This is shown in the following example:

```
$Computer = "FileServer01"
$Member = "Operator"
$GroupName = "Backup Operators"
([ADSI]"WinNT://$Computer/$GroupName,group").Add("WinNT://$Member")
```

You can also add a domain group to a local group by replacing the user's name with the group name in the $Member variable.

Removing users from local groups requires exactly the same syntax as adding users. The only difference is that the Remove() method is called. The following example removes the user contoso\bartb from the local group Power Users on the server Exch2010:

```
$Computer = "Exch2010"
$Member = "bartb"
$Domain = "Contoso"
$GroupName = "Power Users"
([ADSI]"WinNT://$Computer/$GroupName,group").Remove("WinNT://$Domain/$Member")
```

You modify a user account much the same as you modify a group. As a security precaution, many organizations rename the built-in administrator account to attempt to prevent unauthorized access. The following example renames the Administrator account on the server FileServer01 to ServerAdmin, sets the description of the account to Local Administrative User, and sets the password to never expire. This final step is accomplished by modifying the UserFlags property of the user object. The UserFlags property is modified by using the inclusive bitwise OR operator –bor. Notice that the Rename() method must be called before the other methods.

```
$Computer = "FileServer01"
$UserName = "Administrator"
$DONT_EXPIRE_PASSWD = 0x10000
#Use the symbolic constant "DONT_EXPIRE_PASSWD" as it is
#easier to see what we are doing than the hexadecimal version
$User = ([ADSI]"WinNT://$Computer/$UserName")
$User.Rename("ServerAdmin")
$User.Description = "Local Administrative User"
$User.UserFlags = $User.UserFlags.Value -bor $DONT_EXPIRE_PASSWD
$User.SetInfo()
```

Note

For more information on the various user flags, see http://msdn.microsoft.com/en-us/library/ aa772300%28v=VS.85%29.aspx. ∎

Creating and Deleting Local Users and Groups

Creating and deleting local users and groups can be accomplished with the [adsi] type accelerator in much the same manner as modifying existing accounts. The methods used are the `Create()` and `Remove()` methods. The `Create()` method requires that the `SetInfo()` method be called directly afterward, because the `Create()` method creates the object only in memory.

The following example creates the new group WMI Users on the computer Exch2010, and sets the description to WMI Users for the server. Notice the seemingly redundant use of the `Setinfo()` method. This is required because the object does not exist on the computer until after the initial `SetInfo()` call.

```
$Computer = "Exch2010"
$Group = ([ADSI]"WinNT://$Computer").Create("Group", "WMI Users")
$Group.SetInfo()
$Group.Description = "WMI Users for the server"
$Group.SetInfo()
```

The following example creates the new user wmiaccount on the server Exch2010 and sets the password, description, and full name as indicated:

```
$Computer = "Exch2010"
$User = ([ADSI]"WinNT://$Computer").Create("User", "wmiaccount")
$User.SetPassword("P@ssw0rdZero")
$User.SetInfo()
$User.Description = "WMI User for the server"
$User.FullName = "WMI User"
$User.SetInfo()
```

Local users and groups are considered children of the computer, so when removing these accounts, you reference the `Children` property of the computer. Unlike the `Create()` method, the `Remove()` method removes the object from the computer directly; there is no need to call the `SetInfo()` method. The following two examples remove the local user wmiaccount and group WMI Users from the computer Exch2010:

```
$Computer = "Exch2010"
$User = "wmiaccount"
([ADSI]"WinNT://$Computer,computer").Children.Remove("WinNT://$Computer/$User")
$Computer = "Exch2010"
$Group = "Wmi Users"
([ADSI]"WinNT://$Computer,computer").Children.Remove("WinNT://$Computer/$Group")
```

Configuring Remote DCOM

The Distributed Component Object Model (DCOM) allows communication between objects on different computers on a LAN or WAN, or over the Internet. Accessing WMI on remote computers requires that you have the proper permissions to use DCOM and WMI on the remote computer.

Viewing DCOM Permissions

You can view DCOM permissions on a local computer or on a remote computer by querying a registry key. The key is in the HKEY_Local_Machine hive, in the path Software\ Microsoft\Ole, and is a binary value known as MachineLaunchRestriction. Because the value is a binary value, you cannot merely read the value and make sense of it. Locally, the cmdlet Get-ItemProperty retrieves the data; however, you will need to convert it to a Win32 security descriptor using the BinarySDToWin32SD() method of the Win32_SecurityDescriptorHelper class, which is part of the System.Management .ManagementClass class. The following example returns the binary data in the MachineLaunchRestriction value on the local machine. As you can see from the small sample shown, the data returned is a seemingly meaningless bunch of numbers.

```
(Get-ItemProperty -Path HKLM:\SOFTWARE\Microsoft\Ole\).MachineLaunchRestriction
1
0
4
128
120
...
```

Because viewing the DCOM permissions is accomplished by reading the registry, and reading a registry remotely can be accomplished with the Get-WmiObject cmdlet, I will use this method in the following examples, which will work locally or remotely. The following simple example expands on the previous example, converting the binary value in MachineLaunchRestriction to a Win32 security descriptor. This example returns only which accounts have permission to access DCOM on the server Server01. It does not return what specific permissions those accounts have.

```
$strcomputer = "Server01"
$ConverterObject = @{
TypeName = "System.Management.ManagementClass"
ArgumentList = "Win32_SecurityDescriptorHelper"
}
$Reg = [WMIClass]"\\$strcomputer\root\default:StdRegProv"
$DCOM = $Reg.GetBinaryValue(2147483650,`
"software\microsoft\ole","MachineLaunchRestriction").uValue
$Converter = New-Object @ConverterObject
$DCOMDescriptor = ($Converter.BinarySDToWin32SD($DCOM)).Descriptor
foreach ($DACL in $DCOMDescriptor.dacl)
{
$Permission = ($DACL.Trustee).Name
Write-Output "$Permission has DCOM permission on $strcomputer"
}
```

You can display the specific DCOM access permissions each account has by parsing the discretionary access control list (DACL) objects returned from the previous example. These DACLs contain an access mask, which will need to be converted from the binary form to be readable. You can use a hashtable to hold the possible values, and use Windows PowerShell's bitwise and comparison operator to convert the Win32 security descriptor. The hashtable looks like this:

```
$DCOMConversion = @{}
$DCOMConversion.Add(0x2,"Local Launch")
$DCOMConversion.Add(0x4,"Remote Launch")
$DCOMConversion.Add(0x8,"Local Activation")
$DCOMConversion.Add(0x10,"Remote Activation")
```

An individual DACL access mask may be 19. Using the bitwise and operator would show that the account has `Remote Activation` and `Local Launch` permissions to DCOM. The typical DCOM security descriptor will have multiple DACLs listed. As you can see in the previous example, you use a loop to gather information on each DACL.

Note

If you need a refresher on the bitwise and comparison operator, see the help topic `Get-Help about_Comparison_Operators`. ∎

The script in Listing 9-2 returns the accounts that have DCOM and WMI permission and the specific permission granted on a computer of your choosing. The script, when run without parameters, returns data for the local computer. When run with the optional `Computer` parameter, the script returns DCOM permissions for the remote computer specified.

LISTING 9-2

Get-DCOMPermission.ps1

```
Param (
[string] $Computer = ".",
[System.Management.Automation.PSCredential] $Credential = $null
)
$DCOMConversion = @{}
$DCOMConversion.Add(0x2,"Local Launch")
$DCOMConversion.Add(0x4,"Remote Launch")
$DCOMConversion.Add(0x8,"Local Activation")
$DCOMConversion.Add(0x10,"Remote Activation")
$WMIConversion = @{}
$WMIConversion.Add(0x1,"Enable")
$WMIConversion.Add(0x4,"Full Write")
$WMIConversion.Add(0x2,"Method Execute")
$WMIConversion.Add(0x8,"Partial Write Rep")
$WMIConversion.Add(0x20,"Remote Enable")
$WMIConversion.Add(0x10,"Write Provider")
$WMIConversion.Add(0x20000,"Read Control")
$WMIConversion.Add(0x40000,"Write Dac")
```

continues

LISTING 9-2   *(continued)*

```
$ConverterObject = @{
TypeName = "System.Management.ManagementClass"
ArgumentList = "Win32_SecurityDescriptorHelper"
}
$ACLObject = @{
Property = "Computer","Name","Type","Permission"
}
$WmiObject = @{
ComputerName = "$Computer"
Namespace = "root/cimv2"
Class = "__SystemSecurity"
}
if ($Credential)
{
$Object = @{
List = $True
Namespace = "root\default"
ComputerName = $Computer
Credential = $Credential
}
$Filter = @{
FilterScript = {$_.name -eq "StdRegProv"}
}
$Reg = Get-WmiObject @Object | Where-Object @Filter
$Security = Get-WmiObject @WmiObject -Credential $Credential
}
else
{
$Reg = [WMIClass]"\\$Computer\root\default:StdRegProv"
$Security = Get-WmiObject @WmiObject
}
$DCOM = $Reg.GetBinaryValue(
2147483650,"software\microsoft\ole",
"MachineLaunchRestriction").uValue
$Converter = New-Object @ConverterObject
$binarySD = @($null)
$result = $Security.PsBase.InvokeMethod("GetSD",$binarySD)
$DCOMDescriptor = ($Converter.BinarySDToWin32SD($DCOM)).Descriptor
$WMIDescriptor = ($converter.BinarySDToWin32SD($binarySD[0])).Descriptor
$RightsCollection = @()
foreach ($DCOMDACL in $DCOMDescriptor.dacl)
{
if ($DCOMDACL.AceType -eq 0)
{
$Perms = @()
```

```
foreach ($key in $DCOMConversion.keys)
{
if ($DCOMDACL.AccessMask -band $key)
{
$Perms += $DCOMConversion[$key]
}
}
$Perm = ($Perms | ForEach-Object -Process {$_.ToString()}) -join ","
$Permission = ($DCOMDACL.Trustee).Name
$PermsObject = "" | Select-Object @ACLObject
$PermsObject.Computer = $Computer
$PermsObject.Name = ($DCOMDACL.Trustee).Name
$PermsObject.Type = "DCOM"
$PermsObject.Permission = $Perm
$RightsCollection += $PermsObject
}
}
foreach ($DACL in $WMIDescriptor.dacl)
{
if ($DACL.AceFlags -eq 0)
{
$Perms = @()
foreach ($key in $WmiConversion.keys)
{
if ($DACL.AccessMask -band $key)
{
$Perms += $WMIConversion[$key]
}
}
$Perm = ($Perms | ForEach-Object -Process {$_.ToString()}) -join ","
$PermsObject.Computer = $Computer
$PermsObject.Name = ($DACL.Trustee).Name
$PermsObject.Type = "WMI"
$PermsObject.Permission = $Perm
$RightsCollection += $PermsObject
}
}
Return $RightsCollection
```

If you need to pass credentials to the remote computer, you can use the optional Credential parameter. The following example retrieves the DCOM permissions from the computer Server01 using the credentials of the user contoso\johnb:

```
Get-Credential -Credential contoso\johnb
.\Get-DCOMPermission.ps1 -Computer "Server01" -Credential $cred
```

The following example retrieves the DCOM permissions from the computer `Mailbox01` using the credentials of the current user:

```
.\Get-DCOMPermission.ps1 -Computer "Mailbox01"
```

Granting a Domain User Remote DCOM Access

By default, DCOM is enabled for members of the local administrators group. Running scripts with this level of permission could provide a huge security risk. Granting a domain user account remote DCOM access allows data gathering without exposing the servers to this security risk.

The script in Listing 9-3 configures DCOM and WMI permissions on the server `Exch2010` to allow the domain user `contoso\burtb` to run WMI queries in the `root\cimv2` namespace and perform other tasks via remote DCOM. This example could easily be modified to provide WMI access to other namespaces and to operate on multiple computers. This example requires that the type accelerators from Listing 9-1 be loaded prior to running the example.

LISTING 9-3

Set-DCOMPermission Script

```
function Get-Sid
{
Param (
$DSIdentity
)
$ID = New-Object -TypeName System.Security.Principal.NTAccount($DSIdentity)
return $ID.Translate([System.Security.Principal.SecurityIdentifier]).toString()
}
$Server = "Exch2010"
$regHive = [reghive]"LocalMachine"
$sid = Get-Sid "contoso\burtb"
$keyName = "software\microsoft\ole"
$ValueName = "MachineLaunchRestriction"
$SDDL = "A;;CCWP;;;$sid"
$DCOMSDDL = "A;;CCDCRP;;;$sid"
$regKey = [regkey]::OpenRemoteBaseKey($regHive,$Server)
$DCOMKey = $regKey.OpenSubKey($keyName,$True)
$DCOM = $DCOMKey.GetValue($ValueName)
$SecurityObject = @{
ComputerName = $Server
Namespace = "root/cimv2"
Class = "__SystemSecurity"
}
$Security = Get-WmiObject @SecurityObject
$ConverterObject = @{
```

```
TypeName = "System.Management.ManagementClass"
ArgumentList = "Win32_SecurityDescriptorHelper"
}
$Converter = New-Object @ConverterObject
$binarySD = @($null)
$result = $security.PsBase.InvokeMethod("GetSD",$binarySD)
$outsddl = $converter.BinarySDToSDDL($binarySD[0])
$outDCOMSDDL = $converter.BinarySDToSDDL($DCOM)
$newSDDL = $outsddl.SDDL += "(" + $SDDL + ")"
$newDCOMSDDL = $outDCOMSDDL.SDDL += "(" + $DCOMSDDL + ")"
$WMIbinarySD = $converter.SDDLToBinarySD($newSDDL)
$WMIconvertedPermissions = ,$WMIbinarySD.BinarySD
$DCOMbinarySD = $converter.SDDLToBinarySD($newDCOMSDDL)
$DCOMconvertedPermissions = ,$DCOMbinarySD.BinarySD
$result = $security.PsBase.InvokeMethod("SetSD",$WMIconvertedPermissions)
$DCOMKey.SetValue($ValueName, $DCOMbinarySD.binarySD)
```

Summary

In this chapter, you learned to manage Windows services and processes locally and remotely. You examined how to read and write to the registry on the local computer as well as remote computers. You examined and modified network settings, discovered and retrieved performance counters, and extended your knowledge of the registry to allow you to modify regional settings on remote computers. You learned to manage local groups and users on remote computers. Finally, you also examined DCOM permissions on the local and remote computers.

In the next chapter, you work with Active Directory. You learn the prerequisites for installing the module. Once your computer meets the requirements, you load the module and learn to query Active Directory objects. You administer users and groups, and manage service accounts and organizational units. You also examine password policies.

Managing Active Directory

When Active Directory was released with Windows Server
2000, it was immediately obvious that the GUI would not
be enough for administrators. A series of command-line
tools, resource kits, and even a COM scripting interface were released
over the years to help people automate their tasks. Activities such as
cleaning up stale objects, moving objects that meet specific criteria
between containers, bulk importing new users from other feeds,
or exporting data for reporting purposes are just a few of the many
types of tasks that make great candidates for automation. Although
the command-line tools have existed for years, it is no surprise that
administrators who deal with Active Directory day to day were some
of the earliest adopters of Windows PowerShell.

Windows PowerShell 1.0 was released with a type accelerator for
the COM interface known as the Active Directory Scripting Interface
(ADSI) in order to provide immediate scripting support for Active
Directory within Windows PowerShell. Though ADSI and the
underlying .NET classes that manage Active Directory provide a
workable solution, it is far from being Windows PowerShell-centric.
The interface does not have easy-to-use cmdlet names that follow the
verb-noun syntax, it does not offer a Windows PowerShell provider,
it does not have any native pipeline support, and it requires you to
understand the syntax and inner workings of ADSI. It was obvious that
these flaws created a gap in the Windows PowerShell-Active Directory
story. Fortunately for the Windows PowerShell community, this gap
was filled by the ActiveRoles Management Shell from Quest software,
which could not only manage Active Directory, but could interface with
Quest's ActiveRoles Server to provide additional functionality. This
shell, also known affectionately by administrators as the "Quest tools,"
has become the standard snap-in for managing Active Directory with
Windows PowerShell.

IN THIS CHAPTER

**Installing Remote Server
Administration Tools and
cmdlets**

**Finding objects in Active
Directory**

Managing users and groups

**Manipulating objects and
organizational units**

Scripting password policies

**Using the ActiveRoles
Management Shell**

With the release of Windows Server 2008 R2, Microsoft has finally provided its own set of cmdlets and a provider that enables you to manage Active Directory. This chapter focuses on using these newer cmdlets with only a small section dedicated to the ActiveRoles Management Shell.

Note

All three of the methods of managing Active Directory with Windows PowerShell are worth learning. Each has advantages and disadvantages. Unfortunately, covering all three methods would require a complete book. In order to provide focus for this chapter, we only look at one of the three methods in detail. Because Active Directory is a Microsoft product, it makes sense to use the Microsoft module as the method of choice. As you will soon see, strict requirements make these cmdlets unusable in certain Active Directory environments; it's at least important to know that the ActiveRoles Management Shell exists for this reason. The end of this chapter provides a brief glance at how it is used. ∎

Installing and Using the Cmdlets

The Active Directory cmdlets come within a module. The method for installing it differs depending on whether you are using a client or server version of Microsoft Windows. Before doing anything, however, it's important to understand the prerequisites for the computer on which the module is getting installed and for Active Directory.

Prerequisites

The `ActiveDirectory` module can be installed on:

- Windows Server 2008 R2 Standard
- Windows Server 2008 R2 Enterprise
- Windows Server 2008 R2 Datacenter
- Windows 7 Professional
- Windows 7 Ultimate

Caution

You cannot install the module on Windows Server if you are installing it on the command line–only version of Windows Server 2008 R2, Server Core. ∎

To install the module on your computer, you must have Windows PowerShell and the .NET 3.5.1 Framework installed on your computer.

To use the module in a Windows Server 2008 R2 domain, you must have the Active Directory Web Service (ADWS) running on a domain controller in your environment. If you want to use the module against a Windows Server 2008 or a Windows Server 2003 domain, you will need to download and install the Active Directory Management Gateway Service on one of your servers.

To use the module on a Windows 7 computer, you must have at least one Windows Server 2008 R2 domain controller in your domain.

Note

These requirements are what cause many administrators to continue to use the ActiveRoles Management Shell from Quest. The Quest tools are much more flexible with their operating system and domain requirements, and they do not require any special web services on a server in your domain. ∎

A Word About Remoting

Because the `ActiveDirectory` module can be installed only on certain versions of Windows 7 and Windows Server 2008 R2, remoting is essential if you want to use the module on any other Windows operating system. It is also necessary if you want to use the module on Windows 7 to manage a domain that does not have a 2008 R2 domain controller. The `ActiveDirectory` module is a great candidate to be used with implicit remoting so that you can create a local proxy module that will connect through a remoting session via WinRM to run the module on a remote server whenever you load the module on your computer. This technique was discussed in Chapter 2. This will give you a way to load the module on any computer that has Windows PowerShell 2.0 even if that computer does not meet the requirements for installation.

Cross-Reference

For more information on the WinRM technique, review Chapter 2, "What's New in Windows PowerShell V2." ∎

Installation

The `ActiveDirectory` module is a part of the Remote Server Administration Tools (RSAT), which is provided by Microsoft. These tools are available as a feature without requiring installation on Windows Server 2008 R2, but need to be manually installed on Windows 7. In addition, the technique required to enable the module differs slightly depending upon which operating system you are using.

Enabling the Module on Windows Server

The installation of the `ActiveDirectory` module can be performed three ways on any of the supported versions of Windows Server:

1. It is installed by default whenever you install the AD DS or AD LDS server roles.

2. It is installed automatically whenever you use `dcpromo.exe` to create a domain controller.

3. It can be installed manually with the Remote Server Administration Tools (RSAT) feature on Windows Server 2008 R2.

Cross-Reference

You can perform the manual installation of the RSAT feature with the `Add-WindowsFeature` cmdlet that comes with the `ServerManager` module discussed in Chapter 8, "Performing Basic Server Management":

```
Add-WindowsFeature RSAT-AD-PowerShell
```
∎

Installing the Module on Windows 7

To install the module on Windows 7, you'll need to download and install RSAT for Windows 7 from the Microsoft website. After RSAT is installed, you will need to enable the feature by performing the following steps:

1. **Click Start ➢ Control Panel** to open the Control Panel window.
2. **Click Programs** to switch to the Programs section of the Control Panel.
3. Underneath Programs and Features, **click Turn Windows Features On or Off.** The Windows Features dialog box opens.
4. **Expand Remote Server Administration Tools ➢ Role Administration Tools ➢ AD DS and AD LDS Tools.**
5. **Select Active Directory Module for Windows PowerShell**.
6. **Click OK**.

Loading the Module

After the module is installed, you can load it into your Windows PowerShell session with:

```
Import-Module ActiveDirectory
```

Using the Active Directory Provider

After you import the `ActiveDirectory` module into your Windows PowerShell session, a PSDrive named `AD:\` is automatically created for you that binds to your authenticated domain. If you would like to connect to another domain, an ADAM instance, or an Active Directory Lightweight Directory Services (AD LDS) instance, you can use `New-PSDrive` to do so. For example, the following will create a new drive called PSBibleAD that uses the domain controller named DC1. It makes use of the splatting technique to pass parameters to a cmdlet that was discussed in Chapter 2.

```
$Arguments = @{
  Name = 'PSBibleAD'
  PSProvider = 'ActiveDirectory'
  Root = '//RootDSE/'
  Server = 'DC1'
}
New-PSDrive @Arguments
```

Browsing the drive is as simple as browsing the filesystem. You can use `Set-Location` or `cd` as well as `Get-ChildItem` or `dir`. You can even use `Move-Item` or `move` to move objects between containers, and you can use `md` or `mkdir` to assist in creating containers or organizational units. Here's an example of how you might interact with the provider using the default `AD:\` drive that is created when you load the module.

```
cd ad:
dir
```

Name	ObjectClass	DistinguishedName
home	domainDNS	DC=home,DC=psbible,DC=com
Configuration	configuration	CN=Configuration,DC=home,DC=psbibl...
Schema	dMD	CN=Schema,CN=Configuration,DC=home...
DomainDnsZones	domainDNS	DC=DomainDnsZones,DC=home,DC=psbib...
ForestDnsZones	domainDNS	DC=ForestDnsZones,DC=home,DC=psbib...

```
cd '.\DC=home,DC=psbible,DC=com'
dir
```

Name	ObjectClass	DistinguishedName
Builtin	builtinDomain	CN=Builtin,DC=home,DC=psbible,DC=com
Computers	container	CN=Computers,DC=home,DC=psbible,DC...
Domain Controllers	organizationalUnit	OU=Domain Controllers,DC=home,DC=p...
ForeignSecurityPr...	container	CN=ForeignSecurityPrincipals,DC=ho...
Infrastructure	infrastructureUpdate	CN=Infrastructure,DC=home,DC=psbib...
LostAndFound	lostAndFound	CN=LostAndFound,DC=home,DC=psbible...
Managed Service A...	container	CN=Managed Service Accounts,DC=hom...
NTDS Quotas	msDS-QuotaContainer	CN=NTDS Quotas,DC=home,DC=psbible,...
Program Data	container	CN=Program Data,DC=home,DC=psbible...
System	container	CN=System,DC=home,DC=psbible,DC=com
Users	container	CN=Users,DC=home,DC=psbible,DC=com

```
md 'OU=SQLServers'
```

Name	ObjectClass	DistinguishedName
SQLServers	organizationalUnit	OU=SQLServers,DC=home,DC=psbible,D...

```
cd '.\CN=Computers'
dir
```

Name	ObjectClass	DistinguishedName
SERVER1	computer	CN=SERVER1,CN=Computers,DC=home,DC...
SHAREPOINT1	computer	CN=SHAREPOINT1,CN=Computers,DC=hom...
SQL1	computer	CN=SQL1,CN=Computers,DC=home,DC=ps...

```
move '.\CN=SQL1' '..\OU=SQLServers'
```

Note

You may have noticed that moving between the containers and organizational units (OUs) is not quite as straightforward as you might expect. You need to specify `CN=` or `OU=` along with the name of object you would like to browse to when using `cd` or `Set-Location`. Because you need to use the equal sign in these container names, you must enclose everything in quotes. This makes tab completion essential when moving between containers in the directory. For example, `'cd CN=[tab]'` cycles through all of the containers in your current directory.

As essential as this is, it is also impossible to use tab completion for any container outside of ones in the current directory because the nature of an AD path is to have the subfolders first in the string. Take the following path as an example: `AD:\OU=SQLServers,DC=home,DC=psbible,DC=com`. It would be impossible to type `cd AD:\OU=[tab]` to cycle through anything but OUs underneath the root of `AD:\` because at the time you hit Tab, the only information you have given the parser about the location of potential OUs is the `AD:\` that begins the path. ∎

Querying Active Directory

Though the Active Directory provider is nice for browsing the directory, it falls short in much of the functionality administrators require when scripting against Active Directory. Fortunately, the `ActiveDirectory` cmdlets pick up where the provider leaves off.

Users, Groups, and Computers

The primary purpose of many Active Directory scripts is to interact with users, groups, or computers. Many tasks require you to interact with more than just one. The `ActiveDirectory` module provides a series of `Get` cmdlets to help you work with all of the objects in Active Directory.

The Get-AD Cmdlets

Three specific cmdlets enable you to query users, groups, and computers: `Get-AdUser`, `Get-ADGroup`, and `Get-ADComputer`. Each of these cmdlets has an identical set of parameters. At their simplest, you may use only the `Identity` parameter to find a single object if you know its exact name:

```
Get-ADUser -Identity 'Administrator'
```

The `Identity` parameter is a positional parameter. This means that if you omit the parameter name, you are implying that the argument passed should be supplied to the `Identity` parameter. For example, you can retrieve the Domain Admins group by running the following line of code:

```
Get-ADGroup 'Domain Admins'
```

The versatility of this parameter is impressive. Besides the `sAMAccountName`, you can pass a `dn`, the `objectSid`, or the `objectGUID` of the object you would like to retrieve.

```
Get-ADComputer 'CN=DC1,OU=Domain Controllers,DC=home,DC=psbible,DC=com'
Get-ADUser 'S-1-5-21-3032037283-1324540821-3147598018-1114'
Get-ADUser '7df539b8-589b-4e8f-a9eb-78b6b0c9be0b'
```

Searching with Filters

Whether you need to query the directory for a single object or multiple objects, the `Filter` parameter provides you with an efficient way to search for objects in Active Directory. When you use the `Filter` parameter, the processing of the search occurs on the server. This is a much better technique to find what you are looking for than returning all of the objects to your Windows PowerShell session and then piping them to `Where-Object` for Windows PowerShell to do the processing.

A filter can be enclosed in either quotes or brackets, and it must consist of a specific syntax. Fortunately, the syntax is very similar to something you would find if `Where-Object` was used. The following is an example of a simple filter that finds all computers that are running a server version of Windows:

```
Get-ADComputer -filter { OperatingSystem -like 'Windows Server*'}
```

The `Filter` parameter can also take a single asterisk to mean include everything. For example, the following line returns all groups in AD:

```
Get-ADGroup -Filter *
```

Filters can be enclosed in parentheses, and their logic can be joined together with either `-and` or `-or`:

```
Get-ADUser -Filter {(sn -eq 'Snover') -or (title -like 'C*O')}
```

The parentheses and operators in a filter may consist of multiple lines. For example, the following bit of code shows how you can format a complex filter to make it look a little bit nicer. The filter in the example will retrieve all user accounts that have been created in the last five days in the state of New York that have an office phone number that starts with 212 or 718.

```
$date = (Get-Date).AddDays(-5)
Get-ADUser -Filter {
  (whenCreated -gt $date) -and (
    (state -eq 'NY') -and (
      (OfficePhone -like '212-*') -or
      (OfficePhone -like '718-*')
    )
  )
}
```

Table 10-1 shows some of the different operators that are supported within a filter.

TABLE 10-1

Filter Operators

Operator	Description
-eq	Equal to
-ne	Not equal to
-lt	Less than
-gt	Greater than
-le	Less than or equal to
-ge	Greater than or equal to
-like	The same as -eq, but supports asterisks as wildcards
-notlike	The same as -ne, but supports asterisks as wildcards
-bor	Bitwise or
-band	Bitwise and
-not	Not (exclamations do not work in filters)

To view all of the information available about filtering in Active Directory with the cmdlets, you should read through the contents of Get-Help about_ActiveDirectory_Filter.

Note

Filtering could take up an entire chapter in this book. The module's implementation of filtering is what makes these cmdlets stand out, so it is important to read through this particular bit of help documentation. One thing that becomes obvious very quickly is that filtering is much more intuitive and easier to learn with the **ActiveDirectory** module's syntax than the traditional syntax found in LDAP queries. Many of the examples shown in **Get-Help about_ActiveDirectory_Filter** are there to show you just how much easier it is. ∎

If you need to use an LDAP filter for any reason, you can still do so with the cmdlets by using the LDAPFilter parameter:

```
Get-ADUser -LDAPFilter '(&(name=A*)(lastLogon>=128812906535515110))'
```

Controlling the Scope of a Search

The ActiveDirectory provider works very nicely with the Get cmdlets. If you are working in a container or organizational unit, the cmdlets search all sublevels underneath your current level. For example, the following retrieves all users found in the Offices OU and any sub-OUs:

```
cd 'ad:\OU=Offices,DC=home,DC=psbible,DC=com'
Get-ADUser -Filter *
```

If you want to specify another starting point for your search without changing location within the provider, you can do so by using the `SearchBase` parameter. For example, the following retrieves exactly the same information as the above code.

```
Get-ADUser -Filter * -SearchBase 'OU=Offices,DC=home,DC=psbible,DC=com'
```

In addition, you can limit the scope of how deep the searching should go with the `SearchScope` parameter. The following example restricts the search to only the Offices OU. If a user exists in this OU, the user will be returned. Any locations underneath this OU, for example a NewYork or California OU, will not be searched.

```
Get-ADUser -Filter * -SearchScope OneLevel
```

Working with Properties

Each of the `Get` cmdlets has a `Properties` parameter that enables you to specify the properties you are interested in retrieving about the object from AD. By default, each of the cmdlets in the preceding section gets a subset of all of the properties that are available for each object it retrieves. You can force the cmdlets to return all of the properties for an object or set of objects by using an asterisk in the `Properties` parameter:

```
Get-ADGroup -Identity PSBible -Properties *
```

Though this is useful for exploring objects in the shell, it is inefficient to do this for multiple objects if you do not actually need all of the properties. By specifying the exact properties you care about, you can greatly increase the speed of your scripts. The following line shows how you can get the name and title for all users in your Active Directory:

```
Get-ADUser -Filter * -Properties name,title
```

Note

A few properties are retrieved regardless of what is passed to the `Properties` parameter: `DistinguishedName`, `Enabled`, `GivenName`, `Name`, `ObjectClass`, `ObjectGUID`, `SamAccountName`, `SID`, `Surname`, and `UserPrincipalName`. It is not necessary to specify these properties when using the `Properties` parameter; however, it will not return an error so it is safe to specify them for the purpose of consistency within your scripts. If you truly only wanted specific properties, you would need to pipe your command into a `Select-Object` to ensure that only the properties you specified are returned in your script. ■

Get-ADObject

On some occasions, you may be searching for objects that cross the boundaries of the object classes. For this reason, there is also a generic `Get-ADObject` you can use to return more than one type of object. For example, the following section of code returns all of the users and groups that have names that start with the letter *a*:

```
Get-ADObject -Filter {
  (
    (ObjectClass -eq 'group') -or
```

```
        (ObjectClass -eq 'user')
    ) -and (
        (Name -like 'a*')
    )
}
```

You can also use the `Get-ADObject` cmdlet to return things that aren't users, groups, or computers. In other words, it acts as a generic tool to retrieve objects regardless of their object class.

Querying Group Membership

When scripting against Active Directory, two group membership tasks are very common. The first is the ability to find the groups that an object belongs to, and the second is the ability to find all of the users that belong to a specific group.

Getting the Groups an Object is a Member of

You can get the groups that an Active Directory object belongs to in two ways. First, you can ask for the `MemberOf` property when you use one of the `Get` cmdlets:

```
Get-ADUser jsnover -Properties MemberOf
```

This returns all groups that are in the `MemberOf` attribute in LDAP, but it has two drawbacks. First, you will only receive the distinguished name (DN) for the groups. Second, it will miss at least one key group, Domain Users.

The alternative to using LDAP is to use `Get-ADPrincipalGroupMembership`. This cmdlet not only gets you the missing group, but also retrieves the actual object you would normally get from `Get-ADGroup`. This allows you to use the return objects further down in a Windows PowerShell pipeline. It also allows you to pipe users, computers, service accounts, or other groups to it in order to find out what groups they belong to. Here's an example of how the cmdlet may be used. Both lines do exactly the same thing.

```
Get-ADPrincipalGroupMembership -Identity JohnW

Get-ADUser JohnW |Get-ADPrincipalGroupMembership
```

You can also pipe the groups into `Get-ADGroup` to get additional properties for the groups, as shown in following example. It returns the name of each group along with the date the group was created.

```
Get-ADUser JohnW |
    Get-ADPrincipalGroupMembership |
    Get-ADGroup -Properties whenCreated |
    Select name,whencreated
```

Although you can pipe a whole set of objects to `Get-ADPrincipalGroupMembership`, it is more common to be able to process multiple objects in a `foreach` loop in order to maintain a reference to the original object. The following example shows this technique. It will get all users in the domain and create a CSV file that lists a user with every group that they are a member of.

```
$report = @()
foreach ($user in (Get-ADUser -filter *)) {
  $groups = $user |Get-ADPrincipalGroupMembership
  foreach ($group in $groups) {
    $report += New-Object psobject -Property @{
      User = $user.name
      Group = $group.name
    }
  }
}
$report |export-csv d:\report.csv -Encoding ASCII -NoTypeInformation
```

If you need to find out what groups a user belongs to in another domain, you can use the ResourceContextServer parameter to specify a server in that domain.

```
Get-ADUser johnW |
  Get-ADPrincipalGroupMembership -ResourceContextServer dc1.domain2.com
```

Getting Members of a Group

There is an LDAP property called Member that you can retrieve from a query to retrieve all of the members of a group. Just like the results of the MemberOf property, it returns a list of all distinguished names. If the DN is the only bit of information you care about, it's a very easy way to get the immediate members of a group:

```
Get-ADGroup NYC -Properties Member
```

The ActiveDirectory module also provides a cmdlet called Get-ADGroupMember that you can use to retrieve the object version of the members of a group. For example, the following code retrieves the name and object type for all members of the group named NY.

```
Get-ADGroupMember -Identity NY |select name,objectClass
```

You can pipe group objects to Get-ADGroupMember. For instance, the following line does the same thing as the last example:

```
Get-ADGroup NY |Get-ADGroupMember |select name,objectClass
```

The most important switch is the Recursive. It is used to get all of the nested members within a group. For example, in the following line, if there is a group within the NY group called NYC that has user objects in it, it will return all of the users in NYC as well as any users who are directly in the NY group:

```
Get-ADGroup NY |Get-ADGroupMember -Recursive
```

Caution

When you use the `Recursive` switch, the cmdlet goes through every group that the object is a member of, and then every group those groups are members of, all the way through the hierarchy. One small caveat to be careful of is that when `Get-ADGroupMember` is used with the `Recursive` switch, it will return an actual group object only if there are no members within that particular group. If there are members within the group, it returns the direct member within them, and then recursively goes through any additional groups. In nearly all scenarios, this is actually what you want, but if you need to retrieve all of the group names, even if they have members, you will need to write a bit of custom code to do that. ■

User and Group Administration

Finding users, groups, and group membership is useful for reporting, but it doesn't do much in terms of automation. In this section, you look at how you can create, modify, and delete user and group objects in Active Directory with the `ActiveDirectory` module.

Creating Users and Groups

New users are created with `New-ADUser`. At the very minimum, a user can be created and enabled with a valid password by running the following bit of code:

```
$pass = ConvertTo-SecureString 'P@ssw0rd1' -AsPlainText -Force
New-ADUser jack -AccountPassword $pass -Enabled $true
```

You may use additional parameters to specify AD attribute information during the creation of the user:

```
New-ADUser kate -AccountPassword $pass -Enabled $true -PostalCode 11211
```

The splatting technique will help you maintain scripts that use this cmdlet with a long list of parameters:

```
$Arguments = @{
  Name = 'hurley'
  AccountPassword = $pass
  Enabled = $true
  PostalCode = '10016'
  Office = 'NYC'
  Department = 'Windows Engineering'
}
New-ADUser @Arguments
```

If you want to use an existing user as a template, you may do so by piping a user object returned from `Get-ADUser` into `New-ADUser`:

```
$user = Get-ADUser hurley -Properties PostalCode,Office,Department
$user |New-ADUser -Name ben -SamAccountName ben -AccountPassword $pass
```

It is not possible for Get-ADUser to have a parameter for every possible property you would like to set. If you need to set an attribute during the creation of a user and a parameter does not exist for that attribute, you may use the OtherAttributes parameter. This is useful for custom and uncommon attributes. In the following example, you can see how the OtherAttributes parameter works. You should note that the title attribute actually has a parameter. Even though this is the case, you can still specify the attribute name in the OtherAttributes parameter. This makes the OtherAttributes parameter flexible enough to handle all of the attributes for an object.

```
$atts = @{
  msTsAllowLogon = $true
  title = 'CEO'
}
New-ADUser sawyer -AccountPassword $pass -Enabled $true -OtherAttributes $atts
```

As you have seen with many of the other cmdlets, the New-ADUser cmdlet is sensitive to the context of the provider. You can browse to the location in AD where you would like to create the user prior to using New-ADUser to have that user created in the location you have browsed to:

```
cd 'AD:\OU=NY,OU=Offices,DC=home,DC=psbible,DC=com'
New-ADUser jacob -AccountPassword $pass -Enabled $true
```

You can also specify the path where the user should be created by using the Path parameter:

```
$path = 'OU=NY,OU=Offices,DC=home,DC=psbible,DC=com'
New-ADUser MrEcho -AccountPassword $pass -Enabled $true -Path $path
```

Groups are similarly created with New-ADGroup. This cmdlet may be called minimally with the Name and GroupScope parameter. The Name parameter is positional and does not need to be specified.

```
New-ADGroup Dharma1 -GroupScope Universal
```

The following example shows the most common set of parameters used with New-ADGroup:

```
$arguments = @{
  Name = 'Dharma2'
  DisplayName = 'The Swan'
  Description = 'Where the button is pushed'
  GroupScope = 'Global'
  GroupCategory = 'Security'
  Path = 'OU=NY,OU=Offices,DC=home,DC=psbible,DC=com'
}
New-ADGroup @arguments
```

Both the New-ADUser and the New-ADGroup cmdlets support a PassThru parameter. This parameter returns the object you have just created. It is useful if there is more you need to do with the user or group after you have created it. For example, you could display the information to the screen so that the operator of the script can verify that what was created is what was expected.

```
$group = New-ADGroup Dharma3 -GroupScope 'DomainLocal' -PassThru
"Group Created: {0}" -f $group.name
"Group Scope: {0}" -f $group.GroupScope
"Group Category: {0}" -f $group.GroupCategory
```

Modifying Properties

The database of information stored within Active Directory is often heavily relied on by multiple systems within a company. Because of this, it's very important that organizations keep their Active Directory attributes up to date. This can be a tedious task without the help of scripting. The `ActiveDirectory` module gives you a very flexible way of scripting logic into changes that you may need to make.

User properties are modified, created, or deleted with `Set-ADUser`, and group properties are managed by `Set-ADGroup`. Both cmdlets are similar in how they work. The main difference is that each cmdlet has its own set of properties to help you work with the common properties you will find for the object. For example, to convert a group into a global group, you would run the following.

```
Set-ADGroup Dharma1 -GroupScope 'Global'
```

Here's an example that uses `Set-ADUser`. It sets the `Office` attribute to NY for all users that are found underneath the NY OU.

```
cd 'AD:\OU=NY,OU=Offices,DC=home,DC=psbible,DC=com'
$users = Get-ADUser -Filter *
foreach ($user in $users) {
    $user |Set-ADUser -Office 'NY'
}
```

The `Instance` parameter is used to modify a changed object that was returned from `Get-ADUser` or `Get-ADGroup`.

```
$group = Get-ADGroup Dharma2 -Properties DisplayName,Description
$group.DisplayName = 'The Orchid'
$group.Description = 'Turn the wheel and come home'
Set-ADGroup -Instance $group
```

For attributes that do not have parameters, you can pass a hash table to the `Replace` parameter. You can also use the `Clear` parameter to specify that an attribute should be set to nothing.

```
Set-ADUser sawyer -Clear title -Replace @{msTsAllowLogon = $false}
```

The Add and Remove parameter can be used for attributes that take multiple values.

```
Set-ADUser sawyer -Add @{otherTelephone = '555-1212','555-1234'}
Set-ADUser sawyer -Remove @{otherTelephone = '555-1234'}
```

Note
Even though this section focuses on users and groups, it should be noted that computer objects have identical cmdlets to help you manage them. Just as there is a Get-ADComputer, there is also a New-ADComputer and Set-ADComputer. ■

Working with Group Membership

You can modify group memberships within the administrative tool entitled Active Directory Users and Computers in two different ways. You can either double-click a group and add or remove users to that group, or double-click a user and add or remove groups from that user's membership. The ActiveDirectory module provides cmdlets that let you use both of these approaches in Windows PowerShell.

Adding and Removing Members of a Group

The cmdlets provided to enable you to add or remove users from a given group are Add-ADGroupMember and Remove-ADGroupMember. The following two lines of code show how this cmdlet can be used on its own or through the pipeline:

```
Add-ADGroupMember Dharma1 -Members jack
Get-ADGroup Dharma1 |Add-ADGroupMember -members kate,hurley
```

The following example shows how you can use Remove-ADGroupmember. When this cmdlet is used, it will normally prompt you for confirmation that you want to perform the task. You may override this prompt by specifying the Confirm parameter with the value $false. The exact syntax for this is -Confirm:$false.

```
Remove-ADGroupMember Dharma1 -Members jack -Confirm:$false
```

This final example shows a solution to a real-world problem. It removes all of the members of a group and then adds those users to another group.

```
$group = Get-ADGroup Dharma1
$members = $group |Get-ADGroupMember
$group |Remove-ADGroupMember -Members $members -Confirm:$false

Add-ADGroupMember Dharma2 -Members $members
```

Adding and Removing Groups from a User

The cmdlets provided to enable you to add or remove groups from a user or set of users are Add-ADPrincipalGroupMembership and Remove-ADPrincipalGroupMembership. For example, the following uses Add-ADPrincipalGroupMembership to add a user to two groups.

```
Add-ADPrincipalGroupMembership sawyer -MemberOf Dharma1,Dharma2
```

The following example shows how `Remove-ADPrincipalGroupMembership` may be used. It specifically removes a user from all groups except the Domain Users group.

```
$user = Get-ADUser sawyer
$groups = $user |Get-ADPrincipalGroupMembership |where {
  $_.name -ne 'Domain Users'
}
$user |Remove-ADPrincipalGroupMembership -MemberOf $groups -Confirm:$false
```

Common Tasks

When dealing with users and groups in Active Directory, you may choose to add some automation for a few common tasks.

Enabling and Disabling Accounts

You already know that you can set any AD attribute, including the `Enable` attribute, using the `Set` cmdlets. There is, however, an easier way to go about enabling or disabling an account. The `ActiveDirectory` module comes with an `Enable-ADAccount` cmdlet you can use to enable any AD account in your domain with the exception of an Active Directory snapshot or a read-only domain controller. The syntax for this cmdlet is very straightforward. It can be used with the `Identity` parameter or you can pipe an object retrieved with one of the `Get` commands to it:

```
Enable-ADAccount -Identity TheKraken
Get-ADUser TheKraken |Enable-ADAccount
```

Conversely, you can disable accounts using `Disable-ADAccount` with identical syntax:

```
Disable-ADAccount -Identity TheKraken
Get-ADUser TheKraken |Disable-ADAccount
```

Unlocking Users

Unlocking an account is as simple as enabling or disabling an account. You use the `Unlock-ADAccount` cmdlet to do this:

```
Unlock-ADAccount -Identity TheKraken
Get-ADUser TheKraken |Unlock-ADAccount
```

Resetting Passwords

Earlier in this chapter, you saw how you can create a new user and pass that user a default password. Though you could use this technique with the `Set-ADUser` cmdlet, the `ActiveDirectory` module gives you an easy way to do this with the `Set-ADAccountPassword` cmdlet. This cmdlet can be used by an end user to change his own password.

```
$oldpass = Read-Host -Prompt "Enter Old Password" -AsSecureString
$newpass = Read-Host -Prompt "Enter New Password" -AsSecureString
Set-ADAccountPassword $env:username -OldPassword $oldpass -NewPassword $newpass
```

`Set-ADAccountPassword` can also be used by an administrator to reset a password:

```
$pass = ConvertTo-SecureString 'P@ssw0rd1' -AsPlainText -Force
Set-ADAccountPassword JohnW -NewPassword $pass -Reset
```

Here is a real-world example that shows how an administrator can change a password for all the users in an OU:

```
$pass = Read-Host -Prompt "Enter Password" -AsSecureString
cd 'AD:\OU=NY,OU=Offices,DC=home,DC=psbible,DC=com'
Get-ADUser -Filter * |Set-ADAccountPassword -NewPassword $pass -Reset
```

Creating Reports with Search-ADAccount

A few queries are so common to an Active Directory administrator that the `ActiveDirectory` module has provided a single cmdlet to perform them all. Table 10-2 shows a list of parameters you can use to have the `Search-ADAccount` perform a specific query. It also shows any required supporting parameters.

TABLE 10-2

Possible Queries Using Search-ADAccount

Parameter	Query
AccountDisabled	Finds all disabled accounts
AccountExpired	Finds accounts where the account's expiration date has passed
AccountExpiring	Finds accounts that are expiring in a given timeframe or a specific date
AccountInactive	Finds accounts that have not logged in within a given timeframe or a specific date
LockedOut	Finds all accounts that are locked out
PasswordExpired	Finds all accounts that have expired passwords
PasswordNeverExpires	Finds all accounts that have a password that is not configured to expire

Here are some examples of how you can use `Search-ADAccount`. The first one retrieves a list of all computer accounts that are locked out.

```
Search-ADAccount -LockedOut -ComputersOnly
```

The following example retrieves a list of all of the disabled accounts and then pipes them into Enable-ADAccount. The effect is that it enables all the disabled accounts in Active Directory. It should be obvious, but this one is probably not one you want to run in production.

```
Search-ADAccount -AccountDisabled |Enable-ADAccount
```

AccountExpiring and AccountInactive require the use of either the DateTime parameter or TimeSpan. In addition, any query can be limited to computers or users only by using the appropriate ComputersOnly or UsersOnly switch. The following two lines show all the users that have not logged in since January 1, 2011, and list all the accounts that are expiring after 10 days:

```
Search-ADAccount -AccountInactive -DateTime '1/1/2011' -UsersOnly
```

```
Search-ADAccount -AccountExpiring -TimeSpan 10
```

Managed Service Accounts

Many companies have policies in place that ensure that all service accounts have their passwords reset at regular intervals. This can be an administrative nightmare because in most organizations, every service requires its own password. In addition, there is the potential that the act of changing a service account's password may accidentally bring down production systems if a password is not set in the appropriate place for the service.

Microsoft's solution to this problem is a new feature included with Windows Server 2008 R2: managed service accounts. These accounts are special user accounts in Active Directory that perform automated password resets while updating the appropriate location within a server to ensure that the passwords are never out of synch with the services that are configured to use them. Currently, the ActiveDirectory module with Windows PowerShell is the only way you can install one of these accounts on a computer; there is no GUI available.

Creating Service Accounts

The first step in using a service account is to create one within your Active Directory. You do this with the New-ADServiceAccount cmdlet:

```
New-ADServiceAccount 'Sqlserv1'
```

Installing Service Accounts on a Computer

Once the account is created, it can be installed on the computer that will use the service account with the Install-ADComputerServiceAccount cmdlet. This cmdlet must be run on the computer that will use the account. If the following were run on Server1, it would install the Sqlserv1 account on that computer so that it can be used to run services:

```
Install-ADServiceAccount Sqlserv1
```

Using a Managed Service Account

After a service account is installed, it can be used to start any service running on a computer. Within the properties of a service in `services.msc`, the service account is simply specified in the Log On tab with the syntax `domain\username$` with a blank password, as shown in Figure 10-1.

Configuring a service to use a managed service account

Even though the password and the coordination of the password changes on the computer that is using it will forever be managed by Active Directory, there may be occasions when you want to force a password to be changed. If so, you can run `Reset-ADServiceAccountPassword` on the computer that has the service account installed to force a password change.

Managing Organizational Units

Organizational units (OUs) make up the structure of the directory within Active Directory. They can be used to set policies on objects, to create logical groupings of objects, or to set layers of security on the objects that they contain. This section looks at how you can create these structures and maneuver the objects within them.

Moving Active Directory Objects

Earlier in the chapter, you saw a quick example of how to move a computer object using the `ActiveDirectory` provider. Here is a sample as a refresher:

```
cd 'ad:\OU=NY,OU=Offices,DC=home,DC=psbible,DC=com'
move .\CN=jack .\OU=NYC
```

The `ActiveDirectory` module also provides a `Move-ADObject` cmdlet to facilitate moving objects around the directory.

```
Move-ADObject jack -TargetPath 'OU=NY,OU=Offices,DC=home,DC=psbible,DC=com'
```

You can also use `Move-ADObject` in the pipeline after a `Get-ADUser` command.

```
$target = 'OU=NYC,OU=NY,OU=Offices,DC=home,DC=psbible,DC=com'
Get-ADUser jack |
  Move-ADObject -TargetPath $target
```

The pipeline support also works nicely for a large set of users. For example, the following moves all users in the NY OU into the NYC OU:

```
cd 'ad:\OU=NY,OU=Offices,DC=home,DC=psbible,DC=com'
Get-ADUser -Filter * -SearchScope OneLevel |
  Move-ADObject -TargetPath $target
```

You can use the `Server` parameter when you want to transfer the object to another domain.

```
$arguments = @{
  Identity = 'jack'
  Server = 'server2.psbible2.com';
  TargetPath = 'CN=User,DC=home,DC=psbible2,DC=com'
}
Move-ADObject @arguments
```

Creating Organizational Units

Earlier in this chapter, you briefly saw how to create an OU using the provider:

```
cd 'ad:\OU=NYC,OU=NY,OU=Offices,DC=home,DC=psbible,DC=com'
md 'OU=Brooklyn'
```

In addition, the `New-ADOrganizationalUnit` cmdlet can also be used:

```
cd 'ad:\OU=NYC,OU=NY,OU=Offices,DC=home,DC=psbible,DC=com'
New-ADOrganizationalUnit Bronx
```

If you would rather not use the provider, you can specify the target location with the `Path` parameter:

```
$location = 'OU=Brooklyn,OU=NYC,OU=NY,OU=Offices,DC=home,DC=psbible,DC=com'
New-ADOrganizationalUnit Greenpoint -Path $location
```

The following example shows some of the additional parameters you can specify when using `New-ADOrganizationalUnit`:

```
$arguments = @{
  Name = 'Williamsburg';
```

```
    Path = $location;
    City = 'Williamsburg'
    Country = 'USA'
    PostalCode = '11211'
    State='NY'
    ManagedBy = 'jack'
}
New-ADOrganizationalUnit @arguments
```

New-ADOrganizationalUnit also support the Instance parameter. This allows you to use another OU as a template.

```
$ou = Get-ADOrganizationalUnit -Filter {
  Name -eq 'Williamsburg'
} -Properties ManagedBy,Country,State

New-ADOrganizationalUnit Bushwick -Path $location -Instance $ou
```

Removing Active Directory Objects

Removing objects is very straightforward with the Active Directory cmdlets. For every cmdlet you have seen that uses the verb New, there is a corresponding Remove cmdlet that can remove the object:

- Remove-ADUser

- Remove-ADComputer

- Remove-ADGroup

- Remove-ADObject

- Remove-ADOrganizationalUnit

Caution
The only concern you may have when removing an object with one of these cmdlets is that the object may be configured to prevent accidental deletion. If that is the case, you will need to use Set-ADObject to replace the ProtectedFromAccidentalDeletion attribute to $false before you use the Remove cmdlet. ∎

Password Policies

Password policies are security features within Active Directory that enable you to control the usage and characteristics of passwords within an organization. This includes things like the length of the password as well as how long it takes before a password expires. With Windows Server 2008 domains, you can now specify fine-grained policies that affect only specific users or groups of users. The creation and management of these policies can be a bit convoluted because they require you to create objects with specific properties that have names like msDS-LockoutObservationWindow. Without Windows PowerShell, this is traditionally done through the LDAP editing tool provided by Microsoft called ADSI edit.

Microsoft has compensated for the lack of tools to manage password policies with the `ActiveDirectory` module by providing a series of cmdlets that enable you to work with both default and fine-grained password policies.

Viewing Password Policies

If you would like to retrieve a password policy, you can use `Get-ADDefaultDomainPasswordPolicy` and `Get-ADFineGrainedPasswordPolicy`. Here is a sample of what these look like when they are run:

```
Get-ADDefaultDomainPasswordPolicy
```

```
ComplexityEnabled            : True
DistinguishedName            : DC=home,DC=psbible,DC=com
LockoutDuration              : 00:30:00
LockoutObservationWindow     : 00:30:00
LockoutThreshold             : 0
MaxPasswordAge               : 42.00:00:00
MinPasswordAge               : 1.00:00:00
MinPasswordLength            : 7
objectClass                  : {domainDNS}
objectGuid                   : cffdf13d-3888-4902-9442-db8a84eeca4c
PasswordHistoryCount         : 24
ReversibleEncryptionEnabled  : False
```

```
Get-ADFineGrainedPasswordPolicy passpol1
```

```
AppliesTo                    :
{CN=jack,OU=NYC,OU=NY,OU=Offices,DC=home,DC=psbible,DC=com}
ComplexityEnabled            : False
DistinguishedName            : CN=passpol2,CN=Password Settings
Container,CN=Syst
em,DC=home, DC=psbible,DC=com
LockoutDuration              : 00:30:00
LockoutObservationWindow     : 00:30:00
LockoutThreshold             : 0
MaxPasswordAge               : 42.00:00:00
MinPasswordAge               : 1.00:00:00
MinPasswordLength            : 4
Name                         : passpol2
ObjectClass                  : msDS-PasswordSettings
ObjectGUID                   : e6708d2e-4861-47ea-8ece-df3dca4e9d9f
PasswordHistoryCount         : 12
Precedence                   : 20
ReversibleEncryptionEnabled  : True
```

If you would like to retrieve the password policy that a particular user is using, you can use the following line to retrieve the resultant policy for the user:

```
Get-ADUserResultantPasswordPolicy jack
```

Note

Alternatively, if you want to view what users or groups are using a particular policy, you can see their DNs underneath `AppliesTo` in the policy that is returned by `Get-ADFineGrainedPasswordPolicy`. If you would like to easily see more information about those users and groups, you can pipe the policy into `Get-ADFineGrainedPasswordPolicySubject`. ■

Creating a Fine-Grained Policy

Fine-grained policies are created with `New-ADFineGrainedPasswordPolicy`. At the minimum, you must specify a name for the policy and the precedence for the policy. Policy preferences are used to determine which policy overrides another. Precedence is generally entered in increments of 10 with the lowest number receiving the highest priority.

```
New-ADFineGrainedPasswordPolicy passpol1 -Precedence 10
```

If you want to apply the policy to a user or a group, you can use the `Add-FineGrainedPasswordPolicySubject` cmdlet to do so. The following example adds the passpol1 policy to a group named group1 and all of the users underneath the NYC OU:

```
Add-ADFineGrainedPasswordPolicySubject passpol1 -Subjects group1

cd 'AD:\OU=NYC,OU=NY,OU=Offices,DC=home,DC=psbible,DC=com'
Get-ADUser -Filter * |Add-ADFineGrainedPasswordPolicySubject passpol1
```

Modifying Password Policies

Password policies can be changed by piping a policy into the appropriate cmdlet for the policy type you are changing. Default domain-based policies are changed with `Set-ADDefaultDomainPasswordPolicy` and fine-grained policies are set with `Set-ADFineGrainedPasswordPolicy`. Here are two examples that show how you can change a password policy with these cmdlets:

```
Get-ADDefaultDomainPasswordPolicy |
   Set-ADDefaultDomainPasswordPolicy -PasswordHistoryCount 10

Get-ADFineGrainedPasswordPolicy caspol1 |
   Set-ADDefaultDomainPasswordPolicy -MaxPasswordAge 40
```

`Set-ADFineGrainedPasswordPolicy` also accepts an `Instance` parameter to allow you to modify an existing policy that is retrieved with `Get-ADFineGrainedPasswordPolicy`.

```
$policy = Get-ADFineGrainedPasswordPolicy caspol1
$policy.LockoutThreshold = 5
$policy.LockoutObservationWindow = (New-TimeSpan -Minutes 15)
Set-ADFineGrainedPasswordPolicy -Instance caspol1
```

If you need to add or remove users or groups from a fine-grained policy, you can use Add-
FineGrainedPasswordPolicySubject and Remove-FineGrainedPasswordPolicySubject.
If you need to remove a fine-grained policy altogether, you can use Remove-
ADFineGrainedPasswordPolicy.

Managing the Rest of Active Directory

I have discussed the foundation for what an administrator needs to query and manage
Active Directory objects. For the most part, Active Directory is managed by finding an
appropriate object and modifying the relevant properties for that object. For example, if
you wanted enable the Global Cache, you could do the following:

```
cd 'ad:\CN=Configuration,DC=home,DC=psbible,DC=com'
Get-ADObject -Filter {Name -eq 'NTDS Settings'} |
    Set-ADObject -Replace @{options='1'}
```

Many tasks can be accomplished by finding an attribute and setting it to the appropriate
value even if there is also an ActiveDirectory cmdlet that performs a specific task. For
example, the Enable-ADAccount enables an Active Directory object. This could also be
achieved by setting the Enabled property of an object to $true. A few additional cmdlets
not discussed in this chapter perform some specific tasks that are worth mentioning. In
addition, two Move cmdlets are available to help you manage domain controllers. Table 10-3
lists these additional cmdlets and their descriptions.

TABLE 10-3

Additional Active Directory cmdlets

Cmdlet	Description
Clear-ADAccountExpiration	Clears the expiration date for an Active Directory account
Enable-ADOptionalFeature	Enables an Active Directory optional feature: for example, Recycle Bin
Disable-ADOptionalFeature	Disables an Active Directory optional feature
Get-ADOptionalFeature	Gets one or more Active Directory optional features
Get-ADAccountAuthorizationGroup	Gets the accounts token group information
Get-ADForest	Gets an Active Directory forest
Get-ADRootDSE	Gets the root of a directory server information tree
Move-ADDirectoryServer	Moves a directory server in Active Directory to a new site
Move-ADDirectoryServerOperation MasterRole	Moves operation master roles to an Active Directory directory server

In addition to the cmdlets listed in the table, an additional set of cmdlets is available to control the replication of passwords to read-only domain controllers:

- `Add-ADDomainControllerPasswordReplicationPolicy`
- `Get-ADDomainControllerPasswordReplicationPolicy`
- `Get-ADDomainControllerPasswordReplicationPolicyUsage`
- `Remove-ADDomainControllerPasswordReplicationPolicy`

Managing Active Directory with the ActiveRoles Management Shell

ADSI and Quest's ActiveRoles Management Shell were mentioned during the introduction to this chapter. Though you can easily brush aside ADSI for the purpose of this book, there is no way to talk about Windows PowerShell and Active Directory without showing a few examples of the ActiveRoles Management Shell. In environments where the Active Directory Web Service (ADWS) is not yet running on a server in your domain, it is likely that you will want to use the ActiveRoles Management Shell from Quest to perform many of the tasks discussed in this chapter.

Installing the Cmdlets

The snap-in can be downloaded for free from Quest's website at www.quest.com/ powershell/activeroles-server.aspx.

After it is installed, it can be loaded with:

```
Add-PSSnapin Quest.ActiveRoles.ADManagement
```

Caution
At the time of writing, this was the snap-in name. Always read through the documentation of a third-party module or snap-in because it is possible for the names or installation instructions to change. ■

Using the Cmdlets

The ActiveRoles Management Shell has a set of cmdlets similar to those in the `ActiveDirectory` module. `Get-QAD` commands look and act nearly identical to their `Get-AD` counterparts. One thing that is different is that the Quest tools do not come with a provider. Another difference is with their implementation of filtering. Most of the `Get` commands in the ActiveRoles Management Shell have a parameter for common attributes like `Department`, `LastName`, or `City`. These parameters accept wildcards within them. So even though you lose the robust filtering that mimics Windows PowerShell that you get with the `ActiveDirectory` module, you can still do `-like` filters by using wildcards within your parameters with the Quest tools. If you need to perform any other type of filtering on objects that are not within the parameter set, you can still use LDAP filters to find what you are looking for.

Here are some examples of tasks that you have already seen with the `ActiveDirectory` module. To retrieve a user named jack, you would use the `Get-QADUser` cmdlet:

```
Get-QADUser jack
```

In order to retrieve a computer object by specifying its DN, you would do this:

```
Get-QADComputer 'CN=DC1,OU=Domain Controllers,DC=home,DC=psbible,DC=com'
```

If `Get-QADUser` is called by itself with no parameters, it will retrieve all of the users in the domain:

```
Get-QADUser
```

Wildcards are supported in `Get-QADUser`. This line gets all users whose name begins with the letter *u*:

```
Get-QADUser u*
```

Wildcard support exists in the parameters that represent AD attributes. For example, the following gets all users whose `Department` attribute has the word *engineering* in it:

```
Get-QADUser -Department *engineering*
```

If you need to connect to another domain, you can use the `Service` parameter to specify another domain or domain controller:

```
Get-QADUser domain2\user -service dc1.domain2.com
```

You can retrieve the common reports that were returned by `Search-ADAccount` in the `ActiveDirectory` module by using the same `Get-QADUser` with specific switches:

```
Get-QADUser -NotLoggedOnFor 60
Get-QADUser -ExpiredFor 7
```

Pipeline support is just as robust in the Quest tools as it is in the `ActiveDirectory` module. For example, the following line enables all disabled users:

```
Get-QADUser -Disabled |Enable-QADUser
```

In order to display all of the properties for a user, you must use the `IncludeAllProperties` switch parameter of `Get-QADUser`. You must also specify `Select *` to see all of these properties after they are retrieved.

```
Get-QADUser jack -IncludeAllProperties |Select *
```

`Set-QADUser` is used to modify a user object. For example, the following will populate the `Office` attribute for users in the NYC OU:

```
$searchroot = 'OU=NYC,OU=NY,OU=Offices,DC=home,DC=psbible,DC=com'
Get-QADUser -SearchRoot $searchroot |Set-QADUser -Office NYC
```

Viewing users in a group is accomplished with the Get-QADGroup cmdlet:

```
Get-QADGroup dharma1 |select -ExpandProperty Members
Get-QADGroup dharma1 |select -ExpandProperty NestedMembers
Get-QADGroup dharma1 |select -ExpandProperty AllMembers
```

You can find out which groups a user belongs by inspecting the MemberOf, NestedMemberOf, and AllMemberOf properties of the user objects that are returned by Get-QADUser:

```
Get-QADUser jack |select -ExpandProperty MemberOf
Get-QADUser jack |select -ExpandProperty NestedMemberOf
Get-QADUser jack |select -ExpandProperty AllMemberOf
```

If you want to add a user to a group, you could do this:

```
Get-QADUser jack |Add-QADMemberOf -Group Dharma1
```

You can move a group to a new container with Move-QADObject:

```
Get-QADGroup dharma1
   |Move-QADObject 'OU=NYC,OU=NY,OU=Offices,DC=home,DC=psbible,DC=com'
```

To remove a user, call Remove-QADObject. The following code suppresses the confirmation prompt by setting the Confirm parameter to $false:

```
Get-QADUser jack |Remove-QADObject -Confirm:$false -Force
```

Summary

In many environments, Active Directory is the foundational directory that core services in IT rely upon. Whether it is used for file and print security, web authentication, or as a corporate directory of user information, Active Directory drives much of what you see in the enterprise. Windows PowerShell gives you a way to automate many of the common tasks that administrators are responsible for daily. Combined with the other powerful features that Windows PowerShell provides, Active Directory can also be used as a reporting tool or a powerful logic-driven engine that manipulates data.

In the next chapter, you look closely at one of the core Microsoft features that leverages Active Directory extensively, Group Policy.

Managing Group Policy

Throughout Part III of this book, you have seen many of the new modules that were introduced with Windows Server 2008 R2 that provide you with a Windows PowerShell way to work with server components that are traditionally very tricky or impossible to script against. Group Policy is another example of this. Prior to 2008 R2, Group Policy could be scripted via an API or a COM interface. With the release of 2008 R2, you can now use the Windows PowerShell module that is installed with the Group Policy Management Console (GPMC).

IN THIS CHAPTER

Installing the Group Policy
    Management Console cmdlets

Querying Group Policy Objects
    and creating reports

Automating the creation and
    manipulation of Group Policy
    Objects

Working with Group Policy
    Object backups

Managing Group Policy Object
    security

Installing and Using the Cmdlets

The `GroupPolicy` module is directly attached to the GPMC. To install the module on a computer, you must install or enable the GPMC on that computer.

Enabling the Module on Windows Server 2008 R2

To use the `GroupPolicy` module on Windows Server 2008 R2, you can install the module and the GPMC by running the following two lines of code:

```
Import-Module ServerManager
Add-WindowsFeature GPMC
```

Installing the Module on Windows 7

For Windows 7, you must download and install the Remote Server Administration Tools (RSAT). You can download these tools from `www.microsoft.com/download/en/details.aspx?id=7887`. After you have installed RSAT, you can enable the GPMC feature by performing the following steps:

1. **Click Start ➢ Control Panel.** The Control Panel window opens.
2. **Click Programs.** Switch to the Programs section of the Control Panel.
3. Underneath Programs and Features, **click Turn Windows Features On or Off.** The Windows Features dialog box opens.
4. **Expand Remote Server Administration Tools and then Feature Administration Tools.**
5. **Select Group Policy Management Tools.**
6. **Click OK.**

A Word about Remoting

If you are using any other operating system, your only option is to install the module on a computer that meets the requirements and then configure WinRM to allow remote connections. The `GroupPolicy` module is an excellent candidate to be used with implicit remoting so that you can load a wrapper module locally, but have it connect without effort to the computer that is configured with WinRM.

Cross-Reference
Chapter 2, "What's New in Windows PowerShell V2," discusses this technique. ■

Once the module is installed, you can load it into your Windows PowerShell session with:

```
Import-Module GroupPolicy
```

Getting Policy Information

You can view information about Group Policy with a series of cmdlets that use the verb `Get`.

Group Policy Objects (GPOs)

A few cmdlets are available to help you get information about the GPOs in your domain. Depending on the level of information, you might use one or a combination of these cmdlets.

Getting Basic Information about a GPO

You can retrieve basic information about GPOs in a domain by using Get-GPO. It returns information that is found in the Details pane of the GPO within the GPMC. This includes things like the description, owner, and time the policy was last modified. This cmdlet can be used with the GUID or the name of a GPO you would like to retrieve by using the GUID or Name parameter, respectively. You can also retrieve all of the GPOs in the domain by using the All switch parameter. Unfortunately, wildcards are not supported, so there is no way to filter for GPO names when you only know a part of the name. To do this type of filtering, you would need to use the All switch and then pipe it into a Where-Object. The following example shows how you can use this cmdlet and includes an example of this filtering technique.

```
Get-GPO -Name 'Default Domain Controllers Policy'
Get-GPO -GUID '6ac1786c-016f-11d2-945f-00c04fb984f9'
Get-GPO -All
Get-GPO -All |Where {$_.DisplayName -like 'Default*'}
```

Note

All but two of the cmdlets that come with the module (Copy-GPO and Get-GPResultantSetOfPolicy) have a Server and a Domain parameter. These parameters can be used to specify an alternate domain or domain controller. This chapter does not focus on using these parameters, but it is important to note that they are available. ■

Getting a Detailed Report of Information about a GPO

To get detailed information about the settings within a GPO, you can use Get-GPOReport. This cmdlet retrieves an HTML or XML report that displays all of the settings that are configured by the GPO. When this cmdlet is used to create an HTML report, the report is identical to the one you see within the GPMC when looking at the settings for a GPO. The cmdlet takes an optional Path parameter so that you can specify a filename to create. Here is an example of how this cmdlet can be used to generate an HTML report for the Default Domain Policy:

```
Get-GPOReport 'Default Domain Policy' -ReportType HTML -Path c:\gporeport.html
```

If nothing is specified in the Path parameter, it displays the report to the screen. The following command illustrates how you can send the XML report to the screen. The example also shows that you can use the pipeline to generate reports about GPOs retrieved using Get-GPO.

```
Get-GPO 'psbible' |Get-GPOReport -ReportType XML
```

Caution

The Path parameter of Get-GPOReport does not operate as you would expect it to. If you specify only a filename, it will create the file in c:\windows\system32 regardless of where you are in the FileSystem provider. Because of this, you must ensure that you specify a full path name when using the Path parameter. ■

Getting Specific Values for Changes Made by a GPO

Though registry policy and preference information is shown when using `Get-GPOReport`, the `GroupPolicy` module offers specific cmdlets to help you view and set most of these values. This gives you an interface to create and script dynamic policies. It will even let you work with registry-based policies without having to create a custom ADMX file (an XML representation of a set of Group Policy configurations).

Note

Using the Windows PowerShell cmdlets to modify GPO settings is a double-edged sword. It is great that you can do it, but it does not work nicely with the ADMX files that specify which registry a setting affects. There is no way to find out which key a particular setting like "Prohibit Adding Items to the desktop" changes through the cmdlets. You must know this information by reading through the ADMX and ADML (language resource) files. This makes querying this information difficult because you must specify the key you are affecting when using the cmdlets in this section.

Similarly, if you create a registry-based policy that does not exist in any of the ADMX files, it is not possible to edit that policy through the GPMC. In essence, you would be creating an orphaned setting just as you would if you deleted an ADMX file that is in use. ∎

You can retrieve information about the registry-based policies configured within a GPO by using `Get-GPRegistryValue`. It requires you to know which key you are modifying within the policy. The following example shows how you can use the cmdlet to find all of the settings configured for Active Desktop.

```
$key = 'HKCU\Software\Microsoft\Windows\CurrentVersion\Policies\ActiveDesktop'
Get-GPO psbible |
  Get-GPRegistryValue -key $key |
    select ValueName, PolicyState, Value |Format-Table -AutoSize
```

```
ValueName                PolicyState Value
---------                ----------- -----
NoDeletingComponents         Set     1
NoAddingComponents           Set     1
NoEditingComponents          Set     1
NoComponents                 Set     1
```

```
# Get just the value of the NoComponents setting
get-gpo psbible |
  Get-GPPrefRegistryValue -Context User -Key $key -ValueName NoComponents |
    Select -ExpandProperty Value
```

```
1
```

In addition to using traditional registry-based policies, you can also use the Windows PowerShell cmdlets to get and modify registry settings within the GPO's registry preferences section. `Get-GPPrefRegistryValue` is used to retrieve information about these settings. It requires you to know the registry key the policy is affecting as well as the context in which the preference exists. Context can be either `User` or `Computer`. The following example illustrates how this cmdlet is used:

```
$key = 'hkcu\Software\Policies\Microsoft\Windows\Control Panel'
Get-GPO psbible |
  Get-GPPrefRegistryValue -Context User -Key $key |
  Select Order, ValueName, Action, Value |
  Format-Table -AutoSize


Order ValueName                  Action Value
----- ---------                  ------ -----
    1 ScreenSaveIsSecure         Create 1
    2 ScreenSaveIsSecure         Update 1
```

Note

If you are not familiar with preference policies, they are a new feature that was added to Group Policy with Windows Server 2008. They are Microsoft's answer to the growing problem of unmanageable logon scripts. They provide you with a way to set such things as drive mappings, INI file settings, shortcuts, and registry settings. They allow you to specify the order in which these items are updated to give you control over which GPOs have higher priorities for these specific configurations. With the `GroupPolicy` cmdlets, you can only modify the registry settings preferences. ∎

Group Policy Links

To see what GPOs are applied to a particular container, you can use `Get-GPInheritance`. This cmdlet takes a positional parameter called `Target` that lets you specify a distinguished name (DN) for the container in question. This cmdlet returns an object that has a `GpoLinks` and an `InheritedGpoLinks` property that contain the names of all of the GPOs applied to this container. The following code snippet shows how to use this cmdlet to retrieve the GPOs that are applied to an OU.

```
$ou = Get-GPInheritance 'OU=NYC,OU=NY,OU=USA,dc=home,dc=psbible,dc=com'
$ou


Name                   : NYC
ContainerType          : OU
Path                   : ou=theisland,dc=home,dc=toenuff,dc=com
GpoInheritanceBlocked  : No
GpoLinks               : {psbible1}
InheritedGpoLinks      : {psbible2, Default Domain Policy}
```

You can also use this with `Get-GPO` to display information about the GPOs that are linked to the container.

```
$ou.InheritedGpoLinks |foreach {
  Get-GPO $_.DisplayName
} |select DisplayName, ModificationTime


DisplayName                              ModificationTime
-----------                              ----------------
psbible2                                 10/24/2010 7:02:12 PM
Default Domain Policy                    5/1/2011 4:48:06 PM
```

Resultant Set of Policy (RSOP)

If you would like to see what policies are applied to a particular user, computer, or both, you can use `Get-GPResultantSetOfPolicy`. This cmdlet requires you to specify the full name of a file with the `Path` parameter where the RSOP report can be saved. You can create either an HTML or XML version of the RSOP by using the mandatory parameter `ReportType`. Listing 11-1 shows how this cmdlet can be used.

Cross-Reference

Listing 11-1 makes use of the splatting technique that was discussed in Chapter 2, "What's New in Windows PowerShell V2," to pass a large set of parameters to a cmdlet. ■

LISTING 11-1

Using Get-GPResultantSetOfPolicy to Create RSOP Reports

```
# Create the html report in the current directory: $pwd
$report = Join-Path $pwd RSOP_user1.html

# Generate an HTML RSOP report for user1
Get-GPResultantSetOfPolicy -User user1 -ReportType HTML -Path $report

# Generate an XML RSOP report for computer1
$report = Join-Path $pwd RSOP_comp1.xml
Get-GPResultantSetOfPolicy -Computer comp1 -ReportType XML -Path $report

# Create an RSOP report for user1 on comp1
$report = Join-Path $pwd RSOP_comp1user1.html
$params = @{
  Path = $report
  User = user1
  Computer = comp1
  ReportType = HTML
}
Get-GPResultantSetOfPolicy @params
# View the report in your browser
Start-Process $report
```

Creating and Configuring GPOs

In addition to retrieving information, the `GroupPolicy` module enables you to create and make changes to GPOs. Table 11-1 shows a list of the cmdlets that are used to perform these types of tasks.

TABLE 11-1

Cmdlets Used to Manipulate GPOs

Name	Description
New-GPO	Creates a GPO
New-GPLink	Links a GPO to a site, domain, or OU
Rename-GPO	Renames a GPO's display name
Set-GPLink	Allows you to enable, disable, enforce, or specify the link order for the GPO
Set-GPInheritance	Blocks or unblocks inheritance for a specified domain or OU
Set-GPRegistryValue	Applies a registry-based policy to a GPO
Set-GPPrefRegistryValue	Applies a registry preference item to a GPO
Remove-GPO	Removes a GPO
Remove-GPLink	Removes a link
Remove-GPRegistryValue	Removes a registry-based policy from a GPO
Remove-GPPrefRegistryValue	Removes a registry preference item from a GPO

Here are a few examples that show how these cmdlets can be used. The following line creates a new GPO with New-GPO:

```
$gpo = New-GPO psbible1 -Comment 'An automated gpo'
```

The following illustrates how you can use Set-GPRegistryValue to create a registry-based policy for the GPO you created above that prevents a user from deleting items from his or her Active Desktop:

```
$key = 'HKCU\Software\Microsoft\Windows\CurrentVersion\Policies\ActiveDesktop'
$gpo |
  Set-GPRegistryValue -Key $key -ValueName NoComponents -Value 1 -Type Dword
```

The following sets a registry value as a registry preference item under the user configuration:

```
$params = @{
  Key = 'HKCU\Software\PSBible'
  Context = 'User'
  ValueName = 'OffOn'
  Value = 1
  Type = 'DWord'
  Action = 'Create'
  Order = '1'
}
$gpo |Set-GPPrefRegistryValue @params
```

The next two lines apply the GPO to an OU with `New-GPLink`:

```
$link = $gpo |
    New-GPLink -Target 'OU=USA,DC=home,DC=psbible,DC=com' -LinkEnabled 'Yes'
```

The following section uses `Set-GPInheritance` to block inheritance of policies on the NY organizational unit:

```
$target = 'OU=NY,OU=USA,DC=home,DC=psbible,DC=com'
Set-GPInheritance -Target $target -IsBlocked 'No'
```

The next line uses `Set-GPLink` to set the priority order for the link and mark it as enforced. Marking the GPO as enforced will override the inheritance set at the NY OU.

```
$link |Set-GPLink -Order 1 -Enforced 'Yes'
```

Here is an example of how you can use `Rename-GPO` to rename a GPO. In this case, the `psbible1` policy is being renamed to `psbible1.markedfordelete`.

```
Get-GPO psbible1 |Rename-GPO -TargetName psbible1.markedfordelete
```

The following line shows how you can use the Windows PowerShell pipeline to filter for a specific set of GPOs. In this command, it will return all of the GPOs that have the words `.markedfordelete` at the end of their `DisplayName`. The pipeline then passes these objects to `Remove-GPO` so that they will be deleted.

```
Get-GPO -All |Where {$_.DisplayName -like '*.markedfordelete'} | Remove-GPO
```

Note

The `GroupPolicy` cmdlets are sometimes inconsistent with the Windows PowerShell way of doing things. For example, the use of `'Yes'` and `'No'` for things like the `LinkEnabled` parameter of `New-GPLink` would seem more natural if the parameter were a switch or a Boolean. These are generally not complex things to take note of, but they do require you to take a moment to understand a module or snap-in's specific syntax. ■

Backing Up and Restoring GPOs

The `GroupPolicy` module provides the `Backup-GPO` cmdlet to enable you to back up one or more GPOs in your domain. For example, you can back up all of the GPOs in your domain with one line of code:

```
Get-GPO -All |Backup-GPO -Path '\\server1\gpobackups'
```

The `Restore-GPO` cmdlet is used to restore from these backups. Restoring all of the GPOs in a domain from the most recent backup is also one line of code.

```
Restore-GPO -Path '\\server1\gpobackups' -All
```

To restore a single GPO, you can use the `Name` parameter of `Restore-GPO`. The following line will restore the psbible GPO from the most recent backup found in \\server1\gpobackups.

```
Restore-GPO -Path '\\server1\gpobackups' -Name psbible
```

If there is a specific backup you would like to restore from, you can supply the backup ID to `Restore-GPO` by using the `BackupId` parameter.

```
$id = '00003D27-F9E6-4C59-BF69-938E5AE43D05'
Restore-GPO -Path '\\server1\gpobackups' -BackupId $id
```

In addition, you can use `Import-GPO` to restore a GPO with a new name. This final example restores the last backup of the psbible GPO and restores it with the name psnew.

```
$dir = '\\server1\gpobackups'
Import-GPO -Path $dir -BackupGpoName psbible -TargetName psnew -CreateIfNeeded
```

Group Policy Security

The `GroupPolicy` module provides two cmdlets to work with permissions on GPOs:

- `Get-GPPermissions`
- `Set-GPPermissions`

Getting Security Information

Retrieving permissions for a GPO is as simple as piping a GPO object into `Get-GPPermissions`. Two common sets of parameters are used with this cmdlet. You can either specify the `All` parameter to get all of the users and groups associated with the GPO:

```
get-gpo psbible |Get-GPPermissions -All
```

Or you can use `TargetName` and `TargetType` to specify the Active Directory (AD) name and the type of AD object it is. Valid arguments for the `TargetType` parameter are `User`, `Computer`, or `Group`.

```
get-gpo psbible |
    Get-GPPermissions -TargetType Group -TargetName 'group1'
```

Setting Permissions

`Set-GPPermissions` requires that you specify a `TargetName` and `TargetGroup`. It also requires you to pass the level of security you are granting with the `PermissionLevel` parameter. Valid arguments for this parameter are:

- `GpoRead`
- `GpoApply`

- `GpoEdit`
- `GpoEditDeleteModifySecurity`
- `None`

If you use `Set-GPPermissions` to replace a permission for a user, group, or computer that grants less access than the object already has, you must also use the `Replace` switch parameter. Listing 11-2 shows an example of how you can use this cmdlet to grant and revoke access for a group to read a GPO.

LISTING 11-2

Using Set-GPPermissions to Grant and Revoke Access to a GPO

```
$gpo = get-gpo psbible

# Grant access to allow the group1 group to read the psbible gpo
$params = @{
  TargetName = 'group1';
  TargetType = 'group';
  PermissionLevel ='GpoRead';
}
$gpo |Set-GPPermissions @params

# Revoke access for the group1 group from the psbible gpo
$params = @{
  TargetName = 'group1';
  TargetType = 'group';
  PermissionLevel ='None';
  Replace = $true;
}

$gpo |Set-GPPermissions @params
```

Summary

Group Policy provides a way to control almost all aspects of your server and desktop configurations within your domains. The `GroupPolicy` module provides an easy way to view what GPOs are in place and what settings they are using. Although it requires a bit of extra digging to determine the registry settings you are interested in, the cmdlets provide you with a method to automate changes to group policies that you can easily incorporate into your change control process. In addition, the information that is exposed can be used with the Windows PowerShell logic to provide you with a way to script cleanups, consolidations, and migrations of group policies between users, groups, and containers.

This brings us to the end of Part III on Windows Server and some of the core services that are shipped with it. In Part IV, you will look at how you can use Windows PowerShell to manage the diverse server applications that run on Windows Server. The next chapter begins that journey with a discussion of how to use Windows PowerShell in managing Microsoft Exchange.

Part IV

Server Applications

IN THIS PART

Chapter 12
Managing Microsoft Exchange
Server

Chapter 13
Managing SQL Server 2008 R2

Chapter 14
Managing Microsoft SharePoint
2010 Server

Chapter 15
Managing Internet Information
Services 7

Chapter 16
Managing System Center
Operations Manager 2007 R2

Chapter 17
Managing Microsoft Deployment
Toolkit 2010

Chapter 18
Managing Citrix XenApp 6

Chapter 19
Managing Citrix XenDesktop 5

Managing Microsoft Exchange Server

With the release of Microsoft Exchange Server 2007, Microsoft made the decision to use Windows PowerShell for all management tasks. Although the Exchange Management Console is still available, all tasks run in the console actually run Windows PowerShell scripts in the background.

As part of the installation of any Exchange role on Exchange Server 2007 or Exchange Server 2010, the Exchange Management Tools are also installed.

Installing the Cmdlets on a Workstation

Microsoft Exchange Server can be managed by logging in to an Exchange Server directly or via remote desktop services. In my opinion, this opens up your organization to potential security risks, because you will most likely be logging in to the server with an account that has administrator privileges on that server. For this reason, I always recommend installing the Microsoft Exchange Management Tools on your local workstation. If your workstation is not running one of the supported operating systems, you can either upgrade the operating system or investigate one of the freely available virtual machine solutions such as VMware Player or VirtualBox. These solutions are outside the scope of this book.

Exchange Server 2010 introduces remote management via Windows PowerShell Remoting. This resolves the security issue inherent with logging in to the Exchange server directly, but is not without problems, as explained later.

IN THIS CHAPTER

Installing cmdlets locally

Managing permissions in the Exchange organization

Administering Exchange objects

Managing Exchange databases

Using filters to limit results

Managing Exchange remotely

Working with Exchange Web Services

Microsoft Exchange Server 2007

You can install just the Management Tools for Exchange Server 2007 on an administrator's workstation from the Exchange Server DVD (64-bit) or by downloading the tools from Microsoft (32-bit).

To manage Exchange Server 2007, your management workstation can run Microsoft Windows XP or Microsoft Windows Server 2003, in 32-bit or 64-bit format, and either Windows PowerShell Version 1 or Version 2.

Microsoft Exchange Server 2007 Service Pack 1 adds Microsoft Windows Vista and Microsoft Windows Server 2008 to the supported operating systems for the Exchange Management Tools.

Microsoft Exchange Server 2007 Service Pack 3 adds Windows 7 and Microsoft Windows Server 2008 R2 to the supported operating systems list.

Note

Visit `http://technet.microsoft.com/en-us/library/bb232090(EXCHG.80).aspx` for more information on installing the Management Tools for Exchange 2007.

You can download the 32-bit tools from `www.microsoft.com/downloads/en/details.aspx?familyid=6BE38633-7248-4532-929B-76E9C677E802&displaylang=en#AffinityDownloads`. ∎

Once the Exchange Server 2007 Management Tools are installed, you can start the tools by clicking Start ➢ Programs ➢ Microsoft Exchange Server 2007, and choosing Exchange Management Shell. You can also load the Exchange Server 2007 cmdlets by adding the snap-ins to an existing PowerShell session. Because there are two snap-ins for Exchange Server, I use the wildcard character "*" to add them both at once:

```
Add-PSSnapIn -Name Microsoft.Exchange.*
```

Microsoft Exchange Server 2010

The Microsoft Exchange Server 2010 tools do not need to be installed on the administrator's workstation; you can manage Exchange Server 2010 by importing the Exchange session into Windows PowerShell Version 2 and connecting to an Exchange server. This is covered later in the chapter, in the "Managing Microsoft Exchange Server Remotely" section.

You can install the Exchange Server 2010 Management Tools on your administrator workstation if you are running the 64-bit version of one of the following operating systems:

- Microsoft Windows Vista with SP2
- Microsoft Windows 7
- Microsoft Windows Server 2008 with SP2
- Microsoft Windows Server 2008 R2

You can install the Exchange Server 2010 Management Tools on the administrator workstation by following the steps described at `http://technet.microsoft.com/en-us/library/bb232090.aspx`.

Installing the Management Tools locally does bring some benefits:

- You don't need to create a session; it is created as you start the Management Tools.
- You don't need to specify the Exchange server to connect to; the tools connect to the closest Exchange server the Management Tools find.
- The Exchange server will return rich Exchange objects, as opposed to Windows PowerShell objects. This can be important, as you will see later.

Once the Exchange 2010 Management Tools are installed, you can start them by clicking Start ➤ Programs ➤ Microsoft Exchange Server 2010, and choosing Exchange Management Shell.

What's New in Microsoft Exchange Server 2010

Exchange Server 2010 introduces Role Based Access Control (RBAC). RBAC is the new permission model for Exchange Server. As part of starting the shell or console, the shell checks for permissions based on the RBAC, providing only the cmdlets appropriate to the roles you have been assigned.

Except for servers running the Edge Transport role, all Exchange Server 2010 management is done via remote shell — even if you are physically connected to the Exchange server.

In Exchange Server 2010, you can enable audit logging and track who made changes to the organization and when. When audit logging is enabled, the default logs all Exchange cmdlets except `Get-*` and `Search-*` cmdlets.

Exchange Server 2010 enables you to add or remove values in multi-valued properties with a single command.

Exchange Server 2010 includes more than 255 new Exchange cmdlets; and a few have been dropped, notably the cmdlets related to storage groups.

Note

For the rest of this chapter, I am going to operate on the assumption that you are loading the Exchange Management Shell with no other snap-ins, with Windows PowerShell Version 2 installed. I will be using splatting to break long script lines into shorter lines. For a refresher on splatting, see the section "Splatting" in Chapter 2, "What's New in Windows PowerShell V2." If you have Windows PowerShell Version 1, and cannot upgrade your management workstation to Version 2, you will have to "de-splat" the scripts. A simple example is:

```
$User =@{
Identity = "a*"
```

```
Resultsize = "Unlimited"
SortBy = "Name"
}
Get-User @User
```

The equivalent Version 1 string would be:

```
Get-User -Identity a* -ResultSize Unlimited -SortBy Name ■
```

Managing Microsoft Exchange Server Permissions

Managing either Exchange Server 2007 or Exchange Server 2010 requires that you have been assigned the proper permissions. Permissions are managed differently in each version. Exchange Server 2007 permissions may initially seem easier to manage than Exchange Server 2010 permissions, but I highly recommend you take the time to learn the new Role Based Access Control that is introduced with Exchange Server 2010 because the permission model is far more granular than in Exchange Server 2007.

Microsoft Exchange Server 2007

To administer objects in Exchange Server 2007, you will need to be a member of at least one of the following roles:

- **Exchange Organization Administrators:** People in this role have the highest permissions on all properties for the whole Exchange organization.

- **Exchange Recipient Administrators:** People in this role have full permission to manage all properties and objects for mailboxes, contacts, users, groups, dynamic distribution groups, and public folders within the Exchange organization.

- **Exchange View-Only Administrators:** People in this role can view all Exchange objects within the organization, but cannot modify them.

- **Exchange Server Administrators:** People in this role can manage a particular Exchange server.

- **Exchange Public Folder Administrators:** People in this role can only administer public folders. This role was added in Exchange Server 2007 Service Pack 1.

Note

To view a list of administrators and the roles assigned to them, use the `Get-ExchangeAdministrator` cmdlet. Running the `Get-ExchangeAdministrator` cmdlet on its own provides a list of all administrators and their roles.

To view a list of only Exchange Organization Administrators, you can pipe the output of the `Get-ExchangeAdministrator` cmdlet to the `Where-Object` cmdlet:

```
Get-ExchangeAdministrator | Where-Object {$_.Role -eq "OrgAdmin"}
```

You can use the same concept to show all administrators except View-Only Administrators:

```
Get-ExchangeAdministrator | Where-Object {$_.Role -ne "ViewOnlyAdmin"} ■
```

To add an administrator to a group, use the `Add-ExchangeAdministrator` cmdlet, passing the `Identity` of the administrator and the most permissive `Role` the administrator should have:

```
Add-ExchangeAdministrator -Identity contoso\karl -Role RecipientAdmin
```

Possible roles are `OrgAdmin`, `RecipientAdmin`, `ViewOnlyAdmin`, `PublicFolderAdmin`, or `ServerAdmin`. For the `ServerAdmin` role, the cmdlet has an additional required parameter: the `Scope`, which is the server that the administrator will be a server administrator on. The following example assigns the user `contoso\ben` to the `ServerAdmin` role on the server Exch01:

```
Add-ExchangeAdministrator -Identity contoso\ben -Role ServerAdmin -Scope Exch01
```

Microsoft Exchange Server 2010

Exchange Server 2010 introduces Role Based Access Control (RBAC). Within this permission model, permissions across the organization can be more granularly applied. For instance, Exchange Server 2010 provides nearly 60 built-in roles for granting permissions, and you can create your own roles as well. The `Get-ExchangeAdministrator` cmdlet from Exchange Server 2007 is no longer available in Exchange Server 2010. The equivalent cmdlet is the `Get-RoleGroup` cmdlet. There are additional cmdlets for managing roles as well.

Note

A full explanation of RBAC is beyond the scope of this chapter. For a complete explanation, see "Understanding Role Based Access Control" on TechNet at `http://technet.microsoft.com/en-us/library/dd298183.aspx`. ■

Use the `Add-RoleGroupMember` cmdlet to add an administrator to a role group. The following example adds the Active Directory account `John` to the `Recipient Management` role. This allows John to create or modify recipients in Exchange Server 2010.

```
Add-RoleGroupMember -Identity "Recipient Management" -Member John
```

If you are not in the `ManagedBy` property of the role group, but are in the `Organization Management` role group, you can force the addition by adding the optional `BypassSecurityGroupManagerCheck` parameter. The following example adds the Active Directory account `John` to the `Recipient Management` role without requiring you to be in the `ManagedBy` property of the role group:

```
$RoleGroupmember = @{
Identity = "Recipient Management"
Member = "John"
BypassSecurityGroupManagerCheck = $true
}
Add-RoleGroupmember @RoleGroupmember
```

You can also add a universal security group to a role group. The following example adds the members of the security group `Accounting Administrators` to the `Recipient Management` role group:

```
$RoleGroupMember = @{
Identity = "Recipient Management"
Member = "Accounting Administrators"
}
Add-RoleGroupMember @RoleGroupMember
```

With Exchange Server 2010, however, you have the ability to set up fine-grained role groups, so you could create a role group named Accounting Recipient Management, and allow that role group to only manage objects in the Accounting organizational unit. Look for more on managing role groups later in the chapter.

Administering Objects

One of the first functions you should become familiar with in the Exchange Management Shell is the `Get-ExCommand` function. This function takes no parameters, and returns all Exchange cmdlets. The `Get-ExCommand` function is actually a wrapper for the Windows PowerShell cmdlet `Get-Command`, returning only Exchange cmdlets. The default data returned includes the command type, name, and definition for each cmdlet. Because the output of `Get-ExCommand` will most likely not fit your Exchange Management Shell, I recommend piping the output of the `Get-ExCommand` function to the `Select-Object` cmdlet, specifying to return only the name of the cmdlets.

This next example, run in an Exchange Management Shell, returns all available Exchange cmdlets, sorted by verb:

```
Get-ExCommand | Select-Object -Property Name
PS> Get-ExCommand | Select-Object -Property Name

Name
----
Add-ADPermission
Add-AvailabilityAddressSpace
Add-ContentFilterPhrase
Add-DistributionGroupMember
Add-ExchangeAdministrator
Add-IPAllowListEntry
Add-IPAllowListProvider
Add-IPBlockListEntry
Add-IPBlockListProvider
Add-MailboxPermission
Add-PublicFolderAdministrativePermission
Add-PublicFolderClientPermission
```

```
Clean-MailboxDatabase
Clear-ActiveSyncDevice
Connect-Mailbox
...
```

When run in an Exchange Management Shell, the following code returns all available Exchange Server cmdlets, sorted by noun. As you will recall, Windows PowerShell cmdlets are named with a verb-noun pair. The example script line sorts the Exchange Server cmdlets by the object they operate on — all the mailbox cmdlets sort together, as do the user, group, database, and so on.

```
Get-ExCommand | Sort-Object -Property Noun | Select-Object -Property Name
```

```
PS> Get-ExCommand | Sort-Object -Property Noun | Select-Object -Property Name

Name
----
New-AcceptedDomain
Set-AcceptedDomain
Remove-AcceptedDomain
Get-AcceptedDomain
Test-ActiveSyncConnectivity
Remove-ActiveSyncDevice
Clear-ActiveSyncDevice
Get-ActiveSyncDeviceStatistics
Export-ActiveSyncLog
Set-ActiveSyncMailboxPolicy
Remove-ActiveSyncMailboxPolicy
New-ActiveSyncMailboxPolicy
Get-ActiveSyncMailboxPolicy
...
```

Unfortunately, Microsoft changed the output of the `Get-ExCommand` function in Exchange Server 2010. You will have to do a little more work to get the same functionality the Exchange Server 2007 Management Shell provides. The following example, when run in either version of the shell, returns all available cmdlets, sorted by noun. In the case of Exchange Server 2010, the list of cmdlets depends on your Exchange role.

```
$ExCommands = @{}
$Sort = @{
Property = "Value"
}
$Select = @{
Property = "Key"
}
Get-ExCommand | ForEach-Object {$ExCommands.Add($_.Name,$_.Name.Split("-")[1])}
$ExCommands.GetEnumerator() | Sort-Object @Sort | Select-Object @Select
>> $ExCommands.GetEnumerator() | Sort-Object @Sort | Select-Object @Select
>>

Key
---
```

```
New-AcceptedDomain
Set-AcceptedDomain
Get-AcceptedDomain
Remove-AcceptedDomain
Test-ActiveSyncConnectivity
Clear-ActiveSyncDevice
Remove-ActiveSyncDevice
Get-ActiveSyncDeviceStatistics
Export-ActiveSyncLog
Remove-ActiveSyncMailboxPolicy
New-ActiveSyncMailboxPolicy
Set-ActiveSyncMailboxPolicy
Get-ActiveSyncMailboxPolicy
...
```

In either version, you can also tailor the output of the `Get-ExCommand` function by passing a string to the cmdlet showing what sort of Exchange command you are looking for. These following two examples, though very similar, return different data. The first example returns all Exchange cmdlets that end in `Mailbox`, and the second example returns all Exchange cmdlets that contain `Mailbox` in the name.

```
Get-ExCommand *Mailbox
Get-ExCommand *Mailbox*
```

You can get help for each of the Exchange Server roles by passing the `Role` parameter to the `Get-Help` cmdlet. The following example shows the available mailbox cmdlets:

```
Get-Help -Role *Mailbox*
Get-Help -Role *ClientAccess*
```

The remaining server roles are `Hub`, `UnifiedMessaging`, and `Edge`. Additionally, you can get role-specific help for the administration roles `OrgAdmin`, `SrvAdmin`, `RcptAdmin`, `WinAdmin`, and `ReadOnly`.

As with all strings passed to the `Role` parameter of the `Get-Help` cmdlet, the roles need to be enclosed with asterisks (*).

Note

Besides roles, you can get help for components and functionality. To see valid values for components and functionality, see Tables 7 and 8 on `http://technet.microsoft.com/en-us/library/aa997174(EXCHG.80)` `.aspx`. ∎

The four main recipient objects in Exchange (distribution group, mailbox, mail contact, and mail user) share common verbs — `Enable`, `Disable`, `New`, `Remove`, `Get`, and `Set`.

For these four recipient types, `Enable`, `Disable`, `Get`, `Set`, and `Remove` operate on existing Active Directory objects. The lone exception is `New`, which creates objects in Active

Directory while creating the Exchange object. The `Get-*` cmdlets are inherently read-only; you cannot make any changes using only `Get-*` cmdlets.

`Disable-*` cmdlets in all cases remove Exchange attributes from an Active Directory object, whereas `Remove-*` cmdlets delete the Active Directory object.

Armed with this knowledge, you can start reviewing information about recipients almost immediately. You can get a list of all mailboxes within the domain with the `Get-Mailbox` cmdlet:

```
Get-Mailbox
```

The `Get-Mailbox` cmdlet takes multiple optional parameters designed to provide just the mailboxes you are interested in. Among those parameters is the `ResultSize` parameter. You can set the result size to any number, or use `Unlimited` to retrieve all mailboxes that match the query:

```
Get-Mailbox -ResultSize Unlimited
```

The result size defaults to 1,000 objects, so if you do not expect more than 1,000, you can leave the parameter off. Using the optional parameters, you can limit the results to mailboxes on a server or database, or within an organizational unit (`Server`, `Database`, and `OrganizationalUnit`), or you can select a specific mailbox with the `Identity` parameter:

```
Get-Mailbox -Identity Contoso\bob
```

Perhaps the most powerful parameter that the `Get-Mailbox` cmdlet takes is the `Filter` parameter. With the `Filter` parameter, you can refine the results that the Exchange server returns based on many Active Directory attributes. This filtering is performed on the Exchange server as opposed to piping results to the `Where-Object` cmdlet, which filters results after the Exchange server sends them to the shell. See "Using Filters" later in this chapter for more on filtering.

The remaining `Get-*` cmdlets operate in much the same way, returning data on mail contacts, mail users, users, distribution groups, dynamic distribution groups, and recipients.

Note

Except for the public folder cmdlets, `New-*` and `Remove-*` cmdlets require that you have the proper Exchange permissions as well as Account Operator permissions in the Active Directory container in which the object will be created or from which it will be removed, as do `Set-*` cmdlets that modify Active Directory attributes. Although the `New-*` cmdlets do not normally require the `Alias` or `OrganizationalUnit` parameters, I recommend that you always specify these parameters, and all my samples will use them. ∎

Administering Recipients

To administer recipients, you will need to be in at least the `RecipientAdmin` role in Exchange 2007 or an equivalent role in Exchange 2010 such as the `Recipient Management` role.

Recipients in Exchange are mailboxes, contacts, users, groups, and dynamic groups. Exchange 2007 and 2010 provide cmdlets that operate on only Exchange attributes of existing Active Directory objects and cmdlets that create or modify Active Directory objects.

Administering Mailboxes

Use the `Enable-Mailbox` cmdlet to create a mailbox for a current Active Directory object, passing the required parameters `Identity` and `Database`. The following example mail-enables the Active Directory object `contoso\bob`, storing the mailbox on the database described as `ExchServer01\EXDB01`:

```
$Mailbox = @{
Identity = "contoso\bob"
Database = "ExchServer01\EXDB01"
}
Enable-Mailbox @Mailbox
```

Tip

If you do not specify a server as part of the `database` parameter when running the `Enable-Mailbox` cmdlet, the Exchange Management Shell attempts to find the database on the local machine. The `database` parameter takes a `GUID`, `database name`, `server\database`, or `server\storagegroup\database`. You will not need the storage group name unless you have multiple databases on the server with the same name. ■

To enable multiple mailboxes, you can use the `Enable-Mailbox` cmdlet in a loop, if you have a comma-separated value (`.csv`) file known as `c:\users.csv` that contains the following:

```
Identity,Database
"Contoso\Bob","ExchServer01\EXDB-01"
....
"Contoso\Sherry","ExchServer02\EXDB-02"
```

You could mail-enable each listed account by running the following code:

```
foreach ($user in Import-Csv -Path C:\users.csv)
{
Enable-Mailbox -Identity $User.Identity -Database $User.Database
}
```

You can also enable multiple mailboxes by getting a list of Active Directory accounts that do not have associated mailboxes and piping them to the `Enable-Mailbox` cmdlet. The following sample finds all accounts in the `Accounting` organizational unit that are of the type `User` and pipes the output to the `Enable-Mailbox` cmdlet, which creates mailboxes in the `AccountingDB` database. Mailboxes are assigned an email address based upon the recipient template that applies to the mailbox.

```
$User = @{
OrganizationalUnit = "Accounting"
RecipientTypeDetails = "User"
```

```
ResultSize = "Unlimited"
}
Get-User @User | Enable-Mailbox -Database "ExchServer03\AccountingDB"
```

Tip

Exchange Server 2007 assigns the user principal name prefix as the alias for the mailbox, whereas Exchange Server 2010 uses the common name, replacing all non-ASCII characters with question marks (?), and removing spaces. Thus, Johnson, Bob gives an alias of `Johnson?Bob`. You can specify an alias while you are enabling the mailbox. Exchange Server 2010 Service Pack 1 and newer reverts to the behavior provided by Exchange Server 2007. ■

To enable a mailbox and specify the alias, you use the `Alias` parameter. The following example mail-enables the Active Directory object `Contoso\Bob` on the database described as `ExchServer01\EXDB01`, and sets the mailbox alias to `bobj`:

```
$Mailbox = @{
Identity = "Contoso\Bob"
Database = "ExchServer01\EXDB01"
Alias = "bobj"
}
Enable-Mailbox @Mailbox
```

Creating a mailbox and associated Active Directory account is nearly as easy as mail-enabling an existing account. If you are not working in a split permissions model, the `New-Mailbox` cmdlet operates as the `Enable-Mailbox` cmdlet did, with the additional required parameters of `Password`, `UserPrincipalName`, and `Name` (which is the display name). The following example creates the Active Directory object `smitschke` in the Users container, while creating a mailbox on the mailbox server `ExchServer02`, in the `EXDB2` mailbox database:

```
$password = ConvertTo-SecureString -String "NewPass91" -AsPlainText -Force
$Mailbox = @{
UserPrincipalName = "smitschke@contoso.com"
Database = "ExchServer02\EXDB2"
Name = "Mitschke, Sherry"
Password = $password
}
New-Mailbox @Mailbox
```

As shown, the password must be passed as a secure string. You can do it the way I have shown, or read input from the keyboard as:

```
$password = Read-Host -Prompt "Please enter a valid password" -AsSecureString
```

Optionally, you can specify an organizational unit for the user account with the `OrganizationalUnit` parameter. The next example creates the Active Directory object `smitschke@contoso.com` in the organizational unit `OU=Users,OU=Apps,DC=contoso,DC=com`, on the mailbox server `ExchServer02` in the mailbox database `EXDB2` and with a display name of `Mitschke, Sherry`. This example uses the password from the preceding example:

```
$Mailbox = @{
UserPrincipalName = "smitschke@contoso.com"
Database = "ExchServer02\EXDB2"
Name = "Mitschke, Sherry"
Password = $password
OrganizationalUnit = "OU=Users,OU=Apps,DC=contoso,DC=com"
}
New-Mailbox @Mailbox
```

You can add or change an address or change other Exchange attributes for an existing mailbox by using the Set-Mailbox cmdlet. The following example adds a new email address, bobj@contoso.com, to the mailbox Contoso\Bob:

```
$NewAddress = @{
Identity = "Contoso\Bob"
PrimarySmtpAddress = "bobj@contoso.com"
EmailAddressPolicyEnabled = $false
}
Set-Mailbox @NewAddress
```

To change the address, you need to wait for Active Directory replication and remove the old address. The example in Listing 12-1 sets the primary SMTP address for the mailbox bobj to bojohnson@contoso.com. After setting the new address, there will be at least two SMTP addresses. Use a do . . . while loop to get the mailbox email addresses until the PrimarySmtpAddress is not equal to the newAddressString. Once the PrimarySmtpAddress matches the NewAddressString, you set the variable $Addresses to the current email addresses. You then remove all addresses that have a prefix string indicating that they are SMTP addresses, and are not the PrimarySmtpAddress from the $Addresses variable. Finally, you use the Set-Mailbox cmdlet to apply the EmailAddresses to the variable $Addresses.

LISTING 12-1

Changing an Email Address for a Mailbox in Exchange 2007

```
$User = "bobj"
$NewAddressString = "bojohnson@contoso.com"
$NewAddress = @{
Identity = $User
PrimarySmtpAddress = $NewAddressString
EmailAddressPolicyEnabled = $False
}
Set-Mailbox @newAddress
$Select = {
Property = "PrimarySmtpAddress"
}
do{$address = Get-Mailbox -Identity $User | Select-Object @Select}
```

```
while ($address.PrimarySmtpAddress.ToString() -ne $NewAddressString)
$Mailbox = Get-Mailbox -Identity $User
$Addresses = $Mailbox.EmailAddresses
$Mailbox.EmailAddresses | ForEach-Object {
if (!$_.IsPrimaryAddress -and ($_.PrefixString -eq 'SMTP')) {
$Addresses -= $_}}
Set-Mailbox -Identity $User -EmailAddresses $Addresses
```

This script works in Exchange Server 2007 or Exchange Server 2010, but as mentioned in the "What's New in Microsoft Exchange Server 2010" section, you can now add or remove values in multi-valued properties with a single command. This is shown in Listing 12-2, which accomplishes the same email address change as the previous script, in an Exchange Server 2010 Management Shell:

LISTING 12-2

Changing an Email Address for a Mailbox in Exchange 2010

```
$AddressesBefore = @{
Identity = "bobj"
}
$User =  Get-Mailbox @AddressesBefore
$SetAddress = @{
Identity = $AddressesBefore["Identity"]
EmailAddressPolicyEnabled = $False
PrimarySmtpAddress = "bojohnson@contoso.com"
}
Set-Mailbox @SetAddress
$RemoveAddresses = @{
Identity = $AddressesBefore["Identity"]
EmailAddresses = @{Remove = $User.EmailAddresses}
}
Set-Mailbox @RemoveAddresses
```

Notice the final `Set-Mailbox` call removes all previous email addresses at once.

To disable a mailbox, you can use either the `Disable-Mailbox` or `Remove-Mailbox` cmdlets. The following example removes the Exchange attributes from the account `smitschke` and marks the mailbox for deletion while leaving the Active Directory object:

```
Disable-Mailbox -Identity smitschke
```

To remove the Active Directory object `bobj` and mark the mailbox for deletion, use the following code:

```
Remove-Mailbox -Identity bobj
```

In both cases, for as long as the deleted mailbox retention period lasts, the disconnected mailbox can be reconnected to an existing Active Directory account that does not currently have an associated mailbox. The deleted mailbox retention period is explained further in the "Managing Databases" section of the chapter.

To reconnect the mailbox, you use the aptly named `Connect-Mailbox` cmdlet. This cmdlet takes the required parameters `Identity` and `Database`. Optional parameters allow you to choose which Active Directory account to connect the mailbox to, set the `alias`, and apply managed folder policies. You can also specify that the mailbox is a resource account.

If you do not specify the `User` parameter, Exchange searches Active Directory for a matching account based on the `LegacyExchangeDN` and `Display Name` of the disconnected mailbox. If Exchange is not able to find a matching account, the mailbox is not reconnected. Not specifying the user can potentially be a problem, because the matching account might not be the account you expect. To verify the account before connecting the mailbox, add the `ValidateOnly` parameter. Further optional parameters allow you to bypass confirmation or to simulate the action.

Unlike most of the recipient cmdlets, the `Identity` parameter does not accept an alias, because the disconnected mailbox does not have an alias. Instead, you can use the mailbox `GUID`, `DisplayName`, or `LegacyExchangeDN`.

This example connects the mailbox for Johnson, Bob to the existing Active Directory account on the mailbox database `ExchServer01\ExchDB`:

```
Connect-Mailbox -Identity "Johnson, Bob" -Database "ExchServer01\ExchDB"
```

The following example shows what Active Directory account the mailbox for Johnson, Bob would be connected to. Note that even though you set the `ValidateOnly` parameter, you still need to pass the required parameter `Database`.

```
$Connect = @{
Identity = "Johnson, Bob"
Database = "ExchServer01\ExchDB"
}
Connect-Mailbox $Connect -ValidateOnly | Select-Object SamAccountName
```

The following code connects the mailbox Mitschke, Sherry to the Active Directory account contoso\sherry:

```
$Connect = @{
Identity = "Mitschke, Sherry"
User = "contoso\sherry"
Alias = "sherrym"
}
Connect-Mailbox @Connect
```

You cannot use the `Connect-Mailbox` cmdlet to create an Active Directory account and connect the mailbox to that account simultaneously. If an Active Directory account does not already exist, you'd need to create one in a separate step.

You can get a list of disconnected mailboxes by using the `Get-MailboxStatistics` cmdlet and using client-side filtering for mailboxes that have a disconnect date. The following example returns all mailboxes on the server `ExchServer1` that have been disconnected. Details shown are the display name, disconnect date, database where the mailbox exists, and mailbox GUID.

```
$Server = @{
Server = "ExchServer1"
}
$Object = @{
FilterScript = {$_.DisconnectDate -ne $null}
}
$Format =@{
Property = "DisplayName","DisconnectDate","Database","MailboxGuid"
AutoSize = $True
}
Get-MailboxStatistics @Server | Where-Object @Object | Format-Table @Format
```

The following example returns all mailboxes on all Exchange servers that have been disconnected. Details shown are the display name, disconnect date, server name, and database where the mailbox exists.

```
$Object = @{
FilterScript = {$_.DisconnectDate -ne $null}
}
$Select =@{
Property = "DisplayName","DisconnectDate","Database"
}
Get-MailboxServer | Get-MailboxStatistics | Where-Object @Object `
| Select-Object @Select
```

You may notice that recently disconnected mailboxes are not included in the output. To view recently disconnected mailboxes, you can run the `Clean-MailboxDatabase` cmdlet before the `Get-MailboxStatistics` cmdlet. The `Clean-MailboxDatabase` cmdlet takes the required parameter `Identity`, which accepts pipeline input. This cmdlet scans Active Directory for mailbox objects that have been disconnected and which are not yet marked as disconnected in Microsoft Exchange. These mailboxes are then marked as disconnected. You can clean all mailbox databases at once by piping the output of the `Get-MailboxDatabase` cmdlet to the `Clean-MailboxDatabase` cmdlet:

```
Get-MailboxDatabase | Clean-MailboxDatabase
```

You can also clean all the databases on a specific server by using the `Server` parameter of the `Get-MailboxDatabase` cmdlet:

```
Get-MailboxDatabase -Server Exch2010 | Clean-MailboxDatabase
```

To clean a specific database, pass the database name to the cmdlet. The first line in the following code cleans a database on Exchange Server 2007, whereas the second cleans a database on Exchange Server 2010:

```
Clean-MailboxDatabase -Identity "Exchsvr\Ex2007DB"
Clean-MailboxDatabase -Identity Ex2010DB
```

Moving Mailboxes

Moving mailboxes is significantly different in Exchange Server 2007 and Exchange Server 2010. Mailbox moves in Exchange Server 2007 are performed synchronously, whereas mailbox moves in Exchange Server 2010 are performed asynchronously. Additionally, *dumpster data*, otherwise known as recoverable deleted items, is not moved in Exchange Server 2007, whereas it is moved in Exchange Server 2010.

Moving an Exchange Server 2007 mailbox causes user interruption. The mailbox is inaccessible while it is being moved. Additionally, the mailbox is moved from the source database to the administrative workstation, and then to the target database.

Moving a mailbox in Exchange Server 2010 is only an inconvenience to users. The users will need to restart their client after the move is completed, as the mailbox is copied from one database to another. Once the mailbox exists on the target database, it is deleted from the source database. Mailboxes are moved directly from the source database to the target database by the Exchange Mailbox Replication service. Additionally, users may access their mailbox while it is being moved.

Moving a mailbox from Exchange Server 2007 Service Pack 2 to Exchange Server 2010 works the same way as moving mailboxes within Exchange Server 2010.

Moving Mailboxes in Microsoft Exchange Server 2007

To move a mailbox in Exchange Server 2007, you use the `Move-Mailbox` cmdlet, passing the required parameters `Identity` and `TargetDatabase`. The following example moves the mailbox for `bobj` to the database `ex2007db1` on server `Exchsvr1`, after prompting for confirmation:

```
$Move = @{
Identity = "bobj"
TargetDatabase = "Exchsvr1\ex2007db1"
}
Move-Mailbox @Move
```

The `Move-Mailbox` cmdlet takes an optional parameter, `BadItemLimit`, which defaults to 0; any bad items will cause the move to fail if the parameter is not set. A bad item, otherwise known as a corrupted item, is any item in the mailbox database that cannot be read. This could be an email message, contact, calendar item, etcetera. The following example moves the mailbox for `bobj` to the database `ex2007db1` on server `Exchsvr1`, ignoring up to 40 bad items, after prompting for confirmation:

```
$Move = @{
Identity = "bobj"
TargetDatabase = "Exchsvr1\ex2007db1"
BadItemLimit = 40
}
Move-Mailbox @Move
```

Tip

To avoid being prompted for confirmation, add the `Confirm` parameter to any cmdlet that accepts it as:
`Confirm: $False` or, in a script block used for splatting, as `Confirm = $False`. ■

Moving Mailboxes in Microsoft Exchange Server 2010

To move a mailbox in Exchange Server 2010, use the `New-MoveRequest` cmdlet, passing the
`Identity` and `TargetDatabase` required parameters. At this point, the `New-MoveRequest`
cmdlet looks like it's nothing more than a renamed `Move-Mailbox`. The cmdlet returns
almost immediately, however. This is because the Mailbox Replication service, which runs
on all Client Access Servers, is processing the move request in the background. Unlike the
`TargetDatabase` parameter in Exchange Server 2007, Exchange Server 2010 takes only a
database GUID or database name.

This example requests that the Client Access Server move the mailbox for `bobj` to the
database `Ex2010db`:

```
New-MoveRequest -Identity bobj -TargetDatabase Ex2010DB
```

You can move a list of mailboxes in a loop or by piping the output of one of the `Get-*`
cmdlets to the `New-MoveRequest` cmdlet. This example requests that the Client Access
Server move all mailboxes that match `*mitschke` to the database `Ex2010db`:

```
$Mailbox = @{
Identity = "*mitschke"
}
$Move = @{
TargetDatabase = "ExchServer01\Ex2010db"
}
Get-Mailbox @Mailbox | New-MoveRequest @Move
```

Finally, this example requests that the Client Access Server move all mailboxes for users in
the specified organizational unit to the database `Ex2010db`:

```
$Mailbox = @{
OrganizationalUnit = "OU=Users,OU=Apps,DC=contoso,DC=com"
}
Get-Mailbox @Mailbox | New-MoveRequest -TargetDatabase Ex2010db
```

Like the `Move-Mailbox` cmdlet, the `New-MoveRequest` cmdlet takes the optional parameter `BadItemLimit`, which defaults to 0; if there are any bad items, the move will fail. If you set the `BadItemLimit` to more than 50, you also have to pass the `AcceptLargeDataLoss` switch parameter.

The following example modifies the previous example to allow 50 bad items, and allows large data loss:

```
$Mailbox = @{
Identity = "*mitschke"
}
$Move = @{
TargetDatabase = "Ex2010db"
BadItemLimit = 50
AcceptLargeDataLoss = $True
}
Get-Mailbox @Mailbox | New-MoveRequest @Move
```

To see the status of the move request, you use the `Get-MoveRequest` cmdlet. This example shows the status of the move request for `bobj`:

```
Get-MoveRequest -Identity bobj
```

You can also run the `Get-MoveRequest` cmdlet with no parameters to see the status of all move requests, or specify the status of move requests you are interested in with the `MoveStatus` parameter. This example returns all move requests that are completed:

```
Get-MoveRequest -MoveStatus Completed
```

If you have been performing move requests for a while, you will see multiple completed requests. Valid status values for the `MoveStatus` parameter are shown in the following list:

- `AutoSuspended`
- `Completed`
- `CompletedWithWarning`
- `CompletionInProgress`
- `Failed`
- `InProgress`
- `None`
- `Queued`
- `Suspended`

Once you have requested a move using the `New-MoveRequest` cmdlet, you cannot request a new move for that mailbox without removing the existing move request. This is true even for completed moves. To remove move requests, use the `Remove-MoveRequest` cmdlet.

The first line in the following code removes the single move request for the user bobj. The second example removes all completed move requests.

```
Remove-MoveRequest -Identity bobj
Get-MoveRequest -MoveStatus Completed | Remove-MoveRequest
```

One of the results might show "Failed" — there are multiple reasons a move request can fail. To view the reason for a failed move, use the Get-MailboxStatistics cmdlet with the optional IncludeMoveReport switch parameter. The following example displays the move report for the mailbox bobj:

```
(Get-MailboxStatistics -Identity bobj -IncludeMoveReport).MoveHistory
```

Another parameter of the Get-MailboxStatistics cmdlet is IncludeMoveHistory, which shows a less detailed view of the move. This is handy for keeping track of the original database for a mailbox. You can use this information if you need to restore a mailbox for a user and aren't sure what database the mailbox existed on.

This example shows the most recent move information for the mailbox bobj, followed by as many move requests as possible, up to the configured limit. Details returned are the SourceDatabase, TargetDatabase, and the CompletionTimeStamp.

```
$Statistics = @{
Identity = "bobj"
IncludeMoveHistory = $True
}
$Object = @{
Property = "SourceDatabase","TargetDatabase","CompletionTimeStamp"
}
(Get-MailboxStatistics @Statistics).MoveHistory | Select-Object @Object
```

To limit the results to only the most recent move, add the First parameter to the Select-Object cmdlet, with a value of 1. The next example is identical to the preceding one, with the exception that only the most recent move is displayed:

```
$Statistics = @{
Identity = "bobj"
IncludeMoveHistory = $True
}
$Object = @{
Property = "SourceDatabase","TargetDatabase","CompletionTimeStamp"
First = 1
}
(Get-MailboxStatistics @Statistics).MoveHistory | Select-Object @Object
```

By default, Exchange Server 2010 stores the move history for the previous two moves. Each move history takes approximately 300 KB and is stored in a hidden folder in the associated mailbox. You can change the number of move histories by editing an XML file on each Exchange Server 2010 Client Access Server. This file is named `MSExchangeMailboxReplication.exe.config` and is located in the `Bin` folder on the Client Access Server(s). The following script displays the current number of move histories for each Exchange Server 2010 Client Access Server in your organization:

```
foreach ($server in Get-ExchangeServer | Where-Object {
$_.AdminDisplayVersion -like "Version 14*" -and $_.ServerRole -like "*Client*"})
{
$serverName = $server.Name
$hive ="LocalMachine"
$keyName = "SOFTWARE\Microsoft\ExchangeServer\v14\Setup"
$valueName = "MsiInstallPath"
$regHive = [Microsoft.Win32.RegistryHive]$hive
$regKey = [Microsoft.Win32.RegistryKey]::OpenRemoteBaseKey($regHive,$serverName)
$moveConfigPath = "\\$serverName\"
$moveConfigPath += ($regKey.OpenSubKey($keyName)).GetValue("MsiInstallPath")
$moveConfigPath += "Bin\MSExchangeMailboxReplication.exe.config"
$moveConfigPath = $moveConfigPath.Replace(":","$")
$xml = [xml](get-content $moveConfigPath)
$numberOfMoves = $xml.configuration.LastChild.MaxMoveHistoryLength
Write-Output -InputObject "$serverName is set to keep $numberOfMoves moves"
}
```

You can modify the number of move histories saved by each Client Access Server by adding three lines to the preceding script, changing the 4 to the actual number you want:

```
$newMoveHistory = "4"
$xml.configuration.LastChild.MaxMoveHistoryLength = $newMoveHistory
$xml.Save($moveConfigPath)
```

Listing 12-3 provides the complete script.

LISTING 12-3

Modifying the Move History to Retain Information on Four Moves

```
foreach ($server in Get-ExchangeServer | Where-Object {
$_.AdminDisplayVersion -like "Version 14*" -and $_.ServerRole -like "*Client*"})
{
$serverName = $server.Name
$hive = "LocalMachine"
$keyName = "SOFTWARE\Microsoft\ExchangeServer\v14\Setup"
$valueName = "MsiInstallPath"
$regHive = [Microsoft.Win32.RegistryHive]$hive
$regKey = [Microsoft.Win32.RegistryKey]::OpenRemoteBaseKey($regHive,$serverName)
$moveConfigPath = "\\$serverName\"
```

```
$moveConfigPath += ($regKey.OpenSubKey($keyName)).GetValue("MsiInstallPath")
$moveConfigPath += "Bin\MSExchangeMailboxReplication.exe.config"
$moveConfigPath = $moveConfigPath.Replace(":","$")
$xml = [xml](get-content $moveConfigPath)
$numberOfMoves = $xml.configuration.LastChild.MaxMoveHistoryLength
Write-Output "$serverName is set to keep $numberOfMoves moves"
$newMoveHistory = "4"
$xml.configuration.LastChild.MaxMoveHistoryLength = $newMoveHistory
$xml.Save($moveConfigPath)
$xml = [xml](get-content $moveConfigPath)
$numberOfMoves = $xml.configuration.LastChild.MaxMoveHistoryLength
Write-Output -InputObject "$serverName is now set to keep $numberOfMoves moves"
}
```

Managing Contacts

The `Enable-MailContact` cmdlet mail-enables existing contact objects. This cmdlet requires that you pass the `Identity` and `ExternalEmailAddress` parameters. The following example mail-enables the existing contact `Curt Johnson` with an external email address of `cjohnson@powershell.com`:

```
$MailContact = @{
Identity = "Curt Johnson"
ExternalEmailAddress = "cjohnson@powershell.com"
}
Enable-MailContact @MailContact
```

As with the `Enable-Mailbox` cmdlet, if you do not specify an alias, Exchange creates one for you. In my experience, the alias will be the common name of the contact with spaces removed and replacing all non-ASCII characters with question marks (?). Thus, `Johnson, Bob` gives an alias of `Johnson?Bob`, and `Tyler Jones` gives an alias of `TylerJones`. This behavior is the same in Exchange Server 2007 and Exchange Server 2010.

The `New-MailContact` cmdlet creates a new contact in Active Directory, and mail-enables it. This cmdlet requires the `Name` and `ExternalEmailAddress` parameters. As with the `Enable-MailContact` cmdlet, Exchange creates an alias if you do not specify one. Additionally, unless specified, the display name for the contact will be the `Name` you specified.

The following example creates the new contact `Jones, Kent` with an alias of `kjones` and a display name of `Jones, Kent` in the `Contacts` container of the `Marketing` organizational unit:

```
$MailContact = @{
Name = "Jones, Kent"
ExternalEmailAddress = "kjones@powershell.com"
OrganizationalUnit = "Contoso.com/Marketing/Contacts"
Alias = "kjones"
}
New-MailContact @MailContact
```

You can change an address for an existing email contact with the `Set-MailContact` cmdlet, passing the parameters `Identity`, `ExternalEmailAddress`, and `EmailAddressPolicyEnabled`. The `EmailAddressPolicyEnabled` parameter must be set to `$False`.

The following example changes the external email address for the contact `Ted Jones` to `tedjones@powershell.com`, and disables the email address policy that applies to the contact (if any):

```
$MailContact = "Ted Jones"
$NewAddressString = "tedjones@powershell.com"
$NewAddress = @{
Identity = $MailContact
ExternalEmailAddress = $NewAddressString
EmailAddressPolicyEnabled = $False
}
Set-MailContact @NewAddress
```

Existing email contacts can be disabled or deleted with the `Disable-MailContact` or `Remove-MailContact` cmdlets. As always, you can bypass the confirmation prompt by specifying the `Confirm = $False` parameter.

The following example disables the email contact for `Jones, Kent`. Changing the last line to `Remove-MailContact @MailContact` deletes the email from Active Directory:

```
$MailContact = @{
Identity = "Jones, Kent"
Confirm = $false
}
Disable-MailContact @MailContact
```

Administering Users

Mail-enabled users are similar to mail-enabled contacts in that mail sent to either sends to an external domain instead of a local Exchange mailbox. Mail-enabled contacts have no login accounts in Active Directory, whereas mail-enabled users do have the ability to log in to Active Directory.

You can mail-enable existing user accounts by using the `Enable-MailUser` cmdlet with the required parameters `Identity` and `ExternalEmailAddress`.

The following example mail-enables the account `jdoll`, and sets the external email address to `jdoll@nowhere.com`:

```
$MailUser = @{
Identity = "jdoll"
ExternalEmailAddress = "jdoll@nowhere.com"
}
Enable-MailUser @MailUser
```

As with the `Enable-Mailbox` cmdlet, if you do not specify an internal SMTP address, Exchange assigns one for you. In this case, the primary SMTP address will be the external email address, and Exchange will assign a secondary email address that matches the email address policy.

You can create and mail-enable a new user with the `New-MailUser` cmdlet as shown in the following example. The example creates the mail-enabled user `Ed Johnson` with an external email address of `ed@external.com`, and a user principal name of `ed@contoso.com`. This account will be created in the Users container. As seen in the section on creating mailboxes, you create a password via the `Read-Host` cmdlet:

```
$Password = Read-Host "Enter password" -AsSecureString
$User =@{
Name = "Ed Johnson"
ExternalEmailAddress = "ed@external.com"
UserPrincipalName = "ed@contoso.com"
Password = $Password
}
New-MailUser @User
```

Optionally, you can pass an organizational unit for the user account with the `OrganizationalUnit` parameter, and an alias with the `Alias` parameter, as shown in the following example. I recommend always specifying the organizational unit and alias.

```
$Password = Read-Host "Enter password" -AsSecureString
$User =@{
Name = "Ed Johnson"
ExternalEmailAddress = "ed@external.com"
UserPrincipalName = "ed@contoso.com"
Password = $Password
OrganizationalUnit = "OU=Users,OU=Apps,DC=contoso,DC=com"
Alias = "ejohnson"
}
New-MailUser @User
```

Once again, you will need to have Account Operator permissions in Active Directory to use the `New-MailUser` or `Remove-MailUser` cmdlets.

Changing the email address is as easy as with a mailbox, with the exception that you can change the primary SMTP address or the external email address, or both. The primary SMTP address is used inside the organization, and the external email address is where mail is delivered. The external email address is specified with the `ExternalEmailAddress` parameter.

The following example adds the external email address `emcray@federalbank.com` to the mail user and sets the primary SMTP address to `emcray@contoso.com`. As with mailboxes, you need to wait for Active Directory replication to be complete to remove the old address.

```
$User = @{
Identity = "Erik Mcray"
PrimarySmtpAddress = "emcray@contoso.com"
EmailAddressPolicyEnabled = $false
ExternalEmailAddress = "emcray@federalbank.com"
}
Set-MailUser @User
```

In the next example, the code adds the external email address emcray@federalbank.com to the mail user and sets the primary SMTP address to emcray@contoso.com. The example then uses a do...while loop to wait for Active Directory to recognize the email address change. Finally, the example removes the old email addresses.

```
$User = @{
Identity = "Erik Mcray"
PrimarySmtpAddress = "emcray@contoso.com"
EmailAddressPolicyEnabled = $false
ExternalEmailAddress = "emcray@federalbank.com"
}
Set-MailUser @User
do{$address = Get-MailUser -Identity $User["identity"]}
while ($address.PrimarySmtpAddress.ToString() -ne $User["PrimarySmtpAddress"])
$MailUser = Get-MailUser -Identity $user["identity"]
$Addresses = $MailUser.EmailAddresses
$MailUser.EmailAddresses | ForEach-Object {
if (!$_.IsPrimaryAddress -and ($_.PrefixString -eq 'SMTP')){
$Addresses -= $_}}
$SetUser = @{
Identity = $user["identity"]
EmailAddresses = $Addresses
}
Set-MailUser @SetUser
```

Because mail-enabled users are User objects, you can modify Active Directory attributes with the Set-User cmdlet exactly as you could with mailboxes. The following example sets the Company, StreetAddress, City, StateOrProvince, and PostalCode for the user Erik Mcray:

```
$User = @{
Identity = "Erik Mcray"
Company = "Federal Bank"
StreetAddress = "129 South Pine"
City = "Memphis"
StateOrProvince = "TN"
PostalCode = "38115"
}
Set-User @User
```

The `Set-User` cmdlet sets Active Directory attributes. As such, you need Account Operator permissions in the Active Directory container. You use the `Set-MailUser` cmdlet to set Exchange attributes for the object.

As you could with mailboxes, you can disable or remove a mailuser if you have Account Operator permissions. The first line in the following code removes Exchange attributes from the user object, and the second one deletes the user object:

```
Disable-MailUser -Identity ejohnson -Confirm:$False
Remove-MailUser -Identity ejohnson -Confirm:$False
```

Administering Groups

Microsoft Exchange Server provides two different kinds of groups: distribution groups and dynamic distribution groups. *Distribution Groups* have static membership, managed by one or more people. These people would normally not have any sort of Exchange management permission. For instance, an `AccountingUsers` distribution group would normally be set up so the membership is managed by someone in the accounting department.

As the name implies, *dynamic distribution groups* have their membership created dynamically. These groups are, in effect, created each time an email is sent to them.

Administering Distribution Groups

Note

For the purpose of this book, I am not going to distinguish between mail-enabled security groups and true distribution groups. ∎

Groups in Exchange Server 2007 and Exchange Server 2010 must be universal groups before you can mail-enable them. You cannot use the `Enable-DistributionGroup` cmdlet to change a group from a global or domain local group to a universal group. If you attempt to mail-enable a group that is not a universal group, you will receive an error: "The group that you want to mail-enable is not a universal group. Only a universal group can be mail-enabled."

The following example mail-enables the existing universal group `SafetyTeam` with a display name of `Safety Team` and an email address generated by the applicable email address policy:

```
Enable-DistributionGroup -Identity "SafetyTeam" -DisplayName "Safety Team"
```

You can specify the email address with the additional parameter `PrimarySmtpAddress`. The following example mail-enables the existing universal group `MarketingGroup`, with a display name of `Marketing Group` and a primary SMTP address of `marketing@contoso.com`:

```
$DistributionGroup = @{
Identity = "MarketingGroup"
DisplayName = "Marketing Group"
PrimarySmtpAddress = "marketing@contoso.com"
}
Enable-DistributionGroup @DistributionGroup
```

If you have Account Operator permissions in the Active Directory container where the group exists, you can convert a group to a universal group by using the Set-Group cmdlet and passing the required parameter Identity and the switch parameter Universal. The following example converts the existing group SalesTeam to a universal group:

```
Set-Group -Identity SalesTeam -Universal
```

If you have Account Operator permissions, you can create and mail-enable a distribution group in Exchange 2007 with the New-DistributionGroup cmdlet, passing the required parameters Name, Type (Distribution or Security), and SamAccountName.

This example creates the distribution group Accounting in the Users container with the DisplayName of Accounting, and an Alias of accounting:

```
$DistributionGroup = @{
Type = "Distribution"
Name = "Accounting"
SamAccountName = "accounting"
}
New-DistributionGroup @DistributionGroup
```

The New-DistributionGroup cmdlet in Exchange 2010 requires only the Name parameter. The following example creates a distribution group named Legal, also in the Users container with the DisplayName and Alias of Legal. In Exchange Server 2010, the group type will be Distribution unless specified with the optional Type parameter.

```
$DistributionGroup = @{
Name = "Legal"
}
New-DistributionGroup @DistributionGroup
```

As with all of the New-* recipient cmdlets, I recommend you specify the optional parameters OrganizationalUnit and Alias. I also recommend you use the optional parameter ManagedBy, because the cmdlet sets a default to the person running the cmdlet in Exchange Server 2010 and leaves ManagedBy blank in Exchange Server 2007. The account listed in the ManagedBy attribute can add and remove members from the group, but is not a member of the group on creation. Additionally, I recommend you set the DisplayName parameter.

An Exchange Server 2007 example script would look like this:

```
$DistributionGroup = @{
Type = "Distribution"
Name = "accounting"
DisplayName = "Accounting"
SamAccountName = "accounting"
Alias = "accountants"
OrganizationalUnit = "contoso.com/Accounting/Groups"
ManagedBy = "contoso\jballard"
}
New-DistributionGroup @DistributionGroup
```

The equivalent Exchange Server 2010 script would be:

```
$DistributionGroup = @{
Name = "accounting"
DisplayName = "Accounting"
Alias = "accountants"
OrganizationalUnit = "contoso.com/Accounting/Groups"
ManagedBy = "contoso\jballard"
}
New-DistributionGroup @DistributionGroup
```

Note that a SamAccountName was not specified for the group in Exchange Server 2010. In this case, the group defaults to using the name for the SamAccountName. The SamAccountName is used for clients running operating systems prior to Windows 2000.

You can add members to distribution groups with the Add-DistributionGroupMember cmdlet, passing the required parameters Identity and Member, where identity is the group, and member is the object to add to the group. The following example adds the mailbox associated with the Active Directory account jballard to the distribution group accounting:

```
$DistributionGroupMember = @{
Identity = "accounting"
Member = "jballard"
}
Add-DistributionGroupMember @DistributionGroupMember
```

You can also pipe the results of a Get-Mailbox cmdlet to the Add-DistributionGroupMember cmdlet to add all the results to the group at once. The following example adds all mailboxes in the Accounting organizational unit to the Accounting distribution group:

```
$Mailbox = @{
OrganizationalUnit = "Accounting"
}
$DistributionGroupMember = @{
Identity = "Accounting"
}
Get-Mailbox @Mailbox | Add-DistributionGroupMember @DistributionGroupMember
```

You can remove members from a distribution group with the Remove-DistributionGroupMember cmdlet, once again passing the required parameters Identity and Member. The following example removes the object associated with the Active Directory account jballard from the distribution group Accounting:

```
Remove-DistributionGroupMember -Identity Accounting -Member jballard
```

You can view the members of a group with the Get-DistributionGroupMember cmdlet, which has only one required parameter, the Identity. The following example shows all members of the Accounting distribution group:

```
Get-DistributionGroupMember -Identity Accounting
```

As with users and mailboxes, you can disable or remove distribution groups using the Disable-DistributionGroup or Remove-DistributionGroup cmdlets. As always, the Disable-DistributionGroup cmdlet leaves the Active Directory object, whereas the Remove-DistributionGroup cmdlet removes the Active Directory object. Once again, the Remove-DistributionGroup cmdlet requires that you have Account Operator permissions on the Active Directory container. Both cmdlets require the Identity parameter, which takes the group's alias, display name, or name, among other values.

The first line in the following code removes the Exchange attributes from the Active Directory object, and the second removes the Active Directory object:

```
Disable-DistributionGroup -Identity Accounting
Remove-DistributionGroup -Identity Accounting
```

Oddly enough, there is no built-in Exchange cmdlet for finding groups a mailbox is a member of. For this, you need to rely on Active Directory. The following example shows all groups that jballard is a direct member of, and shows both security and distribution groups:

```
$Member = "(&(objectClass=person)(name=jballard))"
(([adsisearcher] $Member).FindOne()).Properties.memberof
```

Administering Dynamic Distribution Groups

Dynamic distribution groups are different from distribution groups in that their membership is defined each time a mail message is sent to the group. The membership is defined by an Active Directory query, which is created when the group is created. You can modify the query after the group is created as well.

To create a dynamic distribution group, you use the New-DynamicDistributionGroup cmdlet, which requires the parameters Name and either RecipientFilter or IncludedRecipients. Modifying a dynamic distribution group is accomplished with the Set-DynamicDistributionGroup cmdlet, which requires the Identity parameter.

Some of the parameters of these two cmdlets are mutually exclusive because they belong to different parameter sets. If you use one, you cannot use the other. These are shown in Table 12-1.

TABLE 12-1

Parameter Sets for the DynamicDistributionGroup Cmdlets

If you use this parameter	You cannot use these parameters
RecipientFilter	IncludedRecipients
	ConditionalCompany
	ConditionalCustomAttribute1 through 15
	ConditionalDepartment
	ConditionalStateOrProvince

The following example creates a dynamic distribution group named Building 50 Users with a recipient filter that finds all mail-enabled Active Directory objects with Building 50 in the Office attribute:

```
$DynamicDistributionGroup = @{
Name = "Building 50 Users"
Alias = "Building50"
DisplayName = "Building 50 Users"
RecipientFilter = {Office -eq "Building 50"}
OrganizationalUnit = "Contoso.com/Groups/DynamicGroups"
}
New-DynamicDistributionGroup @DynamicDistributionGroup
```

You can restrict the membership of the dynamic distribution group to include specific mailboxes with an extended filter. The following example creates a dynamic distribution group named Building 50 Users with a recipient filter that finds all mailboxes with Building 50 in the Office attribute:

```
$Filter = {
Office -eq "Building 50" -and RecipientTypeDetails -eq "usermailbox"
}
$DynamicDistributionGroup = @{
Name = "Building 50 Users"
Alias = "Building50"
DisplayName = "Building 50 Users"
RecipientFilter = $Filter
}
New-DynamicDistributionGroup @DynamicDistributionGroup
```

As an alternative to the RecipientFilter parameter, you can use the IncludedRecipients parameter. This parameter accepts multiple recipient types, separated by a comma. Along with the IncludedRecipients parameter, you can use any of the conditional parameters, which cannot be used with the RecipientFilter parameter.

IncludedRecipients "MailboxUsers, MailUsers" finds any mail-enabled objects that are either mailboxes or mail users. ConditionalDepartment "Accounting,Finance" finds any Active Directory objects with the department of Accounting or Finance.

Put together, the two parameters find all mailboxes and mail users in the Accounting or Finance department. The following example creates a new dynamic distribution group named Finance & Accounting Users containing all mailboxes and mail users in the Finance or Accounting department:

```
$Recipients = "MailboxUsers, MailUsers"
$Department = "Accounting","Finance"
$DynamicDistributionGroup = @{
Name = "Finance & Accounting Users"
Alias = "Finance&Accounting"
```

```
DisplayName = "Finance & Accounting"
IncludedRecipients = $Recipients
ConditionalDepartment = $Department
}
New-DynamicDistributionGroup @DynamicDistributionGroup
```

Additional conditional parameters include ConditionalCompany, ConditionalStateOrProvince, and ConditionalCustomAttribute1 through ConditionalCustomAttribute15. These work the same as the ConditionalDepartment parameter. Any strings passed to these parameters with a comma separating them are treated as OR filters. That is, ConditionalCompany "Contoso","Contoso Sales" would find objects with Contoso or Contoso Sales in the Company field.

Verifying the membership of a dynamic distribution group is a two-step process. First, you set a variable to the group using the Get-DynamicDistributionGroup cmdlet, and then you pass that variable to the Get-Recipient cmdlet. The following example shows which mail-enabled objects would receive an email message sent to the dynamic distribution group Building 50 Users at the moment the check is done. Any mail-enabled objects with an office attribute of Building 50 added after this check will also receive mail sent to the group. Likewise, any mail-enabled object that no longer has an office of Building 50 will no longer receive email sent to the group.

```
$Building50 = Get-DynamicDistributionGroup -Identity "Building 50 Users"
Get-Recipient -RecipientPreviewFilter $Building50.RecipientFilter
```

Verifying the group membership is a good step to perform immediately after creating the dynamic distribution group, because it will verify that the filter works as you expected. If the verification step returns results that you did not expect, you can set a new filter with the Set-DynamicDistributionGroup cmdlet. This cmdlet requires the Identity parameter, and whatever parameter you wish to change.

However, if the current filter uses the RecipientFilter parameter, you cannot add filters that are not allowed with that parameter (any of the conditional parameters, or the IncludedRecipients parameter).

You can see the current filter for the dynamic distribution group using the Identity parameter and passing the name of the group. The following example shows the filter for the dynamic distribution group Building 50 Users:

```
$Group = "Building 50 Users"
$Filter = "RecipientFilter"
(Get-DynamicDistributionGroup -Identity $Group |
Select-Object $Filter).RecipientFilter
```

You can modify an existing dynamic distribution group using the Set-DynamicDistributionGroup cmdlet. The following example sets the ManagedBy attribute for the dynamic distribution group Building 50 Users to contoso\ceverhart, and adds an email address, `Building50@contoso.com`. If you want to remove the old address, you will need to modify the code in Listing 12-1.

```
$DynamicDistributionGroup = @{
Identity = "Building 50 Users"
PrimarySmtpAddress = "Building50@contoso.com"
ManagedBy = "contoso\ceverhart"
EmailAddressPolicyEnabled = $false
}
Set-DynamicDistributionGroup @DynamicDistributionGroup
```

You can also set the filter for the dynamic distribution group by specifying the proper parameters and values to the `Set-DynamicDistributionGroup` cmdlet. The following example sets the `ManagedBy`, `PrimarySmtpAddress`, and `RecipientFilter` for the dynamic distribution group `Building 50 Users`:

```
$DynamicDistributionGroup = @{
Identity = "Building 50 Users"
PrimarySmtpAddress = "Building50@contoso.com"
ManagedBy = "contoso\ceverhart"
EmailAddressPolicyEnabled = $false
RecipientFilter = {Office -eq "Building 50"}
}
Set-DynamicDistributionGroup @DynamicDistributionGroup
```

You can remove a dynamic distribution group with the `Remove-DynamicDistributionGroup` cmdlet. This example removes the dynamic distribution group `Finance & Accounting Users`:

```
$Group = @{
Identity = "Finance & Accounting Users"
Confirm = $false
}
Remove-DynamicDistributionGroup @Group
```

Note

There is no `Disable-DynamicDistributionGroup` cmdlet. All `Disable-*` cmdlets remove Exchange attributes from an Active Directory object. Dynamic distribution groups have no function in Active Directory, and couldn't exist without Exchange, thus, if there were a `Disable-DynamicDistributionGroup` cmdlet, it would be functionally equivalent to the `Remove-DynamicDistributionGroup` cmdlet. ∎

Managing Resource Mailboxes

Resource mailboxes are mailboxes with several additional attributes and with an extra requirement — the Active Directory account must be disabled. Resource mailboxes can be rooms, equipment, or shared mailboxes.

Room mailboxes are mainly used to schedule an area, such as a conference room or an office. *Equipment mailboxes* are best used for items that are not tied to a specific location such as projectors, laptops, company vehicles, and other such items. *Shared mailboxes* are ideal in situations where you have multiple people in a department responsible for answering mail sent to one address, such as marketing@contoso.com.

Managing resource mailboxes is exactly like managing mailboxes, with the added parameter of the resource type. In all cases, the type is a switch parameter.

This parameter can be set to Room, Equipment, or Shared. The following example enables the account Area 51 and sets it to a room:

```
$Mailbox = @{
Identity = "Area 51"
Database = "ResourceDb"
Room = $true
}
Enable-Mailbox @Mailbox
```

If the account is not disabled before running the Enable-Mailbox cmdlet, the error "The user's Active Directory account must be logon-disabled for linked, shared, or resource mailbox" will be returned. If you have Account Operator permissions in the Active Directory container that contains Area 51, you can disable the account with a combination of the [adsisearcher] and [adsi] type accelerators. *Type accelerators* are a shortcut to an underlying .NET type name. In this case, System.DirectoryServices.DirectorySearcher and System.DirectoryServices.DirectoryEntry, respectively. This example disables the Active Directory account and enables the Equipment mailbox Projector 1:

```
$user = ((([adsisearcher]"(&(objectClass=person)(name=Projector 1))").FindOne())
$account=[adsi]$user.Path
$account.PsBase.InvokeSet("AccountDisabled", $true)
$account.SetInfo()
$Mailbox = @{
Identity = "Projector 1"
Database = "ResourceDb"
Room = $True
}
Enable-Mailbox @Mailbox
```

You can create and mail-enable a resource mailbox with the New-Mailbox cmdlet. This example creates the logon-disabled Active Directory object truck in the organizational unit resources, and mail-enables it as an Equipment mailbox:

```
$Mailbox = @{
Name = "Delivery Truck"
UserPrincipalName = "truck@contoso.com"
DisplayName = "Parts Delivery Truck"
Alias = "truck"
OrganizationalUnit = "contoso.com/resources"
Database = "ResourceDb"
Equipment = $true
}
New-Mailbox @Mailbox
```

Note that when you are creating a new resource mailbox with associated Active Directory account, you do not need to provide a password. As the account is disabled, a password is not needed.

You can convert an existing mailbox to a room or equipment mailbox with the `Set-Mailbox` cmdlet, passing the `Type` parameter. The following example converts the existing mailbox `Car 54` to the type `Equipment`:

```
$Mailbox = @{
Identity = "Car 54"
Type = "Equipment"
}
Set-Mailbox @Mailbox
```

Valid options for the `Type` parameter are `Room`, `Equipment`, `Shared`, and `Regular`. The type `Regular` converts the mailbox back to a user mailbox, and enables the Active Directory account.

Disabling or removing a resource mailbox is exactly the same as performing the same operation on a user mailbox. When a resource mailbox is disabled, the Active Directory account remains disabled. If you want to then enable the account as a user mailbox, you will need to enable the Active Directory account.

Managing Public Folders

Public folders are unlike the other recipient types in that they do not have an entry in Active Directory unless or until they are mail-enabled. Once mail-enabled, all public folder objects can be found in the `Microsoft Exchange System Objects` organizational unit. Additionally, you cannot create and mail-enable a public folder with a single cmdlet as you can the other recipients. Thus, mail-enabling a new public folder is inherently a two-step process:

1. Create the public folder.
2. Mail-enable the public folder.

You create a public folder with the `New-PublicFolder` cmdlet passing the required parameter `Name`. The following example creates the folder `Legal` under the root public folder, also known as `IPM_SUBTREE`:

```
New-PublicFolder -Name Legal
```

You can specify the path for the new folder using the `Path` parameter. The following example creates the folder `Sales` in the `Marketing` folder under the root public folder:

```
$PublicFolder = @{
Name = "Sales"
Path = "\Marketing"
}
New-PublicFolder @PublicFolder
```

You can mail-enable an existing public folder with the `Enable-MailPublicFolder` cmdlet. This cmdlet has the required parameter of `Identity`. The following example mail-enables the `Sales` public folder using the email address policy that applies:

```
$MailPublicFolder = @{
Identity = "\Marketing\Sales"
}
Enable-MailPublicFolder @MailPublicFolder
```

You can pipe the `New-PublicFolder` cmdlet to the `Enable-MailPublicFolder` cmdlet to create and mail-enable a folder at once. The following example creates a new folder named `District 3 Calendar` under the `\Marketing\Sales` folder, and mail-enables it:

```
$PublicFolder = @{
Name = "District 3 Calendar"
Path = "\Marketing\Sales"
}
New-PublicFolder @PublicFolder | Enable-MailPublicFolder
```

Oddly enough, the `Enable-MailPublicFolder` cmdlet does not allow you to specify the email address for a folder. To specify the address, you must use the `Set-MailPublicFolder` cmdlet, passing the `Identity`, `PrimarySmtpAddress`, and `EmailAddressPolicyEnabled` parameters.

Optionally, you can specify the parameters `Alias` and `DisplayName` for the public folder. I recommend that you always specify these parameters. The following example adds the email address `district3@contoso.com` to the public folder `District 3 Calendar`, sets the alias to `district3`, and the display name to `District 3 Sales Calendar` while preventing the email address policy from being applied. Note that there will already be an email address for the folder, because the `Enable-MailPublicFolder` cmdlet does not disable the email address policy.

```
$PublicFolder = @{
Identity = "\marketing\Sales\District 3 Calendar"
Alias = "district3"
PrimarySmtpAddress = "district3@contoso.com"
EmailAddressPolicyEnabled = $False
DisplayName = "District 3 Sales Calendar"
}
Set-MailPublicFolder @PublicFolder
```

If you'd rather not have the default email address as an additional email address, you will need to remove it. The following example builds upon the previous example, and uses the method introduced in Listing 12-1 to change the SMTP address for the mail-enabled public folder `District 3 Calendar` to `district3@contoso.com`, removing all other SMTP addresses:

```
$PublicFolder = @{
Identity = "\marketing\Sales\District 3 Calendar"
Alias = "district3"
```

```
PrimarySmtpAddress = "district3@contoso.com"
EmailAddressPolicyEnabled = $false
DisplayName = "District 3 Sales Calendar"
}
Set-MailPublicFolder @PublicFolder
do{$address = Get-MailPublicFolder -Identity $PublicFolder.Identity}
While ($address.PrimarySmtpAddress -ne $PublicFolder.PrimarySmtpAddress)
$folder = Get-MailPublicFolder -Identity $PublicFolder.Identity
$Addresses = $folder.EmailAddresses
$folder.EmailAddresses | ForEach-Object {
if (!$_.IsPrimaryAddress -and ($_.PrefixString -eq 'SMTP')) {
$Addresses -= $_}}
Set-MailPublicFolder -Identity $PublicFolder.Identity -EmailAddresses $Addresses
```

You can disable or remove a public folder using the cmdlets Disable-MailPublicFolder or Remove-PublicFolder. As previously mentioned, public folders do not have an entry in Active Directory unless they are mail-enabled. Thus, the Disable-MailPublicFolder cmdlet removes the Active Directory object. The public folder still exists, however, and retains all data stored in it.

The Remove-PublicFolder cmdlet removes the public folder and all data stored in the folder.

Both cmdlets require the Identity parameter, and accept the optional Confirm switch parameter. If you do not specify Confirm = $False, you will be prompted for confirmation.

The following example removes the email address information from the public folder District 3 Calendar:

```
$PublicFolder = @{
Identity = "\marketing\Sales\District 3 Calendar"
Confirm = $False
}
Disable-MailPublicFolder @PublicFolder
```

The Remove-PublicFolder cmdlet removes all data from the public folder, and removes the folder from all servers in the organization. If the folder has subfolders, you need to specify the switch parameter Recurse. This parameter causes the cmdlet to remove the specified folder and all subfolders.

The next example deletes all the data from the public folder District 3 Calendar and all subfolders:

```
$PublicFolder = @{
Identity = "\marketing\Sales\District 3 Calendar"
Confirm = $False
Recurse = $True
}
Remove-PublicFolder @PublicFolder
```

If you only want to remove the folder from one or more servers, you will need to use the `Set-PublicFolder` cmdlet to manage replicas.

Note

When working with a public folder database, the Exchange Server 2010 documentation indicates that you can use the server name as part of the `Identity` parameter as `Server\Database`. In my experience, that is incorrect. In Exchange Server 2010, the name of the public folder database must be unique within the organization, so you only need to specify the database name. In the Exchange Server 2007 Management Shell, you can specify the `Server\Database` or `Server\StorageGroup\Database` to work with public folder databases. ∎

Public folder replication can be set on a per-folder basis, or at the database level. Managing replication on a per-folder basis can be a good way to minimize replication traffic across the network, while still providing local access to necessary public folders. Imagine you have three mailbox servers, ExMbx01, ExMbx02, and ExMbx03. On ExMbx01, you have a public folder database, PF01, and mailbox databases for the Human Resources department. On ExMbx02, you have a public folder database, PF02, and mailbox databases for Marketing and Research & Development. On ExMbx03, you have another public folder database, PF03, along with mailbox databases for Legal. For the purposes of this example, I am going to use PF01 as the main public folder database, and replicate only a few folders to PF02 and PF03. Setting public folder replication is accomplished with the `Set-PublicFolder` cmdlet, passing the `Replicas` and `ReplicationSchedule` parameters.

The following example sets replication for the folder Marketing to the database PF02 on the server ExMb02 to run from 1 minute after midnight on Monday until 1 minute before midnight on Friday. The folder R&D will replicate to the same server and database as Marketing, but will follow the default schedule of the database. The Legal folder will replicate to the database PF03 on the server ExMbx03 every day of the week.

```
$PublicFolder = @{
Identity = "\Marketing"
Replicas = "PF02"
ReplicationSchedule = "Monday.00:01-Friday.23:59"
}
$PublicFolder2 = @{
Identity = "\R&D"
Replicas = "PF02"
ReplicationSchedule = "Always"
}
$PublicFolder3 = @{
Identity = "\Legal"
Replicas = "PF03"
ReplicationSchedule = "Sunday.12:01 AM-Saturday.11:59 PM"
}
Set-PublicFolder @PublicFolder
Set-PublicFolder @PublicFolder2
Set-PublicFolder @PublicFolder3
```

You can specify the time in 24-hour format, or in 12-hour format. If you use 12-hour format, you need to add AM and PM to the time, with a space between the time and either AM or PM.

If your public folder hierarchy experiences an error in replication, you will need to suspend replication of the public folder content. After troubleshooting the errors, you can resume replication. Suspending or resuming replication is an organization-wide procedure. You use the Suspend-PublicFolderReplication or the Resume-PublicFolderReplication cmdlets to perform this procedure. Note that the public folder hierarchy will continue to replicate while the content replication is suspended.

The Suspend-PublicFolderReplication cmdlet accepts the optional Confirm parameter, allowing you to bypass the confirmation prompt. The following example suspends public folder replication while bypassing the confirmation prompt:

```
Suspend-PublicFolderReplication -Confirm:$False
```

Although the Resume-PublicFolderReplication cmdlet accepts the Confirm parameter, it is not necessary to use it; running the cmdlet with no parameters will resume replication of the public folder content. The following example resumes public folder replication:

```
Resume-PublicFolderReplication
```

You can check to see if public folder replication is suspended with the Get-OrganizationConfig cmdlet. The object you are interested in is the Heuristics flag.

The following example returns only the heuristics information from the Get-OrganizationConfig cmdlet. If replication is suspended, the cmdlet returns SuspendFolderReplication. Otherwise, the cmdlet returns None.

```
(Get-OrganizationConfig).Heuristics
```

You can manually replicate a public folder with the Update-PublicFolder cmdlet, passing the required parameters Server and Identity, where Server is the server to replicate from, and Identity is the folder to replicate.

The following example starts replication of the folder \Legal from the server Exch2010 to all replicas of that folder:

```
$PublicFolder = @{
Identity = "\Legal"
Server = "Exch2010"
}
Update-PublicFolder @PublicFolder
```

Managing Storage Groups

Databases in Exchange Server 2007 are stored within storage groups. In Exchange Server 2010, storage groups no longer exist.

In Exchange Server 2007 Standard edition, you can have up to 5 storage groups and 5 databases. Exchange Server 2007 Enterprise edition allows you to create up to 50 storage groups and 50 databases. Although you can store up to 5 databases in each storage group, there are benefits to keeping each database in its own storage group.

You create a storage group using the New-StorageGroup cmdlet, passing the required parameters of Name and LogFolderPath. If you are running the cmdlet from a workstation, you will also need to pass the Server parameter.

The following example creates the storage group AccountingSG on the server Exch07 and sets the log folder path to D:\AccountingLogs on the Exchange server. Note that the log folder path is set on the storage group — any database in that storage group will share that log folder. This means that if you need to do a recovery for any database in that storage group, replaying the log files will take longer than it would have if you had only one database in the storage group. Thus, I recommend that you have one database per storage group. This is also Microsoft's recommendation.

```
$StorageGroup = @{
Name = "AccountingSG"
LogFolderPath = "D:\Accountinglogs"
Server = "Exch07"
}
New-StorageGroup @StorageGroup
```

You can remove a storage group using the Remove-StorageGroup cmdlet if there are no mailbox or public folder databases saved in the storage group. The Remove-StorageGroup cmdlet takes the required parameter Identity, and prompts for confirmation without the optional Confirm parameter.

If the storage group contains one or more databases, the cmdlet will fail. The following example removes the empty storage group LegalSG without prompting for confirmation. You will receive the warning illustrated in Figure 12-1 that you need to remove the log files, along with the path to the log files.

```
$StorageGroup = @{
Identity = "LegalSG"
Confirm = $false
}
Remove-StorageGroup @StorageGroup
```

FIGURE 12-1

Output of Remove-StorageGroup

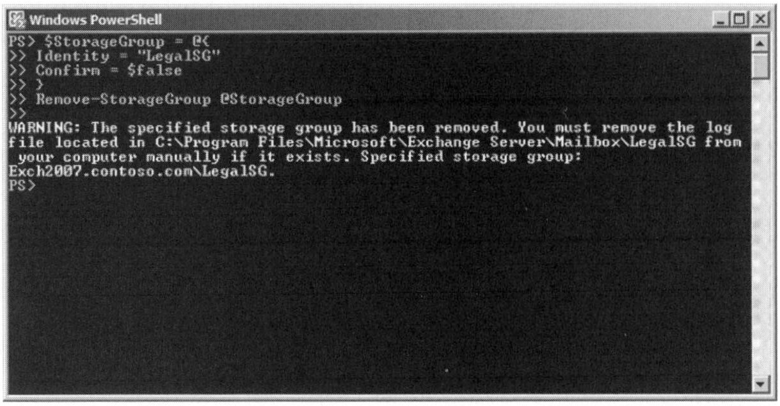

If you are sure that the storage group contains no database and that the log files are not needed, you can remove the log files after removing the storage group by using a combination of the Get-StorageGroup and Remove-Item cmdlets. The following example removes the storage group LegalSG, and deletes all log files and the log file path. Using the if construct prevents the log files from being removed if the Remove-StorageGroup cmdlet fails. Without this, the log files would be deleted regardless of the storage group status.

```
$StorageGroup = @{
Identity = "LegalSG"
Confirm = $false
}
$LogFolderPath = Get-StorageGroup $StorageGroup["Identity"]
if (Remove-StorageGroup @StorageGroup)
{
Remove-Item $LogFolderPath.LogFolderPath -Recurse -Confirm:$False
}
```

Managing Databases

Microsoft Exchange Server stores all mailbox and public folder data in databases. Exchange Server 2007 and earlier stored the databases within storage groups. Mailbox database names within Exchange Server 2007 do not need to be unique. You could name all your mailbox databases MboxDB as long as they were in separate storage groups.

Exchange Server 2010 no longer uses storage groups. Every database in Exchange Server 2010 must have a name that is unique within the organization. The following sections describe how to manage databases in both versions of Exchange Server.

Microsoft Exchange Server 2007

A storage group isn't much good without at least one database (either mailbox or public folder) stored in it, so let's create the mailbox database AccountingDB in the newly created storage group AccountingSG. You will use the New-MailboxDatabase cmdlet, passing the required parameters Name, EdbFilepath, and StorageGroup.

The following example creates the mailbox database AccountingDB in the storage group AccountingSG on the server Exch07. As with the New-StorageGroup cmdlet, if you are running this from a workstation, or a different Exchange server, you will need to specify the specific storage group in the format of server\storage group, the storage group's GUID, or the distinguished name of the storage group.

```
$MailboxDatabase = @{
Name = "AccountingDB"
EdbFilePath = "E:\AccountingDB\AccountingDB.edb"
StorageGroup = "Exch07\AccountingSG"
}
New-MailboxDatabase @MailboxDatabase
```

When you create the mailbox database, it is in an unmounted status. You can mount the database with the Mount-Database cmdlet, passing the required parameter Identity. The following example mounts the existing database Exch07\AccountingSG\AccountingDB on the server Exch07, in the storage group AccountingSG:

```
Mount-Database -Identity "Exch07\AccountingSG\AccountingDB"
```

You can also create and mount the mailbox database at once by piping the New-MailboxDatabase cmdlet to the Mount-Database cmdlet. The following example builds on the New-MailboxDatabase example presented earlier to create the mailbox database specified in the previous example's @MailboxDatabase hashtable and pass the output to the Mount-Database cmdlet:

```
New-MailboxDatabase @MailboxDatabase | Mount-Database
```

Dismounting a mailbox database is accomplished with the aptly named Dismount-Database cmdlet, passing the required parameter Identity. The next example dismounts the Exchange Server 2007 mailbox database AccountingDB in the storage group AccountingSG, on the server Exch07. The example prompts for confirmation. Once again, this prompt can be bypassed by adding the switch parameter Confirm, set to $false.

```
Dismount-Database -Identity "Exch07\AccountingSG\AccountingDB"
```

Microsoft Exchange Server 2010

Creating mailbox databases on Exchange Server 2010 is also accomplished with the New-MailboxDatabase cmdlet. On Exchange Server 2010, the cmdlet requires the Name and Server parameters. The following example creates the mailbox database Ex2010DB on the server Exch2010. After the mailbox database is created, the mailbox database object is piped to the Mount-Database cmdlet, which mounts it.

```
New-MailboxDatabase -Name Ex2010DB -Server Exch2010 | Mount-Database
```

As with the Exchange Server 2007 New-StorageGroup and New-MailboxDatabase cmdlets, if you do not specify the EdbFilePath and LogFolderPath, they will be created in the same folder path as the Exchange binaries, under the Mailbox folder. The following example builds on the previous one, specifying that the EdbFilePath be F:\Ex2010db\ Ex2010db.edb, and the LogFolderPath be F:\Ex2010logs. In this case, the F: drive is a mount point. Otherwise, it's recommended that the EdbFilePath and LogFolderPath be on separate drives.

```
$Database = @{
Name = "Ex2010DB"
Server = "Exch2010"
EdbFilePath = "F:\Ex2010DB\Ex2010DB.edb"
LogFolderPath = "F:\Ex2010Logs"
}
New-MailboxDatabase @Database | Mount-Database
```

Once again, as with Exchange Server 2007, to dismount a mailbox database, you use the Dismount-Database cmdlet with the required parameter Identity.

Because mailbox database names in Exchange Server 2010 must be unique within the organization, you need only pass the mailbox database name in the Identity parameter.

The following example dismounts the Exchange Server 2010 mailbox database Legal without prompting for confirmation:

```
Dismount-Database -Identity Legal -Confirm:$False
```

Finding Mailbox Database White Space

Exchange mailbox databases contain white space after online maintenance is completed. White space is the space that exists in the mailbox database file after items have been deleted. If the mailbox database had grown to 20 GB, and had 2 GB of data deleted, the mailbox database file would still occupy 20 GB of disk space but would have 2 GB of internal space that could be consumed before growing the mailbox database file. These data could be items removed from mailboxes, or mailboxes being moved or deleted.

Finding White Space in Microsoft Exchange Server 2007

In Exchange Server 2007 (and previous), you need to look in the event logs to gather white space information. When online maintenance completes, an event with the ID of 1221 and source of "MSExchangeIS Mailbox Store" is created in the application log. A separate 1221 event is created for each database.

Because the white space is retrieved by viewing the application log, you can do this via the Exchange Management Shell or a generic Windows PowerShell window. You use the Get-WmiObject cmdlet, passing the required parameters Class, ComputerName, and Filter.

Listing 12-4 illustrates how to display the white space for all mailbox databases in your Exchange Server 2007 organization.

LISTING 12-4

Finding Database White Space in Exchange 2007

```
$TimeConversion = [System.Management.ManagementDateTimeconverter]
$StartDate = $TimeConversion::ToDmtfDateTime((Get-Date).AddDays(-1).Date)
$EndDate = $TimeConversion::ToDmtfDateTime((Get-Date).Date)
$Version = @{
FilterScript = {$_.AdminDisplayVersion.major -eq 8}
}
$Action = @{
ErrorAction = "SilentlyContinue"
}
$Servers = Get-ExchangeServer| Where-Object @Version | Get-MailboxServer @Action
Foreach ($MailboxServer in $Servers)
{
$WMIObject = @{
ComputerName = $MailboxServer
Query = @"
Select * from Win32_NTLogEvent Where LogFile='Application'
AND EventCode=1221
AND TimeWritten>='$StartDate'
AND TimeWritten<='$EndDate'
"@
}
$SelectObject = @{
Property = "ComputerName",
@{Name="DB";Expression={$_.InsertionStrings[1]}},
@{Name="FreeMB";Expression={[int]$_.InsertionStrings[0]}}
}
$SortObject = @{
Property = "FreeMB"
Unique = $true
Descending = $true
}
Get-WMIObject @WMIObject | Select-Object @SelectObject | Sort-Object @SortObject
}
```

Finding White Space in Microsoft Exchange Server 2010

In Exchange Server 2010, you no longer need to examine event logs to determine mailbox database white space. This information is available in real time via the Get-MailboxDatabase cmdlet, passing the optional parameter Status.

The following example shows free space for all Exchange 2010 mailbox databases:

```
$Object = @{
Property = "Name","AvailableNewMailboxSpace"
}
Get-MailboxDatabase -Status | Select-Object @Object
```

You can also pass optional parameters to the `Get-MailboxDatabase` cmdlet to limit the output to a specific server or database by using the `Server` or `Database` parameters. The following example shows the free space available for the mailbox database `Legal`:

```
$MailboxDatabase = @{
Identity = "Legal"
Status = $true
}
$Object = @{
Property = "Name","AvailableNewMailboxSpace"
}
Get-MailboxDatabase @MailboxDatabase | Select-Object @Object
```

The following example shows the free space available on each mailbox database on the Exchange Server `EXCH2010`:

```
$MailboxDatabase = @{
Server = "EXCH2010"
Status = $true
}
$Object = @{
Property = "Name","AvailableNewMailboxSpace"
}
Get-MailboxDatabase @MailboxDatabase | Select-Object @Object
```

Discovering Space Used by Disabled Mailboxes

Disabled mailboxes could consume a large amount of your mailbox database space. The following example lists the server, display name, database, size in MB, and disconnected date of all disconnected mailboxes:

```
$Server = @{
Server = @(Get-ExchangeServer)
}
$Object = @{
FilterScript = {$_.DisconnectDate -ne $null}
}
$Select =@{
```

```
Property =
@{Name = 'Server Name';Expression={$_.ServerName}},
@{Name = 'Display Name';Expression={$_.DisplayName}},
"Database",
@{Name='Total Item Size(MB)';Expression={$_.TotalItemSize.Value.ToMB()}},
@{Name='Disconnect Date';Expression={$_.DisconnectDate}},
MailboxGUID
}
foreach ($Server in Get-MailboxServer)
{
Get-MailboxStatistics -Server $Server |
Where-Object @Object | Select-Object @Select
}
```

You can gather information on all disconnected mailboxes on a specific mailbox database by passing that information to the Get-MailboxStatistics cmdlet. The following example lists all disconnected mailboxes on the database Accounting:

```
$Object = @{
FilterScript = {$_.DisconnectDate -ne $null}
}
$Select =@{
Property =
@{Name = 'Server Name';Expression={$_.ServerName}},
@{Name = 'Display Name';Expression={$_.DisplayName}},
"Database",
@{Name='Total Item Size(MB)';Expression={$_.TotalItemSize.Value.ToMb()}},
@{Name='Disconnect Date';Expression={$_.DisconnectDate}},
"MailboxGUID"
}
Get-MailboxStatistics -Database "AccountingDB" |
Where-Object @Object | Select-Object @Select
```

Although I recommend leaving disconnected mailboxes alone until they are automatically purged via the Deleted Mailbox Retention policy, you may need to purge disconnected mailboxes before the retention period expires.

You can do this by combining the Get-MailboxStatistics cmdlet with the Remove-Mailbox cmdlet. The Remove-Mailbox cmdlet requires the parameters Database and StoreMailboxIdentity. The StoreMailboxIdentity should be passed the mailbox GUID for the value.

Suppose you find that the mailbox for Clayton Tarleton occupies 1721 MB in the database AccountingDB, and you want to reclaim that space. You can get the GUID by running Get-MailboxStatistics, filtering by display name.

The following example returns the Display Name, Database, and GUID for the mailbox Clayton Tarleton, as shown in Figure 12-2:

```
$Mailbox = @{
FilterScript = {$_.DisplayName -eq 'Clayton Tarleton'}
}
$List =@{
Property =
@{Name = 'Display Name';Expression={$_.DisplayName}},
"Database",
"MailboxGUID"
}
Get-MailboxStatistics | Where-Object @Mailbox | Format-List @List
```

FIGURE 12-2

Output of Get-MailboxStatistics cmdlet

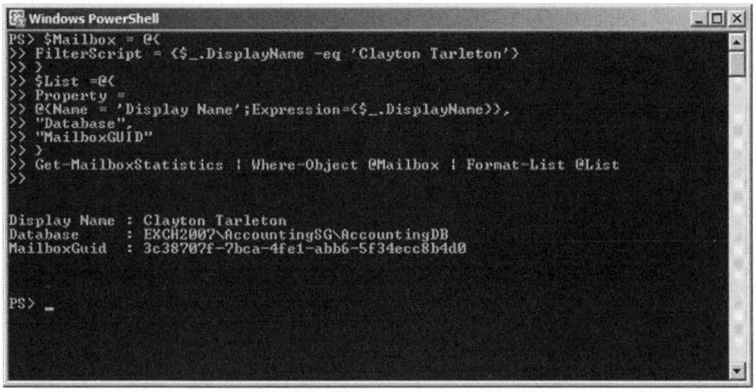

Now that you have the GUID and database, you can call the Remove-Mailbox cmdlet as shown here:

```
$Mailbox = @{
Database = "AccountingDB"
StoreMailboxIdentity = "1fd412bc-71db-446d-a13b-296d6850dd43"
Confirm = $false
}
Remove-Mailbox @Mailbox
```

Alternatively, you can get the mailbox and remove it at once by passing the output of the Get-MailboxStatistics cmdlet to the Remove-Mailbox cmdlet. The following example removes the disconnected mailbox for Clayton Tarleton:

```
$Mailbox = @{
FilterScript = {$_.DisplayName -eq 'Clayton Tarleton'}
}
```

```
$Remove = @{
Process = {Remove-Mailbox
Database = `_.Database
StoreMailboxIdentity = `$_.MailboxGuid
Confirm = $False
}
}
Get-MailboxStatistics | Where-Object @Mailbox | ForEach-Object @Remove
```

As you can see, the `Remove-Mailbox` cmdlet works in a `ForEach-Object` loop. This means you can easily modify the previous example to remove all disconnected mailboxes on a specific mailbox database or mailbox server by changing the `Get-MailboxStatistics` criteria.

Managing Quotas

New mailbox databases have default mailbox quotas that may be too large for your organization. By default, the `IssueWarningQuota` is set to 1.9 GB, the `ProhibitSendQuota` is set to 2 GB, and the `ProhibitSendReceiveQuota` is set to 2.3 GB.

You can view the current quotas with the `Get-MailboxDatabase` cmdlet, sending the output through either the `Select-Object` or `Format-List` cmdlet. The following example shows the `IssueWarningQuota`, `ProhibitSendQuota`, and `ProhibitSendReceiveQuota` on the Exchange Server 2007 mailbox database `Exch07\AccountingSG\AccountingDB`. The same script run against an Exchange Server 2010 mailbox database returns the previous three quotas, along with the `RecoverableItemsQuota` and `RecoverableItemsWarningQuota`. All of these quotas can be set on the mailbox database level, or on individual mailboxes.

```
$MailboxDatabase = @{
Identity = "Exch07\AccountingSG\AccountingDB"
}
Get-MailboxDatabase @MailboxDatabase | Select-Object -Property *quota*
```

The following example sets the specified quotas on the `AccountingDB` database to 200, 210, and 220 MB. You can specify the limits in KB, MB, GB, or as just integers. If you specify an integer value without a multiplier, the value will be applied as bytes.

```
$MailboxDatabase = @{
Identity = "Exch07\AccountingSG\AccountingDB"
IssueWarningQuota = "200MB"
ProhibitSendQuota = "210MB"
ProhibitSendReceiveQuota = "220MB"
}
Set-MailboxDatabase @MailboxDatabase
```

As mentioned, Exchange Server 2010 adds the `RecoverableItemsQuota` and `RecoverableItemsWarningQuota` to the list of quotas that can be configured. These quotas manage the dumpster data for the mailbox database, or an individual mailbox. By default, the `RecoverableItemsWarningQuota` is set to 20 GB and the `RecoverableItemsQuota` is set to 30 GB on each mailbox database. These quotas are not enabled on individual mailboxes by default.

The following example sets the mailbox quotas for all mailboxes on the Legal database to 100, 110, and 120 MB, and sets the RecoverableItemsWarningQuota and RecoverableItemsQuotas to 10 GB and 20 GB, respectively.

```
$MailboxDatabase = @{
Identity = "Legal"
IssueWarningQuota = "100MB"
ProhibitSendQuota = "110MB"
ProhibitSendReceiveQuota = "120MB"
RecoverableItemsWarningQuota = "10GB"
RecoverableItemsQuota = "20GB"
}
Set-MailboxDatabase @MailboxDatabase
```

Along with the quota limits, you can set the QuotaNotificationSchedule, which determines when users are notified that their mailbox limit(s) have been exceeded. The following example adds Monday from 1:00 to 1:15 p.m. to the existing notification schedule:

```
$Database = "WIN-DKV0RVOVBJS\AccountingSG\AccountingDB"
$Quota = (Get-MailboxDatabase -Identity $Database).QuotaNotificationSchedule
$Quota += "Monday.13:00-Monday.13:15"
Set-MailboxDatabase -Identity $Database -QuotaNotificationSchedule $Quota
```

The day for the QuotaNotificationSchedule can be set using names as I have or the integers 0 through 6, where 0 represents Sunday.

Knowing this allows you to create a notification schedule in a ForEach-Object loop. The following example sets the notification schedule for the mailbox database AccountingDB in the storage group AccountingSG on the server Exch2007 to send out notifications between 11:00 and 11:15 p.m. on a daily basis:

```
$Database = "Exch2007\AccountingSG\AccountingDB"
0..6 | ForEach-Object {$Quota += @("$_.11:00 PM-$_.11:15 PM")}
$MailboxDatabase = @{
Identity = "$Database"
QuotaNotificationSchedule = "$Quota"
}
Set-MailboxDatabase @MailboxDatabase
```

The following example sets the notification schedule for all databases on the Exchange server Exch2007 to run between 1:00 and 1:15 a.m. on a daily basis:

```
0..6 | ForEach-Object {$Quota += @("$_.01:00-$_.01:15")}
$Database = @{
QuotaNotificationSchedule = $Quota
}
Get-MailboxDatabase -Server Exch2007 | Set-MailboxDatabase @Database
```

You can pipe the results of the Get-MailboxDatabase cmdlet without using the Server parameter to the Set-MailboxDatabase cmdlet to modify all mailbox databases on that version of Exchange at once.

Another limit that can be set on the database or mailbox level is the deleted item retention. The default is to keep 14 days of deleted items. You can set the retention period on a database with the Set-MailboxDatabase cmdlet using the required parameter Identity and the optional parameter DeletedItemRetention. The following example sets the DeletedItemRetention period on all mailbox databases on the server Exch2007 to 21 days, 0 hours, 0 minutes, and 0 seconds. The format for the retention period is days.hours:minutes:seconds.

```
$DB = @{
DeletedItemRetention = "21.00:00:00"
}
Get-MailboxDatabase -Server Exch2007 | Set-MailboxDatabase @DB
```

You can set the deleted item retention period for any mailbox or mailbox result set with the Set-Mailbox cmdlet, passing the RetainDeletedItemsFor parameter. The following example sets the deleted item retention period for all mailboxes in the organizational unit Accounting to 45 days, 12 hours, 0 minutes, and 0 seconds:

```
$mailbox = @{
OrganizationalUnit = "Accounting"
}
$retention = @{
RetainDeletedItemsFor = "45.12:00:00"
}
Get-Mailbox @mailbox | Set-Mailbox @retention
```

Retention for deleted mailboxes is set on the database level, once again using the Set-MailboxDatabase cmdlet, along with the MailboxRetention parameter. By default, deleted mailboxes are retained for 30 days. You can set the retention period on an individual mailbox database by specifying the Identity parameter, or pass a Get-MailboxDatabase result set to the Set-MailboxDatabase cmdlet.

The following example, when run in either the Exchange Server 2007 or Exchange Server 2010 Management Shell, sets all mailbox databases on that version of Exchange to use a deleted mailbox retention period of 45 days. If you have a mix of Exchange Server 2007 and Exchange Server 2010, you will need to run the script on both.

```
Get-MailboxDatabase | Set-MailboxDatabase -MailboxRetention "45.00:00:00"
```

Interestingly, both Exchange Server 2007 and Exchange Server 2010 have a parameter that you can pass to the Get-MailboxDatabase cmdlet that will display information about the databases on either version. The following example, when run from an Exchange Server 2010 Management Shell, shows the mailbox retention and identity for each mailbox database:

```
$Object = @{
Property = "MailboxRetention","Identity"
}
Get-MailboxDatabase -IncludePreExchange2010 | Select-Object @Object
```

The parameter on Exchange Server 2007 is, appropriately, `IncludePreExchange2007` — contrary to its name, it displays Exchange Server 2010 mailbox database information. In both versions of the shell, you can abbreviate the parameter to `IncludePreExchange` to allow one script to run on either version.

The following example, when run from either Exchange Server 2007 or Exchange Server 2010 management shells, shows the mailbox retention period and identities for all mailbox databases on either version. In an Exchange Server 2007 Management Shell, depending on your warning preference, you may see warnings for each Exchange Server 2010 mailbox database indicating that the database is corrupted. You can safely ignore these warnings.

```
$Object = @{
Property = "MailboxRetention","Identity"
}
Get-MailboxDatabase -IncludePreExchange | Select-Object @Object
```

If you configure replication to allow a subset of folders to be replicated for performance issues as described in the "Managing Public Folders" section, you might want to also set the default public folder database for mailbox databases on the affected servers as well. You do this with the `Set-MailboxDatabase` cmdlet, passing the required parameter `Identity` and the optional parameter `PublicFolderDatabase`. The following example sets the default public folder database for the mailbox database `MarketingDB` to `PF02`:

```
$MailboxDatabase = @{
Identity = "MarketingDB"
PublicFolderDatabase = "PF02"
}
Set-MailboxDatabase @MailboxDatabase
```

If you replicate an entire public folder structure to more than one server, you can set all mailbox databases to a specific public folder database by piping the output of the `Get-MailboxDatabase` cmdlet to the `Set-MailboxDatabase` cmdlet. The following example sets the default public folder database for every mailbox database on the server `Exch2010` to `PF02`:

```
$Server = "Exch2010"
$Database = @{
PublicFolderDatabase = "PF02"
}
Get-MailboxDatabase -Server $Server | Set-MailboxDatabase @Database
```

Managing Microsoft Exchange Server Remotely

As mentioned at the beginning of the chapter, you do not need to install the Exchange Server 2010 Management Tools locally to manage Exchange Server 2010. You can create a remote session to an Exchange Server 2010 server running any role except the Edge Transport role. Your management workstation will need to be running Windows PowerShell Version 2 or above, and TCP port 80 will need to be open from your workstation to the Exchange server.

If you are not logged in to your workstation with Exchange Administrator privileges, you will need to pass credentials. Run the following command:

```
$UserCredential = Get-Credential
```

In the dialog box that opens, type the username and password of an administrator account that has access to administer the Exchange 2010 server you want to connect to, and then click OK. Once the password is entered, you can open the connection to Exchange Server 2010 by running the following command:

```
$PSSession = @{
ConfigurationName = "Microsoft.Exchange"
ConnectionUri = "http://Exch2010.contoso.com/PowerShell/"
Authentication = "Kerberos"
Credential = $UserCredential
}
$Session = New-PSSession @PSSession
```

In this case, Exch2010.contoso.com is the fully qualified domain name of one of your Exchange servers. You now import the Windows PowerShell session into your Windows PowerShell console by running the following command:

```
Import-PSSession -Session $Session
```

You can add the session initialization to your profile to start the Exchange session each time you load Windows PowerShell if you'd like. The complete script to add to your $profile is:

```
$UserCredential = Get-Credential
$PSSession = @{
ConfigurationName = "Microsoft.Exchange"
ConnectionUri = "http://Exch2010.contoso.com/PowerShell/"
Authentication = "Kerberos"
Credential = $UserCredential
}
$Session = New-PSSession @PSSession
Import-PSSession -Session $Session
```

If you will be starting Windows PowerShell as a user who already has Exchange permissions, you can skip the `Get-Credential` step. The complete script to add this version to your profile is:

```
$PSSession = @{
ConfigurationName = "Microsoft.Exchange"
ConnectionUri = "http://Exch2010.contoso.com/PowerShell/"
Authentication = "Kerberos"
}
$Session = New-PSSession @PSSession
Import-PSSession -Session $Session
```

Although this is a supported configuration, I would discourage it for all but basic administration of the Exchange organization.

If you are running an operating system that will support the installation of the Exchange Server 2010 Management Tools, I would highly recommend that you install them locally.

As previously mentioned, if you are running Windows PowerShell with a remote Exchange session, the objects returned will be Windows PowerShell objects, instead of Exchange objects. A simple example of this is the `Get-Mailbox` cmdlet.

In a native Exchange Server 2010 Management Shell, you can retrieve the white space of a database and convert that number to bytes, kilobytes, megabytes, gigabytes, terabytes, or a string. The returned object is of the type `Microsoft.Exchange.Data .ByteQuantifiedSize`.

In a remote session, the returned object is a `System.String`, which you will have to manipulate to be useful.

The following script, when run in a native Exchange Server 2010 Management Shell, returns the available new mailbox space for the database `Ex2010DB` in megabytes:

```
$Database = @{
Identity = "Ex2010DB"
Status = $true
}
(Get-MailboxDatabase @Database).AvailableNewMailboxSpace.ToMB()
```

The same script, when run in a remote session, returns the error shown in Figure 12-3.

FIGURE 12-3

Results of Get-MailboxDatabase in remote session

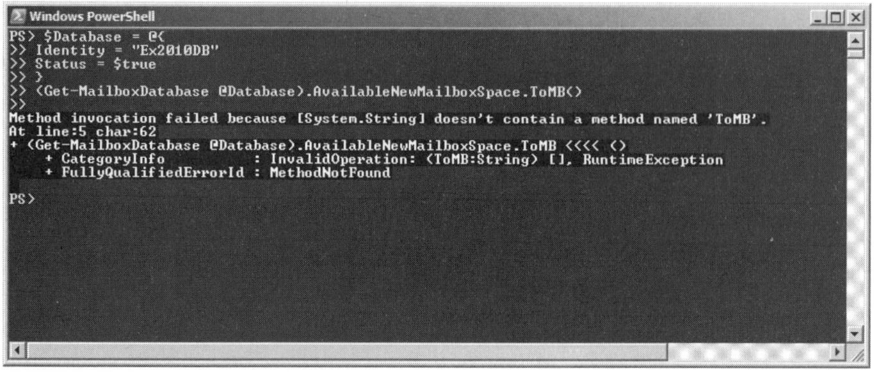

If you remove ToMb() from the preceding script, it will run and return data. The available new mailbox space will be a string, which you can manipulate with the ToString() method. In my environment, the following example returns a string showing the free space number and quantifier:

```
Get-MailboxDatabase @Database).AvailableNewMailboxSpace).Split("(")[0]
```

Although this example of the difference between the native Exchange Management Shell and a remote session may seem trivial, converting a string to a numeric value can be problematic. Additionally, besides the scripts in this chapter, many of the scripts you will find online for Exchange Server 2010 rely on the Exchange objects. Any script that you find online that depends on the Exchange objects will fail with often cryptic errors when run in a remote session.

Email Address Policies

Email address policies stamp an email address on each recipient object as it is created, and whenever the policy is applied, unless the recipient object's attribute EmailAddressPolicyEnabled is set to False.

You can create an email address policy with the New-EmailAddressPolicy cmdlet, passing the required parameters Name, IncludedRecipients, and EnabledEmailAddressTemplates. The following example creates a new email address policy named PowerShell Email Policy, which includes all recipients, sets the priority to lowest, and sets the email address to an SMTP address of %1g%s@powershell.com:

```
$EmailAddressPolicy = @{
Name = "PowerShell Email Policy"
IncludedRecipients = "AllRecipients"
```

```
Priority = "Lowest"
EnabledEmailAddressTemplates = "SMTP:%1g%s@powershell.com"
}
New-EmailAddressPolicy @EmailAddressPolicy
```

The `%1g` and `%s` variables are defined in Table 12-2.

TABLE 12-2

Variables for the Email Address Policy

Variable	Definition
%g	First Name (Given Name)
%i	Middle Initial
%s	Last Name (Surname)
%d	Display Name
%m	Exchange Alias
%xg	Uses x number of letters of the first name
%xs	Uses x number of letters of the last name

You can also create an email address policy that applies only to mailboxes in the Marketing department by specifying the `ConditionalDepartment` parameter, and setting the `IncludedRecipients` parameter to `MailboxUsers`. The following example creates the previously specified email address policy, with an email address of `firstinitiallastname@marketing.powershell.com`:

```
$EmailAddressPolicy = @{
Name = "Marketing Mailbox Email Policy"
IncludedRecipients = "MailboxUsers"
ConditionalDepartment = "Marketing"
Priority = "Lowest"
EnabledEmailAddressTemplates = "SMTP:%1g%s@marketing.powershell.com"
}
New-EmailAddressPolicy @EmailAddressPolicy
```

By default, email address policies are applied only to new recipients. If you want to apply the policy to existing recipients, you will need to use the `Update-EmailAddressPolicy` cmdlet, passing the required parameter `Identity`. The following example applies the `Marketing Mailbox Email Policy`:

```
Update-EmailAddressPolicy -Identity "Marketing Mailbox Email Policy"
```

In a pure Exchange Server 2010 environment, you can create an email address policy for recipients in specific organizational units by specifying the `RecipientContainer` parameter. The following example creates the email address policy `Sales Mailbox Email Policy`, which includes `AllRecipients` in the organizational unit `OU=Sales,DC=contoso,DC=com`. The email address policy has a `Priority` of `Lowest`, and uses the email address template of `%1g%s@sales.contoso.com`.

```
$EmailAddressPolicy = @{
Name = "Sales Mailbox Email Policy"
IncludedRecipients = "AllRecipients"
RecipientContainer = "OU=Sales,DC=contoso,DC=com"
Priority = "Lowest"
EnabledEmailAddressTemplates = "SMTP:%1g%s@sales.contoso.com"
}
New-EmailAddressPolicy @EmailAddressPolicy
```

The `RecipientContainer` parameter can be specified as the organizational unit's distinguished name or canonical name, or a domain name.

If you discover that an email address policy is configured incorrectly, you can modify it with the `Set-EmailAddressPolicy` cmdlet, passing the required parameter `Identity`, and whichever parameters you wish to change. The following example modifies the marketing mailbox email policy to apply to all recipients, instead of only applying to mailboxes:

```
$EmailAddressPolicy = @{
Identity = "Marketing Mailbox Email Policy"
IncludedRecipients = "AllRecipients"
}
Set-EmailAddressPolicy @EmailAddressPolicy
```

You can view the properties for an email address policy with the `Get-EmailAddressPolicy` cmdlet. The following example displays all properties of the `Marketing Mailbox Email Policy` in a list:

```
$EmailAddressPolicy = @{
Identity = "Marketing Mailbox Email Policy"
}
Get-EmailAddressPolicy @EmailAddressPolicy | Format-List -Property *
```

Interoperating with Earlier Versions of Microsoft Exchange

Several of the `Set-*` cmdlets in Exchange Server 2007 and Exchange Server 2010 require the target object to be of the same Exchange version as the management shell you are working with. In Exchange Server 2007, for instance, to work with a distribution group that has an Exchange version of 2003, you will need either to use the Exchange Server

2003 tools, or to upgrade the distribution group to Exchange Server 2007. Once an object is upgraded to the current version, it cannot be managed by the previous version of the Exchange Management Tools. Thus, if you have a diverse management team, you will want to be sure everyone has upgraded their Management Tools to the newer version before upgrading the objects, or upgrade them as needed.

Exchange Server 2003 and previous used LDAP filters to define dynamic distribution groups, email address policies, address lists, and global address lists.

Exchange Server 2007 and newer use OPATH filters to define these objects, and for filterable parameters for the Exchange cmdlets (covered later in the chapter in "Using Server-Side Filters").

Note

Microsoft has posted an LDAP-to-OPATH conversion script on the EHLO blog: `http://msexchangeteam .com/files/12/attachments/entry442867.aspx`. ∎

Microsoft Exchange Server 2007

In Exchange Server 2007, you can upgrade address lists, dynamic distribution groups, email address policies, and global address lists.

Before upgrading address lists and email address policies, you will want to update the filters that create the policies and lists. Exchange Server 2003 and previous use LDAP filtering to create email address policies and address lists, whereas Exchange Server 2007 and 2010 use OPATH filtering. Updating the filters that create default policies and lists is easy to do; custom policies and lists will take more work.

The default Email Address Policy matches all recipient objects, so it is very easy to update. You will not need to write a custom OPATH filter for this. The following example prompts for confirmation before upgrading the default policy. If you want to bypass confirmation, you can add the switch parameter `ForceUpgrade`.

```
$EmailAddressPolicy = @{
Identity = "Default Policy"
IncludedRecipients = "AllRecipients"
}
Set-EmailAddressPolicy @EmailAddressPolicy
```

The following example performs the same upgrade as the previous example, without prompting for confirmation:

```
$EmailAddressPolicy = @{
Identity = "Default Policy"
IncludedRecipients = "AllRecipients"
ForceUpgrade = $true
}
Set-EmailAddressPolicy @EmailAddressPolicy
```

The following example upgrades the default Address List All Users without prompting for confirmation:

```
$AddressList = @{
Identity = "All Users"
IncludedRecipients = "MailboxUsers"
ForceUpgrade = $true
}
Set-AddressList @AddressList
```

This example upgrades the default Address List All Groups without prompting for confirmation:

```
$AddressList = @{
Identity = "All Groups"
IncludedRecipients = "MailGroups"
ForceUpgrade = $true
}
Set-AddressList @AddressList
```

Finally, this example upgrades the default Address List All Contacts without prompting for confirmation:

```
$AddressList = @{
Identity = "All Contacts"
IncludedRecipients = "MailContacts"
ForceUpgrade = $true
}
Set-AddressList @AddressList
```

Once an object is upgraded, you cannot manage it from Exchange Server 2003 or earlier tools.

Microsoft Exchange Server 2010

In Exchange Server 2010, you can upgrade address lists, distribution groups, dynamic distribution groups, email address policies, global address lists, mail contacts, and mail users.

When you attempt to modify one of these objects that has an Exchange version prior to 2010, you will be prompted to upgrade the object. The following example, run from an Exchange Server 2010 Management Shell against an Exchange Server 2007 Distribution Group, produces the confirmation prompt shown in Figure 12-4:

```
$DistributionGroup = @{
Identity = "AccountingGroup"
MaxReceiveSize = "5MB"
}
Set-DistributionGroup @DistributionGroup
```

FIGURE 12-4

The results of attempting to modify an object stamped with an earlier Exchange version

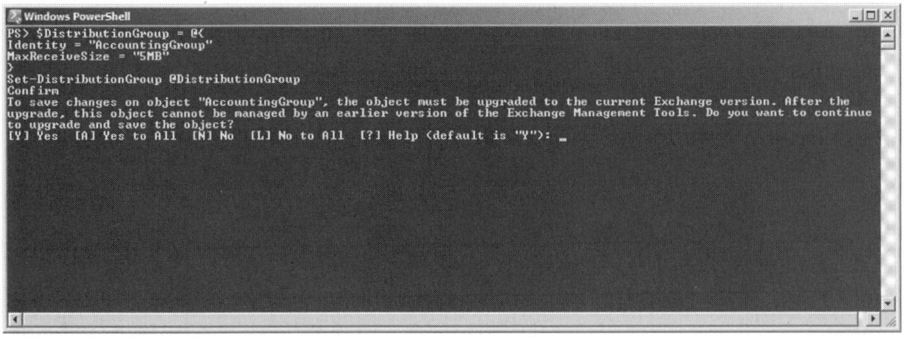

You use the associated `Set-*` cmdlet, with the `ForceUpgrade` parameter to bypass the upgrade prompt:

```
$DistributionGroup = @{
Identity = "AccountingGroup"
MaxReceiveSize = "5MB"
ForceUpgrade = $True
}
Set-DistributionGroup @DistributionGroup
```

If all Exchange administrators have upgraded their Management Tools to the Exchange Server 2010 version, you can upgrade all distribution groups at once. The following example finds all distribution groups that are not of the current version and upgrades them to Exchange Server 2010. You can substitute any of the associated `Get/Set` cmdlet pairs to upgrade any of the objects that are upgradeable.

```
$DGroup = @{
Filter = {ExchangeVersion -lt "0.10 (14.0.100.0)"}
}
Get-DistributionGroup @DGroup | Set-DistributionGroup -ForceUpgrade
```

The `Filter` parameter is explained in the next section.

You can use a similar filter to update all mail contacts and mail users. The following example upgrades all mail contacts to Exchange Server 2010:

```
$MailContact = @{
Filter = {ExchangeVersion -lt "0.10 (14.0.100.0)"}
}
Get-MailContact @MailContact | Set-MailContact -ForceUpgrade
```

The following example upgrades all mail users to Exchange Server 2010:

```
$MailUser = @{
Filter = {ExchangeVersion -lt "0.10 (14.0.100.0)"}
}
Get-MailUser @MailUser | Set-MailUser -ForceUpgrade
```

The address lists can be upgraded with the examples from the "Microsoft Exchange Server 2007" section.

Using Filters

Filtering refers to limiting the results returned from a cmdlet. You can filter the output of any cmdlet on the client with the Where-Object cmdlet. Many Exchange cmdlets accept the Filter parameter, which performs the filtering on the Exchange server before returning the data to the management shell.

These two forms of filtering are known as client-side and server-side filtering. I describe both in the following sections.

Using Client-Side Filters

You can filter the output of any cmdlet by sending the output down the pipeline and through the Where-Object cmdlet. This is called *client-side filtering* because the cmdlet returns all available objects to the client before sending them to the Where-Object cmdlet.

An example of this would be retrieving all mailboxes with an email address in the powershell.com domain. You can do this by sending the output of the Get-Mailbox cmdlet to the Where-Object cmdlet. The following example retrieves all mailboxes within your recipient scope, and then sends every one of those objects down the pipeline to the Where-Object cmdlet, where only objects with an email address at powershell.com are output. On larger domains, this is very inefficient. In my domain, with approximately 15,000 mailboxes, this takes 380 seconds to return 353 mailboxes.

```
$Mailbox = @{
ResultSize = "Unlimited"
}
$Object = @{
FilterScript = {$_.emailaddresses -like "*powershell.com"}
}
Get-Mailbox @Mailbox | Where-Object @Object
```

An example that more clearly shows the problem with client-side filtering is looking for one specific email address within the organization. An email address can be assigned to any of the recipient types, so the quickest way to search for an email address is via the `Get-Recipient` cmdlet.

The following example, when run in my domain with approximately 30,000 recipients, takes 196 seconds to return the single mailbox that matches the specific email address. You might wonder why I included the `ResultSize unlimited` parameter. This is needed in any organization with more than 1,000 recipient objects, because the Exchange Management Shell defaults to returning only 1,000 objects.

```
$Recipient = @{
ResultSize = "Unlimited"
}
$Object = @{
FilterScript = {$_.emailaddresses -eq 'kmitschke@powershell.com'}
}
Get-Recipient @Recipient | Where-Object @Object
```

Remember that filtering with the `Where-Object` cmdlet requires that the Exchange server first return all objects to the client. However, as mentioned, the output of any cmdlet can be filtered via the `Where-Object` cmdlet.

Using Server-Side Filters

Many Exchange Server 2007 and Exchange Server 2010 `Get-*` cmdlets accept the optional `Filter` parameter. Wherever there is a `Filter` parameter, I recommend its use. The equivalent `Get-Mailbox` script from the client-side filtering section is:

```
$Mailbox = @{
ResultSize = "Unlimited"
Filter = {EmailAddresses -like "*@powershell.com"}
}
Get-Mailbox @Mailbox
```

In my domain, with the same approximately 15,000 mailboxes, this takes 11 seconds to return 353 mailboxes.

The equivalent `Get-Recipient` script from the client-side filtering section, rewritten to a server-side filter, would be:

```
Get-Recipient -Filter{EmailAddresses -eq 'kmitschke@powershell.com'}
```

In my domain, this test took 0.08 seconds to return the single object.

Any time you can use a server-side filter, the data will be returned more quickly than if you had used the equivalent `Where-Object` filter.

You can combine conditions in a filter using the standard logical operators `-and`, `-or`, `-xor`, and `-not`.

Note

You can get a list of properties for the `Filter` parameter from Microsoft TechNet.

For Exchange Server 2007 Service Pack 1 through Exchange Server 2010, see `http://technet.microsoft.com/en-us/library/bb738155(EXCHG.80).aspx`.

If you are still running Exchange Server 2007 RTM, see `http://technet.microsoft.com/en-us/library/bb430744(EXCHG.80).aspx`. ∎

The `Get-Mailbox` cmdlet does not accept the property `Company` for the `Filter` parameter. However, the `Get-User` cmdlet does. Further, the `Get-User` cmdlet accepts the property `RecipientType` for the `Filter` parameter. This enables you to get a list of all mailboxes in a specified company. The following example displays all user mailboxes that are identified as in the company `Contoso`:

```
$User = @{
ResultSize = "Unlimited"
Filter = {Company -eq "Contoso" -and RecipientType -eq "UserMailbox"}
}
Get-User @User
```

Suppose you wanted to set all mailboxes for users in the company `Contoso` to have a warning, prohibit send, and prohibit send receive quota of 1.5, 2, and 2.5 GB, respectively. You can accomplish this by passing the results of the previous `Get-User` example to the `Set-Mailbox` cmdlet, as shown here:

```
$User = @{
ResultSize = "Unlimited"
Filter = {Company -eq "Contoso" -and RecipientType -eq "UserMailbox"}
}
$Mailbox = @{
IssueWarningQuota = 1.5GB
ProhibitSendQuota = 2GB
ProhibitSendReceiveQuota = 2.5GB
}
Get-User @User | Set-Mailbox @Mailbox
```

Managing Recipient Scope

By default, the Exchange Management Shell is set to operate in a Domain scope — the shell connects to a domain controller, and operates on objects in that domain. This means that you can view or modify only objects in the domain controller's domain.

You can set the recipient scope to operate in a Forest scope, which connects the shell to a Global Catalog. This enables you to view or modify any object within the forest. Any modifications are written to a domain controller in the correct domain, and then replicated to the Global Catalog. This could cause your view of the object to be out of date, due to replication latency.

Managing Scope in Microsoft Exchange Server 2007

Managing recipient scope in Exchange Server 2007 is accomplished by modifying an Exchange Management Shell variable called $AdminSessionADSettings.

To view the current recipient scope, you need only enter $AdminSessionADSettings in the Exchange Management Shell. The relevant parameter is the ViewEntireForest parameter. This is a Boolean parameter, and defaults to $False. To manage objects across the forest, you need to set the value to $True. The following example sets the recipient scope to the forest level:

```
$AdminSessionADSettings.ViewEntireForest = $True
```

You may also want to hard-code the global catalog server, configuration domain controller, or preferred domain controllers. The following three lines set the global catalog, configuration domain controller, and preferred domain controllers:

```
$AdminSessionADSettings.PreferredGlobalCatalog = "GC1"
$AdminSessionADSettings.ConfigurationDomainController  = "DC1"
$AdminSessionADSettings.PreferredDomainControllers = "DC3","DC2"
```

A final property of the $AdminSessionADSettings variable is the DefaultScope. This property is null if you are in forest scope. If you are in domain scope, you can set this parameter to allow the Exchange Management Shell to only manage objects within a certain organizational unit. The following example sets the scope for the Exchange Management Shell to modify objects only in the Accounting organizational unit:

```
$AdminSessionADSettings.DefaultScope = "Contoso.com/Accounting"
```

If you set the DefaultScope, ViewEntireForest is set to null. Likewise, if you set ViewEntireForest to True, the DefaultScope will be null.

Any changes you make to the $AdminSessionADSettings variable while in the Exchange Management Shell are valid for only that session. If you want them to persist across sessions, you will need to load them in your $Profile script.

Managing Scope in Microsoft Exchange Server 2010

Recipient scope in Exchange Server 2010 is managed with the Active Directory cmdlets Get-AdServerSettings and Set-AdServerSettings.

Use Get-AdServerSettings to view the current settings. Get-AdServerSettings takes no parameters. The cmdlet returns more data than can be viewed onscreen, however, so you should pipe the cmdlet to the `Format-List` cmdlet. The following example returns the current Active Directory server settings:

```
Get-AdServerSettings | Format-List
```

To modify the Active Directory server settings, you use the `Set-AdServerSettings` cmdlet, passing the parameter or parameters that you want to modify.

As with Exchange Server 2007, you can set preferred domain controllers, the configuration domain controller, the preferred global catalog server, the recipient scope, and the forest/ domain scope. The following example sets the recipient scope to forest level:

```
Set-AdServerSettings -ViewEntireForest $True
```

The following example sets the recipient scope to forest level, and sets the configuration domain controller, global catalog, and preferred domain controllers:

```
$AdServerSettings = @{
ViewEntireForest = $true
ConfigurationDomainController = "DC1"
PreferredGlobalCatalog = "GC1"
SetPreferredDomainControllers = "DC3","DC2"
}
Set-AdServerSettings @AdServerSettings
```

As with Exchange Server 2007, you can restrict the shell to manage objects in only a specific organizational unit with the `RecipientViewRoot` parameter. The following example sets the scope for the Exchange Management Shell to modify objects only in the `Accounting` organizational unit:

```
Set-AdServerSettings -RecipientViewRoot "Contoso.com/Accounting"
```

If you set the `RecipientViewRoot`, the `ViewEntireForest` is set to `False`. Likewise, if you set `ViewEntireForest` to `True`, the `RecipientViewRoot` will be `null`.

Any changes you make to the Active Directory server settings while in the Exchange Management Shell will be valid for only that session. If you want them to persist across sessions, you will need to load them in your `$Profile` script.

Managing Role Based Access Control

Exchange 2010 provides 11 default management role groups. These role groups should be sufficient if you centrally manage Exchange. If, however, you want to delegate management to separate management groups, you will want to create your own role groups.

Suppose you want to create a role group to allow the universal security group
AccountingServiceDesk to manage recipients in the Accounting organizational unit.
You use the New-RoleGroup cmdlet, passing the required parameters Name, Roles, Members,
and RecipientOrganizationalUnitScope.

The following example creates the role group Accounting, and assigns the role group
to the AccountingServiceDesk global security group, allowing that group to create
mailboxes and mail-enabled public folders. The accounting help desk will only be able to
perform these tasks on recipients in the Accounting organizational unit.

```
$RoleGroup = @{
Name = "Accounting"
Roles = "Mail Recipient Creation","Mail Enabled Public Folders"
Members = "AccountingServiceDesk"
RecipientOrganizationalUnitScope = "Accounting"
}
New-RoleGroup @RoleGroup
```

You can get a list of current role groups with the Get-RoleGroup cmdlet. The following
example shows the name and assigned roles for all current role groups:

```
Get-RoleGroup | Format-List -Property Name, Roles
```

If you want to add a management role to a current role group, universal security group,
user, or management role assignment policy, you use the New-ManagementRoleAssignment
cmdlet. The required parameters for this cmdlet depend on the target. For a universal
security group or role group, the required parameters are SecurityGroup and Role. In the
case of a role group, SecurityGroup is the name of the role group.

The following example adds the Retention Management role to the existing role group
Accounting:

```
$ManagementRoleAssignment = @{
SecurityGroup = "Accounting"
Role = "Retention Management"
}
New-ManagementRoleAssignment @ManagementRoleAssignment
```

You can verify that the role was added with the Get-RoleGroup cmdlet, specifying the
Identity parameter:

```
Get-RoleGroup -Identity Accounting | Format-List -Property Name, Roles
```

As mentioned in the "Microsoft Exchange Server 2010" subsection of the "Managing
Microsoft Exchange Server Permissions" section, you can add a specific user or users to a
role group with the Add-RoleGroupMember cmdlet. Conversely, to remove a user or users
from a role group, you use the Remove-RoleGroupMember cmdlet, passing the required

parameters `Identity` and `Member`. The following example removes the user `John` from the role group `Recipient Management`:

```
$RoleGroupmember = @{
Identity = "Recipient Management"
Member = "John"
}
Remove-RoleGroupmember @RoleGroupmember
```

You can add the switch parameter `Confirm = $False` to prevent being prompted for confirmation on the member removal.

Additionally, as with the `Add-RoleGroupMember` cmdlet, you can specify the optional switch parameter `BypassSecurityGroupManagerCheck` to perform the modification if you are not in the `ManagedBy` property of the role group. The following example removes the member `John` from the role group `Recipient Management`, without prompting for confirmation, and will not fail if you are not in the `ManagedBy` property of the role group:

```
$RoleGroupmember = @{
Identity = "Recipient Management"
Member = "John"
Confirm = $false
BypassSecurityGroupManagerCheck = $true
}
Remove-RoleGroupmember @RoleGroupmember
```

You can see a list of current members of a particular role group with the `Get-RoleGroupMember` cmdlet, passing the `Identity` parameter. The following example lists all members of the role group `Recipient Management`:

```
Get-RoleGroupMember -Identity "Recipient Management"
```

You can pass the output of the `Get-RoleGroup` cmdlet to the `Get-RoleGroupMember` cmdlet to get a list of all members of all role groups. The following example lists all members of all role groups:

```
Foreach($group in Get-RoleGroup)
{
$Member = Get-RoleGroupMember $group | Select-Object -Property Name
Write-Host -NoNewline -Object Group: $group.Name has members: $Member.Name`n
}
```

Note

For more information on role groups, see TechNet: **http://technet.microsoft.com/en-us/library/ dd298183.aspx.** ∎

Introducing Microsoft Exchange Web Services

Microsoft has included programming APIs with every version of Exchange Server, and Exchange Server 2007 and Exchange Server 2010 are no different in that respect. In Exchange Server 2000 and Exchange Server 2003, Microsoft provided CDO and WebDAV.

In Exchange Server 2007, WebDAV is still supported, but deprecated. Microsoft provided Exchange Web Services for Exchange Server 2007 and Exchange Server 2010. Starting with Exchange Server 2007 Service Pack 1, Microsoft also provides the Exchange Web Services Managed API.

The managed API enables you to directly manipulate mailbox or public folder contents, among other tasks, within a .NET Framework. This means that you can create, modify, or view items in mailboxes with Windows PowerShell.

Before you can use the API, you need to download it from www.microsoft.com/downloads/en/details.aspx?displaylang=en&FamilyID=c3342fb3-fbcc-4127-becf-872c746840e1.

Once you have downloaded and installed the Managed API, you can start using it from Windows PowerShell. Because the Managed API does not include cmdlets, you work with it by loading the DLL.

Suppose you need to change the name of a folder in all mailboxes in the Sales department from Leads to Sales Leads. Depending on users to modify their folders is problematic at best.

Using the Exchange Web Services Managed API and Windows PowerShell, you can easily accomplish this task.

Note

The Exchange Web Services Managed API does not rely on the Exchange Management Shell. You can use either Windows PowerShell or the Exchange Management Shell if you do not need to gather data from the Exchange infrastructure, such as mailbox names. ■

The first step in any script utilizing Exchange Web Services is to load the DLL. Currently, the version of the DLL is 1.1. You will need to modify the $path to match the actual version you download:

```
$path = "$env:ProgramFiles\Microsoft\Exchange\Web Services\1.1"
$dllpath = "$path\Microsoft.Exchange.WebServices.dll"
Add-Type -Path $dllpath
```

Once you have the DLL loaded, you need to create an Exchange Server object. If you are running Exchange Server 2010, you can do this as:

```
$EWSObject = @{
TypeName = "Microsoft.Exchange.WebServices.Data.ExchangeService"
}
$EWSService = New-Object @EWSObject
```

If you are running Exchange Server 2007 Service Pack 1, however, you will need to set the version:

```
$EWSObject = @{
TypeName = "Microsoft.Exchange.WebServices.Data.ExchangeService"
ArgumentList = "Exchange2007_SP1"
}
$EWSService = New-Object @EWSObject
```

Now that you have the service, you need to populate the `AutoDiscoverUrl`. The `AutodiscoverUrl` is set by passing an email address. You can hard-code an `AutoDiscoverUrl` as:

```
$EWSService.AutoDiscoverUrl("email@contoso.com")
```

If you do not want to hard-code the email address into the `AutoDiscoverUrl`, you can get the email address of the current logged-in user, and use that for the `AutoDiscoverUrl`:

```
$Identity = [System.Security.Principal.WindowsIdentity]::GetCurrent()
$bind = "LDAP://<SID=" + $Identity.User.Value.ToString() + ">"
$User = [ADSI]$bind
$EWSService.AutoDiscoverUrl($User.mail.ToString())
```

If you do not want to use AutoDiscover, or cannot for some reason, such as not being logged in to the domain, you can hard-code the service URL:

```
$EWSservice.Url = "https://webmail.contoso.com/EWS/Exchange.asmx"
```

Finally, if you do not want to use the credentials of the logged-in user, you can pass a username and password to the EWS Service:

```
$Object = @{
TypeName = "System.Net.NetworkCredential"
ArgumentList = ("user","password","domain")
}
$EWSService.Credentials = New-Object @Object
```

Now the service is complete, so you can use it.

You need the email address for each mailbox you want to modify. If you have the Exchange Management Shell loaded, you can get the email addresses for everyone in the Marketing department with the `Get-Recipient` cmdlet:

```
$Recipient = @{
Filter = {Department -eq "Sales" -and RecipientTypeDetails -eq "UserMailbox"}
}
$Address = @{
Property = "PrimarySmtpAddress"
}
$Mailboxes = @(Get-Recipient @Recipient | Select-Object @Address)
```

Now that you have the list of email addresses, and have created the service, you can bind to each mailbox and change the folder name:

```
$PropObject = @{
TypeName = "Microsoft.Exchange.WebServices.Data.PropertySet"
}
$PropSet = New-Object @PropObject
foreach ($Mailbox in $Mailboxes)
{
$Email = $Mailbox.PrimarySmtpAddress.ToString()
$RootFolderID = `
New-Object -TypeName Microsoft.Exchange.WebServices.Data.FolderId `
-ArgumentList `
([Microsoft.Exchange.WebServices.Data.WellKnownFolderName]::MsgFolderRoot`
,$Email)
$Root = `
[Microsoft.Exchange.WebServices.Data.Folder]::Bind($EWSService,$RootFolderID)
$View = New-Object Microsoft.Exchange.WebServices.Data.FolderView(10000)
$View.Traversal = [Microsoft.Exchange.WebServices.Data.FolderTraversal]::Deep
$View.PropertySet = $Propset
$Response = $Root.FindFolders($View)
foreach ($folder in $Response.Folders)
{
if ($folder.DisplayName -eq "Leads")
{
Write-Output "Found Marketing Deals on $Email"
$folder.DisplayName = "Sales Leads"
$folder.Update()
}
}
}
```

The complete script to change the name of a folder in all mailboxes in the `Sales` department from `Leads` to `Sales Leads` is shown in Listing 12-5. This example uses the credentials of the current user.

LISTING 12-5

Changing a Folder Name in a List of Exchange Mailboxes

```
$path = "$env:ProgramFiles\Microsoft\Exchange\Web Services\1.1"
$dllpath = "$path\Microsoft.Exchange.WebServices.dll"
Add-Type -Path $dllpath
$EWSObject = @{
TypeName = "Microsoft.Exchange.WebServices.Data.ExchangeService"
}
$PropObject = @{
TypeName = "Microsoft.Exchange.WebServices.Data.PropertySet"
}
$EWSService = New-Object @EWSObject
$PropSet = New-Object @PropObject
$Identity = [System.Security.Principal.WindowsIdentity]::GetCurrent()
$bind = "LDAP://<SID=" + $Identity.user.Value.ToString() + ">"
$User = [ADSI]$bind
$EWSService.AutodiscoverUrl($User.mail.ToString())
$Recipient = @{
Filter = {Department -eq "Sales" -and RecipientTypeDetails -eq "UserMailbox"}
}
$Address = @{
Property = "PrimarySmtpAddress"
}
$Mailboxes = @(Get-Recipient @Recipient | Select-Object @Address)
foreach ($Mailbox in $Mailboxes)
{
$Email = $Mailbox.PrimarySmtpAddress.ToString()
$RootFolderID = `
New-Object -TypeName Microsoft.Exchange.WebServices.Data.FolderId `
-ArgumentList `
([Microsoft.Exchange.WebServices.Data.WellKnownFolderName]::MsgFolderRoot`
,$Email)
$Root = `
[Microsoft.Exchange.WebServices.Data.Folder]::Bind($EWSService,$RootFolderID)
$View = New-Object Microsoft.Exchange.WebServices.Data.FolderView(10000)
$View.Traversal = [Microsoft.Exchange.WebServices.Data.FolderTraversal]::Deep
$View.PropertySet = $Propset
$Response = $Root.FindFolders($View)
foreach ($folder in $Response.Folders)
{
if ($folder.DisplayName -eq "Leads")
{
Write-Output -InputObject "Found Marketing Deals on $Email"
$folder.DisplayName = "Sales Leads"
$folder.Update()
}
}
}
```

If you are only concerned with folders at the root of the mailbox, you can eliminate the `$View.Traversal = [Microsoft.Exchange.WebServices.Data.FolderTraversal]::Deep` line from the preceding examples.

If you routinely work with Exchange Web Services, you can create a function in your `$profile` script to allow you to easily load the DLL and create the references. The following example loads the DLL and creates references using the currently logged-in user. This example is specific to Exchange Server 2010. Remember to modify the sample if you have Exchange Server 2007 Service Pack 1 or newer, or if you want to pass credentials.

```
function Load-EWS
{
$path = "$env:ProgramFiles\Microsoft\Exchange\Web Services\1.1"
$dllpath = "$path\Microsoft.Exchange.WebServices.dll"
Add-Path -Path $dllpath $EWSObject = @{
TypeName = "Microsoft.Exchange.WebServices.Data.ExchangeService"
}
$EWSService = New-Object @EWSObject
$Identity = [System.Security.Principal.WindowsIdentity]::GetCurrent()
$bind = "LDAP://<SID=" + $Identity.User.Value.ToString() + ">"
$User = [ADSI]$bind
$EWSService.AutoDiscoverUrl($User.mail.ToString())
}
```

Once you have this function in your `$profile` script, you can use the Exchange Web Services API by calling the function, and then whatever Exchange Web Services API calls you need to make. Remember to dot-source the function.

Note

For more information on working with Windows PowerShell and the Exchange Web Services Managed API, see http://msdn.microsoft.com/en-us/library/dd633696.aspx. ∎

Summary

In this chapter, you explored how to manage Exchange recipient objects, databases, and permissions. You also took a look at using Exchange Web Services to manage data within mailboxes.

You learned how to manage Exchange Server 2010 via Windows PowerShell Version 2 remote consoles. You also learned why I recommend that the Exchange Management Tools be loaded on a local workstation as opposed to logging in to an Exchange server via either remote desktop or remote Windows PowerShell.

Finally, you explored using filters to limit results, and explored the two kinds of filters. You saw the difference between client-side and server-side filters, and why server-side filters are more efficient.

In the next chapter, you explore managing SQL Server with Windows PowerShell. Important concepts include querying and adding data to databases, discovering information about the databases, and learning about SQL Server itself.

Managing SQL Server 2008 R2

S oftware systems have many interdependent moving parts. These parts might include operating systems, databases, and applications. The historical challenge of managing this type of system was that each part of a software system required a different mechanism to communicate with the component. A database might need T-SQL, application code might require C#, and the operating system may require a command-line scripting language. Managing these varied components required either multiple people with unique skill sets or people who were capable of learning multiple languages. Either way, it was a challenge.

In Windows PowerShell, we have a single language that can be used to interact with an operating system, an application, or a database. This is a huge benefit for anyone who wears multiple hats in their organization. Windows PowerShell enables IT professionals to develop a single skill set that can help bridge the gap between each area of the system. This level of flexibility and control over my environment is why Windows PowerShell is my favorite topic to teach and write on. This chapter focuses on how to leverage Windows PowerShell in a SQL Server environment and covers tasks that can be made more efficient and reusable in both development and administration processes.

IN THIS CHAPTER

Basics of SQL Server management

Querying and inserting data

Getting information from SQL Server

Scripting and automation

Using SQL Server agent jobs

PowerShell Basics for SQL Server

Whether it be using Windows PowerShell and adding in SQL functionality or using *SQL PowerShell (SQLPS)*, the SQL Server specific mini-shell of Windows PowerShell, there is a lot of value to be had by learning to use PowerShell in a SQL Server environment. SQL Server

2008 and 2008 R2 have only five PowerShell cmdlets; however, increasing the number of cmdlets is already being addressed in the next release of SQL Server, SQL Server 2012. With SQL Server, you have several distinct approaches available to access the same information. They fall into the following categories:

- Windows PowerShell cmdlets
- SQL Server cmdlets
- WMI
- SMO (SQL Management Objects)
- Other .NET classes

SMO are a highly customized group of .NET objects that are purpose-built for working with SQL Server. They can be very confusing to use at first, so this chapter uses examples that show how to get exactly the same information using SMO, Provider, and cmdlets. Because SQL Server 2008 has only five cmdlets available, sometimes the SMO must be used to perform everyday tasks. The community CodePlex project SQLPSX (`http://sqlpsx .codeplex.com/`) is a collection of scripts that enables you to access the SMO more simply. At the time of this writing, 163 advanced functions and 2 cmdlets are available in SQLPSX.

Keep in mind that SQL Server is not a single product; it is a suite of products. As such, some products like MDS (Master Data Services) have had cmdlets built for them, whereas other products like SSRS (SQL Server Reporting Services) have not. The cmdlets for Master Data Services are out of scope for this book.

The examples included in this chapter are based on functionality in SQL Server 2008 (and SQL Server 2008 R2) unless otherwise specified. To work with SQL Server in Windows PowerShell, you need to have SQL Server Management Studio (SSMS) 2008 or SSMS 2008 R2 installed.

Note

If you don't have access to the install media, you can download and install SQL Server 2008 R2 Express with Advanced Services from `http://www.microsoft.com/download/en/details .aspx?displaylang=en&id=25174`. ■

The installation of SSMS contains the required .NET assemblies and the Windows PowerShell features that you will be working with throughout this chapter. The documentation states that you can install some downloads off the Feature Pack; however, I have found that simply installing SSMS 2008 or SSMS 2008 R2 is much more reliable.

Even though the version of SSMS used here is 2008, the examples also work on SQL Server 2005 instances and their databases.

Note

The examples demonstrated in this chapter use a default instance of SQL Server as well as a named instance of SQL Server. "R2" is the name of the named instance. Both instances used to produce these examples are the R2 version of SQL Server 2008.

Some of the examples use a database called SandBox. If you don't have a database on your `localhost\R2` instance, you can create one quickly by running the following PowerShell code:

```
Invoke-Sqlcmd -ServerInstance "LocalHost\R2" -Database "master" -Query "
CREATE DATABASE SandBox"
```

In addition, a few Windows PowerShell functions are referenced that are available for download from the TechNet Script Center Repository. This site is a freely available resource where other users have posted scripts that they have developed. The site for this repository is: `http://gallery.technet.microsoft.com/scriptcenter/2fdeaf8d-b164-411c-9483-99413d6053ae.` ■

Managing SQL Server Services

Before getting started with what SQL Server brings to the Windows PowerShell table, this section takes a quick look at something you can do with Windows PowerShell and SQL Server right away. You can use the `Get-Service` cmdlet to look for installed SQL Server services on your local or remote machines.

In the following code sample, you'll see that I piped the output to the `Where-Object` cmdlet to filter down to just the `"SQL*"` services on the machine. It's important to note that I used the `DisplayName` property coming back from the `Get-Service` cmdlet because several of the services don't actually start with the name SQL when you use the `Name` property. Keep in mind that if you had a service installed that just happened to begin with the letters *SQL*, it would be returned as well.

```
Get-Service -ComputerName "localhost" |
Where {$_.DisplayName -like "SQL*"} |
Select MachineName, Name, DisplayName, Status, ServiceName |
Format-Table -AutoSize
```

If you are working through these examples at home on your laptop, the `-Force` switch is a handy feature to be aware of. It is used in a situation where you want to restart a service that has a dependent service. For example, the main SQL Engine has a service called SQL Agent that can only run when the parent (SQL Engine) service is already running, making it dependent. Normally, when you try to restart the SQL Server (Engine) service from the Services window, it gives an error if it's already running. In Windows PowerShell, if you use the `-Force` switch, it will go ahead and stop and start the dependent service for you after it stops and starts the parent service.

```
Get-Service -Name *SQL* | Where-Object {$_.Name -eq "MSSQLSERVER"} |
Restart-Service -Force
```

This type of granular control over common SQL Server operations is an example of why Windows PowerShell is a great option for anyone who needs to interact with one or multiple instances or databases.

There are two additional ways to affect services using Windows PowerShell. These include the `Get-WMIObject` cmdlet and the SMO itself.

The following example returns information about each SQL Server service using `Get-WMIObject`:

```
Get-WmiObject -Query "
SELECT * FROM win32_service WHERE DisplayName LIKE '%SQL%'
" -ComputerName localhost |
SELECT DisplayName, Name, PathName, ServiceType, StartName, SystemName |
Sort DisplayName |
Format-Table -AutoSize
```

The following example returns information about the service using SMO:

```
 [System.Reflection.Assembly]::LoadWithPartialName("Microsoft.SqlServer.Sql↵
WmiManagement") | Out-Null
$SMOWmiserver = New-Object ('Microsoft.SqlServer.Management.Smo.Wmi.Managed↵
Computer') "LOCALHOST"

<#These just act as some queries about the SQL Services on the
machine you specified.#>
$SMOWmiserver.Services |
Select name, type, ServiceAccount, DisplayName, Properties, StartMode, Start↵
upParameters |
Format-Table
```

Note

Although the preceding SMO example for retrieving information about services has been provided in the interest of comprehensiveness, using it will likely present performance issues when compared to the performance of `Get-Service` or `Get-WMIObject`. Avoid using this code whenever possible. If you've inherited code that evaluates service information using SMO, consider rewriting it using either the `Get-Service` cmdlet or `Get-WMIObject`.

The exception to this practice is when you need to change the account that the SQL Server service is running under. In this case, SMO is required. For more information, see the MSDN article at `http://technet .microsoft.com/en-us/library/ms345578.aspx`. ∎

Working with Snap-ins

SSMS 2008 and SSMS 2008 R2 both come with a pair of cmdlets for working with SQL Server. The `SqlServerCmdletSnapin100` snap-in contains two cmdlets: `Invoke-SQLcmd` and `Invoke-PolicyEvaluation`. The `SqlServerProviderSnapin100` snap-in, which is primarily known for making your SQL Server traversable just like any drive on your machine, brings in three more cmdlets: `Convert-UrnToPath`, `Encode-SqlName`, and `Decode-SqlName`. To use these snap-ins, run the following lines of code for each snap-in, respectively:

```
Add-PSSnapin SqlServerCmdletSnapin100;
Add-PSSnapin SqlServerProviderSnapin100
```

Note

You can download the `SQLServerProviderSnapin100` snap-in from the Microsoft SQL Server 2008 R2 Feature Pack at www.microsoft.com/download/en/confirmation.aspx?id=16978. ∎

When you open up the Integrated Scripting Environment (ISE) and run `Get-PSDrive`, you'll see a list of drives and providers on your machine. Once you add the `SqlServerProviderSnapin100` snap-in (`Add-PSSnapin SqlServerProviderSnapin100`), you will notice a new drive called `SQLServer:\`. You can do a `CD` (Change Directory) or `Set-Location` over to the `SQLServer:\` drive. From there, you have six options, which are basically logical subfolders of the `SQLSERVER:\` object:

- `SQL`
- `SQLPolicy`
- `SQLRegistration`
- `DataCollection`
- `Utility`
- `DAC`

When you navigate under the `SQL\` directory, you can begin navigating your SQL Servers and instances just as though they were any other directory on your machine. The really exciting thing is that you are not limited to just the instances on your local machine; by default, you will be able to access any instance for which you have permissions.

One thing to keep in mind when working with the `SQLServer:\` Provider is that you don't actually have to set your location (via `CD` or `Set-Location`) into the SQLServer Provider to be able to use it and pull information out of it. In fact, staying outside of the provider itself can often be a much less frustrating way to work with SQL Server. When you're inside the SQL Server 2008 or 2008 R2 version of the SQLServer Provider, things like tab completion, also known as command completion, don't behave as you would expect and can lead to frustration.

```
Get-ChildItem SQLServer:\SQL\LocalHost  | select name, version
```

Working with Assemblies

When writing scripts, I try to avoid loading assemblies directly in the script. I prefer to leverage functions that have already loaded the necessary assembly for me. This is because using functions rather than assemblies generally results in cleaner, more concise code. The assemblies that you are most likely to work with in the current version of SQL Server are:

- `Microsoft.SqlServer.SMO`
- `Microsoft.SqlServer.SMOExtended`
- `Microsoft.SqlServer.SqlWmiManagement`
- `Microsoft.SqlServer.ConnectionInfo`

Changing the Service Account

With SQL Server 2005 through 2008 R2 running on Windows 2008 or Windows 2003, you must use SQL Server Configuration Manager if you need to change the account the service is running under. When you use the SQL WMI Management class to change a SQL Server service account, service account security changes required by SQL Server are also addressed.

Note

See `http://blogs.msdn.com/b/dtjones/archive/2010/12/15/changing-service-account-amp-service-account-password.aspx` for a detailed explanation. ∎

Having the ability to programmatically make this type of change allows you to affect multiple instances without having to access multiple user interfaces, and it also enables you to schedule a change during off hours while you're not even there.

The following code shows how to change the service account for the SQL Server engine:

```
#Load the SqlWmiManagement assembly off of the DLL
[System.Reflection.Assembly]::LoadWithPartialName("Microsoft.SqlServer.SqlWmi↵
Management") | Out-Null
$SMOWmiserver = New-Object ('Microsoft.SqlServer.Management.Smo.Wmi.Managed↵
Computer') "LocalHost"
#Suck in the server you want

<#Specify the "Name" (from the query above) of the one service whose
Service Account you want to change.#>
$ServiceToChange=$SMOWmiserver.Services | where {$_.name -eq "MSSQLSERVER"}
#Make sure this is what you want changed!
#Check which service you have loaded first
$ServiceToChange

$UName="DomainName\UserName"
$PWord="YourPassword"

$ServiceToChange.SetServiceAccount($UName, $PWord)
#Now take a look at it afterwards
$ServiceToChange
```

Querying SQL Server

Querying SQL Server is very straightforward with Windows PowerShell. The simplest way to write T-SQL (Transact SQL) within Windows PowerShell is to load the `SqlServerCmdletSnapin100` snap-in and pass your query to `Invoke-SQLcmd`. There are two options for `Invoke-SQLcmd`. You can pass a query in a quoted string to the `–Query` parameter, or you can pass in the name and location of a `.sql` file to the `–InputFile` parameter for the cmdlet to run.

Using a Quoted String to Query SQL Server

The most direct way to query SQL Server with Windows PowerShell is to use `Invoke-SQLcmd` and a quoted string. Imagine that you are using SSMS, and you have a very basic query of `sys.dm_db_partition_stats` because you want to identify the number of pages on disk for each of your tables. The SQL would look like this:

```
SELECT * FROM sys.dm_db_partition_stats;
```

To run the same query from Windows PowerShell, you place the SELECT statement within a quoted string and identify that string as a query by using the `–Query` parameter. You will need to provide the server instance information to define which instance is being queried. This is accomplished with the `–ServerInstance` parameter. Optionally, you can provide a database name with the `–Database` parameter, along with the `–Username` and `–Password` credentials that will allow you to access the instance. Keep in mind that if you do not provide a database name, the default database tied to the account you are logged in with will be used, as defined within the security of the instance you are connecting to. If no username and password are provided, your current login credentials are used.

```
Invoke-SQLcmd -ServerInstance "Localhost\R2" -Database "master" -Query "
SELECT * FROM sys.dm_db_partition_stats"
```

Using Variable Expansion

One of the major benefits of running T-SQL queries from Windows PowerShell is the ability to leverage variable expansion. Anyone who's ever suffered through writing dynamic SQL will see the beauty of being able to cleanly provide a parameter to a query. Assume that you're running a process that determines the table to query at runtime. Within T-SQL, you'd have to concatenate a variable into a string and carefully ensure that correct syntax is maintained. With variable expansion, this is not a concern. Simply assign the table name to a variable, and include it in the query. At runtime, Windows PowerShell will expand the variable into the value it was set to as long as it is contained within a double-quoted string, producing a syntactically correct query to pass to SQL Server.

```
$table = 'sys.databases'
Invoke-SQLcmd -ServerInstance "Localhost\R2" -Database "master" -Query "
SELECT * FROM $table"
```

The query that is actually passed to the database is:

```
SELECT * FROM sys.dm_db_partition_stats
```

Note

Should you use single quotes or double quotes? Minor but very impactful differences exist between using a quoted string with a variable and without a variable. If the query does not contain a variable, it can be encapsulated in single quotes, such as `'SELECT * FROM sys.dm_db_partition_stats'`. However, if a parameter is provided as part of the query string, the query needs to be wrapped in double quotes, as in `"SELECT * FROM $table"`. ∎

Running Queries Against Multiple Servers

Windows PowerShell variable expansion greatly simplifies the process of passing parameters into a quoted string. The real benefit is realized when you want to run the same query against multiple servers using a single code block. Imagine that you're collecting information from a Data Management View (DMV), `sys.dm_os_wait_stats`. Using a variable and a `foreach` loop, you can query the same view on each instance and return the results to the console:

```
$MultipleServers = '127.0.0.1', 'LocalHost'

Foreach($Server in $MultipleServers)
{
Invoke-SQLCmd -Query "
SELECT * FROM sys.dm_os_wait_stats" -ServerInstance $Server -Database "master"
}
```

What is happening in this example is that as the `foreach` loop iterates through each value assigned to `$MultipleServers`, it passes the value into `$Server`. The query is passed to SQL Server, and each result set is returned to the console.

Returning Data into a Datatable

When data is returned by `Invoke-SQLCmd`, the result set comes back in an array of data rows, whether it is 1 row or 400,000 rows. Unless you are only viewing the results or the result set contains only one row, the result set often needs to be converted to a datatable. If the results need to be pushed into a SQL Server table, HTML table, or if you need to combine result sets, it is much simpler to interact with a datatable than an array. While you can use the `WriteToServer` method of `SQLBulkCopy`, you may find it easier to move the results into the datatable so that you have more flexibility later on in your processes. The following example illustrates that, by default, the results are returned in an array. The `GetType()` method displays the result set type, which is `System.Array`.

```
$dbSizes = Invoke-SQLcmd -Query "
sp_databases" -Database master -ServerInstance "LocalHost\R2"
$dbSizes;
$dbSizes.GetType()
```

Piping the results to the `Out-DataTable` function, as shown in the next code sample, converts the result set from an array to a datatable. This function, written by Chad Miller and available in the TechNet Script Center Repository, is available at http://gallery .technet.microsoft.com/scriptcenter/4208a159-a52e-4b99-83d4-8048468d29dd.

```
$dbSizes = Invoke-SQLcmd -Database master -ServerInstance "LOCALHOST\R2" `
-Query "sp_databases" | Out-DataTable
$dbSizes;
$dbSizes.GetType()
```

Finally, ADO.NET can be used to execute a query or stored procedure and return the results directly into a datatable without having to call the third-party function `Out-DataTable`. However, this is quite a bit more code to achieve the same result:

```
$conn = New-Object System.Data.SqlClient.SqlConnection("Data Source=↵
LocalHost\R2; Initial Catalog=master; Integrated Security=SSPI")
$conn.Open()
$cmd1 = $conn.CreateCommand()
$cmd1.CommandType = [System.Data.CommandType]::StoredProcedure
$cmd1.CommandText ="sp_databases"
$data = $cmd1.ExecuteReader()
$dt = new-object "System.Data.DataTable"
$dt.Load($data)
$dt | Format-Table
$conn.Close()
```

Using an Input File to Query SQL Server

In some situations, you want to deploy database objects that you have developed, or just want to run a query that you have saved. When you need to reuse a query or load database objects, the query or set of queries can be saved as a `.sql` file. Much like a quoted string, it can be referenced by `Invoke-SQLcmd`. But instead of using the `-Query` parameter with a quoted string, the query file is referenced and the `-InputFile` parameter is provided. The following example passes the query stored within `SavedQueryFile.sql` file to SQL Server:

```
Invoke-SQLcmd -ServerInstance "Localhost\R2" -Database "AdventureWorks" `
-InputFile "SavedQueryFile.sql"
```

Note

You have other options for querying SQL Server from Windows PowerShell, such as building a connection string and opening a connection to SQL Server using ADO.NET objects, but that takes significantly more code than **Invoke-SQLcmd**. In practice, a common reason to avoid the ADO.NET approach is because it is not only harder to read, but also harder to troubleshoot and transition to other developers. ∎

Loading Data

The previous section covered how to get data out of a SQL Server database. This section takes the next step and addresses how to get data into a database by using different types of data to load: SQL Server data and non-SQL Server data, as well as data contained in an array or datatable.

Note

The use of PowerShell instead of Windows PowerShell indicates the capabilities of both Windows PowerShell and SQLPS. ∎

Loading SQL Server Data

Loading data into SQL Server with PowerShell can be pretty simple. In fact, if you already have your table created and your INSERT statement formed, all you have to do is leverage Invoke-SQLcmd and away you go. In the following example, you create a basic table in the SandBox database that was mentioned at the beginning of this chapter. You insert two rows with the next PowerShell statement. Finally, you execute a statement to retrieve all the rows from the table to verify that the rows were inserted correctly:

```
Invoke-SQLcmd -ServerInstance "LocalHost\R2" -Database "SandBox" -Query "
CREATE TABLE [dbo].[FoundSQLServers](
  [ServerName] [varchar](128) NULL,
  [InstanceName] [varchar](128) NULL,
  [IsClustered] [varchar](5) NULL,
  [VersionNumber] [varchar](64) NULL
) ON [PRIMARY]"

Invoke-SQLcmd -ServerInstance "LocalHost\R2" -Database SandBox -Query "
INSERT INTO dbo.FoundSQLServers
VALUES
('PoShSQL', 'R2', 'No', '10.50.1600.1'),
('PoShSQL', 'DENALI', 'No', '11.0.1103.9')"

Invoke-SQLcmd -ServerInstance "LocalHost\R2" -Database SandBox -Query "
SELECT ServerName, InstanceName, IsClustered, VersionNumber
  FROM dbo.FoundSQLServers"
```

For those times when you don't yet have a SQL statement to call, you can form your INSERT statement by using variable expansion in the pipeline. In this approach, you compose the VALUES for the INSERT and add only one row of data at a time as it comes in off the pipeline. This approach can be ideal in situations where you are collecting one or only a few lines of data at a time before you move to another object to start the collection process again. An example of that type of behavior is when you connect to one instance, grab a row, insert it into a table, and then move on to another table, as shown in the following code sample:

```
[Microsoft.SqlServer.Management.Smo.SmoApplication]::EnumAvailableSqlServers() |
foreach {

Invoke-SQLcmd -ServerInstance "LocalHost\R2" -database SandBox -query "
INSERT INTO dbo.FoundSQLServers
VALUES ('$($_.Server)', '$($_.Instance)', '$($_.IsClustered)',
'$($_.Version)')"

          }
```

Once the data is inserted into dbo.FoundSQLServers, you can query it using:

```
Invoke-SQLcmd -ServerInstance "LocalHost\R2" -database SandBox -query "
SELECT ServerName, InstanceName, IsClustered, VersionNumber
   FROM dbo.FoundSQLServers"
```

Loading Non-SQL Server Data

The whole point of using Windows PowerShell in a SQL Server environment is that you can integrate querying and manipulating data into an overall process seamlessly. Once you've queried data, the next step is to do something with that output. You can load data produced by Windows PowerShell into SQL Server using an input file, array, or with ADO.NET and a datatable.

The following example shows how to load data from an input file named InsertRows.sql:

```
invoke-sqlcmd -InputFile "C:\temp\InsertRows.sql" `
-database master -serverinstance "LOCALHOST\R2"
```

Arrays are notoriously difficult to use for loading data because they must be parsed to pull the data out field by field. However, if an array is all you have to work with, it can be done. You can use the SQLBulkCopy class to load data into a SQL Server table from a datatable. Neither of these options is covered in this book.

Getting SQL Server Information

Most people think that keeping up to date with patches and service packs is only important for security reasons. It's not. For example, Microsoft used Service Pack 2 of SQL Server 2008 to retrofit/allow SQL Server 2008 instances to work with Utility Control Point, a feature introduced in SQL Server 2008 R2.

Just as vital is maintaining the same patch version in your Production, QA, and Development environments. Because more people tend to have direct access to servers in lower environments, it's completely possible for someone to install a patch accidentally. If a developer builds a local copy of the database on the server, he or she might be running the latest service pack (or not). While you can easily see the connection, you're probably not going to want to log in to every single developer's workstation one at a time inside of SSMS.

Getting Version Information

In T-SQL, you can determine the version of the SQL Server instance you're connected to by running:

```
SELECT @@version;
```

The challenge in evaluating instance versions and recording them somewhere lies in the fact that in order for the query to run, you must be connected to the instance. With Windows PowerShell, you're able to use the SMO to retrieve the same information. The benefit of this method is that you can iterate through multiple instances by using a foreach loop.

```
[System.Reflection.Assembly]::LoadWithPartialName("Microsoft.SqlServer.SMO") |
Out-Null
$SQLInstance=New-Object Microsoft.SqlServer.Management.Smo.Server "LocalHost\R2"
$SQLInstance |Format-Table -Property name, version, Product
```

Getting Service Pack Information

Obtaining the service pack level from your SQL instance is just as easy as retrieving the version. All you need to do is snag the ProductLevel property from the server instance object:

```
[System.Reflection.Assembly]::LoadWithPartialName("Microsoft.SqlServer.SMO") |
Out-Null
$SQLInstance= New-Object↵
    Microsoft.SqlServer.Management.Smo.Server "LOCALHOST\R2"
$SQLInstance | Format-Table -Property name, version, ProductLevel –AutoSize
```

Getting Instance Uptime Information

Gathering the uptime of a SQL Server instance has become easier in more recent versions. SQL Server 2005 provided the Data Management View (DMV) sys.dm_os_sys_info, which had a column called ms_ticks that you could use to calculate server uptime. Unfortunately, the word "calculate" in that last sentence was very accurate; ms_ticks contains the number of milliseconds that have elapsed since the last time that the instance was started. You then needed to subtract all those milliseconds from the current date and time to figure out when the instance started.

In SQL Server 2008, there is a column called sqlserver_start_time that provides the date and time the instance started without forcing you to go through the process of writing the code to do the calculation yourself.

To store the data, you'll need a table:

```
Invoke-SQLcmd -ServerInstance "LOCALHOST\R2" -Database "Sandbox" -Query "
CREATE TABLE [dbo].[InstanceUpTime](
  [ServerName] [nvarchar](128) NULL,
  [InstanceName] [nvarchar](128) NULL,
  [sqlserver_start_time] [datetime] NOT NULL,
  [CheckedOn] [datetimeoffset](7) NOT NULL
) ON [PRIMARY]"
```

To gather the uptime information, you need to connect to one instance, grab the information, store it in a variable, then connect to a different instance and insert it into a table. If you're pulling the information from a SQL Server 2005 instance, it is best to go ahead and convert the values into an actual date and time that the instance started. Here's what that would look like:

```
Invoke-SQLcmd -ServerInstance "LOCALHOST\R2" -Database "Sandbox" -Query "
INSERT INTO InstanceUpTime
SELECT @@SERVERNAME AS 'ServerName',
  @@SERVICENAME AS 'InstanceName',
  DATEADD(S, ((-1) * ([ms_ticks]/1000)), GETDATE()) AS 'sqlserver_start_time',
  SYSDATETIMEOFFSET() AS 'CheckedOn'
  FROM sys.dm_os_sys_info"
```

Grabbing the information from a SQL Server 2008 instance can be done with a slightly different approach:

```
Invoke-SQLcmd -ServerInstance "LOCALHOST\R2" -Database "Sandbox" -Query "
INSERT INTO InstanceUpTime
SELECT @@SERVERNAME AS 'ServerName',
  @@SERVICENAME AS 'InstanceName',
  sqlserver_start_time,
  SYSDATETIMEOFFSET() AS 'CheckedOn'
  FROM sys.dm_os_sys_info"
```

Finally, insert the data into a log table:

```
Invoke-SQLcmd -ServerInstance "LOCALHOST\R2" -Database "Sandbox" -Query "
INSERT INTO InstanceUpTime
VALUES
(
'$($UTValues.ServerName)',
'$($UTValues.InstanceName)',
'$($UTValues.sqlserver_start_time)',
'$($UTValues.CheckedOn)'
)"
```

Gathering Performance Counters

Gathering SQL Server performance counters is very straightforward in SQL Server 2005 and above thanks to the `sys.dm_os_performance_counters` DMV. Through the DMV, you are able to access over 800 SQL Server–specific performance counters for that instance plus 31 performance counters per database that you have running on your instance. This is great, but it comes with a caveat the size of the great state of Texas: `sys.dm_os_performance_counters` only exposes performance counters for the instance of SQL Server that you are connected to when you run a `SELECT` against it. What if you want to grab performance counters from another instance of SQL Server on the same machine or performance counters from the server itself? That's where Windows PowerShell comes in handy.

The components of the SQL Server Business Intelligence Stack, SSIS, SSAS, and SSRS, each have their own performance counters. These performance counters are not exposed by `sys.dm_os_performance_counters`. However, they are available through Windows PowerShell.

Windows PowerShell enables you to easily discover and collect all the counters from the operating system, and once they are converted to a datatable, they are easily stored in a CSV, Excel spreadsheet, or my personal favorite, a table inside of SQL Server. In other chapters, you learned how to discover what counters are available and retrieve large blocks of them. With SQL Server, the easiest way to discover them is to run the following T-SQL query:

```
SELECT [object_name], counter_name
FROM sys.dm_os_performance_counters;
```

Alternatively, you can use the following PowerShell code to retrieve the same information:

```
<# All SQL Server Counters #>
Get-Counter -listset SQLSERVER* | ForEach-Object {$_.CounterSetName, $_.Paths} |
 Format-Table -AutoSize
```

As you have learned in other chapters, the easiest way to capture multiple performance counters at once is to create a hashtable with an array of items as shown here:

```
$CountersList = @(
'\SQLServer:Buffer Manager\Page life expectancy',
'\SQLServer:Buffer Manager\Page reads/sec',
'\SQLServer:Buffer Manager\Page writes/sec',
'\SQLServer:Buffer Manager\Page lookups/sec',
'\SQLServer:Buffer Manager\Free list stalls/sec',
'\SQLServer:Buffer Manager\Total pages',
'\SQLServer:Buffer Manager\Database pages',
'\SQLServer:Buffer Manager\Reserved pages',
'\SQLServer:Buffer Manager\Stolen pages',
'\SQLServer:Buffer Manager\Lazy writes/sec',
'\SQLServer:Buffer Manager\Readahead pages/sec',
'\SQLServer:Buffer Manager\Checkpoint pages/sec'
)
```

Once you have your list of counters, you can start collecting them on a timed interval and for a specific period of time:

```
Get-Counter -SampleInterval 10 -MaxSamples 360 -Counter $CountersList
```

Once that is accomplished, what you have is a lot of information that doesn't appear to be very useful. The counters come back in a format that is not very readable. In fact, they look nothing like you would expect. That's because they need to be translated into a datatable so they are formatted on the screen as you'd expect. This also lets you save the collected counters more cleanly. To get the results into the datatable, you'll need to separate the results from each sampling. A foreach loop can handle that simply.

Note

Other methods for "shredding" your results exist. Although the other methods may in fact be faster as far as converting and then storing the data, they are not nearly as concise as the method described here. If you are collecting performance counters from tens or hundreds of servers, you probably want to have a look at http://sqlblog.com/blogs/aaron_bertrand/archive/2011/01/31/how-i-use-powershell-to-collect-performance-counter-data.aspx. ■

Regardless of the method you use to run an ad hoc query of performance counters, you may not have the time to figure everything else out. Use the Out-DataTable function to convert the output captured in the variable $CountersList into a datatable. You can pipe your variable into this function using the following code:

```
$CounterResults = Get-Counter -SampleInterval 2 -MaxSamples 10 `
-Counter $CountersList
foreach($CounterStats in $CounterResults)
{
$CounterRecords += $CounterStats.CounterSamples | Out-DataTable
}
```

Once you have the results in the datatable, you're now ready to start saving them to a SQL table. Although CSV and Excel are great for doing quick work analysis, you should store the data in a SQL table to allow quick access to the historical information. When you store the data, make sure to retain the name of the machine that the counters came from. Even if you're only capturing one machine right now, you'll need this information if you add counters from another server.

For the sake of this example, I have created a very basic SQL table:

```
CREATE TABLE [dbo].[CounterSamples](
  [Path] [varchar](256) NULL,
  [InstanceName] [varchar](128) NULL,
  [CookedValue] [varchar](50) NULL,
  [RawValue] [varchar](50) NULL,
  [SecondValue] [varchar](100) NULL,
  [MultipleCount] [varchar](50) NULL,
```

```
        [CounterType] [varchar](256) NULL,
        [Timestamp] [varchar](50) NULL,
        [Timestamp100NSec] [varchar](50) NULL,
        [Status] [varchar](50) NULL,
        [DefaultScale] [varchar](50) NULL,
        [TimeBase] [varchar](50) NULL
    ) ON [PRIMARY]
```

The following is a simple example of how to dump the counters to a SQL table. It uses `Write-DataTable`, a publicly available Windows PowerShell function, written by Chad Miller, which can be downloaded from the TechNet Script Center Repository: http://gallery .technet.microsoft.com/ScriptCenter/2fdeaf8d-b164-411c-9483-99413d6053ae/.

```
Write-DataTable -ServerInstance "LOCALHOST\R2" -Database CentralInfo `
-TableName CounterSamples -Data $CounterRecords

Invoke-SQLcmd -ServerInstance "LOCALHOST\R2" -Database SandBox -Query "
SELECT Path,
  InstanceName,
  CookedValue,
  RawValue,
  SecondValue,
  MultipleCount,
  CounterType,
  Timestamp,
  Timestamp100NSec,
  Status,
  DefaultScale,
  TimeBase
  FROM [dbo].[CounterSamples]" | Format-Table
```

Going out and gathering this data is a good first step, but you will likely have reason to tell a particular machine or set of machines to collect their counters locally and then send the results to a central point once they are done. This book has taught you how to use Windows PowerShell remote jobs for this type of thing. This chapter covers how to use the scheduling engine inside of SQL Server, called SQL Agent.

Note

For more information on Windows PowerShell jobs, look at the content help topics `about_jobs`, `about_job_details`, and `about_remote_jobs`. ∎

When using SQL Server 2008 or 2008 R2, I tend to shy away from using Windows PowerShell in a job step at all. Though SQL Server recognizes Windows PowerShell as a valid language, it unfortunately uses the SQLPS implementation of Windows PowerShell (using the now deprecated `Make-Shell`), which does not allow you to import modules or use all of the awesome features of Windows PowerShell V2. I often avoid using

SQLPS by simply calling `PowerShell.exe -NonInteractive -File c:\scripts\` `NameOfSomeScriptSQLAgentHasAccessTo.ps1` as the only syntax in my job step.

Caution

An important note about using Windows PowerShell in SQL Agent job steps is that the account the SQL Agent Service is running under must be a domain account if you want to be able to do things like send an email with your results or connect to another machine. The domain account must also have file access to wherever the `.PS1` script file it is about to run resides. Although this type of permission requirement is second nature to experienced SQL administrators, even I got tripped up by this for a bit because when I first develop scripts on my local machine, it is running under a low-privileged non-domain account. ∎

Scripting Objects

Scripting objects in SQL Server can be deceivingly easy with Windows PowerShell. The deception comes in when you're using the Provider and you want to script out the DROP and CREATE statements. If you don't need the DROP statement, however, it's the greatest thing since Jeffrey Snover!

Note

If the Snover reference is lost on you, check out the following link: `http://www.microsoft.com/` `presspass/exec/de/snover/default.mspx`. ∎

When you're scripting with the Provider, what you're doing is grabbing a complete object (a table, an index, a database, a linked server, logins) and then executing the script *method* on that object.

First, you navigate to the directory where your object lives inside of your SQL Server:

```
CD SQLSERVER:\sql\LocalHost\Default\DATABASES\ADVENTUREWORKS\TABLES
```

Next, you actually script out your object:

```
$PTH = Get-Item Production.TransactionHistory
$PTH.Script()
```

In the previous two lines of script, notice that you used the `Get-Item` cmdlet to grab your table named `TransactionHistory`, which is in the `Production` schema. You then created a variable called `$PTH` to hold the table and its properties. On the next line, you used the `.script()` method on your object to script it out. To find out if an object has a `.script()` method, just pipe the object to `Get-Member`:

```
Get-Item Production.TransactionHistory | Get-Member
```

Scripting out all the tables in a database is very simple. In the next example, you cycle through the tables one at a time; as you do, you build a unique filename for each table that you want to script out and store that in the variable $k. You will need to have followed the CD step above and have a directory named `temp` on the `C:\` drive of your machine.

```
foreach ($tbl in Get-ChildItem )
{
$k="C:\Temp\$($tbl.Schema).$($tbl.name)_table.SQL"
$tbl.Script() > $k
}
```

The downside to this approach is that it doesn't include the Primary Keys, Foreign Keys, Indexes, Default Constraints, and so on that you will need to fully re-create the entire database schema. You could CD to the child directory of each table and script out the child objects, but thankfully, the SMO already provides another feature to accomplish this.

To retrieve all of the objects in a database, you have to load an assembly and fire up a new server object that you'll let the SMO define. Then, grab one of the databases on the instance. From there, you'll be able to grab the specific objects you want to script out. When you go to script them out, you now have a large number of options to choose from. As you set these different options, most of them are basically adding things that will ultimately be included in your final script. Things like setting `Options .ClusteredIndexes` to $true are pretty clear and return the results you would expect. A CREATE statement for the clustered index will be included in the script if the table in fact has a clustered index.

When you set the `Options.ScriptDrops` to $true, however, you get a completely unexpected result. You end up with only the DROP statement itself, which doesn't make any sense at all if you're trying to generate a script that drops and re-creates objects. To get the DROP statement in addition to the CREATE statement, you use another *scripter* object to generate the DROP statement separately.

```
$ScriptDrops = New-Object↵
    ('Microsoft.SqlServer.Management.Smo.Scripter') ($SMOserver)
```

By my count, there are 78 different scripter options in SQL Server 2008 R2. To see a full list of them, open up your standard Windows PowerShell window and run the following:

```
[System.Reflection.Assembly]::LoadWithPartialName↵
    ("Microsoft.SqlServer.SMO") | out-null
$server = "LOCALHOST\R2"
$scriptr = New-Object↵
    ('Microsoft.SqlServer.Management.Smo.Scripter') ($SMOserver)
$scriptr.Options
```

You should end up with a list that looks something like this:

```
FileName                         :
Encoding                         : System.Text.UnicodeEncoding
DriWithNoCheck                   : False
IncludeFullTextCatalogRootPath   : False
```

```
            BatchSize                               : 1
            ScriptDrops                             : False
            TargetServerVersion                     : Version80
            TargetDatabaseEngineType                : Standalone
            AnsiFile                                : False
            AppendToFile                            : False
            ToFileOnly                              : False
            SchemaQualify                           : True
            IncludeHeaders                          : False
            IncludeIfNotExists                      : False
            WithDependencies                        : False
            DriPrimaryKey                           : False
            DriForeignKeys                          : False
            DriUniqueKeys                           : False
            DriClustered                            : False
            DriNonClustered                         : False
            DriChecks                               : False
            DriDefaults                             : False
            Triggers                                : False
            Bindings                                : False
            NoFileGroup                             : False
            NoFileStream                            : False
            NoFileStreamColumn                      : False
            NoCollation                             : False
            ContinueScriptingOnError                : False
            IncludeDatabaseRoleMemberships          : False
            Permissions                             : False
            AllowSystemObjects                      : True
            NoIdentities                            : False
            ConvertUserDefinedDataTypesToBaseType   : False
            TimestampToBinary                       : False
            AnsiPadding                             : False
            ExtendedProperties                      : False
            DdlHeaderOnly                           : False
            DdlBodyOnly                             : False
            NoViewColumns                           : False
            Statistics                              : True
            SchemaQualifyForeignKeysReferences      : False
            ClusteredIndexes                        : False
            NonClusteredIndexes                     : False
            AgentAlertJob                           : False
            AgentJobId                              : True
            AgentNotify                             : False
            LoginSid                                : False
            FullTextIndexes                         : False
            NoCommandTerminator                     : False
            FullTextStopLists                       : False
            NoIndexPartitioningSchemes              : False
            NoTablePartitioningSchemes              : False
```

```
                   IncludeDatabaseContext        : False
                   FullTextCatalogs              : False
                   NoXmlNamespaces               : False
                   NoAssemblies                  : False
                   PrimaryObject                 : True
                   DriIncludeSystemNames         : False
                   Default                       : True
                   XmlIndexes                    : False
                   OptimizerData                 : False
                   NoExecuteAs                   : False
                   EnforceScriptingOptions       : False
                   NoMailProfileAccounts         : False
                   NoMailProfilePrincipals       : False
                   NoVardecimal                  : True
                   ChangeTracking                : False
                   ScriptDataCompression         : True
                   ScriptSchema                  : True
                   ScriptData                    : False
                   ScriptBatchTerminator         : False
                   ScriptOwner                   : False
                   Indexes                       : False
                   DriIndexes                    : False
                   DriAllKeys                    : False
                   DriAllConstraints             : False
                   DriAll                        : False
```

Listing 13-1 creates a function that produces a separate `.sql` file for each object defined: Tables, Views, Stored Procedures, and User Defined Functions. It builds in a DROP statement in case the object already exists. The collection of files will be written to `C:\TEMP\ Databases\<Database Name>\<Date & Time>\<Object Type>`.

LISTING 13-1

Script-DBObjectsIntoFolders Function

```
function Script-DBObjectsIntoFolders([string]$dbname, [string]$server){
[System.Reflection.Assembly]::LoadWithPartialName("Microsoft.SqlServer.SMO") |
Out-Null
$SMOserver = New-Object ('Microsoft.SqlServer.Management.Smo.Server') `
-ArgumentList $server
$db = $SMOserver.databases[$dbname]

$Objects = $db.Tables
$Objects += $db.Views
$Objects += $db.StoredProcedures
$Objects += $db.UserDefinedFunctions

<#Build this portion of the directory structure out here in case
```

```
  scripting takes more than one minute.#>
$SavePath = "C:\TEMP\Databases\" + $($dbname)
$DateFolder = Get-Date -Format yyyyMMddHHmm
New-Item -Type directory -Name "$DateFolder" -Path "$SavePath"

foreach ($ScriptThis in $Objects | where {!($_.IsSystemObject)}) {
#Need to Add Some mkDirs for the different $Fldr=$ScriptThis.GetType().Name
$scriptr = New-Object ('Microsoft.SqlServer.Management.Smo.Scripter') `
($SMOserver)
$scriptr.Options.AppendToFile = $True
$scriptr.Options.AllowSystemObjects = $False
$scriptr.Options.ClusteredIndexes = $True
$scriptr.Options.DriAll = $True
$scriptr.Options.ScriptDrops = $False
$scriptr.Options.IncludeHeaders = $True
$scriptr.Options.ToFileOnly = $True
$scriptr.Options.Indexes = $True
$scriptr.Options.Permissions = $True
$scriptr.Options.WithDependencies = $False
<#Script the Drop too#>
$ScriptDrop = new-object ('Microsoft.SqlServer.Management.Smo.Scripter') `
($SMOserver)
$ScriptDrop.Options.AppendToFile = $True
$ScriptDrop.Options.AllowSystemObjects = $False
$ScriptDrop.Options.ClusteredIndexes = $True
$ScriptDrop.Options.DriAll = $True
$ScriptDrop.Options.ScriptDrops = $True
$ScriptDrop.Options.IncludeHeaders = $True
$ScriptDrop.Options.ToFileOnly = $True
$ScriptDrop.Options.Indexes = $True
$ScriptDrop.Options.WithDependencies = $False

<#This section builds folder structures.
  Remove the date folder if you want to overwrite#>
$TypeFolder=$ScriptThis.GetType().Name
if ((Test-Path -Path "$SavePath\$DateFolder\$TypeFolder") -eq "true")
       {"Scripting Out $TypeFolder $ScriptThis"}
else {new-item -type directory -name "$TypeFolder" -path "$SavePath\↵
$DateFolder"}
$ScriptFile = $ScriptThis -replace "\[|\]"
$ScriptDrop.Options.FileName = "" + $($SavePath) + "\" + $($DateFolder) + `
"\" + $($TypeFolder) + "\" + $($ScriptFile) + ".SQL"
$scriptr.Options.FileName = "$SavePath\$DateFolder\$TypeFolder\$ScriptFile.SQL"
#This is where each object actually gets scripted one at a time.
$ScriptDrop.Script($ScriptThis)
$scriptr.Script($ScriptThis)
} #This ends the loop
} #This completes the Script-DBObjectsIntoFolders function
```

To call this function, use the following statement:

```
Script-DBObjectsIntoFolders "ADVENTUREWORKS" "LocalHost\R2"
```

Note

If you're interested in learning more about this particular example, you can read more at the Hey, Scripting Guy! Blog: `http://blogs.technet.com/b/heyscriptingguy/archive/2010/11/04/use-powershell-to-script-sql-database-objects.aspx.` ∎

Scheduling Windows PowerShell SQL Server Agent Job Steps

Scheduling PowerShell tasks to run in SQL Agent has a few quirks that you need to be aware of in order to be successful. In SQL Server 2008, when creating a job step, you can now select a type of "PowerShell." Running PowerShell code inside SQL Agent 2008 and 2008 R2 comes with a few boundaries, the most painful of which is SQLPS.exe itself. SQLPS is a mini-shell or closed shell. It doesn't have the extensibility that Windows PowerShell does.

Note

For more information on SQLPS and why it is likely to change in the next version of SQL Server, read the following MSDN article: `http://blogs.msdn.com/b/powershell/archive/2008/06/23/sql-minishells.aspx` ∎

The other major limitation is the same as any other SQL Agent job you have created in the past; you are constrained by the rights of the service account that SQL Agent is running under. If your service account is running under Local System and the Windows PowerShell task that you set up is trying to copy a file to another server, it will fail because you won't have the required permissions. Likewise, if you try to send an email via your company's Exchange server and SQL Agent isn't running under a domain account, the job is not going to be able to send the email.

In future versions of SQL Server, SQL Agent will have a fully functional version of Windows PowerShell that is more consistent with the OS version you're already using while still implementing the SQLSERVER Provider by default when you launch it.

When you run scripts through SQL Agent, they cannot be interactive. You can't have anything that requires user input on the local machine. If your job requires using interaction, it will hang and have to be shut down manually.

An additional limitation of running PowerShell steps inside of SQL Agent jobs for SQL Server 2008 and SQL Server 2008 R2 is that you cannot import modules. If you want to bring in outside functionality, you will have to include it in the script that you are running.

Oftentimes, an easier approach to running SQLPS from SQL Agent is to simply call `Powershell.exe` from inside of a Windows PowerShell Type Step.

Getting Space Usage Information

Gathering information about space used and space available is a vital task in any environment. So common, in fact, that it is one of the most written about and discussed topics about Windows PowerShell in SQL Server. In addition to knowing how much space is used on a drive, you also need to know how much space each table in the database is taking up. In this section, you learn how to evaluate volume space usage as well as database space usage.

Getting Volume Space Usage

A lot of Windows PowerShell examples focus on gathering space for local disks. The issue with this approach is that it misses the measurement of mount points, which have become very prevalent in clustered SQL Server instances. The code below finds mount points on a Windows Server:

```
Function Get-DisksSpace ($ServerName, $unit= "GB")
{
$measure = "1$unit"

Get-WmiObject -ComputerName $ServerName -query "
SELECT SystemName, Name, DriveType, FileSystem, FreeSpace, Capacity, Label
  FROM Win32_Volume
 WHERE DriveType = 2 or DriveType = 3" |
SELECT SystemName, `
Name, `
@{Label="SizeIn$unit";Exp={"{0:n2}" -f($_.Capacity/$measure)}}, `
@{Label="FreeIn$unit";Exp={"{0:n2}" -f($_.freespace/$measure)}}, `
@{Label="PercentFree";Exp={"{0:n2}" -f(($_.freespace/$_.Capacity)*100)}}, `
Label
}#Get-DisksSpace
```

To call the function `Get-DisksSpace`, simply provide it with a name of a server that you want to interrogate and discover the disk space usage on. By default, it will return results in gigabytes. You can optionally pass `"MB"` to the function and it will return the value in megabytes.

```
Get-DisksSpace LocalHost MB
```

Getting Database Space Usage

A lot of options exist for gathering space information about a database. However, the need for information doesn't stop there. Knowing the remaining capacity of each data file is vital to making sure you aren't going to run out of space unexpectedly. If you have 20 GB of total space free throughout the database, that's not going to do you a lick of good if your Transaction Log file is down to 0 MB free.

Note

Databases need a minimum of two files: a data file and a log file. You only need one log file, and having more than one does you no good, because the engine will write to only one transaction log file at a time. On the other hand, you can often benefit from having more than one Data File. Data Files belong to File Groups, and there can be more than one Data File per File Group. However, this is not a common scenario because you can only control which File Group a table is written to, not the individual Data File. The very first Data File is always in the Primary File Group and it ends with an `.mdf` extension. Subsequent Data Files can be part of the Primary File Group (although they shouldn't) and should end with a file extension of `.ndf`. Log files will end with an `.ldf` extension.

When creating a database that you expect to grow larger than 10 GB, it's a good habit to go ahead and create a Secondary File Group and make that the Default File Group for tables. The reason for this is that the Primary File Group holds all the definitions for all tables regardless of which File Group they were created on. It also holds all of the information for any Service Broker Queues as well as several other items. Setting up this Secondary File Group gives you the opportunity to put your tables on a separate set of disks than all of your database objects that will be going into the Primary File Group by default. This may seem excessive for just a 10-GB database, but if it's expected to grow to 100 GB, you'll be glad you went to the trouble of setting up your data files properly in the first place. ∎

All that being said, to gather database space usage information, you can use several different approaches. The following sections cover the Provider, cmdlet, and the SMO.

Getting Database Space Usage with the Provider

With the Provider, you don't even have to navigate inside of the SQLSERVER provider directory to collect the information. You can just run `Get-ChildItem` to gather the information. On top of that, you can switch the database context and even switch instances and servers all while staying at the `C:\` prompt. The following example returns the size, data space usage, index space usage, and space available for the AdventureWorks database:

```
$AdvWrks = Get-Item SQLSERVER:\sql\LocalHost\R2\DATABASES\ADVENTUREWORKS
$AdvWrks |
Format-Table -Prop Size DataSpaceUsage,IndexSpaceUsage,SpaceAvailable -Auto
```

Beyond collecting data for one database, you can also collect the statistics for multiple databases. In the event you want to collect the data for a production database and a staging database, you can store the results in variables as you switch through the Provider.

```
dir SQLSERVER:\sql\LocalHost\R2\DATABASES |
Format-Table -Prop Name,Size,DataSpaceUsage,IndexSpaceUsage,SpaceAvailable -Auto
```

Getting Database Space Usage with the Cmdlet

Gathering space usage information with the cmdlet can use a relatively tiny amount of code depending on what you're looking for. You have the option to collect overall data and log file space usage information, or you can return more granular data, evaluating the space usage for each data file in the database independently. The following code sample returns information about database files used by the AdventureWorks database.

```
Invoke-SQLCmd -ServerInstance "LocalHost\R2" -database "AdventureWorks" -query "
SELECT [file_id],
       [type_desc],
       [name],
       ([size] * 8) as 'SizeInKB',
       [physical_name]
   FROM [AdventureWorks].[sys].[database_files]"
```

Getting Database Space Usage with the SMO

Finally, for completeness, have a look at how to do this with the SMO:

```
[System.Reflection.Assembly]::LoadWithPartialName("Microsoft.SqlServer.SMO") |
Out-Null
$SMOserver = New-Object ('Microsoft.SqlServer.Management.Smo.Server') `
"LocalHost\R2"
$SMOserver.databases |
Format-Table -Prop Name,Size,DataSpaceUsage,IndexSpaceUsage,SpaceAvailable -Auto
```

Getting Table Space Usage

You can approach the challenge of retrieving table space information from two different angles: from the Provider or the SMO.

Getting Table Space Usage with the Provider

Using the Provider is just like grabbing properties off a file in a directory. With the Provider, all you have to do is a simple Get-ChildItem (aliased as dir), and then filter the results by piping them to Format-Table and specifying only the properties you want to display. Tables have approximately 60 properties that you can look at.

```
dir SQLSERVER:\sql\LocalHost\R2\DATABASES\ADVENTUREWORKS\TABLES |
Format-Table -Property Schema, Name, DataSpaceUsed, IndexSpaceUsed, RowCount
```

Getting Table Space Usage with the SMO

The SMO route is a little more involved. The assembly must be loaded and a new SQL Server object instantiated. Then, the instance that you want to interrogate must be passed to the object. From there, a new variable, $db, is created to name the database that is evaluated. Once the variable is populated, the properties that you want to return are passed in. At this point, the table properties are piped to `Format-Table`, just as in the Provider example.

```
[System.Reflection.Assembly]::LoadWithPartialName("Microsoft.SqlServer.SMO") |
Out-Null
$SMOserver = New-Object ('Microsoft.SqlServer.Management.Smo.Server') `
"LocalHost\R2"
$db = $SMOserver.databases["AdventureWorks"]
$db.Tables | Format-Table -Property `
Schema, Name, DataSpaceUsed, IndexSpaceUsed, RowCount -AutoSize
```

In addition to retrieving space information, you may want to know whether or not the table is partitioned, and if so, what the partition scheme is. The `PhysicalPartitions` and `PartitionScheme` properties can come in handy here. To get an answer for whether or not the table is partitioned, you can call the `IsPartitioned` property on the table.

Managing Registrations in SQL Server Management Studio

Registered Servers (abbreviated as Reg.S) is one of the two things that got me hooked on Windows PowerShell. (The other is SQLPSX.) Registered Servers is an often overlooked feature, usually by people who do not need to administer a high number of SQL Server instances. However, benefits of Reg.S can be realized even if you're only working with a few instances.

Registered Servers can be confused with Central Management Servers (CMS) because CMS is located within the Registered Servers pane in SQL Server Management Studio (SSMS). Though both are used for keeping track of a list of servers, there are some major differences to know about. Reg.S is a local XML file that contains a list of connections, instances, and other information. CMS is intended to be a central place where everyone can reference a list of all SQL Server instances in an organization. CMS works only for connections to instances made with integrated authentication. Reg.S allows you to define connections using either SQL Authentication or integrated authentication. SQL Authentication is when a username and password are provided to authenticate on the server. Integrated authentication is when your Windows credentials are used to establish a connection in SQL Server. In addition, CMS does not limit how many servers can be defined as the "central" server, which can lead to confusion. Reg.S avoids this problem by being locally hosted. If you want more than one database administrator to have the same list of instances, just copy the Reg.S XML file using `Copy-Item` and distribute it. Of course, once it is installed on an individual's machine, there is no synchronization mechanism between XML files.

The great news is that both CMS and Reg.S are accessible through Windows PowerShell once you add the SQL Provider:

```
Add-PSSnapin SqlServerProviderSnapin100
```

After you add the snap-in, you have two options to access either the registered servers or the centrally managed servers. The first option is to CD (Change Directory) to SQLServer:\ SQLRegistration and then examine the directory to see what instances are available:

```
CD SQLSERVER:\SQLRegistration
dir | Select PSChildName
```

One quirk to keep in mind is that names contain spaces, so you'll always need to reference them with single ticks, such as 'Database Engine Server Group' or 'Central Management Server'.

The second option for using Reg.S or CMS within Windows PowerShell is to stay within whatever working directory you're already in and query the SQLServer Provider using the full path.

Note

When working with SSMS 2008 or 2008 R2, I tend to avoid navigating within the SQLSERVER Provider because tab-expansion doesn't function within the provider. The second option described, staying in the filesystem provider and providing the path as part of the query, is the way I usually work with Reg.S or CMS. If, by the time you are reading this, you have already installed the 2012 version of SSMS and are using that provider, you likely will be able to disregard this technique. ■

Regardless of the route your organization takes to manage and organize a group of instances, you will be able to take advantage of this stored connection information through Windows PowerShell. In the next two sections, you learn how to leverage Reg.S and CMS to query multiple servers with a single Windows PowerShell script.

Caution

When you fire up the ISE or some other Windows PowerShell editor and load the SQL Provider snap-in, Windows PowerShell loads and caches your registered servers file and CMS. Getting this list to refresh during the session is inconsistent at best. I've seen it refresh intermittently, but do not know what triggers it. Usually, just closing SSMS and reopening it does the trick. ■

Leveraging Registrations to Query Multiple Registered Servers

When working with registered servers, I spend the vast majority of my time leveraging them to query multiple instances. Once the Reg.S file is created, I rarely add or modify an instance as part of my daily routine. The best approach is to break your registrations down into a set of server groups that fit your querying pattern. Place instances into groups based on how often they need to be queried together. For example, a Production group might contain all of your Production instances, while a Development group might contain all of your Development instances.

Note

You can organize your instances into server groups (folders). You can register the same instance multiple times under different credentials. If you do this within the same folder, the instances must have different names. However, if you create registrations to the same instance, with different credentials and under different server groups, you can use the same name. This is mostly a blessing if you're organized and remember to leverage it. It will turn into a curse if you forget it or don't organize well. Invest some thought into how you organize your registered servers, and you'll be able to reap the benefits of well-organized server groups. ∎

In the following example, you interrogate the list of instances in a server group called LocalInstances, grabbing any instances in the server group, while filtering to exclude any subgroup names, and placing those objects into a single variable called $InstanceList. Next, you enter a foreach loop and iterate through the list of instances, placing each one into a new variable called $instance. The query is then run against each instance as it is handled by the foreach loop. One key point to note is that you supply the name property of the $instance variable to the -ServerInstance parameter of Invoke-SQLCmd. This is easy to forget when working with a parameterized instance name. With this particular example, you will end up with a result set based on querying the sys.dm_os_sys_memory DMV in each instance.

```
$InstanceList = dir -Recurse `
SQLSERVER:\SQLRegistration\'Database Engine Server Group'\LocalInstances\ |
Where {$_.Mode -ne "d"}

foreach($instance in $InstanceList)
{
  Invoke-SQLcmd -ServerInstance $instance.name -Database master -Query "
  SELECT * FROM sys.dm_os_sys_memory"
}
```

Taking the example a little further, you can run a query against every database within each instance in your server group. This can be extremely useful when trying to deploy code or trying to audit where particular user permissions have been deployed to.

```
$InstanceList = dir -Recurse `
SQLSERVER:\SQLRegistration\'Database Engine Server Group'\LocalInstances\ |
Where {$_.Mode -ne "d"}
foreach($instance in $InstanceList)
{
  $dbs = Invoke-SQLcmd -ServerInstance $instance.name -Database master -Query "
  SELECT * FROM sys.databases"
```

```
foreach($db in $dbs)
{
  Invoke-SQLcmd -ServerInstance $instance.name -Database $db.name -Query "
  SELECT @@SERVERNAME AS 'InstanceName',
  DB_NAME(DB_ID()) AS 'DatabaseName',
  name,
  principal_id,
  type,
  type_desc,
  default_schema_name
  is_fixed_role  FROM sys.database_principals" | ft
}
}
```

In addition to using registered servers within Windows PowerShell, you can modify the registered server directly. One of the things registered servers allows you to do is set a custom color to appear at the bottom of the query pane when a query window is opened starting from a given registered server. In the following example, the color of the registered server is changed in SSMS:

```
$AnInstance = dir -Recurse `
SQLSERVER:\SQLRegistration\'Database Engine Server Group'\LocalInstances\ |
Where {$_.Mode -ne "d"} | select -First 1

$AnInstance.CustomConnectionColorArgb
$AnInstance.CustomConnectionColorArgb = '-65536'
$AnInstance.Alter()
```

Leveraging Registrations to Query Multiple Central Management Servers

Registered servers provide a great way to organize and categorize database instances on your local machine. Central Management Servers (CMS) provides very similar organizational capabilities, but the information is stored on a central server rather than in a local XML file. To get some ideas on how to leverage CMS and Windows PowerShell, check out the following article: http://johnsterrett.com/2011/05/12/passed-my-sqluniversity-powershell-midterm/.

Summary

In this chapter, you learned how to leverage Windows PowerShell in a SQL Server environment. You've learned ways to streamline and speed up common management and monitoring tasks. In addition to Windows PowerShell cmdlets, you have learned about the

CodePlex project SQLPSX and myriad options for interacting with SQL Server via Windows PowerShell.

I recommend that you install the next version of SQL Server as soon as it is released. There are huge advantages to the SMO updates included in this new release that will make PowerShell an even better option for anyone managing SQL Server.

In the next chapter, you learn about managing Microsoft SharePoint. Key concepts include accessing data, deploying SharePoint solutions, backing up and restoring data, and managing the configuration of SharePoint.

Managing Microsoft SharePoint 2010 Server

T he SharePoint product team at Microsoft made a huge investment in Windows PowerShell. The SharePoint 2010 Management Shell and snap-in that are installed with Microsoft SharePoint Server 2010 contain 531 cmdlets. That is more than double what the core Windows PowerShell language has. This is yet another statement from Microsoft that Windows PowerShell is the future — and that future is now.

SharePoint has provided some level of command-line administration with tools like `stsadm.exe` since Windows SharePoint Services 2.0. However, with Windows PowerShell, the product team in Microsoft was able to leverage the existing SharePoint .NET library to provide access to components of SharePoint that have traditionally been available only to developers. Requirements such as automating tasks against document libraries and lists are now in the scope of a SharePoint administrator's work, along with the more traditional tasks like backing up and restoring configurations and sites.

Installing and Using the Cmdlets

The cmdlets for SharePoint are included with Microsoft SharePoint Server 2010. During an installation of SharePoint Server, the required snap-in is automatically installed. In addition to the snap-in, there is also a shortcut that is created in your Start menu for the SharePoint 2010 Management Shell that will load the snap-in for you.

IN THIS CHAPTER

Using the SharePoint object model

Accessing data in SharePoint

Deploying SharePoint solutions

Managing workflows

Backing up and restoring data

Managing the configuration of SharePoint

SharePoint 2010 Management Shell

After the installation of SharePoint, you can load the SharePoint 2010 Management Shell by clicking Start ➤ All Programs ➤ Microsoft SharePoint 2010 Products ➤ SharePoint 2010 Management Shell. Alternatively, you can load the cmdlets into an existing Windows PowerShell session or script by running the following lines of code:

```
Add-PSSnapin Microsoft.SharePoint.PowerShell
$host.Runspace.ThreadOptions = "ReuseThread"
```

Note

`$host.Runspace.ThreadOptions = "ReuseThread"` is an option that is new in PowerShell Version 2. It is suggested when using the SharePoint cmdlets, and it is loaded by default when you load the SharePoint 2010 Management Shell through the Start Menu. This option is configured by default if you are using the PowerShell ISE. ∎

Before digging into how to use the shell, it is worth examining a couple of elements that are unique to the SharePoint cmdlets.

PipeBind Parameters

When you use `Get-Help` on most of the cmdlets, you will see that many of the parameters have a suffix called `PipeBind`:

```
Get-Help New-SPSite -Parameter Template

...
-Template <SPWebTemplatePipeBind>
...
```

These parameters are designed in a way either to allow you to pass the string name for the value you would like to send to the cmdlet or it can optionally take an object of the type specified before the `PipeBind` suffix. For example, the `Template` parameter in the preceding code can be passed an `SPWebTemplate` object that is retrieved from a corresponding `Get-SPWebTemplate` cmdlet, or it can just be passed the name of the template you would like to use.

SPAssignment

The SharePoint cmdlets that retrieve `SPWeb`, `SPSite`, or `SPSiteAdministration` objects from the SharePoint server can use up large amounts of memory. Because of this, the SharePoint cmdlets provide their own memory management that ensures that data in memory is released immediately after they are called. This means that if you set a variable to an object that is retrieved from SharePoint, the SharePoint system may be queried every time you use the variable. This can be extremely inefficient if you are doing something like adding multiple document libraries or lists to an `SPWeb` object. You can override this behavior within a script by using the `Start-SPAssignment` cmdlet. When this cmdlet is used with the `Global` switch, as shown below, it ensures that all of the objects are retained in memory until the script closes or `Stop-SPAssignment` is called with the `Global` switch.

```
Start-SPAssignment -Global
```

Caution

If you choose to use **Start-SPAssignment,** it is extremely important that you eventually call **Stop-SPAssignment** or you may experience memory issues due to the improper disposal of the SharePoint objects. ■

Remoting with SharePoint

Many of the cmdlets built into the SharePoint snap-in revolve around using the SharePoint object model that is built on .NET. This library requires you to access the underlying objects from the server where SharePoint is installed. Because of this, the SharePoint snap-in is a great candidate for PowerShell remoting.

Cross-Reference

Read more about remoting in Chapter 2, "What's New in Windows PowerShell V2." ■

Limitations of the SharePoint Cmdlets

There is a slight problem, however, with using remoting to access the snap-in on a SharePoint server. The problem is that the objects that are used by the SharePoint object model require you to authenticate against them with your credentials. Unfortunately, this is not possible with the default authentication because the WS-Man service does not have the ability to pass your credentials by default to any other service. The solution is to enable CredSSP authentication so that WS-Man can delegate your credentials through to the SharePoint objects.

Memory Limits in WS-Man

Another WS-Man configuration you should be aware of when thinking about enabling Windows PowerShell remoting on a SharePoint server is the memory limit. By default, the memory limit is set to 150 MB. Some of the SharePoint cmdlets can use up much more memory than this. You can configure WS-Man to use up to 1 gigabyte of memory by running the following command on the server:

```
Set-Item WSMan:\localhost\Shell\MaxMemoryPerShellMB 1000
```

Caution

Think the memory limits through carefully. You must be sure that this memory is available to use on the server. Taking 1 gigabyte of RAM to use for remoting means that you have 1 gigabyte less RAM to use for SharePoint. ■

Automating Site Administration

SharePoint provides many services, but the most visible and the most tangible is the site. You may be using sites for collaboration, meetings, as an internal portal, an externally facing web presence, or as an application front end. Regardless of how you are using SharePoint, it goes without saying that, as a SharePoint administrator, you have created and configured at least one site. If you are in a large environment, it could be tens of thousands. Either way, the SharePoint cmdlets provide you with an easy way to automate the tasks of working with sites.

Creating Site Collections

Sites are created using the `New-SPSite` cmdlet. At a bare minimum, the cmdlet requires a URL for the site as well as a primary owner for the site. You can use a series of optional parameters that mirror the Central Administration page for creating new site collections. The following code is a sample of the most common set of parameters used to automate the task of creating a new site collection. This example makes use of the splatting technique you learned about in Chapter 2 to pass a set of parameters defined in a hashtable to a cmdlet:

```
$template = Get-SPWebTemplate |where {$_.Title -eq 'Team Site'}
$arguments = @{
  Url = 'http://server1/sites/psbible';
  OwnerAlias = 'psbible\Tome';
  SecondaryOwnerAlias = 'psbible\JGoslin';
  Template = $template;
  Name = 'Author Team Site';
}
New-SPSite @arguments
```

Note

If you're unsure of the exact name of a template, you can use `Get-SPWebTemplate` on its own to see a list of all the templates installed in your SharePoint server. ■

Connecting to Sites

You can retrieve sites by using `Get-SPSite`. By itself, the command returns 20 sites. You can use the Limit parameter to change this default behavior. The following returns all of the sites in your environment:

```
Get-SPSite -Limit All
```

To retrieve a particular site, however, you must pass a value to the `Identity` parameter that is either the site's URL or its GUID. The `Identity` parameter is positional. This means that the parameter name `Identity` does not need to be specified when the cmdlet is used. For example, to retrieve the team site created in the previous section, you could run the following:

```
Get-SPSite http://server1/sites/psbible
```

Removing Sites

You can remove sites in two ways. You can either invoke the `Delete()` method on an `SPSite` object like this:

```
$site = Get-SPSite http://server1/sites/psbible
$site.Delete()
```

or you can use the `Remove-SPSite` cmdlet:

```
Remove-SPSite http://server1/sites/psbible
```

Using SharePoint Lists

SharePoint lists make up sets of data that are stored within SharePoint. It should be no surprise that it is common for a script that works with SharePoint data to retrieve or manipulate data in a SharePoint list.

SharePoint lists are managed through the SharePoint object model through the `SPWeb` object. You can retrieve an `SPWeb` object for a site by using the `Get-SPWeb` cmdlet:

```
$web = Get-SPWeb http://server1/sites/psbible
```

Browsing Lists

With an `SPWeb` object in hand, you can access the lists contained within it by using the `Lists` property of the object. For example, to see the name and description for each list in an `SPWeb` object, you would run the following:

```
$web.Lists |select title, description
```

Caution

When you are viewing list data, by default, an enormous amount of content is returned if you do not specify the exact properties you want to view with **Select-Object**. This can result in poor performance in your SharePoint scripts. If you are unsure of which properties you need returned, you can always pipe the lists into **Get-Member** to see what is available first. ■

To gain access to a specific list, you can use the following line to return the list based on its name. This line returns the task list for the site:

```
$list = $web.Lists[Tasks]
```

Viewing List Data

To look at the data within a list, you need to inspect the `Items` property of the list. For example, if you wanted to see the items in the task list that was retrieved in the preceding line of code, you would use the following code:

```
foreach ($item in $list.Items) {
  New-Object psobject -Property @{
    Title = $item.Item("Title");
    Status = $item.Item("Status");
  }
}
```

```
Status                    Title
------                    -----
Not Started               Finish the SharePoint chapter
Not Started               Celebrate
```

Note

Lists can be strange to work with at times. In the preceding example, you would think that you could just do `$list.Items |select Title, Status`. That will not work because the **Status** property is not exposed in the base object. That is why you need to use the **Item()** method to expose the underlying fields.

If you are looking at code on the Web, you may also see the **Item()** method removed for something like `$item["Status"]`. Both of these do exactly the same thing.

One final caveat to be aware of is that the value passed to the **Item()** method is case-sensitive. ∎

Updating List Data

If you want to update an item in a list, it is a three-step process. First, set a variable to the item you would like to update. Second, update the item's values appropriately. Finally, call the `Update()` method on the item. For example, if you wanted to set the first element in the task list to a status of started, you would do the following:

```
$item = $list.Items[0]
$item.Item("Status") = "Started"
$item.Update()
```

Adding Items to a List

You can add an item to a list by invoking the `Add()` method on the `Lists` collection. This returns an `SPListItem` object that you can modify. Once you have everything added with the values you want, you invoke the `Update()` method on the item:

```
$item = $list.Items.Add()
$item["Title"] = 'Go Shopping'
$item.Update()
```

Working with Views

You can access views in a list through the `Views` property of an `SPList` object. To see all of the views in a list, you would run the following line of code:

```
$list.Views | select Title
```

Modifying Views

Changing a view uses a similar process to changing a list item. You must first retrieve the view you would like to change, make the changes, and then invoke the `Update()` method. For example, if you wanted to remove the priority column from the "All Tasks" view, you would do the following:

```
$view = $list.views.Item("All Tasks")
$view.ViewFields.Delete('Priority')
$view.Query = '<OrderBy><FieldRef Name="Status" /></OrderBy>'
$view.Update()
```

This sample shows the two properties that are most commonly touched when you create or modify a view. `ViewFields` contains the columns that are shown in the view, and `Query` shows a Collaborative Application Markup Language (CAML) filter that is applied to the set of data in the list.

Creating Views

You can create views by invoking the `Add()` method on the `Views` collection. This method requires you to pass it a name, the list of columns in the view, the CAML query, the number of rows to show in the view, and whether the view has the option to see more data on other pages over the row limit.

```
$views = $list.views
$viewName = 'Completed Tasks'
$viewFields = New-Object System.Collections.Specialized.StringCollection
$viewFields.Add('Title')
$viewFields.Add('Assigned To')
$query = @'
<Where>
  <Eq>
    <FieldRef Name="Status" />
    <Value Type="Text">Completed</Value>
  </Eq>
</Where>
'@
$rowlimit = 128
$paged = $true
$defaultView = $false
$views.Add($viewName,$viewFields,$query,$rowlimit,$paged,$defaultView)
```

Creating Lists

You can create a list by invoking the `Add()` method on the `Lists` collection of an `SPWeb` object. Creating a list requires you to specify one of the existing list templates to create the list from.

```
$template = [Microsoft.SharePoint.SPListTemplateType]::GenericList
$web = Get-SPWeb http://server1/sites/psbible
$lists = $web.Lists
$lists.Add("Servers","List of servers and IPs",$template)
```

List Settings

Once the list is created, you'll want to modify its settings to meet your requirements. You can modify any of the properties on the `SPList` object and then call the `Update()` method when you are done. For example, the following adds two columns to the new list you created and adds the list to the Quick Launch area of the site:

```
$list = $lists.Item("Servers")
$required = $true
$type = [Microsoft.SharePoint.SPFieldType]::Text
$list.Fields.Add("ServerName",$type,$required)
$list.Fields.Add("IP Address",$type,$required)
$list.OnQuickLaunch = $true
$list.update()
```

Managing Permissions

The process to configure permissions for a SharePoint list is a multistep procedure:

1. Break inheritance on the `SPList` by invoking the `BreakRoleInheritance()` method.

2. Run the `Update()` method on the `SPList` to apply the changes to inheritance.

3. Create an `SPRoleAssignment` object for a `SiteUser` or a `SiteGroup` object that exists in the `SPWeb` object for the site.

4. Add a role to the `SPRoleAssignment` object.

5. Add the `SPRoleAssignment` object to the `RoleAssignments` collection of the `SPList`.

6. Run the `Update()` method on the `SPList` object to apply the changes.

The following illustrates this process:

```
$web = Get-SPWeb http://server1/sites/psbible
$list = $web.Lists.Item("Servers")

$copypermsfromparent = $false
$list.BreakRoleInheritance($copypermsfromparent)
```

```
$list.Update()

$role = $web.RoleDefinitions.Item("Full Control")
$user = $web.SiteUsers.Item("home\Administrator")

$assignment = New-Object Microsoft.SharePoint.SPRoleAssignment ($user)
$assignment.RoleDefinitionBindings.Add($role)

$list.RoleAssignments.Add($assignment)
$list.Update()
```

Managing Document Libraries

Document libraries are a special type of list object that enable you to store files within your SharePoint site. In addition to the standard list properties, they also may contain a hierarchy of folders to allow you to categorize and store documents in a logical structure.

Creating Libraries

You create a document library the same way that you create any list. The only difference is that the SPListTemplateType you use to create the list should be DocumentLibrary.

```
$template = [Microsoft.SharePoint.SPListTemplateType]::DocumentLibrary
$web = Get-SPWeb http://server1/sites/psbible
$lists = $web.Lists
$lists.Add("Windows PowerShell Scripts","Repository of scripts",$template)
```

Navigating Folders

Folders exist within the Folders collection of an SPList object. These folders exist in this single collection regardless of their depth within the document library. To understand where the folder actually lives, you should inspect the Url property of the folder. The URL will be a relative path that includes the name of the document library itself. For example, this is the output of a document library named Windows PowerShell Scripts that has a folder named SharePoint Scripts with two subfolders of its own:

```
$list.Folders |select Name, Url |Format-List
Name : SharePoint Scripts
Url  : Windows PowerShell Scripts/SharePoint Scripts

Name : List Scripts
Url  : Windows PowerShell Scripts/SharePoint Scripts/List Scripts

Name : Site Scripts
Url  : Windows PowerShell Scripts/SharePoint Scripts/Site Scripts
```

If you happen to know the relative path for a folder, you can access it directly by invoking the `GetFolder()` method on the `SPWeb` object. For example, to retrieve the `SharePoint Scripts` folder you saw in the preceding output, you would do this:

```
$folder = $web.GetFolder('Windows PowerShell Scripts/SharePoint Scripts')
```

Creating Folders

You can create a folder by invoking the `Add()` method on the `Folders` collection of an `SPList` object. For example, to add a folder named `SharePoint Scripts` to the `Windows PowerShell Scripts` document library, you would do the following:

```
$web = Get-SPWeb http://server1/sites/psbible
$list = $web.Lists.Item("Windows PowerShell Scripts")

$type = [Microsoft.SharePoint.SPFileSystemObjectType]::Folder
$folder = $list.Folders.Add("", $type, "SharePoint Scripts")
$folder.update()
```

Downloading Documents

Downloading documents from a document library requires you to open up a binary stream of data from the file in the library. The technique used to convert that stream to a file on disk involves using some of the .NET classes that are found in `System.IO` namespace. Normally in Windows PowerShell, you can steer clear of these types of interactions with .NET because so many good cmdlets exist to help you handle things like reading and writing to disk. However, in this particular case, you must use them to save the binary stream of data to disk.

To create the binary stream, you must first get the `SPFile` object for the file you would like to download. The easiest way to do this is to supply the relative URL path to the `GetFile()` method of the `SPWeb` object. The alternative is to find the file by traversing the `Files` collection of an `SPFolder` object. Either way, after you have retrieved the `SPFile` object, you can invoke the `OpenBinary()` method to create the binary stream. The following example puts this all together for you by downloading a script named `s1.ps1` in the `Windows PowerShell Scripts` document library underneath the `SharePoint Scripts` folder:

```
$web = Get-SPWeb http://server1/sites/psbible

$file = $web.GetFile('Windows PowerShell Scripts/SharePoint Scripts/s1.ps1')
$bytes = $file.OpenBinary()

$downloadpath = Join-Path c:\download $file.name
$filemode = [System.IO.FileMode]::Create
$filestream = New-Object System.IO.FileStream ($downloadpath, $filemode)

$filestream.Write($bytes, 0, $bytes.Count)
$filestream.Close()
```

Uploading Documents

Files can be added to an `SPFolder` object by invoking the `Add()` method of the `Files` collection. For example, to dump the contents of `Get-Process` to a text file and then upload it to the folder named `Data` that exists within the `Windows PowerShell` folder, you would do the following:

```
Get-Process |Out-File processes.txt
$file = Get-ChildItem processes.txt

$web = Get-SPWeb http://server1/sites/psbible
$folder = $web.GetFolder('Windows PowerShell Scripts/Data')

$folder.Files.Add($file.name, $file.OpenRead())
```

Creating a Web Application

You create a SharePoint web application by running `New-SPWebApplication`. The following example shows how this cmdlet can be used with a common set of parameters:

```
$arguments = @{
  Name = 'Dilbert';
  Port = 80;
  URL = 'http://dilbert';
  ApplicationPool = 'DilbertAppPool';
  ApplicationPoolAccount = 'NetworkService';
}
New-SPWebApplication @arguments
```

Note

`New-SPWebApplication` has a number of parameters that you are not seeing in this example. Every option you have when creating a web application through SharePoint Central Administration is available to the Windows PowerShell cmdlet. If you require one of the options outside of the common ones listed in this example, look through the `Get-Help` documentation for `New-SPWebApplication`. ∎

Deploying Developer Code

The SharePoint snap-in provides an administrator with a series of cmdlets to help install and uninstall web parts and other types of solutions to and from a SharePoint farm. Solution files need to be added to SharePoint with `Add-SPSolution`:

```
Add-SPSolution c:\webparts\Cal.wsp
```

Once the solution is added, it can be installed to a web application with `Install-SPSolution`:

```
Install-SPSolution Cal.wsp -WebApplication http://server1 -GacDeployment
```

If a solution is no longer needed, it can be uninstalled with `Uninstall-SPSolution`:

```
Uninstall-SPSolution Cal.wsp -WebApplication http://server1
```

Once the solution is uninstalled from every web application it was installed on, it can be removed by retrieving the solution with `Get-SPSolution` and then piping it into `Remove-SPSolution`:

```
Get-SPSolution Cal.wsp |Remove-SPSolution
```

Administering Workflows

The workflow engine in SharePoint Server 2010 may be leveraged by developers, administrators, or power users of SharePoint. The SharePoint cmdlets provide a way to automate or interactively work with workflows.

Manually Kicking Off Workflows

Some workflows need to be manually started on an item in order for them to launch. Or perhaps you have an automatic workflow that was stopped and needs to be restarted. Workflows are started by using the `WorkflowManager` object that exists in an `SPSite` object. There is a `StartWorkflow()` method you can invoke to manually start a workflow. The method takes three arguments: a workflow association that exists on the list where the item exists, the `SPItem` object, and any string arguments that need to be passed to the workflow. Here's an example of how you can create an item in a list named Tasks and then start a workflow named `ApproveTasks`:

```
$web = Get-SPWeb http://server1/sites/psbible
$list = $web.Lists.Item("Tasks")
$item = $list.Items.Add()
$item["Title"] = 'Take a break'
$item.Update()

$wf = $item.ParentList.WorkflowAssociations |where{$_.Name -eq 'ApproveTasks'}
$wfarguments = ""
$site = $web.Site
$workflowmanager = $site.WorkflowManager
$workflowmanager.StartWorkflow($item,$wf,$wfarguments)
```

Monitoring Workflows

The `WorkFlowManager` object contains an overall view from the site level of all of the workflows on your system. Listing 14-1 shows a function called `Get-SPRunningWorkflows` that accepts an `SPList`. It returns the `SPWorkflowObjects` for the items that have active workflows.

LISTING 14-1

Get-SPRunningWorkflows — Retrieves All Active Workflows on Items in a List

```
function Get-SPRunningWorkflows {
  param(
    [Parameter(Mandatory=$true,Position=0,ValueFromPipeline=$true)]
    [Microsoft.SharePoint.SPList]$List
  )
  $web = $list.ParentWeb
  $site = $web.Site
  $workflowmanager = $site.WorkflowManager
  if ($workflowmanager.CountWorkflows($list)) {
    $items = $list.Items |where {$_.Workflows}
    foreach ($item in $items) {
      $workflowmanager.GetItemActiveWorkflows($item)
    }
  }
}
```

The function in Listing 14-1 can be called with the following code to retrieve information about the Tasks list in the psbible site:

```
$web = Get-SPWeb http://server1/sites/psbible
$list = $web.Lists.Item('Tasks')
$list |Get-SPRunningWorkflows |select ItemName,InternalState, Created
```

```
ItemName                         InternalState Created
--------                         ------------- -------
Trip to Tahiti                         Running 7/4/2011 12:12:32 AM
Amex Bill Payment                      Running 7/1/2011 10:32:54 PM
```

Cancelling Workflows

To cancel a workflow, you must invoke the RemoveWorkflowFromListItem() method of the WorkFlowManager object. This method accepts an SPWorkflowObject. This is the same type of object that is returned by the Get-SPRunningWorkflows function created in Listing 14-1. Because of this, you can run the following code to remove all of the active workflows on the Tasks list:

```
$web = Get-SPWeb http://server1/sites/psbible
$list = $web.Lists.Item('Tasks')
$site = $web.Site
$workflowmanager = $site.WorkflowManager
foreach ($workflow in ($list |Get-SPRunningWorkflows)) {
    $workflowmanager.RemoveWorkflowFromListItem($workflow)
}
```

Backing Up and Restoring

Backing up and restoring SharePoint data has traditionally been a bit convoluted. Ask anyone who has ever had to manually restore a SharePoint 2003 site from a set of SQL backups, and you will understand after an hour-long discussion on the topic. Fortunately, SharePoint has come a long way, and the cmdlets that allow you to interact with the backups empower you to easily manage your SharePoint backup strategy. In this section, you learn how you can back up and restore the configuration database, SharePoint farms, site collections, lists, and libraries.

The Configuration Database

You can back up the configuration database using the Backup-SPConfigurationDatabase cmdlet with the Directory parameter pointing to the location in which you would like to store the backup files. If SharePoint's instance of SQL is on its own server, you must specify a UNC path to a share that your service accounts for both SQL and SharePoint have write access to. Backup-SPConfigurationDatabase can be run multiple times to the same backup directory; it creates a new folder named sbrxxxx each time it is run with an incremented value for xxxx.

```
Backup-SPConfigurationDatabase -Directory \\server1\backups
```

You can query the history of all backups in a directory by using the Get-SPBackupHistory cmdlet. The ID for the backups is stored in the SelfID property. This property is required to restore the configuration.

```
Get-SPBackupHistory -Directory \\server1\backups -ShowBackup |
  select SelfId,ConfigurationOnly
SelfId                                          ConfigurationOnly
------                                          -----------------
931dffbb-ad69-4cb8-ac41-6d55b17d70f2                         True
```

Note

Get-SPBackupHistory contains data about both backups and restorations. You can optionally use either the ShowBackup or ShowRestore switch to retrieve only one or the other. ∎

The configuration database can be restored using Restore-SPFarm with the ConfigurationOnly switch. This cmdlet also requires the directory where the backup is stored along with the backup ID of the backup you wish to restore from. For example, to restore the backup that was retrieved in the preceding example, you would do the following:

```
$arguments = @{
  BackupID = '931dffbb-ad69-4cb8-ac41-6d55b17d70f2';
  Dir = '\\server1\backups';
  ConfigurationOnly = $true;
  RestoreMethod = 'OverWrite'
}
Restore-SPFarm @arguments
```

Farms

`Backup-SPFarm` is used to back up a SharePoint farm. It requires a `Directory` parameter to specify the location where the backup files will be created. If SharePoint's instance of SQL is on its own server, you must specify a UNC path to a share that your service accounts for both SQL and SharePoint have write access to. You must also specify a value for the `BackupMethod` parameter. This parameter accepts either `Full` or `Differential` to indicate the type of backup that should be performed.

```
Backup-SPFarm -Directory \\server1\backups -BackupMethod Full
```

If `Backup-SPFarm` is run with the `ShowTree` switch parameter, it lists out all of the components that will be backed up by the command:

```
Backup-SPFarm -ShowTree
```

You can specify which components within the farm you would like to back up by using the `Item` parameter. For example, to perform a differential backup on `WSS_Administration`, you would run the following:

```
$item = 'Farm\WSS_Administration'
$dir = '\\server1\backups'
Backup-SPFarm -Directory $dir -BackupMethod Differential -Item $item
```

Restoring a farm is a nearly identical process to how a SharePoint configuration is restored. The only difference is that during the restoration of a farm, you should not use the `ConfigurationOnly` switch parameter when using `Restore-SPFarm`. Here is an example of what a restoration command might look like:

```
$arguments = @{
  BackupID = 'a698ed30-d0e3-43a1-909e-cdf23e9418a6';
  Dir = '\\server1\backups';
  RestoreMethod = 'OverWrite'
}
Restore-SPFarm @arguments
```

Site Collections

Sites can be backed up by using the `Backup-SPSite` cmdlet. This cmdlet takes an `SPSite` object or the URL for the site as the positional parameter. It requires you to specify a path with the `Path` parameter, and it can, alternatively, use a switch named `UseSqlSnapshot` if your database server supports SQL snapshots. When using a snapshot, the backup will occur without any danger of locking out users during the backup. When the backup is completed, the snapshot is deleted. If this switch is not used, the site will become read-only for the duration of the backup. Alternatively, you can use the `NoSiteLock` switch parameter to ensure that the site stays in read-write mode for the duration of the backup. This, however, is not recommended by Microsoft if the site is being used during the backup.

```
$site = Get-SPSite http://server1/sites/psbible
$datestamp = (Get-Date).tostring('yyyyMMdd')
$path = "c:\backups\psbible.$datestamp.bak"
```

`Backup-SPSite $site -Path $path`Sites **can be restored by using the** `Restore-SPSite` **cmdlet:**

```
$site = Get-SPSite http://server1/sites/psbible
Restore-SPSite $site -Path c:\backups\psbible.20110703.bak
```

Lists and Libraries

Lists and document libraries can be backed up using the `Export-SPWeb` cmdlet. The cmdlet requires the URL or the GUID for the `SPWeb` object as well as a relative path where the list exists in SharePoint.

```
$weburl = "http://server1/sites/psbible"
$datestamp = (Get-Date).tostring('yyyyMMdd')
$path = "c:\backups\tasklist.$datestamp.bak"
$taskurl = "/sites/psbible/Lists/Tasks"
Export-SPWeb $weburl -Path $path -ItemUrl $taskurl
```

A few optional parameters are worth mentioning with `Export-SPWeb`:

- **NoFileCompression:** Leaves the data uncompressed in the backup location.
- **IncludeVersion:** Accepts the values `LastMajor` (default), `CurrentVersion`, `LastMajorandMinor`, or `All`.
- **IncludeUsersSecurity:** Copies the security permissions for the list into the backup.
- **UseSqlSnapshot:** Uses a SQL snapshot to create the backup. This is identical to the process that occurs when this parameter is used with `Backup-SPSite`.

The backup files created by `Export-SPWeb` can be restored to a website using `Import-SPWeb`:

```
$web = Get-SPWeb http://server1/sites/psbible
$path = "C:\backups\tasklist.20110704.bak"
Import-SPWeb $web -Path $path
```

Search and Timer Jobs

The SharePoint cmdlets give you interfaces to manage many aspects of search. This section looks specifically at how you can manage the search crawls that index the data within a SharePoint server.

Modifying Crawls

To retrieve the information about the crawls that are configured, you must first get the object that represents the search service itself. The cmdlet used to retrieve this object is `Get-SPEnterpriseSearchServiceApplication`:

```
$searchapp = Get-SPEnterpriseSearchServiceApplication
```

The crawls that are configured are retrieved by piping the search service application into `Get-SPEnterpriseSearchCrawlContentSource`:

```
$searchapp |Get-SPEnterpriseSearchCrawlContentSource
```

Name	Id	Type	CrawlState	CrawlCompleted
Local SharePo...	2	SharePoint	Idle	7/4/2011 12:27:32 AM

To modify a crawl, you first need to get the crawl you are looking for. The `Identity` parameter of `Get-SPEnterpriseSearchCrawlContent` enables you to specify the crawl name you are looking to retrieve:

```
$name = 'Local SharePoint Sites'
$crawl = $searchapp |Get-SPEnterpriseSearchCrawlContentSource -Identity $name
```

When modifying a crawl, you will generally need to modify either the addresses you are crawling or the schedule. Both of these can be modified and updated with a `SharePointContentSource` object that is returned from the `Get-SPEnterpriseSearchCrawlContentSource` cmdlet. The following adds a new root site to the crawl:

```
$crawl.StartAddresses.Add("http://server1/sites/psbible")
$crawl.Update()
```

To change the interval at which an incremental crawl occurs, you can use the following:

```
$crawl.IncrementalCrawlSchedule.RepeatInterval = 40
$crawl.Update()
```

Kicking Off Crawls

In addition to retrieving information about a crawl and changing its behavior, you can also perform a few methods to control the status of a crawl:

- `PauseCrawl()`
- `ResumeCrawl()`
- `StopCrawl()`
- `StartFullCrawl()`
- `StartIncrementalCrawl()`

Each of these methods can be called on a crawl object like this:

```
$crawl.StartFullCrawl()
```

Summary

This chapter has only scratched the surface of what is possible when using Windows PowerShell to manage Microsoft SharePoint Server 2010. You've seen a set of tasks that are extremely useful to administrators, but you haven't even seen one-fifth of the cmdlets released by Microsoft. If only one thing is certain, it is that SharePoint server will be running on Windows PowerShell for many years to come.

In the next chapter, you continue the exploration of Windows PowerShell on Microsoft's web platform as you explore how you can automate deployments and tasks on Internet Information Services 7.

## CHAPTER 3

Managing Internet Information Services 7

Internet Information Services (IIS) is the collection of web, FTP, and SMTP services that is shipped with Microsoft's Windows server and desktop operating systems. IIS 7.0 was shipped with Windows Server 2008 and Windows Vista. IIS 7.5 is being shipped with Windows Server 2008 R2 and Windows 7. The Windows PowerShell cmdlets and provider that are used with IIS 7 give you complete control over the web and FTP services available in IIS.

The Windows PowerShell provider and cmdlets give you a robust way of managing web services. Automating management and deployment tasks for IIS is useful for a variety of reasons:

- Controlling the configuration of IIS through scripts allows for less administrator error when moving changes made in development into testing and production environments.

- Using Windows PowerShell as a deployment method for websites means that your code can easily extend to any IIS 7 server. This technique, along with virtualization and cloud technologies, can be used to spin up new servers on demand to meet your processing and bandwidth needs.

- IIS 7 is one of the roles available to Windows Server Core (the stripped-down command line–only version of Windows 2008). Windows Server 2008 R2 added the ability to host .NET code and Windows PowerShell. Although you can use the IIS management tools to manage an IIS server remotely, the fact that the server itself can only be managed via command line at the console makes Windows PowerShell very attractive.

IN THIS CHAPTER

Installing the necessary components

Browsing IIS

Scripting deployments

Managing IIS

Digesting log files

Extending Windows PowerShell to manage IIS 7 script deployments and changes

Managing services and configuration backups

Working with IIS logs

Installing the Necessary Components

The cmdlets that are used to manage IIS 7 come in both snap-in and module form. Starting with Windows Server 2008 R2 and Windows 7, the `WebAdministration` module is installed automatically when you install IIS 7.5. Windows Server 2008 and Windows Vista (SP1 and higher) require you to install the `WebAdministration` snap-in that is available on Microsoft's website (in both x86 and x64 formats) in order to manage IIS 7.0.

Note
You can download the `WebAdministration` snap-in from `www.iis.net/download/PowerShell`. ∎

Installing the Snap-in

If you are using Windows Vista or Windows Server 2008 (not R2), you will need to install the `WebAdministration` snap-in in order to use the cmdlets. The snap-in is installed with a standard .msi installation package that you must run as an administrator. The installation registers the appropriate DLLs for you. The snap-in works with both Windows PowerShell 1.0 and Windows PowerShell 2.0.

Installing the Web Server Role

The method used to install the web server role varies depending on whether you are running the Server or Desktop version of Windows.

Microsoft Windows Server 2008

If you are using Windows Server 2008 R2, the `WebAdministration` module is installed automatically when installing IIS. IIS 7 can be installed through the Server Manager GUI on Windows Server 2008 and Windows Server 2008 R2:

1. **Click Start ⇨ All Programs ⇨ Administrative Tools ⇨ Server Manager.** Server Manager opens up with a connection to the local server.

2. **Right-click Roles and select Add Role.** The Add Roles Wizard opens up to the Before You Begin page.

3. **Click Next.** You are brought to the Web Server (IIS) page in the wizard.

4. **Click Next.** You are brought to the Select Role Services page.

5. **Select the options you would like to install.** As long as you select any of the IIS components, the `WebAdministration` module will be installed if you are installing IIS on a Windows Server 2008 R2 server.

6. **Click Next.** You see the Confirm Installation Selections screen, where you can review your choices.

7. **Click Install.** Then wait for the installation to be completed.

8. **Click Close.**

In addition to the GUI method, you can also install the Web Server role with the `Add-WindowsFeature` cmdlet that comes with the `ServerManager` module discussed in Chapter 7. The following line installs the minimal amount of IIS features required to install the `WebAdministration` module:

```
Add-WindowsFeature Web-Server
```

Note
All of the Windows features that can be installed for the Web Server (IIS) role begin with the prefix `Web`. You can get a complete listing by using `Get-WindowsFeature Web*`. ■

Microsoft Windows Desktop Operating System
If you are using Windows 7, the `WebAdministration` module is installed with IIS. IIS is installed on Windows 7 and Windows Vista by turning on the Internet Information Services feature:

1. **Click Start ➪ Control Panel.** The Control Panel window opens.
2. **Click Programs.**
3. **Click Turn Windows Features On or Off.** The Windows Features dialog box opens up.
4. **Select Internet Information Services and click OK.**

Loading the WebAdministration Cmdlets and Provider

The technique for loading the cmdlets depends on whether you are using the IIS 7.0 snap-in or the IIS 7.5 module.

Using the IIS 7.0 Snap-in
You can load the `WebAdministration` snap-in with:

```
Add-PSSnapin WebAdministration
```

Using the IIS 7.5 Module
You can load the `WebAdministration` module with:

```
Import-Module WebAdministration
```

Making Your Scripts Generic
If you are unsure whether the computer that is running your script will have the module or snap-in installed, you can use the following snippet of code to ensure that the proper version is loaded at the beginning of your IIS scripts.

```
if (Get-Module -ListAvailable WebAdministration) {
  Import-Module WebAdministration
} elseif (Get-PSSnapin -Registered -EA SilentlyContinue WebAdministration) {
```

```
        Add-PSSnapin WebAdministration
    } else {
    Write-Error "Cannot find the WebAdministration cmdlets"
    exit
    }
    # Add your IIS code here
```

Note

When you use `WebAdministration` to manage IIS on Windows Vista and Windows 7, you are required to run an elevated Windows PowerShell session by right-clicking the Windows PowerShell icon and selecting Run as Administrator. ∎

Installing the WMI Provider

IIS 7 also has a method to manage IIS via Windows Management Instrumentation (WMI). To use the WMI classes, you must install the IIS Management Scripts and Tools feature from either Server Manager (Windows Server 2008) or the Add/Remove Windows Features functionality in Windows Vista and Windows 7. You can install this feature with `Add-WindowsFeature` as follows:

```
    Add-WindowsFeature Web-ScriptingTools
```

Note

The `WebAdministration` cmdlets and provider are so simple that the chances are very high that you will never install the WMI provider. That is, unless you expect to script against SMTP. The `WebAdministration` cmdlets do not give interfaces to managing SMTP, whereas the WMI provider does. The SMTP service is not integrated into IIS 7; SMTP continues to use IIS 6 as its foundation. This internal design is hidden from you, but it explains why there are no Windows PowerShell interfaces to working with SMTP in the `WebAdministration` provider and cmdlets. ∎

The WMI provider is created within its own namespace in WMI. To use the `Get-WmiObject` cmdlet, you will need to specify `root\WebAdministration` with the `-Namespace` parameter. For example, to look at the `VirtualDirectory` class, you would use the following command:

```
    Get-WmiObject -Namespace root\WebAdministration VirtualDirectory
```

The `WebAdministration` namespace contains more than 400 classes. You can view them all with the following command:

```
    Get-WmiObject -Namespace root\WebAdministration -List
```

Note

Although it is possible to manage IIS via WMI via Windows PowerShell, this chapter does not go into those details. This chapter focuses on managing IIS 7 with the Windows PowerShell provider and cmdlets. ∎

Browsing IIS:\

The WebAdministration module and snap-in come with a Windows PowerShell provider called WebAdministration that can be used to browse, create, modify, and delete items within IIS. When the module or snap-in is loaded, a default WebAdministration drive is created called IIS:\.

You can browse to the IIS:\ drive by using either Set-Location or its alias cd. The root of IIS:\ has three folders, which are visible when using Get-ChildItem or dir:

- **AppPools:** Application Pools
- **Sites:** Web and FTP Sites
- **SSLBindings:** A collection of sites that are configured with certificates to use SSL

```
cd IIS:
dir
```

```
Name
----
AppPools
Sites
SslBindings
```

```
Get-ChildItem .\Sites
```

Name	ID	State	Physical Path	Bindings
Web Site 1		Started	%SystemDrive%\inetpub\wwwroot	http *:80: https *:443:

```
cd .\AppPools
dir
```

Name	State	Applications
Classic .NET AppPool	Started	
DefaultAppPool	Started	Default Web Site /CertSrv

```
dir IIS:\SslBindings
```

IP Address	Port	Store	Sites
192.168.1.100	443	MY	Default Web Site

393

Scripting Deployments and Changes

Scripting new deployments within IIS becomes a breeze with Windows PowerShell. Once you work out all of the requirements for an application, you can automate the process to build web farms or testing environments for your sites.

Scripting configuration changes is an excellent technique you can use to reduce the risk of making changes to production web servers. You can work out your script in a development environment, test it in a QA environment, and then push that change to production.

Using New-Item

The `New-Item` cmdlet enables you to create the following types of items within `IIS:\` via the `WebApplication` provider:

- **AppPool:** This is an object that represents an application pool. It is the default type that is created when `New-Item` is used within `IIS:\AppPools\`.
- **Site:** This is a website item. It is the default type for `New-Item` within `IIS:\Sites\`. Within websites, you can create the following types using `New-Item`:
  - **Application:** A directory in a website that is specified to run an application, for example, .NET-enabled directories.
  - **VirtualDirectory:** A directory in a website that is a virtual directory.
- **SslBinding:** This item represents the collection of properties that make up an SSL binding. This is the default type for `IIS:\SslBindings\`.

To create items of the type `Application` or `VirtualDirectory`, you must use the dynamic parameter `Type` that is available only when `New-Item` is called within the `WebAdministration` provider.

`New-Item` also has two additional dynamic parameters when used with this provider. These parameters only exist for `New-Item` when they are used within the IIS provider.

- **PhysicalPath:** Used to specify the physical path for a website, virtual directory, or application.
- **Bindings:** Used to specify the protocol, address, port, and host headers associated with a website. The `Bindings` property takes a hash or collection of hashes with two name/value pairs:
  - **Protocol:** The web protocol for the binding, for example, HTTP or HTTPS.
  - **BindingInformation:** This is three bits of information separated by colons:
    - **IP Address:** The IP address to bind to. Asterisks can be used as a wildcard to specify a range of addresses. A single asterisk represents any IP address.
    - **Port:** The port the site should use.

- **Host header:** A host header that signifies that the site should respond to requests when a specific hostname is used. This value can be left blank to associate the site with any hostname.

Creating Sites

Websites and FTP sites can be created very easily with the WebAdministration snap-in or module. As you will see throughout this chapter, there is often both a provider and direct cmdlet way of performing these tasks.

Using the Provider

The following example illustrates how you can create a website using New-Item. Prior to using the New-Item cmdlet, it will create the underlying directory structure if it does not already exist. It also shows you how to use the Bindings parameter to add two bindings to the site.

```
$dir = 'C:\inetpub\wwwroot\PowerShellBible'
if (!(Test-Path $dir)) {
  md $dir
}
$bindings = @()
$bindings += @{protocol='http';bindinginformation='192.168.1.100:8080:'}
$bindings += @{protocol='https';bindinginformation='*:443:'}

New-Item IIS:\Sites\PowerShellBible -PhysicalPath $dir -Bindings $bindings
```

Using New-Website

The WebAdministration module also provides a cmdlet called New-Website that creates a site without needing to use the provider. New-Website has the following parameters worth noting:

- **Name:** Name of the website.
- **ID:** Optional parameter that allows you to specify a unique ID for the site.
- **Port:** The port that will be used for the site.
- **IPAddress:** The IP address for the site.
- **HostHeader:** The hostname that the site will respond to.
- **ApplicationPool:** The application pool that the site will use.
- **Ssl:** This is a switch that enables https as the protocol for the site.

The following example illustrates how this cmdlet is used:

```
$dir = 'C:\inetpub\wwwroot\PSBible'
if (!(Test-Path $dir)) {
  md $dir
}
```

```
$params = @{
  Name='PowerShellBible'
  Port=443
  IPAddress='*'
  HostHeader = 'powertoe.wordpress.com'
  PhysicalPath=$dir
  ApplicationPool='AppPool1'
  SSL=$true
}
New-Website @params
```

Note

When using the `New-Website` cmdlet to create a website, you cannot specify multiple bindings. When using the SSL switch, the website will be created with an HTTPS binding only. This can easily be addressed after the website has been created, but you should be aware of the differences between `New-Item` and `New-Website` if you expect to script deployments of IIS sites. ∎

Using New-WebFTPSite

FTP sites are created with `New-WebFtpSite`. This cmdlet is identical to `New-WebSite` except that it does not have an `ApplicationPool` or `SSL` parameter.

Creating Virtual Directories

Virtual directories are web folders within a site that point to a folder that is outside of a site's normal directory structure. They are used to point a site directory to another folder on the server, including those that exist on separate disks.

Using the Provider

Here is an example of how to use `New-Item` in the `WebAdministration` provider to create a virtual directory. The example creates a directory in the PowerShellBible website that is pointing to the D drive of the server.

```
cd IIS:\Sites\PowerShellBible\
New-Item Data -Type VirtualDirectory -PhysicalPath d:\
```

Using New-WebVirtualDirectory

Virtual directories can also be created with the `New-WebVirtualDirectory` cmdlet. The relevant parameters are:

- **Name:** Name of the virtual directory.

- **Application:** If the application is omitted, the virtual directory will be created at the root of the site.

- **PhysicalPath:** The directory must already exist on the filesystem.

- **Site**

Here is an example of how this cmdlet can be used.

```
$dir = 'C:\virtualdir1'
if (!(Test-Path $dir)) {
  md $dir
}
$params = @{
  Name='VirtualDir1'
  Site='PowerShellBible'
  PhysicalPath = $dir
}
New-WebVirtualDirectory @params
```

Caution

Even though many of the parameters are optional in the WebAdministration cmdlets, omitting certain parameters may cause you problems. For example, creating a virtual directory without specifying a physical path will make IIS Manager think you have a corrupted configuration when you try to browse to the virtual directory. A good rule of thumb is to supply parameters for each item of information that you normally supply to the GUI when you perform the same function manually. ∎

Creating Web Applications

Creating a web application directory is a very simple process whether you use the provider or the cmdlet. The cmdlet methods within IIS are generally more robust and easier to read and modify in scripts, but it is really just personal preference.

Using the Provider

The following example converts a directory in the PowerShellBible website into an application folder via the WebAdministration provider.

```
cd IIS:\Sites\PowerShellBible
md App #Creates the App directory on the file system
New-Item App -Type Application -PhysicalPath (Get-Item .\App).fullname
```

Note

The function mkdir and its alias md is one of the only FileSystem functions that work in the WebAdministration provider. You cannot copy, delete, or write to files using the IIS:\ drive. If you need to access the files within the websites, you will need to run Get-Item to return the underlying object (as illustrated in the previous example) or use the FileSystem drives that you normally use to manage files on disk. ∎

Using New-WebApplication

Application folders can also be created with the New-WebApplication cmdlet. The parameters of importance are:

- **Name:** Name of the application directory.
- **PhysicalPath:** The path on the filesystem to the directory that will contain the web application. The directory must already exist.

- **Site:** The site where the application folder will be created.
- **ApplicationPool:** The application pool that the web application will use.

The following shows an example of how to use this cmdlet:

```
$dir = 'C:\inetpub\wwwroot\PSBible\app1'
if (!(Test-Path $dir)) {
  md $dir
}
$params = @{
  Name='App1'
  Site='PowerShellBible'
  PhysicalPath = $dir
  ApplicationPool='AppPool1'
}
New-WebApplication @params
```

Creating Application Pools

Application pools encapsulate applications and sites into groups of worker processes. Whether you are creating these application pools via the provider or the cmdlet, only one line of code is required.

Using the Provider

Creating application pools is very straightforward using New-Item.

```
New-Item IIS:\AppPools\PowerShellBible
```

Using New-WebAppPool

This method is also very straightforward. The cmdlet takes a positional parameter that represents the name of the new application pool.

```
New-WebAppPool PowerShellBible
```

Configuring SSL

Setting up SSL is a multistep process:

1. You must have a certificate installed that you can use for the binding.
2. You must create a web binding on a website using New-WebBinding that uses the HTTPS protocol.
3. You create an SSL binding in IIS:\SslBindings specifying the allowed IP addresses and the certificate you would like to use.

The following example shows how to perform the above steps.

```
New-WebBinding -Name 'PSBible' -Protocol https -Port 443  -IPAddress 0.0.0.0
cd IIS:\SslBindings
$cert = Get-Item cert:\LocalMachine\My\734A6B9F621496813276A7134D64BFEFA5FF5C11
$cert |New-Item 0.0.0.0!443
```

Note

This example uses the IP address 0.0.0.0 for both the SSL and web binding. The 0.0.0.0 address is used to specify all IP addresses for this server. ■

Using the Provider to Make Changes

Once items have been created, you can use the cmdlets that you use with any Windows PowerShell provider to get information and remove and modify the underlying objects: Get-Item, Remove-Item, Get-ItemProperty, Set-ItemProperty, New-ItemProperty, and Clear-ItemProperty. It's worth highlighting a few examples of how you can modify items in the provider.

In order to bind a site to an application pool, you can use Set-Item as follows:

```
$website = Get-Item IIS:\Sites\PSBible
$website |Set-ItemProperty-Name ApplicationPool-Value PSBible
```

Here is an example of how you can remove all of the existing web bindings and then create a new one.

```
$website |Clear-ItemProperty -Name bindings
$binding = @{protocol='http';bindinginformation='*:80:www.wiley.com'}
$website |Set-ItemProperty -Name bindings -Value $bindings
```

This example modifies the queue length for an application pool and then recycles that pool.

```
$pool = Get-Item IIS:\AppPools\PSBible
$pool.queueLength = 3000
$pool.Recycle()
```

Here is an example of how you can grab one of the properties returned by Get-ItemProperty:

```
Get-ItemProperty .\DefaultAppPool |Select -ExpandProperty processmodel
```

This example shows how you can use Set-ItemProperty to modify the properties of an application pool. The following two lines of code set a username and password for the application pool to run as:

```
$properties = @{userName='domain\IIS_pool'; password='password';identitytype=3}
Set-ItemProperty IIS:\AppPools\PSBible -name processmodel -value $properties
```

The following line of code is a useful one that moves the location where log files are stored from a site to a new directory:

```
Set-ItemProperty IIS:\Sites\PSBible -Name LogFile.Directory -Value 'd:\Logs'
```

Finally, here is an example of using `Remove-Item`. The following code deletes a website:

```
Remove-Item IIS:\Sites\PSBible
```

Removing IIS Objects with the Cmdlets

In addition to using `Remove-Item` to delete IIS objects within the `IIS:\` drive, each `New-WebIISObject` cmdlet also has a corresponding `Remove-WebIISObject` that can be used. For example, the cmdlet used to create websites is `New-Website` and the cmdlet used to delete a website is `Remove-Website`.

Advanced WebConfiguration Settings

Not all configurations are exposed to the `WebAdministration` provider. Some settings require you to use the `WebConfiguration` cmdlets. These cmdlets work with the provider to expose more information about the IIS objects.

To understand how these cmdlets work, it's important to realize that these settings are maintained within XML files in a series of layers. For example, a website will get its configuration from a combination of the `machine.config`, the global `web.config`, the `applicationHost.config`, and finally through the `web.config` that belongs to the site. The cmdlets use XPath queries to find the locations you are looking to view and change.

To view these settings, you use `Get-WebConfiguration` and `Get-WebConfigurationProperty`.

Viewing Web Configuration Settings

`Get-WebConfiguration` uses the following important parameters:

- **PSPath:** This is the location you would like to get information from. It can be a location in the `IIS:\` drive or you can use `webroot`, `apphost`, or *computer name*.
- **Filter:** This is the `XPath` query filter. Wildcards (*) are supported.
- **Location:** This specifies the delegation level you are looking at. This is important only when pushing changes back into the configuration because it allows you to override a configuration that is locked from a parent configuration file.

The following is a snippet of XML that is taken from a `machine.config`:

```
<configProtectedData defaultProvider="RsaProtectedConfigurationProvider">
  <providers>
    <add name="RsaProtectedConfigurationProvider"
type="System.Configuration.RsaProtectedConfigurationProvider, ↵
System.Configuration,
```

```
Version=2.0.0.0, Culture=neutral, PublicKeyToken=b03f5f7f11d50a3a"↵
description="Uses
RsaCryptoServiceProvider to encrypt and decrypt"
keyContainerName="NetFrameworkConfigurationKey" cspProviderName=""
useMachineContainer="true" useOAEP="false"/>

    <add name="DataProtectionConfigurationProvider"
type="System.Configuration.DpapiProtectedConfigurationProvider,↵
System.Configuration,
Version=2.0.0.0, Culture=neutral, PublicKeyToken=b03f5f7f11d50a3a"↵
description="Uses
CryptProtectData and CryptUnProtectData Windows APIs to encrypt and decrypt"
useMachineProtection="true" keyEntropy=""/>
  </providers>
</configProtectedData>
```

To view the `configProtectedData` section for the PowerShellBible website, you would use the following code:

```
cd IIS:\Sites\PowerShellBible
Get-WebConfiguration -Filter /configProtectedData |select *
```

```
defaultProvider       : RsaProtectedConfigurationProvider
providers             : Microsoft.IIs.PowerShell.Framework.ConfigurationElement
PSPath                : MACHINE/WEBROOT/APPHOST/Default Web Site
Location              :
ConfigurationPathType : Location
ItemXPath             : /configProtectedData
IsLocked              : True
OverrideMode          : Inherit
OverrideModeEffective : Allow
SectionPath           : /configProtectedData
Attributes            : {defaultProvider}
ChildElements         : {providers}
ElementTagName        : configProtectedData
Methods               :
Schema                :
Microsoft.IIs.PowerShell.Framework.ConfigurationElementSchema
```

According to the output, there are `ChildElements` that refer to the `<providers>` section of the XML. There is also an attribute called `defaultProvider`. To browse all of the `<add>` elements within `<providers>`, you could use a filter like this:

```
Get-WebConfiguration -Filter /configProtectedData/providers/*
```

Caution

Looking at the preceding filter, you would think that using a filter like `/*` would return all configurations. Unfortunately, it does not. Due to the way the XPath queries work, you will need to look at the `/*` and `/*/*` filters to see everything that is available. ■

To look at the `defaultProvider` attribute, you can inspect what is returned from `Get-WebConfiguration` using:

```
(Get-WebConfiguration /configProtectedData).defaultprovider
```

As an alternative, you can also use the `Get-WebConfigurationProperty` cmdlet. `Get-WebConfigurationProperty` has the same parameters as `Get-WebConfiguration` with the addition of a `-Name` parameter to specify the property you would like to view:

```
Get-WebConfigurationProperty /configProtectedData ↵
-Name defaultprovider|
  Select Value
```

Modifying Configuration Settings

Sections are added to a configuration using `Add-WebConfiguration` and `Add-WebConfigurationProperty`. For example, if you wanted to add a new filename to the default files for the site, you could do the following.

```
$filter = '/system.webServer/defaultDocument/files'
Add-WebConfiguration $filter -AtIndex 0 -value @{value="default.html"}
```

Caution

You must be mindful of case-sensitivity when working with these XML configuration files. The filter listed in this example is very specific. ■

Sections are modified using `Set-WebConfiguration` and `Set-WebConfigurationProperty`. The following example shows how you can use `Set-WebConfiguration`. The snippet redirects the PowerShellBible site to `wiley.com`.

```
cd IIS:\Sites\PowerShellBible
Set-WebConfiguration system.webServer/httpRedirect -Value @{
  enabled=$true
  destination="http://wiley.com"
  exactDestination=$true
  httpResponseStatus="Permanent"
}
```

This final example shows how to use the `Set-WebConfigurationProperty`. Specifically, it shows you how to change the CGI timeout value for the PowerShellBible site.

```
cd IIS:\Sites
$filter = '/system.webserver/cgi'
Set-WebConfigurationProperty $filter -name timeout -Value '00:20:00' `
  -Location 'PowerShellBible'
```

Caution

In the last example, if you run the Set-WebConfigurationProperty cmdlet from IIS:\Sites\PowerShellBible, you will receive the following error: "This configuration section cannot be used at this path. This happens when the

section is locked at a parent level." By executing this one level up, `IIS:\Sites\`, and specifying the `-Location` parameter, you are able to explicitly override this locked setting. ∎

Working with IIS Modules

In addition to the `WebConfiguration` cmdlets, there are a few cmdlets that are designed to work with IIS 7 modules:

- `Disable-WebGlobalModule`
- `Enable-WebGlobalModule`
- `Get-WebGlobalModule`
- `Get-WebManagedModule`
- `New-WebGlobalModule`
- `New-WebManagedModule`
- `Remove-WebGlobalModule`
- `Remove-WebManagedModule`
- `Set-WebGlobalModule`
- `Set-WebManagedModule`

The cmdlets that refer to the global modules have a module type of Managed when looking at the modules with IIS Manager. The cmdlets are very straightforward in their usage. For example, the `Get` cmdlets will retrieve all of the modules, or you can specify a module name you would like to view information about. All the cmdlets take the name of the module by using the `Name` positional parameter. For example, the following will disable the `AnonymousAuthenticationModule`:

```
Disable-WebGlobalModule AnonymousAuthenticationModule
```

There are not many properties you can set when creating or modifying a module. Typically, the managed modules can point to a new type or precondition while the global modules can be pointed to a new DLL by using the Image property. The following example shows how you can modify a global and managed module:

```
Set-WebManagedModule UrlMappingsModule -Type PSBible.Mappings
Set-WebGlobalModule IsapiModule -Image c:\customisapi.dll
```

Managing IIS

In addition to scripting deployments and changes to sites, Windows PowerShell can also be used to perform administrative tasks for IIS. This may be something as simple as controlling the state of IIS services or performing backups or restorations of configuration settings.

Controlling IIS Services

Application pools, websites, and the underlying Windows services of IIS can all be controlled via Windows PowerShell.

Starting and Stopping Pools and Sites

You have already seen that the provider exposes methods on application pools to allow things like stopping, starting, and recycling. You can also use the `Stop()` and `Start()` methods on the objects returned by `Get-Item` when using the cmdlet against items in the `IIS:\Sites` container:

```
(Get-Item IIS:\sites\PowerShellBible).Stop()
(Get-Item IIS:\sites\PowerShellBible).Start()
```

In addition to the preceding technique, there are six cmdlets to help you start and stop sites and application pools:

- `Stop-WebSite`
- `Start-WebSite`
- `Stop-AppPool`
- `Start-AppPool`
- `Stop-WebItem`
- `Start-WebItem`

You can use the cmdlets by themselves:

```
Stop-WebSite PowerShellBible
Start-WebSite PowerShellBible
```

Or you can pipe the provider objects into the cmdlets:

```
Get-ChildItem IIS:\sites\ |Stop-WebSite
Get-Item IIS:\sites\PowerShellBible |Start-WebSite
```

The `Start-WebItem` and `Stop-WebItem` cmdlets can be used with either an application pool or a site.

Note

Actually, the **AppPool** and **WebSite** stop and start cmdlets are just wrappers to **Start-WebItem** and **Stop-WebItem**. When you call **Start-WebSite**, it looks for an item in **IIS:\sites** with the name you are passing it, and then it pipes it into **Start-WebItem**. Similarly, the **Start-AppPool** cmdlet does the same thing, but it looks in **IIS:\AppPools**. ∎

Starting and Stopping IIS Services

While discussing starting and stopping items, it's also important to note that no WebAdministration cmdlets stop and start IIS because the cmdlets built into Windows

PowerShell V2 already have cmdlets that do this for you. The only problem is that there is more than one service controlled via `iisreset` in IIS 7: W3WSVC, WAS, and IISADMIN (installed only if you are using components of IIS 6). You could write a set of functions that would handle this natively in Windows PowerShell, but there's really no reason to because `IISReset.exe` works fine from within Windows PowerShell — even within a remoting session.

Caution

There is a small issue with **IISReset** in Windows 7. If you run **IISReset** from a Windows PowerShell ISE window, it will work without problem, but if you run it from a regular Windows PowerShell window, it will return unsuccessfully without an error. The workaround is to use **start iisreset** instead. ∎

Determining the State of a Site or Pool

The cmdlets and methods you can use to stop and start sites and application pools work regardless of the state the item is in prior to you calling the start or stop methods. In other words, if you call `Start-WebSite` on a site that is already running, it will not do anything, but it will not fail, either. Even though this logic is built into the cmdlets, you may still be interested in looking at the state for verification or reporting purposes within your script.

As with stopping and starting, you can do this in multiple ways with the `WebAdminstration` provider and cmdlets. You can use the cmdlets `Get-WebSiteState`, `Get-WebAppPoolState`, or `Get-WebItemState` the same way you use the stop and start cmdlets. You also have the ability to inspect the state property of a website or app pool item returned from the `Get-Item` cmdlet. For example, each of these will show you the same thing:

```
Get-WebAppPoolState PowerShellBible

(Get-Item IIS:\AppPools\PowerShellBible).State

$pool = Get-Item IIS:\AppPools\PowerShellBible
$pool.state

$pool = Get-Item IIS:\AppPools\PowerShellBible
$pool | Get-WebAppPoolState

$pool = Get-Item IIS:\AppPools\PowerShellBible
$pool | Get-WebItemState
```

If you would like to retrieve the state of all of the app pools, you can use either of the following lines of code:

```
Get-ChildItem IIS:\AppPools\ |Get-WebItemState
Get-WebAppPoolState
```

Backing Up and Restoring Configurations

If you would like to back up your entire IIS configuration, you can do so with `Backup-WebConfiguration` *BackupName*. This creates a folder in `$env:windir`

`\System32\inetsrv\backup` with the name you supplied to the cmdlet. The data in the backup directory can be restored with `Restore-WebConfiguration` *BackupName*. You should ensure that IIS is stopped prior to running the restoration or you will get errors.

Digesting Log Files

Reading IIS log files can be a cumbersome task if it needs to be done manually. Though a lot of tools are available to help you make sense of IIS logs, it's important to note that Windows PowerShell truly excels at this type of data manipulation. There is a slight trick to the technique in order to get the header information, but once that is determined, the process is very simple.

ConvertFrom-Csv

To let `ConvertFrom-Csv` turn each line of the log file into a Windows PowerShell object, you must first determine the header of the log from the line that begins with `#Fields:`. Once that is obtained, you can pass a single space character to the `-Delimiter` property of the cmdlet. Listing 15-1 is a complete script that uses this technique to parse the log file into Windows PowerShell objects.

LISTING 15-1

Parsing an IIS Log File

```
$site = 'IIS:\sites\PowerShellBible'

#The logfile.directory configuration usually has an environment variable
#Passing it to cmd will get the full path
$log = cmd /c echo (Get-Item $site).logfile.directory

#Get the log file path
$log = Join-Path $log ("W3SVC" + (Get-Item $site).id)

#Get the full path to the log file
$log = Join-Path $log "u_ex$yesterday.log"

$header = @()
$logentries = get-content $log |foreach {
  #Read the log file and look for the first line that has Fields#
  if ($header.count -eq 0 -and $_ -match '\#Fields: ([\s\S]+)') {
    #Split the line by a single space to get the header properties
    #for the log file
    $header = $matches[1] -split '\s'
  }
  else {
    #Make sure the line does not begin with a comment symbol
```

```
   if ($_ -notmatch '^#') {
     #Convert the line into PowerShell objects from a
     #space delimited file
     $_ |ConvertFrom-Csv -Header $header -Delimiter ' '
   }
 }
}
#Display the entries to the screen
$logentries
```

Filtering Tips

Once you have the log entries as Windows PowerShell objects, you can use the filtering, sorting, and formatting cmdlets you are familiar with. For example, if you wanted to filter for a list of 404 errors, you could use Where-Object or its alias where:

```
$logentries |where {$_.$("sc-status") -eq 404}
```

Sorting can be done by using the Sort-Object cmdlet or its alias sort:

```
$logentries |sort time-taken
```

You could just as easily use Export-CSV or ConvertTo-HTML. For example, the following creates an HTML report that shows the date/time along with the client's IP address and browser type. It uses Out-GridView so that you can more easily sort or filter the entries manually:

```
$logentries |Out-GridView
$logentries |select date,time, 'cs(User-Agent)', c-ip |
  ConvertTo-Html |
  Out-File c:\report.html
Start c:\report.html
```

Summary

As is the case with most things in Windows PowerShell, there are often multiple ways to accomplish tasks with the WebAdministration module and snap-in. The path you choose doesn't really matter. The important thing to realize is that you have everything you need to automate, manage, and report on your IIS servers directly within Windows PowerShell.

The next chapter looks at how you can use PowerShell to help manage System Center Operations Manager.

Managing System Center Operations Manager 2007 R2

T he command shell that comes with System Center Operations Manager 2007 R2 (OpsMgr) provides the means to perform many tasks you might normally perform in the OpsMgr Operations console from the command line instead. It also provides a convenient way to perform bulk administration and recurring tasks that would be labor-intensive or simply not possible from the console user interface. To successfully launch the command shell, you must be a member of an Active Directory security group with membership in the Operations Manager Administrators user role. All OpsMgr command shell instances connect directly to the OpsMgr Root Management Server (RMS), and the connection will fail without OpsMgr Administrator privileges.

Exploring the Available Cmdlets

The OpsMgr command shell contains 87 product-specific cmdlets for managing an Operations Manager 2007 (OpsMgr) deployment. The first cmdlet you may want to try is `Get-OperationsManagerCommand`, which returns a list of all the cmdlets contained in the OpsMgr Windows PowerShell snap-in. Once you have the list of cmdlets for OpsMgr in hand, you can use `Get-Help` (with the `-Full`, `-Detailed`, or `-Examples` switch parameters) to retrieve syntax and examples to help you get started writing your own command shell scripts when no sample exists.

By loading the OpsMgr Windows PowerShell snap-in, you can access any of these cmdlets in a Windows PowerShell script. In fact, one of the most common uses of the OpsMgr command shell is for bulk administrative tasks that cannot be easily performed in the Operations

IN THIS CHAPTER

Exploring Operations Manager cmdlets

Processing alerts in bulk

Automating maintenance mode

Discovering, deploying, and managing agents and network devices

Exploring discovered inventory

Working with overrides

Creating monitoring scripts in Windows PowerShell

Where to find and share Windows PowerShell scripts for Operations Manager

console. Such scripts are often configured as part of a scheduled task to run on a recurring basis. To connect to an OpsMgr management group from a Windows PowerShell script, you must first load the OpsMgr Windows PowerShell snap-in, specify the root management server, and set the working location to `OperationsManagerMonitoring` using the `Set-Location` cmdlet. Inserting the following code snippet at the beginning of any OpsMgr Windows PowerShell script enables you to run the script from any Windows PowerShell session or as part of a scheduled task. Just replace the name of the root management server (RMS) assigned to the `$rootMS` variable with the name of your RMS.

```
$RootMS = "myrms.contoso.com"
Add-PSSnapin "Microsoft.EnterpriseManagement.OperationsManager.Client" `
-ErrorVariable errSnapin;
Set-Location "OperationsManagerMonitoring::" -ErrorVariable errSnapin;
New-ManagementGroupConnection -ConnectionString:$rootMS -ErrorVariable `
errSnapin;
Set-Location $rootMS -ErrorVariable errSnapin;
```

When configuring a script to run as a scheduled task, make sure the user account used to run the script has Administrator rights in the target OpsMgr environment.

Working with Alerts

Alerts are the basis for most of your daily administrative effort in OpsMgr. When an alert is raised, it has to be determined if the alert is actionable; in other words, "Does this alert represent a real problem?" If so, the next step is to review the product knowledge contained in the alert to determine the root cause and identify an appropriate resolution. Sometimes, error conditions may occur repeatedly over an extended period of time. Occasionally, interruptions in network connectivity or application failures can result in a large number of non-actionable alerts called an *alert storm*. In these last two situations, the OpsMgr cmdlets provide a way to easily identify which alerts are occurring most often in your OpsMgr deployment, as well as how to process alerts in bulk. In this section, you learn how to work with OpsMgr alerts using the Windows PowerShell cmdlets that come with the OpsMgr command shell.

Processing Alerts in Bulk

Because many thousands of alerts can be generated in large environments (or any environment under the wrong circumstances), bulk processing of alerts is one of the most common uses of the OpsMgr command shell. Because the number of objects you are working with can be so large, the syntax you use to query OpsMgr is very important. For example, the following query for alerts will be successful only if there are no more than a few thousand alerts:

```
get-alert | where-object {($_.Name –like "File group*") -and `
($_.ResolutionState -eq 0)}
```

This next example performs the same task as the previous line of code, but in a way that will run much faster in larger environments, even when tens of thousands of open alerts are present:

```
Get-Alert -Criteria "Name Like 'File group%' AND ResolutionState=0"
```

Note

When using the –Criteria parameter, bear in the mind that, unlike a string comparison using Where-Object, the Criteriavalue is case-sensitive. ■

The reason behind the performance difference is that when the -Criteria parameter is used, the value passed is provided directly to the SQL Server database, and only the relevant data is returned. This reduces the objects that must be passed all the way back to the Windows PowerShell console. A Where-Object clause is the equivalent of a select * statement in SQL — all the results are returned and then sorted. The -Criteria statement is equivalent to a select * … where statement in SQL, returning only the data of interest. When coupled with the Resolve-Alert cmdlet, you can close alerts in bulk as well. This following code offers an easy way to remove open alerts based on the criteria of your choice:

```
Get-Alert -Criteria "Name Like 'Script%' AND ResolutionState=0" `
   | Resolve-Alert
```

This method is commonly used to close aging non-actionable alerts (like the common "script or executable failed to run" error) or alerts generated in an alert storm (such as when network connectivity results in large numbers of alerts due to the transient condition). Depending on your requirements, you can schedule this script in Task Scheduler to run automatically.

A common question from OpsMgr administrators is, "How can I retrieve a list of the most common alerts in my environment?" Retrieving a list of the most commonly occurring alerts may seem like a simple task, but it can be quite challenging due to the differences between the way rules and monitors function. Rules that generate alerts typically generate a single alert, and until that alert is closed, no additional alerts are created. Instead, the RepeatCount property of the alert is incremented. Retrieving the most commonly occurring alerts based on their RepeatCount property in reality presents the most commonly occurring rule-generated alerts, as shown in this example, which returns the 10 most common alerts:

```
Get-Alert | Sort-Object -Property RepeatCount -Descending | Select-Object `
   -Property Name,RepeatCount,MonitoringObjectPath -First 10
```

Monitors work much differently. Because monitors are state-aware, monitor-generated alerts for a single monitor do not repeat — they are in a resolution state of New (when the error condition occurs) or Resolved (when the error condition is improved and the alert is closed). The RepeatCount for monitor-generated alerts is always zero.

Creating a single combined report to present top alerts across rules or monitors requires tabulating repeated occurrences in a consistent manner by counting occurrences grouping them on alert ID. The sample script in Listing 16-1 (written by Andreas Zuckerhut) uses an in-memory DataTable for storage and tabulation of both rule and monitor-generated alerts. The results are written to a comma-separated value file `c:\TopAlerts.csv`.

Note

You can find the original source and related information at **www.systemcentercentral.com/ BlogDetails/tabid/143/IndexId/50372/Default.aspx**. ■

LISTING 16-1

TopAlerts.ps1 Script

```
#Create Datatable

$AlertTable = New-Object System.Data.DataTable "AlertTable"
$AlertTable.Columns.Add((New-Object System.Data.DataColumn ID,([string])))
$AlertTable.Columns.Add((New-Object System.Data.DataColumn Name,([string])))
$AlertTable.Columns.Add((New-Object System.Data.DataColumn AlertCount,([int])))
$AlertTable.Columns.Add((New-Object System.Data.DataColumn IsMonitorAlert,`
([string])))
foreach ($Alert in (Get-Alert))

{

  #Check if Alert exists already.

  $AlertExists = $False

  foreach ($Row in $AlertTable.Rows)

  {

    if ($Row.ID -eq $Alert.MonitoringRuleId.ToString())

    {

        $AlertExists = $True

        #In case it does, we just merge the Repeatcount
        $Row.AlertCount = $Row.AlertCount + ($Alert.RepeatCount + 1)

    }
  }

  if ($AlertExists)
```

```
    {

    }

    else

    {

        #If the Alert doesn't exist, add it to the DataTable.
        $NewRow = $AlertTable.NewRow()
        $NewRow.ID = $Alert.MonitoringRuleId.ToString()
        $NewRow.Name = $Alert.Name
        $NewRow.AlertCount = ($Alert.RepeatCount + 1)
        $NewRow.IsMonitorAlert = $Alert.IsMonitorAlert
        $AlertTable.Rows.Add($NewRow)

    }
}


$AlertTable = ($AlertTable | Sort-Object -Property AlertCount -Descending)

$AlertTable | Select-Object -First 10 | Export-Csv –path c:\TopAlerts.csv`
    -NoTypeInformation
```

The output of this script, a "Top 10 Alerts Report," is shown in Figure 16-1.

FIGURE 16-1

Default troubleshooting packs

	A	B	C	D
1	ID	Name	AlertCount	IsMonitorAlert
2	4d837281-97d5-413a-92db-01ffa391d236	Run As Account does not exist on the target system or does not have enough permissions	29697	FALSE
3	1a033455-8867-236c-5ae1-34b7f63ce2e6	WMI Probe Module Failed Execution	144	FALSE
4	53272049-e12e-30b4-c451-a6c77b32ec50	OleDB: Results Error	82	FALSE
5	09561b23-513f-be75-03df-b8a28e17e5f6	Virtual machine error	8	TRUE
6	b17a04e5-634c-fbf2-f1e9-b81baf37e4b3	Operational Data Reporting failed	7	FALSE
7	029d253d-5593-c127-1d5a-ea4a8b179297	Percentage of Committed Memory in Use is too high	7	TRUE
8	c72731b1-eb45-a86a-ba4f-1e43460e6cc4	Script or Executable Failed to run	6	FALSE
9	b59f78ce-c42a-8995-f099-e705dbb34fd4	Health Service Heartbeat Failure	1	TRUE
10	308c0379-f7f0-0a81-a947-d0dbcf1216a7	Failed to Connect to Computer	1	TRUE
11	eb666a69-f035-6f3f-3c47-00a9f7aa9a57	Health Service Unloaded System Rule(s)	1	TRUE

Updating Custom Fields in Alert Properties in Bulk

OpsMgr alerts include a number of read-write fields, including `Owner`, `TicketId`, `ResolutionState`, and 10 custom fields, named `CustomField1` through `CustomField10`.

OpsMgr administrators routinely use these to store values to support a number of integration scenarios, such as result status of an Opalis Integration Server workflow to correct an error condition, or to store categorization information for alert forwarding through the OpsMgr Connector Framework.

Although it is not always convenient to update these fields from an existing OpsMgr workflow (rule, monitor, or discovery), you can use Windows PowerShell to update these fields on a schedule or on demand when the situation warrants. The following sample script writes the computer principal name to CustomField1 and the name of the management pack containing the workflow that generated the alert in CustomField2. The Update() method at the end of the script writes the user-defined reason for the update presented on the History tab in alert properties.

```
#Retrieve open alerts
foreach ($alert in Get-Alert -Criteria 'PrincipalName is not null `
and ResolutionState = 0')

{
  #Update custom fields
  $alert.CustomField1 = $alert.PrincipalName
  $alert.ResolutionState = 1
  if ($alert.IsMonitorAlert -eq $False) { $alert.CustomField2 = `
((Get-Rule $alert.MonitoringRuleId).GetManagementPack()).DisplayName
  }
  else {
    $alert.CustomField2 = (Get-Monitor
$alert.ProblemId).GetManagementPack().DisplayName
  }
  $alert.Update("Alert update via Windows PowerShell")
}
```

The output of this script is shown in Figures 16-2 and 16-3.

FIGURE 16-2

Updated Alert Properties (Custom Fields tab)

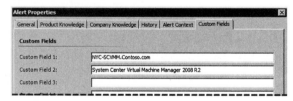

FIGURE 16-3

Updated Alert Properties (History tab)

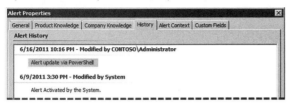

Automating Maintenance Mode

Placing a computer or other objects into maintenance mode instructs OpsMgr to stop monitoring and stop alerts for these objects for the duration indicated. Among recurring administrative tasks that require automation, maintenance mode is perhaps the most common. Fortunately, you can make short work of this using the OpsMgr cmdlets for PowerShell.

Adding and Removing Objects and Groups

When you place an object into maintenance mode in OpsMgr 2007, the object you specify "and all contained objects" are placed into maintenance mode by default. When you put a group object into maintenance mode, this means that OpsMgr automatically places all the objects contained in the group into maintenance mode as well.

When executing group maintenance mode, you are not restricted to groups of computers. You can place groups of objects of any type(s) into maintenance mode (health service, SQL databases, IIS websites, and so on) to avoid alerts being raised during scheduled application maintenance.

The script shown in Listing 16-2 places a group and all contained objects into maintenance mode. Download this script from the book's website and run it from a command prompt using the following syntax specifying the target group and root management server:

```
.\StartMaint.ps1 -GroupName 'Test Group' -rootMS 'myrms.contoso.com'
```

LISTING 16-2

StartMaint.ps1 Script

```
param ($groupName, $rootMS, $MMLength)

#Load OpsMgr snap-in and connect to RMS
Add-PSSnapin "Microsoft.EnterpriseManagement.OperationsManager.Client"
```

continues

LISTING 16-2 *(continued)*

```
Set-Location "OperationsManagerMonitoring::"
$MG = New-ManagementGroupConnection -ConnectionString $rootMS
if($MG -eq $null)
{
Write-Host "Failed to connect to $rootMS"
return
}

Set-Location $rootMS

$startTime = Get-Date
$endTime = $startTime.AddHours($MMLength)
$GroupName = Get-MonitoringClass | Where-Object {$_.DisplayName -eq $groupName}
$GroupID = Get-MonitoringObject $GroupName.Id

New-MaintenanceWindow -StartTime $startTime -EndTime $endTime `
-Reason"ApplicationInstallation" -Comment none -MonitoringObject $GroupID
```

If you need to remove a group from maintenance mode earlier than expected, you can do so on demand, using the `StopMaintenanceMode()` method. However, to end maintenance mode, you have to explicitly specify in the script that maintenance mode should be ended for all contained objects as well by specifying a `TraversalDepth` of recursive.

The script in Listing 16-3 removes a group and all contained objects from maintenance mode. Download this script from the book's website. Run it from a command prompt using the following syntax and specifying the target group and root management server:

```
.\StopMaint.ps1 -GroupName 'Test Group' -rootMS 'myrms.contoso.com'
```

LISTING 16-3

StopMaint.ps1 Script

```
param ($groupName, $rootMS)

#Load the Operations Manager snapin and connect to the Root Management Server
add-pssnapin "Microsoft.EnterpriseManagement.OperationsManager.Client";
Set-Location "OperationsManagerMonitoring::";
$mgConn = New-ManagementGroupConnection -connectionString:$rootMS;
if($mgConn -eq $null)
```

```
{
[String]::Format("Failed to connect to RMS on '{0}'",$rootMS)
return
}

Set-Location $rootMS

$MonitoringClassCG = Get-MonitoringClass | `
Where-Object {$_.DisplayName -eq $groupName}
$MonitoringGUID = Get-MonitoringObject $MonitoringClassCG.Id

$MonitoringGUID.StopMaintenanceMode([DateTime]::Now.ToUniversalTime(),`
[Microsoft.EnterpriseManagement.Common.TraversalDepth]::Recursive)
```

Tip

A very common mistake in group maintenance mode scripts is a lot of extra code to enumerate the members of the group and to put each of these objects into maintenance mode explicitly. Because the default behavior of maintenance mode is to include "object and all contained objects," this is unnecessary and places additional performance overhead on the RMS. ■

Automating Client-Side (Remote) Maintenance Mode

A common complaint of about maintenance mode in OpsMgr is that it requires server administrators to have some knowledge of OpsMgr, because maintenance mode is initiated either through the OpsMgr console UI or through the command shell.

Client-side maintenance mode (sometimes called remote maintenance mode) solutions eliminate this requirement. *Client-side maintenance mode* refers to a custom solution that allows server administrators to place servers into maintenance mode directly from the Windows computer on which they are about to perform maintenance without opening the Operations console or running a Windows PowerShell script directly. Though multiple methods exist to achieve this objective, all versions have some high-level components in common:

- A custom management pack that installs a small application (usually an HTML application) on the desktop. The application allows the server administrator to start or end maintenance mode for the server, as well as set maintenance mode duration. When the server administrator requests to start or end maintenance mode, the requested maintenance settings are written to a Windows event in the Operations Manager Event Log.

- Rules running on the agent that detect the "Maintenance Mode ON" and "Maintenance Mode OFF" events and trigger a response on the RMS.

- A Windows PowerShell maintenance mode script (hosted on the RMS) that places the computer, health service, and health service watcher in maintenance mode when triggered by the rule (running on the server) that detects the maintenance mode request.

Tip

To prevent any alerts from being raised during maintenance mode on a computer, three objects must be placed into maintenance mode in OpsMgr: the computer object, the health service, and the health service watcher. In the R2 release of OpsMgr 2007, a change was introduced in the maintenance mode feature. Now, when a computer is placed into maintenance mode, the health service and health service watcher objects for the computer are placed into maintenance mode automatically. ■

The following simple Windows PowerShell script is used to place a computer (and thus health service and health service watcher) into maintenance mode. With some simple modifications, it can be extended to facilitate client-side maintenance mode.

```
param($rootMS,$urlName,$minutes,$comment,$reason)
Add-PSSnapin "Microsoft.EnterpriseManagement.OperationsManager.Client" `
-ErrorVariable errSnapin

Set-Location "OperationsManagerMonitoring::" -ErrorVariable errSnapin
New-ManagementGroupConnection -ConnectionString $rootMS -ErrorVariable errSnapin
Set-Location $rootMS -ErrorVariable errSnapin


$ComputerName = (Get-MonitoringClass -Name Microsoft.Windows.Computer) | `
Get-MonitoringObject | Where-Object {$_.DisplayName -eq $urlName}

$startTime = Get-Date
$endTime = $startTime.AddMinutes($minutes)

"Putting URL into maintenance mode"
New-MaintenanceWindow -StartTime $startTime -endTime $endTime `
-MonitoringObject $ComputerName -comment$comment -Reason $reason
```

Note

You can download a working example of client-side maintenance mode from Derek Harkin's OpsMgr blog at http://derekhar.blogspot.com/2009/11/new-agent-maintenance-mode.html. ■

Deploying and Configuring OpsMgr Agents and Network Devices

Agent installation and configuration are tasks generally associated with the OpsMgr Operations console UI. However, many recurring tasks are associated with agent deployment configuration. The good news is, whether you want to configure heartbeat, agent proxy, agent failover settings, or even agent deployment, these tasks can all be automated with Windows PowerShell.

Configuring Agent Failover Without AD Integration

The Active Directory integration feature, which is used to assign agent failover settings in OpsMgr, provides a means to control primary and failover management server assignments for agent-managed computers. However, some organizations require granularity in agent failover assignment that is not easily achieved through an Active Directory–integrated assignment. With a little help from the `Get-Agent`, `Get-ManagementServer`, and `Set-ManagementServer` cmdlets, agent failover settings can be updated in bulk on demand.

The sample script shown next sets the primary and failover management servers for the specified agent(s). To run this script, update the `$rootMS` variable with the name of your RMS, and update `$PriMS` and `$SecMS` with the names of the primary and failover management servers. To specify which agents will be updated, change the value of the query criteria assigned to the `$agent` variable.

```
$rootMS= "opsmgr.contoso.com"
#Initializing the OpsMgr Powershell provider and Connecting to Mgmt Group
Add-PSSnapin "Microsoft.EnterpriseManagement.OperationsManager.Client" `
-ErrorVariable errSnapin
Set-Location "OperationsManagerMonitoring::" -ErrorVariable errSnapin
New-ManagementGroupConnection -ConnectionString $rootMS -ErrorVariable errSnapin
Set-Location $rootMS -ErrorVariable errSnapin


# Retrieve a list of agents and assign to variable $agent
# In this example, all servers with server name starting with 'FS'
$agents = Get-Agent -Criteria "Name LIKE 'FS%'" # set variables for primary `
and secondary management servers.
# make sure the WHERE clause in each one-liner below matches only 1 MS!
$PriMS = Get-ManagementServer | Where-Object {$_.Name -eq 'ms1.contoso.com'}
$SecMS = Get-ManagementServer | Where-Object {$_.Name -eq 'ms2.contoso.com'}


#Loop through list of agents and update primary and failover MS settings
ForEach ($agent in $agents) {
Set-ManagementServer -PrimaryManagementServer $PriMS `
-AgentManagedComputer $agent -FailoverServer $SecMS | Out-Null
}
```

Managing SNMP Device Failover

In OpsMgr, Simple Network Management Protocol (SNMP)–enabled devices are monitored through an SNMP GET for the `SysName` property issued from a proxy agent every 2 minutes. If the proxy agent responsible for monitoring the network device goes down, the SNMP devices polled by this agent will not be assigned to a new proxy agent automatically. Because this proxy agent can be simply an agent on a managed computer or from a management server, how you assign new proxy agent settings depends on whether the proxy agent is a managed computer or a management server.

If the proxy agent is a managed computer, the following script changes the proxy agent for the network device of your choice to a new agent-managed computer you designate:

```
param($rootMS,$proxyAgent, $deviceName)

#connect to mgmt group

Add-PSSnapin  Microsoft.EnterpriseManagement.OperationsManager.Client
Set-Location  OperationsManagerMonitoring::
New-ManagementGroupConnection -ConnectionString $serverName
Set-Location $ServerName

#Retrieve all our monitored network devices
$netDevices = Get-RemotelyManagedDevice | Where-Object {$_.Name `
-like $deviceName}

#Retrieve agent that will serve as proxy agent
$proxy = Get-Agent | Where-Object {$_.PrincipalName -like $proxyAgent }

#Sets the proxy of all network devices to the specified proxy server
Set-ProxyAgent -ProxyAgent $proxy -Device $netDevices
```

Download this script from the book's website, run it from a Windows PowerShell prompt on a computer with the OpsMgr command shell installed, and pass the needed parameters from any Windows PowerShell prompt as shown here:

```
.\snmpproxy.ps1 -RootMS "opsmgr.contoso.com" -ProxyAgent "svr1.contoso.com" `
-DeviceName '10.1.1.1'
```

If the proxy agent you want to assign is a management server or gateway server, the syntax you use to retrieve the proxy agent details must be updated to retrieve the correct computer. The syntax to run the script is the same as the previous script, but the method within the script used to retrieve the proxy agent has been modified to retrieve the designated management server rather than a managed computer.

```
param($rootMS,$proxyAgent, $deviceName)

#connect to mgmt group
$ServerName=$rootMS
Add-PSSnapin  Microsoft.EnterpriseManagement.OperationsManager.Client
Set-Location  OperationsManagerMonitoring::
New-ManagementGroupConnection -ConnectionString:$serverName;
Set-Location $ServerName

#Retrieve all our monitored network devices
$netDevices = Get-RemotelyManagedDevice | Where {$_.Name -like $deviceName}

#Retrieve agent that will serve as proxy agent
```

```
$mea=" Microsoft.EnterpriseManagement.Administration"
$crit=New-Object -Type "${mea}.ManagementServerCriteria("Name = '$proxyagent'")"

#Sets the proxy of all network devices to the specified proxy server
Set-ProxyAgent -ProxyAgent $proxy -Device $netDevices
```

Caution

When updating primary and failover settings for OpsMgr agents, be absolutely certain the management server and/or gateways specified in the script are in fact reachable from the network segments where agents reside. If you specify a management server that is inaccessible due to firewall or routing restrictions, you can leave agents in an orphaned state. Reversing this condition requires updating settings locally on all affected agents. ■

Automating Agent Discovery and Deployment

Though System Center Essentials 2010 (SCE) has a scheduled discovery feature to enable automated daily discovery of new computers on the network, this feature is not available in OpsMgr due to the other enterprise deployment options available. However, if you would like to discover new servers on your network on a scheduled basis, this is entirely possible with Windows PowerShell. In fact, by using LDAP queries to scope the search, you can filter the discovery within Active Directory to ensure agents are deployed only to the desired computers.

Automating discovery and agent deployment for Windows computers in Windows PowerShell involves the following high-level steps:

1. Define an LDAP query to scope the computer discovery (using the `New-LdapQueryDiscoveryCriteria` cmdlet and LDAP query language).

2. Start the discovery of the target computer from the specified management server (using `Start-Discovery`, taking the LDAP query as input).

3. Upon successful discovery, perform a push-install of the agent from the specified management server to target computer (using `Install-Agent`).

The script shown in Listing 16-4 discovers the specified computer (represented by `$targetAgent`) in the specified domain using the specified management server (represented by `$targetMS`). Upon successful discovery, the agent binaries are pushed from the management server to the target computer and installed.

Running the script in Listing 16-4 discovers computer `webserver1` in the `contoso` domain using management server `mgmtsvr1.contoso.com` and deploys the agent using the push deployment method:

```
.\WindowsDiscovery.ps1 -RootMS 'rms.contoso.com' -Domain 'contoso' `
-TargetMS 'mgmtsvr1.contoso.com' -TargetAgent webserver1
```

LISTING 16-4

WindowsDiscovery.ps1 Script

```
Param ($rootMS,$Domain,$targetMS,$targetAgent)

#Initialize the OpsMgr Provider
Add-PSSnapin Microsoft.EnterpriseManagement.OperationsManager.Client

# Set the location to the root of the provider namespace.
Set-location OperationsManagerMonitoring::

#create a connection to the Management Group
New-ManagementGroupConnection $rootMS

#change the path
Set-location $rootMS

#configure LDAP query setting
$ldap_query = New-LdapQueryDiscoveryCriteria -Domain $Domain `
 - LdapQuery "(sAMAccountType=805306369)(name=$targetAgent*)"

#configure discovery setting
$windows_discovery_cfg = New-WindowsDiscoveryConfiguration    `
- LdapQuery $ldap_query

# discoveryresults
$discovery_results = Start-Discovery -ManagementServer (Get-ManagementServer | `
where {$_.Name -eq "$targetMS"}) -WindowsDiscoveryConfiguration `
$windows_discovery_cfg

#install agents based on the criteria of your search in the -targetMS parameter
Install-Agent -ManagementServer (Get-ManagementServer | Where-Object `
{$_.Name -eq "$targetMS"}) `
-AgentManagedComputer $discovery_results.CustomMonitoringObjects
```

This script can be extended to accept a list of computers as input to perform discovery in batch. However, be careful not to perform more than a few computers at a time to avoid overloading your management group.

Verifying Agent Load Balance Across Management Servers

Balancing the agent load across management servers is an important factor in ensuring server utilization is optimized. However, agent load-balancing across management groups is not performed automatically, so periodically checking the agent count across all management servers can shed light on disparities in agent load.

The following example retrieves a count of agents grouped by the primary management server to which they report. Download this script from the book's website, and run the script from any Windows PowerShell prompt on a server with the OpsMgr Windows PowerShell snap-in installed. Before you do, change the value of $rootMS to the name of your RMS.

```
$rootMS = "nyc-omcm.contoso.com"
#Initialize the OpsMgr Provider
Add-PSSnapin "Microsoft.EnterpriseManagement.OperationsManager.Client"
Set-Location  "OperationsManagerMonitoring::"

#set Management Group context to the provided RMS
New-ManagementGroupConnection -ConnectionString $rootMS
Set-Location $rootMS

#Retrieve list of agents
$agent = Get-Agent | Sort-Object -Property Name

#Output a list of management servers and agent count for each
$agent | Group PrimaryManagementServerName -NoElement | Sort Name `
| Select-Object Name, Count | Export-Csv -NoTypeInformation `
-Path c:\agents.csv
```

Exploring Discovered Inventory Data

You can explore the objects discovered by OpsMgr using the Operations console. However, you can also explore the discovered inventory in your OpsMgr deployment using Windows PowerShell and learn a few things about object types (classes), their base classes, and any relationships that cannot be viewed in the graphical user interface (GUI). Exploring discovered inventory via Windows PowerShell will give you insight into management pack internals you cannot gain from the console GUI.

Enumerating Classes and Discovered Instances

You can explore the discovered inventory in your OpsMgr deployment from the command shell. You can retrieve a class or classes with the Get-MonitoringClass cmdlet:

```
Get-MonitoringClass | Where-Object {$_.Name -eq `
"Microsoft.Windows.Server.Computer"}
```

To retrieve instances of the class that have already been discovered by OpsMgr, simply pipe the output to Get-MonitoringObject:

```
Get-MonitoringClass -Name "Microsoft.Windows.Server.Computer" |
Get-MonitoringObject
```

Much like classes in the .NET world, every class in OpsMgr is derived from a base class and inherits all the properties of the base class. For example, the Windows Server class (`Microsoft.Windows.Server.Computer`) is derived from the base class Windows Computer (`Microsoft.Windows.Server.Computer`). The following script enumerates all the classes derived from a specified class using the `GetDerivedMonitoringClass()` method:

```
#Replace Microsoft.Windows.Computer with the class of your choice
$Class = 'Microsoft.Windows.Computer'


$DerivedClasses = (get-monitoringclass | where {$_.Name -eq `
"$Class"}).GetDerivedMonitoringClasses()

    Write-Host "The following are derived classes of $Class   "
    Write-Host " "

foreach ($DerivedClass in $DerivedClasses) {
    Write-Host "Class Name:" $DerivedClass.DisplayName "(" $DerivedClass.Name ")"
}
```

Figure 16-4 displays the output of the sample, enumerating classes of the `Microsoft .Windows.Computer` (Windows Computer) class.

FIGURE 16-4

Enumeration of derived classes

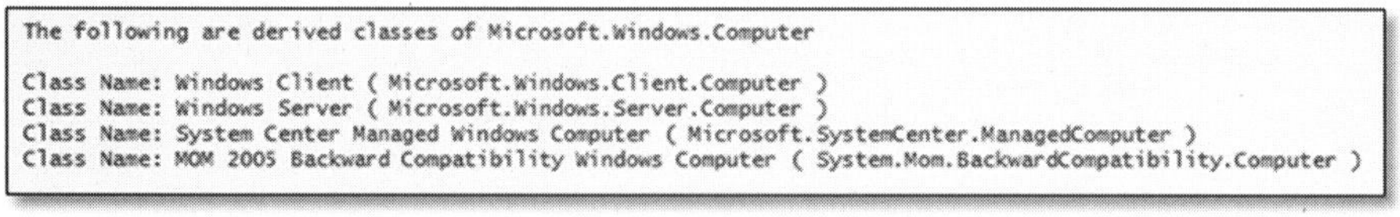

```
The following are derived classes of Microsoft.Windows.Computer

Class Name: Windows Client ( Microsoft.Windows.Client.Computer )
Class Name: Windows Server ( Microsoft.Windows.Server.Computer )
Class Name: System Center Managed Windows Computer ( Microsoft.SystemCenter.ManagedComputer )
Class Name: MOM 2005 Backward Compatibility Windows Computer ( System.Mom.BackwardCompatibility.Computer )
```

With a couple of small changes, you can enumerate the derived classes *recursively*, meaning that the derived classes of derived classes will be enumerated as well, all the way down the class hierarchy. The output will be multiple collections of derived classes, grouped by the base class from which they are derived.

```
#Replace system.entity with the class of your choice
$Class = 'Microsoft.Windows.Server.Computer'

Write-Host Report for derived classes of $Class
Write-Host "==============================================================="


$DerivedClasses = (get-monitoringclass | where {$_.Name -eq `
"$Class"}).GetDerivedMonitoringClasses()
```

```
foreach ($DerivedClass in $DerivedClasses) {
    Write-Host " "
    Write-Host "Derived classes based on " $DerivedClass.DisplayName "(" `
$DerivedClass.Name ")"
    Write-Host "The following classes are derived from " `
$DerivedClass.DisplayName ":"
   (get-monitoringclass -Name $DerivedClass ).GetDerivedMonitoringClasses() | `
select DisplayName, Name
}
```

Figure 16-5 displays the output of the sample, enumerating classes of the `Microsoft.Windows.Computer` (Windows Computer) class.

FIGURE 16-5

Recursive enumeration of derived classes

```
Report for derived classes of Microsoft.Windows.Server.Computer
===============================================================

Derived classes based on  Windows Domain Controller ( Microsoft.Windows.Server.DC.Computer )
The following classes are derived from  Windows Domain Controller :

Derived classes based on  Virtual Server ( Microsoft.Windows.Cluster.VirtualServer )
The following classes are derived from  Virtual Server :

Derived classes based on  Windows Server 2000 Computer ( Microsoft.Windows.Server.2000.Computer )
The following classes are derived from  Windows Server 2000 Computer :

Derived classes based on  Windows Server 2003 Computer ( Microsoft.Windows.Server.2003.Computer )
The following classes are derived from  Windows Server 2003 Computer :

Derived classes based on  Windows Server 2008 Computer ( Microsoft.Windows.Server.2008.Computer )
The following classes are derived from  Windows Server 2008 Computer :

DisplayName                                              Name
-----------                                              ----
Windows Server 2008 Core Computer                        Microsoft.Windows.Server.2008.Core.Computer
Windows Server 2008 Full Computer                        Microsoft.Windows.Server.2008.Full.Computer
Windows Server 2008 R2 Computer                          Microsoft.Windows.Server.2008.R2.Computer

Derived classes based on  Virtualization Candidate Computer ( Microsoft.Virtualization.2008.VirtualizationCandidateComputer )
The following classes are derived from  Virtualization Candidate Computer :
```

Tip

Classes are sometimes referred to as object types or targets, depending on where you look in the OpsMgr UI and product documentation. Just remember that no matter which is used, they all have the same meaning in OpsMgr terms. ■

Enumerating Monitored Objects and Relationships

You can use the `GetMonitoringRelationshipClasses()` method to explore the relationships between classes in Operations Manager. Given a target class, this method returns all the relationships for which the target class is either the source or the target. Again, nothing fancy, but this simple function does provide an easy way to enumerate relationships without opening multiple management packs in the MPViewer utility or the Management Pack (MP) Authoring console.

As with enumeration of derived classes, you can extend this function to enumerate all child classes and their relationships *recursively*.

```
function GetRelationships {
  param ($Class)
    (Get-MonitoringClass | -Name $Class).GetMonitoringRelationshipClasses()| `
      Format-List DisplayName,Description
    #call the function specifying target class in quotes


}
GetRelationships "Microsoft.SQLServer.DBEngine" | Select-Object DisplayName,Name
```

Figure 16-6 displays the output of the sample, enumerating classes of the `Microsoft.Windows.Computer` (Windows Computer) class.

FIGURE 16-6

Enumeration of class relationships

```
GetRelationships "Microsoft.SQLServer.DBEngine"


DisplayName : SQL Database Engine Hosts SQL Database
Description :

DisplayName : Instance Group Contains All Instances of SQL DBEngine
Description :
```

Windows PowerShell and the Command Notification Channel

OpsMgr notification capabilities include a command notification channel that can be used to launch batch files, scripts, and command-line utilities. Though this is one of the less commonly used notification channels, it can be very useful when email notification is not your desired delivery format. This section explores how to use the command channel to extend the off-the-shelf notification functionality in OpsMgr using Windows PowerShell in the command notification channel.

Performing Simple Event and Log File Creation from the Command Channel

For test environments or auditing purposes, you can use Windows PowerShell in the OpsMgr command channel to log alert details of your choosing to a text file — a notification log of sorts. The script in Listing 16-5 logs key details of an OpsMgr alert to a text file when called from a command notification channel. You can download this script from the book's website.

LISTING 16-5

NotificationEventLog.ps1 Script

```
#Verify log file exists...if not, create it
if(Test-Path -Path c:\scripts\mylog.txt -PathType Leaf)
{
    "File c:\scripts\mylog.txt already exists."
}
else
{
  $file = New-Item -ItemType file 'c:\scripts\mylog.txt'

  $info = "----Alert generated at $DateTime----"
  $info += "$AlertName`n$AlertDesc`n$MngdEntity`n$Severity "
  $info += "----End of alert----"

  $info | Out-File -FilePath $file
}
```

Implementing this script as part of an OpsMgr command notification channel and subscription requires completing the following configuration tasks:

1. Download this script from the book's website and save to a directory on the RMS (`c:\scripts` is used in this example) as PoshLog.ps1.

2. Configure a command notification channel in the OpsMgr Operations console.

3. Configure a notification subscription that utilizes the command notification channel.

Once you have completed step 1, the command notification subscription should be configured similar to the image in Figure 16-7, using the values shown here.

FIGURE 16-7

Command channel configuration for Windows PowerShell

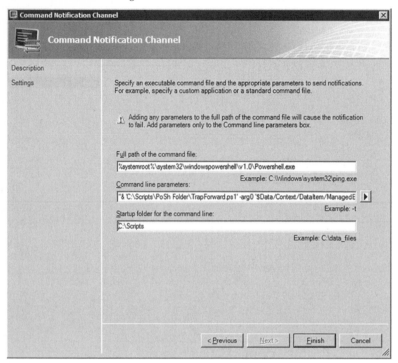

Full path of the command file:

```
c:\windows\system32\windowspowershell\v1.0\powershell.exe
```

Command-line parameters:

```
-Command "& C:\Scripts\PoshLog.ps1" `
-DateTime $Data/Context/DataItem/DataItemCreateTimeLocal$ `
-AlertName $Data/Context/DataItem/AlertName$ `
-AlertDesc $Data/Context/DataItem/AlertDescription$ `
-MngdEntity $Data/Context/DataItem/ManagedEntityFullName$ `
-Severity $Data/Context/DataItem/Severity$ `
```

Startup directory:

```
C:\Scripts
```

Once you have entered these values and saved your changes, configure a notification subscription for the alert sources, resolution states, severities, and priorities of your choice.

Note

For detailed steps on how to create a notification command channel in OpsMgr, see `http://technet`
`.microsoft.com/en-us/library/dd440871.aspx`.

For detailed steps on how to configure an OpsMgr notification subscription, see `http://technet`
`.microsoft.com/en-us/library/dd440889.aspx`. ■

To test your work, create an error condition to trigger an alert on one of the monitored
computers in your test environment.

Forwarding SNMP Traps with Windows PowerShell

The SNMP trap-forwarding functionality present in Microsoft Operations Manager 2005
(MOM) was not carried forward to OpsMgr 2007. Though this was not a widely used
feature, it is one that is definitely missed by more than a few organizations relying on
OpsMgr to deliver alert data to other monitoring and reporting systems.

Fortunately, this problem can be resolved using the command notification channel, a
command-line trap generator (like `trapgen.exe`, available at `http://www.ncomtech.`
`com/trapgen.html`), and Windows PowerShell. The script shown in Listing 16-6 forwards
OpsMgr alert details to the SNMP trap receiver. You can download this script from
`www.wiley.com/go/WindowsPowerShellBible`. You will need to update the IP addresses
of the RMS and remote trap receiver to which traps should be sent.

LISTING 16-6

TrapForward.ps1 Script

```
Param($DateTime, $AlertName, $AlertDesc, $MngdEntity, $Severity )

#==================================================================
#Retrieve the monitoring object
#==================================================================
$object = Get-MonitoringObject -Id $Param0

#==================================================================
#Assign XPath replacements to variables (for later trap construction)
#==================================================================

#Target Trap Catcher (Destination for the trap)
$Param0 = "-s 7 -d 192.168.1.50"

#RMS IP Address (Source of the trap)
$Param1 = "-i 192.168.1.20"

#SNMP Community String
```

continues

LISTING 16-6 *(continued)*

```
$Param2 = "-c public"

#Notification Timestamp
$Param3 = "$DateTime"

#RMS Server Name
$Param4 = "rms.contoso.com"

#Alert Name
$Param6 = "$AlertName"

#Class Name...Full Display Name (ManagedEntity)
$Param7 = "$MngdEntity"

#Alert Description
$Param8 = "$AlertDesc"

#Severity
$Param9 = "$Severity"

#==================================================
#Construct the trapgen command line and send trap
#==================================================

#The following two lines are actually one single line
$cmdLine = "c:\tools\trapgen.exe $Param1 $Param2 $Param3 `
$Param4 $Param5 $Param6 $Param7 $Param8 $Param9"

#Run TrapGen.exe with parameters created above
Invoke-Expression -Command $cmdLine | Out-Null
```

Implementing this script as part of an OpsMgr command notification channel and subscription requires completing the following configuration tasks:

1. Download this script from the book's website and save to a directory on the RMS (c:\scripts is used in this example) as TrapForward.ps1. Be sure to update the IP addresses of RMS and remote trap receiver as mentioned previously.

2. Copy trapgen.exe to a directory on the RMS (c:\tools is used in this example).

3. Configure a command notification channel in the OpsMgr Operations console.

4. Configure a notification subscription that utilizes the command notification channel, using the following settings:

Full path of the command file:

```
c:\windows\system32\windowspowershell\v1.0\powershell.exe
```

Command-line parameters:

```
-Command "& C:\Scripts\TrapForward.ps1" `
-DateTime $Data/Context/DataItem/DataItemCreateTimeLocal$ `
-AlertName $Data/Context/DataItem/AlertName$ `
-AlertDesc $Data/Context/DataItem/AlertDescription$ `
-MngdEntity $Data/Context/DataItem/ManagedEntityFullName$ `
-Severity $Data/Context/DataItem/Severity$ `
```

Startup directory:

```
C:\Scripts
```

Once you have entered these values and saved your changes, configure a notification subscription for the alert sources, resolution states, severities, and priorities of your choice.

To test your work, create an error condition to trigger an alert on one of the monitored computers in your test environment.

Overrides

Workflows (rules, monitors, overrides, and so on) in OpsMgr can be modified (tuned) through *overrides*. The parameters made available for modification by the management pack author (the overridable parameters) can be modified for a specific object (instance), a group of objects, or all instances of the class targeted by the workflow. Over time, the creation of overrides can make determining the source of the settings tedious for OpsMgr administrators. In the most dynamic OpsMgr environments (such as those of service providers and hosters), the need often arises to create overrides programmatically to keep up with new monitored objects being introduced to the environment. Fortunately, the OpsMgr cmdlets make all of this possible.

Retrieving and Converting Overrides into Readable Reporting Format

When troubleshooting unexpected behavior or an unhealthy environment, OpsMgr administrators may want to see which workflows have overrides applied, and the settings of each. You can retrieve the existing overrides for all management packs in an OpsMgr environment by retrieving all management packs and passing the list to the `Get-Override` cmdlet:

```
Get-ManagementPack | Get-Override
```

With a Where-Object clause, you can target the query to overrides for a specific management pack:

```
Get-ManagementPack -Name 'Microsoft.SQLServer.2008.Monitoring' | `
Get-Override
```

Unfortunately, the `Context` and `ContextInstance` of the override (at minimum) are not clear when overrides are retrieved in this way, making it impossible to determine the target object type and instance to which the override was applied.

If you would like to export all overrides from multiple management packs into a single report including all the details of the override (property, target, value), Windows PowerShell requires a couple of extra steps to match a name to the GUIDs presented in the default output. The sample script in Listing 16-7, written by Daniele Muscetta (Microsoft) and enhanced by MVP Pete Zerger, goes beyond the available cmdlets to retrieve the Display Name of the `Context` and `ContextInstance` to provide a user-friendly report of the overrides present in an OpsMgr environment.

LISTING 16-7

Export Overrides into an Overrides Report

```
#define the path you want to export the CSV files to
$exportpath = "c:\scripts\export\"

#gets all UNSEALED MAnagement PAcks
$mps = Get-ManagementPack | Where-Object {$_.Sealed -eq $false}

#loops thru them
foreach ($mp in $mps)
{
  $mpname = $mp.Name
  Write-Host "Exporting Overrides info for Management Pack: $mpname"

  #array to hold all overrides for this MP
  $MPRows = @()

  #Gets the actual override objects
  $overrides = $mp | Get-Override

  #loops thru those overrides in order to extract information from them
  foreach ($override in $overrides)
  {

      #Prepares an object to hold the result
      $obj = New-Object System.Management.Automation.PSObject

      #clear up variables from previous cycles.
```

```
    $overrideName = $null
    $overrideProperty = $null
    $overrideValue = $null
    $overrideContext = $null
    $overrideContextInstance = $null
    $overrideRuleMonitor = $null

    # give proper values to variables for this cycle for output.
    $name = $mp.Name
    $overrideName = $override.Name
    $overrideProperty = $override.Property
    $overrideValue = $override.Value
    trap { $overrideContext = ""; continue } $overrideContext = `
    $override.Context.GetElement().DisplayName
      trap {$overrideContextInstance=""; continue} $overrideContextInstance `
      = (Get-MonitoringObject -Id $override.ContextInstance).DisplayName

    if ($override.Monitor -ne $null){
        $overrideRuleMonitor = $override.Monitor.GetElement().DisplayName
    } elseif ($override.Discovery -ne $null){
        $overrideRuleMonitor = $override.Discovery.GetElement().DisplayName
    } else {
        $overrideRuleMonitor = $override.Rule.GetElement().DisplayName
    }

    #fills the current object with those properties
    #$obj = $obj | Add-Member -MemberType NoteProperty `
- Name overrideName - Value $overrideName - PassThru
    $obj = $obj | Add-Member -MemberType NoteProperty `
- Name overrideProperty - Value $overrideProperty - PassThru
    $obj = $obj | Add-Member -MemberType NoteProperty `
- Name overrideValue - Value $overrideValue - PassThru
    $obj = $obj | Add-Member -MemberType NoteProperty `
- Name overrideContext - Value $overrideContext - PassThru
    $obj = $obj | Add-Member -MemberType NoteProperty `
- Name overrideContextInstance - Value $overrideContextInstance - PassThru
    $obj = $obj | Add-Member -MemberType NoteProperty `
- Name overrideRuleMonitor - Value $overrideRuleMonitor - PassThru
    $obj = $obj | Add-Member -MemberType NoteProperty `
- Name MPName - Value $name - PassThru
    $obj = $obj | Add-Member -MemberType NoteProperty `
- Name overrideName - Value $overrideName - PassThru


    #adds this current override to the array
    $MPRows = $MPRows + $obj
}

#Store up the overrides for all packs to a single variable
```

continues

LISTING 16-7 (continued)

```
    $MPRpt = $MPRpt + $MPRows

}
    #exports cumulative list of overrides to a single CSV

    $filename = $exportpath + "overrides.csv"
    $MPRpt | Export-CSV -path $filename -NoTypeInformation
```

Creating Overrides Programmatically

In large and active environments, you may want to create overrides programmatically when a rule is found to be causing large numbers of alerts. The sample script in Listing 16-8 creates an override that sets the Enabled property of the matching rule name assigned to the $rule variable to False (which disables the rule). By specifying an unsealed management pack in the $mp variable, you can save the override to a dedicated overrides management pack rather than to the Default Management Pack.

Download this script from the book's website and run from an Operations Manager command shell prompt.

LISTING 16-8

Rule Override Creation Script

```
$SourceMP = Get-ManagementPack | Where-Object { $_.Name -match `
'Microsoft.SQLServer.2008.Monitoring' }
$mp = Get- ManagementPack | Where-Object {$_.FriendlyName -match 'SQL 2008 `
Overrides' }
#This does successfully retrieve the MP.
$rule = Get-Rule -ManagementPack $SourceMP | Where-Object { $_.Name -match `
'Microsoft.SQLServer.2008.NumberDeadlocksPerSecond' }
$Target = Get-MonitoringClass | Where-Object { $_.Name -match `
'Microsoft.SQLServer.2008.DBEngine' }

$override = New-Object `
Microsoft.EnterpriseManagement.Configuration.Management`
PackRulePropertyOverride($mp,'DeadlockOverride')

# Casting some of the generic types needed by the monitor override properties `
using reflection (::op_Implicit())

$Rule = [Microsoft.EnterpriseManagement.Configuration.ManagementPackElement
```

```
Reference``1[Microsoft.EnterpriseManagement.Configuration.ManagementPackRu
le]]::op_Implicit($Rule);

$override.Rule = $Rule
$Override.Property = 'Enabled'
$override.Value = 'false'
$override.Context = $Target
$override.DisplayName = 'Disable deadlock monitoring for SQL 2008'
$mp.Verify()
$mp.AcceptChanges()
```

Notifications

You can do some reporting and bulk processing on notification subscriptions with relative ease by using the command shell. With the `Get-Notification` cmdlet, reporting on notification subscription configuration is possible, and with `Enable-Notification` and `Disable-Notification`, you can enable or disable notification subscriptions without launching the Operations console.

Enabling and Disabling Notifications

When maintenance operations are being undertaken for your network infrastructure, you may want to disable the notification subscriptions used to send email notifications of alert conditions to avoid filling your Inbox with non-actionable alerts. To disable all enabled notification subscriptions, use the following code:

```
Get-NotificationSubscription | Where-Object {$_.Enabled -eq $true} |
Disable-NotificationSubscription
```

When the event is complete and you are ready re-enable notification, you can do so with the `Enable-NotificationSubscription` cmdlet. To enable all disabled notification subscriptions, use the following code (which looks very similar to the code used to disable the subscriptions):

```
Get-NotificationSubscription | Where-Object {$_.Enabled -eq $false} |
Enable-NotificationSubscription
```

Working with Notification Recipients

With the `Get-NotificationSubscription` cmdlet, you can specify the recipients on a notification subscription:

```
Get- NotificationSubscription | Format-List DisplayName,`
@{Label="Criteria";Expression={$_.Configuration.Criteria}}
```

Note

You can also use Windows PowerShell to update the recipients in an OpsMgr notification subscription, as shown in the blog post "Operations Manager - Set email address for a notification device" at `http://cornasdf.blogspot.com/2009/06/operations-manager-set-email-address.html`. ∎

Monitoring Scripts in Windows PowerShell

OpsMgr uses modules in management packs to define workflows. Originally, with the release of OpsMgr 2007 R2, Microsoft introduced a new module that made using Windows PowerShell much more efficient. The new efficiency comes from the fact that a single Windows PowerShell instance is opened on the agent and is shared by all monitored scripts, rather than a unique instance being launched for each. Since the introduction of this feature, the use of Windows PowerShell for monitoring functions (rather than just administration) in OpsMgr management packs has become commonplace.

You can create custom two-state and three-state monitors for OpsMgr in Windows PowerShell to support a variety of custom monitoring scenarios where no native management pack exists. The sample script in Listing 16-9 verifies availability of a remote FTP site. Replace the username and password with a read-only user account in order to safely implement this script for a live site.

LISTING 16-9

Two-State FTP Site Availability Monitor Script

```
#Instantiate OpsMgr Scripting API and create a Property Bag
$api = New-Object -ComObject 'MOM.ScriptAPI'
$bag = $api.CreatePropertyBag()

# Get the object used to communicate with the server.
$Request = [System.Net.WebRequest]::Create("ftp://ftp.mydomain.com/mydir/")
$Request.Method = [System.Net.WebRequestMethods+Ftp]::ListDirectoryDetails

# This example assumes the FTP site uses anonymous logon.
# Username/password not real
$Request.Credentials = New-Object System.Net.NetworkCredential "myuser",`
"MyPassword"

$Response = $Request.GetResponse()
$ResponseStream = $Response.GetResponseStream()

# Read and display the text in the file
$Reader = New-Object System.Io.StreamReader $Responsestream
```

```
[System.Console]::Writeline($Reader.ReadToEnd())

# Display Status
"Download Complete, status:"
$response.StatusDescription

if ($response.StatusDescription -match '226'){
  #Write-Host "We hit a TRUE match"
  $bag.AddValue("State","GOOD")
  #Submit Property Bag
  $bag
    }
else {
  #If not exists STATE=BAD
  #Write-Host "We hit a False match"
  $bag.AddValue("State","BAD")

  #Submit Property Bag
  $bag
  }

# Close Reader and Response objects
$Reader.Close()
$Response.Close()
```

Note

A few management pack authoring tutorials on the Internet demonstrate how to incorporate a Windows PowerShell-based monitoring script into a unit monitor using the OpsMgr Management Pack Authoring Console. The two most comprehensive are shown here.

For detailed steps on how to implement a two-state unit monitor for OpsMgr containing a Windows PowerShell script, see "How to create a monitor based on a Windows PowerShell script" on the Microsoft TechNet website at `http://technet.microsoft.com/en-us/library/ff381420.aspx`.

OpsMgr MVP Stefan Koell wrote a four-part series on how to implement a two-state unit monitor in Windows PowerShell at `www.systemcentercentral.com/BlogDetails/tabid/143/IndexId/50085/Default.aspx`. ∎

Sample OpsMgr Scripts and Other Community Resources

A handful of sites on the Internet have sizable collections of Windows PowerShell scripts for OpsMgr, as well as sources of free assistance as you write and customize scripts for your own environment.

Where to Find and Share Samples on the Web

By using the examples of experienced PowerShell scripters as a starting point, you can reuse and customize existing scripts to suit your specific need. A couple of great sources of Windows PowerShell scripts for OpsMgr are available on the Internet.

The first is the community website System Center Central (`www.systemcentercentral .com`). One of the community members maintains a list of all the OpsMgr-related Windows PowerShell scripts he can find on his "Master collection of PowerShell scripts" page at `www.systemcentercentral.com/BlogDetails/tabid/143/IndexID/60930/Default.aspx`.

You can also find a number of scripts directly from the OpsMgr Product Team at Microsoft, but these are spread out in a couple of different places. Good starting points include the following TechNet blog sites:

- Boris Yanushpolsky's blog at `http://blogs.msdn.com/b/boris_yanushpolsky/`
- Jonathan Almquist's blog at `http://blogs.technet.com/b/jonathanalmquist/`

Finally, the community code repository Poshcode.org has a few scripts under the "SCOM" and "OpsMgr" categories at `www.poshcode.org`.

Good sources for Windows PowerShell scripts are popping up all the time, so keep an eye out for new sources on OpsMgr-related blogs and Twitter.

Where to Find Free Support on Authoring Windows PowerShell Scripts for OpsMgr

Sometimes, sample scripts just are not enough and you need an expert. When you need a helping hand, a number of great support forums exist where you can get free help with your script authoring efforts. The most active locations for discussions specific to OpsMgr 2007 R2 are shown here.

The Extensibility forum on the OpsMgr TechNet Forums is well-tended by OpsMgr scripting experts from Microsoft and the community. You can find it at `http://social.technet .microsoft.com/Forums/en-US/operationsmanagerextensibility/threads`.

You can always find help from the PowerShell TechNet Forums, which is perhaps the most active support forum in the world for Windows PowerShell assistance. You can find it at `http://social.technet.microsoft.com/Forums/en-US/winserverpowershell/ threads`. Be mindful that these scripting experts may not be OpsMgr experts, so be patient when posting here!

Finally, System Center Central (`www.systemcentercentral.com/tabid/60/tag/ Forums+Operations_Manager/Default.aspx`) is a community site well-tended by OpsMgr specialists with advanced Windows PowerShell scripting skills, so you can generally get ample assistance there as well.

Please be mindful of forum etiquette when posting to these sources. Participants are generally supporting the community for free on a best-effort basis, so response time, verbosity, and accuracy of the answers you receive may vary.

Summary

In this chapter, you explored the available OpsMgr cmdlets to automate recurring and bulk administrative tasks in OpsMgr 2007 R2.

You learned how to report on the top alerts in your OpsMgr deployment. You also explored how to parse and update alerts in bulk, with due attention to performance optimization in your Windows PowerShell scripts.

You explored the options for automating maintenance mode in OpsMgr, including maintenance mode for agents, maintenance mode for groups, and even maintenance mode remotely from agent-managed computers.

You learned how to fully automate the discovery of Windows computers and then automate deployment of the OpsMgr agent to discovered computers. You also investigated the options for determining the load distribution of agents in your OpsMgr environment, as well as how to redistribute the load of Windows agents and monitored network devices across multiple management servers.

You worked with Windows PowerShell scripts to explore discovered inventory in your OpsMgr environments to provide greater visibility into the monitored objects and how these objects are related. You then explored how to report on the overrides present in your OpsMgr deployment, as well as how to automate the creation of new overrides using Windows PowerShell.

Finally, you learned how to write monitoring scripts for OpsMgr in Windows PowerShell and where to go for sample scripts and online support when you need a helping hand.

Next, you learn to leverage Windows PowerShell in your Microsoft Deployment Toolkit 2010 (MDT) task sequences to enhance your deployment capabilities.

Managing Microsoft Deployment Toolkit 2010

M icrosoft Deployment Toolkit (MDT) is Microsoft's solution for automating the delivery of Windows 7 and Windows Server 2008 R2. MDT is actually a "Solution Accelerator" from Microsoft. Solution Accelerators are tools that are provided by Microsoft for free and are fully supported. This chapter covers MDT 2010 Update 1.

IN THIS CHAPTER

Creating deployment shares

Adding applications

Adding drivers

Creating task sequences

Generating media

Installing and Using the Cmdlets

The MDT PowerShell snap-in is installed as part of the overall MDT installation and does not require any special installation procedure. The snap-in is certified to work with both Windows PowerShell and Windows PowerShell V2.

To enable remote management, install MDT on a workstation to install the snap-in. You can then add the remote Deployment Share by specifying the UNC path to the remote Deployment Share folder.

MDT does not create a shortcut for launching the snap-in, so you will need to load it manually:

```
Add-PSSnapIn -Name Microsoft.BDD.PSSnapIn
```

If you use the snap-in often, you can create a console file to load it from a shortcut, or you can add it to your profile to have it always loaded.

Cross-Reference

Read more about adding items to your profile in "Customizing Windows PowerShell with Profiles" in Chapter 1, "Introduction to Windows PowerShell." ■

Exploring the MDT Windows PowerShell Provider

The MDT snap-in includes a Windows PowerShell provider called `MDTProvider` that is used to present the Deployment Share as a Windows PowerShell drive. It enables you to navigate the Deployment Share as you would a file system or registry. The following code snippet demonstrates the ability to change to the Applications directory and list the contents as you would a folder on your file system.

```
Set-Location DS001:\
Get-ChildItem

Name
----
Applications
Operating Systems
Out-of-Box Drivers
Packages
Task Sequences
Selection Profiles
Linked Deployment Shares
Media

Set-Location .\Applications
Get-ChildItem

Name
----
Microsoft Security Essentials 2.0.657.0
```

Each object in this Provider has its own corresponding properties. Just as a file has a `length` property that indicates its size, an MDT application has a `version` property that indicates the version of the software. The properties are covered in more detail in other chapters, but it is important to remember that they exist, because in certain cases, the Provider is the only way to change the properties.

Using the GUI to Create Your Scripts

The Deployment Workbench, MDT's graphical console, has an excellent facility built into it that helps you develop automated solutions against MDT. At the end of most of the wizards, there will be a button labeled View Script. If you click this button, Notepad opens with the actual Windows PowerShell script needed to duplicate the action you just completed with the wizard. You can use this to duplicate the configuration on another system or use it as a base to explore different options.

Creating and Populating the Deployment Share

In MDT, the *deployment share* is the physical repository for all the media and configuration information for the deployment environment. The deployment share is a folder, usually on a server, that MDT and clients use to deploy operating systems and software.

Initializing the Deployment Share

In Listing 17-1, you create the folder in which you are going to store the Deployment Share. Then, you use New-PSDrive to create the Deployment Share using the MDTProvider. Instead of a specialized cmdlet for creating a Deployment Share, the developers of the cmdlets chose to use the Provider framework.

LISTING 17-1

Creating the Deployment Share

```
Mkdir "S:\Shared\MDTDeploymentShare"
New-PSDrive -Name "DS001" `
  -PSProvider "MDTProvider" `
  -Root "S:\Shared\MDTDeploymentShare" `
  -Description "MDT Deployment Share" `
  -NetworkPath "\\Procyon\MDTDeploymentShare$" `
  -Verbose |
  Add-MDTPersistentDrive -Verbose
```

New-PSDrive is the built-in command for creating Windows PowerShell drives. Normally, this command just creates a shortcut to a file system or a registry location. In this case, it not only creates a shortcut to a Deployment Share, but it also creates the share. When you call New-PSDrive specifying the PSProvider parameter with MDTProvider and there is not an existing Deployment Share at that location, it proceeds with the code to initialize the Deployment Share. This includes setting up the basic structure of the Deployment Share.

The NetworkPath parameter is a custom parameter that allows you to specify the share path that clients will use to connect to the Deployment Share. The cmdlet creates this network share so that it is available to clients. To connect to a remote Deployment Share, simply use the UNC path to the share.

Note

The NetworkPath parameter is a custom parameter that is specific to the MDT Provider type. It is not discoverable with Get-Help or Get-Command. ■

The Add-MDTPersistentDrive cmdlet registers the new Deployment Share into your profile so that it is automatically reopened either by the Deployment Workbench or by issuing the `Restore-MDTPersistentDrive` cmdlet in Windows PowerShell. When you reopen Windows PowerShell at a later time, you can simply load the module and execute `Restore-MDTPersistentDrive` to restore all of the Deployment Shares that you had opened. To permanently remove a Deployment Share so that it should not be opened again, the `Remove-MDTPersistentDrive` is the command you want.

Creating the MDT Database

MDT also includes the ability to utilize a database for configuration settings that can be used in various deployment scenarios. The database is essentially a centralized version of the `CustomSettings.ini` file used to store configuration information.

Before creating the database, you have to create a share on your SQL Server system. This is required to make a Windows integrated security connection from Windows PE. The Windows PE image first needs to establish a secure connection to the server and uses this share access to accomplish that.

To create the database, you use the `New-MDTDatabase` cmdlet, specifying the SQL Server, database, and share name. Other parameters can be used to specify connection details such as port and connection method. The relevant parameters are as follows:

- **Path:** Path to the deployment share.
- **SQLServer:** Name of the SQL Server.
- **Instance:** Name of the SQL Server instance.
- **Port:** The TCP/IP port number for the SQL Server instance.
- **NetLib:** The network library that is used for communication. "DBNMPNTW" for Named Pipes and "DBMSSOCN" for TCP/IP Sockets.
- **Database:** The name of the database that will be created.
- **SQLShare:** The file share that will be used for authentication by Windows PE.

The following command shows an example of the cmdlet accepting some of the default values for parameters, which are not specified:

```
New-MDTDatabase -Path "DS001:\" `
  -SQLServer SQLServer `
  -Database MDT `
  -SQLShare MDTShare
```

Importing Operating Systems

What good would a deployment solution be if you didn't have any operating systems to deploy? Your next step is to add the operating systems to the Deployment Share. In Listing 17-2, you see two different types of operating systems that can be imported into your Deployment Share. Although not shown in this example, you can also import images from a Windows

Deployment Services (WDS) server. The first line of the listing imports the Windows 2008 R2 operating system from the expanded DVD source files, and the second example imports a custom Windows 7 image file in the Windows Imaging Format (WIM).

Note

When you import the Windows 7 and Windows 2008 R2 operating systems, you will notice numerous entries in the Operating Systems tab in the Deployment Workbench. This is because Microsoft puts every edition of a product on a single DVD. When you import the operating systems, you will have an entry for each edition. ■

LISTING 17-2

Adding Operating Systems

```
Import-MDTOperatingSystem -Path "DS001:\Operating Systems" `
  -SourcePath "S:\Software\Operating Systems\2008R2" `
  -DestinationFolder "Windows Server 2008 R2" `
  -Verbose
Import-MDTOperatingSystem -Path "DS001:\Operating Systems" `
  -SourceFile "S:\Software\Operating Systems\custom.wim" `
  -DestinationFolder "Windows 7 x64 (Custom)" `
  -Verbose
```

For this cmdlet, you should note the following relevant parameters:

- **Path:** Path to the deployment share
- **SourcePath:** Path to the operating system source files
- **DestinationFolder:** Name of the folder that should be created in the Deployment Share for the operating system
- **Move:** Switch indicating that the files should be moved instead of copied

When you execute this cmdlet, MDT pulls the operating system files and extracts and copies them to the Deployment Share. During this process, you will see a progress bar indicating the current status of the task.

The operating system entries in the Provider do not contain any properties you can set, but you can retrieve properties of the operating systems like Size, Build, and Language for reporting.

Importing Device Drivers

After importing the operating systems, you now need to import drivers to make all of that hardware work properly. Listing 17-3 shows how to add drivers to the Deployment Share. This listing adds the drivers from our company's driver repository.

LISTING 17-3

Adding Drivers

```
Mkdir "DS001:\Out-of-Box Drivers\Laptops"
Import-MDTDriver -Path "DS001:\Out-of-Box Drivers\Laptops" `
  -SourcePath "\\Server\Drivers\" -Verbose
```

MDT starts at the specified path and navigates through it and every child folder, searching for drivers, including ones located within .cab files. It then imports each driver into the Deployment Share. This saves time because you don't have to add each driver individually. MDT detects the driver type and what hardware it is applicable to.

Although you could easily add all drivers into a single folder, that could end up unwieldy. By separating the drivers into manageable folders, you can separate the drivers, which will be immensely helpful when you need to create media and limit the driver detection to speed up the build process. You could even create targeted driver folders that only contain drivers for targeted hardware platforms.

The Driver entries do not contain any settable properties, but you can retrieve properties of the drivers like Manufacturer, Version, Platform, and Plug-And-Play IDs.

Importing Applications

In MDT, there are three basic types of applications that are available to your deployed operating systems, with source files, without source files, and bundles. Each of these types is explored within this section, and you learn how to use Windows PowerShell to add them to your deployment share.

With Source Files

Now, you will add the applications. For this step, you use the Import-MDTApplication cmdlet. In Listing 17-4, you add the Microsoft Security Essentials antivirus software. For the cmdlet, you specify the information identifying the software as well as the command line to install the software and where to get the source files from. The DestinationFolder indicates where on the disk the package will exist. The Path is what node the application will exist in within the Deployment Workbench.

The relevant parameters for this example are:

- **Path:** Path to the deployment share.
- **Enable:** Whether the application is available to deployment wizards.
- **Name:** Name of the application.
- **ShortName:** Name of the folder in which the application resides.
- **Version:** Version number of the application.
- **Publisher:** Publisher of the application.

- **Language:** Language of the application.

- **CommandLine:** The complete command line that is used to install the application.

- **WorkingDirectory:** The relative directory to perform the installation from.

- **ApplicationSourcePath:** The folder containing the source files for the application you are importing.

- **DestinationFolder:** This is the physical folder on the file system where the source files should be placed. This is not the same as what is shown in the Deployment Share.

LISTING 17-4

Adding Software with Source Files

```
$MDTApplication = @{
  Path = "DS001:\Applications"
  Enable = "True"
  Name = "Microsoft Security Essentials 2.0.657.0"
  ShortName = "Microsoft Security Essentials"
  Version = "2.0.657.0"
  Publisher = "Microsoft"
  CommandLine = "mseinstall.exe /s /runwgacheck"
  WorkingDirectory = ".\Applications\Microsoft Security Essentials 2.0.657.0"
  ApplicationSourcePath = "\\DFS\Share\Microsoft\Security Essentials"
  DestinationFolder = "Microsoft Microsoft Security Essentials 2.0.657.0"
  Verbose = $True
}
Import-MDTApplication @MDTApplication
```

The interesting thing to note with this example is that some of these properties such as Version, Publisher, and Language are not actually parameters of the cmdlet. They are the properties of the application object itself as demonstrated in the following code:

```
Get-ItemProperty '.\Microsoft Microsoft Security Essentials 2.0.657.0'
```

```
PSPath                 : Microsoft.BDD.PSSnapIn\MDTProvider::DS001:\Applications\
  Microsoft Microsoft Security Essentials 2.0.657.0
PSParentPath           : Microsoft.BDD.PSSnapIn\MDTProvider::DS001:\Applications
PSChildName            : Microsoft Microsoft Security Essentials 2.0.657.0
PSDrive                : DS001
PSProvider             : Microsoft.BDD.PSSnapIn\MDTProvider
guid                   : {3d569334-a0e5-4b9b-84a4-1fa1c952f4fc}
hide                   : False
enable                 : True
Comments               :
CreatedTime            : 1/17/2011 10:20:42 PM
CreatedBy              : MILKYWAY\Meson
LastModifiedTime       : 1/22/2011 12:48:08 PM
```

```
LastModifiedBy      : MILKYWAY\Meson
DisplayName         : Microsoft Security Essentials
ShortName           : Microsoft Security Essentials
Version             : 2.0.657.0_biteme
Publisher           : Microsoft
Language            :
Source              : .\Applications\Microsoft Microsoft Security Essential
CommandLine         : mseinstall.exe /s /runwgacheck
WorkingDirectory    : .\Applications\Microsoft Security Essentials 2.0.657
UninstallKey        :
Reboot              : True
SupportedPlatform   : {}
Dependency          : {}
```

To modify the parameters after creation, you use `Set-ItemProperty` like this:

```
Set-ItemProperty -Path ".\Microsoft Microsoft Security Essentials 2.0.657.0" `
  -Name Version `
  -Value "2.0.657.01"
```

In this example, you set the `Version` property of the application object.

Without Source Files

If you maintain a central storage repository and don't want to copy all of your files into the Deployment Share, you can add the link to the software without actually copying the software. The difference between Listing 17-5 and Listing 17-4 is the addition of the `NoSource` parameter. This tells MDT not to copy the software and to leave it in its current location.

LISTING 17-5

Adding Software Without Source Files

```
$MDTApplication = @{
  Import = $True
  MDTApplication = $True
  Path = "DS001:\Applications\Required"
  Enable = $true
  Name = "Citrix ICA Client"
  ShortName = "ICA Client"
  Version = "12.0"
  Publisher = "Citrix"
  Language = "English"
  CommandLine = "\\DFS\Share\Citrix\CitrixOnlinePluginWeb.exe /silent"
  WorkingDirectory = ""\\DFS\Share\Citrix"
  NoSource = $true
  Verbose = $true
}
import-MDTApplication @MDTApplication
```

Caution

If you add the software without copying the source files, you must guarantee that the account used for the installation has the required permissions to access the software. ∎

Bundles

The third application type that can be added is a bundle. Bundles are not actually software that is installed on a system, but merely a collection of software. For example, Listing 17-6 creates a bundle that represents all of the required software packages for your environment. Envision this as all the software that must be loaded on each and every computer in your environment. You could add each individual component, but it is much easier to add a single bundle.

Adding a Bundle

```
Import-MDTApplication -Name "Required Software" `
  -ShortName Required `
  -Bundle `
  -Dependency "{3d569334-a0e5-4b9b-84a4-1fa1c952f4fc}"
```

Dependency indicates which software in the deployment share is contained in the bundle. In this case, the value listed here is the GUID of the Microsoft Security Essentials software that added to the Deployment Share in Listing 17-4. You could just as easily have used a script to dynamically populate the GUID(s).

Creating Task Sequences

Now, you have all of the components required to deploy your operating system in your MDT environment. You just need to give it the instructions so that everything can be connected. You do this with Task Sequences. *Task Sequences* are the steps or instructions for deploying the operating systems and applications, and performing whatever custom scripts are needed.

In Listing 17-7 you create a Task Sequence for deploying a Windows 7 operating system. You specify the required parameters for the sequence, including the operating system.

Creating a Task Sequence

```
$MDTTaskSequence = @{
Path = "DS001:\Task Sequences"
Name = "Windows 7 Ultimate Base Build"
Template = "Client.xml"
Comments = ""
ID = "Win7_Build"
```

continues

LISTING 17-7 *(continued)*

```
Version = "1.0"
OperatingSystemPath = "DS001:\Operating Systems\↵
  Windows 7 ULTIMATE in Windows 7 x64 install.wim"
FullName = "Windows User"
OrgName = "Windows Org"
HomePage = "about:blank"
ProductKey = "XXXXX-XXXXX-XXXXX-XXXXX-XXXXX"
AdminPassword = "password"
Verbose = $true
}
Import-MDTTaskSequence @MDTTaskSequence
```

The template field is used to specify the deployment template for the task sequence. Templates are XML files that describe all of the steps required to complete the task sequence. Some templates are included with the product and are described in Table 17-1.

TABLE 17-1

Task Sequence Template

Name	File	Description
Sysprep and Capture	CaptureOnly.xml	Captures only an image of the reference computer
Standard Client Task Sequence	Client.xml	Creates the default task sequence for deploying operating system images to client computers, including desktop and portable computers
Standard Client Replace Task Sequence	ClientReplace.xml	Backs up the system entirely, backs up the user state, and wipes the disk
Custom Task Sequence	Custom.xml	Creates a customized task sequence that does not install an operating system
Standard Server Task Sequence	Server.xml	Creates the default task sequence for deploying operating system images to server computers
Litetouch OEM Task Sequence	LTIOEM.xml	Preloads operating system images on computers in a staging environment prior to deploying the target computers in the production environment (typically by a computer OEM)
Post OS Installation Task Sequence	StateRestore.xml	Performs installation tasks after the operating system has been deployed to the target computer

Most of these templates can be used as is for system deployment. However, as you progress, you will want to define custom templates to perform such tasks as installing software. If you use any of the provided templates, you only need to specify the filename to the `Template` property. For custom templates, you will need to specify the full path to the template file.

Managing the Deployment Share

Now that you have created the deployment share and have added operating systems and applications, you need to be able to perform maintenance on your deployment share.

Configuring the Deployment Share

Once you have created your Deployment Share, you then need to configure it. If you have been looking around, you might have noticed that there is no cmdlet for configuring the Deployment Share, or any component for that matter. This is where the MDT custom Windows PowerShell Provider comes in.

For each component in the MDT Deployment Share, custom properties are exposed via the Windows PowerShell Provider. For example, to see all of the Deployment Share properties, execute:

```
Get-ItemProperty DS001:\
```

When you execute the command, you will get a listing similar to Figure 17-1.

FIGURE 17-1

Deployment share properties

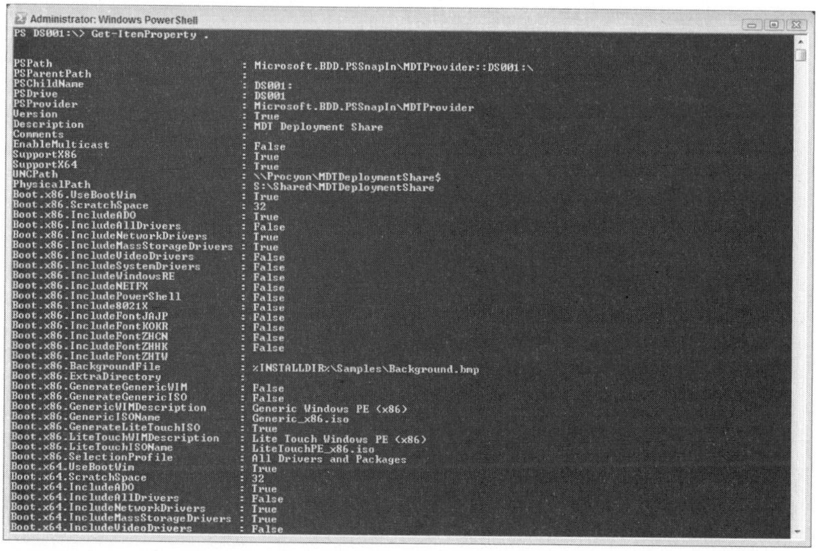

Each property listed is associated with the Deployment Share and corresponds to a property that is accessible from the Deployment Toolkit. For example, there is a property, Boot.x86 .BackgroundFile, which corresponds to the image that is used for the background in the Windows PE image. Your company wants to use a customized image instead of the default image. You can simply use the following command to make the change:

```
Set-ItemProperty -Path DS001:\ `
  -Name Boot.x86.BackgroundFile `
  -Value "\\Server\Images\Custom.bmp"
```

The change is made immediately; however, you may have to close and reopen the Deployment Toolbox console if you have it open in order for it to recognize the changes. There is also no documentation provided for each property. If you want to know more, you will have to match the property to the corresponding entry in the Deployment Toolbox and then use the help to get the information.

Note

If you receive the message "The MDT Drive is being opened" when you open the drive or try and set a property, make sure you opened the PowerShell console as an administrator. The following code snippet can be used to verify:

```
$User = [Security.Principal.WindowsIdentity]::GetCurrent()
$UserPrincipal = New-Object Security.Principal.WindowsPrincipal $user
$UserPrincipal.IsInRole([Security.Principal.WindowsBuiltinRole]::Administrator) ■
```

Updating the Deployment Share

When you update the deployment tool files, such as those included from the Windows Automated Installation Kit (AIK), you need to update your Deployment Share to include those files. Also, if you tweak any of the Windows PE files, you need to regenerate the boot files. To accomplish this, use the Update-MDTDeploymentShare cmdlet, specifying the Windows PowerShell Provider path to the Deployment Share:

```
Update-MDTDeploymentShare -Path DS001:\
```

Note

The boot media is not created when you create the Deployment Share, so you have to update the Deployment Share at least once before you can deploy any operating systems. ■

Managing Media

Once the deployment share has been created and populated, you need to create the media. The media will contain the bootable image that will build your target systems.

Creating Media

MDT enables you to generate media images that contain all or a subset of the Deployment Share contents so that you can perform stand-alone deployments from removable media when access to the Deployment Share does not exist or is very poor.

The first step is to create the media entry in the Deployment Share as demonstrated in Listing 17-8. The relevant parameters for this example are:

- **Path:** The location within the Deployment Share's logical structure.
- **Name:** Name you want to give to your media location.
- **SelectionProfile:** The content you want copied to the media when you generate. Possible values are Everything, Nothing, Sample, All Packages, All Drivers, All Drivers and Packages.
- **SupportX86:** Whether or not you want to generate 32-bit boot image.
- **SupportX64:** Whether or not you want to generate 64-bit boot image.
- **GenerateISO:** Whether or not you want to generate the boot ISO. If you didn't make any changes that need to be updated, excluding this step can shorten the update process.
- **ISOName:** If you chose to generate the ISO, this is the name that you want given to the ISO.

LISTING 17-8

Creating the Deployment Media

```
$item = @{
Path = "DS001:\Media"
Name = "MEDIA001"
Comments = ""
Root = "S:\Media"
SelectionProfile = "Everything"
SupportX86 = "True"
SupportX64 = "True"
GenerateISO = "True"
ISOName = "LiteTouchMedia.iso"
Verbose = $True
}
New-Item @item
```

Generating Media

When you "create media," the boot images aren't actually created. You are essentially just creating a record of the media location and its properties in the deployment share as well as creating a blank folder structure. To actually generate the media, you need to perform another step:

```
Update-MDTMedia -Path "DS001:\Media\Media001"
```

`Update-MDTMedia` performs the work of copying all of the data and generating boot images as described when you created the media. Once you complete this step, the media is ready to be burned to removable media.

When you add applications, drivers, or any other content to your Deployment Share, you are going to want to update your media to make sure those updates get pushed out. The following line iterates through all of the media in the Deployment Share and updates each of the media locations:

```
Get-ChildItem -Path DS001:\Media |
    ForEach-Object { Update-MDTMedia -Path DS001:\Media\$($_.Name) }
```

Depending on your environment, this is probably a good line to add to your scripts whenever you update the Deployment Share so that you can be assured that at least the media share is up-to-date. You still have to burn new media, of course.

Summary

In this chapter, you explored the Microsoft Deployment Toolkit and how to manage it with Windows PowerShell. Starting with creating a deployment share, you progressed through adding operating systems and applications. Finally, you generated the media to build your target systems.

In the next chapter, you learn about the Citrix XenApp 6 platform. XenApp is Citrix's solution for server-based computing and provides enhancement to Microsoft's Remote Desktop Services.

Managing Citrix XenApp 6

The Citrix XenApp product line has undergone many name changes over the years, but at its core, it has remained the same. XenApp is still the leader in the server-based computing arena.

In XenApp 6, the original programming interface (MFCOM) was discarded in favor of Windows PowerShell. Now, any automation performed is done with Windows PowerShell.

IN THIS CHAPTER

Managing administrators

Creating and modifying published resources

Gathering information from users' sessions

Controlling servers

Installing and Using the Cmdlets

Citrix XenApp 6 comes with three snap-ins that are used to manage the product:

- `Citrix.Common.Commands`
- `Citrix.Common.GroupPolicy`
- `Citrix.XenApp.Commands`

`Citrix.Common.Commands` is a generic snap-in that is supplied with several Citrix products. It contains cmdlets for working with various aspects of the environment, but not specifically targeted at XenApp. For example, the majority of the cmdlets interact with the Citrix tracing facility. These cmdlets would be extremely useful if you interact with the diagnostics facility in your environment.

`Citrix.Common.GroupPolicy` is different from the other snap-ins because it does not actually contain any cmdlets at all. Its sole purpose is to provide a Windows PowerShell Provider that represents the Citrix Group Policy configuration. It essentially represents the policies like files and folders on a filesystem.

`Citrix.XenApp.Commands` is the workhorse of the snap-ins. It contains all of the cmdlets for interacting with XenApp and is the snap-in that you will work with the most.

What's New in XenApp 6

XenApp 6 is the latest version of the XenApp product line. XenApp 6, which is available only for Windows Server 2008 R2, is a revolutionary new version. For the first time since the product's inception, MFCOM, the XenApp API, is no longer present. Instead, Windows PowerShell has been promoted to the task of providing an interface for programming against XenApp.

If you have developed custom scripts and code for previous versions of XenApp, you have become all too familiar with MFCOM. For those who haven't, MFCOM or MetaFrame COM is a COM-based API for interacting with XenApp. It has done its job of providing methods for automating XenApp components. But it required the use of COM objects, wasn't very intuitive, and required you to deal with interfaces for the different versions.

Beginning natively in XenApp 6 and retroactively for XenApp 5, Citrix introduced Windows PowerShell cmdlets for managing XenApp. In XenApp 6, MFCOM no longer exists, and Windows PowerShell is the official method for managing XenApp components.

Note
You should always download the latest version of the XenApp Windows PowerShell cmdlets from the Citrix Developer network at `http://community.citrix.com/display/xa/XenApp+6+PowerShell+SDK`. ∎

Working with Administrators

In the XenApp environment, three types of administrators exist:

- **Full:** Administrators with full administrative rights over the entire XenApp farm.
- **ViewOnly:** Administrators with read-only rights over the entire XenApp farm.
- **Custom:** Administrators with custom permissions set for individual components of the XenApp farm.

When you add an administrator to the XenApp farm, you make them one of these three types of administrator. `Full` and `ViewOnly` are built-in types that grant a particular right to all components of the XenApp farm. `Custom`, on the other hand, gives you granular control over what actions the administrator can do and on what objects.

Retrieving Administrators

To retrieve the administrators in your XenApp farm, you use the `Get-XAAdministrator` cmdlet. As illustrated in the following code, this cmdlet, executed with no options, lists all the administrators in your farm.

```
Get-XAAdministrator
AdministratorName : MILKYWAY\Meson
AdministratorType : Full
Enabled           : True
FarmPrivileges    :
FolderPrivileges  :


AdministratorName : MILKYWAY\domain users
AdministratorType : ViewOnly
Enabled           : True
FarmPrivileges    :
FolderPrivileges  :


AdministratorName : MILKYWAY\Domain Admins
AdministratorType : Custom
Enabled           : True
FarmPrivileges    : {LogOnConsole}
FolderPrivileges  : {}
```

The privileges are explained later in this chapter, but you can see the three types of administrators. Another useful function of this cmdlet is that you can retrieve the permissions for the currently logged-in user by using the Current parameter. In the following code, execution of this line returns the administrator account for the user running the command. This is useful in determining whether the person running the script has the necessary permissions to perform the tasks defined in the script.

```
Get-XAAdministrator -Current
AdministratorName : MILKYWAY\Meson
AdministratorType : Full
Enabled           :
FarmPrivileges    :
FolderPrivileges  :
```

Adding and Removing Administrators

To add a new administrator, you must use the New-XAAdministrator cmdlet, which accepts the following relevant parameters:

- **AdministratorName:** The name of the administrator that you are adding.
- **AdministratorType:** The type of the administrator. Possible values are Full, ViewOnly, and Custom.
- **Enabled:** Whether the administrator account should be enabled when added.
- **FarmPrivileges:** The farm privileges specified for the administrator account.

Only the AdministratorName is required by the cmdlet. If you just specify the cmdlet with that parameter, it creates a ViewOnly administrator:

```
New-XAAdministrator -AdministratorName "MilkyWay\Domain Users"
```

This command set up the Domain Users group for the domain as administrators with read-only rights to the farm. To create a full administrator, add the `AdministratorType` parameter with the `Full` value:

```
New-XAAdministrator -AdministratorName "MilkyWay\Domain Admins" `
  -AdministratorType Full
```

Now you have an administrator group that is full of administrators of your farm. Privileges are discussed in the "Modifying Privileges" section, but for clarity, I include an example for adding a custom administrator.

For this example, you want to create an administrator that has the ability to log on to the console and view general farm information:

```
New-XAAdministrator -AdministratorName "MilkWay\Domain Users" `
  -AdministratorType Custom `
  -FarmPrivileges ViewFarm, LogOnConsole
```

Removing administrators from a XenApp farm could not be any easier. Executing the `Remove-XAAdministrator` cmdlet with the name of the administrator is all that is needed:

```
Remove-XAAdministrator -AdministratorName "MilkyWay\Domain Users"
```

With this command, you have removed the Domain Users group from the administrators of the farm.

Enabling and Disabling Administrators

There will be some instances when you want to grant and revoke administrator permissions in certain circumstances. For example, you might need to have an administrator account ready for a support organization that can be used only during engagements. To facilitate this type of activity, you can enable and disable administrator accounts.

When you disable an account, you prevent it from being used, but it is still defined so you don't have to redefine it when you need it again. Say that you have a support organization coming in to look at your farm and you need to re-enable their administrator account, which allows them to look at all of your farm details. Use the following line of code:

```
Enable-XAAdministrator "MilkyWay\CitrixSupportOrganization"
```

Now, their account can be utilized to access your farm information. When they are done with the engagement, you need to disable the account so neither they nor anyone else will be able to use it to gain access to your information. Simply call `Disable-XAAdministrator` the same way you called `Enable-XAAdministrator`:

```
Disable-XAAdministrator "MilkyWay\CitrixSupportOrganization"
```

Modifying Privileges

Privileges exist in two forms in XenApp 6. You have farm privileges and folder privileges. *Farm privileges* are privileges whose scope is the entire XenApp farm. *Folder privileges*, however, are privileges that are scoped on certain folders within the XenApp farm.

First, look at farm privileges. Table 18-1 shows the available options for privileges and the corresponding definition. Probably the most important one is the LogOnConsole privilege because your administrator will need that just to open the console to do anything else.

TABLE 18-1

Farm Privilege

Property	Privilege
ViewFarm	View Farm Management
EditZone	Edit Zone Settings
EditConfigurationLog	Edit Configuration Logging Settings
EditFarmOther	Edit All Other Farm Settings
ViewAdmins	View Administrators
LogOnConsole	Log on to the Management Console
LogOnWIConsole	Edit Centrally Configured Web Interface Sites
ViewLoadEvaluators	View Load Evaluators
AssignLoadEvaluators	Assign Load Evaluators
EditLoadEvaluators	Edit Load Evaluators
ViewLoadBalancingPolicies	View Load Balancing Policies
EditLoadBalancingPolicies	Edit Load Balancing Policies
ViewPrinterDrivers	View Printer and Printer Drivers
ReplicatePrinterDrivers	Replicate Printer Drivers

The next type of privilege is folder privileges. These are privileges that are assigned to folders within. They can be assigned to the root of each of three folders — Applications, Servers, and Worker Groups — or they can be applied to subfolders of the respective root folder. Tables 18-2, 18-3, and 18-4 list the privileges for the Applications folder, Servers folder, and Worker Groups folder, respectively.

TABLE 18-2

Applications Folder Privileges

Property	Privilege
ViewApplications	View Published Applications and Content
EditApplications	Publish Applications and Edit Properties
TerminateProcess	Terminate Processes
ViewSessions	View Session Management
ConnectSessions	Connect Sessions
DisconnectSessions	Disconnect Users
LogOffSessions	Log Off Users
ResetSessions	Reset Sessions
SendMessages	Send Messages

TABLE 18-3

Servers Folder Privileges

Property	Privilege
AssignApplicationsToServers	Assign Applications to Servers
ViewServers	View Server Information
EditOtherServerSettings	Edit Other Server Settings
RemoveServer	Move and Remove Servers
TerminateProcess	Terminate Processes
ViewSessions	View Session Management
ConnectSessions	Connect Sessions
DisconnectSessions	Disconnect Users
LogOffSessions	Log Off Users
ResetSessions	Reset Sessions
SendMessages	Send Messages

TABLE 18-4

Worker Groups Folder Privileges

Property	Privilege
ViewWorkerGroups	View Worker Groups
AssignApplicationsToWorkerGroups	Assign Applications to Worker Groups

To illustrate adding privileges, I will use a real-world example. Your organization has a helpdesk and you want to give them the ability to manage user sessions so they can assist users. Listing 18-1 indicates the steps you follow to grant them the necessary rights.

In the first step, you create the administrator account for the Helpdesk Support group, which in this case is the group of users that are in the helpdesk. You may remember from the section on adding administrators that you could specify folder privileges when the account is created. In this example, it is divided into separate statements for clarity.

The second command utilizes Add-XAAdministratorPrivilege to add the ability to log on to the management console. The third command specifies the folder privileges. You could have combined the second and third commands, but they were separated for clarity.

In the third command, you again use the Add-XAAdministratorPrivilege command to add permissions. This time, because you are specifying a folder permission, you must specify a folder path. In this case, you are specifying the Applications folder. For the privileges you are granting the administrator the ability to view sessions, log off users' sessions, reset their sessions, and send messages to users.

LISTING 18-1

Adding Privileges

```
New-XAAdministrator "MilkyWay\HelpDesk Support" -AdministratorType Custom
Add-XAAdministratorPrivilege -AdministratorName "MilkyWay\HelpDesk Support" `
  -FarmPrivileges LogonConsole
Add-XAAdministratorPrivilege -AdministratorName "MilkyWay\HelpDesk Support" `
  -FolderPath "Applications" `
  -FolderPrivileges ViewSessions, LogOffSessions, ResetSessions, SendMessages
```

Note

Folder privileges in XenApp are set up such that they only apply to the folders themselves and not subfolders. In Listing 18-1, you added privileges to the `Applications` folder. However, those privileges would not propagate to child folders. If you add the following code, the privileges will apply to all child folders within the `Applications` folder:

```
$AdminPriv = @{
  AdministratorName = "MilkyWay\HelpDesk Support"
  FolderPrivileges =  "ViewSessions,
                       LogOffSessions,
                       ResetSessions,
                       SendMessages"
}

Get-XAFolder -FolderPath "Applications" -Recurse |  ForEach-Object {
  Add-XAAdministratorPrivilege @AdminPriv  -FolderPath $_
}
```

The privileges will not, however, apply to the `Applications` folder itself, so you still need the statement for the root folder. ∎

Providing Applications

Published applications are the central components to any XenApp farm. Without them, there would be no need for any other component. Three primary types of published applications exist in a XenApp farm:

- Server installed applications
- Content
- Desktops

If you include streamed applications, that adds a couple more Published Application types, but those are beyond the scope of this book.

Retrieving Applications

Retrieving the published applications in your XenApp farm is a very important task, but it is an extremely simple task. Within the Citrix XenApp cmdlets, this is accomplished with the `Get-XAApplication` cmdlet. Simply executing this cmdlet without any parameters returns all details of all the applications in the list. Most of the time, this is way too much information, so you want to retrieve only the properties you want.

```
Get-XAApplication |
    Select-Object DisplayName, Enabled |
    Format-Table -AutoSize
```

This example returns the display name of the application and whether or not it is enabled. You can supply a few options to the `Get-XAApplication` cmdlet to retrieve a subset of applications. Currently, you can specify browser name, folder path, server name, Worker Group, file type name, account, and Load Evaluator name. For other properties, you would use `Select-Object` to filter the results.

Publishing New Applications

To create new published applications of any type, you use the `New-XAApplication` cmdlet. However, each of the different types uses different parameters of the cmdlet so each type is covered in a separate section.

Server Installed Applications

Server installed applications are the published applications that XenApp administrators are most familiar with. In fact, server installed applications are why they are called published applications. Server installed applications are the applications that are installed on the XenApp servers and presented to the users of the farm.

To create a new published application you use `New-XAApplication` with `ApplicationType` specified as `ServerInstalled`. This tells the cmdlet that you are going to create a published application that points to a server installed application. `DisplayName` specifies the name that is displayed for the application. The last required parameter is the `CommandLineExecutable`, which specifies which application to launch. With these parameters specified, you can now create the published application:

```
New-XAApplication -DisplayName "Microsoft Notepad" `
    -ApplicationType ServerInstalled `
    -CommandLineExecutable 'C:\WIndows\System32\notepad.exe'
```

This creates a published application that references Microsoft Notepad. However, this application isn't very useful. You didn't specify where to publish the application from or to whom you want to display the application. Without these items, the published application is disabled. For those options, you use the `ServerNames` and `Accounts` properties:

```
    -ServerNames Server1, Server2 `
    -Accounts "Domain\Domain Users"
```

One last important parameter is `FolderPath`. `FolderPath` indicates in which folder the application should be placed. As you saw earlier, folders are important in assigning privileges, but they also offer much-needed organization to the environment. In this case, you want to place the application into the `Windows Applications` folder:

```
    -FolderPath "Applications\Windows Applications"
```

When you place all of this code together, you end up with Listing 18-2.

LISTING 18-2

Adding a Server Installed Application

```
New-XAApplication -DisplayName "Windows Notepad" `
  -ApplicationType ServerInstalled `
  -CommandLineExecutable 'C:\WIndows\System32\notepad.exe' `
  -ServerNames Server1, Server2 `
  -Accounts "Domain\Domain Users" `
  -FolderPath "Applications\Windows Applications"
```

More than a dozen more parameters are available that allow you to specify everything from the size of the application to audio settings to encryption. If you don't specify these parameters, the application will accept the default setting defined for them.

Note

If you want granular control over each of the settings or want to override the default value for one, check out the help file for New-XAApplication for additional information. ■

Content

Content is not actually an application, but it is content that users access with applications installed on their client workstations. Published content can be documents, websites, or video presentations.

To publish content, you use the New-XAApplication cmdlet, specifying Content as the ApplicationType. For this example, you want to publish a link to your company's intranet site:

```
New-XAApplication -DisplayName "Intranet Website" `
  -ApplicationType Content `
  -ContentAddress "http://intranet.company.com"
  -Accounts "Domain\Domain Users" `
```

You specify the DisplayName and Accounts parameter as you did in the previous example. Unlike the previous example, you don't need to specify ServerNames because nothing is actually launched from any servers. The new parameter in this example is the ContentAddress parameter, which specifies the location of the content you want to publish.

If you want to publish a document to users, you can do so by using a Universal Naming Convention (UNC) path as the ContentAddress.

Desktops

When you want to provide users with a full desktop experience where they can launch their own applications, you create a desktop published application. Listing 18-3 adds a server desktop. In my environment, I always add a published desktop for each server in my farm for administrators.

LISTING 18-3

Creating Published Desktops

```
$ServerName = "Server01"
  New-XAApplication -ApplicationType ServerDesktop `
    -DisplayName "$ServerName Desktop" `
    -FolderPath "Applications/Admin/Desktops" `
    -Description "Admin Desktop for Remote Administration" `
    -ClientFolder "Admin\Desktops" `
    -Accounts "$ServerName\Administrators" `
    -Servernames $Servername
```

By specifying the `ApplicationType` of `ServerDesktop`, you indicate that you are creating a desktop published application. You also specify `DisplayName`, `FolderPath`, `Description`, `Accounts`, and `ServerName`, which you have already seen previously. `ClientFolder` is an option that determines what folder the application is placed in when it is presented to the users.

Modifying Application Properties

You can modify applications with the `Set-XAApplication` cmdlet. It operates very similarly to the `New-XAApplication` cmdlet you saw in the previous section. However, `Set-XAApplication` uses the `BrowserName` to identify which application to modify.

I haven't talked about browser names yet. Browser name is the unique identifier for applications in the XenApp environment. In most cases, it is the same as the display name. However, in cases where the display name is duplicated, the browser name is adjusted so that it is unique. This is most easily demonstrated by duplicating an application.

Importing/Exporting Applications

As a Citrix administrator, there will be many times when you need to back up your applications or move them from one environment to another. With Windows PowerShell, you will not believe how easy it can be. There have been entire applications written for this purpose.

The heart of the solution is based on the `Export-CliXml` and `Import-CliXml` cmdlets, which are a part of the base Windows PowerShell environment. `Export-CliXml` takes a Windows PowerShell object and creates an XML-based representation of that object, which is then saved to an XML file. `Import-CliXml` then takes that XML file and deserializes the XML representation into a Windows PowerShell object. These objects aren't attached to actual physical implementations, so you can't execute the object's methods.

In the following example, you use `Get-XAApplication` to get the list of all applications in your farm. You could easily restrict this list to any subset of applications that you want. You pipe the output of `Get-XAApplication` to `Export-CliXml`, which uses `applications.xml` to store the serialized object:

```
Get-XAApplication | Export-Clixml .\applications.xml
```

Now, you move to your target farm. For this purpose, suppose that you are duplicating your published applications from your production farm to your test farm. You copy the `applications.xml` file to your test farm and then use `Import-Clixml` to deserialize the data into a collection of `Citrix.XenApp.Commands.XAApplication` objects. These objects don't represent any physical entity, but do have all of the properties. By passing them to `New-XAApplication`, you create applications with all of the properties of the previous objects.

```
Import-CliXml .\applications.xml | New-XAApplication
```

Now you have duplicated your published applications on your test farm. But your test farm has its own servers, which are, of course, named differently than your production servers. No problem. You can specify the `ServerNames` property and override the servers from which the applications are published. This will work on any property that the cmdlet supports, such as `Accounts` if you wanted to change who the application was published to.

```
Import-Clixml .\applications.xml | New-XAApplication -ServerNames TestServer
```

Adding and Removing Assigned Accounts

Adding and removing accounts from applications is extremely easy by using the `Add-XAApplicationAccount` and `Remove-XAApplicationAccount` cmdlets, respectively. Each takes the name of the application and the accounts that you want to add or remove.

```
Add-XAApplicationAccount -BrowserName "Windows Notepad" `
  -Accounts "Domain\User"

Remove-XAApplicationAccount -BrowserName "Windows Notepad" `
  -Accounts "Domain\User"
```

Removing and Disabling Applications

To permanently remove an application from a farm, you use the `Remove-XAApplication` cmdlet. It accepts the application's `BrowserName` or you can pass an application object to it.

```
Remove-XAApplication -BrowserName "Windows Notepad"
```

If you just want to disable an application so that users can't utilize it, but don't want to remove it completely, you use `Disable-XAApplication`, specifying the `BrowserName`:

```
Disable-XAApplication -BrowserName "Windows Notepad"
```

Then, when you want to enable it, you use `Enable-XAApplication`:

```
Enable-XAApplication -BrowserName "Windows Notepad"
```

Managing Sessions

Every connection a user creates to a XenApp server results in a session. The XenApp cmdlets allow for the management and thorough reporting of those sessions.

Enumerating Sessions

Now that you have published your applications, you want to know who is using them. For this purpose, you look to the `Get-XASession` cmdlet.

Executing the cmdlet without any options returns all of the sessions in the XenApp farm. Unfortunately, this includes the console sessions as well as any listeners you have configured. Because you only want actual user sessions, you are going to include the `-Farm` switch.

```
Get-XASession -Farm
```

This command returns only actual user-related sessions. The code shows the information returned on one of the sessions in your farm.

```
Get-XASession -Farm

    SessionId             : 3
    SessionName           : ICA-TCP#1
    ServerName            : Atlanta
    AccountName           : Milkyway\Meson
    BrowserName           : Published Desktop
    State                 : Active
    ClientName            : Client
    LogOnTime             : 5/13/2011 9:16:13 AM
    Protocol              : Ica
    VirtualIP             :
    EncryptionLevel       : Basic
    ServerBuffers         :
    ClientIPV4            :
    ClientBuffers         :
    ClientBuildNumber     :
    ColorDepth            : Colors16Bit
    ClientDirectory       :
    ClientProductId       :
    HorizontalResolution  :
    VerticalResolution    :
    ConnectTime           : 5/13/2011 9:16:05 AM
```

```
DisconnectTime             :
LastInputTime              :
CurrentTime                :
ClientCacheLow             :
ClientCacheTiny            :
ClientCacheXms             :
ClientCacheDisk            :
ClientCacheSize            :
ClientCacheMinBitmapSize   :
```

Notice in this example that there are blank entries for some of the properties. This is by design. The Get-XASession cmdlet by default returns all of the properties of the session, but it calculates only some of the values. This is because calculating those properties can be very resource-intensive, especially when you have many sessions. To return those values, you execute the same command with the -Full parameter:

```
Get-XASession -Farm -Full
SessionId                  : 3
SessionName                : ICA-TCP#1
ServerName                 : Atlanta
AccountName                : Milkyway\Meson
BrowserName                : Published Desktop
State                      : Active
ClientName                 : Client
LogOnTime                  : 5/13/2011 9:16:13 AM
Protocol                   : Ica
VirtualIP                  :
EncryptionLevel            : Basic
ServerBuffers              : 0 x 0
ClientIPV4                 : 192.168.1.25
ClientBuffers              : 0 x 0
ClientBuildNumber          : 30
ColorDepth                 : Colors16Bit
ClientDirectory            : C:\PROGRA~2\Citrix\ICACLI~1\
ClientProductId            : 1
HorizontalResolution       : 864
VerticalResolution         : 1536
ConnectTime                : 5/13/2011 9:16:05 AM
DisconnectTime             :
LastInputTime              : 5/13/2011 9:17:11 AM
CurrentTime                : 5/13/2011 9:17:14 AM
ClientCacheLow             : 3145728
ClientCacheTiny            : 32768
ClientCacheXms             : 0
ClientCacheDisk            : 0
ClientCacheSize            : 0
ClientCacheMinBitmapSize   : 0
```

Now you can see all of the values populated. There is a lot of valuable information present about the user's session and client.

If you had to pull all of the sessions every time, you could be wasting a lot of time. This cmdlet has parameters that enable you to specify which records are returned. Currently, you can filter by server name, session ID, browser name, and account. For example, if you wanted to find the sessions that were running Microsoft Word, you could use the following command:

```
Get-XASession -BrowserName "Microsoft Word"
```

Managing Session Processes

Another very powerful cmdlet in the XenApp arsenal is the `Get-XASessionProcess` cmdlet. This cmdlet enables you to retrieve information about the executable the users are running, not just the published applications. The following code shows one process that was returned from the command. As you can see, you can get valuable information about the processes that users are running. With this cmdlet, you have to specify the server name.

```
Get-XASessionProcess -Servername Atlanta
ProcessName            : powershell_ise.exe
ProcessId              : 5164
SessionId              : 0
ServerName             : Atlanta
AccountDisplayName     : Milkyway\Meson
State                  : Unknown
CreationTime           : 5/13/2011 7:59:08 AM
UserTime               : 38704
KernelTime             : 13000
BasePriority           : 8
PeakVirtualSize        : 0
CurrentVirtualSize     : 0
PageFaultCount         : 152877
PeakWorkingSetSize     : 163897344
CurrentWorkingSetSize  : 161873920
PeakPagedPoolQuota     : 570144
CurrentPagedPoolQuota  : 535928
PeakNonPagedPoolQuota  : 50668
PageFileUsage          : 169996288
PrivatePageCount       : 0
PercentCpuLoad         : 2.15
```

These results can be used to monitor your servers and see which processes are consuming large amounts of resources or even track which processes users are running.

Managing Sessions

To disconnect active sessions for a user or group of users, you use the `Disconnect-XASession` cmdlet. Disconnecting users puts their session into a disconnected state, which means that they can reconnect to it at a later time. The following examples demonstrate how you can disconnect users that are using a specified application, users that are logged in to a specified server, or any user or group of users that are passed to the cmdlet:

```
Disconnect-XASession -BrowserName "Microsoft Notepad"
Disconnect-XASession -ServerName "Server1"
Get-XASession -Account "Domain\User" | Disconnect-XASession
```

To reset a session, you use the `Reset-XASession` cmdlet. `Reset-XASession` works exactly the same as `Disconnect-XASession` except that it resets the session. Resetting a session terminates the session so that it is no longer available and a user cannot reconnect to it.

```
Reset-XASession -BrowserName "Microsoft Notepad"
Reset-XASession -ServerName "Server1"
Get-XASession -Account "Domain\User" |
    Reset-XASession
```

Maintaining Servers

The XenApp servers are the workhorses of the XenApp farm. They host and run the applications that users depend on.

Managing Server Logons

When you need to work on one of your XenApp servers, you will need to make sure that no users log on to the server while you are working. You do this by disabling the logons to the server using the `Disable-XAServerLogon` cmdlet. The cmdlet simply takes the name of the server for which you want to disable logons:

```
Disable-XAServerLogon -ServerName TestServer
```

To enable logons, you use the `Enable-XAServerLogon` cmdlet, again specifying the name of the server:

```
Enable-XAServerLogon -ServerName TestServer
```

Note

The problem with disabling access to the servers with this method is that it disables *all* logons. This includes when you try to connect to the server remotely to do the work. A better method that I employ in my production network is to use load-balancing policies.

Create a load-balancing policy that uses a scheduling rule to disallow logins at any part of the day. Then apply that policy to the server, using the method shown in the "Managing Load Evaluators" section later in this chapter. This rule affects only connections that are load-balanced, so you can still remote directly into the server. ■

Getting Server Load

To obtain the numerical load of your servers, you use the `Get-XAServerLoad` cmdlet. Without any parameters, it retrieves the server name and load number for each of your XenApp servers. If you specify a server name, it returns the load only for that specific server.

Managing Load Evaluators

In the XenApp environment, server load is calculated based on a collection of rules. Each rule is evaluated and combined to produce a number in the range of 0 to 10,000 with 0 representing no load and 10,000 representing a full load. When a user launches an application, all servers hosting that application are compared, and the server with the lowest load number receives the connection.

The load evaluator rules can be based on one of the conditions shown in Table 18-5.

TABLE 18-5

XenApp Load Evaluator Rules

Rule	Load Calculation
Application User Load	Based on number of users accessing a specific application
Context Switches	Based on the number of context switches
CPU Utilization	Based on the percentage of CPU utilization
Disk Data I/O	Based on disk data I/O throughput
Disk Operations	Based on the number of disk operations per second
IP Range	Based on the IP address of the client requesting access
Load Throttling	Based on logon operations occurring at time of request
Memory Usage	Based on the available memory
Page Faults	Based on the number of page faults per second
Page Swaps	Based on the number of page swaps per second
Scheduling	Based on the time of the day that the access is being requested
Server User Load	Based on the total number of users on requested server

Getting Load Evaluators

To retrieve load evaluators, you use the `Get-XALoadEvaluator` cmdlet. Without any parameters, you get a listing of all the load evaluators on the system.

```
Get-XALoadEvaluator
```

You can also specify the server name or the browser name to get load evaluators attached to particular servers or applications, respectively.

```
Get-XALoadEvaluator -ServerName MyServer
Get-XALoadEvaluator -BrowserName "Windows Notepad"
```

Creating Load Evaluators

This section does not address every load evaluator type listed in the "Managing Load Evaluators" section. Instead, it addresses the general task of adding load evaluators with a few examples. To find more information about the specific load evaluator rules, consult the Windows PowerShell help file.

When creating new load evaluators, you use the New-XALoadEvaluator cmdlet. After specifying the name and the description of the load evaluator rule, you begin to add the rules. In the following example, you create a load evaluator that allows logins only during business hours. The scheduling rule is different from the rest in that you actually have seven properties that define the rule, one for each day of the week.

```
New-XALoadEvaluator -LoadEvaluatorName "BusinessHours" `
    -Description "Allows logins only during business hours." `
    -SundaySchedule "00:00-00:00" `
    -MondaySchedule "08:00-17:00" `
    -TuesdaySchedule "08:00-17:00" `
    -WednesdaySchedule "08:00-17:00" `
    -ThursdaySchedule "08:00-17:00" `
    -FridaySchedule "08:00-17:00" `
    -SaturdaySchedule "00:00-00:00"
```

In the next example, you create a load evaluator that is an exact duplicate of the Advanced load evaluator that is built into XenApp to illustrate that you can combine any of the rules:

```
New-XALoadEvaluator -LoadEvaluatorName "Copy of Advanced" `
    -Description "Use the Advanced Load Evaluator to limit memory usage,
      CPU utilization, and page swaps on a server for load management."`
    -CPUUtilization 10, 90 `
    -LoadThrottling "High" `
    -MemoryUsage 10, 90 `
    -PageSwaps 0, 100
```

Notice that several of the rules accept two integer values. The first value is the low watermark, which represents no load, and the second value is the high watermark, which represents full load.

Applying Load Evaluators

The load evaluator has been created, and now you need to apply it to your servers. You do this with the Set-XALoadEvaluator cmdlet. To apply it to a list of servers, you can supply the list to the ServerName parameter.

```
Set-XALoadEvaluator  -LoadEvaluatorName "BusinessHours" `
   -ServerName "ATL-1"
```

However, if you want to apply it to a large number of servers, you can just pipe server objects to the cmdlet, which applies the load evaluator to all of the servers in the farm, as shown here:

```
Get-XAServer | Set-XALoadEvaluator -LoadEvaluatorName "Business Hours"
```

Note

Reset-XALoadEvaluator automatically attaches the Default load evaluator to the server(s) specified. I discourage use of the Default load evaluator because it calculates load based only on the number of the users and doesn't take into account what they are doing. If you still want to use the Default load evaluator, I would recommend you still use **Set-XALoadEvaluator** to explicitly change the load evaluator to Default as a clear reminder of your intentions. ■

Changing Server Zones

To change the zone membership of a server, use the Set-XAServerZone cmdlet. The following example changes the Vega-2 server to the Earth Zone:

```
Set-XAServerZone -ServerName Vega-2 -ZoneName Earth
```

Caution

After changing the zone membership of a server, it is important to reboot the server as soon as possible to avoid IMA DataStore corruption. ■

Applying Load-Balancing Policies

Load-balancing policies were added to XenApp to allow administrators to direct users to the least loaded XenApp server hosting published resources based on various filters.

Creating Load-Balancing Policies

Creating a load-balancing policy for XenApp is a multistep operation. The first step involves creating the policy itself using the New-XALoadBalancingPolicy cmdlet. This cmdlet differs from others in that it does not actually do any work; it simply creates a blank policy.

```
$LBPolicy = New-XALoadBalancingPolicy -PolicyName "DRFailover" `
   -Description "DR Failover Policy"
```

Because this policy is used as you work through creating your load-balancing policy, assign it to the $LBPolicy variable. In the next section, you configure the load-balancing policy.

Configuring Load-Balancing Policies

In the previous section, you created the policy. Now, you will configure the policy. The `Set-XALoadBalancingPolicyConfiguration` cmdlet includes several options for configuring streaming options that won't be covered. The parameter that you will be most interested in is the `WorkerGroupPreferences` parameter. This parameter configures the priority of the Worker Groups, which decides the order in which users are directed to the Worker Groups. When a higher-priority Worker Group is unavailable or full, applicable connections are sent to the next-highest Worker Group. When that Worker Group is full or unavailable, connections are sent to the next-highest Worker Group.

```
Set-XALoadBalancingPolicy -PolicyName $LBPolicy `
    -WorkerGroupPreferences "1=MainSite","2=DRSite"
```

In this example, the `MainSite` is the primary Worker Group and has a higher priority; `DRSite` is the lower-priority Worker Group. The next step in the process of creating and configuring load balancing is creating the policy filter.

Applying Filters to Load-Balancing Policies

Load-balancing policies can be applied to users based on a combination of four conditions:

- Access Control
- Client IP Address
- Client Name
- Users

Using Access Control, you are able to load-balance users based on whether or not they come through an Access Gateway or even if they meet defined Access Gateway policies. Client IP Address allows you to direct users based on client IP address. Client Name allows you to direct users based on the name of the client workstation, and Users allows you to direct users based on user accounts or group membership.

Using `Set-XALoadBalancingPolicyFilter`, you apply load-balancing policies to users or devices based on the conditions in the previous list. In this first example, you create a filter based on the IP address of the client.

As with all of the filters, you first have to enable it for it to take effect. Just setting a value does not apply the filter. In this example, setting `ClientIpAddressEnabled` to true enables it and the `AllowedIPAddresses` sets the value:

```
Set-XALoadBalancingPolicyFilter -PolicyName "Internal Users" `
    -ClientIPAddressEnabled $True `
    -AllowedIPAddresses "10.0.0.0-10.255.255.255"
```

Each filter condition also has a global condition that applies to all devices. For example, to match all client devices regardless of the IP address, you would set ApplyToAllClientAddresses to true:

```
Set-XALoadBalancingPolicyFilter -PolicyName "All Users" `
  -ClientIPAddressEnabled $True `
  -ApplyToAllClientAddresses $True
```

Conditions can be combined to apply a policy to a specific subset of clients and/or users. For example, in the following code you use the IP address condition and a user group condition to target a policy to all of your executives that are accessing the system from an internal network:

```
Set-XALoadBalancingPolicyFilter -PolicyName "Internal Executives" `
  -ClientIPAddressEnabled $True `
  -AllowedIPAddresses "10.0.0.0-10.255.255.255" `
  -AccountEnabled $True `
  -AllowedAccounts "Domain\Executives Group"
```

Worker Groups

Worker Groups are collections of XenApp servers that are managed as a single unit. Worker Group membership can be explicit or dynamic, and a single server can be a member of one or more Worker Groups. This provides very powerful capabilities for the management of your XenApp servers.

Adding and Removing Worker Groups

You can add machines in one of three different ways:

- Specifying the names of the farm servers.
- Specifying an Active Directory group that will contain the servers.
- Specifying an Active Directory Organizational Unit that will contain the servers.

When adding a worker group you can actually mix the conditions, such as specifying group and server names. You can also specify more than one condition as shown here:

```
New-XAWorkerGroup -WorkerGroupName MyWorkerGroup `
  -Description "My Worker Group" `
  -FolderPath "WorkerGroups/Testing" `
  -ServerNames "ATL-1" `
  -ServerGroups "OfficeServers" `
  -OUs "OU=Resources,DC=Domain,DC=com", "OU=Servers, DC=Domain,DC=com
```

As you can see, server names, server groups, and Organizational Units are all specified with multiple Organizational Units specified in addition. Also included in this command is the folder path where the Worker Group is created.

Another method for adding a Worker Group is to copy an existing one using `Copy-XAWorkerGroup`. This cmdlet takes an existing Worker Group and creates an exact duplicate. You are able to specify the folder location of the Worker Group, but the name will automatically be the name of the existing Worker Group with a counter added to the end.

```
PS> $WorkerGroup = Copy-XAWorkerGroup -WorkerGroupName MyWorkerGroup `
>> -FolderPath "WorkerGroups\AnotherFolder"
>>
PS> $WorkerGroup.WorkerGroupName
MyWorkerGroup-1
```

You remove worker groups with the `Remove-XAWorkerGroup` cmdlet, which requires only the name of a worker group:

```
Remove-XAWorkerGroup -WorkerGroupName MyWorkerGroup
```

Modifying Worker Groups

You modify worker groups using the `Set-XAWorkerGroup` cmdlet, which allows you to change any of the Worker Group properties except for folder path and name, which are covered next.

To change the description of the worker group, you use the `Description` parameter to set the new description:

```
Set-XAWorkerGroup -WorkerGroup MyWorkerGroup `
   -Description "My New Description"
```

To change the server names, server groups, or Organizational Units, you would use the appropriate parameter and specify your replacement value. One thing to note is that you are replacing the existing value. To add a value, you would need to retrieve the existing value and then add your new value to it. Then reference the resulting value in the cmdlet.

```
$WGServers = (Get-XAWorkerGroup -WorkerGroupName MyWorkerGroup).ServerNames
$WGServers += Vega-2"
Set-XAWorkerGroup -WorkerGroupName MyWorkerGroup `
   -ServerNames $WGServers
```

Changing the folder location of a Worker Group is accomplished with the `Move-XAWorkerGroup` cmdlet. The `ToFolderPath` parameter is used to specify the new folder path:

```
Move-XAWorkerGroup -WorkerGroupName MyWorkerGroup `
   -ToFolderPath "WorkerGroups/NewFolder"
```

To change the name of a Worker Group, use the `Rename-XAWorkerGroup` cmdlet. Here, `NewName` is the name you want to change your Worker Group to:

```
Rename-XAWorkerGroup -WorkerGroupName MyWorkerGroup `
   -NewName MyNewWorkerGroupName
```

Summary

In this chapter, you learned how to use Windows PowerShell to manage your XenApp 6 environment. Starting with administrators, you then proceeded to manage applications, interact with sessions, and maintain servers. Finally, you were introduced to load-balancing policies and worker groups.

In the next chapter, you will be introduced to XenDesktop 5, Citrix's answer to the virtual desktop infrastructure (VDI) arena. A complete re-architecture of the previous version, this version was built with Windows PowerShell in mind from the very beginning.

Managing Citrix XenDesktop 5

The latest version of the Citrix XenDesktop solution is a complete re-architecture of the product. It is no longer based on the standard Integrated Multi-system Architecture (IMA) that has powered the XenApp product for many years. This redesign is touted as being able to scale to much larger enterprise environments than the preceding versions. Another important factor in the redesign is that the management architecture is based completely on Windows PowerShell. Windows PowerShell serves as the backbone for everything you do in the Desktop Studio, the GUI-based configuration utility. And, with a little research, you can effectively manage your XenDesktop environment without even touching the GUI.

IN THIS CHAPTER

Setting up a XenDesktop environment

Managing administrators

Adding collections

Creating policies

Working with hosts

Note

The Citrix XenDesktop 5 product is a specialized product sold by Citrix Systems, Inc. If you do not have this product installed but are interested in following along with this chapter, you can download an evaluation copy at `http://deliver.citrix.com/go/citrix/XDExpress`.

This product supports SQL Server 2008 and 2008 R2 and will not work with earlier versions of SQL Server. ∎

Introducing Citrix XenDesktop 5

To begin your introduction to Citrix XenDesktop 5 and Windows PowerShell, you start by learning how even the graphical management console leverages Windows PowerShell. Next, you investigate the snap-ins that power the functionality. And finally, you learn how to set up and configure your XenDesktop database using Windows PowerShell commands alone.

Examining the Windows PowerShell Tab

Citrix Desktop Studio is the GUI-based configuration utility for managing a XenDesktop environment. When you open the Desktop Studio, you will immediately notice a tab in the main window labeled PowerShell. When you navigate to this tab, you will, at the minimum, see a couple of Windows PowerShell commands that the Desktop Studio used to connect to the XenDesktop installation.

As illustrated in Figure 19-1, every action you perform in the Desktop Studio is recorded and executed using Windows PowerShell to perform the actual commands. The Desktop Studio is just the user-friendly interface. As you perform your daily work, Desktop Studio keeps track of every Windows PowerShell command it executes and keeps track of the commands in the PowerShell tab. You can use it to go back to a prior command to see what the actual Windows PowerShell command is. This is an excellent way of learning the Windows PowerShell cmdlets. You can do your normal work in Desktop Studio and then see how it was done in Windows PowerShell. You can use the Launch PowerShell button in the lower-right corner of the main window, as shown in Figure 19-1, to launch Windows PowerShell and execute the commands right away. All of the XenDesktop snap-ins are automatically loaded.

FIGURE 19-1

The Desktop Studio interface

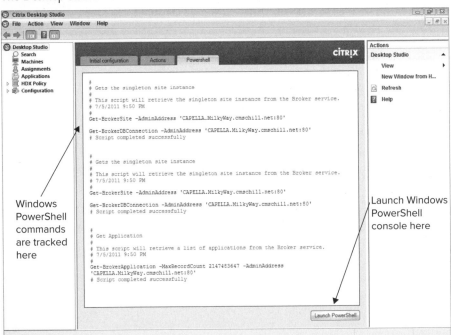

Windows PowerShell commands are tracked here

Launch Windows PowerShell console here

Exploring the Snap-Ins

XenDesktop 5 offers several different snap-ins for managing the XenDesktop environment. The snap-ins each provide a method for managing the various components of the product. Table 19-1 lists all the Citrix-provided snap-ins installed with XenDesktop 5.

TABLE 19-1

XenDesktop Snap-ins

Snap-in	Description
Citrix.ADIdentity.Admin.V1	Manages Active Directory computer accounts.
Citrix.Broker.Admin.V1	This Windows PowerShell snap-in contains cmdlets used to manage the Citrix Broker.
Citrix.Common.Commands	Contains cmdlets for working with various aspects of the Citrix product line. The majority of the cmdlets interact with the Citrix tracing facility.
Citrix.Common.GroupPolicy	Provides a PowerShell Provider that represents the Citrix Group Policy configuration.
Citrix.Configuration.Admin.V1	Stores service configuration information.
Citrix.Host.Admin.V1	Manages hosts and Hypervisor connections.
Citrix.MachineCreation.Admin.V1	Creates new virtual machines.
Citrix.MachineIdentity.Admin.V1	Manages virtual machine storage.
PvsPsSnapIn	Provides functionality for connecting with the Provisioning Services product.

The Citrix.Common.Commands snap-in is a generic Citrix module that is provided with a majority of the Citrix products. It includes the ability to create and manage Citrix CTX traces, among some other functions. I do not cover this module, but if you perform a lot of diagnostic work on your environment, I would recommend that you look at it.

Performing an Automated Environment Setup

Citrix has made every effort to make sure that you can manage and fully automate the entire environment with Windows PowerShell. It even went so far as to enable you to perform the initial setup, including database creation. In this section, you step through the process of performing a basic setup of a XenDesktop environment. The only prerequisite is that you installed the XenDesktop Controller and have a database instance ready for the database.

Setting Parameter Values

In Listing 19-1, you are setting the values for the parameters that are subsequently going to be used to create the environment. You specify the name of the Microsoft SQL Server, the database, and the connection string that will be used to connect to the database, Desktop Controller, Service Group, and License Server.

LISTING 19-1

Setting Your Values

```
# Set all the custom parameters
$SQLServer = "Canopus"
$DatabaseName = "XenDesktopDB"
$DBConnection = `
  "Server=$SQLServer; Initial Catalog=$DatabaseName; Integrated Security=True"
$DesktopController = "Capella"
$ServiceGroup = "XDServiceGroup"
$LicenseServer = "Rigel"
```

Loading Snap-Ins

The next step is to load the Citrix Windows PowerShell snap-ins. You could easily load them one by one, but loading them all at once is simpler and makes sure that they are all loaded.

```
# Load all Citrix Snap-ins
Get-PSSnapin -Name Citrix* -Registered |
  Add-PSSnapin -ErrorAction SilentlyContinue
```

Creating the Database

This section focuses on creating the database that will be used by XenDesktop. First, you define a function called Invoke-SQL that will be responsible for running SQL on the SQL Server. This procedure requires that you have Remoting enabled on your SQL Server.

Cross-Reference

Remoting is covered in the "Remoting" section of Chapter 2, "What's New in Windows PowerShell V2." ■

XenDesktop has six different "components," and each is managed somewhat independently. Each component has a method for retrieving the Transact-SQL statement needed to create the required SQL schema in the database. You have to feed it some parameters to fill in the SQL statement. This includes the name of the database, address of the Desktop Controller, and the name of the Service Group. Because these are going to be common among the different cmdlets, you create $SQLParameters so you don't have to enter the same parameters for each cmdlet.

Note

For whatever reason, the `Citrix.Broker.Admin.V1` module is slightly different than the other modules. For example, whereas the other Schema cmdlets accept `Database` as the `ScriptType` parameter, the Broker module requires `FullDatabase`. When you encounter errors with this module, check the parameters first to make sure that the syntax isn't different. ■

Once you define the parameters, the next step is to get the SQL statements required to set up the schema. Listing 19-2 begins with defining the function for executing the SQL commands. Each module has a cmdlet for retrieving the Transact-SQL. After you store the Transact-SQL into variables, you create a new Remoting session to your SQL Server, which is used for the subsequent statements.

The first SQL statement you execute actually creates the database with the required collation settings. All of these statements, of course, require that you have the appropriate server permissions. After the database is created, you then execute each of the retrieved SQL statements. When you are finished, you have a complete database ready for XenDesktop. Close the Remoting session and proceed to connect XenDesktop to the database.

LISTING 19-2

Creating the Database

```
function Invoke-SQL
{
  param($SQL)
  Invoke-Command -Session $SQLSession -ScriptBlock {
    param($DatabaseName, $SQL) Invoke-SQLCmd -Query $SQL
  } -ArgumentList $DatabaseName, $SQL

}

$SQLParameters = @{
  DatabaseName = $DatabaseName
  AdminAddress = $DesktopController
  ServiceGroupName = $ServiceGroup
}

$AcctDBSQL = Get-AcctDBSchema @SQLParameters -ScriptType Database
$ConfigDBSQL = Get-ConfigDBSchema @SQLParameters -ScriptType Database
$BrokerDBSQL = Get-BrokerDBSchema @SQLParameters -ScriptType FullDatabase
$HypDBSQL = Get-HypDBSchema @SQLParameters -ScriptType Database
$ProvDBSQL = Get-ProvDBSchema @SQLParameters -ScriptType Database
$PVSVMDBSQL = Get-PvsVmDBSchema @SQLParameters -ScriptType Database
$SQLSession = New-PSSession -ComputerName $SQLServer
Invoke-Command -Session $SQLSession -ScriptBlock {
  Add-PSSnapin SqlServerCmdletSnapin100
```

continues

LISTING 19-2   *(continued)*

```
}
Invoke-SQL "Create database [$DatabaseName] collate Latin1_General_CI_AS_KS"
Invoke-SQL $AcctDBSQL
Invoke-SQL $ConfigDBSQL
Invoke-SQL $BrokerDBSQL
Invoke-SQL $HypDBSQL
Invoke-SQL $ProvDBSQL
Invoke-SQL $PVSVMDBSQL
Remove-PSSession $SQLSession
```

Connecting to the Database

Now, the database is completely set up and you just need to connect XenDesktop to the newly created database. With XenDesktop, you can just switch connections from one database to another. First, you have to clear the connection. As shown in Listing 19-3, you do that by setting the DBConnection to $Null, in essence clearing the connection. This step is not needed if you are setting up a brand-new Desktop Controller.

LISTING 19-3

Connecting XenDesktop to the Database

```
# Reset Database Connections
$ConnectionParameters = @{
  DBConnection = $Null
  AdminAddress = $DesktopController
}
Set-ConfigDBConnection @ConnectionParameters
Set-AcctDBConnection @ConnectionParameters
Set-HypDBConnection @ConnectionParameters
Set-ProvDBConnection @ConnectionParameters
Set-PvsVmDBConnection @ConnectionParameters
Set-BrokerDBConnection @ConnectionParameters

# Set Database Connections
$ConnectionParameters = @{
  DBConnection = $DBConnection
  AdminAddress = $DesktopController
}
Set-ConfigDBConnection @ConnectionParameters
Set-AcctDBConnection @ConnectionParameters
Set-HypDBConnection @ConnectionParameters
```

```
Set-ProvDBConnection @ConnectionParameters
Set-PvsVmDBConnection @ConnectionParameters
Set-BrokerDBConnection @ConnectionParameters
```

Configuring Services

The next step involves the configuration of service instances. The code segment in Listing 19-4 may seem a little overwhelming at first, but it's really just two simple steps that are executed for each of the XenDesktop components. The first step registers each component service instance with the configuration service. The second step enables access permissions and configuration service locations to be loaded. This must be performed on new installations to reset the membership and permissions.

LISTING 19-4

Configuring the Services

```
Get-ConfigServiceInstance -AdminAddress $DesktopController |
  Register-ConfigServiceInstance -AdminAddress $DesktopController
Get-HypServiceInstance -AdminAddress $DesktopController |
  Register-ConfigServiceInstance -AdminAddress $DesktopController
Get-AcctServiceInstance -AdminAddress $DesktopController |
  Register-ConfigServiceInstance -AdminAddress $DesktopController
Get-PvsVmServiceInstance -AdminAddress $DesktopController |
  Register-ConfigServiceInstance -AdminAddress $DesktopController
Get-ProvServiceInstance -AdminAddress $DesktopController |
  Register-ConfigServiceInstance -AdminAddress $DesktopController
Get-BrokerServiceInstance -AdminAddress $DesktopController |
  Register-ConfigServiceInstance -AdminAddress $DesktopController

Get-ConfigRegisteredServiceInstance -AdminAddress $DesktopController |
  Reset-ConfigServiceGroupMembership -AdminAddress $DesktopController
Get-ConfigRegisteredServiceInstance -AdminAddress $DesktopController |
  Reset-HypServiceGroupMembership -AdminAddress $DesktopController
Get-ConfigRegisteredServiceInstance -AdminAddress $DesktopController |
  Reset-AcctServiceGroupMembership -AdminAddress $DesktopController
Get-ConfigRegisteredServiceInstance -AdminAddress $DesktopController |
  Reset-PvsVmServiceGroupMembership -AdminAddress $DesktopController
Get-ConfigRegisteredServiceInstance -AdminAddress $DesktopController |
  Reset-ProvServiceGroupMembership -AdminAddress $DesktopController
Get-ConfigServiceInstance -AdminAddress $DesktopController |
  Reset-BrokerServiceGroupMembership -AdminAddress $DesktopController
```

Configuring the License Server

The last part of the script, shown in Listing 19-5, is to configure the license server. For this, you use the `Set-BrokerSite` cmdlet to specify the license server and license types for the installation. Now, your system is ready to further configure.

Configuring Licensing

```
# Configure Licensing
Set-BrokerSite -LicenseServerName $LicenseServer `
  -AppLicenseEdition PLT `
  -DesktopLicenseEdition PLT `
  -Name "XDServiceGroup" `
  -AdminAddress $DesktopController
```

Administrators

In XenDesktop, your administrators are anyone that needs to manage any part of your farm. They range from users who just need to view your environment to you, the full-access administrator.

Explaining Access Control

XenDesktop has five main levels of administrative access, which are accessible via the Desktop Studio GUI. Table 19-2 lists the administration roles that you can assign to users.

Administration Roles

Role	Description
Full administrator	Full administrative rights to manage the entire XenDesktop site.
Read-only administrator	Can see all aspects of the XenDesktop site, but cannot make any changes.
Machine administrator	Owns the catalog and assigns assignment administrators.
Assignment administrator	Takes desktops created by the machine administrator and creates Desktop Groups and assigns users.
Help desk administrator	Performs day-to-day monitoring and maintenance.

When utilizing the Windows PowerShell cmdlets, you have extra granularity over permissions compared with the Desktop Studio. Each Windows PowerShell module has its own administrator. For example, to give administrator access to the hypervisor snap-in, you would use New-HypAdministrator. Each cmdlet supports either full or read-only access.

Creating Administrators

Creating administrators begins with the `New-BrokerAdministrator` cmdlet. In Listing 19-6, you create a full broker administrator by setting `-FullAdmin` to `$True`. This creates a full broker administrator. You also have to grant access to the five snap-ins for the administrator to be able to manage those components.

LISTING 19-6

Creating a Full Broker Administrator

```
$Account = "Domain\User"

# Create Full Administrator
New-BrokerAdministrator -BrokerAdmin $True `
  -Enabled $True `
  -FullAdmin $True `
  -Name $Account `
  -ProvisioningAdmin $True `
  -ReadOnly $False `

New-ConfigAdministrator -Account $Account
New-AcctAdministrator -Account $Account
New-HypAdministrator -Account $Account
New-ProvAdministrator  -Account $Account
New-PvsVmAdministrator -Account $Account
```

In Listing 19-7, you create an assignment administrator. This administrator role creates Desktop Groups and assigns users to those Desktop Groups. The process for creating an assignment administrator is slightly different than a site administrator. In the first section, you create a read-only administrator, an administrator that can only view the environment but not make any changes. Then, with the `Add-BrokerAdministrator` cmdlet, you add the account as an administrator to the `PreExisting` catalog.

LISTING 19-7

Creating an Assignment Administrator

```
$Account = "Domain\User"

# Create a new Assignment Administrator
Set-BrokerAdministrator -BrokerAdmin $True `
  -Enabled $True `
  -FullAdmin $False `
  -Name $Account `
```

continues

487

LISTING 19-7   (continued)

```
    -ProvisioningAdmin $False `
    -ReadOnly $True `

New-ConfigAdministrator -Account $Account -ReadOnly
New-AcctAdministrator -Account $Account -ReadOnly
New-HypAdministrator -Account $Account -ReadOnly
New-ProvAdministrator  -Account $Account -ReadOnly
New-PvsVmAdministrator -Account $Account -ReadOnly

Add-BrokerAdministrator -Name $Account `
  -Catalog 'PreExisting'
```

Catalogs

In XenDesktop, a *catalog* is a collection of machines of the same type. Catalogs can contain both physical and virtual machines with varying levels of management. Table 19-3 lists the five machine types you can use when creating catalogs.

TABLE 19-3

XenDesktop Machine Types

Machine Type	Description
Pooled	Machines are provided to users on a per-session, first-come, first-served basis. Changes are discarded at logoff.
Dedicated	Machines are assigned manually or automatically, and changes are kept after logoff.
Existing	Preexisting virtual machines.
Physical	Physical machines, usually blade PCs hosted in the data center.
Streamed	Machines streamed with Provisioning Services.

Creating Catalogs

In XenDesktop, catalogs are groups of machines that are of the same type. The machine type takes into consideration the type of hosting infrastructure (physical or virtual) and whether user changes are persisted when they log off.

Pooled Catalogs

Pooled machines are dynamic machines that are allocated to users on a per-session, first-come, first-served basis. *Pooled catalogs* utilize the Machine Creation Services introduced in XenDesktop 5 to allow a single disk image to be shared among multiple virtual machines. Any changes made during a session are discarded when the user logs off. Machines are either allocated on a random basis or allocated to the same person on every logon. The latter allocation type is used for certain software licensing requirements.

The first step in creating a functional catalog is to create the broker catalog, which is the actual catalog object itself. In Listing 19-8, you create the catalog. In this example, you set the `AllocationType` to `Random` so that users are given desktops on a random basis. In this step, you also specify the `CatalogKind`, which in this instance is `SingleImage`. `SingleImage` is actually the value used to specify a pooled machine catalog.

LISTING 19-8

Creating a Pooled Catalog

```
$BrokerCatalog = New-BrokerCatalog -AllocationType 'Random' `
   -CatalogKind 'SingleImage' `
   -Description "Windows 7 Ultimate x64" `
   -Name  'Windows 7' `
   -PvsForVM @() `
   -Verbose
```

After creating the catalog, the next step is to create an Identity Pool using the code provided in Listing 19-9. The Identity Pool is used to define the template for which accounts will be created in Active Directory for the desktop catalog. The relevant parameters are as follows:

- **NamingScheme:** The pattern used for the name of the machine. The # symbol is a placeholder and will be replaced with actual values when the machines are created.

- NamingSchemeType: Possible values are numeric or alphabetic. The type determines whether # symbols are replaced with numeric (0–9) or alphabetic (a–z) characters.

- OU: The Organizational Unit where new desktop machine accounts will be placed.

LISTING 19-9

Creating an Identity Pool

```
$IdentityPool = New-AcctIdentityPool `
   -IdentityPoolName 'Std VDI Naming Scheme' `
   -NamingScheme 'VDI-##' `
```

continues

LISTING 19-9   (continued)

```
-NamingSchemeType 'Numeric' `
-OU 'OU=VDI,OU=Desktops,OU=Computers,OU=Resources,DC=domain,DC=com' `
-Domain 'domain.com' `
-AllowUnicode
```

The next step is to create a snapshot that will be used for all of your machines as shown in Listing 19-10. The New-HypVMSnapshot cmdlet is actually a XenDesktop cmdlet that works with the host to create a snapshot of the virtual machine specified by LiteralPath.

Continuing in Listing 19-10, you will create the template for the virtual machine itself. The New-ProvScheme cmdlet creates a new provisioning scheme, or virtual machine (VM) template. For this cmdlet, you specify the following parameters:

- **HostingUnitName:** Name of the hypervisor
- **IdentityPoolName:** Name of the Identity Pool created earlier
- **VMCpuCount:** Number of CPUs to assign
- **VMMemoryMB:** Amount of memory to assign
- **CleanOnBoot:** Whether to reset the VM to its initial condition on restart
- **RunAsynchronously:** Return before task is complete

When you run this cmdlet, XenDesktop makes a copy of the hard disk attached to the virtual machine snapshot and stores it in every storage location referenced by the provisioning scheme. This can be a lengthy task so the next section indicated by the do loop tracks the progress of the provisioning task.

When the task completes, you have the new provisioning scheme that you need to associate with the catalog. This is accomplished with the Set-BrokerCatalog cmdlet, which accepts the provisioning scheme via the PvsForVM parameter. The parameter accepts an array of strings composed of the global unique identifier (GUID) of the hosting unit as well as the GUID of the provisioning scheme itself.

LISTING 19-10

Connecting the Images

```
$SnapShotImage = New-HypVMSnapshot -SnapshotName 'Windows 7 - 20110509' `
  -LiteralPath 'XDHyp:\hostingunits\SOL\UrsaMajor.vm' -Verbose

$ProvTaskID = New-ProvScheme -ProvisioningSchemeName 'Windows 7 Gen Desktop' `
  -HostingUnitName 'SOL' `
```

```
  -IdentityPoolName 'Std VDI Naming Scheme' `
  -VMCpuCount 1 `
  -VMMemoryMB 512 `
  -CleanOnBoot `
  -MasterImageVM $SnapShotImage `
  -RunAsynchronously

do
{
  $ProvisioningTask = (Get-ProvTask $ProvTaskID)
  Write-Progress -Activity $ProvisioningTask.ProvisioningSchemeName `
    -PercentComplete $ProvisioningTask.TaskProgress `
    -Status $ProvisioningTask.TaskState
  Start-Sleep -Seconds 1
} while ($ProvisioningTask.WorkflowStatus -eq 'Running')

$ProvScheme = Get-ProvScheme -ProvisioningSchemeName 'Windows 7 Gen Desktop'
$ProvSchemeGUID = $ProvScheme.ProvisioningSchemeUID.Guid
$ProvSchemeHostingGUID = $ProvScheme.HostingUnitUID.Guid

Set-BrokerCatalog -Name 'Windows 7' `
  -PvsForVM @("$($ProvSchemeGUID):$($ProvSchemeHostingGUID)")
```

In Listing 19-11, you start by creating the Active Directory (AD) accounts using the Identity Pool you created previously. In this example, you start at 10 and create 5 accounts.

The next step is to actually provision the virtual machines. You start by associating the controller address with the provisioning scheme via the Add-ProvSchemeControllerAddress cmdlet. This allows newly created virtual machines to be associated with the controller.

Now you are ready to actually create the machines. For this task, you use the New-ProvVM cmdlet, which actually provisions the virtual machines. You call New-ProvVM, specifying the provisioning scheme name and the AD accounts that the machines will be associated with. This can be a lengthy task, so you again use the RunAsynchronously parameter and follow up with a loop to track the progress of the task.

LISTING 19-11

Creating the Machines

```
$ADAccounts = New-AcctADAccount -IdentityPoolName 'Std VDI Naming Scheme' `
  -StartCount 10 -Count 5

Add-ProvSchemeControllerAddress `
  -ProvisioningSchemeName 'Windows 7 Gen Desktop' `
```

continues

LISTING 19-11   *(continued)*

```
   -ControllerAddress @('CAPELLA.MilkyWay.cmschill.net')


$ProvVMTask = New-ProvVM -ProvisioningSchemeName 'Windows 7 Gen Desktop' `
  -ADAccountName $ADAccounts.SuccessfulAccounts `
  -RunAsynchronously


do
{
  $ProvisioningTask = (Get-ProvTask $ProvVMTask)
  $MachinesCreated = $ProvisioningTask.VirtualMachinesCreatedCount
  $MachinesToCreate = $ProvisioningTask.VirtualMachinesToCreateCount
  Write-Progress -Activity $ProvisioningTask.ProvisioningSchemeName `
      -PercentComplete $($MachinesCreated / $MachinesToCreate) `
      -Status $ProvisioningTask.TaskState
  Start-Sleep -Seconds 1
} while ($ProvisioningTask.WorkflowStatus -eq 'Running')


$ProvisioningTask.CreatedVirtualMachines |
  Lock-ProvVM -ProvisioningSchemeName 'Windows 7 Gen Desktop' `
      -Tag 'Brokered'


$ADAccounts.SuccessfulAccounts | %{
  $AccountSID = $_.ADAccountSid
  $HostedMachineID = Get-ProvVM |
    Where-Object { $_.AdAccountSid -eq $AccountSID } |
    Select-Object -ExpandProperty VMID
  New-BrokerMachine -CatalogUid $BrokerCatalog.UID `
      -HostedMachineId $HostedMachineID `
      -HypervisorConnectionUid 1 `
      -MachineName $_.ADAccountSid
}
```

After the machines are created, you then use `Lock-ProvVM` to lock the machines so they aren't modified accidently. Finally, you loop through each of the AD accounts that were successfully added and retrieve the provisioned virtual machine. You then add that virtual machine to the catalog, thereby registering it and making it available to XenDesktop.

Dedicated Catalogs

Dedicated machines are very much like pooled machines except that changes are not lost when a user logs off. Users are either assigned automatically on launch or manually by an administrator. After the first login, that user will always receive the same desktop. When users log off, their settings are saved and not discarded as they are with the pooled catalog.

In Listing 19-12, you create the machine catalog. The `AllocationType` is `Permananent` and `CatalogKind` is `ThinCloned`.

LISTING 19-12

Creating a Dedicated Pool

```
$BrokerCatalog = New-BrokerCatalog -AllocationType 'Permanent' `
  -CatalogKind 'ThinCloned' `
  -Description 'WIndows 7 Dedicated' `
  -Name 'WIndows 7 Dedicated' `
  -PvsForVM @() `
  -Verbose
```

This step is the only variation from the Pooled machine catalog steps. You can use the remaining steps from the previous example to complete the dedicated catalog.

Existing Catalog

Existing catalogs contain virtual machines that already exist. These virtual machines were created by an external process and are managed manually or by a third-party utility. Adding existing virtual machines to XenDesktop does give some extra control to XenDesktop. One example is power control. You can configure XenDesktop to shut down a virtual machine when a user logs off to conserve power.

The first step, as show in Listing 19-13, is the same as previous examples: create the catalog. In this example, you use the `PowerManaged` value for the `CatalogKind` parameter. The `AllocationType` is, of course, `Permanent` because XenDesktop is not managing the virtual machines.

The next step is to register the machine with the catalog. In previous examples, there were a lot of steps in between. In this example, because XenDesktop is not doing the provisioning, you just need to add the machine to the catalog. For the `New-BrokerMachine` cmdlet, you use the following parameters:

- **CatalogUid:** The unique identifier (UID) for the catalog you want to assign the machine to.
- **HostedMachineID:** This unique identifier for the virtual machine. This is how the machine's hypervisor recognizes it.
- **HypervisorConnectionUid:** This is the UID for the hosting hypervisor in XenDesktop.
- **MachineName:** Name of the AD account for the machine.

Once you add the machine, you need to assign a user to it. The `Add-BrokerUser` cmdlet assigns the user specified by the `Name` parameter and assigns it to the virtual machine identified by the `Machine` parameter. Now, when that user logs in to XenDesktop, he or she will find the machine available.

LISTING 19-13

Creating an Existing Pool

```
$BrokerCatalog = New-BrokerCatalog -AllocationType 'Permanent' `
   -CatalogKind 'PowerManaged' `
   -Description 'Windows 7 Existing' `
   -Name 'Windows 7 Existing' `
   -Verbose

New-BrokerMachine -CatalogUid $BrokerCatalog.UID `
   -HostedMachineId '4a3877cb-991c-4252-8140-c00b6fe4ec57' `
   -HypervisorConnectionUid 1 `
   -MachineName 'Domain\Machine'

Add-BrokerUser -Name 'Domain\User' -Machine 'Domain\Machine'
```

Physical Catalog

Physical catalogs are almost identical to Existing catalogs except that the machines are physical and not virtual. These catalogs, which are not frequently used, are typically used for blade PCs that are in a data center. This situation is typically reserved for high-demand users that need the resources of an actual physical machine.

In Listing 19-14, you see that, in this case, you use `Unmanaged` for the `CatalogKind`. With the `New-BrokerMachine` cmdlet you specify the catalog's UID and machine name, but because this is not a virtual machine, you omit those details. The final step is to assign the machine to the user.

LISTING 19-14

Creating a Physical Pool

```
$BrokerCatalog = New-BrokerCatalog -AllocationType 'Permanent' `
   -CatalogKind 'Unmanaged' `
   -Description 'Windows 7 Physical' `
   -Name 'Windows 7 Physical' `
   -Verbose

New-BrokerMachine -CatalogUid $BrokerCatalog.UID `
```

```
-MachineName 'Domain\Machine'

Add-BrokerUser -Name 'Domain\User' -Machine 'Domain\Machine'
```

Streamed Catalog

A streamed catalog is the type of catalog seasoned XenDesktop administrators are most used to seeing. Such catalogs utilize the Citrix Provisioning Services, which have been an integral part of previous XenDesktop releases.

The first step to creating a streamed catalog is to create the connection to the Provisioning Services (PVS) collection via the `Set-PvsConnection` cmdlet. In this cmdlet, you specify the server and the port as well as the domain.

Note

The `PvsPsSnapIn` module, of which `Set-PvsConnection` is a member, was not developed as well as the rest of the modules included in the XenDesktop 5 product. In fact, it doesn't even follow the same naming convention. Unfortunately, the cmdlets in this module do not have any help files configured for them, so `Get-Help` will not be of any use. ■

Next, you grab the PVS collection that you want to associate your catalog with using `Get-SimplePvsCollection` and specifying your site name as it appears in PVS. The catalog is now created using `New-BrokerCatalog`, specifying that it is a `Pvs` catalog, and supplying the address to the PVS server. At this point, you still haven't associated the catalog with the actual PVS collection.

The next step is to get the devices that are in the PVS collection you specified. You iterate through each of the devices and perform several steps on them. The first step is to get the Active Directory account for the device via the `Get-SimplePvsADAccount` cmdlet. Next, you grab the MAC address for the primary NIC in the device. However, the MAC address associated with the device uses a dash (-) as a separator, whereas you need to have a colon (:) as the separator for the next step. Using the `Get-HypVMMacAddress` cmdlet, and by filtering the output using the MAC address from the previous step, you obtain the ID for the virtual machine. The key thing to note for this statement is that you specified the path to the hypervisor PS provider connection.

With all of the information you collected so far, you can now associate machines with the catalog. Using `New-BrokerMachine`, you specify:

- **CatalogUid:** The ID of the Broker Catalog t§o which you are adding machines
- **HostedMachineId:** The ID of the virtual machine as assigned by the hypervisor of the machine you are adding to the catalog
- **HypervisorConnectionUid:** The ID of the hypervisor connection
- **MachineName:** The SID of the machine's Active Directory account

Once this step is completed, the machines are now available to the Broker Catalog. The code needed to complete these tasks is provided in Listing 19-15.

LISTING 19-15

Creating a Streamed Pool

```
$Server = 'Atlanta'
$Site = 'Site'

Set-PvsConnection -server 'Atlanta' `
  -port 54321 `
  -domain 'MilkyWay.cmschill.net'

$Collection = Get-SimplePvsCollection -siteName @('Site')

$Catalog = New-BrokerCatalog -AllocationType 'Random' `
  -CatalogKind 'Pvs' `
  -Description 'Windows 7 Streamed Desktops' `
  -MachinesArePhysical $False `
  -Name 'Windows 7 Desktops' `
  -PvsAddress 'Atlanta' `
  -PvsDomain 'MilkyWay.cmschill.net'


$Devices = Get-SimplePvsDevice -CollectionId $Collection.CollectionId

$Devices | ForEach-Object {
  $ADAccount = Get-SimplePvsADAccount `
    -domain 'MilkyWay.cmschill.net' `
    -name $_.DeviceName

  $MacAddress = $_.DeviceMac -replace '-',':'

  $VMID = (Get-HypVMMacAddress -LiteralPath 'xdhyp:\connections\Hyper-V' |
    Where-Object { $_.MacAddress -eq $MacAddress }).VMID
  New-BrokerMachine -CatalogUid $Catalog.UID `
    -HostedMachineId $VMID `
    -HypervisorConnectionUid 1 `
    -MachineName $ADAccount.SID `
}
```

Managing Catalogs

Now that your catalogs are created, you will need to manage them. For this purpose, you will use the `Set-BrokerCatalog` cmdlet. Using `Set-BrokerCatalog`, you can modify the following properties of a catalog:

- **Description:** Provides a description of the catalog.
- **MachinesArePhysical:** Indicates whether the machines in the catalog are physical machines. Can only be set if the CatalogKind property is PVS.
- **PvsAddress:** Specifies the address of the Provisioning Server. Can only be set if the CatalogKind property is PVS.
- **PvsDomain:** Specifies the domain of the Provisioning Server. Can only be set if the CatalogKind property is PVS.
- **PvsForVM:** Links the broker catalog to the actual provisioning scheme. Can only be set if the CatalogKind property is PVS.

By specifying the name of the catalog, you can change the properties of a single catalog. For example, the following line of code changes the description for the Windows 7 catalog:

```
Set-BrokerCatalog -Name "Windows 7" -Description "Windows 7 with SP1"
```

If you want to change properties for more than one catalog, you can use the -InputObject parameter to pass multiple catalogs or use the pipeline:

```
Get-BrokerCatalog -AllocationType Permanent |
    Set-BrokerCatalog -Description "Permanent allocated machines."
```

To actually change the name of a catalog, you must use the Rename-BrokerCatalog cmdlet:

```
Rename-BrokerCatalog -Name "Windows 7" -NewName "Windows 7 SP1"
```

Removing Catalogs

Removing catalogs is extremely easy. Simply use the Remove-BrokerCatalog cmdlet. Note that any catalog that contains one or more machines that are part of a Desktop Group cannot be deleted until those machines are removed.

```
Remove-BrokerCatalog -Name "Windows 7" -Description "Windows 7 with SP1"
```

If you want to remove more than one catalog, you can use the -InputObject parameter to pass multiple catalogs or use the pipeline:

```
Get-BrokerCatalog -AllocationType Permanent | Remove-BrokerCatalog
```

Provisioning

Provisioning is the process of taking a single machine image and configuring it to be used by multiple devices. The previous section, "Creating catalogs," covers the task of provisioning images. This section covers additional topics related to provisioning.

Introducing Machine Creation Services

You have already been briefly introduced to Machine Creation Services in the "Pooled catalog" section. Machine Creation Services is the provisioning technology that was introduced in XenDesktop 5. It differs from Provisioning Services in that it utilizes the underlying hypervisor's storage to deliver copies of virtual machines instead of using the network to deliver the information.

Updating Master Images

When you provision a machine, you are creating numerous machines that are based on a point-in-time snapshot of a master image. As time goes by, you will need to update the image and propagate the changes to the client machines. Whether it's a configuration change, software installation, or even the monthly Windows patch cycle, you will need to deploy these changes to the client machines.

For this task, you are going to use the `Publish-ProvMasterVmImage` cmdlet. Assume that you need to update the "Windows 7 Gen Desktop" provisioning scheme that you used earlier in this chapter. The code is provided in Listing 19-16. The first step is to take a snapshot of the virtual machines with all of the changes included with the `New-HypVMSnapshot` cmdlet.

LISTING 19-16

Updating a Master Image

```
$SnapShotName = 'Windows 7 - 20110701'
$ProvScheme = 'Windows 7 Gen Desktop'
$SnapShotImage = New-HypVMSnapshot -SnapshotName $SnapShotName `
  -LiteralPath 'XDHyp:\hostingunits\SOL\UrsaMajor.vm' -Verbose

$ProvTaskID = Publish-ProvMasterVmImage -ProvisioningSchemeName $ProvScheme `
  -MasterImageVM $SnapShotImage -RunAsynchronously

do
{
  $ProvisioningTask = (Get-ProvTask $ProvTaskID)
  Write-Progress -Activity $ProvisioningTask.ProvisioningSchemeName `
    -PercentComplete $ProvisioningTask.TaskProgress `
    -Status $ProvisioningTask.TaskState
  Start-Sleep -Seconds 1
} while ($ProvisioningTask.WorkflowStatus -eq 'Running')
```

Once the snapshot has been taken, call `Publish-ProvMasterVmImage`, specifying the provisioning scheme name and the path of the updated snapshot. Because this is a long-running task, tell it you want to exit and continue running it in the background. You then display a progress bar so you can track the process of the task.

Desktop Groups

Desktop Groups are virtual machines that you allocate to users from catalogs. A number of key facts about Desktop Groups are:

- A Desktop Group can contain virtual machines from one or more catalogs.
- A machine can only belong to a single Desktop Group.
- A user can be granted access to multiple Desktop Groups.
- Multiple users can be granted access to a single virtual machine.
- Using Windows PowerShell, you can actually assign a virtual machine from a Desktop Group to a device instead of a user.

Creating Desktop Groups

Desktop Groups in XenDesktop are sets or collections of virtual machines that are allocated to users. Desktop Groups are created from Broker Catalogs and allow for an abstraction of administration. Your virtualization administrators can allocate and be responsible for the machines themselves, while the assignment administrators can create the Desktop Groups and assign them to users.

In addition to Desktop Groups are Application Desktop Groups. *Application Desktop Groups* are what used to be referred to as *VM Hosted Apps*. For those unfamiliar with this terminology, virtual machines in Application Desktop Groups allow the user to run an application and only be presented with the application. They have no Desktop or Start Menu. Now, with XenDesktop 5, you don't need a special farm for VM Hosted Apps. It is now built into XenDesktop. I cover that feature in this section.

Starting with Listing 19-17, you are going to create a new Desktop Group. For this step, you use the `New-BrokerDesktopGroup` cmdlet. You specify the `Name`, `PublishedName`, and whether the Desktop Group is enabled. Many more parameters for the cmdlet allow you to specify some connection parameters as well.

Once you create the Desktop Group, you need to add machines from an existing Broker Catalog to the Desktop Group. For that purpose, you use the `Add-BrokerMachinesToDesktopGroup` cmdlet. You specify the catalog to pull machines from, the Desktop Group to add them to, and the number of machines to pull.

Now you must add users to your Desktop Group. The first step is to create a new broker user using the `New-BrokerUser` cmdlet. You aren't actually assigning anything. You are just creating a broker object that will be used in the `New-BrokerEntitlementPolicyRule`. With this cmdlet, you create a rule for access. In this case, you specify the Desktop Group's UID and the name of your entitlement rule as well as the group that you want to be able to access the Desktop Group.

Creating and Assigning a Desktop Group

```
New-BrokerDesktopGroup -DesktopKind 'Shared' `
  -Name 'Windows 7 Desktop' `
  -PublishedName 'My Desktop' `
  -Enabled $True `

Add-BrokerMachinesToDesktopGroup -Catalog 'Windows 7 Ultimate' `
  -DesktopGroup 'Windows 7 Desktop' `
  -Count 5

New-BrokerUser -Name 'MILKYWAY\Domain Users'

New-BrokerEntitlementPolicyRule -DesktopGroupUid 2 `
  -Enabled $True `
  -IncludedUsers @('MILKYWAY\Domain Users') `
  -Name 'Windows 7 Desktop_1'
```

Now that you have created the Desktop Group, you need to create policies to define who can access to the Desktop Groups. The following policies control how users can access the Desktop Group as well as what they can do when they are connected.

- **AllowedConnections:** Used to determine whether a connection is coming in through an Access Gateway (AG).

- **AllowedProtocols:** The protocols that a user can use to connect to the resource. If this property is blank, access to the resource is implicitly denied.

- **AllowedUsers:** Users/Groups allowed to access a resource.

- **AllowRestart:** Whether or not a user can restart a desktop to which access is granted.

- **Enabled:** Whether the rule is initially enabled.

- **IncludedDesktopGroupFilterEnabled:** Specifies whether the `IncludedDesktopGroups` filter is enabled.

- **IncludedDesktopGroups:** Specifies the Desktop Groups to which you grant access.

- **IncludedSmartAccessFilterEnabled:** Specifies whether the `IncludedSmartAccessTags` filter is enabled.

- **IncludedSmartAccessTags:** Specifies the Smart Access Tags from the user's connection. Not applicable for non-Access Gateway connections.

- **Name:** Name of the access policy rule.

Listing 19-18 creates two access polices, the first one for access that bypasses an Access Gateway device. The second one creates an access policy for devices that go through an Access Gateway device.

LISTING 19-18

Creating Access Policies

```
New-BrokerAccessPolicyRule -AllowedConnections 'NotViaAG' `
  -AllowedProtocols @('RDP','HDX') `
  -AllowedUsers 'AnyAuthenticated' `
  -AllowRestart $True `
  -Enabled $True `
  -IncludedDesktopGroupFilterEnabled $True `
  -IncludedDesktopGroups @('Windows 7 Desktop') `
  -Name 'Windows 7 Desktop_Direct'

New-BrokerAccessPolicyRule -AllowedConnections 'ViaAG' `
  -AllowedProtocols @('RDP','HDX') `
  -AllowedUsers 'AnyAuthenticated' `
  -AllowRestart $True `
  -Enabled $True `
  -IncludedDesktopGroupFilterEnabled $True `
  -IncludedDesktopGroups @('Windows 7 Desktop') `
  -IncludedSmartAccessFilterEnabled $True `
  -IncludedSmartAccessTags @() `
  -Name 'Windows 7 Desktop_AG'
```

Now that access has been granted by the access policies, you have to control the availability of the Desktop Groups. For this, you are going to use the `New-BrokerPowerTimeScheme` cmdlet to define how many machines are available during certain periods of time. For this, you are going to use the following parameters:

- **Name:** Name of the power time scheme. Must be unique.

- **DaysOfWeek:** When the power time scheme applies. Valid values are Monday, Tuesday, Wednesday, Thursday, Friday, Saturday, Sunday, Weekdays, and Weekend — or a combination of those values.

- **DisplayName:** Name of the power time scheme in Desktop Studio. Must be unique *within* the Desktop Group, but can be duplicated in other Desktop Groups.

- **PeakHours:** A set of 24 Boolean values that represent each hour of the day starting with 00:00 and ending with 00:59. Indicates whether that period of time is considered a peak hour.

- **PoolSize:** A set of 24 Boolean values that represent each hour of the day starting with 00:00 and ending with 00:59. Defines either the absolute number of machines or a percentage of machines that are always to be running.

As you can see from the code in Listing 19-19, you create a power time scheme for business hours, which are defined as 8:00 a.m. to 6:00 p.m. Monday through Friday.

Note

When you use the Desktop Studio, you can manage only two distinct time periods, Weekdays and Weekends. When you use the cmdlets, you can define multiple time schemes. For example, you can define a time scheme for Mondays, Wednesdays, and Fridays. ■

LISTING 19-19

Controlling Availability

```
New-BrokerPowerTimeScheme -DaysOfWeek 'Weekdays' `
  -DesktopGroupUid 2 `
  -DisplayName 'Weekdays' `
  -Name 'Windows 7 Desktop_Weekdays' `
  -PeakHours (0..23 | %{ $_ -gt 8 -and $_ -lt 18 } )
  -PoolSize @(0,0,0,0,0,0,0,0,1,1,1,1,1,1,1,1,1,1,0,0,0,0,0)
```

Creating Application Desktop Groups

Application Groups, as mentioned earlier in this chapter, is the successor to VM Hosted applications. Previously, you had to have a completely separate installation. With XenDesktop 5, the Application Groups feature is built into the product itself. Application Groups allows you to run applications on a desktop operating system, but still present the application to the user. What this means is that you can present to the user Microsoft Outlook, for example, and not have to present the user with a Desktop or Start menu. One such example is an application that is not compatible with Remote Desktop Services, but you still want to present the application to the users without having to give them a desktop and multiple start menus.

Creating an Application Group is very much like creating a Desktop Group, with a few modifications. In Listing 19-20, you create the actual Desktop Group, but this time, you specify `SharedApp` as the `DesktopKind`. The rest of the parameters are the same as when you created the Desktop Group (see Listing 19-17).

LISTING 19-20

Creating and Assigning an ApplicationGroup

```
New-BrokerDesktopGroup -DesktopKind 'SharedApp' `
  -Name 'Windows 7 Application' `
  -OffPeakBufferSizePercent 10 `
```

```
-PeakBufferSizePercent 10 `
-ShutdownDesktopsAfterUse $True `
-TimeZone 'Eastern Standard Time'

Add-BrokerMachinesToDesktopGroup -Catalog 'Windows 7 Ultimate' `
  -DesktopGroup 'Windows 7 Application' `
  -Count 5
```

In Listing 19-21, you create access polices the same way you did in Listing 19-18 for a Desktop Group.

LISTING 19-21

Creating Access Policies

```
New-BrokerAccessPolicyRule -AllowedConnections 'NotViaAG' `
  -AllowedProtocols @('RDP','HDX') `
  -AllowedUsers 'AnyAuthenticated' `
  -AllowRestart $True `
  -Enabled $True `
  -IncludedDesktopGroupFilterEnabled $True `
  -IncludedDesktopGroups @('Windows 7 Application') `
  -IncludedSmartAccessFilterEnabled $True `
  -IncludedUserFilterEnabled $True `
  -Name 'Windows 7 Application_Direct'

New-BrokerAccessPolicyRule -AllowedConnections 'ViaAG' `
  -AllowedProtocols @('RDP','HDX') `
  -AllowedUsers 'AnyAuthenticated' `
  -AllowRestart $True `
  -Enabled $True `
  -IncludedDesktopGroupFilterEnabled $True `
  -IncludedDesktopGroups @('Windows 7 Application') `
  -IncludedSmartAccessFilterEnabled $True `
  -IncludedSmartAccessTags @() `
  -IncludedUserFilterEnabled $True `
  -Name 'Windows 7 Application_AG'
```

Here, in Listing 19-22, you create the time scheme for the Desktop Group the same way you did in Listing 19-19.

503

Controlling Availability

```
New-BrokerPowerTimeScheme -DaysOfWeek 'Weekdays' `
  -DesktopGroupUid 3 `
  -DisplayName 'Weekdays' `
  -Name 'Windows 7 Application_Weekdays' `
  -PeakHours
@($False,$False,$False,$False,$False,$False,$False,$True,$True,
$True,$True,$True,$True,$True,$True,$True,$True,$True,
$False,$False,$False,$False,$False,$False) `
  -PoolSize @(0,0,0,0,0,0,0,0,1,1,1,1,1,1,1,1,1,1,1,0,0,0,0,0)

New-BrokerPowerTimeScheme -DaysOfWeek 'Weekend' `
  -DesktopGroupUid 3 `
  -DisplayName 'Weekend' `
  -Name 'Windows 7 Application_Weekend' `
  -PeakHours
@($False,$False,$False,$False,$False,$False,$False,$True,$True,
$True,$True,$True,$True,$True,$True,$True,$True,$True,
$False,$False,$False,$False,$False,$False) `
  -PoolSize @(0,0,0,0,0,0,0,0,0,0,0,0,0,0,0,0,0,0,0,0,0,0,0,0)
```

When you get around to actually creating the application for the Desktop Group, you have a very important choice to make. You have two cmdlets for creating the application, New-BrokerApp and New-BrokerApplication. New-BrokerApplication is the most complete method for creating the application, but it also requires you to manually specify all of the necessary information. New-BrokerApp performs the following activities for you:

- Creates the access policy rule and adds specified users and/or session conditions
- Associates file-type associations
- Associates with Desktop Group
- Automatically attempts to locate the application icon
- Creates a folder and places the application in that folder

You will use the New-BrokerApp for the examples in this chapter because it is the most efficient way to create the application. In Listing 19-23, you create the application.

Creating the Application

```
New-BrokerApp -DisplayName "Windows PowerShell ISE" `
  -CommandLineExecutable "C:\Windows\System32\WindowsPowerShell\v1.0\↵
```

```
powershell_ise.exe" `
  -Description "Windows PowerShell ISE Script Environment" `
  -CommandLineArguments " " `
  -Enabled $True `
  -WorkingDirectory "C:\Windows\System32\WindowsPowerShell\v1.0" `
  -DesktopGroups 'Windows 7 Application' `
  -Accounts "Milkyway\Domain Users" `
  -ClientFolder "Windows PowerShell"Modifying desktop groups
```

Hosts

In XenDesktop 5, hosts refer to the hypervisor platform that contains the virtual machines you deliver to your users. XenDesktop 5 supports XenServer, Hyper-V, and ESX(i) hypervisors to deliver the virtual machines.

Hosts PSProvider

XenDesktop 5 uses a Windows PowerShell provider to facilitate access to the Hypervisor hosts that are connected to the product. In other words, XenDesktop allows you to navigate the hosts just as you would navigate a filesystem.

The Hypervisor Windows PowerShell Provider is part of the Citrix.Host.Admin .V1 snap-in. When you load the snap-in, you will notice that Get-PSDrive shows a new Windows PowerShell Provider drive named XDHyp of type citrix.host.admin.v1\ Citrix.Hypervisor. When you navigate to this drive, you will notice two subdirectories at this location as show in Figure 19-2.

FIGURE 19-2

Two subdirectories on the Windows PowerShell Provider

Connections

The Connections directory contains the connections that are created between XenDesktop and a specific hypervisor type. In the case of Microsoft Hyper-V, this is the Virtual Machine Manager server. In Citrix XenServer, it is the Resource Pool Master, and in VMWare ESX(i), it is the Virtual Center Server.

HostingUnits

The `HostingUnits` directory contains all of the actual hosting units. Hosting units, which are referred to as Hosts in the Desktop Studio, is a configuration unit that includes the name of the hosting unit, guest networks, and storage used by the hosting unit.

Adding Hosts

Adding connections and hosts to the XenDesktop environment is probably the first step that is done with any XenDesktop environment. Each of the following examples follows the same syntax for adding hosts among the various hypervisor technologies.

XenServer

In Listing 19-24, you are adding a XenServer Resource Pool to your XenDesktop environment. In the first line, you actually use the built-in Windows PowerShell cmdlet `New-Item` to add the hypervisor connection. This is possible due to the capabilities enabled by the Windows PowerShell Provider.

You specify the name of the connection as well as the hypervisor address and the connection type of `XenServer`. Because this is a XenServer Resource Pool, the hypervisor address is the URL to the XenServer Resource Pool.

With the hypervisor connection created, you now add it to XenDesktop by using `New-BrokerHypervisorConnection`. After the hypervisor connection is added, you need to add the hosts.

LISTING 19-24

Adding XenServer Hosts

```
$HyperVisorConnection = New-Item -Path 'xdhyp:\connections' `
  -Name 'MainCampusResourcePool' `
  -HypervisorAddress 'http://192.168.2.118' `
  -ConnectionType 'XenServer' `
  -Username 'root' `
  -Password 'password' `
  -Persist

New-BrokerHypervisorConnection `
  -HypHypervisorConnectionUid $HyperVisorConnection.HyperVisorConnectionUID

New-Item -Path 'xdhyp:\hostingunits' `
  -Name 'CriticalMachineHosting' `
  -HypervisorConnectionName 'MainCampusResourcePool' `
  -RootPath 'xdhyp:\connections\MainCampusResourcePool' `
  -NetworkPath 'xdhyp:\connections\MainCampusResourcePool\Network 0.network' `
  -StoragePath @('xdhyp:\connections\MainCampusResourcePool\Tier I.storage')
```

As you can see, in Listing 19-24, you again use the `New-Item` cmdlet, in this case to add the hosting unit.

For the name, I used `CriticalMachineHosting`. The reason I used this name is to illustrate that although the GUI uses the term "host" for this, it is not really a host. It is really a configuration unit. For example, with the `CriticalMachineHosting` name, you could imagine that the network specified was a priority network with greater bandwidth allocation and that the storage, for example, is on faster disks.

Hyper-V

Listing 19-25 adds a Microsoft Virtual Machine Manager environment to the XenDesktop environment. The first line is very similar to the previous example with XenServer. However, the connection type is `SCVMM` and the hypervisor address is the address of the Virtual Machine Manager controller. After the connection is created, you again utilize `New-BrokerHypervisorConnection` to add the connection to XenDesktop.

In the last step, where you add the hosting unit, you might notice something a little different in the root path as well as the network and storage path. Take the root path. You will notice that after the name of the connection, `Hyper-V`, there is another level, `SOL.host`. This is due to the nature of Virtual Machine Manager. In Virtual Machine Manager, you can have multiple clusters, unlike a single Resource Pool in XenServer. This additional level references the cluster that will be hosting your virtual machines.

LISTING 19-25

Adding Hyper-V Hosts

```
$ConnectionUID = New-Item -Path 'xdhyp:\connections' `
  -Name 'Hyper-V' `
  -HypervisorAddress @('Procyon.MilkyWay.cmschill.net') `
  -ConnectionType 'SCVMM' `
  -Username 'MilkyWay\Administrator' `
  -Password 'password' `
  -Persist

New-BrokerHypervisorConnection `
  -HypHypervisorConnectionUid $ConnectionUID.HypervisorConnectionUid

New-Item -Path 'xdhyp:\hostingunits' `
  -Name 'General VM Hosting' `
  -HypervisorConnectionName 'Hyper-V' `
  -RootPath 'XDHyp:\connections\Hyper-V\SOL.host' `
  -NetworkPath 'XDHyp:\connections\Hyper-V\SOL.host\192.168.2.0_24.network'`
  -StoragePath @('XDHyp:\connections\Hyper-V\SOL.host\VirtualMachines on ↵
SOL.MilkyWay.cmschill.net.storage')
```

ESX(i)

ESX(i) hosts are managed through VMware VCenter in the same way that Hyper-V is managed through Virtual Machine Manager. For the `ConnectionType`, you use `VCenter` to indicate that you are dealing with ESX(i) hosts, as shown in Listing 19-26. The rest of the example is the same as the Hyper-V example.

LISTING 19-26

Adding VMware Hosts

```
$ConnectionUID = New-Item -Path 'xdhyp:\connections' `
  -Name 'VMware' `
  -HypervisorAddress @('https://vcenter.MilkyWay.cmschill.net') `
  -ConnectionType 'VCenter' `
  -Username 'MilkyWay\Administrator' `
  -Password 'password' `
  -Persist

New-BrokerHypervisorConnection `
  -HypHypervisorConnectionUid $ConnectionUID.HypervisorConnectionUid

New-Item -Path 'xdhyp:\hostingunits' `
  -Name 'General VM Hosting' `
  -HypervisorConnectionName 'VMware' `
  -RootPath 'XDHyp:\connections\VMware\SOL.host' `
  -NetworkPath 'XDHyp:\connections\VMware\SOL.host\192.168.2.0_24.network' `
  -StoragePath @('XDHyp:\connections\VMware\SOL.host\VirtualMachines on ↵
SOL.MilkyWay.cmschill.net.storage')
```

Removing Hosts

Removing hosts and connections from XenDesktop is extremely simple and is the same among all hypervisors. To remove a hosting unit, you use the `Remove-Item` cmdlet, as shown here:

```
Remove-Item -Path 'xdhyp:\hostingunits\SOLHost'
```

After this statement, the hosting unit is removed. The next step is to remove the connection:

```
Remove-BrokerHypervisorConnection -Name 'SOL'
Remove-Item -Path 'xdhyp:\connections\SOL'
```

As shown here, you remove the broker connection using
`Remove-BrokerHypervisorConnection` and then you remove the hypervisor connection
itself using `Remove-Item`, just as you did with the hosting unit.

Summary

In this chapter, you explored the Citrix XenDesktop 5 product and how Windows
PowerShell can efficiently manage the environment. XenDesktop 5 was built from the
ground up with Windows PowerShell in mind.

In Part V you look at the use of virtualization. In the next chapter, you will be introduced
to Microsoft's virtualization solution, Hyper-V, which is built into the core Windows Server
2008 R2 operating system.

Part V

Virtualization and Cloud Computing

IN THIS PART

Chapter 20
Managing Hyper-V 2008 R2

Chapter 21
Managing System Center Virtual Machine Manager 2008 R2

Chapter 22
Managing Windows Azure

Chapter 23
Managing VMware vSphere PowerCLI

Managing Hyper-V 2008 R2

H yper-V is Microsoft's entry in the bare metal virtualization market. Although one of the relatively late arrivals in the market, it is a solid virtualization platform that is quickly gaining a foothold in the arena. At the core of Hyper-V is the Windows 2008 R2 kernel that enables administrators to manage Hyper-V with the same familiar tools they already use to manage Windows, including Windows PowerShell.

IN THIS CHAPTER

Using WMI to manage Hyper-V

Introducing the Windows PowerShell Management Library

Controlling virtual machines

Taking and managing snapshots

Hyper-V Management Interfaces

The default management interface provided by Microsoft for interacting with the Hyper-V service is WMI. You may remember WMI from Chapter 6, "Managing and Installing Software," where it was used to perform software-related tasks. This chapter briefly looks at the WMI interface for Hyper-V and its structure. The Windows PowerShell community is very active and is always making improvements. So, in the next section, you look at a project created by the community that augments the WMI interface and makes it easier to use. The rest of the chapter focuses solely on management using this project.

WMI Management Classes

Microsoft's interface for automation of Hyper-V is WMI. There are no native Windows PowerShell cmdlets for managing Hyper-V, but as you discovered in Chapter 6, Windows PowerShell can interact effectively with WMI.

Cross-Reference
For more information on using WMI, refer to Chapter 6, "Managing and Installing Software." ∎

The Hyper-V WMI Provider contains multiple management classes. These classes are present in the `root\virtualization` namespace. Table 20-1 lists the various classes and what component they are directed toward.

TABLE 20-1

Hyper-V WMI Classes

Class	Purpose
`Msvm_ComputerSystem`	Represents physical or virtual computer systems
`Msvm_ImageManagementService`	Represents the virtual media for a virtual machine
`Msvm_Keyboard`	Represents virtual keyboards
`Msvm_SyntheticMouse`	Represents virtual mice
`Msvm_VirtualSwitchManagementService`	Represents the global networking resources
`Msvm_VirtualSystemManagementService`	Represents the virtualization service

To illustrate how you interact with these classes, start by listing all of the computer systems in your Hyper-V environment. To do that, you use the `Msvm_ComputerSystem` class listed previously, as shown in Listing 20-1.

LISTING 20-1

Retrieving Hyper-V Machines

```
Get-WmiObject -ComputerName SOL `
  -Namespace root\virtualization `
  -Class Msvm_ComputerSystem |
    Select-Object ElementName, Description, Caption |
      Format-Table -AutoSize
```

As you can see from the output shown next, listing the class retrieves all of the machines, hosts, and virtual machines in the Hyper-V environment.

```
ElementName  Description                              Caption
-----------  -----------                              -------
Host         Microsoft Hosting Computer System Hosting Computer System
Atlanta      Microsoft Virtual Machine                Virtual Machine
Chicago      Microsoft Virtual Machine                Virtual Machine
NewYork      Microsoft Virtual Machine                Virtual Machine
```

Listing 20-2 actually provides the code necessary to perform an action on a virtual machine. First, you use a WMI query to retrieve a virtual machine with the name you specified. Next, you use the `RequestStateChange` to change the state of the machine to Enabled, which is represented by the value of 2.

Note

The `RequestStateChange` variable values and their corresponding meanings can be obtained from `http://msdn.microsoft.com/en-us/library/cc723874(v=vs.85).aspx`. ■

LISTING 20-2

Starting a Virtual Machine

```
$VM = Get-WmiObject -ComputerName SOL `
  -Namespace root\virtualization `
  -Query "SELECT * FROM Msvm_ComputerSystem WHERE ElementName = 'Atlanta'"

$VM.RequestStateChange(2)
```

Windows PowerShell Management Library for Hyper-V

Managing Hyper-V with WMI, although effective, is sometimes very cumbersome. You already saw that in order to start a virtual machine, you have to first look up a value in a table. A community-driven project called the Windows PowerShell Management Library for Hyper-V, located on the Codeplex site at `http://pshyperv.codeplex.com/`, attempts to make managing Hyper-V much easier than is possible with WMI alone. This project wraps the WMI commands with easier native Windows PowerShell commands that also perform additional error checking.

The project is delivered as a Windows PowerShell module. To install the module, follow these steps:

1. Download the module from the project's website.
2. Unblock the zip file.
    1. Right-click on the file, and click **Properties**.
    2. Under the **General** tab, click the **Unblock** button and click **OK**.

       If you do not see a **Unblock** button, then the file is already unblocked.
3. Extract the zip file to your local drive.
4. Copy the `HyperV-Install` folder to your module's directory and rename it **HyperV**.

Note

You can easily determine your module directories by checking the `PSModulePath` variable.

`Get-Item env:PSModulePath` ∎

Once you have the module in place, you can then use it by importing it with the following command:

```
Import-Module HyperV
```

The Windows PowerShell module is now loaded, and you are able to use it to manage your Hyper-V servers. From this point on, the examples in this chapter use this project unless otherwise noted.

Note

The Windows PowerShell Management Library for Hyper-V is an active community-based project. Details around it may change frequently. Please review the project's website for the most recent documentation: `http://pshyperv.codeplex.com/`. ∎

Managing Hosts

In the "WMI Management Classes" section of this chapter, you connected to a host directly. The Windows PowerShell Hyper-V Library includes a great command for discovering hosts. When you execute `Get-VMHost`, it queries your Active Directory (AD) domain and returns all of the Hyper-V servers registered. You can also specify a parameter to select another domain to search.

Retrieving Information

One of the items of information you might want to know is where the virtual disk files are stored by default. When you add a virtual disk, if you don't specify a location, it is stored in the default location. To find this location, you use the `Get-VHDDefault` function.

Using Show-HypervMenu

Within the project is a very interesting function for managing Hyper-V hosts: `Show-HypervMenu`. The `Show-HypervMenu` function does exactly what it sounds like — it creates a simple text-based menu for managing various settings of your Hyper-V host.

The code below shows the invocation of the function and the initial screen that is displayed. You can see in Figure 20-1 that you have many choices for managing the host as well as manipulating virtual machines. The menu is hierarchical in that as you select different options, you are shown different menus.

```
Show-HyperVMenu -Server SOL
```

FIGURE 20-1

Show-HyperVMenu output

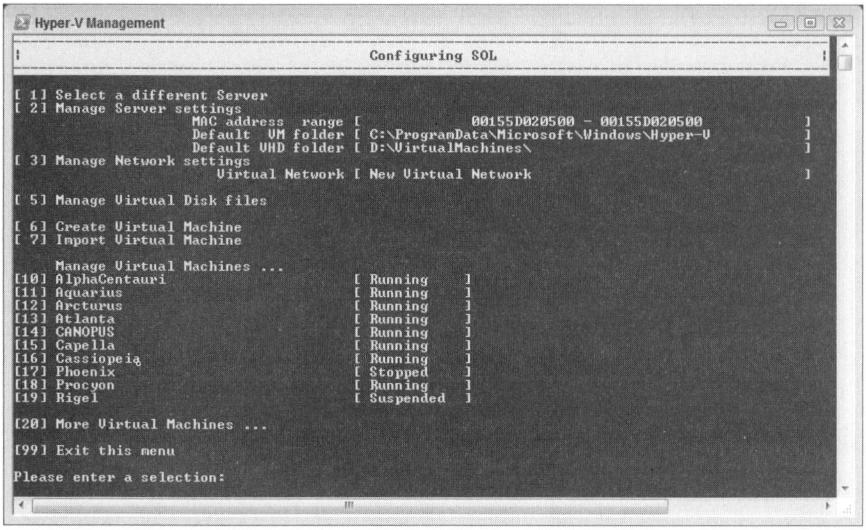

Managing Virtual Machines

In this section, you learn how to create and manage your virtual machines. You also cover controlling the power state of your virtual machine and how to take snapshots. Finally, you learn how you can easily create a disaster recovery plan with only a few lines of code.

Creating and Modifying Virtual Machines

Now you are going to create a new virtual machine. Several steps need to be completed to create a virtual machine that is ready to install a new operating system. Code for these steps is provided in Listing 20-3, which appears after the process is described.

The first step is to create a new virtual machine with the New-VM function. With this function, you create a virtual machine shell. It is configured for the bare minimum resources and does not yet have a hard drive or network connection.

Next, you set the number of CPUs and the memory to values that are adequate for your final operating system. Use the Set-VMCPUCount and Set-VMMemory functions, as well as the virtual machine object that was returned from New-VM to pass to the functions. You add a network interface card (NIC) the same way. Specify which switch you want it attached to as part of the function.

Adding a disk is a little different in this example. The function Add-VMNewHardDisk is actually doing the work of three separate functions. First, you are creating a new virtual disk file on the host that is 40 GB in size. Next, it is creating a drive in the virtual machine's controller. And finally, it is attaching your virtual disk file to the drive.

LISTING 20-3

Creating a New Virtual Machine

```
$Server = SOL
$VM = New-VM -Name Phoenix -Server $Server
Set-VMCPUCount -VM $VM -CPUCount 2 -Server $Server
Set-VMMemory -VM $VM -Memory 4GB -Server $Server
# Requires that the virtual switch already exists!
Add-VMNic -VM $VM -VirtualSwitch '192.168.2.0_24' -Server $Server
Add-VMNewHardDisk -VM $VM -Size 40GB -Server $Server -Fixed $false
```

Controlling Virtual Machines

Now that you have learned how to create a virtual machine, you proceed to managing virtual machines. In the first section, you manage the power state of the virtual machines, including starting, stopping, and shutting down virtual machines. Then, you learn how to take a snapshot of a virtual machine.

Managing Power State

Controlling virtual machines is an easy task with the Hyper-V Windows PowerShell Management Library. To start a virtual machine, you use the Start-VM function. There are two different approaches to calling Start-VM; the first is calling it directly, and the second is by passing a VM object to the function. In the first approach, you specify the virtual machine name and the server on which the virtual machine resides:

```
Start-VM -VM Phoenix -Server SOL -Wait
```

In second approach, you get a virtual machine object and then pass that object to the Start-VM function:

```
Get-VM -VM Phoenix -Server SOL | Start-VM -Wait
```

In each of these approaches, you will notice the usage of the Wait parameter. By default, the function starts the action in the background and then returns, which enables you to proceed in your script while operations are being done. However, most of the time, you will want the action to complete before proceeding. That is when the Wait parameter becomes useful. This parameter also displays a progress bar indicating the ongoing status of the job.

Suspending and stopping virtual machines is accomplished via the Suspend-VM and Stop-VM functions, respectively. These functions operate the same way Start-VM does. Suspending a virtual machine enables you to store the contents of memory to disk and "pause" a virtual machine. Stopping a virtual machine is the same as pulling the physical machine's power cord, which is not a good idea. Instead, you want to gracefully shut down the virtual machine's guest operating system. To accomplish this, you use the `Shutdown-VM` function. The `Shutdown-VM` function works the same way that the previous functions work except that it also takes a `Reason` parameter. When you specify a reason, that information is sent to the guest operating system so that it registers why the operating system was shut down and performs a graceful shutdown.

Working with Snapshots

Snapshots are an important tool in managing your virtual machines and are what make virtual machines so powerful. Within a matter of seconds, you have a point-in-time checkpoint of your virtual machine. No matter what changes you make to the operating system, you can always fall back to that point in time by reverting to that snapshot. Taking a snapshot before a major upgrade or change could save you hours of rebuilding a machine in the event of a failure.

Retrieving Snapshots

`Get-VMSnapshot` enables you to retrieve virtual machine snapshots under a variety of conditions. Simply executing `Get-VMSnapshot` without any additional parameters lists all of the snapshots on a given system:

```
Get-VMSnapshot
```

If you want to get the snapshots for a given virtual machine, you supply the `VM` parameter:

```
Get-VMSnapshot -VM UrsaMajor
```

If you want to retrieve only the latest snapshot for a given virtual machine, add the `Newest` parameter:

```
Get-VMSnapshot -VM UrsaMajor -Newest
```

Taking Snapshots

Now that you can retrieve the snapshots, you need to know how to create them. Using the `New-VMSnapshot` function, you can create snapshots of virtual machines:

```
New-VMSnapshot -VM UrsaMajor -Note "Testing" -Wait -Force
```

In the preceding example, you specify the virtual machine with the `VM` parameter. The `Note` parameter allows you to add notes to the snapshot. It is a good idea to create a detailed note indicating when the snapshot was taken, why it was taken, and for how long it should be kept. The `Wait` parameter tells the function to halt further script execution and display a progress indicator. Finally, the `Force` parameter eliminates the prompting before continuing with the operation.

When you create the snapshot, you will notice that the name of the snapshot consists of the virtual machine name and the time the snapshot was taken. This is very valuable information, but suppose you have a naming scheme that you want to adhere to. There is no way to specify the name of the snapshot, but with some additional work, you can end up with the name you want. As shown in the following code, you create the snapshot the same way you did previously. In the second step, you retrieve that snapshot by using the `Newest` parameter because this will be the latest snapshot of that virtual machine. You then pass that snapshot to `Rename-Snapshot` and specify the name you want. You also specify the `Force` parameter so you don't get prompted:

```
New-VMSnapshot -VM UrsaMajor -Note "Testing" -Wait -Force
Get-VMSnapshot -VM UrsaMajor -Newest |
  Rename-VMSnapshot -NewName "My Snapshot" -Force
```

Removing Snapshots

As time goes by, you are going to want to remove snapshots. They take up valuable space. You remove snapshots with `Remove-VMSnapshot`. The `Remove-VMSnapshot` function differs from the other functions that you have seen. In the previous functions, you could specify a virtual machine and server — and occasionally additional information. With this function, you can specify a snapshot object by parameter or pipeline, but the function itself doesn't accept any parameter directly that identifies the snapshot.

Take a look at a few test cases. The first example included in Listing 20-4 uses `Get-VMSnapshot` to retrieve the latest snapshot for the virtual machine and uses `Remove-VMSnapshot` to remove it. You again specify the `Force` and `Wait` parameters to prevent being prompted to complete the action and to pause further execution until the process is complete.

The second example in the listing uses a function not covered yet, `Choose-VMSnapshot`. This project includes several of these `Choose-*` functions, which present a text menu to allow you to select an object. In this case, you specify a virtual machine and are then presented with a tree view, from which you select the number of the snapshot that you want. This snapshot is then passed to `Remove-VMSnapshot`.

The last example in the listing introduces the `Tree` parameter. The `Tree` parameter directs `Remove-VMSnapshot` to remove the snapshot and all child snapshots.

LISTING 20-4

Removing Snapshots

```
Get-VMSnapshot -VM UrsaMajor -Newest |
  Remove-VMSnapshot -Wait -Force
Choose-VMSnapshot -VM UrsaMajor |
  Remove-VMSnapshot -Wait -Force
Get-VMSnapshot -VM UrsaMajor -Name "My Snapshot" |
  Remove-VMSnapshot -Wait -Tree -Force
```

Implementing Disaster Recovery

Disaster recovery is a huge portion of any system administrator's job, or at least it should be. You are responsible for making sure you can recover any of your systems should you have a failure in any one component. With the Windows PowerShell Management Library for Hyper-V, it is a figurative piece of cake. The library includes a function called `Get-VMBuildScript` that enables you to generate a Windows PowerShell script that will help you rebuild your environment.

In Figure 20-2, `Get-VMBuildScript` is executed for the CANOPUS virtual machine. From the output, you can see that when the function is executed, the output is Windows PowerShell code. The Windows PowerShell code that is outputted enables you to re-create the virtual machine with exactly the same configuration. If you include this script with backups of the virtual disks, you can completely restore your virtual machines on any Hyper-V server.

FIGURE 20-2

Get-VMBuildScript used to re-create a virtual machine

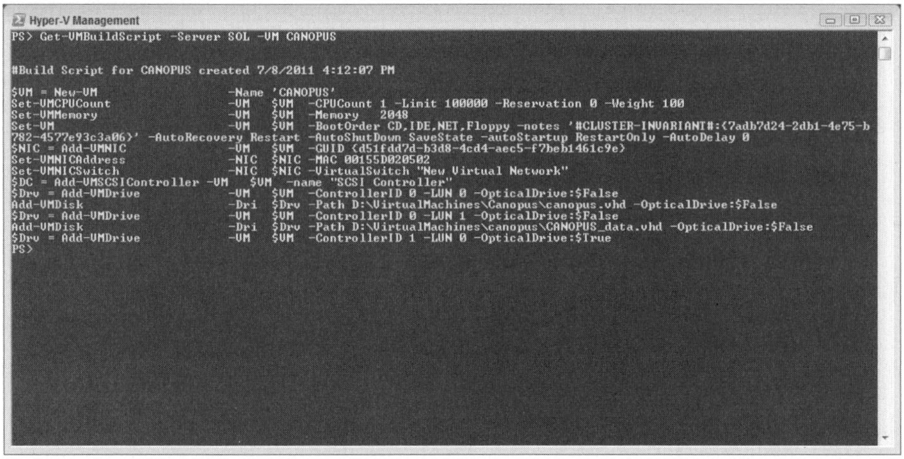

This example specified the virtual machine using the VM parameter. If you omit the parameter, the output will include the code to re-create all of the virtual machines on the server.

Summary

In this chapter, you were introduced to the Hyper-V WMI providers as well as the Windows PowerShell Hyper-V Management Library. You learned how to create and manage virtual machines as well as use snapshots to create point-in-time copies of your virtual machines. The next chapter discusses the System Center Virtual Machine Manager, Microsoft's enterprise management platform for managing Hyper-V environments.

Managing System Center Virtual Machine Manager 2008 R2

IN THIS CHAPTER

Adding Hyper-V hosts to VMM

Attaching clusters to VMM

Creating and controlling virtual machines

Introducing libraries

System Center Virtual Machine Manager (VMM), part of the System Center suite of applications, is Microsoft's solution for managing Hyper-V, Microsoft's virtualization tool in enterprise environments. In this chapter, you explore managing hosts and virtual machines as well as maintaining your VMM library.

Working with System Center Virtual Machine Manager 2008 R2

In this section, you are introduced to the VMM snap-in. In addition, you learn how to back up the VMM database and how to use the VMM Administrator Console to write scripts.

Installing and Loading the Cmdlets

To install the VMM cmdlets on your system, you need to install the VMM Administrator Console. Once you install the VMM Administrator Console, the cmdlets are installed. They are in the `Microsoft .SystemCenter.VirtualMachineManager` snap-in. To load them into your system, you load this snap-in:

```
Add-PSSnapin -Name Microsoft.SystemCenter.VirtualMachineManager
```

The VMM cmdlets are now loaded into your Windows PowerShell session and are available to you.

Backing Up the VMM Database

VMM has a unique cmdlet that enables you to back up your VMM database without having to engage the assistance of your local database administrator. This is accomplished with the `Backup-VMMServer` cmdlet. The first step is to use `Get-VMServer` to get a Virtual Machine Manager server object. That server object is then passed to the `Backup-VMMServer` cmdlet.

```
$VMMServer = Get-VMMServer -ComputerName Procyon
$VMMServer | Backup-VMMServer -Path "D:\Backups\VMM"
```

The `Path` parameter is passed to the cmdlet with the location of where you want to store the backup file. The location specified here is the path relative to the SQL Server that hosts your database and not the Virtual Machine server. To restore the VMM database, you will need to use the `SCVMMRecover.exe` tool directly on the Virtual Machine Manager server.

Using the VMM Administrator Console to Write Scripts

Even using the VMM Administrator Console, you are still using Windows PowerShell. This is because the console is, in fact, based on Windows PowerShell cmdlets. When you execute an action in the GUI, it calls Windows PowerShell cmdlets to do the actual work. This is most evident when you click the View Script button in the summary screen of an action, as you can see in Figure 21-1.

FIGURE 21-1

VMM Administrator Console

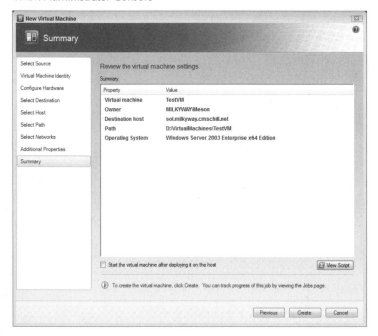

If you click this button, Notepad opens up with the actual scripts that are going to be called to perform the action as shown in Figure 21-2.

FIGURE 21-2

VMM Administrator Console script

```
tmp15B.tmp - Notepad
File  Edit  Format  View  Help
# --------------------------------------------------------------------------------
# New Virtual Machine Script
# --------------------------------------------------------------------------------
# Script generated on Tuesday, July 12, 2011 12:34:25 AM by Virtual Machine Manager
#
# For additional help on cmdlet usage, type get-help <cmdlet name>
# --------------------------------------------------------------------------------


New-VirtualNetworkAdapter -VMMServer Procyon -JobGroup a9bc2172-9566-4f97-9a66-29683e7ef659 -
PhysicalAddressType Dynamic -VirtualNetwork "New Virtual Network" -VLanEnabled $false

New-VirtualDVDDrive -VMMServer Procyon -JobGroup a9bc2172-9566-4f97-9a66-29683e7ef659 -Bus 1 -LUN 0

$CPUType = Get-CPUType -VMMServer Procyon | where {$_.Name -eq "1.20 GHz Athlon MP"}

New-HardwareProfile -VMMServer Procyon -Owner "MILKYWAY\Meson" -CPUType $CPUType -Name "Profile7acf969d-
a66a-469f-a982-a1ae74ddf793" -Description "Profile used to create a VM/Template" -CPUCount 1 -MemoryMB
512 -RelativeWeight 100 -HighlyAvailable $false -NumLock $false -BootOrder "CD", "IdeHardDrive",
"PxeBoot", "Floppy" -LimitCPUFunctionality $false -LimitCPUForMigration $false -JobGroup a9bc2172-9566-
4f97-9a66-29683e7ef659


New-VirtualDiskDrive -VMMServer Procyon -IDE -Bus 0 -LUN 0 -JobGroup a9bc2172-9566-4f97-9a66-29683e7ef659
-Size 40960 -Dynamic -Filename "TestVM_disk_1"

$VMHost = Get-VMHost -VMMServer Procyon | where {$_.Name -eq "sol.milkyway.cmschill.net"}
$HardwareProfile = Get-HardwareProfile -VMMServer Procyon | where {$_.Name -eq "Profile7acf969d-a66a-
469f-a982-a1ae74ddf793"}
$OperatingSystem = Get-OperatingSystem -VMMServer Procyon | where {$_.Name -eq "Windows Server 2003
Enterprise x64 Edition"}

New-VM -VMMServer Procyon -Name "TestVM" -Description "" -Owner "MILKYWAY\Meson" -VMHost $VMHost -Path
"D:\VirtualMachines" -HardwareProfile $HardwareProfile -JobGroup a9bc2172-9566-4f97-9a66-29683e7ef659 -
RunAsynchronously -OperatingSystem $OperatingSystem -RunAsSystem -StartAction NeverAutoTurnOnVM -
StopAction SaveVM
```

Connecting to VMM

When working with the VMM cmdlets, you have a couple of methods for connecting to the VMM Server. One is to pass or specify the server directly. In the previous example, where the VMM database was backed up, Get-VMMServer was used to get a ServerConnection object, which was then passed to the Backup-VMServer cmdlet. You could just as easily have specified the VMMServer property and entered the object variable. You can also specify the server name in which the cmdlet would internally get the ServerConnection object.

Another option is to use an implicit pass-through. If you call Get-VMMServer and get a ServerConnection object, that object is stored in the Windows PowerShell session. It is available until your session is closed. To illustrate, you can rewrite the backup example as follows:

```
Get-VMMServer -ComputerName Procyon
Backup-VMMServer -Path "D:\Backups\VMM"
```

As you can see, you didn't store the connection, nor did you pass it to the backup cmdlet.

Note

The latter method of implicit pass-through is efficient, but I wouldn't recommend using it when you are writing a script. It will make it hard for someone viewing the script to know how you obtained your connection. Without explicitly specifying the connection, there is always a slight chance that something might interfere and switch connections to another server. ∎

Working with Host Servers

In this section, you work with the hypervisor hosts that power VMM. You begin with adding hosts to VMM and proceed to organizing hosts within VMM.

Adding Hosts to VMM

Virtual Machine Manager supports managing three different host types:

- Virtual Server hosts
- Hyper-V hosts
- VMware ESX(i) hosts

Virtual Server is a Windows-based virtualization platform that, unlike Hyper-V, is a service that runs on top of Windows. Its latest version is 2005 R2. VMware ESX(i) hosts are supported via the VMWare VirtualCenter product. Neither Virtual Server nor ESX(i) are considered in this chapter.

Note

If you are adding a host that is not in a domain, such as in a DMZ network, you will first have to install the Virtual Machine Manager agent on those systems. When adding those systems, you have to establish an encryption key and use that key when adding the host. ∎

The code in Listing 21-1 adds your first host to the VMM environment. In the code, you need to pass administrator credentials to the cmdlet that adds the host, so you use `Get-Credential` to store the credential in the `$Credential` variable. The next step is to retrieve the host group that you want to add your host. *Host groups* are virtual folders for you to organize your hosts in VMM. In this example, you are placing your host in the All Hosts group that is the default group in VMM.

The final step is to actually add the host to the VMM Server via the `Add-VMHost` cmdlet. The `Add-VMHost` cmdlet supports several parameters. The primary ones are listed here:

- **VMMServer:** The VMM Server to which you are adding the host.
- **ComputerName:** The name of the host you are adding to the VMM environment.
- **Description:** Optional description used to identify the host.
- **Credential:** Required credential object used to add the host.

- **RemoteConnectEnabled:** Whether you want to allow remote connections to virtual machines on the specified host.
- **VMPaths:** The default location where new virtual machine disks will be added.
- **VMHostGroup:** The host group where the host will be located inside the VMM management environment.
- **AvailableForPlacement:** An indicator of whether or not the host can be used for placement of virtual machines. Set this to false when you don't want virtual machines on the host until later.

Once the `Add-VMHost` cmdlet is executed, it will take a considerable amount of time because the agents are installed on the host. Code execution will be halted until the cmdlet returns. If you want to continue code execution, you can use the `RunAsynchronously` parameter to place the execution in the background. That parameter is not used in Listing 21-1.

LISTING 21-1

Adding a Hyper-V Host

```
$Credential = Get-Credential
$VMHostGroup = Get-VMHostGroup -VMMServer PROCYON |
  Where-Object {$_.Path -eq "All Hosts"}

Add-VMHost -VMMServer PROCYON `
    -ComputerName "sol.milkyway.cmschill.net" `
    -Description "" `
    -Credential $Credential `
    -RemoteConnectEnabled $True `
    -VmPaths "D:\VirtualMachines" `
    -VMHostGroup $VMHostGroup `
    -AvailableForPlacement $True
```

If you add a host that has already had an older version of the VMM agent installed, you might also need to update the agent on the host. Listing 21-2 shows the command for updating the agent on the host just added. Running this cmdlet against a system with the most recent agent version doesn't perform any action. This next listing can be added to any scripts that add new hosts to an environment to make sure they are up-to-date.

LISTING 21-2

Updating a Host Agent

```
$Credential = Get-Credential
Get-VMMManagedComputer -ComputerName "sol.milkyway.cmschill.net" |
  Update-VMMManagedComputer -Credential $Credential
```

Organizing Hosts

To organize your hosts in Virtual Machine Manager, you use host groups. Host groups are organizational containers that enable you to group your hosts in a hierarchical structure inside of VMM.

For this example, you create a new host group and move your newly added server into it. The first step is to get the host object using `Get-VMHost`. Then, you create a new host group called `My Cluster` in the existing `Clusters` host group. Lastly, you use `Move-VMHost` to move the host into your host group.

```
$VMHost = Get-VMHost -ComputerName sol.milkyway.cmschill.net
$HostGroup = New-VMHostGroup -Name  "My Cluster" -ParentHostGroup "Clusters"
Move-VMHost -VMHost $VMHost -ParentHostGroup $HostGroup
```

Managing Clusters

VMM supports highly available virtual machines when deployed on failover clusters. This section covers the cmdlets that interact with clusters. A *failover cluster* is a group of independent servers that interact with each other to provide increased availability of applications and services. Formerly known as *server clusters*, failover clusters are available in Windows Server 2008 Enterprise and Windows Server 2008 Datacenter.

Adding Clusters

Before you can add the host cluster to VMM, you have to create the failover cluster using the Failover Cluster Management tool to create and configure the cluster. Creating and configuring the cluster is not covered in this book. To add the cluster, you use the `Add-VMHostCluster` cmdlet with the following parameters:

- **Name:** Name of your preconfigured failover host cluster
- **Credential:** Required credential object used to add the cluster
- **Description:** Optional description to identify the cluster
- **RemoteConnectEnabled:** Boolean value that indicates whether users can connect to their virtual machines remotely
- **RemoteConnectPort:** Default value for the TCP port when users connect to their virtual machine remotely
- **VMHostGroup:** Virtual directory in the VMM environment where you want your cluster placed
- **JobVariable:** Specifies that job progress is tracked and stored in the variable name specified
- **RunAsynchronously:** Switch that returns control immediately

Listing 21-3 shows the steps for adding a host cluster to the VMM environment. For clarification, note that the `JobVariable` parameter is in no way related to the Windows PowerShell job system. The job functionality discussed here is completely contained within the VMM cmdlets.

LISTING 21-3

Adding a Host Cluster

```
$Credential = Get-Credential
$VMHostGroup = Get-VMHostGroup | Where-Object ($_.Path -eq "Clusters"}
Add-VMHostCluster -Name "HostCluster.domain.com" `
  -Credential $Credential `
  -Description "Hyper-V Failover Cluster" `
  -RemoteConnectEnabled $True `
  -RemoteConnectPort 2179 `
  -VMHostGroup = $VMHostGroup `
  -VMMServer PROCYON `
  -JobVariable "ClusterAddition" `
  -RunAsynchronously

while ($ClusterAddition.status -eq "Running")
{
  Write-Host "Still running…"
  Start-Sleep -Seconds 10
}
Write-Host "Addition complete."
```

When the last statement is executed, the cmdlet actually populates the variable `$ClusterAddition` with an object that represents the job of adding the host cluster. Say you have an additional step that needs to be performed, but only after the cluster is added. You accomplish this by checking the `$ClusterAddition.Status` property to make sure it does not still indicate the job is running.

Caution

Windows PowerShell uses a strong naming convention that uses the module name in addition to the actual cmdlet name to identify cmdlets. This allows for the possibility of having duplicate cmdlet names. This is actually evident with the VMM cmdlets.

The following output demonstrates that the `Microsoft.SystemCenter.VirtualMachineManager` snap-in has a `Get-Job` cmdlet, which is also in the core Windows PowerShell framework. The VMM cmdlet takes priority. If you want to execute the framework version of the cmdlet, you have to execute `Microsoft.PowerShell.Core\Get-Job`.

```
PS> Get-Command -Name Get-Job* |
>> Select-Object Name, ModuleName, CommandType |
```

```
>> Format-Table -Autosize
>>
```

```
Name     ModuleName                                      CommandType
----     ----------                                      -----------
Get-Job  Microsoft.PowerShell.Core                           Cmdlet
Get-Job  Microsoft.SystemCenter.VirtualMachineManager         Cmdlet ■
```

Performing Maintenance on Host Servers

During your normal system administration routine, you will no doubt have to perform work on one of your Hyper-V servers. With a failover cluster and VMM, migrating hosts is an easy task.

The first step is to populate variables with the name of the host you want to perform maintenance on and the host group that contains the cluster that your host belongs to. This example assumes that only your cluster hosts are in the specified host group.

The next step is to iterate through each of the virtual machines on your host. If the virtual machine is running, a set of commands is run; otherwise, nothing is done to a virtual machine that is not running.

With each of the running virtual machines, you get a hashtable of the host ratings. Host ratings are numbers or stars from one to five in half-star increments that indicate the suitability of a host to accept a virtual machine. The following statement retrieves the host ratings in descending order for all hosts that are able to accept the virtual machine:

```
$HostRatings = @(Get-VMHostRating `
  -VM $VM `
  -VMHostGroup $VMHostGroup `
  -IsMigration |
    Where-Object {$_.Rating -gt 0 } |
      Sort-Object -Property Rating -Descending)
```

If there are no available hosts, the script in Listing 21-4 writes an error to screen. Otherwise, the virtual machine is moved to the host with the highest rating, unless it is its current host, in which case it is moved to the next-highest-rated host.

The last step is to reconfigure the host to indicate that is in maintenance mode by setting AvailableForPlacement to $False. Listing 21-4 walks through the steps for migrating all of your virtual machines off your host and then places the host in maintenance mode.

LISTING 21-4

Evacuating a Host

```
$VMHost = "sol.milkyway.cmschill.net"
Get-VMMServer -ComputerName "Procyon"
```

```
$VMHostGroup = Get-VMHostGroup |
  Where-Object {$_.Path -eq 'All Hosts\My Cluster'}


foreach ($VM in (Get-VM -VMHost $VMHost) )
{
  if ( $VM.Status -eq 'Running' )
  {
    $HostRatings = @(Get-VMHostRating -VM $VM `
      -VMHostGroup $VMHostGroup `
      -IsMigration |
        Where-Object {$_.Rating -gt 0 } |
          Sort-Object -Property Rating -Descending)

    if ($HostRatings.Count -eq 0)
    {
      Write-Error "No alternate hosts available."
    }

    if ( $HostRatings[0].VMHost -ne $VMHost )
    {
      Move-VM -VM $VM -VMHost $HostRatings[0].VMHost
    }
    else
    {
      Move-VM -VM $VM -VMHost $HostRatings[1].VMHost
    }
  }
}

Set-VMHost -VMHost $VMHost -AvailableForPlacement $False
```

Working with Virtual Machines

In this section, you interact with virtual machines beginning with the creation of virtual machines. Next, you learn how to modify and control virtual machines. Finally, you learn how to use snapshots.

Creating and Modifying Virtual Machines

Creating a new virtual machine involves several steps. This section breaks the steps down into independent sections that can be placed together to create a new virtual machine.

The first thing you need to do is to create the Hardware Profile. The *Hardware Profile* is used to store the hardware configuration. The first statement in Listing 21-5 gets the CPUType that corresponds to a processor type of a 1.0 GHz Pentium III Xeon. The CPU type represents the characteristics of the processor that your virtual machine requires. VMM uses this value to determine which hosts your virtual machine can exist on. In most cases, you just need a generic CPU, so that is why I selected this value.

LISTING 21-5

Creating the Hardware Profile

```
$CPUType = Get-CPUType -VMMServer PROCYON |
  Where-Object {$_.Name -eq "1.00 GHz Pentium III Xeon"}

$HardwareProfile = New-HardwareProfile -VMMServer PROCYON `
  -Owner "MILKYWAY\Meson" `
  -CPUType $CPUType `
  -Name "ServerDefaultProfile" `
  -Description "Default Server Profile" `
  -CPUCount 2 `
  -MemoryMB 4096 `
  -RelativeWeight 100 `
  -HighlyAvailable $False `
  -NumLock $False `
  -BootOrder "CD", "IdeHardDrive", "PxeBoot", "Floppy"
```

With the CPU type retrieved, you now focus on the Hardware Profile itself. The Hardware Profile enables you to template the general configuration of virtual machines without including the disks or networking. In this example, the profile is named `ServerDefaultProfile`, indicating that you tend to use this profile for all of your servers. The parameters used include:

- **Owner:** Owner of the virtual machine in the form of an Active Directory account.
- **CPUType:** The `CPUType` object retrieved previously.
- **Name:** Name of your Hardware Profile.
- **Description:** Description of your Hardware Profile.
- **CPUCount:** Number of virtual CPUs in your Hardware Profile.
- **MemoryMB:** Amount of memory in megabytes that you want to allocate to your virtual machine.
- **RelativeWeight:** Amount of CPU resources the host can use relative to other virtual machines on the host. For example, a machine with a value of 200 would be granted more resources than a machine with a value of 100.
- **NumLock:** Whether or not the number lock is enabled on the virtual machine.
- **BootOrder:** Order of devices that the virtual machine will boot.

Once you execute this command, you now have a Hardware Profile that you can use to create your virtual machine.

In the next section, you retrieve some information that is needed to create the virtual machine. The first piece of required information is the host, as shown in Listing 21-6. You use `Get-VMHost` to retrieve the object that represents a Hyper-V server named `sol.milkyway.cmschill.net`. This is the server that you want to place your new machine on.

The next bit of information you need is the operating system. Because you are building a new server, you are going to install Windows Server 2008 R2. For this example, select the value of 64-bit edition of Windows Server 2008 R2 Standard. Use `Get-OperatingSystem` to get all the possible operating systems, and then filter out the one you want.

LISTING 21-6

Getting Data

```
$VMHost = Get-VMHost -VMMServer PROCYON |
  Where-Object {$_.Name -eq "sol.milkyway.cmschill.net"}

$OperatingSystem = Get-OperatingSystem -VMMServer PROCYON |
  Where-Object {$_.Name -eq "64-bit edition of Windows Server 2008 R2 Standard"}
```

Now you have all the information you need to create a virtual machine. You can create the virtual machine by using the `New-VM` cmdlet, as shown in Listing 21-7, along with the following parameters:

- **Name:** Displayed name of your virtual machine.
- **Description:** How you describe your virtual machine.
- **OperatingSystem:** Operating system you plan on installing inside the virtual machine.
- **Owner:** Owner of the virtual machine in the form of an Active Directory account.
- **VMHost:** Host object that you retrieved representing the host the virtual machine will be placed on.
- **HardwareProfile:** Your newly created Hardware Profile.
- **StartAction:** What action you want performed on your virtual machine when your host starts. In this case, it's a server, so you always want it to be running.
- **DelayStart:** Number of seconds to wait before starting this virtual machine. Use this value to stagger the startup of virtual machines.
- **StopAction:** Action to perform on a virtual machine when the host for your virtual machine is stopping.

Listing 21-7 provides the code needed to create the virtual machine using the `New-VM` cmdlet and its parameters.

```
LISTING 21-7
```

Creating the Virtual Machine

```
$VM = New-VM -VMMServer PROCYON `
  -Name "MyVM" `
  -Description "My New VM" `
  -OperatingSystem $OperatingSystem `
  -Owner "MILKYWAY\Meson" `
  -VMHost $VMHost `
  -Path "D:\VirtualMachines" `
  -HardwareProfile $HardwareProfile `
  -StartAction AlwaysAutoTurnOnVM `
  -DelayStart 0 `
  -StopAction SaveVM
```

At this point, your virtual machine is not complete. Although you have a virtual machine, it doesn't have any networking or storage capability — and what good is a virtual machine without storage and networking? Beginning in Listing 21-8, you create a new virtual machine network adapter using the `New-VirtualNetworkManager` cmdlet.

```
LISTING 21-8
```

Adding Storage and Networking

```
# $VM is the object created with New-VM
New-VirtualNetworkAdapter -VM $VM `
  -PhysicalAddressType Dynamic `
  -VirtualNetwork "New Virtual Network"

New-VirtualDVDDrive -VM $VM `
-Bus 1 `
-LUN 0

New-VirtualDiskDrive -VM $VM `
-IDE `
-Bus 0 `
-LUN 0 `
-Size 40960 `
-Dynamic `
-Filename "MyVM_disk_1"
```

By setting the `PhysicalAddressType` to `Dynamic`, you tell VMM that you don't care about the virtual MAC address and to generate one on completion. With the `VirtualNetwork` parameter, you indicate that you want your virtual machine to connect to the virtual switch on your "New Virtual Network" network.

In the next two statements, you add storage to the virtual machine. You begin by adding a DVD drive. Using the `New-VirtualDVDDrive` cmdlet, you simply specify the Bus ID and the LUN ID that you want to use. For the hard drive, you use the `New-VirtualDiskDrive`, which requires the Bus ID and the LUN ID as well as a few more parameters. You, of course, specify the size of your virtual disk; in this case, you require a 40 GB drive. You also specify the filename for the virtual disk. The disk will be stored in the default location for the hypervisor.

The last parameter in the cmdlet is the `Dynamic` switch. The `Dynamic` switch tells VMM that you want a dynamic disk. A *dynamic disk* is one that starts as needed and grows as large as it needs to, up to the maximum size. The virtual machine sees the entire space as available.

Note

Dynamic disks enable you to give the space to a virtual machine that it needs to grow. However, if you don't watch it, you can over-allocate your storage and run out of space on your storage devices. If you do use dynamic disks, an excellent exercise for you would be to use Windows PowerShell to create a report showing the total amount of available space and the amount of allocated space. ∎

Removing Virtual Machines

You can remove virtual machines with the `Remove-VM` cmdlet. Removing a virtual machine deletes the record from Virtual Machine Manager and deletes all files associated with the virtual machine. You can specify the name directly or pass a virtual machine object.

```
Remove-VM -VM MyVM
Get-VM | Where-Object {$_.Name -eq 'MyVM'} | Remove-VM
```

Caution

Before removing a virtual machine, make sure that you back up or save any files you need. When you execute this command, the virtual machine files will no longer be available. ∎

Controlling Virtual Machines

Several cmdlets are available for controlling your virtual machines. Table 21-1 lists those cmdlets. As you saw in previous examples, you can specify the virtual machine as a parameter of the cmdlet or via the pipeline. Both examples are shown here:

```
Start-VM -VM MyVM
Get-VM | Where-Object {$_.Name -eq 'MyVM' } | Shutdown-VM
```

TABLE 21-1	

Cmdlets Used to Control Virtual Machine State

Cmdlet	Description
Resume-VM	Resumes paused virtual machines managed by Virtual Machine Manager
SaveState-VM	Saves the state of virtual machines managed by Virtual Machine Manager
Shutdown-VM	Shuts down a running virtual machine managed by Virtual Machine Manager
Start-VM	Starts virtual machines managed by Virtual Machine Manager
Stop-VM	Stops virtual machines managed by Virtual Machine Manager
Suspend-VM	Suspends execution on virtual machines managed by Virtual Machine Manager

Managing Checkpoints

VMM uses checkpoints to allow you to save the state of your virtual machines at any point in time. Generally called snapshots in other products, checkpoints provide a method for taking temporary backups.

Creating Checkpoints

Creating a checkpoint in VMM allows you to create a point-in-time snapshot for a virtual machine. To create a checkpoint in VMM, you will use the New-VMCheckPoint cmdlet as shown in the following code:

```
Get-VMMServer -ComputerName "Procyon"
New-VMCheckPoint -VM "TestVM" `
   -Description "TestVM - SP1 Upgrade"
```

The VM parameter is required and specifies which virtual machine to take a checkpoint on. The Description parameter is optional, but it is recommended to describe the purpose of the checkpoint.

Note

With VMM, you are able to take a maximum of 64 checkpoints. However, checkpoints do take up space, so routinely purging unneeded checkpoints is recommended. ■

Retrieving Checkpoints

Once your checkpoints are created, you need to be able to retrieve them and information about them. Using Get-VMCheckpoint without parameters retrieves all checkpoints registered in the VMM server.

```
Get-VMCheckpoint
```

By specifying the virtual machine using the VM parameter, you retrieve the checkpoints for that virtual machine:

```
Get-VMCheckpoint -VM "TestVM"
```

One additional parameter of interest is the MostRecent parameter. By specifying the MostRecent parameter, you retrieve the most recent snapshot:

```
Get-VMCheckpoint -VM "TestVM" -MostRecent
```

Removing Checkpoints

Removing a checkpoint is an easy task. First, you need to get a reference to a checkpoint using Get-VMCheckpoint, and then pass that to Remove-VMCheckpoint, as illustrated here:

```
Get-VMCheckpoint -VM "TestVM" |
    Remove-VMCheckpoint
```

In this example, you remove all the checkpoints for the specified VM. Alternatively, you could also explicitly specify the checkpoint, as shown here:

```
$Checkpoint = Get-VMCheckpoint -VM "TestVM" -MostRecent
Remove-VMCheckpoint -VMCheckpoint $Checkpoint
```

In this example, you delete the most recent checkpoint for the specified virtual machine.

Restoring Checkpoints

Restoring checkpoints allows you to return a virtual machine to the time at which the checkpoint was taken. In the example here, you restore a machine to the most recent checkpoint for the specified virtual machine:

```
$Checkpoint = Get-VMCheckpoint -VM "TestVM" -MostRecent
Restore-VMCheckpoint -VMCheckpoint $Checkpoint
```

Note

When restoring a checkpoint, it is important to note that any changes made to a machine after the most recent checkpoint will be discarded. If you want to maintain information of the current state, it is important that you take a new checkpoint. ■

Libraries

Virtual Machine Manager libraries are repositories for the storage of virtual machine resources. A library can include:

- Virtual hard disks
- CD/DVD ISO images

- Virtual machine templates
- Stored virtual machines
- Virtual floppy disks
- Hardware and guest profiles
- Sysprep answer files

A library is important because it allows for the central storage and reuse of components among the various hosts of a VMM implementation. In this section, you look at some of the tasks associated with libraries.

Creating a Library

A VMM *library* is a combination of physical media stored on a network share along with data stored in the VMM database. By default, a library is created on your VMM server. For the purpose of this example, assume you want to create a new library on a new server in your datacenter.

On your new server, you completed some previous configurations in preparation. The first thing you did was create a folder structure on your server to hold your files. Then, you shared it as VMM. It can be blank because you just need a file share.

Now, you are ready to create your server. The first step, as you have seen in prior examples, is to get the administrator credentials and store them in a variable. Then, you call Add-LibraryServer, specifying the server name and your VMM server as well as the credentials.

```
$Credential = Get-Credential
Add-LibraryServer -ComputerName Atlanta `
  -VMMServer Procyon `
  -Credential $Credential `
  -AllowUnencryptedTransfers $True
```

You also set AllowUnencryptedTransfers to $True. As you can imagine, that parameter allows transfers to and from the library to occur unencrypted. For this environment, you don't have the security requirement and can use the extra performance from not having to encrypt the data. When this cmdlet is executed, VMM installs the VMM agent on the target server.

Now that the server has been added to the library, you are going to add the share. You use Add-LibraryShare and provide the Universal Naming Convention (UNC) path to the share you created to the SharePath parameter:

```
Add-LibraryShare -SharePath \\Atlanta\VMM `
  -Credential $Credential `
  -Description "VMM Library Share"
```

The library share is now available, but it is empty. You can create folders on your library share and/or copy your files to it. If you have the VMM console opened, you may notice that the files you have placed in the library share aren't visible. That is because VMM needs to update its inventory of the share so it can be displayed. It is periodically updated, so you could just wait. Or you can manually update or refresh the library using `Refresh-LibraryShare`.

Use `Get-LibraryShare` with `Where-Object` to retrieve the library share object, which is then passed to `Refresh-LibraryShare`. This causes VMM to update its inventory of the contents of the physical share.

```
Get-LibraryShare |
  Where-Object {$_.LibraryServer -eq "Atlanta.MilkyWay.cmschill.net" } |
    Refresh-LibraryShare
```

Finding Dependent Objects

As you fill up your library with all of the objects you need to support your environment, you will no doubt accumulate extra components over time. After files have accumulated for a period of time, you will need to clean out your files. First, however, you need to determine whether the objects are in use. VMM provides a cmdlet for this purpose: `Get-DependentLibraryObject`.

In the following example, you use `Get-VirtualHardDisk` to retrieve the hard drives in your library and then select the hard drives that don't have any dependent objects. In this case, a *dependent object* for a hard drive would be a virtual machine that is attached to it. You can replace hard drives with any other library components that you want to review.

```
# Get all hard disks that aren't attached to a virtual machine
Get-VirtualHardDisk |
  Where-Object { (!(Get-DependentLibraryObject $_)) } |
  Select-Object Name

# Get all DVD ISOs that aren't attached to a virtual machine
Get-ISO |
  Where-Object { (!(Get-DependentLibraryObject $_)) } |
  Select-Object Name
```

Summary

In this chapter, you were introduced to Virtual Machine Manager and learned how to use the VMM Administrator Console to help you create your scripts. You learned how to manage hosts and high-availability situations. Finally, you created and managed virtual machines.

In the next chapter, you will be introduced to Microsoft's cloud service, Windows Azure.

Managing Windows Azure

M icrosoft's cloud service offering, Windows Azure, is a robust and extendable infrastructure to host applications that can live in virtual machines (VMs) all over the world. The fact that these systems are dispersed requires not only a delicate hand when it comes to architecting the applications, but also the ability to easily automate tasks like deploying code and scaling the applications to more infrastructure. Although C#, Silverlight, and .NET are the tools being used for the applications that are created in Azure, Windows PowerShell is quickly becoming the automation tool of choice for the Microsoft cloud.

IN THIS CHAPTER

Installing the WASM cmdlets

Scripting Windows Azure deployments

Modifying Windows Azure deployments

Working with Windows Azure logs

Note

When this book was written, the Windows Azure Service Manager (WASM) cmdlets were in Version 1.2. These cmdlets provide a way to do automation tasks like deployments, code changes, configure monitoring, and scaling applications, but it is expected that we will see them grow and mature in future versions. This chapter dives into what is currently available with Version 1.2 of the cmdlets. ∎

Installing and Using the Windows Azure Service Manager Cmdlets

To use the Windows Azure Service Manager (WASM) cmdlets, you must have the following installed on your computer:

- Windows PowerShell
- .NET 3.5 SP1 or higher
- IIS 7 with ASP.NET
- IIS MMC (required by the SDK)
- The Windows Azure software development kit (SDK)

The WASM cmdlet installation files come with a dependency checker that ensures that you have met all of the prerequisites to install the snap-in. If you have not met the requirements, the WASM Configuration Wizard will provide a link to download or install the missing components, as shown in Figure 22-1.

FIGURE 22-1

The WASM dependency checker

Warning

If you use the dependency checker to install the SDK, you will not be able to use the Rescan button to complete the snap-in installation after the SDK installation completes. You must close and rerun the dependency checker in order for it to detect that you have a later version of the SDK than the one originally required. ■

Installing the WASM Cmdlets

You can download the installation files for the WASM cmdlets from the MSDN archive at `http://archive.msdn.microsoft.com/azurecmdlets`.

Once the files are downloaded and extracted to your hard drive (by default, this is to `c:\WASMCmdlets`), you can run `startHere.cmd`. This first loads the dependency checker to help you ensure that your prerequisites are met, followed by the WASM cmdlet installation that installs a snap-in named `AzureManagementToolsSnapIn`.

After the snap-in is installed, you can load it into your Windows PowerShell session with the following:

```
Add-PsSnapin AzureManagementToolsSnapIn
```

Creating and Registering Your Certificate

To control your Windows Azure instance with the WASM cmdlets, you need to create a management certificate for your machine, and then upload it to your instance of Windows Azure. If you have a certificate signed by a certificate authority, you can use that. If you need to create a self-signed certificate, you can do so with the `makecert` utility that is installed with the Windows SDK:

```
.\makecert -r -pe -a sha1 -n CN=Azure -ss My -sky exchange -b 02/28/2011 ↵
-e 12/31/2039 "Azure.cer"
```

Once you have the certificate, you need to upload it to your Azure instance:

1. Log on to `https://windows.azure.com`. This opens the management portal.
2. Click Hosted Services, Storage Accounts & CDN. A new list of tasks is shown in the upper-left corner of the screen.
3. Click Management Certificates. If you have any certificates, they will now be visible in the main pane.
4. Click Add Certificate (see Figure 22-2). The Add New Management Certificate dialog box opens.
5. Choose the Azure subscription instance you plan on managing.
6. Browse to a local copy of your certificate file.
7. Click OK.

FIGURE 22-2

Installing a management certificate in the management portal

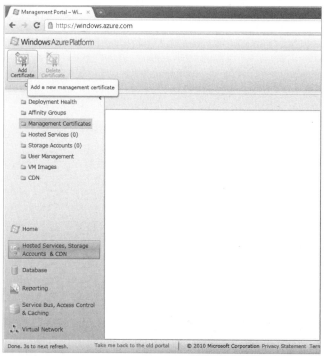

Most of the cmdlets require you to provide this certificate when they are invoked. The best way to do this is to load your certificate into a variable using the certificate provider so that you can use it later:

```
cd cert:\CurrentUser\My\
dir
```

```
        Directory: Microsoft.PowerShell.Security\Certificate::CurrentUser\my


Thumbprint                                Subject
----------                                -------
CC0687153A57C0B1CD30746B43E7C050A9DEFB9E  CN=toenuff
BBED3A8515381C212649868C08E146BD62553856  CN=Azure
```

```
$cert = Get-Item BBED3A8515381C212649868C08E146BD62553856
```

Managing Hosted Services

A *hosted service* is the entry point to a Windows Azure application. It defines which data centers the underlying infrastructure can live in, and it provides a DNS entry point to access any public-facing roles like web services or a web front end. Some applications may take advantage of multiple hosted services, whereas others may build a single deployment in a hosted service that contains all of the roles the application needs. Deployments within a hosted service contain a set of services or roles that can run on a single virtual server. The nature of the cloud means that these sets of roles could be running on one server or they could be running on hundreds of servers. The point is that every one of those hundred servers will be running all of the roles specified by the deployment.

Getting Hosted Service Information

The WASM cmdlets provide two ways of getting hosted services: `Get-HostedServices` and `Get-HostedService`. These cmdlets require you to pass the certificate as well as your Azure account's subscription ID. The following two lines are used to set the variables that you will see in further examples in this section. They must be populated with values that are relevant to your subscription of Azure.

```
$subID = '1741a92f-7f1f-4ed6-921b-90ecc2f3c2cd'
$cert = Get-Item  cert:\CurrentUser\My\CC0687153A57C0B1CD30746B43E7C050A9DEFB9E
```

The `Get-HostedServices` cmdlet returns all of the hosted services that exist in your Azure subscription.

```
Get-HostedServices –Certificate $cert -SubscriptionId $subID
```

`Get-HostedService` retrieves an object that represents a single hosted service. For example, the following retrieves a hosted service named `poshbible`:

```
$serv = Get-HostedService -Certificate $cert -SubscriptionId $subid ↵
-ServiceName 'poshbible'
```

The WASM cmdlets provide proper pipeline support to other cmdlets. You can use `Get-HostedProperties` to see a little bit more information about the affinity groups or data center regions the underlying virtual machines live in. The following shows how you can pipe the object you retrieved from `Get-HostedService` into `Get-HostedProperties`:

```
$serv | Get-HostedProperties
```

Another cmdlet that can be used via the pipeline is `Get-Deployment`. This cmdlet will get information about the code that has been deployed to either the staging or production slot of the hosted service.

```
$serv |Get-Deployment -Slot Production
```

The following shows a quick way to look at the contents of the XML configuration file used by the staging deployment:

```
$serv |Get-Deployment -Slot Staging |Select -ExpandProperty configuration
```

Finally, you can see that Windows PowerShell allows you to use the information retrieved in interesting ways. For example, you can use the `url` property retrieved from `Get-Deployment` to see the URL for the deployment. You can then use `Start-Process` to launch the website automatically in a web browser. The following line of code does this (using the `start` alias for `Start-Process`):

```
start ($serv |Get-Deployment -Slot Production |Select -ExpandProperty url)
```

Starting and Stopping Deployments

Starting and stopping deployments is very straightforward with the `Set-DeploymentStatus` cmdlet. The code needed to start and stop deployments is presented in Listing 22-1. It uses the splatting technique that was discussed in Chapter 2, "What's New in Windows PowerShell V2," to pass arguments to `Get-HostedService`.

Note

It can sometimes be confusing to hear the word *deployment* thrown around the way it is in Windows Azure. It's important to realize that a deployment not only is the code and configuration that makes up a collection of roles or services, but actually represents the roles or services themselves. In the Windows Azure world, setting a deployment to suspended or to run is similar to using **Stop-Service** or **Start-Service** with a collection of services on a server. ■

LISTING 22-1

Using Set-DeploymentStatus to Stop and Start a Deployment

```
$cert = Get-Item   cert:\CurrentUser\My\CC0687153A57C0B1CD30746B43E7C050A9DEFB9E
$serviceargs = @{
  Certificate = $cert
  SubscriptionID = '1741a92f-7f1f-4ed6-921b-90ecc2f3c2cd'
  ServiceName = 'poshbible'
}
$serv = Get-HostedService @serviceargs

# Stop the deployment
$serv |
  Get-Deployment -Slot Staging |
  Set-DeploymentStatus -Status Suspended |
  Get-OperationStatus -WaitToComplete

# Start the deployment
$serv |
  Get-Deployment -Slot Staging |
  Set-DeploymentStatus -Status Running |
  Get-OperationStatus -WaitToComplete
```

Get-OperationStatus

Many of the WASM cmdlets return immediately after they are run without error, but that is not necessarily an indication that the method was successful. The calls made by the cmdlets through the SDK are being done asynchronously. This is by design because many operations may require an excessive amount of time to complete. On the surface, you may be issuing a single command to do something like uploading code to your cloud instance, but the Windows Azure infrastructure may be performing very complex workflows that create new virtual machines, copy code to multiple servers, and manipulate network infrastructure. To find out whether an operation has succeeded, you can use the `Get-OperationStatus` cmdlet to find out the status of a request. Additionally, there is a switch parameter called `WaitToComplete` that you can use to ensure that the entire workload of operations that Azure is performing has been completed prior to continuing.

Deploying New Code

To upload code to Windows Azure, developers must package their project into a service package file (`.cspkg`) with a service configuration file (`.csfg`). When deploying new code to the staging or production slot of the hosted service for the first time, you use the `New-Deployment` cmdlet. This creates a deployment and uploads the package and supporting configuration file to Windows Azure. Listing 22-2 shows a sample of how to use the `New-Deployment` cmdlet.

LISTING 22-2

Creating a New Deployment

```
$cert = Get-Item  cert:\CurrentUser\My\CC0687153A57C0B1CD30746B43E7C050A9DEFB9E
$ServiceArgs = @{
  Certificate = $cert
  SubscriptionID = '1741a92f-7f1f-4ed6-921b-90ecc2f3c2cd'
  ServiceName = 'poshbible'
}

$serv = Get-HostedService @ServiceArgs

$Arguments = @{
  Label = 'PoshBibleSite'                       # Deployment name
  StorageServiceName = 'poshbible'              # Storage account name
  Package = 'd:\PoshBible.cspkg'                # The package to deploy
  Configuration = 'd:\ServiceConfiguration.cscfg' # The config file
}

# This next bit deploys the code
$serv |
  Get-Deployment -Slot Staging |
  New-Deployment @Arguments |
  Get-OperationStatus -WaitToComplete

# Start it up
$serv |
  Get-Deployment -Slot Staging |
  Set-DeploymentStatus -Status 'Running' |
  Get-OperationStatus -WaitToComplete
```

When you want to deploy new or updated code to a hosted service that already contains a deployment, you should use Set-Deployment. Set-Deployment takes the same parameters as New-Deployment, so it's easy to convert the script in Listing 22-2 to an update script by stopping the existing deployment and then changing the line that uses New-Deployment to Set-Deployment:

```
$serv |
    Get-Deployment -Slot Staging |
    Set-DeploymentStatus -Status 'Suspended'
    Get-OperationStatus -WaitToComplete

$serv |
    Get-Deployment -Slot Staging |
    Set-Deployment @Arguments |
    Get-OperationStatus -WaitToComplete
```

Scaling Services

A deployment within a hosted service may consist of one or more virtual machines. These virtual machines can be created and destroyed seamlessly, making it easy to scale applications by adding new virtual machines on demand as more resources are required. This agility is one of the promises that cloud computing offers. Windows PowerShell in concert with the WASM cmdlets provides a way to deliver that promise.

You can use the `Set-DeploymentConfiguration` cmdlet to modify the configuration for a deployment. This cmdlet makes it very easy to add or remove more infrastructure for a Windows Azure application, as shown in Listing 22-3.

LISTING 22-3

Scaling Underlying Infrastructure for a Deployment

```
$cert = Get-Item  cert:\CurrentUser\My\CC0687153A57C0B1CD30746B43E7C050A9DEFB9E
$ServiceArgs = @{
    Certificate = $cert;
    SubscriptionID = '1741a92f-7f1f-4ed6-921b-90ecc2f3c2cd';
    ServiceName = 'poshbible'
}

# The following adds a new server to the deployment in the Production slot
$serv |Get-Deployment -Slot Production |
  Set-DeploymentConfiguration -ScriptConfiguration {
    $_.RolesConfiguration["WebRole1"].InstanceCount += 1
  } |Get-OperationStatus -WaitToComplete
```

Note

It may not be obvious due to the lack of documentation for the `ScriptConfiguration` parameter of `Set-DeploymentConfiguration`, but this script block is giving you a way to modify the value of the configuration property returned by `Get-Deployment`. You can modify any item that lives in the `.cscfg` file that was used for the deployment, but you cannot add new items. `InstanceCount` is the most obvious use of this configuration because it exists in every deployment, but a developer can use this `.cscfg` file to store other information at this level with some effort. ■

Managing Certificates

Using certificates for SSL with Windows Azure is generally handled during development. The developer is able to specify that the endpoint uses HTTPS, specify a port, and choose which certificates to use — all within Visual Studio. Even though the applications are tied to specific certificates, you still need a way to upload these certificates and manage them in the cloud. The WASM cmdlets give you an interface to view, delete, or upload certificates within your hosted service. You can use `Get-Certificate` and `Get-Certificates` to view what certificates have been uploaded to the service host. You can use `Remove-Certificate` to remove a certificate from the service host and `Add-Certificate` to upload a certificate to your hosted service. Listing 22-4 shows how you would automate the task of uploading a certificate to a service host.

LISTING 22-4

Adding a Certificate to a Hosted Service

```
$cert = Get-Item  cert:\CurrentUser\My\CC0687153A57C0B1CD30746B43E7C050A9DEFB9E
$ServiceArgs = @{
  Certificate = $cert
  SubscriptionID = '1741a92f-7f1f-4ed6-921b-90ecc2f3c2cd'
  ServiceName = 'poshbible'
}
$serv = Get-HostedService @ServiceArgs

$serv |Add-Certificate -CertificateToDeploy d:\azure.pfx -Password 'poshbible'
```

Windows Azure Diagnostics

Windows Azure provides you with a way to monitor your application and the underlying servers with log files that can be stored in one of your storage accounts. These logs, also known as buffers, can consist of application trace messages, file-based logs, event viewer messages, performance counters, or messages about the diagnostic monitoring system itself. Windows PowerShell does not give you a way to directly enable monitoring in your applications: however, if a developer has enabled diagnostic monitoring in the Windows Azure application with the `DiagnosticMonitor.Start()` method, you can use Windows PowerShell to modify the configuration of this monitoring on the fly with the WASM cmdlets.

Getting Logging Configuration

The first step to configuring logging is to find the roles that have logging enabled and view their configuration. Listing 22-5 is a script that displays the diagnostic configuration settings for all diagnostic-enabled roles in staging that are configured to use any of your Azure storage accounts. The variable `$BufferNames` contains all of the available logs that can exist within Windows Azure.

LISTING 22-5

Getting Diagnostic Configuration Information

```
$BufferNames = @("DiagnosticInfrastructureLogs","Directories")
$BufferNames += ("Logs","PerformanceCounters","WindowsEventLogs")

$cert = Get-Item  cert:\CurrentUser\My\CC0687153A57C0B1CD30746B43E7C050A9DEFB9E
$ServiceArgs = @{
  Certificate = $cert
  SubscriptionID = '1741a92f-7f1f-4ed6-921b-90ecc2f3c2cd'
  ServiceName = 'poshbible'
}

$serv = Get-HostedService @serviceargs
$deploymentid = ($serv |Get-Deployment -Slot staging).DeploymentId

$serv |Get-StorageServices |foreach {
  $Arguments = @{
  DeploymentId = $deploymentid;
  StorageAccountName = $_.ServiceName
  StorageAccountKey = ($_ |Get-StorageKeys).Primary
  }

  Get-DiagnosticAwareRoles @Arguments |foreach {
    "Web Role: $_"
    "Storage: " + $arguments.StorageAccountName

    $Arguments.RoleName = $_

    Get-DiagnosticAwareRoleInstances @arguments |foreach {
      $Arguments.InstanceId = $_
      foreach ($buf in $BufferNames) {
        $Arguments.BufferName = $buf
        Get-DiagnosticConfiguration @Arguments |select @{
          n='Buffer';e={$buf}
        }, ScheduledTransferPeriod,BufferQuotaInMB, ↵
ScheduledTransferLogLevelFilter, DataSources
      }
    }
  }
}
```

Listing 22-5 uses some new cmdlets you have not seen. They are described in Table 22-1.

TABLE 22-1

Storage and Diagnostic "Get" Cmdlets

Cmdlet	Description
Get-StorageServices	Lists storage services underneath the subscription
Get-StorageKeys	Displays primary and secondary keys for the account
Get-DiagnosticAwareRoles	Lists the roles that have successfully started at least one diagnostic monitor
Get-DiagnosticAwareRoleInstances	Returns the IDs of active role instances where a diagnostic monitor is running
Get-DiagnosticConfiguration	Gets the configuration for a specified buffer

Configuring Logging

You can change the logging configuration for one of the buffers by calling the appropriate Set-* command for the buffer you want to configure. Table 22-2 shows these commands and their corresponding buffer name.

TABLE 22-2

Cmdlets Used to Set Buffer Configurations

Cmdlet	Buffer
Set-InfrastructureLog	DiagnosticInfrastructureLogs
Set-FileBasedLog	Directories
Set-WindowsAzureLog	Logs
Set-PerformanceCounter	PerformanceCounters
Set-WindowsEventLog	WindowsEventLogs

Listing 22-6 shows some examples of how to configure the WindowsEventLogs, Logs, and PerformanceCounters buffers.

LISTING 22-6

Configuring Logging for a Windows Azure Instance

```
$cert = Get-Item  cert:\CurrentUser\My\CC0687153A57C0B1CD30746B43E7C050A9DEFB9E
$ServiceArgs = @{
  Certificate = $cert
  SubscriptionID = '1741a92f-7f1f-4ed6-921b-90ecc2f3c2cd'
  ServiceName = 'poshbible'
}
$serv = Get-HostedService @ServiceArgs

$ArgsMaster = @{
    RoleName = 'WebRole1'
    StorageAccountName = 'poshbible'
    DeploymentId = ($serv |Get-Deployment -Slot staging).DeploymentId
    InstanceId = 'WebRole1_IN_0'
    StorageAccountKey = ($serv |Get-StorageServices |Where {
        $_.ServiceName -eq 'poshbible'
    } |Get-StorageKeys).Primary
}

# This section configures the application and system log to get transferred
# to Azure storage every 60 minutes
$arguments = $argsmaster.Clone()
$arguments.TransferPeriod = 60
$arguments.Eventlogs = ('Application!*','System!*')
Set-WindowsEventLog @arguments

# This section shows how to configure Azure logging to the maximum level
# for debugging.  Data that shows up in these logs are messages from the
# developers of the application via Trace messages
$arguments = $argsmaster.Clone()
$arguments.TransferPeriod = 1
$logLevelFilter = [Microsoft.WindowsAzure.Diagnostics.LogLevel] ::Verbose
$arguments.LogLevelFilter = $logLevelFilterSet-WindowsAzureLog @arguments

# This final section shows how to configure performance counters on an
# Azure instance
$arguments = $argsmaster.Clone()
$arguments.TransferPeriod = 5
$arguments.PerformanceCounters = @()
$arguments.PerformanceCounters += `
New-Object Microsoft.WindowsAzure.Diagnostics.PerformanceCounterConfiguration `
    -Property @{
        CounterSpecifier='\Processor(_Total)\% Processor Time';
        SampleRate=[TimeSpan]::FromSeconds(30)
    }
```

```
$arguments.PerformanceCounters += `
New-Object Microsoft.WindowsAzure.Diagnostics.PerformanceCounterConfiguration `
    -Property @{
        CounterSpecifier='\PhysicalDisk(_Total)\Disk Writes/sec';
        SampleRate=[TimeSpan]::FromSeconds(30)
    }

Set-PerformanceCounter @arguments
```

Forcing Logs to Transfer to Storage

Logging within Windows Azure happens constantly, but the data exists on local storage in your VM. In order for an administrator to see the logs, he or she must transfer the logs to an Azure storage account. Buffers are generally configured to transfer at an interval, as you saw in the previous section, but a transfer can also be forced with `Start-OnDemandTransfer`.

Two additional cmdlets enable you to work with on-demand transfers: `Get-ActiveTransfers` and `Stop-ActiveTransfer`. These cmdlets are necessary because the WASM cmdlets do not clear a transfer when it is complete; you must do this manually. Unfortunately, the cmdlets also do not offer proper pipeline support the way you would expect them to.

Listing 22-7 shows an example of how to force a transfer of the `Directories` buffer, which contains, among other things, the IIS logs. Prior to starting the transfer, the script ensures that any active transfers are first stopped.

LISTING 22-7

Transferring Local Data Logs to Azure Storage

```
$cert = Get-Item  cert:\CurrentUser\My\CC0687153A57C0B1CD30746B43E7C050A9DEFB9E
$serviceargs = @{
  Certificate = $cert
  SubscriptionID = '1741a92f-7f1f-4ed6-921b-90ecc2f3c2cd'
  ServiceName = 'poshbible'
}
$serv = Get-HostedService @serviceargs

# This section gets an active transfer if one exists and
# displays its information to the screen
$argsmaster = @{
  RoleName = 'WebRole1'
```

continues

LISTING 22-7 *(continued)*

```
  StorageAccountName = 'poshbible'
  DeploymentId = ($serv |Get-Deployment -Slot staging).DeploymentId
  InstanceId = 'WebRole1_IN_0'
  StorageAccountKey = ($serv |Get-StorageServices |Where {
    $_.ServiceName -eq 'poshbible'
  } |Get-StorageKeys).Primary
}
$args = $argsmaster.Clone()
$transfer = Get-ActiveTransfers @args
$transfer

# This next section will remove the active transfer we received above
if ($transfer) {
  $args = $argsmaster.Clone()
  $args.TransferId = $transfer.RequestId
  Stop-ActiveTransfer @args
}

# This final section will transfer items found in the directories buffer
# to Azure storage.  If the default configuration is not changed, this will
# include the IIS logs.

$args = $argsmaster.Clone()
$args.DataBufferName = 'Directories'

# The 'From' and 'To' parameters specify the time frame for the log data
# UTC time is the default for every Windows Azure server
$args.From = (Get-Date).ToUniversalTime().AddHours(-5)
$args.To = (Get-Date).ToUniversalTime()

# poshbible is a queue that is created in Azure storage.  You must specify
# this in order to see a status message when using Get-ActiveTransfers
$args.NotificationQueueName = 'poshbible'

Start-OnDemandTransfer @args
```

Summary

Based on Microsoft's investment into cloud computing, it's a safe bet that Windows Azure is here to stay. The Windows Azure Service Management (WASM) cmdlets provide a way to perform many of the management tasks that are available with the Windows Azure

SDK directly from within Windows PowerShell. These cmdlets are young, but you can expect them to mature as Windows Azure and the SDK mature over time. Until then, these cmdlets already make tasks like automating deployments and configuration changes easy. In addition, their ability to configure diagnostics after an application has been deployed is unmatched by any other method currently available from Microsoft.

The next chapter finishes up the exploration of virtualization automation with Windows PowerShell by looking at the cmdlets that are available from one of the earliest third-party adopters of Windows PowerShell: VMware.

Managing VMware vSphere PowerCLI

VMware and Windows PowerShell both received a great boom in support after VMware released its VI toolkit in 2008. This toolkit was a snap-in built on top of Windows PowerShell V1, and as the product matured, it became the standard scripting language for VMware. Though VMware also had a Perl toolkit and an SDK, the Windows PowerShell implementation enabled some administrators to become active scripters almost overnight. VMware had already invested heavily in Windows as its management tier with vCenter; Windows PowerShell has many syntactical elements that make it easy for a Unix administrator or Perl scripter to adopt the language quickly. Add those two facts together, and it is no surprise that Windows PowerShell quickly became the standard for scripting against VMware's products.

IN THIS CHAPTER

Using PowerCLI

Working with ESX hosts

Scripting against virtual machines

Managing vCenter

Installing and Using the Cmdlets

The latest implementation of the cmdlets used to manage VMware is known as vSphere PowerCLI. At the time of writing, PowerCLI is in Version 4.1.1.

Installing PowerCLI

PowerCLI can be installed on most versions of Windows, and it can be used with any version of Windows PowerShell. You can use PowerCLI to manage ESX from Version 3.0.3 and higher (including ESXi), but it requires these hosts to be patched to appropriate versions. It also requires vCenter 2.5 Update 6 if you want to use the cmdlets with vCenter.

To install PowerCLI, you must first download it from VMware's website at
`www.vmware.com/go/powercli`.

The installation of PowerCLI is very straightforward. It simply requires you to run the
downloaded installation file as an administrator.

Loading PowerCLI

After PowerCLI is installed, you can load it by clicking Start ➢ All Programs ➢ VMware ➢
VMware vSphere PowerCLI ➢ VMware vSphere PowerCLI. You can also load the snap-in
into a Windows PowerShell session or script by running the following command:

```
Add-PSSnapin VMware.Vimautomation.Core
```

Connecting to a Host or vCenter Instance

Once the snap-in is loaded, you need to connect PowerCLI to an ESX host or a vCenter
instance. You do this with the `Connect-VIServer` cmdlet:

```
Connect-VIServer vcenter1 -Credential (Get-Credential)
```

In addition to the `Credential` parameter, you can use the `User` and `Password` parameters
to specify a username and password in clear text. You can also omit the credential
completely if you are logged in as a user who has access to the vCenter instance to which
you are trying to connect.

The following example shows a common way of loading the snap-in and connecting to a
vCenter instance within a script. This code is useful during development of a script because
it ensures that you do not waste time trying to load the snap-in or connect to the vCenter
instance more than once.

```
if (!(Get-PSSnapin VMware.Vimautomation.Core -ErrorAction SilentlyContinue)) {
    Add-PSSnapin VMware.Vimautomation.Core
}
if (!$global:DefaultVIServer) {
    Connect-VIServer vcenter1
}
```

Note

The first time you use `Connect-VIServer` more than once in a session, you will be prompted to specify
how you would like this cmdlet to behave when it is used multiple times. You can allow either multiple
simultaneous connections or one connection at a time. PowerCLI uses two global variables to store these
connections: `$global:DefaultVIServer` and `$global:DefaultVIServers`. The code just shown is
designed for PowerCLI instances that are configured to use only one connection at a time.

When you allow multiple connections, your commands will run against each connected instance stored in the `$global:DefaultVIServers` array. If you are using a single instance of vCenter, the chances are high that this is not what you want to do. If you would like to change the behavior, use `Set-PowerCLIConfiguration` to change the `DefaultVIServerMode` value to either single or multiple. ∎

Retrieving Hosts and VMs

PowerCLI offers excellent pipeline support. Many PowerCLI scripts obtain an object or set of objects that represent things, such as a virtual machine (VM) or an ESX/ESXi host, and then pass those objects to another cmdlet that will perform a function on each of them to either get more objects like CD drives on a VM or perform actions like putting an ESX host into maintenance mode. Hosts and VMs are retrieved with `Get-VMHost` and `Get-VM`.

The `Name` parameter of `Get-VM` and `Get-VMHost` is used to specify the name of the VM or host you would like to retrieve. This parameter name does not need to be specified because it is positional. For example, you can retrieve a VM named `vm1` with the following:

```
Get-VM vm1
```

Both `Get-VM` and `Get-VMHost` cmdlets accept wildcards within the `Name` parameter. For example, this gets all hosts that begin with the letter E:

```
Get-VMHost e*
```

Both cmdlets also have a `Location` parameter that can be used to specify a container such as the folder, the datacenter, or the cluster the VM or host belongs to. The following retrieves all VMs from cluster1:

```
Get-VM -Location cluster1
```

If you need to specify multiple clusters, folders, or datacenters, you can do so by passing an array of names to the `Location` parameter. For example, the following code retrieves all the VMs from cluster1, cluster2, and cluster3:

```
Get-VM -Location @('cluster1','cluster2','cluster3')
```

It is very common to perform a Windows PowerShell filter using `Where-Object` or its alias `Where` to retrieve VMs that have specific properties. For example, the following retrieves all VMs on the system that have more than 2 gigabytes of RAM:

```
Get-VM |Where {$_.memoryMB -gt 2048}
```

Most of the cmdlets in PowerCLI have excellent pipeline support. For example, you can get the ESX host that vm1 currently exists on by running the following:

```
Get-VM vm1 |Get-VMHost
```

Managing ESX and ESXi

This section looks at the cmdlets in PowerCLI that are available to manage ESX and ESXi hosts.

Note

For the remainder of this chapter, the name ESX will be used to imply ESX and ESXi. This chapter also focuses mainly on infrastructure that includes a vCenter server. Many of the cmdlets will work without one by connecting directly to a host, but some will not. The rule of thumb is that if you are trying to get information that is only available in vCenter, you probably need a vCenter server in order to get it through PowerCLI. ∎

Putting Hosts in Maintenance Mode

There is rarely a script that modifies an ESX host that does not first have to put the host into maintenance mode. In PowerCLI, this is done by setting the `State` parameter of `Set-VMHost` to `Maintenance`. The following example puts a host named `esx1.psbible.com` into maintenance mode:

```
$vmhost = Get-VMHost esx1.psbible.com
$vmhost |Set-VMHost -State Maintenance
```

Because `Set-VMHost` accepts output from `Get-VMHost` through the pipeline, you can easily put a large set of hosts into maintenance mode. The following does this for all of the hosts in cluster1:

```
Get-VMHost -Location cluster1 |Set-VMHost -State Maintenance -RunAsync
```

Exiting maintenance mode is performed by setting the state of the host to `Connected`. The following code illustrates this. It will exit maintenance mode on all hosts that are currently in maintenance mode.

```
Get-VMHost |
    Where {$_.ConnectionState -eq 'Maintenance'} |
        Set-VMHost -State Connected -RunAsync
```

Note

RunAsync is a parameter that is available for some of the cmdlets in PowerCLI that generally take a long time to complete. By using this parameter, you are telling PowerCLI to initiate the command with vCenter, but then continue to process the rest of the script. If your script does not rely on the action to either fail or succeed before it continues the next set of commands in your script, you should use this parameter. You will find that this cmdlet is very useful when you need to do things like start or stop a large set of VMs. ∎

Inspecting Host Properties

The following code shows all of the properties from the objects that are returned when using `Get-VMHost`:

```
Get-VMHost esx1.psbible.com |Select *
WARNING: 'State' property is obsolete. Use 'ConnectionState' instead.

State                  : Connected
ConnectionState        : Connected
PowerState             : PoweredOn
VMSwapfileDatastoreId  :
VMSwapfilePolicy       : Inherit
ParentId               : ClusterComputeResource-domain-c40
IsStandalone           : False
Manufacturer           : VMware, Inc.
Model                  : VMware Virtual Platform
NumCpu                 : 1
CpuTotalMhz            : 1293
CpuUsageMhz            : 23
MemoryTotalMB          : 2047
MemoryUsageMB          : 833
ProcessorType          : Genuine Intel(R) CPU        U7300  @ 1.30GHz
HyperthreadingActive   : False
TimeZone               : UTC
Version                : 4.1.0
Build                  : 348481
Parent                 : Cluster
VMSwapfileDatastore    :
StorageInfo            : HostStorageSystem-storageSystem-36
NetworkInfo            : esx1:psbible.com
DiagnosticPartition    : mpx.vmhba1:C0:T0:L0
FirewallDefaultPolicy  :
ApiVersion             : 4.1
CustomFields           : {}
ExtensionData          : VMware.Vim.HostSystem
Id                     : HostSystem-host-36
Name                   : esx1.psbible.com
Uid                    : /VIServer=admin@vcenter:443/VMHost=HostSystem-host-36/
```

In addition to these properties, you can get information about the host and the components that the host uses by passing the host into the various Get-* cmdlets within PowerCLI. Table 23-1 lists these cmdlets.

TABLE 23-1

Cmdlets Used to Gather More Information about ESX Hosts

Cmdlet	Description
Get-Annotation	Gets annotations
Get-Datastore	Gets the data stores connected to the host

continues

TABLE 23-1 *(continued)*	
Cmdlet	**Description**
Get-View	Gets the .NET view object for the host
Get-VMHostAdvancedConfiguration	Gets the advanced configuration of the host
Get-VMHostAvailableTimeZone	Gets the time zones that are available on the host
Get-VMHostDiagnosticPartition	Gets the diagnostic partitions on the host
Get-VMHostDisk	Gets information about the disks attached to the host
Get-VMHostFirmware	Gets information about the firmware
Get-VMHostNetwork	Gets information about the host network
Get-VMHostNetworkAdapter	Gets information about the network adapters on the host
Get-VMHostPatch	Gets information about the installed patches on the host
Get-VMHostRoute	Gets the routing table information from the host
Get-VMHostStartPolicy	Gets the start policy for the host
Get-VMHostStorage	Gets information about the storage that is configured on the host
Get-VMHostService	Gets information about the services running on the host
Get-VMHostSysLogServer	Gets the remote syslog servers for the host
Get-VirtualPortGroup	Gets information about the port groups on the host
Get-VirtualSwitch	Gets information about the virtual switches on the host

Managing Storage

Whether it's shared storage or local storage, all aspects of a host's storage configuration can be managed with PowerCLI. Any task that is available within vCenter is also available within Windows PowerShell. For example, to rescan all of the host bus adapters (HBAs) on a host or to rescan the virtual machine file system (VMFS) for additional VMFS volumes, you run the following:

```
$vmhost = Get-VMHost esx1.psbible.com
$vmhost |Get-VMHostStorage -RescanAllHba
$vmhost |Get-VMHostStorage -RescanVmfs
```

Note

You may have noticed that all of the cmdlets that deal with an ESX host are referred to as a VMHost. All of the examples have also been using $vmhost as the variable rather than using $host. The reason that the word *host* is so carefully avoided is because it has special meaning to the core language of Windows PowerShell. In Windows PowerShell, a host is the environment that is running Windows PowerShell. For example, both the Windows PowerShell console and the Windows PowerShell ISE are hosts. The $host variable is a reserved variable that is used to configure and display information about the host you are running your script from. If you try to set $host to a value like the result of Get-VMHost, you will receive an error. ∎

Another set of tasks that is common when dealing with storage is to create, rename, or remove a VMFS. These tasks can be handled by using New-DataStore, Set-Datastore, and Remove-Datastore, as shown in the following lines of code:

```
$vmhost = Get-VMHost esx1.psbible.com

$vmhost |New-Datastore -Nfs -Name NASv1 -NfsHost NAS -Path "/nfs/Nasv1"

$vmhost |Get-Datastore -Name NASv1 |Set-Datastore -Name NASNewName

$vmhost |Get-Datastore -Name NASNewName |Remove-Datastore -Confirm:$False
```

New-Datastore has a different switch parameter for each type of storage system you might create a VMFS on. You can use Nfs, Cifs, or Local to specify which type of storage you are creating with this cmdlet.

Managing Host Networks

Although it is possible to configure almost all aspects of networking with PowerCLI, two requirements seem to manifest more than others when working with vSphere: configuring virtual switches and managing virtual port groups.

Configuring Virtual Switches

Virtual switches can be added, removed, or changed with New-VirtualSwitch, Remove-VirtualSwitch, and Set-VirtualSwitch, respectively. For example, if you wanted to use jumbo frames on your virtual switch, you would need to set the maximum transmission unit (MTU) value to 9000. The following illustrates how you could do this while creating a new virtual switch:

```
Get-VMHost -Location cluster |
    New-VirtualSwitch -Name BibleSwitch -Nic vmnic5 -Mtu 9000 -NumPorts 1024
```

Listing 23-1 shows a script that uses Set-VirtualSwitch to increase the number of ports available to all virtual switches on a cluster. It has some additional logic to put the host into maintenance mode followed by a reboot after the change. The script illustrates how the different elements of PowerCLI can be strung together to perform a change workflow.

LISTING 23-1

Increasing the Number of Ports on a Virtual Switch

```
#Change the number of ports on all vSwitches connected to hosts in cluster1
$vmhosts = Get-VMHost -Location cluster
$vmhosts |
  Get-VirtualSwitch |
    Set-VirtualSwitch -NumPorts 512 -Confirm:$False

# A restart is required for this change to take effect
foreach ($vmhost in $vmhosts) {
  $vmhost |Set-VMHost -State 'Maintenance' |Restart-VMHost -Confirm:$false
  # Wait for the host to come back up before rebooting the next one
  while ((Get-VMHost $vmhost.name).ConnectionState -ne 'Maintenance') {
    Sleep 15
  }
  $vmhost |Set-VMHost -State 'Connected'
}
```

Managing Virtual Port Groups

Virtual port groups are managed by using New-VirtualPortGroup, Remove-VirtualPortGroup, and Set-VirtualPortGroup. For example, to add a port group to a switch named vswitch0 on all hosts in a cluster, you can execute the following:

```
Get-VMHost -Location cluster1 |
    Get-VirtualSwitch -Name vswitch0 |
        New-VirtualPortGroup VLAN20 -VLanId 20
```

The following example shows how you can use Get-VirtualPortGroup along with Remove-VirtualPortGroup through the pipeline. This example will remove the VLAN20 port group from all hosts in cluster1.

```
Get-VMHost -Location cluster1 |
    Get-VirtualPortGroup -Name VLAN20 |
        Remove-VirtualPortGroup -Confirm:$false
```

Configuring NTP Servers

Add-VmHostNtpServer and Remove-VMHostNtpServer are used to add and remove NTP servers from a host's configuration. The following examples show how you can use these cmdlets to add and remove an NTP server from a host:

```
$vmhost = Get-VMHost esx1.psbible.com
# Add an NTP server
$vmhost |Add-VmHostNtpServer '192.168.1.1'
```

```
# Remove the NTP server

$vmhost |Remove-VMHostNtpServer -NtpServer 192.168.1.1 -Confirm:$False
```

Working with Host Profiles

Host profiles were introduced with vSphere 4. They provide the ability to capture the set of configurations a host is using and then apply them to a cluster or another host. These profiles can be applied automatically or they can be used to track which configurations on a host are different from the profile the host is associated with.

Creating a Host Profile

To create a host profile, you need to select a host that will act as a template. The following example shows how to do this with New-VMHostProfile.

```
$vmhost = Get-VMHost esx1.psbible.com
$vmhost |New-VMHostProfile profile1 -Description 'PowerCLI generated'
```

Adding and Removing Profiles from a Host or Cluster

Once the profile is created, you can apply it to either a host or a cluster with Apply-VMHostProfile. When used against a host, this will both configure the host to use the profile and apply its changes unless you use the AssociateOnly parameter. When it is used with a cluster, you must specify the AssociateOnly parameter. For example, to apply a profile named profile1 to a cluster named cluster1, you execute the following two lines of code:

```
$profile = Get-VMHostProfile profile1
$profile |Apply-VMHostProfile -Entity (Get-Cluster cluster1) -AssociateOnly
```

The following illustrates how you can attach and apply the same profile retrieved above with Get-VMHostProfile to a host named esx1.psbible.com.

```
$vmhost = Get-VMHost esx1.psbible.com
$vmhost |Set-VMHost -State Maintenance

$profile |Apply-VMHostProfile -Entity $vmhost

$vmhost |Set-VMHost -State Connected
```

Testing Host Compliance

Test-VMHostProfileCompliance is used to find out whether a host is compliant with its associated profile. This cmdlet returns an object that contains a list of elements that are out of compliance. The following shows how you can use this cmdlet to generate a report that shows the VMHostID along with some information about what is out of compliance for all of your hosts.

```
Get-VMHost |Test-VMHostProfileCompliance |foreach {
  "Host: " + $_.VMHostID
  $_.IncomplianceElementList
}
```

If you would like to apply the changes to make the host compliant with its profile, you must use `Apply-VMHostProfile` with the `ApplyOnly` switch parameter. This is illustrated in the following snippet, which applies the changes required to the esx1.psbible.com host to make it compliant with the profiles that are attached to it:

```
Get-VMHost esx1.psbible.com |
    Set-VMHost -State 'Maintenance' |
        Apply-VMHostProfile -ApplyOnly -Confirm:$False |
            Set-VMHost -State 'Connected'
```

Note

You can suppress any prompts that ask you to confirm whether you really want to do something in PowerCLI by using `-Confirm:$False`. This parameter exists in many of the PowerCLI functions that make changes or remove a component of vSphere. ∎

Backing Up and Restoring Host Profiles

Backing up a profile is done with `Export-VMHostProfile`. For example, the following backs up the profile named profile1 to a file named `profile1.prf`:

```
Get-VMHostProfile profile1 |Export-VMHostProfile profile1.prf
```

You use `Import-VMHostProfile` to restore a profile from a disk backup. The following shows how you can restore the backup file you just created as a new profile named profile2:

```
Import-VMHostProfile profile1.prf -Name profile2
```

Getting Logs

To review log data from an ESX host, you must first connect to the host with `Connect-VIServer`. You can then use `Get-LogType` to show a list of the logs that are available to you, as is shown in the following:

```
Connect-VIServer esx1.psbible.com
Get-LogType
Key                 Summary
---                 -------
hostd               Server log in 'plain' format
messages            Server log in 'plain' format
vpxa                vCenter agent log in 'plain' format
```

To view a log, pass a key name to Get-Log and then inspect the Entries property. For example, to view the hostd log, you would run the following line of code:

```
Get-Log hostd |Select -ExpandProperty Entries
```

To filter the data returned from Get-Log, you can use any of the methods directly within Windows PowerShell like Select-String, Select-Object, or Where-Object. For example, to view the tail of the log, you could use Select-Object or its alias Select with the Last parameter:

```
Get-Log hostd |Select -ExpandProperty Entries |select -Last 20
```

Gathering Performance Data from a Host

Collecting and reviewing performance data is a common task for ESX administrators. PowerCLI provides a few simple ways to gather this data so that it can be exported or analyzed directly within Windows PowerShell. For an ESX host, this data can be gathered from vCenter or it can be collected in real time.

Using Get-Stat to Collect Performance Data from vCenter

The performance data that is collected by vCenter can be queried using Get-Stat. Switch parameters are available to let you specify whether you want to receive Cpu, Disk, Memory, or Network statistics. The following example demonstrates using Get-Stat to look at some CPU data:

```
$vmhost = Get-VMHost esx1.psbible.com
$finish = Get-Date
$start = $finish.addminutes(-2)
$vmhost |Get-Stat -Start $start -Finish $finish -Cpu -IntervalSecs 30
```

MetricId	Timestamp	Value	Unit	Instance
cpu.usagemhz.average	5/29/2011 12:43:33 AM	95	MHz	
cpu.usagemhz.average	5/29/2011 12:43:13 AM	45	MHz	
cpu.usagemhz.average	5/29/2011 12:42:53 AM	350	MHz	
cpu.usage.average	5/29/2011 12:43:33 AM	7.39	%	0
cpu.usage.average	5/29/2011 12:43:13 AM	3.55	%	0
cpu.usage.average	5/29/2011 12:42:53 AM	27.1	%	0
cpu.usage.average	5/29/2011 12:43:33 AM	7.39	%	
cpu.usage.average	5/29/2011 12:43:13 AM	3.55	%	
cpu.usage.average	5/29/2011 12:42:53 AM	27.1	%	

Note

I won't go into this again when I talk about virtual machines or vCenter, but you can also use Get-Stat to get performance data from a VM. If the data is available in vCenter, you can retrieve it with Get-Stat. To view this data about a VM, you would pipe a VM object or collection of VM objects obtained by Get-VM into Get-Stat rather than a VMHost object. ∎

Using esxtop to Collect Real-Time Performance Data from an ESX Host

Esxtop has long been considered one of the essential tools in the utility belt of a VMware engineer. With the release of PowerCLI 4.1.1, you can now use the functionality of esxtop directly from within Windows PowerShell with Get-EsxTop. To do this, you must connect directly to an ESX or ESXi host with Connect-VIServer. Listing 23-2 shows how you can use Get-EsxTop to discover the available counters and then how to retrieve point-in-time data for these counters.

LISTING 23-2

Using Get-EsxTop to Collect Performance Counter Data

```
# Connect to the ESX host
Connect-VIServer esx1.psbible.com -Credential (Get-Credential)

# Display all of the available counters
Get-EsxTop -Counter

# Display the fields collected for the physical memory (PMem) counters
Get-EsxTop -Counter PMem |Select -ExpandProperty Fields

# Collect the point-in-time data from the PMem counter
Get-EsxTop -CounterName PMem |Select *

# A script to collect PMem data about every 5 seconds for a
# little more than a minute
$data = @()
$delay = 5
$iterations = 20
for ($i=0;$i -lt $iterations; $i++) {
  $esxtop = Get-EsxTop -CounterName PMem
  $esxtop |Add-Member Noteproperty -Name Time -Value (Get-Date)
  $data += $esxtop
  Sleep $delay
}
$data |Select * |Export-Csv -Encoding ASCII -NoTypeInformation pmem.csv
```

Managing Virtual Machines

This section looks at how PowerCLI can be used to manage VMs.

Deploying New VMs

You can create VMs in PowerCLI with the New-VM cmdlet. This cmdlet can be used minimally by specifying only a host and a data store where the VM should be created.

```
New-VM -Name VM1 -VMHost esx1.psbible.com -Datastore ds1
```

New-VM has two parameters, VM and Template, which allow you to create the new VM by cloning an existing VM or template in your environment.

```
New-VM -VMHost esx1.psbible.com -VM VM1 -Name VM2 -Datastore ds1
New-VM -VMHost esx1.psbible.com -Template TP1 -Name VM3 -Datastore ds1
```

In addition, if you only need to create the VM containers and you don't care about cloning an existing VM or template's disk, you can create the VM with a template of configurations that are stored in a Windows PowerShell script.

```
$arguments = @{
  Name = 'VM4'
  VMHost = 'esx1.psbible.com'
  Datastore = 'ds1'
  RunAsync = $True
  DiskMB = 16384
  MemoryMB = 2048
  VMSwapfilePolicy = 'InHostDataStore'
  NetworkName = 'VM Network'
  CD = $true
  Floppy = $true
  NumCpu = 1
  OSCustomizationSpec = 'psbiblecustomization' #guest customization template
}
New-VM @arguments
```

Removing VMs

You can remove VMs with Remove-VM. If you want to delete the VM and its disks from the data stores it is using, you must also use the DeletePermanently parameter switch:

```
Get-VM vm1 |Remove-VM -DeletePermanently
```

Working with Virtual Hardware

The process of adding, removing, or modifying virtual hardware components for multiple VMs is extremely tedious when it is done through vCenter. Part of the problem is that vCenter actions take some time to take place, leaving the administrator with a lot of time between clicks. Automation of these types of tasks with PowerCLI makes it much less cumbersome. Rather than having to click through hardware wizards, an administrator can initiate a script and go get a cup of coffee while the VMs are performing tasks like disconnecting all of the floppy and CD drives.

Adding Hardware to a VM

Within PowerCLI, the process for working with virtual hardware is fairly simple. If you want to add hardware, you use Get-VM to find the VMs you want to add the hardware to and then pipe them into the appropriate New cmdlet. For example, to create a new floppy drive for all of your VMs, you could do the following:

```
Get-VM |New-FloppyDrive -StartConnected
```

You can use the following cmdlets to add hardware to a VM:

- New-CDDrive
- New-FloppyDrive
- New-HardDisk
- New-NetworkAdapter

Removing and Modifying Hardware on a VM

Removing or modifying hardware requires you to first retrieve the object you would like to change and then pipe that object into either the Remove or Set cmdlet for that type of hardware. For example, you can remove all of the CD drives from all of your VMs by doing the following:

```
Get-VM |Get-CDDrive |Remove-CDDrive -Confirm:$False
```

You can use the following cmdlets to remove hardware from a VM:

- Remove-CDDrive
- Remove-FloppyDrive
- Remove-HardDisk
- Remove-NetworkAdapter

You can use the following Set cmdlets to modify existing hardware. Each of these also has a corresponding Get cmdlet to enable you to retrieve the object you would like to change.

- Set-CDDrive
- Set-FloppyDrive
- Set-HardDisk
- Set-NetworkAdapter

For example, you use Set-CDDrive to connect a CD drive to an ISO image.

```
Get-VM VM1 | Get-CDDrive |
    Set-CDDrive -IsoPath '[datastore1] boot.iso' -Connected $True -Confirm:$False
```

Here is an example that uses Set-HardDisk to increase the capacity of the first disk in a VM named VM1 by 1 gigabyte.

```
$disks = @(Get-VM vm1 |Get-HardDisk)
$disks[0] |Set-HardDisk -CapacityKB ($disks[0].CapacityKB + (1GB/1KB))
```

Note

The previous example sets the $disks variable to the contents of Get-HardDisk. The way this cmdlet and many other cmdlets work is that it returns one hard disk if there is only one hard disk. If there are multiple hard disks, it returns a collection of hard disks. In this case, @() is used to signify that you want to receive a collection of hard disks even if there is only one hard disk returned. That is why you can then access `$disks[0]`. This is an extremely handy technique when working with cmdlets where it is possible that you may receive either one object or a set of objects. ∎

Managing VM Resource Configuration

Resource configurations are retrieved with `Get-VMResourceConfiguration`. Changes to these configurations are made by piping the configuration into `Set-VMResourceConfiguration`. Here is an example of how you can use these two cmdlets to set the memory reservation for all of your VMs:

```
foreach ($vm in (Get-VM) {
  $vm |Get-VMResourceConfiguration |
    Set-VMResourceConfiguration -MemReservationMB ($vm.MemoryMB/2)
}
```

Updating VM Tools

Updating the VMware tools on a VM is done with `Update-Tools`. This cmdlet mounts the VMware tools, and automatically updates the tools to the latest version.

```
Get-VM VM1 |Update-Tools
```

If the tools are not already installed, you will need to mount the tools with `Mount-Tools` and then execute a silent installation with `msiexec`. Listing 23-3 shows a technique to do this if you have WinRM enabled on the VM.

Cross-Reference

WinRM and Windows PowerShell remoting are discussed in Chapter 2, "What's New in Windows PowerShell V2." ∎

LISTING 23-3

Mounting and Installing VM Tools via Windows PowerShell Remoting

```
$vm = get-vm 'VM1'
$vm |Mount-Tools

$script = {
  $argument '-i "D:\VMware Tools64.msi" ADDLOCAL = ALL /qn'
  [diagnostics.process]::start("msiexec.exe", $args).WaitForExit()
}
Invoke-Command -ComputerName $vm.name -ScriptBlock $script

$vm |Dismount-Tools
```

Starting and Stopping VMs

The power state of VMs can be controlled by piping a VM or a set of VMs into one of the cmdlets listed in Table 23-2. For example, to start all of the VMs on a cluster named `cluster1` you can run the following line:

```
Get-VM -Location cluster1 |Start-VM -RunAsync
```

TABLE 23-2

Cmdlets Used to Control the Power State of a VM

Cmdlet	Description
Start-VM	Starts a VM.
Stop-VM	Turns off the virtual power to a VM. Equivalent to holding down the power button on a physical computer.
Restart-VM	Restarts a VM. Equivalent to hitting the reset button on a physical computer.
Suspend-VM	Puts the VM into a suspended state.
Shutdown-VMGuest	Uses the VM tools to turn off a VM.
Restart-VMGuest	Uses the VM tools to restart a VM.
Suspend-VMGuest	Uses the VM tools to put the VM into a suspended state.

Using Snapshots

Snapshots are used to create very quick point-in-time backups of a VM. PowerCLI provides you with an interface for managing them. Snapshots are created with `New-Snapshot`.

```
$vm = Get-VM vm1
$vm |New-Snapshot -Name pre_sp1 -Description 'Prior to sp1'
```

You can view snapshots by using `Get-Snapshot`. The following line retrieves all the snapshots for the VM we are working with:

```
$vm |Get-Snapshot
```

You can retrieve a specific snapshot by using the `Name` parameter of `Get-Snapshot`. For example, to retrieve the object that represents the snapshot you just created with `New-Snapshot`, you can run the following line:

```
$snapshot = $vm |Get-Snapshot -Name pre_sp1
```

A snapshot can be renamed or its description can be updated with `Set-Snapshot`.

```
$snapshot |Set-Snapshot -Description 'Prior to Service Pack 1'
```

A VM is reverted to a snapshot by using the `Snapshot` parameter of `Set-VM`. The following reverts the VM to the snapshot created at the beginning of this section:

```
$vm |Set-VM -Snapshot $snapshot -Confirm:$False
```

Invoking Scripts

PowerCLI provides a cmdlet called `Invoke-VMScript` that uses the VM tools on the guest (VM) along with the VI Toolkit that is installed with PowerCLI to remotely execute a command or script on a running VM. Though this can also be accomplished using WinRM and Windows PowerShell remoting with `Invoke-Command`, `Invoke-VMScript` can be issued against any guest that is running the VM tools. This includes VMs that are running operating systems other than Windows. The command requires you to specify credentials for both the ESX host and for the guest VM. The following shows an example of how you can use `Invoke-VMScript` to get all of the processes running on a VM named linux1. The script makes use of the fact that the command you wish to run can be passed to the `ScriptText` parameter as a positional parameter.

```
$hcred = Get-Credential
$gcred = Get-Credential
$command = 'ps > /mnt/vol1/proc.txt'
Get-VM linux1 |
   Invoke-VMScript $command -HostCredential $hcred -GuestCredential $gcred
```

Managing vCenter

vCenter is the management layer of the vSphere stack of applications and services from VMware. You have already seen how to use PowerCLI with some of the features, for example, host profiles and collecting vCenter performance statistics about an ESX host, that are available only with a vCenter server. In this section, you will look at some of the additional vCenter components that can be manipulated by PowerCLI.

Clusters

Clusters provide a way of grouping together a set of ESX hosts within vCenter. Although this can be done for security reasons or to apply a common host profile to a set of ESX hosts, clusters are generally used when an administrator wants to take advantage of high availability (HA) or load balancing (DRS).

Clusters are created by using `New-Cluster`.

```
New-Cluster drs1 -DrsEnabled -Location datacenter1
```

Cluster objects can be retrieved and inspected by using `Get-Cluster`. The following two lines retrieve the cluster you created previously and then display its settings to the screen:

```
$cluster = get-cluster drs1
$cluster |Select *
```

You can change a cluster's behavior by piping a cluster object into `Set-Cluster`. For example, to enable HA on the cluster, you can run the following line:

```
$cluster |Set-Cluster -HAEnabled $true -Confirm:$False
```

To add a host to a cluster, you use the `Move-VMHost` cmdlet:

```
get-vmhost esx1.psbible.com |Move-VMHost -Destination $cluster
```

Clusters can also be moved into other datacenters by using `Move-Cluster`:

```
$cluster = Get-Cluster drs1
$cluster |Move-Cluster -Destination (Get-Datacenter dc1)
```

Migrating VMs

The process used to migrate VMs is similar to the process you just looked at to move an ESX host into a new cluster. In the case of VMs, `Get-VM` is used to retrieve the VM and `Move-VM` is used to move the VM. The `Destination` parameter of `Move-VM` is extremely flexible. You can specify a host retrieved by `Get-VMHost`, a folder retrieved by `Get-Folder`, or a resource pool retrieved by `Get-ResourcePool` as the argument for this parameter. For example, you can move a VM to a new host by performing the following line of code:

```
Get-VM vm1 |Move-VM -Destination (Get-VMHost esx1.psbible.com)
```

If vMotion is configured properly and the VM is powered on, then vMotion will be used for the migration of the VM. Similarly, you can use the `Datastore` parameter of `Move-VM` to migrate the VM via Storage vMotion. The following line shows an example of a command that can be used to initiate a migration to new storage:

```
Get-VM vm1 |Move-VM -Datastore (Get-Datastore ds1)
```

If vMotion and Storage vMotion are not configured properly, you would need to shut down a VM prior to issuing the `Move-VM` command against it.

Note

In case you are new to VMWare's technology, vMotion is the ability to migrate a VM from one ESX host to another while the VM is powered on. The technology relies on using shared storage and a network link between the two ESX hosts. The vMotion technology is what makes things like HA and DRS possible.

Storage vMotion is similar to vMotion because it allows you to migrate VMs while they are powered on. In the case of Storage vMotion, this migration occurs to a new set of disks. ■

Managing Folders, Resource Pools, and Datacenters

Folders, resource pools, datacenters, and clusters all have a similar set of cmdlets that help you create, modify, move, and delete them from vCenter. In the "Clusters" section of this chapter, you saw how to use cmdlets to manage clusters. The same techniques for managing clusters can also be applied to the cmdlets in Table 23-3 to manage resource pools and datacenters.

TABLE 23-3

Cmdlets Used to Manage Folders, Resource Pools, and Datacenter Objects in vCenter

Folder Cmdlets	Datacenter Cmdlets	Resource Pool Cmdlets
New-Folder	New-Datacenter	New-ResourcePool
Set-Folder	Set-Datacenter	Set-ResourcePool
Get-Folder	Get-Datacenter	Get-ResourcePool
Move-Folder	Move-Datacenter	Move-ResourcePool
Remove-Folder	Remove-Datacenter	Remove-ResourcePool

Getting Log Data

In the "Getting Logs" section of this chapter, you saw how you can gather log data from an ESX host. The cmdlets used in the examples from this section, Get-LogType and Get-Log, also work when connected to vCenter to retrieve vCenter logs. The following code shows an example of what the output of Get-LogType looks like when connected to a vCenter server:

```
Get-LogType

Key                   Summary
---                   -------
vpxd:vpxd-13.log      vCenter server log in 'plain' format
vpxd:vpxd-14.log      vCenter server log in 'plain' format
vpxd:vpxd-alert-9...  vCenter server log in 'plain' format
vpxd:vpxd-profile...  vCenter server log in 'plain' format
vpxd-profiler:vpx...  vpxd-profiler
```

In addition to this log data, you can also view vCenter events with `Get-VIEvent`. The following code shows how you can use this cmdlet to look at events over the last hour:

```
$finish = Get-Date
$start = $finish.AddHours(-1)
Get-VIEvent -Start $start -Finish $finish |
   Select UserName,FullFormattedMessage |Format-Table -AutoSize
```

```
UserName        FullFormattedMessage
--------        --------------------
Administrator   Task: Initialize powering On
Administrator   Reconfigured VM2 on esx1.psbible.com in dc1
Administrator   Task: Reconfigure virtual machine
Administrator   Removed rp1 on Cluster1 in dc1
Administrator   Task: Delete resource pool
```

Tasks that have occurred recently or are currently taking place can also be retrieved by using `Get-Task`, as shown in the following example. The output shows tasks that are in various states in vCenter.

```
Get-Task
```

```
Name                        State     % Complete Start Time   Finish Time
----                        -----     ---------- ----------   -----------
Destroy_Task                Success          100 06:44:38 PM  06:44:48 PM
CreateClusterEx             Success          100 06:47:52 PM  06:47:53 PM
MoveInto_Task               Error            100 06:48:25 PM  06:48:25 PM
EnterMaintenanceMode_Task   Success          100 06:48:36 PM  06:48:43 PM
MoveInto_Task               Success          100 06:48:45 PM  06:48:45 PM
ExitMaintenanceMode_Task    Running           15 06:48:52 PM
```

Getting Performance Data

You have already seen how you can gather the performance data that is stored in the vCenter database for an ESX host in the "Using Get-Stat to Collect Performance Data from vCenter" section earlier in this chapter. The cmdlet used in this example, `Get-Stat`, can also be used against any object in vCenter that has a performance tab like VMs, clusters, and resource pools. For example, you could retrieve performance data about a VM with the following line of code:

```
Get-VM vm1 |Get-Stat -Memory
```

Everything Else

This chapter has touched on a few common scripting tasks that you may encounter when working with vSphere. Though it's by no means a comprehensive look into what is possible with PowerCLI, it should provide you with enough practical examples and information to begin your journey into automating VMware.

In addition to what you have looked at, PowerCLI also has the ability to manage the following aspects of vSphere:

- vApps
- vCenter alarms
- vCenter Update Manager
- vCenter permissions and roles
- vCenter questions
- DRS

Note

For more information on these topics or any of the topics covered in this chapter, you can review VMWare's documentation: `www.vmware.com/support/developer/PowerCLI/index.html`. ∎

Summary

PowerCLI enables Windows PowerShell users to manage their VMware virtual infrastructure. When comparing this set of cmdlets to others that you have looked at in this book, it is apparent that a lot of thought was put into how the cmdlets interact with each other through the pipeline. The fruit of this effort is that VMware has provided us with an easy and intuitive command-line interface to vSphere.

This brings us to the end of our exploration of virtualization and cloud infrastructure. In the next part of this book, you take a look beyond the console at some other components of Windows PowerShell that can help an administrator deliver a polished set of scripts.

Part VI

Beyond the Console

IN THIS PART

Chapter 24
Creating User Interfaces

Chapter 25
Using the Windows PowerShell ISE

Creating User Interfaces

This chapter shows you how you can create a user interface (UI) using Windows PowerShell. It looks first at what you can do, UI-wise, at the text mode console and then introduces Windows Forms and how to create a form using Windows PowerShell. You look at some of the key elements that you can add to a form, including button, textbox, and label controls, and how you can use these to create a simple share viewer application GUI. You then look at PrimalForms as a tool that can help you to lay out a form. The chapter finishes with a look at other ways to create UIs.

A *user interface* is a set of features that an end user accesses in order to use and operate an application. At the command line, UIs tend to be fairly basic. By comparison, a graphical user interface, or GUI, is a much richer Windows application, complete with buttons, boxes, and so on.

For Windows PowerShell, the most commonly used UIs are the Windows PowerShell console and the Windows PowerShell ISE. Although these are fine for users that fully understand Windows PowerShell, giving the command line to less experienced users may cause some degree of confusion and user resistance.

IN THIS CHAPTER

Using text mode user interface

Creating a simple UI in Windows PowerShell using Windows Forms

Working with Windows Forms controls

Using Windows PowerShell and PrimalForms

Working with other UI mechanisms

Working with Text Mode UI

A text mode UI for a Windows PowerShell script is usually pretty simplistic — you code the script to ask the user for the relevant information and then display a result. The idea is to hide the details of scripts and how Windows PowerShell works from an end user who just is using your script.

Text mode does not offer a lot of options for building a UI. Users can enter data in only a few ways: they can call your script using parameters, you can code requests for information that they type in at runtime, or they can provide a file that contains the necessary information. The next example provides a look at some of the ways you can create a UI to get user credentials for use by a script.

Getting Credentials

For many scripts, users may need to supply specific user credentials because their own logon credentials may not be adequate. Using the principles of lowest privilege, a user may log in to his or her system using fairly low-privilege credentials and then run a script or run a cmdlet using elevated credentials. `Get-WmiObject`, for example, is a cmdlet that supports a `-Credential` parameter.

The most common way to get credentials is to use the `Get-Credential` cmdlet and prompt the user for the domain, user ID, and password. These can then be stored in a variable that is supplied to the relevant cmdlet or profile at runtime.

For example, suppose you want to get the BIOS information from a remote system, using different credentials than you are currently logged on with. You could do the following:

```
$cred = Get-Credential
Get-WmiObject -Class Win32_Bios -Computer Cookham11 -Credentials $cred
```

When you use this approach, Windows PowerShell displays a standard Windows dialog box where the user can enter the credentials. You can see the PowerShell session and the credentials dialog box in Figure 24-1.

FIGURE 24-1

Getting credentials

Getting Strings

A key feature of a UI is its ability to get data from a user that is acted upon by your script. For example, you might want to obtain a user's age. With Windows PowerShell, you use Read-Host to read input from the console. For example:

```
$Age = Read-Host -Prompt "Enter your age: "
```

This statement first displays "Enter your age:" at the console, then assigns what was read to the variable $Age. By default, Read-Host returns a string. To return a number, you cast the result of Read-Host to a number using an explicit type declaration as follows:

```
[int] $Age = Read-Host "Enter your age"
```

There is only one small problem with this approach, which is that the user could enter something other than a number. If so, then Windows PowerShell generates a runtime exception. To get around this, you can code a Try/Catch block like this:

```
while ($True) {
   try {[int] $Age=Read-Host "Enter Your age"
   break}
catch{ "Not a number - try again"}}
```

Validating Input

Another key aspect of a good UI is that it ensures the data entered and passed to your string is valid and not malicious. For the most part, users are responsible and attempt to input correct values when prompted by a script. But not all users do this all the time. Some users can accidentally enter invalid data; other, less nice people do it deliberately as many organizations have learned (after a successful hack attack) to their detriment.

If you start from the premise that all user input is intentionally evil until proven otherwise and proceed from there, you are less likely to have problems. As shown earlier, there are easy ways to detect and code around these issues, but they require some thought and (usually) some extra code.

You can validate data with Windows PowerShell in two broad ways. First, you can write code to examine each bit of data that is entered and reject all invalid data. The second way is to use attributes and have Windows PowerShell check that function (and cmdlet) parameters have acceptable values.

As you examine the data, you should use the try/catch approach noted earlier. This will catch some errors that would otherwise cause your script to abort when converting the string returned by Read-Host into the value type you want it to be.

You should also write Windows PowerShell code to check any input for both formatting and to check that it makes good business sense (for example, ensuring age is, say, greater than or equal to 18 and less than 65).

To both get and validate the age value, you could do something like this:

```
function Get-Age {
while ($True) {
  try {
    [int] $age = Read-Host "Enter your age"
    if ($age -ge 18 -and $age -le 65) {break}
    Write-Host "Age must be between 18 and 65 - please reenter" }
  catch{ "Not a number - Please reenter"}
}
return $age
```

An alternative way of validating numbers and dates is to use the .NET TryParse() method, which exists for a number of .NET value types (for example, Int32 and DateTime). This method takes a string and attempts to convert it into a number or date. The method returns either an error (if the string cannot be parsed successfully, or it returns the parsed value). For example, you could do this:

```
while ($true) {
  try {
    [int] $age = 0
    [int] $number = Read-Host "Enter your age: "
    $result = [System.Int32]::TryParse($number, [ref] $number);
    If ($result) {
      If ($age -ge 18 -and $age -le 65) {break}
      Write-Host "Age must be between 18 and 65"
      Write-Host "Please reenter"}
    }
  catch { "Not a number - Please reenter"}
}
```

This might seem to be overkill, but the more hard validation you do on user input, the less the likelihood of bad data being used leading to bad results.

With a bit of work, you can create a text-mode UI for your product, which may be fine for those users who are experienced at the command line. No matter who you are writing a UI for, you still need to validate any input before using it. If you have less experienced users or you need to do something a bit more, then you need to write additional code, or consider moving the UI to be a GUI.

Building a Simple UI in Windows PowerShell Using Windows Forms

Text-mode UIs are acceptable where the amount of data the user is expected to input is small and where the probability of successful entry of data is high. For other scenarios, a richer Windows-based GUI solution is called for — a full window, with spaces for user entry being explicitly coded in. This window might display information it knows about (or deduces), then allow the end user to enter extra information or to override the script-generated values (that is, where the script has not guessed user intentions wisely enough).

You can use two Windows technologies to achieve this: Windows Forms and Windows Presentation Foundation (WPF). Windows Forms is an older technology but is more than adequate for building simple GUIs. The following section looks at how you can use Windows Forms to build simple GUIs with Windows PowerShell.

Using Windows Forms

Windows Forms is a .NET component that enables you to create GUI-like forms that you use to gather and display information. This makes using your scripts appear much more like a Windows application than using the raw console for input and output.

Creating a GUI using Windows Forms can produce great results, but it can end up being quite a lot of work if the GUI is particularly complex. Try to keep things as simple as possible, and if you can't avoid complexity, consider using more powerful tools, such as PrimalForms, which is covered later in this chapter. Of course, you should always consider whether you are writing a real application and, therefore, should be using a lower-level language like C# or VB.NET and richer development tools such as Microsoft's Visual Studio.

Building a GUI with Windows Forms — the Basics

With Windows Forms, you work with two main objects:

- **Forms:** These are windows that you can display. Typically, for most simple UIs, you just have one form.
- **Controls:** These are objects you place on the form and use to capture and display information.

Using Windows Forms, you must first develop code that creates a form. You then create each control, specify handlers that do things when the user accesses the form at runtime, and then attach the control to the form. When you have completed adding the necessary controls to your form, you can display the form with which the user can interact.

Like many parts of .NET, the .NET assembly needed for Windows Forms exists on your computer, but is not loaded by default. That's simple to overcome by loading the relevant assembly explicitly in your script, like this:

```
[
Add-Type -Assembly System.Windows.Forms
```

Once you have loaded the Windows Forms assembly, you next create the form, with basic sizes and with other properties set. Once created in memory, you show a form using the form's ShowDialog() method:

```
# Create form
$form= New-Object -TypeName Windows.Forms.Form
```

```
$form.Width  = 500
$form.Height = 200
$form.Text   = "My first Windows Forms application"
# Now show the form as dialog box.
$form.ShowDialog()
```

This code brings up a window, as shown in Figure 24-2.

Basic Windows form

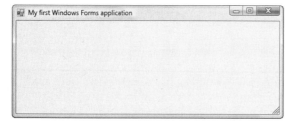

This is not yet a useful GUI, but it does represent a starting point. The form has a basic size, and you can use normal Windows handling to resize it. You close the form by clicking the X in the upper-right corner.

To make the form more useful, you need to add and configure controls as you see in the next section.

Using Windows Forms Controls

Once you have your basic form created, you need to add controls to make the form useful. *Controls* are objects that you add to your form to make the form useful. Typical form controls include a label control, a button control, and a textbox control.

Note
There are many more form controls available. You can read more at http://msdn.microsoft.com/en-us/ library/3xdhey7w.aspx. ∎

Label Control
A label control puts a simple label onto the form. Typically, you place the label next to some input control, to tell the user what the input box is to be used for. Or you can use a label control to display a message inside a form.

Incorporating a label control takes several steps. First, you need to create the control, in memory, by using New-Object and specifying the control name. Next, you need to add the control to a form, and finally, you need to make the control visible on the form.

Like other controls, the label control has a large number of properties to make the control fit your particular purpose. You can set its size, location on the form, color, and so on. Some of the properties of the label control are objects in their own right. Continuing the example form, you create and add a label control like this:

```
# Load System.Windows.Forms
Add-Type -AssemblyName "System.Windows.Forms"

# Create form
$form= New-Object -TypeName Windows.Forms.Form
$form.width  = 500
$form.height = 200
$form.text   = "My first windows forms application"

# Create a label control
# Set label location, text, size, etc.
$label = New-Object -TypeName Windows.Forms.Label
$label.Location = New-Object -TypeName Drawing.Point -ArgumentList 100,75
$label.Size = New-Object -TypeName Drawing.Point -ArgumentList 100,50
$label.text = "Computer Name: "
$label.font = "Comic Sans"

# Now make label visible and add it to the form
$form.Controls.Add($label)
$label.Visible = $true

# Finally, show the form as dialog box.
$form.ShowDialog()
```

You can see the results of this form and control in Figure 24-3.

FIGURE 24-3

A label control

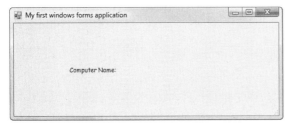

This is a small improvement over the form shown in Figure 24-2, but it needs more controls to make the form useful to an end user.

Button Control

The button control places a push-down button on the form, which enables the user to click the button to perform some action. .NET does the clever stuff to make the button look like it's actually being pushed and released by your mouse click.

Like the Label control, to make use of a button control, you first create the control and set properties. The code to do this is as follows:

```
# Create a button control
$button = new-object windows.forms.button
$button.text = "Push To Close Form."
$button.width = 150
$button.location = new-object drawing.point 100,100
```

Once you have created the control, you define a button handler. The handler is code that runs, for example, when the button is pushed. Once defined, you attach the handler to the control and then attach the button control on the form, using this code:

```
# Define Button Click handler
$button_OnClick = {
  $label.Text = "Closing!!"
  Start-Sleep -Seconds 1
  $form.Close()}

# Add the script block
$button.Add_Click($button_Onclick)

$form.Controls.Add($button)
```

The complete code now looks like this:

```
# Load System.Windows.Forms
Add-Type -AssemblyName System.Windows.Forms

# Create form
$form= New-Object -TypeName Windows.Forms.Form
$form.width  = 500
$form.height = 200
$form.text   = "My first windows forms application"

# Create a label control
# Set label location, text, size, etc.
$label = New-Object -TypeName Windows.Forms.Label
$label.Location = New-Object -TypeName Drawing.Point -ArgumentList 100,50
$label.Size = New-Object -TypeName Drawing.Point -ArgumentList 100,50
$label.Text = "Computer"
$label.Font = "Comic Sans"

# Now make label visible and add it to the form
```

```
$label.Visible = $true
$form.Controls.Add($label)

# Now create a button
$button = New-Object -TypeName Windows.Forms.Button
$button.Text = "Push To Close Form."
$button.Width = 150
$button.Location = New-Object -TypeName Drawing.Point 100,100

# Define Button Click handler
$button_OnClick = {
  $form.Close()}

# Add the script block
$button.Add_Click($button_OnClick)

$form.Controls.Add($button)

# Finally, show the form as dialog box.
$form.ShowDialog()
```

Once you add the button control, the form is now marginally more useful. Figure 24-4 shows the button you created, which you can use to close the form.

FIGURE 24-4

Using a button control

This form is still not very useful, but hopefully, you can see the basic approach to adding more controls to your form: you create the control, define properties, define a handler, and then attach the handler to the control and the control to the form.

Textbox Control

You can use the textbox control to create a box on your form where the user can enter text. The idea is that you display a textbox, and the user enters text into the textbox and clicks a button. The button handler can then take the text in the textbox and do something useful with it.

589

A textbox control is very similar in usage to a button control. To create a textbox, you would do the following:

```
# Create a text box to get computer name and add to form
$text1 = New-Object -TypeName Windows.Forms.Textbox
$text1.location = New-Object -Typename System.Drawing.Point `
  -ArgumentList 150, 50
$text1.text= "Localhost"
$text1.font= "Courier New"
$text1.visible = $true
$form.Controls.Add($text1)
```

As with the label control, you first create the control and work out its location on the form. You then set some properties — in this example, some default text and the font to display the text. For some controls, you can define handlers that define what happens when you click a control — each control can respond to a number of user actions. With the control defined, you add it to the form. You would add this code anywhere before the ShowForm. Then, you move on to the next control. Most controls follow a similar pattern.

Thus far in the examples, you've created a very simple form with a couple of controls. Now, complete the application, which is a GUI for displaying computer shares on a given machine.

To create this application, you can take the preceding snippets and turn them into a GUI. You need to add the textbox control for the user to enter the name of the computer, a button to get the shares from that computer entered, and a button to close the form. Also, the form needs a further label control, where you place the details of the shares for the user to view. Finally, you need to add some code to the button handler that takes the name of the computer and uses WMI to get the shares and display them nicely in the label control.

Listing 24-1 provides the complete code for creating a basic share viewer UI.

LISTING 24-1

Creating a Share Viewer UI

```
# Share Viewer GUI

# Load System.Windows.Forms
Add-Type -AssemblyName System.Windows.Forms

# Create form
$form= New-Object -TypeName Windows.Forms.Form
$form.width  = 600
$form.height = 650
$form.text   = "My Share Viewer UI"

# Create a "computer name" label control
# Set label location, text, size, etc.
$label1 = New-Object -TypeName Windows.Forms.Label
```

```
$label1.Location = New-Object -TypeName Drawing.Point -ArgumentList 50,50
$label1.Text = "Computer Name:"
$label1.Font = "Comic Sans"
$label1.Visible = $true


# Add it to the form
$form.Controls.Add($label1)


# Create a text box to get computer name and add to form
$text1 = New-Object -TypeName Windows.Forms.TextBox
$text1.Location = New-Object -TypeName System.Drawing.Point `
  -ArgumentList 150, 50
$text1.Text= "Localhost"
$text1.Font= "Courier New"
$text1.Visible = $true
$form.Controls.Add($text1)


# Create a label to output stuff
$label2 = New-Object -TypeName Windows.Forms.Label
$label2.Location = New-Object -TypeName Drawing.Point -ArgumentList 50,100
$label2.Width = 500
$label2.Height = 360
$label2.Text = ""
$label2.Font = "Courier New"
$label2.Visible = $true
$form.Controls.Add($label2)


# Create a button to get the shares
$button1 = New-Object Windows.Forms.Button
$button1.Text = "Push To Get Shares"
$button1.Width = 150
$button1.Location = New-Object -TypeName Drawing.Point -ArgumentList 350,50

# Define Getting Shares Button Click handler
$button1_OnClick = {
  $label2.Text = "Shares on $($text1.text):`n"
  $shares = Get-Wmiobject -Class win32_share -computer $text1.text |
    where {$_.Type -eq 0}
  foreach ($share in $shares)
    {
      $label2.Text += "{0,-25}  {1}`n" -f $share.Name, $share.Path
    }
    }

# Add the script block handler
$button1.Add_Click($button1_Onclick)
$form.controls.add($button1)

# Now create a button to close window
```

continues

LISTING 24-1   *(continued)*

```
$button2 = New-Object -TypeName windows.forms.button
$button2.Text = "Push To Close Form"
$button2.Width = 150
$button2.Location = New-Object -TypeName drawing.point -ArgumentList 160,550

# Define Button Click handler
$button2_OnClick = {
  $form.Close()}

# Add the script block handler
$button2.Add_Click($button2_Onclick)
$form.Controls.Add($button2)

# Finally, show the form as dialog box.
$form.ShowDialog()
```

When you run the script, you produce a nice dialog box that, when used, creates what you see in Figure 24-5.

FIGURE 24-5

Completed share viewer UI

Like almost any UI in Windows, you could take this mini-application a lot further. You could add controls to the form that enable the user to add new shares to a system, or that enable the user to remove a share. You could provide an additional form to enable the user to enter credentials that WMI could use to obtain the share information from remote computers. You could define additional handlers for, say, the button control that changes the color of the text whenever you hover over the button (and reverts back to the original color when you stop hovering over the button). Each of those additional features is simply more of the same: you define an additional control, determine where the control goes on the form, set some properties to the controls, define control handlers, and then add the control to the form.

Of course, you can end up writing a full-blown Windows application, and there have been several of these. However, using the out-of-the-box tools (Windows PowerShell and Notepad or the ISE) is not the most efficient method for creating rich GUI applications, if for no other reason than there is no built-in design functionality.

In the examples set out here, I had to play around a bit to get the controls into the right place, ensure the form was the right size, and so on. Tools such as Sapien's PrimalForms make these tasks significantly simpler.

Using Windows PowerShell and PrimalForms

As noted earlier, using Notepad (or even Windows PowerShell ISE) to develop a GUI takes time and a bit of guesswork. For writing full-blown Windows applications, you may be better off using traditional application development methods; that is, writing the application in C# and using Visual Studio. Though you can write applications using Windows PowerShell, it may not always be the best approach for IT professionals.

But there are likely to be many occasions where Windows PowerShell is the right tool for creating your GUI, but where you have multiple controls that need to be accurately placed on one or even more forms. One tool you can use to help you do this is Sapien's PrimalForms.

PrimalForms is a commercial tool that enables you to create visual Windows PowerShell-based applications and UIs that you can then easily package and distribute. At the time of this writing, the full version was selling for US$299 from the website. Though not free, the savings in time make this a very useful tool for developing simple Windows PowerShell-based GUIs. Sapien also ships a free Community edition with less functionality that might be enough for some simple use cases. PrimalForms has a good script editor for you to edit your script as well as a forms designer to make designing your script simple and quick.

Note

PrimalForms has a wealth of other features, as described in Sapien's website (`www.sapien.com/software/primalforms#`). You can also download a fully functional time-bombed evaluation copy.

For more information on the Community edition, see Sapien's blog article at: `www.sapien.com/blog/2011/06/07/where-did-the-free-community-tools-go/.` ∎

Before you can really begin to exploit the richness of PrimalForms, you need to understand the basics of using Windows Forms with Windows PowerShell. If you are likely to create administrative GUIs, then PrimalForms is a great tool to have — but there is a learning curve!

Note

Microsoft has produced extensive documentation on its MSDN site that describes Windows Forms, the controls, which you should be familiar with before starting to use PrimalForms. You can start here: `http://msdn.microsoft.com/en-us/library/aa983655%28VS.71%29.aspx.` ∎

When you run PrimalForms, you get a nice forms designer that you can use to lay out your form and to set default properties for the controls on your form(s). You can then look at the script that PrimalForms generates as you add and update controls. From the script editor, you can add code as needed — for example, to handle a button click, and so on.

You can see the PrimalForms UI in Figure 24-6.

FIGURE 24-6

The PrimalForms UI

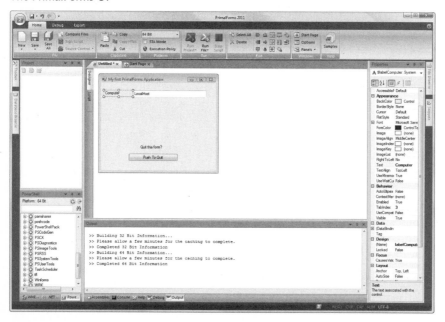

Once you have completed your design work, you can save your form and script and begin to use it. And to make things simple for the end user, you can package your script in an .exe file, which will keep your users from changing the code.

Using Windows Presentation Foundation

You have any number of alternative ways of developing user interfaces — with touch, graphics, and sound. You could, for example, use a Braille tablet to display information to users who are blind (and read braille), and you could use sound or some sort of touch-sensitive surface as a way of capturing input. Most of these options are probably more appropriate for use in developing full applications rather than just creating administrative user interfaces. However, it is worth mentioning them so you are aware of the options available to you.

The only other UI mechanism worth mentioning in the context of simple UI development is Microsoft's Windows Presentation Foundation, or WPF.

Windows Forms has been a part of the .NET Framework for a considerable time. With .NET 3.0 (released as part of the roadmap to Windows Vista), Microsoft introduced a new technology for creating user interfaces — WPF. WPF is a much richer display technology than Windows Forms, although much of this richness may not be of much use or interest to the IT professional. Developers, on the other hand, love WPF as a UI on which to build great graphic applications!

In terms of key features, WPF utilizes DirectX for output support, making it more suitable for later graphics cards. WPF also attempts to provide separation between the UI itself and the business logic behind it. In does this, in part, by the use of Extensible Application Markup Language, XAML (pronounced "zamel") for describing the UI with separate code to handle the business logic. The intention here is that you get great UI designers to use advanced tools to create the layout and render that in XAML. Then, the application developer must code the business logic, and you're done.

Note
You can learn more about XAML and WPF on the Web, including a good introduction at Wikipedia at http://en.wikipedia.org/wiki/Windows_Presentation_Foundation. ∎

Using WPF with Windows PowerShell requires you to first author the UI in XAML. With Windows Forms, you did that in code; but with WPF, you need some good way to author XAML. You can use Notepad, but it's a lot of work. All in all, WPF is a lot more work because there are no built-in tools to help you. Moreover, PrimalForms does not support WPF.

Though there is no equivalent to PrimalForms for WPF yet (that is, tools to create WPF with Windows PowerShell), there have been some community efforts around WPF. As part of the Windows 7 Resource Kit, Microsoft published WPK, a WPF toolkit for Windows PowerShell.

You can get WPK as part of the larger Windows PowerShell Pack Windows 7 Resource Kit release. You can download the whole Windows PowerShell Pack at `http://archive.msdn .microsoft.com/Windows PowerShellPack`.

Work on this concept has continued, and three Windows PowerShell superstars, James Brundage, Doug Finke, and Joel Bennett, have produced an updated version of WPK known as ShowUI. You can get ShowUI from `http://showui.codeplex.com/` as a free download.

Summary

In this chapter, you looked at some ways to create a user interface for a Windows PowerShell script. You first looked at UIs from the text mode console. There's not a great deal you can do here, mainly due to the restrictions of the console itself. You also looked at some ways to validate the input you might encounter.

You then looked at using Windows Forms to build a GUI, and you looked at how you could use Windows Forms and Windows PowerShell to create a simple network-aware share viewer. You then looked at a third-party product, PrimalForms, that makes writing Windows Forms GUIs much simpler. The chapter finished with an overview of Windows Presentation Foundation.

In the next chapter, you look at the Windows PowerShell ISE.

Using the Windows PowerShell ISE

You first learned about the Windows PowerShell Integrated Scripting Environment, or ISE, in Chapter 2. This chapter provides more details about the ISE. First, you explore the basics of the ISE, including the screen layout and menu structure. Next, you look at the ISE profile and review the debugging features in ISE. You then look at the ISE object model and how you can add new menu items to the ISE. Finally, you look at some alternatives to the ISE.

IN THIS CHAPTER

Examining the ISE

Using the ISE

Debugging scripts using the ISE

Extending the ISE

Finding alternatives to the ISE

Key Features of the ISE

The ISE is a graphical Windows PowerShell console and a basic development environment. The ISE is a Microsoft-developed host application for Windows PowerShell V2. You can see the ISE in Figure 25-1.

FIGURE 25-1

The ISE

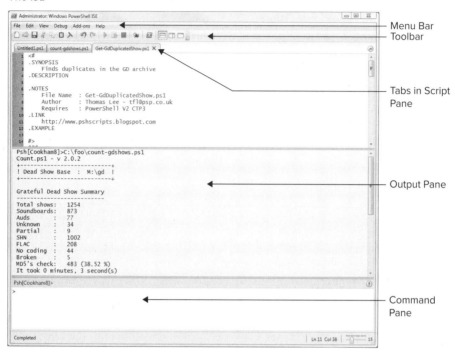

The ISE enables you to run commands and develop scripts and modules in a single Windows GUI. Although similar to the Windows PowerShell console, the ISE offers additional features including script and module editing, multiline editing, syntax coloring, support for Unicode and right-to-left languages, and a rich extensibility/customization model.

Screen Layout

The ISE uses the traditional Windows application menu and toolbar and has no Ribbon. As you can see in Figure 25-1, several key elements make up the ISE:

- **Menu bar:** The traditional Windows application menu bar offering File, Edit, View, Debug, and Help windows by default. The menu bar can be extended to add an additional Add-ons menu.

- **Toolbar:** A Windows applications toolbar offering a variety of functions.

- **Script pane:** A pane in which you can open multiple files for editing and/or execution. The toolbar provides tools that enable you to run a script, run part of a script, and so on. Each file is opened in a separate tab, allowing you to have any number of scripts or other files open for editing. Windows PowerShell provides color-coded syntax for scripts, modules, and manifests. You can also create Remote PowerShell tabs with ISE.

- **Output pane:** Where ISE sends output resulting from either a command entered into the Command pane or output from a running script.

- **Command pane:** Where you enter Windows PowerShell commands, much as you would do in the Windows PowerShell console. Just type the command and see the output in the Output pane.

ISE Menu Bar

The ISE menu bar provides five menu items. They are listed here, and are covered in more depth in the sections that follow:

- **File menu:** Provides basic file-level operations, including opening/saving files

- **Edit menu:** Provides the basic script-editing features used to edit a script in the Script pane

- **View menu:** Provides a number of controls over what you see in the ISE, including the location of the various panes and the ability to zoom in/out or go to a particular tab in the Script pane

- **Debug menu:** Provides script-debugging functions used when you are debugging a script using ISE

- **Help menu:** Provides access to the ISE help file (keyboard shortcut: F1)

Menu items are context-sensitive. Some options, for example, the items in the Debug menu, are available only under specific circumstances (for example, when you are running and debugging a script).

Executing some menu items brings up standard Windows dialog boxes (for example, Find, Replace, and Save) and thus should be very familiar. Executing other menu options simply runs a Windows PowerShell command as though you'd entered it in the command panel. The ISE displays output in the Output pane.

ISE File Menu

The File menu is similar to the File menu in other Windows applications. You use the File menu to manage scripts or files you are editing in the Edit pane. You can open/save/run/stop a script from the File menu or open/close `PowerShellTabs`. Table 25-1 provides an explanation of each menu item, its keyboard shortcut, and what it does.

TABLE 25-1

File Menu Items

Menu Item	Keyboard Shortcut	What It Does
New	Ctrl+N	Opens a new script in a new tab in the Script pane given the working name `Untitled1.ps1`.
Open	Ctrl+O	Brings up the Open File dialog box to enable you to select a file to be opened. Each opened file appears in a new tab in the Script pane.
Save As	None	Brings up the Save As dialog box to enable you to select the file associated with the currently selected tab in the Script pane and then save the file.
Run	F5	Runs the script in the currently selected tab in the Script pane.
Run Selection	F8	Runs just the selected text in the currently selected tab in the Script pane.
Stop Execution	Ctrl+Break	Stops the currently running script.
Close	Ctrl+F4	Offers to save the current script, if it's unsaved. If you agree, or if the script is already saved, the script tab is closed.
New PowerShell Tab	Ctrl+T	Creates a new instance of Windows PowerShell in a new tab. This menu option creates a new `PowerShellTab` in the script pane.
Close PowerShell Tab	Ctrl+Shift+R	Closes the currently selected PowerShell tab in the ISE. If any scripts are unsaved, ISE prompts to save all of them.
New Remote PowerShell Tab	Ctrl+Shift+P	Brings up the New Remote PowerShell tab dialog where you specify a machine and username. Then, ISE enters a remote session to the machine.
Exit	Alt+F4	Quits ISE. If any files in the Script pane have unsaved edits, ISE prompts you to save them or to discard the changes.

ISE Edit Menu

Like the File menu, the ISE Edit menu should be very familiar to you. The ISE Edit menu provides you with basic text-editing features you can use when editing a script in the Script pane. You can also use the ISE Edit menu to organize the look and feel of the ISE's layout — putting the Script pane on the right, increasing/decreasing text font size, and so on. The individual items in the Edit menu are shown in Table 25-2.

TABLE 25-2

Edit Menu Items

Menu Item	Keyboard Shortcut	What It Does
Undo	Ctrl+Z	Undoes the last edit action.
Redo	Ctrl+Y	Redoes the last undone action.
Cut	Ctrl+X	Cuts the currently selected text in the currently selected script in the Script pane into the clipboard. This selected text is also placed in the clipboard so you can later copy it to another place.
Copy	Ctrl+C	Copies the selected text into the clipboard.
Paste	Ctrl+V	Pastes the text in the clipboard into the current script.
Find in Script	Ctrl+F	Brings up the Find dialog, enabling you to find a word or a regular expression.
Find Next in Script	F3	Finds the next occurrence of a string or regular expression in the current script.
Find Previous in Script	Shift+F3	Finds the previous occurrence of a string or regular expression in the current script.
Replace in Script	Ctrl+H	Brings up the Replace dialog, enabling you to find a text string, and replace it with another.

ISE View Menu

The ISE View menu provides a mechanism to adjust the overall ISE window and its components. You can, for example, hide or reveal the toolbar, move panes around, and so on. Table 25-3 explains the items on the View menu.

TABLE 25-3

ISE View Menu Items

Menu Item	Keyboard Shortcut	What It Does
Show Toolbar	None	Shows or hides the toolbar
Show Script Pane	Ctrl+R	Shows or hides the Script pane
Command Pane Up	None	Enables you to move the Command pane to be above the Script pane or back to its default location

continues

TABLE 25-3 *(continued)*

Menu Item	Keyboard Shortcut	What It Does
Show Script Pane Top	Ctrl + 1	Shows the Script pane at the top of the ISE
Show Script Pane Right	Ctrl + 2	Shows the Script pane to the right of the ISE
Show Script Pane Maximized	Ctrl + 3	Maximizes the Script pane, hiding the Command and Output panes
Go to Script Pane	Ctrl + I	Moves focus to the currently selected script in the Script pane (for example, to resume script editing)
Go to Command Pane	Ctrl + D	Moves focus to the Command pane (for example, to enter more commands)
Go to Output Pane	Ctrl + Shift + O	Moves focus to the Output pane (for example, to view output of a previous command)
Zoom In	Ctrl + +	Increases font size of text in the Script, Command, and Output panes
Zoom Out	Ctrl + -	Decreases font size of text in the Script, Command, and Output panes

ISE Debug Menu

The ISE Debug menu (see Table 25-4) provides a number of features to help you run and debug a script. When you need to debug a script, the Debug menu enables you to create/ toggle/turn off breakpoints in a set of scripts. The ISE Debug menu provides a subset of the debugging commands provided in the console and, in a couple of cases, just calls a debugging cmdlet.

TABLE 25-4

ISE Debug Menu Items

Menu Item	Keyboard Shortcut	What It Does
Step Over	F10	Executes the current statement, then stops at the next statement. If the current statement has a call to a function or script, Windows PowerShell runs that script or function.
Step Into	F11	Executes the current statement, then stops at the next statement. If the current statement has a call to a function or script, Windows PowerShell steps into that function or script instead.

Menu Item	Keyboard Shortcut	What It Does
Step Out	Shift+F11	Steps out of the current function/script and continues up one level in the call stack. Any skipped statements are executed, but are not stepped through. If the debugger is running at the top level, then that script is completed (unless there are further breakpoints set).
Run/Continue	F5	Runs, or continues, the current script.
Stop Debugger	Shift+F5	Stops the execution of the current script.
Toggle Breakpoint	F9	Turns a breakpoint on/off at the current location in the selected script in the Script pane.
Remove All Breakpoints	Ctrl+Shift+F9	Removes all breakpoints.
Enable All Breakpoints	None	Enables all breakpoints, including those previously disabled.
Disable All Breakpoints	None	Disables all breakpoints. ISE remembers these breakpoints, which can be enabled later.
List Breakpoints	Ctrl+Shift+L	Executes `Get-PsBreakpoint` and displays output in the Output pane.
Display Call Stack	Ctrl+Shift+D	Calls `Get-PsCallStack` and displays the results in the Output pane.

ISE Add-ons Menu

This menu is optional. By default, you do not see this menu when you enter ISE. However, by using the ISE's customization features, you can add new menus simply and easily.

ISE Toolbar

The ISE toolbar, shown in Figure 25-2, provides single-click access to a variety of 17 commonly used functions within the ISE.

FIGURE 25-2

The ISE toolbar

The tools in the ISE toolbar provide another way of invoking common ISE functions — most of the toolbar items can be invoked by a keyboard shortcut, a menu item, or Windows PowerShell cmdlets. The ISE toolbar functions (working left to right) and their keyboard and menu/cmdlet counterparts are as follows:

- **New:** Clicking this toolbar button creates a new, empty script in the currently selected PowerShell tab (equivalent to Ctrl+N or File ⇨ New).

- **Open:** Invokes the Open dialog to enable you to choose a file to open (equivalent to Ctrl+O or File ⇨ Open).

- **Save:** Saves the active script in the currently selected PowerShell tab (equivalent to Ctrl+S or File ⇨ Save).

- **Cut:** Cuts the selected text to the Windows clipboard (equivalent to Ctrl+X or Edit ⇨ Cut).

- **Copy:** Cuts the selected text to the Windows clipboard (equivalent to Ctrl+C or Edit ⇨ Copy).

- **Paste:** Pastes the contents of the clipboard into the currently active script (equivalent to Ctrl+V or Edit ⇨ Cut).

- **Clear Output Pane:** Clears all the text from the Output pane (equivalent to `Clear-Host` cmdlet).

- **Undo:** Undoes the previous edit operation (equivalent to Ctrl+Z or Edit ⇨ Undo).

- **Redo:** Reapplies the last undone edit operation (equivalent to Ctrl+Y or Edit ⇨ Redo).

- **Run Script:** Runs the currently selected script (equivalent to F5 or Debug ⇨ Run/Continue).

- **Run Selection:** Runs the text currently selected in the active script (equivalent to F8).

- **Stop Execution:** Stops the execution of any running scripts (equivalent to Shift+F5 or Debug ⇨ Stop Debugger).

- **New Remote PowerShell Tab:** Brings up the New Remote PowerShell Tab dialog to enable you to select a computer (and username) on which to open a new PowerShell tab. After prompting, this toolbar item runs `New-PsSession` specifying the computer name and credential parameters you entered.

- **Start PowerShell.exe:** Runs a new copy of `PowerShell.exe` in a separate console window (equivalent to Ctrl+Shift+P or File ⇨ Start PowerShell.exe).

- **Show Script Pane Top:** Shows the Script pane at the top of the ISE (the default position). This is equivalent to Ctrl+1 or View ⇨ Show Script Pane Top.

- **Show Script Pane Right:** Shows the Script pane to the right of the ISE (equivalent to Ctrl+2 or View ⇨ Show Script Pane Right).
- **Show Script Pane Maximized:** Shows the Script pane maximized in the ISE window (equivalent to Ctrl+2 or View ⇨ Show Script Pane Maximized).

ISE Script Pane

The ISE Script pane is where you can open different script tabs to edit and execute scripts. The Script pane is tabbed, with one tab per open script. Each tab in the Script pane provides an edit box in which you edit your script. You use the traditional Windows features you are used to including — Cut/Paste/Insert, Undo/Redo — to edit the text. Once you have completed your edits, you can run or debug your script and finally use the Save/Save As feature to save your script.

You can change Windows PowerShell's default theme to enable different background/foreground colors in the Script pane, and you can affect how the script parser colors different syntax elements. The details of syntax and Script pane customization are discussed later in this chapter. But it's relatively simple to change your default ISE view into something that looks entirely different.

ISE Command Pane

The ISE Command pane enables you to input commands for immediate execution within the ISE. Like the console, you can enter any command/pipeline and so on, and see the output — with the ISE, the output is in the Output pane.

When focused on the Command pane, you can use the up and down arrows to scroll backward through the command history. You can also cut/copy/paste text to/from the clipboard. You can also change the default colors of the default Command pane.

ISE Output Pane

The ISE Output pane is where ISE sends output. That output can be the result of running a script or scripts, or from entering a command from the Command pane. In general, you can't do much with the Output pane aside from:

- Adjust where/whether you see the Output pane
- Select and copy text to the Windows clipboard
- Alter the appearance of the Output pane (foreground/text colors)

PowerShell Tabs

A PowerShell tab represents a separate Windows PowerShell runspace, with separate scripts that you can use against that runspace. This enables you to run scripts in separate and independent environments, although this is not a common task. You can see a screenshot of the ISE with several PowerShellTabs open in Figure 25-3.

FIGURE 25-3

Multiple PowerShell tabs

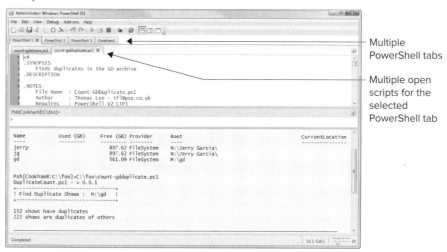

Multiple
PowerShell tabs

Multiple open
scripts for the
selected
PowerShell tab

As you can see from Figure 25-3, the ISE enables you to have more than one PowerShell tab open focused on either the local or a remote machine. When you have multiple PowerShell tabs open, the ISE displays a row of PowerShell tabs (for all the open PowerShell tabs), and below the currently selected/active PowerShell tabs, a set of tabs for the scripts open in the currently selected PowerShell tab. As you can see in Figure 25-3, three local and one remote PowerShell tabs are open with the current PowerShell tab having two open scripts.

By default, ISE names new local tabs PowerShell *n* (where *n* depends on the count of the tabs). Remote tabs are named using the machine name the remote session connects to (Cookham1 in this case). If you do not like these names as you work, you can easily change them (and a whole lot more) using the ISE scripting model described in this chapter.

A PowerShell tab can target the local machine or you can also open a remote PowerShell tab whose scripts are focused on a remote system. When you open a new remote PowerShell tab, the ISE prompts you for a machine and a username for the remote system, then runs the Enter-PSSession cmdlet specifying the computer and domain you just entered. The ISE connects to the remote machine, which requires you to enter your password when prompted. Having multiple PowerShell tabs is a handy feature that avoids needing to have multiple open PowerShell remote sessions in the console. Using multiple PowerShell tabs is an advanced feature that in most cases you don't use — but it's very handy!

Modifying the ISE Layout

As noted, the ISE enables you to alter the layout of the panes within the ISE. There's no means in the ISE to undock any of the panes or other UI elements and have them float — all the UI elements live inside the ISE window.

The independent options you have for customizing the layout are:

- Show the Script pane at the top of the ISE, or to the right of the ISE. When the Script pane is at the right, the Command and Output panes are stacked to the left of the Script pane.

- Have the Command pane above or below the Script pane.

- Hide the Script pane or maximize it. If you maximize the Script pane, the Command and Output panes are hidden.

- Whether to show the toolbar.

- The relative sizes of each of the panes.

Using the ISE

You can use the ISE either as an alternative to using the Windows PowerShell console or as an interactive development tool to develop and maintain Windows PowerShell scripts. And for the more adventurous, you can extend the ISE by both adding new menu items and by creating ISE-specific functions that operate on the Output or Script panes.

The ISE as an Alternative to the Windows PowerShell Console

When used as a console alternative, you type your commands into the Command pane and Windows PowerShell sends output to the ISE Output pane. You can also use the ISE's script-editing features to edit scripts and related files. Should the need arise to do debugging, you can use the full Windows PowerShell debugging toolset directly at the command line as with the Windows PowerShell console. For more common debugging scenarios, you can also use the GUI debugging features, as shown in Table 25-4.

Using the ISE to Edit Windows PowerShell Scripts/Modules

The ISE can be useful as a basic development environment. You can edit a script or module (or any other text-based file such as an XML file) using the Script pane and then run that file by clicking the toolbar button, and so on. As you saw earlier, you can edit every script or other file open in the Script pane using familiar Windows commands.

When editing, you also get the benefit of syntax coloring. The parser recognizes 19 separate language tokens. You direct the ISE to display each token in potentially different foreground colors (against a common background color) or use the ISE default colors. With syntax coloring you can easily see the start of common typing errors, such as a nonterminated string.

ISE Profile Files

Like the Windows PowerShell console itself, the ISE has four profile files, which are executed when you start up the ISE. Profile files are useful to help you customize your ISE environment at startup. With the ISE, you have the following profiles:

- **AllUsersAllHosts:** `C:\Windows\System32\WindowsPowerShell\v1.0\profile.ps1`.
- **AllUsersCurrentHost:** `C:\Windows\System32\WindowsPowerShell\v1.0\Microsoft.PowerShellISE_profile.ps1`.
- **CurrentUserAllHosts:** `C:\Users\tfl\Documents\WindowsPowerShell\profile.ps1`.
- **CurrentUserCurrentHost:** `C:\Users\tfl\Documents\WindowsPowerShell\Microsoft.PowerShellISE_profile.ps1`.

The ISE profiles are the same as the profiles used in `PowerShell.exe`, with the exception of the actual filenames of the "current host" profiles. The filenames for the current host profiles use a script filename of `Microsoft.PowerShellISE.ps1` as opposed to `Microsoft.PowerShell.ps1` for the Windows PowerShell console profiles.

Note

It is tempting to use all of the profile files, but for most uses, you can probably use just two: the all users/all hosts profile and the per-user per-host profile. If you are making use of the ISE and are customizing it, you might want an all users/current host to customize the ISE. ∎

Like the Windows PowerShell console, the ISE dot-sources these profile files, if they exist. Because they are run dot-sourced, the functions, providers, modules, snap-ins, variables, and so on defined in the profile files persist as you start up your ISE session.

Having separate ISE `CurrentHost` profiles enables you to include ISE-specific scripting logic so as to customize the ISE environment. This includes adding new menu items to the ISE menu bar and creating ISE-specific functions that can help with editing or debugging inside the ISE.

Like other profile files, the four ISE profile files are just text files saved with a `.ps1` extension — in other words, simply four more Windows PowerShell scripts.

Debugging with the ISE

Chapter 2 discussed debugging features added to Windows PowerShell Version 2 console. The ISE includes most of these debugging features via menu items and keyboard shortcuts. And of course, you can enter all the Windows PowerShell debugging commands directly into the ISE Command pane as you did with the Windows PowerShell console.

Setting and Using Breakpoints in the ISE

A key debugging feature is the ability to set a breakpoint — some point in your script's execution when you want Windows PowerShell to stop and let you look at what your script is doing and has done. Windows PowerShell ISE, like the Windows PowerShell console, enables you to set three types of breakpoints:

- **Line breakpoint:** Sets a breakpoint at some line/column of a script
- **Command breakpoint:** Sets a breakpoint prior to calling some command or function
- **Variable break point:** Sets a breakpoint when a variable is used

You use a line breakpoint to set a breakpoint at a particular line in a script. The breakpoint is set at the line and column position (if specified) in a script. When executing the script, with debugging enabled, Windows PowerShell stops just before the execution of the commands at the line (and column) you specified. You can set a line breakpoint using the command line, the keyboard, and the menu. You can also set multiple breakpoints in several different scripts.

You use a command breakpoint to set a breakpoint before a particular command is executed. A command can be a function or a cmdlet. When debugging, Windows PowerShell breaks whether the command was executed via a script, or entered from the command line.

You use variable breakpoints to set a breakpoint on a variable that is used, updated, or created. You can set the variable breakpoint for Write (execution stops immediately before a value is written to the specified variable), Read (where execution stops where the variable is read), Write (where execution stops when the variable is written) or ReadWrite (where the breakpoint is triggered on any access to the variable).

Debugging

Using the debugging features provided by the ISE is relatively straightforward. In addition to the debugging functions provided by the Windows PowerShell console, the ISE just offers you keyboard shortcuts and GUI access to some of the more useful Windows PowerShell debug features.

Debugging in the ISE involves running a script, and having Windows PowerShell stop execution at certain defined points known as breakpoints in the script or set of scripts being debugged. Debugging can be as simple as just running a single script, evaluating its output, refining it, and running it again. In more complex situations, you may have a suite of interrelated scripts you are integrating. In those cases, you might want to set a breakpoint in defined places in one or more scripts, or set a breakpoint whenever a variable changes. All in all, debugging is easier using the ISE, when compared to using the Windows PowerShell console.

Extending the ISE

The ISE has a rich and easy-to-use extension model. It consists of a set of nine related .NET object types, bound via a single root object ($PsISE). The object model enables you to:

- **Customize the ISE appearance:** You can access key aspects of each pane to change the color scheme and layout. For example, you could change the font in the edit window to Courier New, 16 point, and tell the ISE to display the text in the Output pane in white on a dark blue background.

- **Enhance the functionality of ISE:** You can create additional menus and shortcuts to enable you to add functionality to the ISE. For example, you could add a menu item to save the current script using ASCII (rather than Unicode).

- **Automate tasks:** With the ISE, you can create menu items or shortcuts to run scripts that automate actions that you commonly perform. For example, you could create a shortcut and/or a menu item to digitally sign the current script and then move the script from your local work folder to a production folder on your release server.

The ISE object model was designed both to provide access to the customization features of the ISE and to make it simple for the end user to access the extensibility. The ISE object model provides a single root object, $PsISE, that holds the whole object model at runtime. Thus, you can use Get-Member (and tab completion) to discover the components of the object model for yourself. This also eliminates the need for you to use constructors and New-Object — when you start ISE, $PsISE (the ISE root object) is created, which gives you access to the full object model. You can then customize the environment via profiles to add menus, add shortcuts, affect the look/feel, and so on.

To customize ISE in these ways, you just need to assign the appropriate values to the $PsISE object or call $PsISE methods. You have two broad ways to do this:

- **Add the relevant code to the ISE's profile file(s):** You can use either the per host or user ISE profiles. Running ISE and just entering notepad $profile is quick and easy.

- **Develop scripts or functions that you can invoke as needed:** These scripts could reside in your home folders, or you could add functions and/or import modules in your ISE profile.

With Windows PowerShell, you can accomplish the customization in the way most sensible to you. For example, you might add a couple of simple customizations into the $profile (for example, to change the color of error and warning messages) and then import a module that adds menu items (and additional functions) you can access while using the ISE. You have considerable flexibility. In the following sections, you learn how you can customize the ISE.

Overview of the ISE Object Model

The ISE object model is a wonderful example of how Windows PowerShell can simplify the access to a complex set of objects (namely, the whole look/feel of the ISE). The ISE extension model is very rich, but everything you need to access this rich set of objects is contained in the variable $PsISE. Thus, you can manage every aspect of customizing ISE simply by using $PsISE! Let's take a more detailed look at what's inside this object.

The ISE object model consists of nine objects in the `Microsoft.PowerShell.Host.ISE` namespace, as shown in Figure 25-4. These objects are as follows:

- **ISEEditor object:** Represents the Output pane and Command pane, which enables customization of these panes. An example is $PsISE.CurrentFile.Editor.

- **ISEFile object:** Enables access to files open in the ISE, including saving the file and access to the editor functions. Example: $PsISE.CurrentFile.

- **ISEFileCollection object:** Represents all the currently open files opened in a given instance of ISE. Example: $PsISE.PowerShellTabs.Files.

- **ISEMenuItem object:** Represents a menu item in the Add-ons menu. Examples: $PsISE.CurrentPowerShellTab.AddOnsMenu and $PsISE .CurrentPowerShellTab.AddOnsMenu.Submenus[0].

- **ISEMenuItemCollection object:** A collection of all the menu items. Example: $PsISE.CurrentPowerShellTab.AddOnsMenu.Submenus.

- **ObjectModelRoot object:** This object gives you access to the components of the object model. When ISE starts, it creates and populates the variable $PsISE.

- **ISEOptions object:** Represents ISE options settings. Examples: $PsISE.Options and $PsISE.Options.DefaultOptions.

- **PowerShellTab object:** Represents a single PowerShellTab. Examples: $PsISE .CurrentPowerShellTab and $PsISE.PowerShellTabs[0].

- **PowerShellTabCollection object:** A collection of the currently open PowerShell tabs.

FIGURE 25-4

The ISE object model

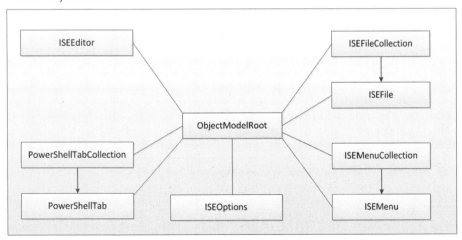

ISEEditor Object

The ISEEditor object provides access to the ISE's editing functions and properties. The editing functions are exposed as methods you can call on an ISEEditor object. The Command pane and Output pane are ISEEditor objects you can address via the $PsISE variable.

The methods in the ISEEditor object are:

- **Clear():** Clears the text in an editor window.
- **EnsureVisible (int LineNumber):** Scrolls the relevant editor window to ensure that the specified line is visible.
- **Focus():** Sets the focus to the specific editor.
- **GetLineLength(int LineNumber):** Gets the length of the specified line.
- **InsertText (string Text):** Replaces or inserts the specified text at the caret position in the specified editor. If the editor has text currently selected, then this method replaces text; otherwise, the text is inserted.
- **Select(int StartLine, int StartColumn, int EndLine, int EndColumn):** This method selects the text between the start line/column and the end line/column.
- **SetCaretPosition(int LineNumber, int ColumnNumber):** Sets the caret position after the specified line number and column.

The properties of this object are:

- **CaretColumn:** Gets the column corresponding to the caret position
- **CaretLine:** Gets the line corresponding to the caret position
- **LineCount:** Gets a count of the number of lines in the editor window
- **SelectedText:** Gets the text that is currently selected in an editor window
- **Text:** Gets all the text in an editor window

Note

For more information on this object, see http://msdn.microsoft.com/en-us/library/dd819438 .aspx. ∎

ISEFile Object

The ISEFile object represents a file in the ISE. This object enables you to access and manage files that are open within the ISE.

The methods of the ISEFIle object are:

- **Save(System.Text.Encoding SaveEncoding):** This method saves the file in a particular encoding (for example, [System.Test.Encoding]::Ascii).
- **Save():** Saves the file (using whatever encoding is currently in place).
- **SaveAs(string FileName):** Saves the file to the specified filename, with a default encoding of UTF-16.

- **SaveAs(String FileName, System.Text.Encoding SaveEncoding):** Saves file with the specified filename and using the specified text encoding.

The properties of the `ISEFile` object are:

- **DisplayName:** Contains the display name of this file
- **Editor:** Gets the `editor` object for this file
- **Encoding:** Gets the original encoding for this file (returned as a `System.Type.Encoding` object)
- **FullPath:** Gets a string representing the full path for any opened file
- **IsSaved:** A Boolean that returns true if the file has been saved or false if there are unsaved changes
- **IsUntitled:** A Boolean that returns true if the file has not been given a title

ISEFileCollection Object

The `ISEFileCollection` object represents a collection of `ISEFile` objects. A given PowerShell tab, for example, contains a `FileCollection` object that represents the files open in that PowerShell Tab.

The `ISEFileCollection` object contains no properties, and the following methods:

- **Add():** Creates a new file in the collection. The file is untitled and contains no text.
- **Add(string FullPath):** Adds the specified file to the collection. The file is initially untitled and contains the text contained on the specified file.
- **Remove(Microsoft.PowerSHell.Host.ISE.ESEFile File):** Removes (closes) the specified file. Files to be removed need to have been saved; otherwise, this method throws an exception when called.
- **Remove(Microsoft.PowerSHell.Host.ISE.ESEFile File, Boolean Force):** Removes the specified file (closes it) from the collection. The `Force` parameter tells the ISE to remove the file even if it's been changed but has not been saved.
- **SetSelectedFile(Microsoft.PowerShell.Host.ISE.ISEFile selectedFile):** Sets the filename as the one selected (so you can invoke further methods on the file).

ISEMenuItem Object

This class represents individual menu items that you have added to the ISE.

This class has no methods and the following three properties:

- **DisplayName:** This gets the display name of the Add-ons menu item.
- **Action:** This gets the script block that is executed by a menu item if that menu item is clicked (or the shortcut invoked).
- **Shortcut:** This property gets the shortcut that invokes a given menu item, if any.

ISEMenuItemCollection Object

This class represents a collection of ISEMenuItem objects. One such collection is the $PsISE.CurrentPowerShellTab.AddOnsMenu.Submenus object that you can use to customize the menus in the ISE.

This object has one method: Add (string DisplayName, System.Management .Automation.ScriptBlock action, System.Windows.Input.KeyGesture shortcut). This method adds a menu to the ISE Add-ons menu and returns an ISEMenuItem.

The Add method can be used like this:

```
$menuAdded =
$PsISE.CurrentPowerShellTab.AddOnsMenu.SubMenus.Add(`
  "_Service",{Get-Service},"Alt+S")
```

When adding a menu, you can add an *accessor*, or fast index into the menu item, by adding an underscore (_) somewhere in the displayName parameter. After adding the menu item, you can select Alt+A to select the Add-ons menu and then type **S** to select the Services menu. Had you made the displayName Ser_vice, typing Alt+A then V would have run the script block.

ObjectModelRoot Object

This object is the root object for all ISE customization. When the ISE starts, it creates a variable, $PsISE, which contains an instance of this class that contains all the aspects of the ISE object model. You use this class instance, $PsISE, for all customization of ISE.

The ObjectModelRoot object has the following properties (and no methods):

- **CurrentFile:** This property represents the file currently open and in focus.
- **CurrentPowerShellTab:** This property gets the PowerShell tab that has focus.
- **Options:** This property contains the options needed to change the look and feel of the ISE.
- **PowerShellTabs:** This property is a collection of all the PowerShell tabs open in the ISE. In most cases, there will only be one PowerShell tab open, but you can open more.

The $PsISE variable greatly simplifies writing extensions or modifying the look and feel of ISE. You modify the look and feel of ISE mainly by operating on the Options and PowerShellTabs properties. Extensions that operate on an open file will involve using the CurrentFile or some part of PowerShellTabs property. You add menu items by managing the $PsISE.CurrentPowerShellTab.AddOnsMenu property.

ISEOptions Object

The ISEOptions object contains a variety of options you can manipulate to customize the ISE. Examples include $PsISE.Options and $PsISE.Options.DefaultOptions.

The ISEOptions object contains two methods:

- **RestoreDefaults():** This method restores the options to their default setting.
- **RestoreDefaultTokenColors:** This method resets the token colors, used to color the text in an edit window(s), to their defaults.

The ISEOptions object also contains a number of properties that reflect specific colors and options that define the look and feel of the ISE. These options are described in more detail in Table 25-5.

TABLE 25-5

ISE Options Accessed from $PsISE.Options

Option	Use
ShowToolBar	A Boolean that tells the ISE to display the toolbar (or not).
TokenColors	This is an array of all color values to be applied to syntax items when displayed in the ISE's editor.
DefaultOptions	This is a set of read-only properties representing the default ISE options.
FontSize	The font size used to display text in all three ISE panes.
FontName	The font name of the font used to display text in all three ISE panes.
ErrorForegroundColor	The foreground color of error text.
ErrorBackgroundColor	The background color of error text.
WarningForegroundColor	The foreground color of warning text.
WarningBackgroundColor	The background color of warning text.
VerboseForegroundColor	The foreground color of verbose output text.
VerboseBackgroundColor	The background color of verbose output text.
DebugForegroundColor	The foreground color of debug text.
DebugBackgroundColor	The background color of debug text.
OutputPaneBackgroundColor	The Output pane's background color.
OutputPaneTextBackgroundColor	The Output pane's background text color.
OutputPaneForegroundColor	The Output pane's foreground text color.

continues

TABLE 25-5 *(continued)*	
Option	Use
CommandPaneBackgroundColor	The Command pane's background text color.
ScriptPaneBackgroundColor	The Script pane's background text color.
ScriptPaneForegroundColor	The Script pane's foreground text color.
ShowWarningForDuplicateFiles	ISE will show a warning if a duplicate file is detected.
ShowWarningBeforeSavingOnRun	Set to display a warning that the script will be saved before it is run.
UseLocalHelp	Whether to use online or local help.
CommandPaneUp	Set to 1 (or $true) to have the Command pane displayed on top of the Output pane.

PowerShellTab Object

The PowerShellTab object is actually a set of objects that relate to a single Windows PowerShell runspace within the ISE. The $PsISE.CurrentPowerShellTab is one instance of this class.

A PowerShellTab contains a single method: Invoke(System.Management.Automation .ScriptBlock script). This method executes a script block in another PowerShell tab (that is, not the one from which it's run).

A PowerShellTab contains the following properties:

- **AddOnsMenu:** This property gets the Add-ons menu for a particular PowerShellTab.

- **CanInvoke:** This is a Boolean that indicates whether a script can be invoked with the Invoke method of this class.

- **Command Pane:** This property gets the CommandPane object for this PowerShellTab.

- **DisplayName:** This property allows you to get and set the name of this PowerShellTab. You will only see the name in the ISE UI if there is more than one PowerShellTab open.

- **ExtendedScript:** A Boolean you can get and set to tell the ISE whether to hide or show the Script pane for this PowerShellTab.

- **Files:** A collection object representing all the files open in this PowerShellTab.

- **Output:** This object is the Output pane of the current PowerShellTab.

- **Prompt:** This gets the prompt on the Command pane of the current PowerShellTab.

- **StatusText:** Gets the status text for the current PowerShellTab.

PowerShellTabCollection Object

This object is the collection of `PowerShellTab` objects open in the current ISE. The `$PsISE` `.PowerShellTabs` is a `PowerShellTabCollection` object you use for customizing the ISE.

The `PowerShellTabCollection` object contains three methods:

- **Add():** Adds a new `PowerShellTab` to the collection and returns the tab that was added by this method.
- **SetSelectedPowerShellTab(Microsoft.PowerShell.Host.ISE.PowerShellTab psTab):** This selects the PowerShell tab indicated by `pstab`.
- **Remove(Microsoft.PowerShell.Host.ISE.PowerShellTab psTab):** This method removes the tab specified by `pstab`.

What's in $PsISE

As noted, the `$PsISE` variable is created when Windows PowerShell ISE starts. `$PsISE` has four useful properties, each of which is a rich object in its own right!

- **CurrentFile:** This is an object of type `ISEFile` that is the current file being edited in the Script pane. From here, you can deal with saving a file (if unsaved), and get the file's name and encoding. The `CurrentFile`'s `Editor` property enables you to do a limited set of edit functions (in this case, on the current file), including Select/Cut/ Paste of text.
- **CurrentPowerShellTab:** This is an object of type `PowerShellTab` and provides access to the details of the current PowerShell tab, including the files, and the Editor, Command, and Output panes. The `Files` property is the collection of files open in the current PowerShell tab.
- **Options:** This object of type `ISEOptions` allows you access to the ISE's color scheme and general layout. You can also access the default options and color scheme should you wish to revert to the default.
- **PowerShellTabs:** This is a collection of all the `PowerShellTabs` open in this invocation of ISE, and includes the `CurrentPowerShellTab`.

To customize the ISE, you use the `$PsISE` object and drill down to the appropriate part for the customization you wish to do.

Changing the Look and Feel of ISE

As noted earlier in the chapter, you can customize the ISE's look and feel. For example, you can make panes visible or you can move the panes around inside the ISE's primary window. You can also change the colors that ISE uses to display both individual panes and to display the various language tokens within the Script pane (for example, coloring a cmdlet name differently than a text string, and so on).

To change the look and feel of the ISE, you either use the menu items noted earlier, or use script code to manipulate the `$PsISE.Options` object. This object exposes all the options for changing screen colors, and the overall layout. The options provided are defined in Table 25-5.

The `$PsISE.Options` object also contains two useful methods: `RestoreDefaultTokenColors` and `RestoreDefaults`. The former resets just the token colors previously set by modifying `$PsISE.Options.TokenColors`. The latter resets all the options back to ISE's default settings.

Within the ISE editor panes, ISE can color each language token in a script differently. This coloring is based on ISE having parsed the script into individual tokens and then using the color scheme set in `$PsISE.Options.TokenColors`. The default color scheme used by ISE provides a good starting point, but as with so many things, colorings are highly personal.

Listing 25-1 provides a simple script that uses the `TokenColors` and other ISE customization properties to re-create the Unix VIM Editor's blackboard theme.

Note

Because this book is printed in black and white, you can't see the colors, but run the script on your system to see this interesting colorizing scheme. ∎

LISTING 25-1

Create the Unix VIM Editor Blackboard Theme

```
# Change ISE to resemble VIM Blackboard
# From script at http://pshscripts.blogspot.com
# Set font name and size
$PsISE.Options.FontName = 'Courier New'
$PsISE.Options.FontSize = 16
# Set colors for output pane
$PsISE.Options.OutputPaneBackgroundColor     = '#FF000000'
$PsISE.Options.OutputPaneTextBackgroundColor = '#FF000000'
$PsISE.Options.OutputPaneForegroundColor     = '#FFFFFFFF'
# Set colors for command pane
$PsISE.Options.CommandPaneBackgroundColor    = '#FF000000'
# Set colors for script pane
$PsISE.options.ScriptPaneBackgroundColor    ='#FF000000'
# Set colors for tokens in Script Pane
$PsISE.Options.TokenColors['Command'] = '#FFFFFF60'
$PsISE.Options.TokenColors['Unknown'] = '#FFFFFFFF'
$PsISE.Options.TokenColors['Member'] = '#FFFFFFFF'
$PsISE.Options.TokenColors['Position'] = '#FFFFFFFF'
$PsISE.Options.TokenColors['GroupEnd'] = '#FFFFFFFF'
$PsISE.Options.TokenColors['GroupStart'] = '#FFFFFFFF'
$PsISE.Options.TokenColors['LineContinuation'] = '#FFFFFFFF'
$PsISE.Options.TokenColors['NewLine'] = '#FFFFFFFF'
$PsISE.Options.TokenColors['StatementSeparator'] = '#FFFFFFFF'
$PsISE.Options.TokenColors['Comment'] = '#FFAEAEAE'
$PsISE.Options.TokenColors['String'] = '#FF00D42D'
$PsISE.Options.TokenColors['Keyword'] = '#FFFFDE00'
$PsISE.Options.TokenColors['Attribute'] = '#FF84A7C1'
$PsISE.Options.TokenColors['Type'] = '#FF84A7C1'
```

```
$PsISE.Options.TokenColors['Variable'] = '#FF00D42D'
$PsISE.Options.TokenColors['CommandParameter'] = '#FFFFDE00'
$PsISE.Options.TokenColors['CommandArgument'] = '#FFFFFFFF'
$PsISE.Options.TokenColors['Number'] = '#FF98FE1E'
```

To restore the default token colors, you could call the `RestoreTokenColors` method noted by using the following code:

```
$PsISE.options.RestoreTokenColors()
```

To restore all the ISE settings, run:

```
$PsISE.Options.RestoreDefaults()
```

Adding Functionality to the ISE

You can also use the ISE object model to add new functionality to the ISE. This involves using other parts of the `$PsISE` object's `PowerShellTabs`, `CurrentPowerShellTab`, or `CurrentFile` properties. Things you can do include parsing the Output pane looking for particular bits of output; loading or saving several scripts; adding text, for example, a code snippet, into an edit window; and so on. To add functionality, you'll most likely be using either the `$PsISE` `.CurrentPowerShellTab`, the `$PsISE.CurrentFile`, or the `$PsISE.PowerShellTabs`.

The `$PseIse.PowerShellTabs` gives you access to all the open PowerShell tabs, and the `$PsISE.CurrentPowerShellTab` gives you access to the currently selected PowerShell tab. Both objects contain `PowerShellTab` objects, which contain the properties shown in Table 25-6.

TABLE 25-6

PowerShellTab Object Contents

Property Name	Property Contents
AddOnsMenu	Read-only property that contains the current Add-on menus for this `PowerShellTab`
CanInvoke	Specifies whether a script can be invoked with the `Invoke` method
CommandPane	Read-only property that contains the Command pane's `editor` object
DisplayName	Enables you to get/set the name of the PowerShell tab
ExpandedScript	Specifies whether the Script pane is hidden or visible (expanded)
Files	A collection of the script files open in the `PowerShellTab`
Output	Gets the current Output pane
Prompt	Gets the current prompt text
StatusText	Gets the current status text

Sample Windows PowerShell ISE Add-On

In the previous sections, you've seen some of the many things you can do to enhance the ISE. A better and richer example is the Windows PowerShell ISE module that Microsoft released as part of the Windows 7 Resource kit.

The IsePack is a set of 39 additions to the ISE, in the form of extra menu items and additional script functions. The IsePack also provides shortcut key sequences to access most of the additions. Here are four specific additions provided by IsePack:

- **Add-InlineHelp (Alt+H):** This function (and shortcut) places a basic autohelp snippet at the caret position into the edit window currently in focus. If you are creating a new function or script, either executing the function name or hitting Alt+H adds the basic documentation. You can, of course, modify the information Add-InlineHelp adds by editing the Add-InlineHelp.ps1 file. The IsePack has three related functions (and shortcuts): Add-ForEachStatement (Ctrl+Shift+F), Add-IfStatement (Ctrl+Shift+I), and Add-SwitchStatement (Ctrl+Shift+S).

- **Search-Bing (Ctrl+B):** This function first looks for highlighted text in any of the panes currently in use in the current PowerShell tab and then runs a Bing search against that text. This is a fantastic lookup tool when you are using new (to you) classes, or possibly unfamiliar properties. This is highly useful if you want to search for an error message, or for more details on a class, property, method, and so on. With a few minutes of work, you can also create a Search-Google shortcut if you prefer Google as your search engine.

- **Show-Member:** This script cmdlet displays a searchable gridview table that contains the members of an object. If you are dealing with a number of new objects, this script may be preferable to using Get-Member (which sends the output to the console).

- **Export-FormatView:** This script cmdlet takes an object, and produces display XML for the properties you specify. If you are using applications such as Lync or Exchange, where you would like the default display of an object (for example, a CSUser object for Lync) to be different, you can create the necessary display XML by using this script, then take the resulting output, and call UpdateFormatData in your profile to persist this new view of your data.

Third-Party Alternatives to the ISE

The Windows PowerShell ISE is a good basic development environment with good customization features. It has the benefit of being "in the box" (or nearly). Thus, you can use it on any of the supported Windows Client versions, although for some versions of Windows Server, it's a separate install (and isn't supported on any Server Core installation).

Several third-party alternatives to ISE are shown in Table 25-7.

TABLE 25-7

Third-Party ISE Alternatives

Company Name	Product	URL for More Information
Idera	PowerShell Plus	`www.idera.com/products/powershell/powershell-plus/`
Itripoli	Admin Script Editor	`www.itripoli.com/ise.asp`
Sapien	Primal Script	`www.primaltools.com/products/info.asp?p=PrimalScript`
Quest	PowerGui (Pro)	`www.quest.com/powershell/powergui.aspx,` and `www.quest.com/PowerGUIPro/`

Idera's PowerShell Plus is a commercial product with a free, fully functional 30-day evaluation download available from the website. PowerShell Plus provides an advanced GUI for Windows PowerShell, with a wealth of learning and productivity features. PowerShell Plus supports snippets, and enables you to find and download script samples from a variety of sources. You can also upload your scripts to community Windows PowerShell repositories.

Itripoli's AdminScript Editor (ASE) is a commercial product that comes in three separate editions. You can also download a 45-day trial version that contains most of the features. ASE provides a number of wizards to help you create rich scripts faster and, like the ISE, has a customizable look and feel. The Pro version of ASE adds in a number of features including an integrated debugger and script signing.

Sapien's Primal Script has been around for a while, and has been enhanced to cater to Windows PowerShell. Primal Script is part of a set of Sapien tools aimed at a variety of IT pros and developers. Primal Script is a commercial product and has a 45-day free edition you can download from the company's website. Primal Script enables you to edit VBScript, Jscript, and Windows PowerShell scripts in a single environment and includes packaging tools to help distribute your scripts.

PowerGui, from Quest, comes in two versions. The freeware version contains a rich set of tools, including an integrated editor and debugger. The Pro version includes the ability to use Windows PowerShell from mobile devices as well as integrated version control.

All these products provide great tools for those involved in heavy scripting work, but the tools are not free. For the occasional scripter, the freeware version of PowerGui or, of course, ISE might suit better.

Tip

Although many of these third-party products are commercial, they all have free trial versions you can download and try out. You should take some time to look at the products and find out the ones that make you the most productive in developing and managing Windows PowerShell scripts. ■

Summary

In this chapter, you looked at Windows PowerShell's ISE. You first looked at the screen components and how the default screen is laid out, and you saw how you can change the layout using the menus (and via ISE's customization features).

The chapter showed how you could use the ISE to access Windows PowerShell and run commands just as you can with the Windows PowerShell console. You also saw the ISE's debug facilities and editing facilities that can assist you in developing and debugging scripts.

You saw how you can extend the ISE. You learned about the ISE's object model and how you can change the look and feel of the ISE as well as develop add-ons to improve your productivity.

The chapter ended with a look at some of the alternatives to the ISE, both free and commercial.

This is the last chapter in the book. Throughout the many hundreds of pages of text, the four authors have labored hard to bring you great content, lots of tips and tricks, and as much knowledge as we could put down on paper. Now, it's up to you to take your knowledge, leverage it, and move forward with Windows PowerShell. We wish you the very best as you move forward. Should you get stuck at any point, please don't hesitate to find us online and let us know how we can help. We're not hard to find!

So, go for it!

Index

Symbols and Numbers

$ (dollar sign), indicating variables, 13–14

= (assignment operator), 13–14

1:1 remoting, 46

-? switch, cmdlet help, 11

64-bit Windows platforms
  assigning values to variables, 14
  creating software baselines, 155
  installing Management Tools for Exchange
      2007, 182
  installing Management Tools for Exchange
      2010, 182–183
  listing software installed on your machine, 154
  server migration, 182

A

abbreviations, cmdlet parameters, 9

about_Scopes help file, 39

Access Control filter, XenApp load-balancing policies,
    474–475

access control lists. See ACLs (access control lists)

AccessMask definitions, share permissions, 128–131

accessors, ISEMenuItemCollection object, 614

$AccessRight variable
    $, 85–86

AccessType parameter, Set-Share
    Permission, 135

AccountExpiring parameter, Search-ADAccount, 246

AccountInactive parameter, Search-ADAccount, 246

accounts, in Active Directory
    enabling and disabling, 244
    managed service, 246–247
    resetting passwords, 244–245
    unlocking users, 244

accounts, modifying XenApp, 465–466

Accounts parameter, New-XAAapplication, 463–464

ACEs (Access Control Entries), current share
    permissions, 128–131

AceType, current share permissions, 128–131

ACLs (access control lists)
    cmdlets retrieving or modifying, 123

modifying registry permissions, 137–139
    setting up remoting, 48

-Action parameter, Register-*Event, 62

Active Directory
    ActiveRoles Management Shell, 253–255
    agent failover in OpsMgr, 419
    cmdlets, 230–232
    enabling and disabling accounts, 244
    group membership, 243–244
    mailboxes and accounts, 280–281
    managed service accounts, 246–247
    managing rest of, 252–253
    noun prefixes for cmdlets, 8
    organizational units, 247–249
    overview of, 229–230
    password policies, 249–252
    pooled machines, 491–492
    properties, 242–243
    provider, 232–234
    querying group membership, 238–240
    querying users, groups, and computers, 234–238
    resetting passwords, 244–246
    resource mailboxes, 302–303
    unlocking users, 244
    users and groups, 240–242

Active Directory Scripting Interface (ADSI), 229

Active Directory Web Service (ADWS), 230–232

ActiveDirectory module
    Active Directory provider, 232–234
    AD group membership, 238–240
    cmdlets, 230–232
    group membership, 243–244
    modifying properties, 242–243
    moving objects, 248
    password policies, 249–252
    querying users, groups, and computers, 234–238
    users and groups, 240–242

ActiveRoles Management Shell
    defined, 229
    installing ActiveDirectory module, 231
    managing Active Directory, 253–255

ActiveSheet property, Excel, 108

`Add()` method
 collection of ports, 144
 e-mail attachments, 117
 Excel charts and graphs, 112–113
 Excel workbooks, 107
 Excel worksheets, 108
 hyperlinks, 100
 `ISEMenuItemCollection` object, 614
 local users and groups, 219
 Outlook folders, 115
 SharePoint document library folders, 380
 SharePoint document library
   items, 381
 SharePoint list items, 376
 SharePoint list views, 377
 SharePoint lists, 378
 tables to Word documents, 101–102
 Word documents, 98
`AddAccessRule()` method, registry, 139
`Add-ADGroupMember` cmdlet, Active Directory, 243
`Add-ADPrincipalGroupMembership` cmdlet, Active
   Directory, 243–244
`Add-BrokerAdministrator` cmdlet, XenDesktop, 486
`Add-BrokerMachinesToDesktopGroup` cmdlet,
   XenDesktop, 499–500
`Add-BrokerUser` cmdlet, XenDesktop, 493
`Add-Certificate` cmdlet, WASM, 549
`AddDefaultScopeRule()` method, Windows 7, 80
`Add-DistributionGroupMember` cmdlet, Exchange, 297
`Add-ExchangeAdministrator` cmdlet, Exchange, 275
`Add-FineGrainedPassword`
   `PolicySubject` cmdlet, AD, 251–252
`Add-InlineHelp (Alt-H)` function, IsePack, 620
`Add-LibraryServer` cmdlet, VMM, 538
`Add-LibraryShare` cmdlet, VMM, 538–539
`Add-MDTPersistentDrive` cmdlet, MDT, 443–444
Add-ons menu, ISE, 603, 614
`Add-PSSnapin` cmdlet
 defined, 35
 MDT cmdlets, 441–442
 server migration snap-in, 180
 VMM cmdlets, 523
`Add-RoleGroupMember` cmdlet, 275, 333–334
`Add-SPSolution` cmdlet, SharePoint, 381
`AddStore()` method, Office, 115
`Add-Type` cmdlet, share permissions, 132–133
`AddUserScopeRule()` method, Windows 7, 80
`Add-VMHost` cmdlet, VMM, 526–527
`Add-VMHostCluster` cmdlet, VMM, 528–529

`Add-VmHostNtpServer` cmdlet, PowerCLI, 564
`Add-VMNewHardDisk` function, Hyper-V, 517–518
`Add-WebConfiguration` cmdlet, IIS, 402
`Add-WebConfigurationProperty` cmdlet, IIS, 402
`Add-WindowsFeature` cmdlet
 installing RSAT, 231
 `Migration` feature, 180
 `WebAdministration` module, 391
 Windows Backup, 174
`Add-WindowsFeature` cmdlet, Windows Server
   2008, 167–169
`Add-XAAdministratorPrivilege` cmdlet, XenApp,
   461–462
`Add-XAApplicationAccount` cmdlet, XenApp,
   465–466
adhoc sessions, creating, 48
admin GUIs, Windows PowerShell in, 7–8
`AdministratorName` parameter, `New-XAAdministrator`,
   457–458
administrators
 Exchange Server 2007 roles, 274
 managing privileges, 459–462
 Windows PowerShell as task platform for, 5–6
 XenApp, 456–458
 XenDesktop, 486–488
`AdministratorType` parameter, `New-XAAdministrator`,
   457–458
`$AdminSessionADSettings` variable, 331
ADSI (Active Directory Scripting Interface), 229
[adsi] type accelerator
 creating and deleting local users, 220–221
 managing local accounts, 219
 modifying local users and groups, 219–220
advanced functions
 cmdlet binding, 55–56
 comment-based help, 54–55
 overview of, 52–53
 splatting, 56
Advanced Query Syntax, 89–91
`AdvancedSearch()` method, 118–119
ADWS (Active Directory Web Service), 230–232
agents, OpsMgr
 automating discovery and deployment, 421–422
 configuring failover without AD integration, 419
 managing SNMP device
   failover, 419–421
 overview of, 418
 verifying load across management servers, 422–423
agents, updating VMM host, 527

alerts, OpsMgr
  overview of, 410
  preventing during maintenance mode, 418
  processing in bulk, 410–413
  updating custom fields in alert properties, 413–415
aliases
  cmdlet, 9
  email contact, 291
  mail distribution group, 296–297
  mail public folder, 304–305
  mail user, 293
  reconnecting mailboxes, 284
  specifying mailbox, 281
All parameter, Get-GPO, 259
AllUsersAllHosts profile, 40–41, 608
AllUsersCurrentHost profile, 40–41, 608
alternation, in scripts, 24–25
AnswerFile parameter, Invoke-Troubleshooting
    Pack, 73–74
Application Desktop Groups, 499, 502–505
Application object
  adding text to Word documents, 99
  in Office, 96–97
  printing, 106
  Word documents, 98
application pools
  creating, 398
  determining state, 405
  starting and stopping, 404–405
  using provider to change, 399–400
applications
  binding to existing, 97
  creating new, 97
  importing in MDT, 446–449
  published. See published applications, Xen App
applications folder privileges, XenApp 6, 460
ApplicationType parameter, New-XAAapplication,
    463–465
AppLocker, Windows Server 2008 R2, 186–187
ApplyOnly parameter, Apply-VMHostProfile, 565
ApplyQuickStyleSet() method, Word, 104
Apply-VMHostProfile cmdlet, PowerCLI, 565–566
AppointmentItem, Outlook, 117–118
AppPool, IIS, 394
AppPools folder, IIS:\, 393
architecture, remoting, 46–48
arithmetic operators, 14
arrays
  discovering currently indexed folders, 77–78

iteration and, 27–30
  loading data with, 351
assemblies, SQL Server, 345–346
Assignment administrator, XenDesktop, 486–488
assignment operators, 14–15
AssociateOnly parameter, Apply-VMHostProfile, 565
attachments, adding email, 117
audit logging, Exchange Server 2010, 273
authentication, CMS vs. Registered Servers, 366
AutoDiscoverUrl, EWS, 336
Autofilter() method, Excel, 112
automating tasks, ISE, 610
AzureManagementToolsSnapIn, 542

B
backup and restore. See also Windows Backup
  Group Policy Objects, 264–265
  host profiles, 566
  IIS configurations, 405–406
  SharePoint data, 384–386
  VMM database, 524
backup target, new backup jobs, 174
Backup-Features, Windows Backup, 174
Backup-GPO cmdlet, Group Policy, 264
Backup-SPConfigurationDatabase cmdlet,
    SharePoint, 384
Backup-SPFarm cmdlet, SharePoint, 384
Backup-SPSite cmdlet, SharePoint, 385–386
Backup-Tools, Windows Backup, 174
Backup-VMMServer cmdlet, VMM, 524
Backup-WebConfiguration BackupName,
    IIS, 405–406
BadItemLimit parameter, Exchange, 286–288
baselines, software, 155–157
Best Practice Analyzer scans
  locally, 169–172
  overview of, 169
  remotely, 172–173
BestPractices module, 168–169
betas, V2, 43–44
BinarySDToWin32SD() method, DCOM, 222
binding, to existing applications, 97
Bindings parameter, New-Item within IIS, 394–395
blogs, PowerShell, 13
break statement, alternation in scripts, 26–27
breakpoints
  debugging cmdlets, 32, 65–66
  ISE, 609

`BreakRoleInheritance()` method, SharePoint list permissions, 378

broker catalog, pooled catalogs, 489

`BrowserName`, XenApp, 465–467

browsing

    directory with Active Directory provider, 232–234

    `IIS:\`, 393

    SharePoint lists, 375

`$BufferNames`, 549–550

bullets, Word, 99–100

bundles, adding, 449

Bus ID, VM storage, 535

business logic, as script component, 24

button control, Windows Forms, 588–589

`BypassSecurityGroupManagerCheck` parameter, `Remove-RoleGroupMember`, 334

C

C# language, Windows PowerShell, 7

calculated properties, hashtables, 22–23

case-insensitivity/sensitivity, 17

catalogs, XenDesktop

    dedicated, 492–493

    existing, 493–494

    machine types, 488

    managing, 496–497

    overview of, 488

    physical, 494–495

    pooled, 489–492

    removing, 497–498

    streamed, 495–496

CEC (Common Engineering Criteria), 6

cells, Excel worksheets, 108–111

Central Management Servers (CMS), 366–367, 369

certificates, WASM, 542–543, 548–549

`ChangeStartMode()` method, disabling services, 206

`ChartObjects( )` method, Excel worksheet, 112–113

charts, Excel, 112–113

checkpoints, VMM, 536–537

`CheckSpelling( )` method, Word, 105

`Choose-VMSnapshot` function, 520

Citrix XenApp 6

    adding/removing administrators, 457–458

    adding/removing assigned accounts, 466

    enabling/disabling administrators, 458

    getting server load, 471

    importing/exporting published applications, 465–466

    installing and using cmdlets, 455–456

    load balancing policies, 473–475

    load evaluator management, 471–473

    managing privileges, 459–462

    modifying published application properties, 465

    publishing new applications, 463–465

    removing/disabling applications, 466–467

    retrieving administrators, 456–457

    retrieving published applications, 462–463

    server logon management, 470

    server zone management, 473

    sessions management, 467–470

    types of administrators, 456

    types of published applications, 462

    what's new in, 456

    worker groups, 475–477

Citrix XenDesktop 5

    administrators, 486–488

    automating environment setup, 481–486

    catalogs, 488

    dedicated catalogs, 492–493

    Desktop Groups, 499–505

    existing catalogs, 493–494

    hosts, 505–509

    managing catalogs, 496–497

    overview of, 479

    physical catalogs, 494–495

    pooled catalogs, 489–492

    provisioning, 497–499

    removing catalogs, 497–498

    snap-ins, 481

    streamed catalogs, 495–496

    Windows PowerShell tab, 480

`Citrix.Common.Commands` snap-in, 455, 481

`Citrix.Common.GroupPolicy` snap-in, 455

`Citrix.XenApp.Commands` snap-in, 456

`Class` parameter

    finding database white space, 312–313

    retrieving share permissions, 127–130

classes

    defined, 14

    enumerating discovered instances, 423–425

    Hyper-V WMI, 513–515

    overview of, 9–10

`Clean-MailboxDatabase` cmdlet, Exchange, 285–286

`Clear-ItemProperty` cmdlet, IIS, 399

Client IP Address filter, XenApp load-balancing, 474–475

Client Name filter, XenApp load-balancing, 474–475

client-side filtering, 328–329
client-side maintenance mode,
        OpsMgr, 417–418
$ClusterAddition variable, 529
clusters, failover, 528–531
cmdlet binding, 55–56
cmdlets
    Active Directory, 230–232, 252–253
    ActiveRoles Management Shell, 253–255
    AppLocker, 186
    backup job, 174–175
    BestPractices module, 169
    breakpoint-related, 32, 65–66
    building GUI administration tools as, 7
    consuming and producing objects, 9–10
    database space usage, 365
    debugging, 32
    discovery-related, 10–12
    ESX host, 561–562
    Exchange Server 2010, 272–273
    Group Policy Objects, 263
    IIS 7 modules, 403
    loading WebAdministration, 391–392
    MDT, 441–442
    OpsMgr, 409–410
    overview of, 8–9
    PowerCLI, 557–559
    process, 207
    PsSnapin, 34–35
    server migration, 180–182
    SharePoint, 371–373
    transaction, 64
    V2 features for, 67
    VM power states, 572
    VM states, 535–536
    VMM, 523
    Windows Azure, 541–542, 551
    Windows Backup, 174
    Windows Backup limitations, 179–180
    Windows services, 203–206
    XenApp 6, 455–456
CMS (Central Management Servers), 366–367, 369
Collect() method, Office scripts, 97
collections, iteration and, 27–30
collisions, avoiding in cmdlets, 8
color coding, syntax, 30–31
COM (Component Object Model), 96, 456. See also
        Office 2010
command breakpoints, ISE, 609

command notification channel, OpsMgr
    events and log files, 427–429
    forwarding SNMP traps, 429–431
    Windows PowerShell and, 426
Command pane, ISE
    customizing screen layout, 607
    defined, 599–600
    overview of, 605
command-line
    debugging in V2 from, 65–66
    management with Windows Server 2003, 4–5
    managing services, 203–206
comment-based help, 54–55
Common Engineering Criteria (CEC), 6
community
    OpsMgr, 437–439
    Windows PowerShell, 12–13
    Windows PowerShell Management Library for
            Hyper-V, 515–516
    Windows Presentation Foundation, 595
Community Technology Preview (CTP) releases, V2, 43–44
ComObject parameter, New-Object, 97
Compare-Object cmdlet, Windows Desktop, 156
comparison operators
    case sensitivity instances, 17–18
    overview of, 15
    wildcards and regular expressions, 16
Component Object Model (COM), 96, 456. See also
        Office 2010
computer object, maintenance mode, 418
ComputerName parameter
    command-line services, 203–204
    database white space, 312–313
    event log data, 195–198
    hotfixes, 195
    listing software remotely, 153–155
    performance counters, 218
    processes, 207
    processes on multiple servers, 207–208
    server migration, 184
    share permissions, 127–131, 135
    stopping processes on remote servers, 208
computers
    ActiveRoles Management Shell, 253–255
    modifying properties within AD, 243
    querying AD, 234–238
conditional execution, scripts, 24–25
ConditionalDepartment parameter,
        New-EmailAddressPolicy, 323

configuration, discovering server, 189–191

configuration database, SharePoint, 384

Confirm parameter

    Dismount-Database, 310–311

    Move-Mailbox, 287

    Remove-StorageGroup, 308

    Resume-PublicFolderReplication, 307

    Suspend-PublicFolderReplication, 307

Connect() method, scheduled tasks on servers, 191

connections

    configuring XenDesktop, 484–485

    to host or vCenter instance, 559–560

    to VMM server, 525–526

Connections directory, XenDesktop, 505–506

Connect-Mailbox cmdlet, Exchange, 284–285

Connect-VIServer cmdlet, PowerCLI, 558, 566, 568

ContactItem, Outlook, 118–119

contacts, Exchange Server, 278–279, 291–292, 326–328

containers, 234

contains operator, 15

content, published applications, 464

Content property, Word, 98–99

ContentAddress parameter, New-XAApplication, 464

context-sensitivity, ISE menu bar items, 599

controls, Windows Forms

    button control, 588–589

    defined, 585

    label control, 586–587

    textbox control, 589–590

    using, 58

ConvertFrom-Csv cmdlet, IIS log files, 406–407

ConvertFromDateTime() method, 200

ConvertToDateTime() method, 199

ConvertTo-HTML, IIS log files, 407

Convert-UrnToPath cmdlet, SQL Server, 345

Copy() method, Word, 103

Copy-XAWorkerGroup cmdlet, XenApp, 475

Counter parameter, Get-Counter cmdlet, 217–218

$CountersList variable, 355

Create method, Win32_Process class, 158

CreateItem() method, Outlook, 117, 118

Create() method, local users and groups, 221

Create-MigrationFolder script, 181–182

Credential parameter, Connect-VIServer, 559–560

credentials

    adding hosts to VMM, 526–527

    checking hotfixes on multiple computers, 194–195

    managing scheduled tasks, 191–192

    modifying backup schedule, 179

    PowerCLI cmdlets, 559–560

    text mode UI, 582

    VMM library, 538

CSearchManagerClass class, Windows Search, 77–79

.csfg file, 546, 548

.cspkg file, 546

.csv (comma-separated value), Enable-Mailbox, 280

CTP (Community Technology Preview) releases, V2, 43–44

Ctrl+B (Search-Bin) function, IsePack, 620

CurrentRegion property, range object, 113

CurrentTimeZone property, Win32_OperatingSystem class, 198

CurrentUserAllHosts profile, ISE, 608

CurrentUserCurrentHost profile, 40–41, 608

CurrentUsersAllHosts profile, 40–41

Custom administrators, 456–458

customization

    of ISE, 610, 614–615

    with profiles, 39–41

Cut() method, Word, 103

D

DACLs (discretionary access control lists), DCOM, 222–223

Data Files, database, 364

Data Management View (DMV), 352, 354

Database parameter

    Connect-Mailbox, 284

    Enable-Mailbox, 280

databases

    automating XenDesktop setup, 482–485

    creating MDT, 444

    finding mailbox white space, 311–313

    managing, 309–311

    space usage data in SQL Server, 363–365

    storage groups for, 308–309

datatable, SQL Server query, 348–349

date, retrieving and setting, 198–201

DaysOfWeek parameter, New-BrokerTimeScheme, 501, 504

DCOM (Distributed Component Object Model)

    defined, 153

    domain user remote access, 226–227

    overview of, 221

    viewing permissions remotely, 222–226

Debug menu, ISE, 599, 602–603

debugging
    from command line in V2, 65–66
    error handling with, 31–32
    with ISE, 602–603, 608–609
    at ISE command line using Windows
        PowerShell, 607
Decode-SqlName cmdlet, SQL Server, 345
dedicated catalogs, XenDesktop, 488, 492–493
default handler, opening file with, 91–92
DefaultScope property, $AdminSessionAD
        Settings, 331
Delete() method
    Excel worksheets, 108
    Outlook items, 116
    removing SharePoint sites, 375
Deleted Mailbox Retention policy, 314
DeletedItemRetention parameter, Set-
        MailboxDatabase, 318
DeleteTask() method, 193–194
DenyTSConnections, Remote Desktop, 147–148
dependency checker, WASM cmdlets, 542
Dependency parameter, Import-MDTApplication, 449
dependent objects, finding in VMM library, 538
deployment, Windows Azure, 545–546
Deployment Share, MDT
    adding device drivers to, 445–446
    adding operating systems to, 444–445
    configuring, 451–452
    creating media, 452–453
    generating media, 453–454
    initializing, 443–444
    updating, 452
Desktop Groups, XenDesktop
    creating, 499–502
    creating Application Groups, 502–505
    overview of, 499
Desktop Studio, XenDesktop, 480
desktops, creating published applications, 464–465
Destination parameter, server migration, 184
DestinationFolder, Import-MDTApplication, 446–447
development
    SharePoint code, 381–382
    Windows PowerShell, 5
    Windows PowerShell V2, 43–45
device drivers, importing in MDT, 445–446
diagnostics, Windows Azure, 549–554
Diagnostics folder, scripts, 71
directory, browsing AD, 234
DirectoryEntry class, local accounts, 219–221

DirectX, WPF utilizing, 595
Disable-* cmdlets, Exchange Server, 278–279
Disable-ADAccount cmdlet, AD, 244
Disable-DistributionGroupMember cmdlet,
        Exchange, 298
Disable-Mailbox cmdlet, Exchange, 283–284
Disable-MailContact cmdlet, Exchange, 292
Disable-MailPublicFolder cmdlet, Exchange, 305
Disable-MailUser cmdlet, Exchange, 295
Disable-Notification cmdlet, OpsMgr, 435
Disable-PsBreakpoint cmdlet, 32
Disable-PSBreakpoint cmdlet, 65
Disable-PSRemoting cmdlet, servers, 174
Disable-XAAdministrator cmdlet, XenApp 6, 458
Disable-XAApplicationAccount cmdlet, XenApp 6,
        466–467
Disable-XAServerLogon cmdlet, XenApp 6, 470
disaster recovery, implementing, 521
Disconnect-XASession cmdlet, XenApp 6, 469–470
discovered inventory data, OpsMgr, 423–426
discovery, in OpsMgr
    automating agent, 421–422
    inventory data, 423–426
discovery-related cmdlets, 10–12
discretionary access control lists (DACLs), DCOM,
        222–223
Dismount-Database cmdlet, 310–311
DisplayName parameter
    Get-Service, 343
    New-BrokerTimeScheme, 501–502, 504
    New-XAApplication, 463–464
    Set-MailPublicFolder, 304–305
distinguished name (DN), AD group membership,
        238–239
Distributed Component Object Model. See DCOM
        (Distributed Component Object Model)
distribution groups, Exchange Server
    administering, 295–298
    dynamic, 298–301
    types of, 295
    upgrading Exchange 2010, 326–328
    verbs for, 278–279
DLL
    adding folders to index, 79–81
    automating Outlook tasks without security
        prompt, 114
    discovering currently indexed folders, 77
    removing folders from index, 82–83
    Windows Search, 77

DMV (Data Management View), 352, 354

DN (distinguished name), AD group membership, 238–239

DNS settings, remote network configuration, 214–216

do until/ do while loop, iteration, 28

document libraries, SharePoint, 379–381, 386

documentation

    automating Word, 98

    help files, 7

documents, Word

    adding tables, 101–102

    adding text, 98–99

    creating header and footer, 102

    creating hyperlinks, 100–101

    creating or opening, 98

    inserting images, 101

    searching text, 102–103

    working with bullets, 99–100

Domain parameter, GroupPolicy module, 259

domain profile, firewalls, 139–143

Domain Users, AD group membership, 238–239

DomainProfile key, checking firewall remotely, 143–144

downlevel systems

    adding Windows PowerShell to, 37

    V2 on, 45

dumpster data, moving in Exchange Server, 286

dynamic disks, adding to VMs, 535

dynamic distribution groups, Exchange Server, 295, 298–301

E

EdbFilepath parameter, New-MailboxDatabase, 310–311

Edit menu, ISE, 599, 600–601, 607

else clause, alternation in scripts, 25

e-mail. *See also* Outlook

email address

    changing for mailbox in Exchange Server, 282–283

    policies, 322–324

    upgrading, 325–326

EmailAddressPolicyEnabled parameter, 292

EmailAddressPolicyEnabled parameter, 304

Enable-ADAccount cmdlet, AD, 244, 246

Enable-DistributionGroup cmdlet, Exchange, 295

Enable-Mailbox cmdlet, Exchange, 280–285

Enable-MailContact cmdlet, Exchange, 291–292

Enable-MailPublicFolder cmdlet, Exchange, 304

Enable-MailUser cmdlet, Exchange, 292–295

Enable-Notification cmdlet, OpsMgr, 435

Enable-NotificationSubscription cmdlet, OpsMgr, 435

Enable-PsBreakpoint cmdlet, 32

Enable-PSBreakpoint cmdlet, 65

Enable-PsRemoting cmdlet, 48

Enable-PSRemoting cmdlet, 173

Enable-XAAdministrator cmdlet, XenApp 6, 458

Enable-XAApplicationAccount cmdlet, XenApp 6, 467

Enable-XAServerLogon cmdlet, XenApp 6, 470

Encode-SqlName cmdlet, SQL Server, 345

EndKey() method, Word, 99

Enter-PsSession cmdlet, 49

enumeration

    discovering currently indexed folders, 78

    using tab completion to see values in, 101

environment setup, XenDesktop, 481–486

$Env:WinDir\Diagnostics\System variable, 75

equipment mailboxes, 301–303

error handling

    with advanced IDE, 30–31

    debugging, 31–32

    nonterminating errors, 33–34

    overview of, 30

    as script component, 24

    with Set-StrictMode cmdlet, 31

    trapping runtime errors, 32–33

    with Try/Catch/Finally in V2, 66–67

error messages, script execution policy, 38

-ErrorAction parameter, nonterminating errors, 34

-ErrorVariable parameter, nonterminating errors, 34

ESX and ESXi hosts

    adding to VMM, 526–527

    adding to XenDesktop, 508

    configuring NTP servers, 564–565

    configuring virtual switches, 563–564

    connecting to, 558–559

    gathering performance data from, 567–568

    getting logs, 566–567

    host profiles, 565–566

    in maintenance mode, 560

    managing virtual port groups, 564

    overview of, 560

    properties, 560–562

    retrieving in PowerCLI, 559

    storage, 562–563

Esxtop, 568

event logs, 195–198

events
  defined, 9
  OpsMgr, 427–429
  in V2, 61–62
EWS (Exchange Web Services), 335–339
Excel spreadsheets
  charts and graphs, 112–113
  creating and opening, 107
  filtering data, 112
  searching, 113
  sorting data, 111–112
  working with cells, 108–111
  worksheets, 107–108
exception handling. *See* error handling
Exchange Organization Administrators, 274
Exchange Public Folder Administrators, 274
Exchange Recipient Administrators, 274
Exchange Server. *See* Microsoft Exchange Server
Exchange Server Administrators, 274
Exchange View-Only Administrators, 274
Exchange Web Services (EWS), 335–339
Execute() method, Word, 102–103
execution policy, 37–39
existing catalogs, XenDesktop, 488, 493–494
Explorer object, Outlook folders, 114
export overrides into overrides report, 432–434
Export-CliXml cmdlet, 155–157, 465–466
Export-Csv cmdlet, 123, 407
Export-FormatView, IsePack, 620
Export-SmigServerSetting cmdlet, server migration, 183–184
Export-SPWeb cmdlet, 386
Export-VMHostProfile cmdlet, PowerCLI, 566
expressions
  case sensitivity vs. insensitivity, 17–18
  overview of, 16
  wildcards and regular, 16–17
extension model, ISE, 610, 614
ExternalEmailAddress parameter, Outlook, 291–294

F

failover clusters, 528–531
fan-in remoting, 46
fan-out remoting, 46
farm privileges, XenApp 6, 459
-Farm switch, Get-XASession, 467–468
FarmPrivileges parameter, New-XAAdministrator, 458

farms, SharePoint backup and restore, 385
FeatureId parameter, server migration, 183
features
  discovering for server migration, 182–183
  exporting in server migration, 183–184
  importing in server migration, 184–186
  Windows Server 2008, 167–169
File Groups, database, 364
File menu, ISE, 599–600
files and folders
  database, 364
  file extensions, 87–88
  Get-Acl managing permissions for, 123
  IIS:\, 393
  migrating, 181–182
  NTFS permissions for, 124–127
  Outlook, 114–115
  public, 303–307
  share permissions for. *See* share permissions
  SharePoint document libraries, 379–380
  Windows Search. *See* Windows Search, managing
  Xen App 6 folder privileges, 459–462
files and folders, Windows 7
  counting specific type of files, 88
  finding empty folders, 89
  listing unique file extensions, 87–88
  opening file with default handler, 91–92
  searching with Windows Search, 89–91
  setting security, 84–86
FileType parameter, Get-AppLockerFile Information, 186
$Filter hash, 79
Filter parameter
  Get-Mailbox cmdlet, 279
  IIS Get-WebConfiguration, 400–403
  querying AD, 235–236
  upgrading Exchange 2010, 327
  using filters, 328–330
FilterHashTable parameter, event logs, 196–198
filtering
  Active Directory, 235–236
  Excel, 112
  GPO names, 259
  IIS log files, 407
  XenApp load-balancing policies, 474–475
Find() method
  contacts in Outlook, 118
  filters accepted by, 118–119
  spreadsheets, 113

Find property, Word, 102

Find-Files function, Windows Search, 89–90

FindNext() method, contacts in Outlook, 118

fine-grained password policies, AD, 251

floppy disks, Microsoft IBM PCs, 3–4

folders. *See* files and folders; files and folders, Windows 7

fonts
  controlling cell, 110–111
  in Word document, 104

footer, in Word, 102

for loop, iteration, 27–28

Force parameter
  New-VMSnapshot, 519
  Remove-VMSnapshot, 520

-Force switch, SQL Server services, 343

ForceUpgrade parameter, upgrading Exchange, 325–327

foreach loop, AD group membership, 238–239

foreach statement, iteration, 28–29

ForEach-Object cmdlet, iteration, 28–30

format operator, 15

Format-List cmdlet
  for details on troubleshooting pack, 72–73
  formatting output, 20–21
  formatting with hashtables, 22–23
  piping Get-Acl through to, 123–125
  retrieving current registry permissions, 136–137
  validating network configuration remotely, 214

FormatString hashtable key, 22

Format-Table
  formatting output, 20–21
  formatting with hashtables, 22–23
  getting table space usage, 365–366

formatting output
  cells, 110–111
  default, 19–20
  with hashtables, 21–22
  overview of, 18–19
  text, 103–105
  using Format-Table and Format-List, 20–21

Format-Wide cmdlet, 21

forms, in Windows Forms, 585–586

forums, PowerShell user, 13

FTP sites, creating, 396

Full administrator
  XenApp 6, 456–458
  XenDesktop, 486–488

-Full parameter, Get-XASession, 468

functions
  customizing ISE, 610
  V2 new advanced, 52–56
  Windows Search, 89–90

G

GC (garbage collector) class, 97

Get-* cmdlets, Exchange Server, 278–279

Get-Acl cmdlet
  file and folder security, 84–85
  managing permissions, 123
  modifying NTFS permissions, 126–127
  registry settings, 135–136
  retrieving current NTFS permissions, 124–125
  retrieving current registry permissions, 136–137

GetActiveObject method, binding to applications, 97

Get-AD cmdlets
  controlling scope of search, 236–237
  Get-ADObject cmdlet, 237–238
  group membership, 238–240
  querying AD, 234–235
  searching with filters, 235–236
  working with properties, 237

Get-ADComputer cmdlet, AD, 243

Get-ADDefaultDomainPasswordPolicy cmdlet, AD, 250

Get-ADFineGrainedPasswordPolicy cmdlet, AD, 250–251

Get-ADGroup cmdlet, AD, 238

Get-ADGroupMember cmdlet, AD, 239–240

Get-ADObject cmdlet, AD, 237–238

Get-ADPrincipalGroupMembership cmdlet, AD, 238

Get-AdServerSettings cmdlet, Exchange, 331–332

Get-ADUser cmdlet, AD, 248

Get-ADUserResultantPasswordPolicy cmdlet, AD, 250–251

Get-Agent cmdlet, OpsMgr, 419

Get-AppLockerFileInformation cmdlet, AppLocker, 186

Get-BpaModel cmdlet, Windows Server, 169–171

Get-BpaResult cmdlet, Windows Server, 169

Get-BrokerCatalog cmdlet, XenDesktop, 496–497

Get-Certificate cmdlet, WASM, 549

Get-Certificates cmdlet, WASM, 549

Get-ChildItem cmdlet
  counting types of files, 88
  database space usage, 364
  finding empty folders, 89
  listing troubleshooting packs, 71–72

listing unique file extensions, 87–88
modifying file/folder security, 86
modifying NTFS permissions, 126–127
retrieving NTFS permissions, 125
retrieving registry permissions, 136–137
Get-Command cmdlet, 11–12
Get-CommandLine function, 160–161
Get-ComputerRestorePoint cmdlet, 157–158
Get-Counter cmdlet, servers, 217–218
Get-Credential cmdlet
    adding hosts to VMM, 526–527
    scheduled tasks, 191
    text mode UI, 582
    Windows Backup, 179
GetDefaultFolder() method, Outlook, 115
Get-DependentLibraryObject cmdlet, VMM, 538
Get-Deployment cmdlet, 545
GetDerivedMonitoringClass() method, OpsMgr, 424
Get-DisksSpace function, SQL Server, 363
Get-DistributionGroupMember cmdlet, Exchange, 297–298
Get-DynamicDistributionGroup cmdlet, Exchange, 300
Get-EventLog cmdlet, 195–198
Get-ExchangeAdministrator cmdlet, 274–275
Get-ExCommand function, Exchange, 276–278
GetFile() method, SPWeb object, 380
Get-FirewallSetting function, 141–143
GetFolder() method, scheduled tasks, 192–193
GetFolder() method, SharePoint document library
    folders, 380
Get-GPInheritance cmdlet, 261
Get-GPO cmdlet, 259, 261
Get-GPOReport cmdlet, 259
Get-GPPermissions cmdlet, 265–266
Get-GPRegistryValue cmdlet, 260–261
Get-GPResultantSetOfPolicy cmdlet, 262
Get-Help cmdlet
    Exchange Server, 278
    OpsMgr cmdlets, 409
    overview of, 11
    PipeBind parameters in SharePoint, 372
Get-HostedProperties cmdlet, 545
Get-HostedService cmdlet, 544–545
Get-HostedServices cmdlet, 544–545
Get-HotFix cmdlet, 84, 194
Get-HypVMMacAddress cmdlet, XenDesktop, 495
Get-Item cmdlet, SQL Server, 357
Get-ItemProperty cmdlet
    DCOM permissions, 222
    making changes with provider, 399

MDT Deployment Share, 454
    using local registry provider, 210
Get-Job cmdlet, 51
Get-LibraryShare cmdlet, VMM, 538
Get-LogType cmdlet, PowerCLI, 566–567
Get-Mailbox cmdlet, Exchange,
    279, 297, 328–330
Get-MailboxDatabase cmdlet, Exchange, 285, 313,
    316–319, 321–322
Get-MailboxStatistics cmdlet, Exchange, 285, 289,
    314–316
Get-MailContact cmdlet, Exchange, 327–328
Get-ManagementServer cmdlet, agent failover in
    OpsMgr, 419
Get-Member cmdlet, 12, 610
Get-MonitoringClass cmdlet, OpsMgr, 423–424
Get-MonitoringObject cmdlet, OpsMgr, 423–424
GetMonitoringRelationshipClasses() method,
    OpsMgr, 425–426
Get-MoveRequest cmdlet, Exchange, 288–289
GetNameSpace() method, Outlook folders, 114
GetNetworkCredential() method, scheduled tasks,
    191–192
Get-Notification cmdlet, OpsMgr, 435
Get-NotificationSubscription cmdlet,
    OpsMgr, 435
Get-OperatingSystem cmdlet, VMM, 533
Get-OperationsManagerCommand cmdlet, 409
Get-OperationStatus cmdlet, WASM hosted
    services, 546
Get-OrganizationConfig cmdlet, 307
Get-Override cmdlet, OpsMgr, 431–434
Get-Process cmdlet, 101–102, 207–208
Get-PsBreakpoint cmdlet, 32
Get-PSBreakpoint cmdlet, 65
Get-PsCallStack cmdlet, 32
Get-PsProvider cmdlet, 64
Get-PsSnapin cmdlet, 35
Get-QAD cmdlets, 253–255
Get-RDPConnection function, Remote Desktop,
    148–149
Get-Recipient cmdlet
    client-side filtering, 329
    dynamic distribution groups, 300
    Exchange Web Services, 337
    server-side filtering, 329
Get-RoleGroup cmdlet
    Exchange permissions, 275
    RBAC, 333
Get-RoleGroupMember cmdlet, RBAC, 334

`GetRunningTasks()` method, scheduled tasks, 191, 193

`Get-Service` cmdlet, 203–205, 343–344

`Get-SharePermission` script, 130–131

`Get-SimplePvsADAccount` cmdlet, XenDesktop, 495

`Get-SimplePvsCollection` cmdlet, XenDesktop, 495

`Get-SmigServerFeature` cmdlet, server migration, 182–183, 185

`Get-Snapshot` cmdlet, PowerCLI, 572

`Get-SPBackupHistory` cmdlet, SharePoint, 384

`GetSpellingSuggestions()` method, application objects, 105

`Get-SPEnterpriseSearchCrawlContentSource` cmdlet, SharePoint, 387

`Get-SPEnterpriseSearchServiceApplication` cmdlet, SharePoint, 387

`Get-SPRunningWorkflows()` function, 382–383

`Get-SPSite` cmdlet, SharePoint, 374–375

`Get-SPSolution` cmdlet, SharePoint, 382

`Get-SPWeb` cmdlet, SharePoint, 375

`Get-Stat` cmdlet, PowerCLI, 567

`Get-TroubleshootingPack` cmdlet, 72–73

`Get-User` cmdlet, server-side filtering, 330

`Get-VHDDefault` function, Hyper-V, 516

`Get-VirtualHardDisk` cmdlet, VMM, 538

`Get-VM` cmdlet, PowerCLI, 559, 569–570

`Get-VMBuildScript` function, Hyper-V, 521

`Get-VMCheckPoint` cmdlet, VMM, 536

`Get-VMHost` cmdlet
   PowerCLI, 559–562
   VMM, 528, 533

`Get-VMHostProfile` cmdlet, PowerCLI, 565–566

`Get-VMMServer` cmdlet, VMM, 524, 525–526

`Get-VMResourceConfiguration` cmdlet, PowerCLI, 571

`Get-VMSnapshot` function, Hyper-V, 519–520

`Get-WBBackupSet` cmdlet, Windows Backup, 177

`Get-WBBackupTarget` cmdlet, Windows Backup, 179

`Get-WBDisk` cmdlet, Windows Backup, 175–176

`Get-WBJob` cmdlet, Windows Backup, 176–177

`Get-WBPolicy` cmdlet, 177–178, 180

`Get-WBProfile` cmdlet, Windows Backup, 178–179

`Get-WBSchedule` cmdlet, Windows Backup, 178

`Get-WBVolume` cmdlet, Windows Backup, 175–176

`Get-WebAppPoolState` cmdlet, IIS, 405

`Get-WebConfiguration` cmdlet, IIS, 400–403

`Get-WebConfigurationProperty` cmdlet, IIS, 402–403

`Get-WebItemState` cmdlet, IIS, 405

`Get-WindowsFeature` cmdlet, Windows Server 2008 R2, 167–168

`Get-WinEvent` cmdlet, event logs, 195–198

`Get-WmiObject` cmdlet
   command-line services, 203
   database white space, 311–313
   date and time, 198–201
   DCOM permissions, 222
   network configuration, 215–216
   server configuration, 189–191
   share permissions, 127–128, 132–133
   software using WMI, 152–153
   SQL Server services, 344
   stopped services set to start automatically, 205–206
   stopping processes on remote servers, 208

`Get-XAApplication` cmdlet, XenApp, 462–463

`Get-XAAdministrator` cmdlet, XenApp, 456–457

`Get-XAApplication` cmdlet, XenApp, 465–466

`Get-XALoadEvaluator` cmdlet, XenApp, 471–472

`Get-XAServerLoad` cmdlet, XenApp, 471

`Get-XASession` cmdlet, XenApp, 467–468

`Get-XASessionProcess` cmdlet, XenApp, 469

GPMC (Group Policy Management Console), 257

GPOs (Group Policy Objects)
   backing up and restoring, 264–265
   basic information, 259
   creating and configuring, 262–264
   detailed reports, 259
   links, 261
   Resultant Set of Policy, 262
   values for changes made by, 260–261

graphical user interface. *See* GUI (graphical user interface)

graphs, Excel, 112–113

`Group` parameter, server migration, 183

Group Policy
   AppLocker, 187
   GPOs. *See* GPOs (Group Policy Objects)
   implicit remoting for, 258
   overview of, 257
   remoting on several machines, 174
   script execution policy, 39
   security, 265–266
   snap-in for Citrix, 455
   Windows 7, 258
   Windows Server 2003, 5
   Windows Server 2008 R2, 257

Group Policy Management Console. *See* GPMC (Group Policy Management Console)

Group Policy Objects. *See* GPOs (Group Policy Objects)

`Group-Object` cmdlet
    counting specific types of files, 88
    listing unique file extensions, 87–88
`GroupPolicy` module
    enabling on Server 2008 R2, 257
    Group Policy. *See* Group Policy
    remote connections, 258
    `Server` and `Domain` parameters, 259
    Windows 7, 258
groups
    adding and removing in OpsMgr, 415–417
    automating maintenance mode, 415–417
    Exchange distribution, 295–298
    Exchange dynamic distribution, 298–301
    upgrading Exchange 2007, 326
groups, Active Directory
    ActiveRoles Management Shell, 255
    automating tasks, 244–246
    creating, 240–241
    creating and deleting local users, 220–221
    membership, 243–244
    modifying local users, 219–220
    modifying properties, 242
    querying, 234–238
    querying membership, 238–240
    viewing password policies, 250–251
GUI (graphical user interface)
    administration tools, 7–8
    creating scripts in MDT, 442
    death knoll of management by, 5
    management with Windows NT, 4
    management with Windows Server 2003, 4–5
    user interface vs., 581
    in Windows PowerShell. *See* Windows Forms
`GUID` parameter, `Get-GPO` cmdlet, 259

H

hardware, virtual, 569–570
Hardware Profile, creating virtual machines, 531–533
hashtables
    formatting output with, 21–22
    in manifest modules, 59
    splatting using, 56
`header`, Word documents, 102
health service, maintenance mode, 418
health service watcher, during maintenance mode, 418
Help
    `Get-Help`. *See* `Get-Help` cmdlet

    topics, 7
    XenDesktop administrator for, 486–488
Help menu, ISE, 599
highlighting text, 104
histories, mailbox move, 289–291
`HKEY_CURRENT_USER` registry hive
    `Get-Acl` and `Set-Acl` cmdlets, 135–136
    reading registry, 209–210
    regional settings on multiple computers, 218–219
`HKEY_LOCAL_MACHINE` registry hive
    enabling Remote Desktop, 147–148
    `Get-Acl` and `Set-Acl` cmdlets, 135–136
    reading registry, 209–210
    viewing DCOM permissions, 222
`HNetCfg.FwMgr`, firewalls, 140–146
`HNetCfg.FwOpenPort`, firewalls, 144–146
Hopper, Grace, 31
host groups, VMM, 526–527, 528
host profiles, ESX, 565–566
`$host` variable, 563
hosted services, WASM
    adding certificates, 548–549
    deploying new code, 546–547
    `Get-OperationStatus`, 546
    getting information, 544–545
    overview of, 544
    scaling infrastructure for deployment, 548
    starting and stopping deployments, 545–546
`HostingUnits` directory, XenDesktop, 506
`$host.Runspace.ThreadOptions = "ReuseThread"`, 372
hosts
    ESX and ESXi. *See* ESX and ESXi hosts
    server maintenance with, 530–531
    in VMM, 526–528
    in Windows PowerShell, 563
hosts, Hyper-V
    adding to VMM, 526–527
    adding to XenDesktop, 507–508
    managing, 516–517
    performing maintenance on, 530–531
hosts, XenDesktop
    adding, 506–508
    defined, 505
    PS provider, 505–506
    removing, 508–509
hotfix status
    checking in Windows 7, 84
    checking server for, 194–195

HTTP/S, remoting architecture, 47
hyperlinks, in Word documents, 100–101
Hyper-V 2008 R2
    creating and modifying virtual machines, 517–518
    disaster recovery, 521
    host management, 516–517
    hosts. *See* hosts, Hyper-V
    management interfaces, 513–515
    power state management, 518–519
    script module, 58
    snapshots, 519–520
    Windows PowerShell Management Library for, 515–516

I

IBM PC, 3–4
ICMP (Internet Control Message Protocol) settings, firewalls, 140
IDE (Interactive Development Environment), error handling, 30–31
Identity parameter
    Add-DistributionGroupMember, 297
    Clean-MailboxDatabase, 285–286
    Connect-Mailbox, 284
    Disable-DistributionGroupMember, 298
    Disable-MailPublicFolder, 305
    Dismount-Database, 310–311
    Enable-Mailbox, 280
    Enable-MailContact, 291
    Enable-MailUser, 292–293
    Get-DistributionGroupMember, 297–298
    Get-SPSite, 375
    Move-Mailbox, 286–287
    New-MoveRequest, 287–288
    Remove-DistributionGroupMember, 297, 298
    Remove-MailPublicFolder, 305
    Remove-StorageGroup, 308
    Set-DynamicDistributionGroup, 300
    Set-Group cmdlet, 296
    Set-MailboxDatabase, 318–319
    Set-MailContact, 292
    Set-MailPublicFolder, 304
    Update-EmailAddressPolicy, 323–324
    Update-PublicFolder, 307
Identity Pool, for pooled catalogs, 489–490
Idera's PowerShell Plus, 621
if statements, alternation in scripts, 24–25

IIS (Internet Information Services) 7
    advanced WebConfiguration settings, 400–403
    backing up and restoring configurations, 405–406
    browsing IIS:\, 393
    configuring SSL, 398–399
    controlling services, 404–405
    creating application pools, 398
    creating sites, 395–396
    creating virtual directories, 396–397
    creating web applications, 397–398
    digesting log files, 406–407
    IIS:\, 393–394
    installing necessary components, 390–392
    overview of, 389
    removing objects with cmdlets, 400
    scripting new deployments and changes, 394
    using New-Item cmdlet, 394–395
    using Provider to make changes, 399–400
IISReset in Windows 7, 404
IMA (Integrated Multi-system Architecture), 479
images
    adding to Word documents, 101
    importing from WDS, 445
    provisioning, 497–499
implicit modules, 59–61
implicit remoting, 50, 231
Import-CliXml cmdlet, 156, 465–466
Import-GPO cmdlet, 264–265
importing
    applications in MDT, 446–449
    device drivers in MDT, 445–446
    features in server migration, 184–186
    operating systems in MDT, 444–445
    ServerManager module, 167
    troubleshooting scripts, 71
    XenApp published applications, 465–466
Import-MDTApplication cmdlet, 446–449
Import-MDTOperatingSystem cmdlet, 445
Import-Module cmdlet
    importing ServerManager module, 167
    importing troubleshooting scripts, 71
Import-Module HyperV command, 516
Import-PsSession cmdlet
    creating implicit modules, 59–61
    implicit remoting, 50
Import-SmigServerSetting cmdlet, server migration, 184–186
Import-SPWeb cmdlet, SharePoint, 386
Import-VMHostProfile cmdlet, PowerCLI, 566

`Include` parameter, server migration, 184

`IncludeAllSubFeature` parameter, `Add-WindowsFeature`, 168

`IncludedRecipients` parameter, Exchange, 299, 322–324

`IncludeMoveHistory` parameter, Exchange, 289

`IncludeMoveReport` parameter, Exchange, 289

`IncludePreExchange2007` parameter, Exchange, 319

index
    adding folders to, 79–81
    discovering current folders, 77–79
    re-indexing search catalog, 82–84
    removing folders from, 82–83

information, in SQL Server, 351–353, 363–366

inheritance
    file and folder security, 86
    SharePoint list permissions, 378

inheritance flags, 124, 137

input
    querying SQL Server using, 349
    validating text mode UI, 583–584

`INSERT` statement, loading SQL Server data, 350–351

`Install` method, `wmiclass`, 158

`Install-ADComputerServiceAccount` cmdlet, service accounts, 246

installation
    `ActiveDirectory` module, 230–232
    IIS 7 components, 390–392
    managed service accounts, 246
    Management Tools for Exchange 2007, 272
    PowerCLI, 557–558
    Server Core, 45
    software, 157–159
    SQL Server 2008 R2, 342
    SSMS, 342
    WASM cmdlet, 542
    Windows PowerShell, 36–39

`Install-SPSolution` cmdlet, SharePoint, 381

instance uptime information, SQL Server, 352

integrated authentication, CMS and Registered Servers, 366

Integrated Scripting Environment. *See* ISE (Integrated Scripting Environment)

IntelliSense, 31

Interactive Development Environment (IDE), error handling, 30–31

Internet Control Message Protocol (ICMP) settings, firewalls, 140

Internet Information Services. *See* IIS (Internet Information Services) 7

Interop DLL, for Windows Search, 77

interoperability, versions of Exchange, 324–328

inventory data, exploring in OpsMgr, 423–426

`Invoke-BpaModel` cmdlet, 170

`Invoke-BpaModel` cmdlet, Windows Server, 169

`Invoke-Command` cmdlet
    installing software remotely, 154–155, 158–159
    remoting using, 48–49
    stopping processes on remote servers, 208

`Invoke-Item` cmdlet, 91–92

`InvokeMethod( )` method, remote servers, 208

`Invoke-PolicyEvaluation` cmdlet, SQL Server, 344

`Invoke-SQL` function, XenDesktop, 482–484

`Invoke-SQLcmd` cmdlet
    instance uptime information, 352
    loading non-SQL Server data, 351
    loading SQL Server data, 350–351
    querying SQL Server, 347–349
    SQL Server snap-in, 344

`Invoke-TroubleshootingPack` cmdlet, 73–74

`Invoke-VMScript` cmdlet, VMM, 573

`Invoke-WmiMethod` cmdlet, WMI, 158–159, 215–216

invoking scripts, PowerCLI, 573

IP address, modifying server, 216–217

`IPConfig` parameter, server migration, 184

ISE (Integrated Scripting Environment)
    alternative to Windows PowerShell console, 607
    debugging with, 608–609
    editing Windows PowerShell scripts/modules, 607
    error handling, 31
    extending, 610
    modifying look and feel, 614
    overview of, 597–598
    `Paging` parameter generating error in, 125
    profile files, 608
    `$PsISE`, 617–619
    sample Windows PowerShell add-on, 620
    third-party alternatives to, 620–621
    using, 63

ISE (Integrated Scripting Environment), object model
    `ISEEditor` object, 611
    `ISEFile` object, 612–613
    `ISEFileCollection` object, 613
    `ISEMenuItem` object, 613
    `ISEMenuItemCollection` object, 614
    `ISEOptions` object, 614–616
    `ObjectModelRoot` object, 614
    overview of, 610–611
    `PowerShellTab` object, 616
    `PowerShellTabCollection` object, 617

ISE (Integrated Scripting Environment),
        screen layout
    Add-ons menu, 603
    Command pane, 605
    Debug menu, 602–603
    Edit menu, 600–601
    File menu, 599–600
    ISEEditor object, 612
    menu bar, 599
    modifying, 606–607
    Output pane, 605
    overview of, 598–599
    PowerShell tabs, 605–606
    Script pane, 605
    toolbar, 603–605
    View menu, 601–602
ISEEditor object, ISE, 611, 612
ISEFile object, ISE, 611, 612–613
ISEFileCollection object, ISE, 611, 613
ISEMenuItem object, ISE, 611, 613
ISEMenuItemCollection object, ISE, 611, 614
ISEOptions object, ISE, 611, 614–616
IsePack, 620
IssueWarningQuota, 316–319
Item() method
    Excel worksheet, 107–108
    SharePoint list data, 376
items, Outlook
    AppointmentItem, 117–118
    ContactItem, 118–119
    TaskItem, 119
    working with cells, 116
    working with MailItem, 116–117
Items property, SharePoint list data, 376
iteration, 24, 27–30
Itripoli's ASE (AdminScript Editor), 621

J

job steps, SQL Server, 356–357, 362–363
jobs
    configuring new backup, 174–175
    new in V2, 50–52
    potential glitches of, 52
    working with, 50–52
join operator, 15

K

key-value pairs, FilterHashTable parameter, 196

L

label control, 586–587
language constructs
    expressions, 16–18
    operators, 14–15
    as script component, 24
    variables, 13–14
Launch PowerShell button, XenDesktop, 480
$LBPolicy variable, 473
LDAP, 236
LDAP, Active Directory, 238
libraries
    SharePoint document, 379–381
    VMM, 537–539
licensing, XenDesktop, 485–486
-like operator, expressions, 16
line breakpoints, ISE, 609
links, Group Policy, 261–262
List parameter, server configuration, 189–190
lists, SharePoint
    adding items, 376
    backup and restore, 386
    browsing, 375
    creating, 378
    managing document libraries, 379–381
    managing permissions, 378–379
    modifying settings, 378
    overview of, 375
    updating data, 376
    viewing data, 376
    working with views, 377
List-Scope function, Windows 7, 81
load-balancing
    OpsMgr agents, 422–423
    XenApp policies, 470, 473–475
loading
    SQL Server data, 350–351
    in XenApp, 471
Load-Search function, 79–84
local accounts, 219–221
LocalDateTime property, Win32_OperatingSystem, 198
Location parameter
    Get-VM and Get-VMHost, 559
    Get-WebConfiguration in IIS, 400–403
Lock-ProvVM cmdlet, 492
log files
    creating from OpsMgr command channel, 427–429
    database, 364
    reading IIS, 406–407

reviewing from ESX host, 566–567
as script component, 24
Windows Azure diagnostics, 549–554
LogFolderPath parameter, Mount-Database, 311
logic errors, 30–32
logical operators, 15
logon
    Exchange Server, 271
    XenApp server, 470
LogOnConsole privilege, XenApp 6, 459
LUN ID, VM storage, 535

M

Machine administrator, XenDesktop, 486–488
Machine Creation Services
    pooled catalogs, 489
    provisioning technology, 497
machine types. See catalogs, XenDesktop
MachineLaunchRestriction, DCOM permissions, 222
mail contacts, Exchange Server, 278–279, 291–292,
    326–328
mail users, verbs for, 278–279
mailboxes. See Microsoft Exchange Server 2007
MailItems, Outlook, 116–117
maintenance mode
    automating using OpsMgr, 415–418
    putting ESX hosts in, 560
makecert utility, WASM certificates, 542
managed service accounts, 246–247
management, early days of Windows, 3–5
management interfaces, Hyper-V, 513–515
Management Tools for Exchange 2010, installing,
    272–273
manifest modules, 59
MAPIFolderItem, Outlook, 114–115
master images, provisioning machines, 497–498
-match operator, expressions, 16
MaxSamples parameter, Get-Counter cmdlet, 218
MDT (Microsoft Deployment Toolkit) 2010
    configuring deployment share, 451–452
    creating database, 444
    creating scripts using GUI, 442
    creating Task Sequences, 449–451
    importing applications, 446–449
    importing device drivers, 445–446
    importing operating systems, 444–445
    initializing Deployment Share, 443–444
    installing and using cmdlets, 441–442

managing media, 452–454
updating deployment share, 452
Windows PowerShell provider, 442
MDTProvider (Windows PowerShell provider), 442–444
media, deployment, 452–454
Member parameter, Exchange
    Add-DistributionGroupMember, 297
    Remove-DistributionGroupMember, 297
Member property, AD groups, 239
$Member variable, 220
MemberOf property, Get-AD, 238
membership, querying Active Directory group, 238–240
memory
    limits in WS-MAN, 373–374
    SharePoint cmdlets managing, 372–373
menu bar, ISE, 599
MetaFrame COM (MFCOM), 456
methods
    class, 9–10
    ISEEditor object, 612
    ISEFile object, 612–613
    ISEFileCollection object, 613
    ISEMenuItemCollection object, 614
    ISEOptions object, 614–615
    PowerShellTabCollection object in ISE, 617
MFCOM (MetaFrame COM), 456
Microsoft
    Deployment Toolkit. See MDT (Microsoft
        Deployment Toolkit) 2010
    Excel spreadsheets. See Excel spreadsheets
    Exchange Web Services, 335–339
    noun prefixes for cmdlets in AD, 8
    Office. See Office 2010
    Outlook. See Outlook
    SharePoint Server. See Microsoft SharePoint 2010
        Server
    Windows management in past, 3–5
    Windows Server 2008. See Windows Server 2008 R2
    Word. See Word, automating
Microsoft Exchange Server
    client-side filtering, 328–329
    contacts, 291–292
    databases, 309–313
    discovering space from disabled mailboxes, 313–316
    distribution groups, 295–298
    dynamic distribution groups, 298–301
    email address policies, 322–324
    Exchange Web Services, 335–339
    installing cmdlets on workstation, 271–273

interoperation with earlier versions, 324–328

mailbox administration, 280–286

mailbox resources, 301–303

moving mailboxes, 286–291

objects, 276–279

permissions, 274–276

public folders, 303–307

quotas, 316–319

recipient scope, 330–332

recipients, 279–280

remote management of, 320–322

role base access control, 332–334

server-side filtering, 329–330

storage groups, 308–309

users, 292–295

what's new in 2010, 273–274

Microsoft Exchange Server 2007

changing email address for mailbox, 282–283

databases, 310–311

finding database white space, 312

installing cmdlets, 272

moving mailboxes, 286–287

permissions, 274

scope, 330–331

storage groups, 308–309

upgrading, 325–326

Microsoft Exchange Server 2010

changing email address for mailbox, 283

databases, 310–311

finding database white space, 312–313

GUI administration tools, 7–8

moving mailboxes, 287–291

scope, 331–332

upgrading, 326–328

Microsoft SharePoint 2010 Server

automating site administration, 374–375

back up and restore, 384–386

cmdlets, 371–373

developer code, 381–382

overview of, 371

remoting with, 373–374

search and timer crawls, 386–388

using SharePoint lists. *See* lists, SharePoint

web applications, 381

workflows, 382–383

Microsoft.Win32.RegistryHive

accessing registry remotely, 209

modifying registry permissions remotely, 138

reading registry remotely, 210–211

retrieving registry permissions remotely, 136–137

setting registry values remotely, 212–213

Microsoft.Win32.RegistryKey

accessing registry remotely, 209

modifying registry permissions remotely, 138

reading registry remotely, 210–211

retrieving installed software remotely, 155

retrieving registry permissions remotely, 136–137

setting registry values remotely, 212–213

migration. *See* server migration, Windows Server 2008 R2

Migration feature, 180

modules

adding new cmdlets with, 11

editing with ISE, 607

extending Windows PowerShell, 36

IIS 7 cmdlets for, 403

implicit, 59–61

manifest, 59

OpsMgr workflow, 436–437

overview of, 57

script, 57–58

Windows Server 2008 R2, 165–166

Monad, 5

Monad Manifesto, 5

Most Valuable Professional (MVP) award, 13

Mount-Database cmdlet, Exchange, 310–311

Move() method, Outlook items, 116

Move-ADObject cmdlet, Active Directory, 248

Move-Mailbox cmdlet, Exchange, 286–287

MoveStatus parameter, Get-MoveRequest, 288

ms_ticks column, instance uptime information, 352

MSExchangeMailboxReplication.exe.config file, 290

.msi (Windows Installer), 152–163

MS-PSRP (Windows PowerShell Remoting protocol), 47–48

MS-WSMV (Web Service Management For Vista), 47–48

MVP (Most Valuable Professional) award, 13

N

Name parameter

Get-GPO, 259

Get-Service, 343

New-BrokerTimeScheme, 501–502, 504

New-DistributionGroup, 296–297

New-EmailAddressPolicy, 322–324

New-Mailbox, 281

New-MailboxDatabase, 310

Name property, Excel worksheet, 108

Namespace object, Outlook, 114–115

Namespace parameter, server configuration, 190

naming conventions
    cmdlets, 529–530
    specifying mailbox, 281
    stopping processes, 209

.NET
    accessing registry remotely, 209
    retrieving installed software remotely, 155
    validating input in text mode UI, 584
    Windows Forms. *See* Windows Forms

NetworkPath parameter, New-PSDrive, 443–444

networks
    adding to virtual machine, 534
    device deployment in OpsMgr, 418–423
    host, PowerCLI, 563–564
    validating on remote servers, 213–217

New-* cmdlets, Exchange Server, 278–279

New-ADComputer cmdlet, AD, 243

New-ADFineGrainedPasswordPolicy cmdlet, AD, 251

New-ADGroup cmdlet, AD, 241–242

New-ADOrganizationalUnit cmdlet, AD, 248–249

New-ADServiceAccount cmdlet, AD, 246

New-ADUser cmdlet, AD, 240–241

New-AppLockerPolicy cmdlet, AppLocker,
    186–187

New-BrokerAdministrator cmdlet, XenDesktop, 486

New-BrokerApp cmdlet, XenDesktop, 504–505

New-BrokerApplication cmdlet, XenDesktop,
    504–505

New-BrokerCatalog cmdlet, XenDesktop, 495

New-BrokerDesktopGroup cmdlet, XenDesktop,
    499–500, 502–505

New-BrokerEntitlementPolicyRule cmdlet,
    XenDesktop, 499–500

New-BrokerHypervisorConnection cmdlet,
    XenDesktop, 506–507

New-BrokerMachine cmdlet, Xen Desktop, 493–496

New-BrokerTimeScheme cmdlet, XenDesktop,
    501–502, 504

New-BrokerUser cmdlet, Xen Desktop, 499–500

New-DataStore cmdlet, PowerCLI, 563

New-Deployment cmdlet, WASM, 546–547

New-DistributionGroup cmdlet, Exchange, 296–297

New-DynamicDistributionGroup cmdlet, Exchange,
    298–300

New-EmailAddressPolicy cmdlet, Exchange, 322–324

New-GPLink cmdlet, Group Policy, 263–264

New-GPO cmdlet, Group Policy, 263

New-HypAdministrator cmdlet, XenDesktop, 486

New-HypVMSnapshot cmdlet, Xen Desktop, 490,
    498–499

New-Item cmdlet
    IIS website, 395
    items within IIS:\, 394–395
    New-Website cmdlet vs., 395–396
    virtual directories, 396
    XenServer hosts, 506

New-LdapQueryDiscoveryCriteria cmdlet, OpsMgr,
    421–422

New-Mailbox cmdlet, Exchange, 281, 302

New-MailboxDatabase cmdlet, Exchange, 310–311

New-MailUser cmdlet, Exchange, 293

New-ManagementRoleAssignment cmdlet, RBAC, 333

New-MDTDatabase cmdlet, MDT, 444

New-ModuleManifest cmdlet, manifest modules, 59

New-MoveRequest cmdlet, Exchange, 287–291

New-Object cmdlet, share permissions, 132–133

New-Object cmdlet, Windows Forms, 587

New-ProvScheme cmdlet, Xen Desktop, 490

New-ProvVM cmdlet, Xen Desktop, 491–492

New-PSDrive cmdlet
    Active Directory provider, 232
    initializing deployment share in MDT, 443–444
    registry settings, 136

New-PublicFolder cmdlet, Exchange, 303–304

New-RoleGroup cmdlet, RBAC, 333

New-Snapshot cmdlet, PowerCLI, 572

New-SPSite cmdlet, SharePoint, 374

New-SPWebApplication cmdlet, SharePoint, 381

New-StorageGroup cmdlet, Exchange, 308–309

NewTask() method, servers, 192

New-VirtualDiskDrive cmdlet, VMM, 535

New-VirtualDVDDrive cmdlet, VMM, 535

New-VirtualNetworkManager cmdlet, VMM, 534

New-VirtualPortGroup cmdlet, PowerCLI, 564

New-VirtualSwitch cmdlet, PowerCLI, 563

New-VM cmdlet
    creating VMs in Hyper-V, 517
    creating VMs in PowerCLI, 568–569
    VMM, 533–534

New-VMCheckPoint cmdlet, VMM, 536

New-VMHostProfile cmdlet, PowerCLI, 565–566

New-VMSnapshot cmdlet, Hyper-V, 519

New-WBBackupTarget cmdlet, Windows Backup,
    175–176, 179

New-WBFileSpec cmdlet, Windows Backup, 175–176

New-WBPolicy cmdlet, Windows Backup, 174–176
New-WebApplication cmdlet, IIS, 397–398
New-WebAppPool cmdlet, IIS, 398
New-WebBinding cmdlet, IIS, 398–399
New-WebFtpSite cmdlet, IIS, 396
New-Website cmdlet, IIS, 395–396
New-WebVirtualDirectory cmdlet, IIS, 396–397
New-XAAapplication cmdlet, XenApp, 463–465
New-XAAdministrator cmdlet, XenApp, 457–458
New-XALoadBalancingPolicy cmdlet, XenAPP, 473
New-XALoadEvaluator cmdlet, XenAPP, 472
New-XAWorkerGroup cmdlet, XenAPP, 475
nonterminating errors, 33–34
NoSiteLock parameter, Backup-SPSite, 385–386
NoSource parameter, Import-MDTApplication, 448–449
notifications
    command notification channel. See command notification channel, OpsMgr
    in OspMgr, 435–436
-notlike operator, expressions, 16
-notmatch operator, expressions, 16
nouns, in cmdlets, 8
NTFS permissions, 124–127
NTP server configuration, 564–565

O

ObjectModelRoot object, ISE, 611, 614
objects
    automating maintenance mode
        for, 415–417
    enumerating relationships and monitored, 425–426
    in Exchange Server, 276–278
    finding what is inside with Get-Member, 12
    moving Active Directory, 247–248
    in OpsMgr, 415–417
    overview of, 9–10
    pipeline using, 10
    removing AD, 249
    scripting in SQL Server, 357–362
    using variables to hold, 14
Office 2010
    Application objects, 96–97
    cleaning up scripts, 97
    COM objects, 96
    Excel spreadsheets. See Excel spreadsheets
    OneNote page, 120–121
    Outlook. See Outlook

overview of, 95
    PowerPoint presentation, 119–120
    Word. See Word, automating
OneNote page, 120–121
one-off command, remote machines, 49
Open() method
    Excel workbook, 107
    Word documents, 98
OpenBinary() method, downloading documents, 380
operands, in expressions, 16
operating systems
    importing applications in MDT to, 446–449
    importing device drivers in MDT, 445–446
    importing in MDT, 444–445
Operations Manager. See OpsMgr (System Center Operations Manager) 2007 R2
OperationsManagerMonitoring, OpsMgr, 410
operators
    within AD filters, 235–236
    iteration, 27–30
    as language constructs, 14–15
OpsMgr (System Center Operations Manager) 2007 R2
    adding/removing objects and groups, 415–417
    agents and network devices, 418–423
    alerts, 410–415
    automating maintenance mode, 417–418
    cmdlets, 409–410
    discovered inventory data, 423–426
    monitoring scripts in Windows PowerShell, 436–437
    notifications, 435–436
    overrides, 431–435
    overview of, 409
    sample scripts and community resources, 437–439
    TechNet Forums, 438
    Windows PowerShell and command notification channel, 426–431
OrganizationalUnit parameter, Exchange, 281–282, 293, 296–297
OtherAttributes parameter, New-ADUser, 241
OUs (organizational units)
    creating, 248–249
    moving Active Directory objects, 247–248
    moving between containers and, 234
    specifying for mailbox user, 281–282
Out-DataTable function, SQL Server, 349, 355
Out-Host cmdlet, NTFS permissions, 125
Outlook
    deleting items, 116
    folders, 115

important objects, 113
key objects, 113
moving items, 116
PST files, 115
security, 114
working with `AppointmentItem`, 117–118
working with `ContactItem`, 118–119
working with `MailItem`, 116–117
working with major folders, 114–115
working with subfolders, 115
working with `TaskItem`, 119
`Out-Null` cmdlet, hyperlinks, 100
output
  debug, 32
  enabling verbose, 66
  formatting, 18–21
  `Get-Acl` vs. `Format-List`, 125
  `Get-ExCommand` in Exchange Server, 277–278
  `Get-WmiObject`, 152–153
  Microsoft Office scripts for, 95
  produced by functions, 53
Output pane, ISE, 599–600, 605, 607
overrides
  converting into reporting format in OspMgr, 431–434
  creating programmatically in OpsMgr, 434–435
  modifying workflows, 431

P

`$PackPath` variable, 73, 75
packs, troubleshooting, 71–74
`Paging` parameter, 125
parameter value globbing, 9
parameters
  `Add-VMHost`, 526–527
  `Add-VMHostCluster`, 528–529
  cmdlet, 9
  database for XenDesktop, 482–483
  `DynamicDistributionGroup`, 298–300
  `Export-SPWeb`, 386
  functions taking, 53
  `Get-Mailbox`, 279
  Hardware Profile, 532
  `Import-MDTApplication`, 446–447
  `Import-MDTOperatingSystem`, 445
  `Invoke-TroubleshootingPack`, 73
  `New-ADUser`, 241
  `New-MDTDatabase`, 444

`New-XAAdministrator`, 457–458
VM, 533–534
XenApp worker groups, 476–477
XenDesktop, 482
partial matches, Outlook, 118
`PassThru` parameter, `New-ADGroup` cmdlet, 241–242
`Password` parameter
  `Connect-VIServer`, 559–560
  `Export-SmigServerSetting`, 183
  `New-Mailbox`, 281
  `Send-SmigServerData`, 184
passwords
  Active Directory policies, 249–252
  resetting Active Directory user, 244–245
`Paste()` method, Word documents, 103
`Path` parameter
  `Backup-SPSite`, 385–386
  `Backup-VMMServer`, 524
  `Get-Acl`, 85, 124–125
  `Get-ChildItem`, 71–72
  `Get-GPOReport`, 259
  `Get-SmigServerFeature`, 183
  `New-ADOrganizationalUnit`, 248–249
  `New-ADUser`, 241
  `New-PublicFolder`, 303
  `Set-Acl`, 85
  `Test-AppLockerPolicy`, 187
patterns, currently indexed, 78–79
`PeakHours` parameter, `New-BrokerTimeScheme`, 501–502, 504
performance counters, 217–218, 354–357
performance data, from ESX host, 567–568
`PermissionLevel` parameter, `Set-GPPermissions`, 265–266
permissions
  DCOM, 222–226
  Exchange Server, 273–276
  file, folder and registry, 123
  Group Policy, 265–266
  NTFS, 124–127
  registry, 135–139
  share, 127–131, 132–135
  SharePoint list, 378–379
persistent sessions, 48
physical catalogs, XenDesktop, 488, 494–495
`PhysicalPath` parameter, `New-Item` within IIS provider, 394
`PipeBind` parameters, SharePoint, 372
pipelines, 10

policies
    Active Directory password, 249–252
    Application Desktop Groups access, 503
    AppLocker, 186–187
    backup jobs as, 174–175
    Desktop Groups access, 500–501
    email address, 322–324
    GPOs. *See* GPOs (Group Policy Objects)
    Group Policy. *See* Group Policy
    new backup job, 175–176
    Windows Backup, 175
polling, 61–62
pooled catalogs, XenDesktop, 488, 489–492
PoolSize parameter, New-BrokerTimeScheme,
        501–502
ports, firewall, 144–146
Power CLI. *See* vSphere PowerCLI
power state, controlling VMs, 518–519
PowerPoint presentations, 119–120
PowerShell Community Extension (PSCX), 12
PowerShell Pack, 12–13
PowerShell tabs, ISE, 605–606
PowerShell TechNet Forums, 438
PowerShell_ISE.exe, 38–39, 41
PowerShell.exe, 38–39, 40
PowerShellTab object, ISE, 611, 616, 619
PowerShellTabCollection object, ISE, 611, 617
preference policies, Group Policy, 260–261
prerequisites, ActiveDirectory module, 230–232
PrimalForms, 593–595
Primary File Group, database, 364
PrimarySmtpAddress parameter, Set-
        MailPublicFolder, 304
printing, Word document, 106
PrintOut() method, Word, 106
private profile, firewalls, 139–143
privileges, XenApp 6, 458–461
processes, managing, 207–209
production scripts, Windows PowerShell in, 7–8
ProductLevel property, service pack
        information, 352
profile files, ISE, 608, 610
$profile variable, 40
profiles
    ESX host, 565–567
    firewall, 139–140
    location of, 40–41
    managing in enterprise, 41
    overview of, 39–40

ProhibitSendQuota, 316–319
ProhibitSendReceiveQuota, 316–319
prompts, suppressing in PowerCLI, 565
propagation flags, 124, 138
properties
    ActiveRoles Management Shell, user, 254
    cell, 110–111
    class, 9–10
    ESX host, 560–562
    Filter parameter, 330
    formatting with hashtables using calculated, 22
    Get-AD cmdlets, 237–238
    ISEEditor object, 612
    ISEFile object, 613
    ISEMenuItem object, 613
    listing software using WMI, 153
    MDT Deployment Share, 451–452
    modifying Active Directory, 242–243
    ObjectModelRoot object, 614
    PowerShellTab object in ISE, 616
    $PsISE, 617
    published application, 465
    XenApp 6 privileges, 459–462
Properties parameter, Active Directory, 237
provider
    getting database space usage, 364–365
    getting table space usage, 365
    implementing transactions, 63–64
    installing WMI, 392
    loading for IIS 7, 391–392
    making changes with, 399–400
    overview of, 18
    scripting objects in SQL Server with, 357
    WebAdministration. *See* WebAdministration
        provider
provisioning, XenDesktop, 497–499
proxy agent, OpsMgr, 419–421
PSCX (PowerShell Community Extension), 12
$PsISE (ISE root object) variable
    adding functionality to ISE, 619
    changing look and feel of ISE, 617–619
    customizing ISE, 610
    ISEOptions accessed from, 615–616
    ObjectModelRoot object and, 614
    properties, 617
.psl extension, ISE profile files, 608
PSModulePath variable, module directories, 516
PSPath parameter, IIS, 400–403
PSProvider parameter, MDT, 443–444

PsSnapin
    modules vs., 35
    overview of, 35
    Windows PowerShell community and, 12
PST files, creating, 115
public folders, 303–307
public profile, firewalls, 140
PublicFolderDatabase parameter, Set-
        MailboxDatabase, 319
PublicProfile key, 143–144
published applications, Xen App
    adding/removing assigned accounts, 466
    importing/exporting, 465–466
    properties, 465
    publishing, 463–465
    removing/disabling, 466–467
    retrieving, 462–463
    types of, 462
Publish-ProvMasterVmImage cmdlet, 498–499
PvsForVM parameter, Set-BrokerCatalog, 490
PvsPsSnapIn module, XenDesktop, 495

Q

Query parameter, discovering server
        configuration, 190
querying SQL Server, 347–349
Quest
    AD tools, 12–13, 229, 253–255
    noun prefixes for cmdlets in AD, 8
    PowerGui, 621
Quit() method, Office, 97
QuotaNotificationSchedule, Exchange, 317
quotas, managing mailbox, 316–319
quoted strings, SQL Server queries, 347–348

R

Range() method, cells, 108–110
Range objects
    applying styles in Word, 104
    formatting text in Word, 103
    searching spreadsheets, 113
    sorting data, 111–112
    using fonts in Word, 104
    working with cells, 108–111
RBAC (Role Based Access Control)
    Exchange Server 2010, 273
    Exchange Server 2010 permissions, 275–276

    managing, 332–334
Read-Host cmdlet
    Exchange Server, 281, 293
    text mode UI, 583
reading registry, 209–211
Read-only administrator, XenDesktop, 486–488
Reason parameter, Shutdown-VM, 519
Receive-SmigServerData cmdlet, server migration,
        184, 185–186
recipient scope, 330–332
RecipientContainer parameter, New-
        EmailAddressPolicy, 324
RecipientFilter parameter,
        DynamicDistributionGroup, 298–301
recipients, Exchange Server
    administering, 279–280
    contacts, 291–292
    databases, 309–313
    distribution groups, 295–298
    dynamic distribution groups, 298–301
    mailbox resources, 301–303
    mailboxes, 280–286
    moving mailboxes, 286–291
    overview of, 278–279
    public folders, 303–307
    storage groups, 308–309
    users, 292–295
RecoverableItemsQuota, 316–319
RecoverableItemsWarningQuota, 316–319
Recursive switch, Get-ADGroupMember, 239–240
redemption.dll, 114
redirection operators, 15
Reflection, 10
Refresh-LibraryShare cmdlet, VMM, 538
regional settings, modifying on multiple computers,
        218–219
Registered Servers (Reg.S), 366–369
Register-EngineEvent, 61–62
Register-ObjectEvent, 9, 61–62
RegisterTaskDefinition() method, scheduled
        tasks, 192
Register-WmiEvent, 61–62
registrations, SQL Server, 366–369
registry
    checking firewall status remotely, 143–144
    checking Remote Desktop status, 148–149
    enabling Remote Desktop, 147–148
    information about GPO policies, 260
    managing permissions, 123

modifying settings, 137–139
overview of, 135–136
reading and modifying, 209–211
retrieving current settings, 136–137
setting values, 211–213
transactions in V2, 63–64
viewing DCOM permissions, 222
registry hives, 209–213
Reg.S (Registered Servers), 366–369
regular expressions, 16–17, 26–27
Reindex( ) methods, Catalog interface, 82–84
ReleaseComObject() method, Office, 97
remote DCOM, 221–227
Remote Desktop, 147–149
remote maintenance mode, OpsMgr, 417–418
Remote Procedure Call (RPC), DCOM, 153
Remote Registry service, 155
Remote Server Administration Tools (RSAT), 231
remote servers, 207–208
remote systems
    accessing registry from, 209
    checking firewall is enabled on, 143–144
    installing GroupPolicy module on, 258
    installing software on, 158–159
    listing software on, 153–155
    managing Microsoft Exchange Server
        on, 320–322
    modifying registry permissions on, 138
    retrieving registry permissions on, 136–137
    running Best Practice Analyzer on, 172–173
    status of backup jobs on, 177
remoting
    ActiveDirectory module for, 231
    architecture, 46–48
    enabling on Windows Server 2008 R2, 173–174
    new in V2, 45–50
    serialization, 50
    setting up, 48
    with SharePoint, 373–374
    understanding, 46
    using, 48–50
    V2 features for, 45–46
    working with jobs in, 50–52
Remove cmdlet, AD objects, 249
Remove() method, firewall ports, 144–146
Remove-* cmdlets, Exchange Server, 278–279
RemoveAccessRuleSpecific() method, NTFS
        permissions, 127
Remove-ADGroupMember cmdlet, AD, 243

Remove-ADPrincipalGroupMembership cmdlet,
        AD, 243–244
Remove-BrokerCatalog cmdlet, XenDesktop, 496–497
Remove-BrokerHypervisorConnection cmdlet,
        XenDesktop, 508–509
Remove-Certificate cmdlet, WASM, 549
Remove-DataStore cmdlet, PowerCLI, 563
RemoveDefaultScopeRule() method, Windows
        Desktop, 82
Remove-DistributionGroupMember cmdlet,
        Exchange, 297, 298
Remove-DynamicDistributionGroup cmdlet,
        Exchange, 301
Remove-FineGrainedPassword PolicySubject
        cmdlet, AD, 252
Remove-GPO cmdlet, Group Policy, 263–264
Remove-Item cmdlet
    IIS objects, 400
    XenDesktop hosts, 508–509
Remove-Mailbox cmdlet, Exchange, 283–284, 314–315
Remove-MailPublicFolder cmdlet, Exchange, 305
Remove-MailUser cmdlet, Exchange, 293, 295
Remove-MDTPersistentDrive cmdlet, MDT, 444
Remove() method, local users and groups, 219, 221
Remove-MoveRequest cmdlet, Exchange, 288–289
Remove-PsBreakpoint cmdlet, 32
Remove-PSBreakpoint cmdlet, 65
Remove-PsSnapin cmdlet, 35
Remove-RoleGroupMember cmdlet, RBAC, 333–334
RemoveScopeRule() method, Windows Desktop, 82
Remove-SPSite cmdlet, SharePoint, 375
Remove-SPSolution cmdlet, SharePoint, 382
Remove-StorageGroup cmdlet, Exchange, 308–309
Remove-VirtualPortGroup cmdlet, PowerCLI, 564
Remove-VirtualSwitch cmdlet, PowerCLI, 563
Remove-VM cmdlet
    PowerCLI, 568–569
    VMM, 535
Remove-VMCheckPoint cmdlet, VMM, 536
Remove-VmHostNtpServer cmdlet, PowerCLI, 564–565
Remove-VMSnapshot function, VMM, 520
Remove-WBPolicy cmdlet, Windows Backup, 177
Remove-WindowsFeature cmdlet, ServerManager, 169
RemoveWorkflowFromListItem() method,
        SharePoint, 383
Remove-XAAdministrator cmdlet, XenApp, 458
Remove-XAApplicationAccount cmdlet, XenApp,
        465–466
Remove-XAWorkerGroup cmdlet, XenApp, 476

removing VMs, 569
Rename-GPO cmdlet, Group Policy, 263–264
Rename-XAWorkerGroup cmdlet, XenApp, 477
replication, public folder, 306–307
reports
    creating with Search-ADAccount, 245–246
    detailed GPO, 259
    Microsoft Office scripts for, 95
    override, 432–434
    Resultant Set of Policy, 262
RequestStateChange value, Hyper-V classes, 515
Reset( ) methods, Catalog interface, 82–84
Reset-XALoadEvaluator cmdlet, XenApp, 473
Reset-XASession cmdlet, XenApp, 470
resource configuration, PowerCLI, 571
resource mailboxes, Exchange, 301–303
ResourceContextServer parameter, AD group
    membership, 239
Responding property, Get-Process, 208
Restart parameter, Add-WindowsFeature,
    168–169
Restore Points, installing software, 157–158
Restore-GPO cmdlet, Group Policy, 264–265
Restore-MDTPersistentDrive cmdlet, MDT, 444
Restore-SPFarm cmdlet, SharePoint, 384, 385
Restore-VMCheckPoint cmdlet, VMM, 536
Restore-WebConfigurationBackupName, IIS, 406
Result parameter, Invoke-TroubleshootingPack, 73
Resultant Sets of Policy (RSOP), 262
ResultSize parameter, Get-Mailbox, 279
Resume-PublicFolderReplication cmdlet,
    Exchange, 307
RevertToDefaultScope() method, Windows
    Desktop, 82
Role Based Access Control. See RBAC (Role Based Access
    Control)
Role parameter, RBAC, 333
role services, Windows Server 2008, 167–169
roles
    Exchange Server 2007, 274–275
    Exchange Server 2010, 275–276
    running Best Practice Analyzer locally, 169–170
    Windows Server 2008, 167–169
    XenDesktop administrative access, 486–487
room mailboxes, 301–303
$rootMS variable, 419
RPC (Remote Procedure Call), DCOM, 153
RSAT (Remote Server Administration Tools), 231

RSOP (Resultant Sets of Policy), 262
RuleNamePrefix parameter, New-AppLockerPolicy,
    186–187
RuleType parameter, New-AppLockerPolicy, 186–187
RunAsync parameter, PowerCLI cmdlets, 560
RunAsynchronously parameter, New-ProvVM, 491–492
runtime errors, 30, 32–33

S

SamAccountName parameter, New-DistributionGroup, 296
SampleInterval parameter, Get-Counter, 218
Sapien's Primal Script, 621
Save() method, 106–107, 117–118
SaveAs() method, 107
scheduled tasks
    agent discovery and deployment, 421–422
    PowerShell, 362–363
    server management, 191–194
Schedule.Service object, 191–194
$ScopeRules variable, 78
scopes, Windows Search, 77–78
script modules, 57–58
Script pane, ISE, 599–600, 605, 607
ScriptConfiguration parameter, Set-
    DeploymentConfiguration, 548
scripts
    alternation of, 24–27
    customizing with profiles, 39–41
    definition of, 23–24
    error and exception handling, 30–34
    execution policy and security, 37–39
    IIS changes in, 399–403
    IIS new deployments, 394–399
    ISE customization of, 610
    ISE Debug menu items, 602–603
    ISE debugging of, 608–609
    ISE Edit menu items, 600–601
    ISE editing of, 607
    iteration and, 27–30
    jobs, 51–52
    language of, 6–7
    Microsoft Office and, 95, 97–98
    Office Application objects, 97–98
    in OpsMgr, 436–439
    in PowerCLI, 573
    running remotely, 49–50
    script modules vs., 58

SQL Server objects, 357–362
troubleshooting, 71
VMM Administrator Console and, 524–525
Windows PowerShell, 7–8
ScriptText parameter, Invoke-VMScript, 573
SCVMMRecover.exe, VMM, 524
SDK, Windows Search, 77
search catalog, 77–81
search crawls, Sharepoint, 387–388
$Search variable, 77–79
Search-Bin (Ctrl+B) function, IsePack, 620
searching
    Excel spreadsheets, 113
    for item in Outlook, 118
    text in Word, 102–103
SearchScope parameter, Active Directory, 237
Secondary File Group, database, 364
security
    enabling Remote Desktop, 147–149
    Exchange Server login and, 271
    file and folder. See files and folders, Windows 7
    Group Policy, 265–266
    inheritance and propagation flags for Set-Acl
        cmdlet, 124
    NTFS permissions, 124–127
    Outlook, 114
    overview of, 123
    registry settings, 135–139
    script execution policy and, 37–39
    share permissions. See share permissions
    Windows Firewall. See Windows Firewall
security descriptor
    overview of, 123
    retrieving current NTFS permissions, 125
    viewing DCOM permissions, 222–225
SecurityGroup parameter, New-
        ManagementRoleAssignment in RBAC, 333
Selection property, adding text to Word, 99
Select-Object cmdlet
    finding empty folders, 89
    listing all processes on multiple servers, 207
    listing running services on multiple servers, 204
    listing unique file extensions, 87
    managing Windows Search, 78, 81
    retrieving performance counters, 217–218
    searching with Windows Search, 90
    troubleshooting Windows 7, 72–73
SelfID property, Get-SPBackupHistory, 384
Send-MailMessage cmdlet, Outlook, 117

Send-SmigServerData cmdlet, server migration,
        184–185
serialization, remoting and, 50
Server 2008 R2 Core, 45, 166
server folder privileges, XenApp 6, 460
server installed published applications, Xen App, 463
server management
    discovering server configuration, 189–191
    event logs, 195–198
    hotfix status, 194–195
    scheduled tasks, 191–194
    Server 2008 R2. See Windows Server 2008 R2
    system time, 198–201
server management, advanced
    command-line services, 203–206
    local accounts, 219–221
    overview of, 203
    performance counters, 217–218
    processes, 207–209
    reading registry, 209–211
    regional settings on multiple computers, 218–219
    registry values, 211–213
    remote DCOM, 221–227
    validating networks on remote servers, 213–217
server migration, Windows Server 2008 R2
    discovering what can be migrated, 182–183
    exporting features, 183–184
    importing features, 184–186
    installing cmdlets, 180–182
    overview of, 180
Server parameter
    Get-MailboxDatabase, 285
    GroupPolicy module, 259
    Move-ADObject, 248
    New-StorageGroup, 308
    Update-PublicFolder, 307
ServerConnection object, VMM Server, 525–526
ServerDesktop parameter, New-XAAapplication, 465
ServerManager module, 167–169
ServerName parameter, Set-XALoadEvaluator, 472–473
ServerNames parameter, New-XAAapplication,
        463–464
servers, XenApp
    load evaluators, 471–473
    load-balancing policies, 473–475
    logons, 470
    obtaining numerical load, 471
    worker groups, 475–477
    zones, 473

server-side filtering, 329–330

service accounts, SQL Server, 346

service pack information, SQL Server, 352

services

    configuring XenDesktop, 485

    controlling IIS, 404–405

    managing SQL Server, 343–344

    managing Windows, 203–206

    using managed service account, 247

sessions, remoting using, 48–50

sessions, XenApp, 467–470

Set-* cmdlets, Exchange Server, 278–279

SetAccessRuleProtection() method, registry
    permissions, 139

Set-Acl cmdlet

    defined, 123

    file and folder security, 84–85

    inheritance and propagation flags, 124

    NTFS permissions, 126–127

    registry settings, 135–136

Set-ADAccountPassword cmdlet, AD, 244–245

Set-ADComputer cmdlet, AD, 243

Set-ADDefaultDomainPasswordPolicySubject cmdlet,
    AD, 251

Set-ADFineGrainedPasswordPolicy cmdlet, AD, 251

Set-ADGroup cmdlet, AD, 242–243

Set-ADObject cmdlet, AD, 249

Set-AdServerSettings cmdlet, AD, 331–332

Set-ADUser cmdlet, AD, 242–245

Set-AppLockerPolicy cmdlet, AppLocker, 187

Set-BpaResult cmdlet, Windows Server, 169, 171–172

Set-BrokerCatalog cmdlet, XenDesktop, 490, 496–497

Set-BrokerSite cmdlet, XenDesktop, 485–486

Set-DataStore cmdlet, PowerCLI, 563

Set-Deployment cmdlet, WASM, 546–547

Set-DeploymentConfiguration cmdlet, WASM, 548

Set-DeploymentStatus cmdlet, WASM, 545–546

Set-DistributionGroup cmdlet, Exchange, 326–328

SetDNSSuffixSearchOrder() method, Invoke-
    WmiMethod, 215

Set-DynamicDistributionGroup cmdlet, Exchange,
    300–301

Set-EmailAddressPolicy cmdlet, Exchange, 324–326

Set-GPInheritance cmdlet, Group Policy, 263–264

Set-GPLink cmdlet, Group Policy, 263–264

Set-GPPermissions cmdlet, Group Policy, 265–266

Set-GPRegistryValue cmdlet, Group Policy, 263

Set-Group cmdlet, Exchange, 296

Set-Item cmdlet, IIS, 399

Set-ItemProperty cmdlet, IIS, 398

Set-ItemProperty cmdlet, MDT, 448, 452

Set-Location cmdlet

    browsing IIS:\, 393

    OpsMgr, 410

    using registry provider locally, 210

Set-Mailbox cmdlet, Exchange, 282–283, 303, 330

Set-MailboxDatabase cmdlet, Exchange, 316–319

Set-MailContact cmdlet, Exchange, 292

Set-MailPublicFolder cmdlet, Exchange, 303–306

Set-MailUser cmdlet, Exchange, 294

Set-ManagementServer cmdlet, OpsMgr, 419

Set-PsBreakpoint cmdlet, 32

Set-PSBreakpoint cmdlet, 65

Set-PsDebug cmdlet, 32

Set-PvsConnection cmdlet, XenDesktop, 495

SetRange() method, Word documents, 99

Set-RDPConnection function, Remote Desktop, 147–148

Set-Service cmdlet, Windows services, 203

SetShareInfo() method, Win32_Share class, 132–135

Set-SharePermission script, 132–135

Set-StrictMode cmdlet, error handling, 31

Set-User cmdlet, Exchange, 294–295

Set-VirtualPortGroup cmdlet, PowerCLI, 564

Set-VirtualSwitch cmdlet, PowerCLI, 563–564

Set-VM cmdlet, PowerCLI, 573

Set-VMCPUCount function, Hyper-V, 517

Set-VMHost cmdlet, PowerCLI, 560

Set-VMMemory function, Hyper-V, 517

Set-VMResourceConfiguration cmdlet, PowerCLI, 571

Set-WBPolicy cmdlet, Windows Backup, 178, 179

Set-WBSchedule cmdlet, Windows Backup, 178

Set-WebConfiguration cmdlet, IIS, 402

Set-WebConfigurationProperty cmdlet, IIS, 402–403

SetWsManQuickConfig cmdlet, 48

Set-XAApplication cmdlet, XenApp, 465

Set-XALoadBalancingPolicyConfiguration cmdlet,
    XenApp, 474

Set-XALoadBalancingPolicyFilter cmdlet,
    XenApp, 474

Set-XALoadEvaluator cmdlet, XenApp, 472–473

Set-XAServerZone cmdlet, XenApp, 473

Set-XAWorkerGroup cmdlet, XenApp, 476

share permissions

    access mask definitions, 128

    ACE type definitions, 129

    modifying, 132–135

    retrieving current, 127–131

    understanding, 127

share viewer UI, 590–593

shared mailboxes, 301–303

ShareName parameter

    Get-SharePermission, 130–131

    Set-SharePermission, 135

SharePoint 2010 Management Shell, 372

SharePoint Server. *See* Microsoft SharePoint 2010
      Server

ShowDialog() method, Windows Forms, 585–586

Show-HypervMenu function, 516–517

Show-Member function, IsePack, 620

ShowTree parameter, Backup-SPFarm, 385

ShowUI, 596

Shutdown-VM function, 519

Simple Network Management Protocol (SNMP),
      419–421, 429–431

Simple Object Access Protocol (SOAP), 47–48

site collections

    backing up and restoring SharePoint, 385–386

    creating SharePoint, 374

sites

    automating administration in SharePoint, 374–375

    creating new item in IIS, 394

    determining state of, 405

    starting and stopping, 404–405

Sites folder, IIS:\, 393

SMO (SQL Management Object), 342, 344, 365–366

SMS (Systems Management Server), 4–5

SMTP, WebAdministration and, 392

snap-ins

    SQL Server, 344–345

    Windows PowerShell, 34–36

    Windows Server 2008 R2, 166

    XenApp 6, 455–456

    XenDesktop, 481–482

snapshots

    creating pooled catalogs, 490

    managing VMs, 519–520

    for VMs in PowerCLI, 572–573

SNMP (Simple Network Management Protocol),
      419–421, 429–431

Snover, Jeffrey, 357

SOAP (Simple Object Access Protocol), 47–48

software

    baselines, 155–157

    installing, 157–159

    listing already installed, 152–155

    removing, 159–162

Sort() method, Excel, 111–112

source files

    adding software with, 446–448

    adding software without, 448–449

SourcePath parameter, server migration, 184

space usage, SQL Server, 363–367

spell checking, Word document or String, 105–106

SPFile object, SharePoint document library, 380

splatting

    creating AD users and groups, 240

    defined, 273–274

    overview of, 56

    using Active Directory provider, 232

SPList object

    accessing views, 377

    adding items to SharePoint list, 376

    creating SharePoint libraries, 379–380

    managing permissions, 378–379

    modifying settings, 378

SPListTemplateType, SharePoint libraries, 379–381

split operator, 15

SPRoleAssignment object, SharePoint list
      permissions, 378

SPWeb object, SharePoint lists, 375–381

SPWorkflowObjects, SharePoint, 382–383

SQL Agent

    job steps, 357

    scheduling tasks, 362–363

SQL Authentication, Registered Servers, 366

SQL Management Object (SMO), 342, 344, 365–366

SQL PowerShell (SQLPS), 341, 356–357

SQL Server 2008 R2

    assemblies, 345–346

    changing service account, 346

    getting information, 351–353

    loading data, 350–351

    loading non-SQL Server data, 351

    management basics, 341–343

    performance counters, 354–357

    querying, 347–349

    registrations in SSMS, 366–369

    scheduling tasks to run in SQL Agent, 362–363

    scripting objects, 357–362

    services, 343–344

    snap-ins, 344–345

    space usage information, 363–366

SQL Server Configuration Manager, 346

SQL Server Management Studio (SSMS), 342, 366–369

SQL statements, XenDesktop, 483–484

SQLBulkCopy class, 348, 351

$SQLParameters variable, 482–485
SQLPS (SQL PowerShell), 341, 356–357
SQLPSX, 342
SQLSERVER:\ Provider, 345
sqlserver_start_time column, instance uptime information, 352
SqlServerCmdletSnapin100 snap-in, 344–345, 347
SSL, configuring for IIS, 398–399
SslBindings, IIS, 393–394
SSMS (SQL Server Management Studio), 342, 366–369
StandardProfile key, firewalls, 143–144
start iisreset, Windows 7, 404
Start() method, application pools and sites, 404
Start-AppPool cmdlet, IIS, 404
Start-Discovery cmdlet, OpsMgr, 421
Start-Job cmdlet, 51
Start-OnDemandTransfer cmdlet, WASM, 553
StartService() method, service management, 206
Start-SPAssignment cmdlet, SharePoint, 373
Start-VM function, 518–519
Start-WBBackup cmdlet, Windows Backup, 178
Start-WebItem cmdlet, IIS, 404
Start-Website cmdlet, IIS, 404
StartWorkflow() method, SharePoint, 382
static methods, 9
static properties, 9
Stop() method
    application pools and sites, 404
    running tasks, 193
Stop-ActivateTransfer cmdlet, WASM, 553
Stop-AppPool cmdlet, IIS, 404
StopMaintenanceMode() method, 416–417
Stop-Process cmdlet, on remote servers, 208
Stop-SPAssignment cmdlet, SharePoint, 373
Stop-VM function, Hyper-V, 518–519
Stop-WebItem cmdlet, IIS, 404
Stop-Website cmdlet, IIS, 404
storage
    adding to VM, 534–535
    configuring host in PowerCLI, 562–563
    transferring logs in Windows Azure to, 553–554
    VMM libraries, 537–539
    Windows Azure cmdlets, 551
StorageGroup parameter, New-MailboxDatabase, 310
streamed catalogs, XenDesktop, 488, 495–496
StrictMode, debugging in, 65–66
strings, text mode UI, 583
style sets, Word, 104

styles
    applying to range of cells, 110–111
    applying to Word document, 104
SubFeatures property, Get-WindowsFeature, 168
subfolders, Outlook, 115
subscribing to event, 47–48
Suspend-PublicFolderReplication cmdlet, Exchange, 307
Suspend-VM function, Hyper-V, 518–519
switch statement, alternation in scripts, 25–26
syntax errors, 30–31
System Center Central website, OpsMgr, 438
System Center Configuration Manager, 4–5
System Center Operations Manager. See OpsMgr (System Center Operations Manager) 2007 R2
System Central Virtual Machine Manager. See VMM (Virtual Machine Manager) 2008 R2
System Restore, 157–158
system time, 198–201
Systems Management Server (SMS), 4–5
System.Security.AccessControl. FileSystemAccessRule class, 85–86

T

tab completion, AD, 234
tab-expansion, SQL Server, 367
table space usage, SQL Server, 365–367
tables, adding to Word documents, 101–102
TargetDatabase parameter
    Move-Mailbox, 286–287
    New-MoveRequest, 287–288
Task Sequences, MDT, 449–451
TaskItem, Outlook, 119
tasks
    in Active Directory, 244–246
    on servers, 191–194
    Windows PowerShell automating, 5–6
$TaskService variable, 192–193
TCP protocol, firewall ports, 144–145
TCP/IP, remoting architecture, 47
TechNet Script Center Repository, 343
TechNet Forums, OpsMgr, 438
templates
    creating Active Directory users, 240–241
    Task Sequence, 450–451
    using group policy for execution, 39
    using OUs from, 249
temporary sessions, 48

terminating errors, 33–34

Test-AppLockerPolicy cmdlet, AppLocker, 187

Test-VMHostProfileCompliance cmdlet,
    PowerCLI, 565

text
    adding to Word, 98–99
    converting numbers and dates into, 22
    formatting in Word document, 103–105
    searching in Word document, 102

text mode UI, 581–584

Text property, Word, 98–99

textbox control, 589–590

third-party alternatives
    ISE, 620–621
    PowerShell user forums, 13

time, using system, 198–201

toolbar, ISE, 599, 603–605, 607

transaction support, V2, 63–64

trap statement, runtime errors, 32–33

trap-forwarding, SNMP, 429–431

Tree parameter, Remove-VMSnapshot, 520

troubleshooting, Windows 7, 71–76

Try/Catch block, text mode UI, 583

Try/Catch/Finally, 32–33, 66

TryParse() method, text mode UI, 584

T-SQL (Transact SQL), 347–349, 352

Twitter, PowerShell blogs on, 13

two-state unit monitor, OpsMgr, 437

type accelerators, 209, 302

type operators, 15

Type parameter, Exchange, 296, 303

TypeBackspace() method, Word documents, 99

U

UDP protocol, firewall ports for, 144–146

UI (user interface)
    overview of, 581
    PrimalForms, 593–595
    text mode, 581–584
    Windows Forms, 584–585
    Windows Forms button control, 588–589
    Windows Forms label control, 586–587
    Windows Forms textbox control, 589–593
    Windows Presentation Foundation, 595–596

UNC (Universal Naming Convention), VMM library, 538

Uninstall key, Windows Registry, 154

Uninstall method, wmiclass, 159–161

Uninstall-SPSolution cmdlet, SharePoint, 382

unique file extensions, 87–88

Universal Naming Convention (UNC), VMM library, 538

Universal parameter, Set-Group cmdlet, 296

Universal Time Coordinate format, 200

Unix/Linux pipelines, 10

Unlock-ADAccount cmdlet, AD, 244

Update() method, SharePoint lists, 376–379

Update-EmailAddressPolicy cmdlet,
    Exchange, 323

Update-MDTDeploymentShare cmdlet, MDT, 452

Update-MDTMedia cmdlet, MDT, 453–454

Update-PublicFolder cmdlet, Exchange Server, 307

updates
    custom fields in alert properties, 413–415
    Deployment Share, 452
    email address policy, 323–324
    primary and failover settings for OpsMgr
        agents, 421
    public folders, 307
    SharePoint list data, 376
    VMM host agents, 527
    VMWare tools on VM, 571

Update-Tools cmdlet, VMware, 571

uploading, to SharePoint document library, 381

URLs, indexed folders and, 78

user flags, 220

user input validation, scripts, 24

user interface. See UI (user interface)

User parameter
    Connect-Mailbox, 284
    Connect-VIServer, 559–560
    Set-SharePermission script, 135

UserAuthentication, Remote Desktop, 147–148

UserPrincipalName parameter,
    New-Mailbox, 281

users, Active Directory
    ActiveRoles Management Shell, 253–255
    adding and removing groups, 243–244
    automating tasks, 244–246
    creating, 240–241
    managed service accounts, 246–247
    modifying properties, 242–243
    password policies, 250–251
    querying, 234–238

users, mail
    administering, 292–295
    moving mailboxes interrupting, 286
    upgrading Exchange 2007, 326
    upgrading Exchange 2010, 328

users, managing local accounts, 219–221
Users filter, XenApp, 474–475
UseSqlSnapshot parameter, Backup-SPSite, 385–386
Use-TroubleshootingPack function, 75–76

V

ValidateOnly parameter, Connect-Mailbox, 284
validating input, text mode UI, 583–584
Value parameter, Get-FirewallSetting, 143
Value2 property, cells, 108–110
variable breakpoints, ISE, 609
variable expansion, SQL Server, 347–348
variables
    email address policy, 323
    language constructs, 13–14
vCenter
    clusters, 573–574
    connecting to instance of, 558–559
    log data, 575–576
    managing folders, resource pools and
        datacenters, 575
    migrating VMs, 574
    performance data, 576
verb-noun syntax, of cmdlets, 8–9
$VerbosePreference variable, 66
verbs, for Exchange Server recipient types, 278
version support
    SQL Server, 352
    Windows PowerShell for downlevel OSs, 37
    Windows PowerShell installation, 37
View menu, ISE, 599, 601–602
ViewEntireForest parameter, AD, 331, 332
ViewOnly administrators, 456–457
views
    SharePoint list, 377
    SharePoint list data, 376
Views property, SPList object, 377
virtual directories, 396
virtual hardware, PowerCLI, 569–571
Virtual Machine Manager. See VMM (Virtual Machine
        Manager) 2008 R2
virtual machines. See VMs (virtual machines)
virtual port groups, 564
Virtual Server hosts, adding to VMM, 526–527
virtual switch configuration, 563–564
VM Hosted Groups, 499
VM resource configuration, 571

VMHost, 563
$vmhost variable, 563
VMM (Virtual Machine Manager) 2008 R2
    backing up database, 524
    checkpoints, 536–537
    clusters, 528–530
    connecting to, 525–526
    controlling virtual machines, 535–536
    creating and modifying virtual machines, 531–535
    host servers, 526–528
    installing and loading cmdlets, 523
    libraries, 537–539
    maintenance on host servers, 530–531
    removing virtual machines, 535
    using VMM Administrator Console to write scripts,
        524–525
VMM Administrator Console, 524–525
VMs (virtual machines)
    checkpoints, 536–538
    controlling, 535–536
    creating and modifying, 517–518, 531–535
    gathering performance data with Get-Stat, 567
    power state management, 518–519
    removing, 535
    snapshots, 519–520
VMs (virtual machines), in PowerCLI
    deploying new, 568–569
    invoking scripts, 573
    removing, 569
    resource configuration, 571
    retrieving, 559
    snapshots, 572–573
    starting and stopping, 572
    updating tools, 571
    working with virtual hardware, 569–571
VMware
    ESX and ESXi hosts. See ESX and ESXi hosts
    updating tools on VM, 571
    vSphere PowerCLI. See vSphere PowerCLI
volume space usage, SQL Server, 363
vSphere PowerCLI
    deploying new VMs, 568–569
    ESX and ESXi hosts. See ESX and ESXi hosts
    installing and using cmdlets, 557–558
    invoking scripts, 573
    other features, 576–577
    overview of, 557
    removing VMs, 569
    retrieving hosts and VMs, 559

snapshots, 572–573
starting and stopping VMs, 572
suppressing prompts, 566
updating VMware tools, 571
vCenter management, 573–576
virtual hardware, 569–571
VM resource configuration, 571

W

W32Time Time Service tool, 198
Wait parameter
 New-VMSnapshot, 519
 Remove-VMSnapshot, 520
 Start-VM, 518
Wait-Event cmdlet, 62
WaitForPendingFinalizers() method,
 Office, 97
WaitToComplete parameter, Get-Operation
 Status, 546
WASM (Windows Azure Service Manager)
 certificates, 542–544, 548–549
 cmdlets, 541–542
 diagnostic logging, 549–551
 forcing logs to transfer to storage, 553–554
 hosted services, 544–548
 logging, 551–553
WdBuiltInStyle enumeration, Word
 documents, 104
WDS (Windows Deployment Services), 445
web applications
 IIS, 397–398
 SharePoint, 381
Web Server Role, IIS 7, 390–391
Web Service Management For Vista
 (MS-WSMV), 47–48
Web Services Management layer (WS-MAN), 47–48,
 373–374
WebAdministration module. See IIS (Internet
 Information Services) 7
WebAdministration provider
 application pools, 398
 IIS 7, 391–392
 New-Item cmdlet, 394–395
 not working with SMTP, 392
 virtual directories, 396
 web applications, 397
WebConfiguration cmdlets, IIS 7, 400–403
WebDAV, 335

Where-Object cmdlet
 filters, 328–330
 finding empty folders, 89
 listing Exchange Organization Administrators,
 274–275
 NTFS permissions, 126–127
 overrides in OspMgr, 432
 running services on multiple servers, 204
 server features and roles, 167
 unique file extensions, 87–88
 Windows Search, 78–79
while loop, iteration, 28
white space, mailbox, 311–313
wildcards
 ActiveRoles Management Shell, 254
 alternation in scripts, 26–27
 in parameter value globbing, 9
 regular expressions and, 16–17
Win32_ComputerSystem class, 199–200
Win32_LogicalShareSecuritySetting, 127–131,
 132–133
Win32_NetworkAdapterConfiguration, 213–217
Win32_OperatingSystem class, 198
Win32_Process class, 158–159, 208
Win32_Product class, 152–153
Win32_SecurityDescriptorHelper class, 222–223
Win32_Service class, 205–206
Windows
 management in early days, 3–5
 PowerShell version support, 37
 Windows PowerShell not available for 2000, 37
Windows 7
 ActiveDirectory module, 230–232
 hotfix status, 84
 IISReset issue, 404
 security of files and folders. See files and folders,
 Windows 7
 troubleshooting, 71–76
 V2 features, 44–45
 WebAdministration module, 391
 Windows PowerShell for, 37
 Windows Search. See Windows Search
Windows Azure. See WASM (Windows Azure Service
 Manager)
Windows Backup
 configuring backup jobs, 174–176
 deleting backup jobs, 177
 installing cmdlets, 174
 limitations of cmdlets, 179–180

overview of, 174
scheduling backup jobs, 178–179
starting and stopping backup jobs, 178
status of backup jobs, 176–177
Windows Deployment Services (WDS), 445
Windows Embedded, 37
Windows Firewall
checking status locally, 140–143
checking status overview, 139–140
checking status remotely, 143–144
opening and closing ports, 144–146
Windows Forms
building GUIs with, 585–586
button control, 588–589
label control, 586–587
overview of, 584–585
textbox control, 589–593
working with, 585
Windows Installer Provider, 152
Windows Management Framework Core (WMFC), 37
Windows Management Instrumentation. *See* WMI
(Windows Management Instrumentation)
Windows NT, 4
Windows PowerShell
cmdlets, 8–9
command notification channel in OpsMgr and, 426–431
community, 12–13
development of, 5
discovery-related cmdlets, 10–12
formatting output, 18–23
installing, 36–39
ISE. *See* ISE (Integrated Scripting Environment)
language constructs, 13–18
modules, 36
monitoring scripts in OpsMgr, 436–437
objects, 9–10
overview of, 3
pipeline, 10
in production scripts and admin GUIs, 7–8
profiles, 39–41
scripting. *See* scripts
scripting language, 6–7
snap-ins, 34–36
as task automation platform, 5–6
Windows PowerShell Management Library, Hyper-V,
515–516
Windows PowerShell provider
MDT, 442–444
XenDesktop, 505–506

Windows PowerShell Remoting protocol
(MS-PSRP), 47–48
Windows PowerShell tab, XenDesktop, 480
Windows PowerShell V2, new features
advanced functions, 52–56
debugging from command line, 65–66
development of, 43–45
eventing, 61–62
handling errors with Try/Catch/Finally, 66–67
Integrated Scripting Environment, 63
jobs, 50–52
modules, 57–61
new cmdlets, 67
remoting, 45–50
serialization, 50
transaction support, 63–64
Windows Presentation Foundation (WPF),
595–596
Windows Registry
listing software, 153–154
listing software not installed with `.msi`, 152–153
removing software, 159–161
Windows Remote Management. *See* remoting
Windows Search
adding folders to index, 79–81
discovering which folders are indexes, 77–79
managing, 77
re-indexing search catalog, 82–84
removing folders from index, 81–82
searching with, 89–91
Windows Search SQL syntax, 89–91
Windows Server 2003
`ActiveDirectory` module, 230
management with, 4–5
Windows PowerShell for, 37
Windows Server 2008 R2
`ActiveDirectory` module, 230–232
AppLocker, 186–187
Best Practice Analyzer scans, 169–173
enabling remoting, 173–174
features and roles, 167–169
`GroupPolicy` module, 257
server migration, 180–186
V2 features for, 44–45
web server role for IIS 7, 390–391
Windows Backup. *See* Windows Backup
Windows PowerShell in, 37, 165–166
XenApp 6 only available for, 456
Windows Vista, 37
Windows XP, 37

WinRM service, 47–48
WMFC (Windows Management Framework Core), 37
WMI (Windows Management Instrumentation)
  defined, 151
  discovering server configuration, 189–191
  Hyper-V classes, 513–515
  listing software, 152–153
  managing IIS, 392
  provider for IIS 7, 392
  remote DCOM access for domain users, 226–227
  removing software, 159
  software installation, 158–159
  Windows Server 2003 and, 5
WMI Query Language (WQL), 151, 190
Word, automating
  bullets, 99–100
  content, 98–99
  creating or opening document, 98
  formatting text, 103–105
  headers and footers, 102
  hyperlinks, 100
  inserting images, 101
  overview of, 98
  printing, 106
  saving document, 106–107
  searching for text, 102–103
  spell checking, 105–106
  tables, 101–102

workbooks, Excel, 107–111
worker groups, XenApp 6, 461, 475–477
WorkerGroupPreferences parameter, Set-XALoadBalan cingPolicyConfiguration, 474
WorkflowManager object, SharePoint, 382
workflows
  administering SharePoint, 382–383
  defining in OpsMgr with modules, 436
  modifying in OpsMgr with overrides. *See* overrides
worksheets, Excel, 107–111
workstation, Exchange Server, 271–273
WPF (Windows Presentation Foundation), 595–596
WPK toolkit, 595–596
WQL (WMI Query Language), 151, 190
Write-DataTable function, SQL Server, 356
Write-Debug cmdlet, 32, 66
Write-Verbose cmdlet, 66
WS-MAN (Web Services Management layer), 47–48, 373–374

X

XAML (Extensible Application Markup Language), WPF, 595
XenApp 6. *See* Citrix XenApp 6
XenDesktop 5. *See* Citrix XenDesktop 5
XenServer hosts, 506–507
XmlPolicy parameter, 187